TRACY E. COOPER

PALLADIO'S VENICE

Architecture and Society in a Renaissance Republic

YALE UNIVERSITY PRESS

New Haven & London

PUBLISHED WITH THE ASSISTANCE OF THE GETTY FOUNDATION
AND OF THE PUBLICATIONS COMMITTEE, DEPARTMENT OF ART AND ARCHAEOLOGY,
PRINCETON UNIVERSITY

Designed by Gillian Malpass

Printed in China

Library of Congress Cataloging-in-Publication Data

Cooper, Tracy Elizabeth.

Palladio's Venice : architecture and society in a Renaissance Republic / Tracy E. Cooper.

p. cm.

Includes bibliographical references and index.

ISBN 0-300-10582-7 (cl : alk. paper)

1. Palladio, Andrea, 1508–1580–Criticism and interpretation.
2. Architecture, Renaissance–Italy–Venice. 3. Church architecture–Italy–Venice.
4. Venice (Italy)–Buildings, structures, etc.
I. Palladio, Andrea, 1508–1580. II. Title.

NA1123.P2C66 2005

720'.92–dc22

2004023963

A catalogue record for this book is available from the British Library

Page i   Paolo Veronese, *Annunciation*, overdoor from the Scuola dei Mercanti at Madonna
dell'Orto, Venice, Gallerie dell'Accademia. Detail of fig. 285

Frontispiece   Andrea Palladio, San Giorgio Maggiore, Venice, crossing pier

CONTENTS

ACKNOWLEDGMENTS

A LENGTHY BOOK PROJECT IS LIKE ARCHITECTURE: what we come to experience is the finished product of countless inter-actions, many of which are not visibly evident, but which are no less fundamental to its evolution. Some bear directly on its devel-opment; others provide the indirect support that makes it possible. The author, like the architect, has given a particular design to the ideas of themselves and others, and other hands and minds leave their imprint in its genesis, production, and reception. I have accrued many pleasurable debts over the years of research and writing of this book, and regrettably lack the space here to give all the friends, my family, and the many scholars with whom I have had the fortune to interact my personal acknowledgment of their valuable contributions to my work. There are those, however, without whose assistance this book could not have been realized, and I ask forgiveness in advance if I inadvertently omit anyone from an explicit expression of my appreciation.

First, I should like to single out those scholars who took pre-cious time out of invariably busy schedules to read parts of this book in various – by now unrecognizable – forms and generously offered their comments and support. This book also is a grateful memorial to those who are no longer here but who live on in the ideas that are reflected on these pages. My special gratitude to: Matteo Casini, David Coffin, James Grubb, Marcia Hall, Henry Millon, Debra Pincus, John Pinto, Dennis Romano, Richard Schofield, John Shearman, Helen Tangires.

My primary research was made possible by crucial financial support from several institutions: I have been the fortunate recipi-ent of grants from the Gladys Krieble Delmas Foundation in 2000, 1998, 1992; the Center for Advanced Study in the Visual Arts at the National Gallery of Art in Washington welcomed me back as an Ailsa Mellon Bruce Visiting Senior Fellow in 1997; Temple Uni-versity granted me a study leave in 1997–98, and travel grants in 2000, 1996. The book's production has been generously aided by publication grants from the Getty Trust and from the Publications Committee, Department of Art and Archaeology, Princeton University.

The rewards of research have been greatly enhanced by profes-sional and personal relationships with individuals who have shared their own deep knowledge and expertise with me. For their part in the fabric of my research, in addition to those already named above, I owe thanks especially to the following: the Direzione of the Archivio di Stato di Venezia, and Michela Dal Borgo, Edoardo Giuffreda, Claudia Salmini, Alessandra Sambo, Alessandra Schiavon; Piero Lucchi of the Biblioteca del Museo Civico Correr di Venezia and Umberto LoCascio; Marino Zorzi of the Biblioteca Nazionale Marciana di Venezia and Elisabetta Lugato, Gabriele Mazzucco; Francesco Turio Böhm of Osvaldo Böhm di Venezia; the British Library in London and Stephen Parkin; Cameraphoto Arte di Venezia and Giorgio Santuzzi, Piero Codato, and Massimo Venchierutti; Elizabeth Cropper of the Center for Advanced Study in the Visual Arts at the National Gallery of Art in Washington, and Peter Lukehart, Steven Mansbach, Therese O'Malley, Marianna Shreve Simpson, friends, staff and fellows; the Centro Internazionale di Studi di Architettura Andrea Palladio di Vicenza and Guido Beltramini, Howard Burns, Renato Cevese, and Maria Teresa Pelizzari; Colnaghi's in London and Tim Warner-Johnson; Vittore Branca of the Fondazione Giorgio Cini di Venezia and David Bryant and Franco Novelli; the Gladys Krieble Delmas Foundation and Patricia and George LaBalme; the Fondazione Levi di Venezia and Giulio Cattin, Francesco Passadori, and Franco Rossi; the Index for Christian Art at Princeton University and John Blazejewski; the Institute for Advanced Study in Princeton and Irving and Marilyn Arenberg Lavin; the Istituto per Ricupero ed Educazione di Venezia and Giuseppe Ellero and Silvia Lunardon; Jean-Luc Baroni Ltd. of London and Stephen Ongpin; Janice Powell of the Marquand Library at Princeton University, and staff; the Museo Civico di Vicenza and Aole Adami; the Metropolitan Museum of Art and Andrea Bayer; the National Gallery of Art in Washington and David

Brown, Gretchen Hirschhauer, Nicolas Penny, Douglas Lewis, and Alison Luchs; Neal Turtell of the National Gallery of Art Library in Washington, and Lamia Doumato, Ted Dalziel, and Thomas McGill; the University of Pennsylvania Rare Book and MS Library and John Pollack; the Royal Institute of British Architects in London and James Elwall, Neil Bingham, and Justine Sambrook; Ruth Kamen of the Royal Institute of British Architects Library in London; Sir John Soane's Museum in London and Susan Palmer; Don Antonio Niero of the Seminario Patriarcale di Venezia; Madre Giulia of the Suore Canossiane di Padova; my colleagues in the Department of Art History and Tyler School of Art at Temple University, especially chairs Philip Betancourt, Therese Dolan, and Gerald Silk; Paley Library at Temple University, and Catherine Meaney in Interlibrary Loan; Kim Strommen of Temple University Rome, and Franca Camiz.

The community of Venetian and Renaissance scholars is a particularly lively and interdisciplinary one that inspires the sharing of ideas, along with an *espresso* or over an *ombra e cicchetti*. For those memorable exchanges, I should like to thank in addition to the above: James Ackerman, Bernard Aikema, Nadja Aksamija, Lillian Armstrong, William Barcham, Bruce Boucher, Monica Chojnacka, Stanley Chojnacki, Paula Clarke, Thomas and Maria Saffiotti Dale, Blake DeMaria, Iain Fenlon, Peter Ferguson, Joanne Ferraro, Alejandra Gimenez, Diana Gisolfi, Elizabeth Gleason, Paul Hills, Charles Hope, Peter Humfrey, Holly Hurlbut, Frederick Ilchman, Paul and Beth Kaplan, Benjamin and Judy Kohl, Claudia Kryza-Gersch, Marion Leathers Kunst, Carolyn Kolb Lewis, Oliver Logan, Vittorio Mandelli, Thomas Martin, Louisa Matthew, Sarah McHam, Dulcia Meyers, Edward Muir, John Onians, Catherine Pugliesi, Roger Rearick, Sheryl Reiss, Paola Saffiotti, Juergen and Anne Markham Schulz, Sally Scully, Alan Stahl, Helena Szepe, Bart Thurber, Francesca Toffolo, Deborah Walberg, Alberto Weissmuller, Bronwen Wilson, Wolfgang Wolters, and Barbara Zlamlova. Additionally, I should like to thank the entire family of Gabriele Carraro for their valued and long-standing hospitality.

Finally, there are certain individuals who have been of monumental importance in the realization of this book, for whom these words are an inadequate expression of my deepest gratitude. Gillian Malpass's dedication to the art of the book is evident in the sensitivity brought to the relationships between text and image, and her editorial wisdom has been a sure guide through the book process; at Yale, her able assistants, Sarah Faulks and Emily Angus, have graciously fielded endless enquiries for me; my copy editor, Delia Gaze, must be thanked for a heroic job. Deborah Howard provided astute and insightful multiple readings that saved me from many errors, she has been enormously generous in her encouragement and scholarly collegiality, and her work has been a direct inspiration. Patricia Fortini Brown has been teacher, mentor, friend, and fellow intrepid explorer of La Serenissima, whether sharing in the prosaic aspects of conducting research or producing a book, or discovering another marvel of this endlessly fascinating city, I have benefited immensely from her deep engagement with bringing the cultural past to life. Timothy D. Wardell deserves greater recognition than these words can suggest for his profound contribution to the scope of intellectual inquiry that he has always encouraged through his unflagging personal support and application of great professional expertise, and above all, for his faith in both author and project, which has been the true foundation of this enterprise.

Tracy E. Cooper
August 2004

PREFACE

THE STORY OF ANDREA PALLADIO'S STRUGGLE to establish himself in Venice is a compelling one. Venice in the second half of the sixteenth century was a city in confrontation with the broader changes sweeping the Mediterranean and Europe. This book positions Palladio as an agent of the transformation of that society and its image of itself in the marble and brick of its built environment. He was undeniably one of the most influential architects that western Europe has produced, but his career in Venice has not received the same attention accorded to the works that he produced outside the capital, the splendid villas and palaces that continue to inspire writers and visitors alike. While an image of Venice in the Renaissance is incomplete if we do not include in our vision Palladio's celebrated churches of San Giorgio Maggiore and Il Redentore, these singular monuments represent only a fraction of what Palladio and his supporters hoped to achieve in the city. The author proposes to explain and redress this imbalance in the study of Palladio by focusing on his complete career and production in the city of Venice, from major to minor to unbuilt projects, in order to provide a lens through which the changing culture of this society can be viewed, and to reveal some major themes that affected the development of the nascent profession of the architect.

The interaction between Palladio and his Venetian patrons – some more meaningfully characterized as collaborators, others as peripheral relationships – and between these individuals and institutions, forms the organizing principle of this book. Previous Palladio studies have been structured monographically or typologically, whether focused on the architect's entire career, single buildings, or some combination thereof. The exceptional character of Palladio's production has been matched by the high level of quality in Palladio scholarship dominated by these approaches. The great nineteenth-century biographer of Palladio, Abbot Antonio Magrini, continues to have relevance today due to his perceptive analysis of Palladio's works in the context of his practice, and reliance on evidence ranging from preparatory material to documentary sources.

Heirs to this scholarship range from chronologically organized monographs such as Lionello Puppi's indispensable catalogue raisonné of 1973, usefully brought up to date in 1999 by Donata Battilotti, to Giangiorgio Zorzi's monumental volumes published between 1959 and 1969 of Palladio's works and their available documentation arranged by building type, to the brilliant and accessible study of 1977 by James Ackerman, who identified changing patterns within building typologies with the developments in Palladio's patronage base in the Veneto – his "geo-political architecture" – and more recently to *Andrea Palladio: The Architect in his Time* of 1998 by Bruce Boucher, its contextual account enriched by the photographs of Paolo Marton. Fundamental to the advancement of Palladio scholarship has been the institution of the Centro internazionale di studi di architettura Andrea Palladio in Vicenza, whose active programs of teaching, conferences, and publications have sponsored prestigious journals and conference volumes (*Bollettino*, 1959–87; *Annali*, 1989–; and André Chastel's and Renato Cevese's *Andrea Palladio: Nuovi contributi* of 1990), an ongoing corpus of individual monuments (*Corpus Palladianum*, 1968–, including Elena Bassi on the Carità and Wladimir Timofiewitsch on the Redentore), and the recent scholarly overview of 2000, *Andrea Palladio: atlante di architettura*, organized by location and type by the editors, Guido Beltramini and Antonio Padoan, with an insightful introduction by Howard Burns, and further enhanced by the photographic campaign of Pino Guidolotti.

Apart from this approach in the literature are several exhibition catalogs and connected symposia volumes that celebrated in 1980 the quadricentenary of Palladio's death. By definition, such multi-authored works do not promote a synthetic individual point of view, but constitute an examination of various themes by collections of distinguished scholars. It is almost a requirement of exhibitions on architecture that supplementary material is given attention *in loco aedificium*, which the prescient catalog *Andrea Palladio, 1508–1580: The Portico and the Farmyard* by Howard Burns, with

Lynda Fairbairn and Bruce Boucher, took as an opportunity to explore the contemporary world of Venice during Palladio's time, as did the relevant sections in *Architettura e utopia nella Venezia del cinquecento*, edited by Lionello Puppi. The utopian Palladio, his unrealized projects for Venice, was acknowledged in a later exhibition, *Le Venezie possibili: Da Palladio a Le Corbusier*, edited by Lionello Puppi and Giandomenico Romanelli. The insistence of these seminal catalogs on contextualizing Palladio within his cultural environment in Venice has been influential in the approach taken here. Further, unlike most monographs on architects, the arts that accompanied building programs will be considered as integral to the understanding of Palladio's and his patrons' expressive aims.

The study of patronage as a means to explore more deeply architectural achievement is, of course, not new. The kind of broad examination of individuals and institutions undertaken here for Palladio was successfully applied to the work of Jacopo Sansovino by Deborah Howard in her innovative publication of 1987, *Jacopo Sansovino: Architecture and Patronage in Renaissance Venice* (first published in 1975), which retains its relevance for the insights it offers into the relation between social and economic conditions and architectural style. The contrast to Palladio's situation is illuminating and speaks to the sociological concept of "generations," making this book a successor to her earlier study of the Venice of Sansovino. These two architects, with overlapping careers, occupied different nodes in the historical fabric of Venice, which radically affected the outcome of their individual production and social positions. The Venice of Doge Andrea Gritti with the triumphant Roman *renovatio* carried out by Sansovino for his patrons from the late 1530s to the 1560s was not the same city that Palladio encountered from his entry in the early 1550s to his death in 1580. Palladio's interaction with his patrons reveals the way in which internal and external forces were reshaping Venetian society during the pivotal period of the third quarter of the sixteenth century. This book hopes to make a contribution to the important comparative studies in patronage for this period, notably Oliver Logan's *Culture and Society in Venice, 1470–1790* of 1972 and Michel Hochmann's comprehensive look at the patronage of Venetian painting, *Peintres et commanditaires à Venise (1540–1628)*, of 1992, with a perspective on the architectural culture of Venice. Architecture *mattered* to Renaissance Venetians. It was argued in the highest councils of the government. Debates over control of the imagery of cultural prestige, what Pierre Bourdieu refers to as "symbolic capital," represent a set of decision-making processes offered here as another tool for prosopographical analysis by historians of this period.

The "Myth" of Palladio

The paradox that this book explores is that, for all his fame, Palladio's Venetian career did not live up fully either to his ambitions or to those of his patrons; that their shared project – the re-imaging of the city of Venice in response to the demands and challenges of the period – was more often blocked than advanced. The tensions between forces that valued the continuity of *venezianità* over the adoption of a "new use" (*usanza nuova*) of the classical and its ideals as offered by Palladio provide the dynamics of this conflicted history. Ultimately, Palladio's failures are as telling as his now iconic successes.

The heroic ideal of the successful architect has been the underlying narrative of many monographic studies of Palladio; this book challenges such an uncomplicated conceptualization by employing a historiographical strategy used by historians to deconstruct the "myth of Venice," analyzed by James Grubb in his "When Myths Lose Power: Four Decades of Venetian Historiography" of 1986. If we recognize that rhetoric and ritual were potent devices to shape community perception and ultimately historical reception of institutions (laid out in Edward Muir's influential *Civic Ritual in Renaissance Venice* of 1981, provided with a comparative context by Matteo Casini in 1996, and explored by art historians, notably in the work of Patricia Fortini Brown), Palladio's work in the Serenissima helps us to understand the dynamics of contemporary power as represented in the language of architecture.

Easily the single greatest contributor to the "myth of Palladio" was Palladio himself. This was instituted through the publication of his "bestseller," *I quattro libri dell'architettura* (Venice, 1570), which continues to appear in new editions and translations (such as Robert Tavernor and Richard Schofield's English edition of 1997, with its useful glossary and return to the illustrations of 1570) and still occupies a place on many architects' and historians' bookshelves. Like the "myth of Venice" that propagated an ideal vision of the Republic, Palladio employed a similar approach in his deliberate ideal re-presentation of his actual built designs. This should be understood, however, as conceptually congruent with his intellectual mentality in regards to the theory and practice of architecture, where there is no absolute model but rather invention according to learned principles – a design *process* – allowing a type to suit the decorum of a particular situation (in this case, a printed book).

The foundations of Palladio's architectural production and his reputation were established well before the publication of the *Four Books*. The success of his *terraferma* villas and palaces has contributed to a modern myopia for the entire category of his works that became his greatest achievement in Venice, his ecclesiastical architecture. His church projects are but minimally present in the publication of 1570, although several were already in progress, and then are mentioned only in the text, not presented in the influential illustrations that contributed to the fame of his other projects. The long-pervasive Burckhardtian secular view of the Renaissance has reinforced a dominant concentration on Palladio's domestic architecture, the villas and palaces that represent the bulk of his published examples in the *Four Books*; witness a recent entry in the field, *The Perfect House* by Witold Rybczynski (New York, 2002). Palladio may even be seen as complicit if we consider his inclusion of the monastery of Santa Maria della Carità in Venice under Book Two on the house.

Another contributing factor to the "myth of Palladio" is that his fame is not matched by actual knowledge about his personal identity; his image remains elusive. This book focuses on our knowledge of the "human factor" surrounding this legendary figure and his relationships. Important precedents for understanding Palladio through his *opere minori*, or minor works, were set by Rodolfo Gallo in 1955 and further developed by Howard Burns in 1979. From the tradition of "microstoria" as described by Edward Muir, this study utilizes the range of information that can be gleaned not only from the major "events" of his monumental commissions and important patrons, from the Benedictines at San Giorgio to the Venetian government at Il Redentore, but also looks at the "long duration" of these projects and the nearly anonymous figures that actually built them, to the most routine of architectural practices with which Palladio was engaged, such as the providing of "expert opinion" or estimates, minor projects, and to his less exalted patrons, such as citizens and women.

A significant contribution of this book is the tracing of networks of patronage, going beyond earlier studies to forge previously unrecognized links, made possible by recent historical research. Formerly "invisible" groups have emerged as players through the informal exchange of power. This study builds on new understandings of the relationships between men and women in family groups and the social and legal structures and institutional organizations in sixteenth-century Venice – from the government to the *scuole* and *ospedali*, from convents and monasteries to social organizations such as the Compagnie della Calza – in which patterns of reciprocity between these private and public relationships were established (I am particularly indebted to the recent work of Stanley Chojnacki, Giuseppe Gullino, and Dennis Romano, on the patriciate, and to Patricia Fortini Brown, Brian Pullan, and Monica Chojnacka, on charitable institutions and women, and Matteo Casini, on the Calza, among others). Single studies of Palladio's patrons have formed a necessary foundation for my construction of his networks of alliances (the researches of Pio Paschini, Giangiorgio Zorzi, Rodolfo Gallo, Lionello Puppi, Giuseppe Gullino, Manfredo Tafuri, Antonio Foscari, James Davis, Douglas Lewis, Carolyn Kolb, Peter Humfrey, and Deborah Howard figure prominently), but above all build on the valuable prosopographical analyses of Paul Grendler, Oliver Logan, Peter Laven, and Martin Lowry. These associations help to explain the choices of adoption or rejection of an architect such as Palladio due to his identification with specific individuals and their circles of influence.

The understanding of patronage as a system of obligatory reciprocity is further complicated when we compare political patterns of allegiance – *clientelismo* – to cultural ones – *mecenatismo* (see my publication of 1996 in *The Search for a Patron in the Middle Ages and the Renaissance* on this subject). A claim is made here for Palladio's contribution to the modern role of the architect since his collaboration with particular patrons implies the voluntary reciprocity more usually associated with kinship and friendship (the studies of Sharon Kettering, such as *Patronage in Sixteenth- and Seventeenth-Century France* of 2002, are a model). Modern terminology seems to have inherited such ambiguity in its identification of the "architect" and "client" relationship, reversing the roles, in which the "support" of the client/patron is rewarded by the "benefit" of the creation, a privileging of the creator.

Palladio's construction and performance of the new role of the architect came out of his particular relationships in aristocratic Vicenza (Howard Burns, for example, documents this through the decisions taken on the Basilica, in his article of 1991), but ran into conflict with established practice in Venice (see the characterization of 1980 by Manfredo Tafuri). The research of Michel Hochmann reveals Venice to be among the leading cities in Europe with the largest number of "amateurs" in the sixteenth century, meaning patrons and collectors who felt entitled to make decisions on artistic style. Palladio himself sagely advised that "one must (as I have said) pay particular attention to those who want to build" (*The Four Books of Architecture*, 1570, Bk. 2, ch. 1, 3).

The identification with a specific client base within the Venetian patriciate would shape the opportunities that came to Palladio. Patronage networks in Venice were created through family connections and alliances formed through political and cultural affiliations. Power was distributed through various councils in the Venetian government, a number of which had a say in building projects in the city. Funds were often approved and dispersed based on the opinions of experts. Designs and models would be debated in committee, for important projects even on the floor of the largest governing body, the Great Council, involving leading figures of Venetian public life, including the doge, as Wolfgang Wolters, Juergen Schulz, Umberto Franzoi, and Staale Sinding-Larsen have shown in their work on the Doge's Palace. Palladio's patrons were educated in matters of architecture, and, moreover, were accustomed to having their say. Palladio wryly alludes to this in the continuation of the quote from his *Four Books*, "but the architect is frequently obliged to accommodate himself to the wishes of those who are paying rather than attending to what he should."

Gaetano Cozzi in a publication of 1961 developed an influential model of the political configuration of patronage groups in Venice, from which Palladio's base in the patriciate has been identified as being *papalisti* or Romanist in such important studies of sixteenth-century architecture as Manfredo Tafuri's *Venice and the Renaissance* and Ennio Concina's *A History of Venetian Architecture*, and others. In this book, the cultural alignments of the Venetian patriciate will be explored further to test how allegiances were expressed in architecture and decision-making in the case of Andrea Palladio, and how they ultimately determined the trajectory of his career in the capital.

★   ★   ★

This study does not aim to provide uniform coverage of all of the projects attributed to Palladio while in Venice, but will look in depth at certain monuments, extending to decorative programs that express the intentions of patrons, and Palladio's articulation of those aims in order to depict more fully the broader historical implications of cultural agency. It will concentrate on the dynamics of the social relationships and conditions of production that resulted in major works and the association of Palladio with Venice. Part I will look at the foundation of Palladio's unique identity as an architect based on the specialized humanist education he received first in Vicenza with Giangiorgio Trissino and subsequently with his introduction to the intellectual and social environment of Padua and Venice, where he came into contact with Daniele Barbaro, as well as other members of the Venetian patriciate. Palladio's focused study of the ancients and new scientific methods of enquiry were formed in this milieu and resulted in his first book productions in Venice. Associations with particular academic circles and continued participation in the book trade continued throughout his career, and set him apart from other practitioners of the craft of building. The nature of Venetian patronage is the focus of Part II, beginning with a detailed look at Venetian society in the third quarter of the sixteenth century, a period of enormous change affecting the structure of the family and institutions. In Venice, Palladio confronted a diverse building tradition and historical precedents. This section will cover some of the early types of commissions that he received in the city, including projects that he contemplated for Venetian palace designs and for parish churches. While his expectations for domestic architecture would remain unmet, the broader sphere of ecclesiastical furnishings opened new areas of patronage. As Palladio became more established, he enjoyed an authority that led to his role as an expert, in which his judgments were solicited for his ability to recognize good workmanship, appropriate materials, and decorum of design, a facet of his professional life that will be considered. Palladio's association with a particular set on his arrival in Venice brought him in contact with new patrons, including the celebrated Compagnie della Calza (Companies of the Hose), which reaffirmed his intellectual foundations and would expand his networks leading to a new phase in his career. Part III will turn to Palladio's first major patrons, the patriarchs of Venice and Aquileia. The status of the institution of the patriarchates, the individuals who held these positions and their relationships to Palladio's already established connections will be discussed, since these factors would ultimately influence the success or failure of the building projects, and the programs that would be conceived for them. The monumental façade projects of San Pietro in Castello and San Francesco della Vigna led to a new phase for Palladio, one in which ecclesiastical commissions dominated for the first time. His success in this arena was marked by the prominence of his commissions from monastic patrons, covered in Part IV. Palladio's commissions for the wealthy Benedictines of San Giorgio Maggiore and the Augustinian Lateran Canons of Santa Maria della Carità reflect his understanding of the diverse requirements of patrons. Even while satisfying the complex requirements of these building programs, Palladio evolved designs that developed the classical principles and scientific approach that informed his work. This diversity extended to the projects for the nuns of Santa Lucia and La Celestia, where the interaction with female institutions and their male patrons added a level of intervening complexity, and introduced private interests into the religious environment, patrician and citizen alike. Part V

addresses Palladio's ambitions to achieve an official status as State architect. Although he was unsuccessful in this quest, his stature was acknowledged by several prestigious commissions. It was in this arena that his patronage affiliations were the most politicized, leading by association to disappointments, such as projects for the Rialto bridge competitions, and only partial success in his grand conceptions for the rebuilding of the Doge's Palace. As proposed here, Doge Alvise Mocenigo was instrumental in elevating Palladio and his patrons, that their classical language of architecture supported the expression of a particular program of ideals, leading to such projects as the doge's tomb in Santi Giovanni e Paolo and the ephemeral triumphal arch for the entry of the French king Henri III. Finally, it was Palladio's new prominence in ecclesiastical architecture that would promote his choice as architect for Il Redentore, the votive church to be erected as a pledge of the doge and the State. Part VI describes the charitable institutions that were developing in early modern Venice as society was in the process of redefining relations between Church and State. The buildings that Palladio created for diverse patrons of *scuole* and *ospedali* provided a new syntax for the expression of civic piety in Venice at this critical moment. The conclusion offers an evaluation of Palladio's Venetian accomplishments. In covering the specific types of patronage and extended building projects there is unavoidable overlap among the chapters, and while the content is generally organized to follow Palladio's career, a chronological table is provided for easy clarification. Genealogical charts have also been included to provide visual references for the interrelationships so crucial to the establishment of the architect's networks of patrons. Palladio responded to the singular environment of Venice, and in his approach to architecture, his relationships to his patrons, and the products of those commissions, he not only transformed the fabric of the city, but the status of his profession as well.

NOTE ON ABBREVIATIONS: Venetian names can be very similar and are often distinguished from each other only by patronymic and/or title, or by association with a branch (*ramo*) of a family (*casa*) identified by a particular location. Females are often known only as the daughter of their father. As much of this study is concerned with establishing the relationships of individuals to each other and to Palladio to present a picture of the network of patronage and associations that contributed to his Venetian career, I have tried to include the critical information (where it is known) for individuals necessary to establish their distinctive identities and roles. Titles are both a distinguishing factor and an indication of status, important in the changing social climate in this period, and will be given as the following abbreviations: "K." for Knight (*kavaliere*, or *cavaliere*), "P." for Procurator (*procuratore*), "Dr." for Doctor (*dottore*), so for example, Marc'Antonio Barbaro K. P., indicates that he is both a knight and a procurator. Variant spellings of names in Italian, Venetian, or Latin are given as most frequently encountered for an individual.

PART I

FOUNDATIONS

Palladio was a most extraordinary able and attractive conversationalist, so that he gave the most intense pleasure to the Gentlemen and Lords with whom he dealt.

Paolo Gualdo, "Vita di Andrea Palladio," 1616[1]

INTRODUCTION

ANDREA PALLADIO'S FIRST COMMISSIONS in the unique urban environment of Venice came in the mid-1550s, following public success in Vicenza and on the *terraferma* for both Vicentine and Venetian patrons (fig. 1).[2] His study of the ancients and the development of scientific methods of architectural practice and design would be critical in the formulation of the identity of the modern architect. Palladio first came under the auspices of the Vicentine humanist and aristocrat Count Giangiorgio Trissino in the 1530s, and he was associated with the Venetian scholar and patrician Daniele Barbaro, patriarch-elect of Aquileia, from the 1550s. These two men were crucial in the development of Palladio's intellectual authority, which would provide the foundation for the architect to challenge established practice in Venice and ultimately to transform the profession. Palladio would confirm his status through his involvement with the book trade, most notably with his enduring contribution to architectural theory in his *Four Books of Architecture* (fig. 2).

Palladio was unusual for the period in his professional formation. Born Andrea di Pietro dalla Gondola in 1508, he began as a stonemason's apprentice in his native Padua at the age of 13. Two years later he broke his apprenticeship and went to Vicenza, where he entered the more ambitious Pedemuro workshop and was recognized as a master in 1524. There Palladio come into contact with Giangiorgio Trissino, who was building a villa outside the city at Cricoli between 1532 and 1537, which was to be both a gentleman's residence and the seat of his humanist academy (figs. 3 and 4).[3] That Palladio during this time was taken up by Trissino testifies to his already outstanding talent as a stone carver in the classical language, as well as to his noted amiable and intelligent personality.[4] Although we have little information regarding Palladio's early knowledge, it seems clear that his early Paduan and Vicentine experiences provided him with a practical background in classical architectural form as it was understood in these workshops, and possibly more exposure to Vitruvius than is generally recognized. Through Trissino's guidance, Palladio received more specialized humanist education directed to the studies pertinent to the practice of architecture. He had left the Pedemuro workshop by 1537 and embarked on an independent career. His background and training conform to none of the professional models of the day, neither belonging to a family of masters in the craft of stonecutting, *tagliapietre* (although his father was a miller and supplier of mill stones), and rising through patronage (such as the Sangallo), nor training in the figurative arts and approaching architecture as a master of *disegno* (as with Michelangelo), nor coming to building initially through education as a humanist and theorist (as in Alberti's case). The first distinguishing factor in Palladio's career was the combination of his skilled craft with a specialist intellectual background, achieved through his early initiative and association with such a benefactor as Trissino, who must be credited with recognizing the young stonemason's extraordinary aptitude.

Palladio's reputation was confirmed during the decade of the 1540s in Vicenza and the Veneto. Consequent to his unusual architectural education enhanced in Trissino's humanist ambience, he succeeded in attaining ambitious villa and palace projects, first for Vicentine patrons and then for Venetians on the *terraferma*. It was, however, securing the commission of the Basilica in Vicenza (between 1546 and 1549) that placed Palladio in the company of illustrious architects who had advised on the building: Michele Sanmicheli, Giulio Romano, Sebastiano Serlio, and Jacopo Sansovino (fig. 5).[5] This elevated Palladio beyond the status of a local architect, which his intellectual preparation and consequent social access to fellow humanists would allow him to take advantage of.

In the 1540s Palladio initiated extensive travels, the second important factor in his formation as an architect and intellectual, probably making his first trip to Rome in 1541 in the company of Trissino, who had a house there near the Pantheon. Not long after their initial association, between 1538 and 1540, Trissino had left Vicenza to reside in Padua; from 1540 until his death in 1550

View of the Bacino San Marco from the Piazzetta with Andrea Palladio's church of San Giorgio Maggiore, Isola San Giorgio Maggiore, Venice

3 Attributed to Leandro or Francesco Bassanao, *Portrait of a Man* (*?Andrea Palladio*), Vicenza, Museo Civico

2 (*left*) Andrea Palladio, *I quattro libri dell'architettura*, Venice, Appresso Dominico de' Franceschi, 1570, titlepage

he was frequently at his palace in Venice or at his Murano villa near San Donato. From a variety of sources it has been shown that Palladio joined his mentor whenever his increasingly busy work schedule permitted, both where Trissino resided and on his travels.[6]

Giangiorgio Trissino was the initial catalyst for the academic and aristocratic circles of Padua and Venice that facilitated for Palladio, on a wider stage, the same intellectual and career development as he had in Vicenza. Trissino's extensive contacts would be formative in this regard. Noted scholars, including Lionello Puppi and Manfredo Tafuri, have elaborated on the place of architecture in the broader scheme of ennobling the city of Vicenza and its "neo-feudal aristocracy" shared by Trissino and his fellows. Puppi comments on Trissino's "turning his patriotic fervour to achieving a concrete realization of his desire for glorification . . . spurred on by his unforgettable memories of the splendours of Rome and of the papal court, which he had long frequented."[7] Trissino could claim the regard of such highly placed and influential patrons as several

princes of the church, notably the Medici court of Pope Leo X, with Cardinal Nicolò Ridolfi, and of Pope Clement VII with the cardinal-patriarch of Aquileia, Marino Grimani, and that of the Farnese pope Paul III with Cardinal Ippolito d'Este of Ferrara; Palladio's early biographers recount how fruitful the results of such contacts were for his career.[8]

The earliest dates with which a project can be associated reliably with Venetian patrons on the *terraferma* are around 1542–44, when a villa was built at Bagnolo di Lonigo (near Vicenza) for Vettor di Giovanni Pisani (born 1520), a young member of the San Paternian branch of this important and well-connected patrician family of Venice, probably on the occasion of his marriage in 1542 to Paola di Marco Foscari (fig. 6). The means by which the as yet relatively untried architect came to Vettor's attention have been attributed first to the Pisani family's activities in Vicenza, and second to the likelihood that the 22-year-old Pisani had frequented the ambience of the University of Padua.[9]

4   Vincenzo Catena,
Giangiorgio Trissino, Paris,
Musée du Louvre

The Bagnolo property had been confiscated by Venice from a member of the Vicentine nobility by Vettor's father, Giovanni, in 1523, two years before he became Venetian governor in Vicenza (a post later held by Vettor's youngest brother Daniele in 1562). Giovanni Pisani had also commissioned work from the Pedemuro workshop, where Palladio was employed, in 1528, the year of his death. In the intervening decade, Vettor attained his majority, and Palladio his status as independent architect under the tutelage of Trissino, who transferred at this time to Padua, where a surprising number of Palladio's future Venetian patrons were to be found in the years around 1540.

During his sojourn in Padua, Trissino continued to move in the highest social circles, as he had in Vicenza, which would have brought him into the spheres of its cultured Venetians. The house that he rented in Padua from the Venetian Antonio Mocenigo would later be remodeled by Palladio for Mocenigo's son Leonardo, who would become his patron both for villa properties in the

Veneto and in Venice itself, as we shall see. Trissino had a model in the *mecenatismo* of the Paduan resident Alvise Cornaro, whose *famiglia* included the antiquarian painter-architect Giovanni Maria Falconetto and the dialect playwright Angelo Beolco, "Ruzzante," and who may have hosted the renowned Accademia degli Infiammati.[10] According to Vasari, it was Cornaro who introduced the Roman Renaissance style in architecture in the complex of buildings, the Loggia and Odeo, linked to his Padua residence and at several villas in the nearby Euganean hills (including the Villa dei Vescovi at Luvigliano for the bishops of Padua). In this same period, Girolamo di Giorgio Corner was the resident governor (1539–40), while Cardinal Francesco di Alvise P. Pisani (of the dal Banco branch) was bishop (1524–55) of the city. Not only were these last two Venetian nobles interrelated, but numerous connections can be traced to Palladio's future patrons. Among them in the early 1550s were Corner's son, Giorgio (called "Zorzon"), for whom Palladio would build a villa in Piombino Dese (near Treviso),[11] and

5　Aerial view of Vicenza and city center with the Basilica Palladiana

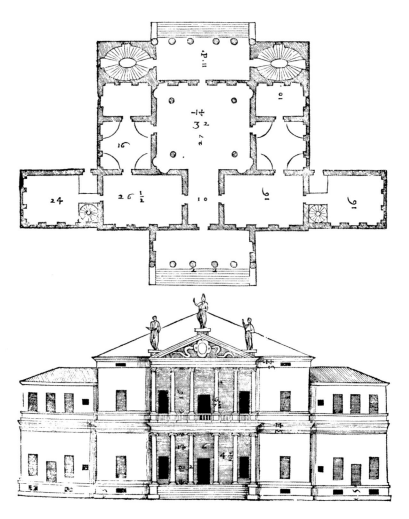

7 (*above*)　Andrea Palladio, Villa Corner at Piombino Dese, *I quattro libri dell'architettura*, Venice, Appresso Dominico de' Franceschi, 1570, lib. 2, cap. 14, 53

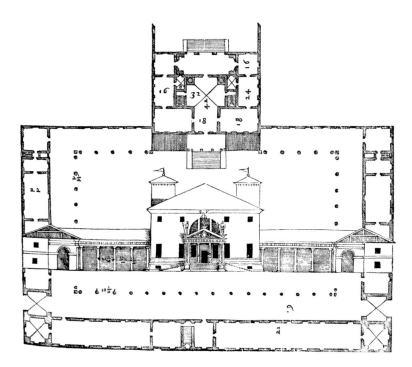

6　Andrea Palladio, Villa Pisani at Bagnolo, *I quattro libri dell'architettura*, Venice, Appresso Dominico de' Franceschi, 1570, lib. 2, cap. 14, 47

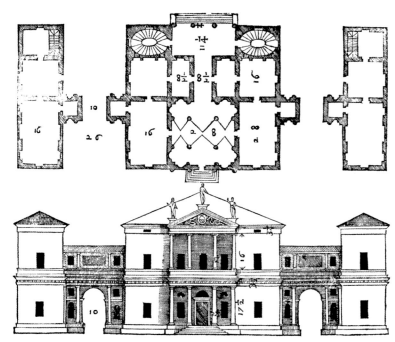

8 (*right*)　Andrea Palladio, Villa Pisani at Montagnana, *I quattro libri dell'architettura*, Venice, Appresso Dominico de' Franceschi, 1570, lib. 2, cap. 14, 52

Francesco di Giovanni Pisani (also dal Banco, whose father was first cousin to the cardinal), for whom Palladio built the extra-urban villa outside the walled town of Montagnana (figs. 7 and 8). Francesco Pisani was close in age to Palladio, and they became friends. The architect later stayed with his patron at the villa and acquired further commissions in Montagnana through his influence.

Few would dispute that the most influential patron for Palladio's career in Venice would be Daniele Barbaro (Venice, 1514–1570), who took his *laurea* in Letters at the University of Padua in 1540 and concurrently was a founding member of the Accademia degli Infiammati.[12] The centrality of Padua's university environment to these Venetians, where it had long brought together intellectual currents not only from inhabitants of the Serenissima, but from elsewhere in Italy and Europe, is indicated in Francesco Pisani's will of 1567.[13] He specifically recommended the value of education to his heirs: "to raise their sons in the fear of God with good manners and good education in the humanities for in this way they will be pleasing to our Lord God and useful to our fatherland." Close ties of consanguinity linked Barbaro through his mother Elena di Alvise P. Pisani dal Banco to the Montagnana and the Bagnolo branches of these other early Venetian patrons of Palladio.[14]

To those familiar with the wealthy families of the Venetian patriciate, the names Pisani and Corner are inescapably linked to the Church, recipients of the great benefices that came with abbeys, bishoprics, and cardinalates. Although some of Palladio's other early aristocratic supporters in Vicenza demonstrated what could be interpreted as crypto-Protestant tendencies, Trissino's connections with the papal court and the Venetian network that Palladio was developing moved distinctly along the lines of Rome.[15] Palladio's studies would naturally lead him to view Venice as the true heir/ess of ancient Rome, an important – and contested – topos in the Republic's ongoing rivalry with the contemporary city of the popes – *Venezia altera Roma*.[16]

9 Titian (workshop of), *Daniele Barbaro*, 1545, Ottawa, National Gallery of Canada, Purchased 1928 (3567)

CHAPTER ONE

PALLADIO AND THE VENETIAN BOOK INDUSTRY

FROM A SHARED IDEAL IN THE ARCHITECTURE and learning of ancient Rome, first inculcated by his mentor, the Vicentine aristocrat Giangiorgo Trissino, to an interest in the new sciences exchanged in the intellectual circles of Venetian patricians such as Daniele Barbaro and Jacopo Contarini, Palladio formed a specific patronage base. The results of their endeavors were realized by means of one of the most important industries in Venice: the book trade. Palladio's growing reputation can be measured by his first publications in 1554; his collaboration on Barbaro's edition of Vitruvius of 1556; the *Four Books*, the treatise published in 1570 that earned him lasting renown; and his commentary of 1575 on Julius Caesar. Palladio himself, rather than the publisher, applied for the privileges that gave him the copyrights on the last title, demonstrating his unique involvement in these ventures.

Trissino's prominence in Paduan cultural circles had already made Palladio's contact with Daniele Barbaro probable, as noted above, since after Barbaro had taken his degree, he had been given the post of superintendent of the building for the Botanic Garden there, a development that would have been of interest to all who pursued the study of science, nature, and architecture.[17] Titian depicted the young scholar at this time, at the age of 30, for the portrait gallery of illustrious men being assembled by Paolo Giovio, bishop of Como (fig. 9). The attribute of the book was a common one of humanist portraits; here, while it is represented almost hidden from view, it acts as the support for the arm that crosses over the body and forms a base for the composition whose apex is the clear gaze of the sitter. From his dress, both the Ottawa portrait and a slightly later version (Madrid, Prado), which shows a more pensive side to Barbaro, would seem to pre-date his title as patriarch-elect of Aquileia.

Exactly how early Barbaro and Palladio began a more sustained association is difficult to pinpoint, whether it began in 1548 before Barbaro's trip to England, or shortly after, but early sources report that they were in Rome together in 1554 ("He [Palladio] traveled there a fifth time with several Venetian Gentlemen who were his special friends"), coming in contact with the papal architects Pirro Ligorio, Jacopo Barozzi da Vignola, and Michelangelo.[18] Since Trissino had died in 1550, this signals the transfer to Barbaro's patronage and an orientation to Venice.

The first concrete project that Palladio produced in Venice was not a building, but rather one that described buildings, or their remains, a guidebook to *L'antichità di Roma*, ("The Antiquities of Rome"), published in 1554 in Rome (by Vincenzo Lucrino) and shortly after in Venice (by Mattio Pagan, 1555). The titlepage for the Venetian edition lays out the themes of Palladio's future career much like an *impresa*: Antiquity, Rome, Ancients and Moderns, Faith (or Religion), Venice; all newly interpreted by the author (fig. 10). Actually, what lies inside the covers follows a long-established format for guides to the "miraculous sights of Rome,"[19] but what concerns us more here is the impression that such a publication would make, which would be associated with its architect author. Often, as here, the illustrations of frontispieces and initials were a part of the stock of the publisher and included their identification not only with mottoes but also with images. Thus the central image of the allegorical figure of "Fede," holding a chalice with the Host and a cross and standing in a landscape in front of a city, makes only a suggestive connection with the author (since Pagan was located "al segno della Fede" in the Frezzaria near San Marco). Palladio's Roman publisher also produced his *Descritione delle chiese . . . in la Città di Roma* ("Description of the Churches of Rome") that same year – a pilgrim's guide updated to follow a more comprehensible itinerary of sacred sites.[20] With these publications, Palladio inserted himself into the Renaissance architectural tradition by establishing his authority on the subject of ancient and

10 Andrea Palladio, *L'antichità di Roma*, Venice, Per Matthio Pagan in Frezaria all'in segna della fide, 1555, titlepage

modern religious architecture. In his remarks to his readers in *L'antichità di Roma*, Palladio demonstrated the method that also underlay his architectural practice, that of checking written authorities (with names ranging from ancient to modern historians) against his own visual observations and measurements, with which he hoped to correct the errors of earlier works (citing *Le cose maravigliose di Roma*).[21] The appearance of this book was not Palladio's first contact with Venice or Venetians, but it was the moment when he moved seriously towards establishing his architectural presence in the capital.

In Venice in 1556 Francesco Marcolini published *I dieci libri dell' architettura*, an Italian edition of Vitruvius' *De architectura libri decem* (*Ten Books on Architecture*), which would definitively supersede its predecessors. It contained a translation and extensive commentary by Daniele Barbaro (figs. 11 and 12), whose titlepage verso coat of arms (argent, a circlet gules) emblematically echoes the authorial identification on the titlepage. Barbaro acknowledged the contribution of Palladio:

> For the designs of the important illustrations I used the works of Messer Andrea Palladio, architect of Vicenza, who of all those whom I have known personally or by hearsay, has according to the judgment of excellent men best understood the true architecture, having not only grasped its beautiful and subtle principles, but also practiced it, whether in his most delicate and exquisite drawings of plans, elevations and sections, or in the execution and erection of many and superb buildings both in his own country and elsewhere; works which vie with the ancients, enlighten his contemporaries, and will arouse the imagination of those who come after us.[22]

Since the illustrated architectural book was to play so crucial a part in Palladio's work and reputation, it is worthwhile to consider the context of its production, especially since his previous two guidebooks relied solely on text. Venice was also home to the first illustrated edition of Vitruvius in 1511; this was by Fra Giocondo, and it joined other contemporary efforts in the circle of Bramante and Raphael to master some of the difficult passages of the Latin text, such as the problem of reconstructing the house of the ancients. Cesare Cesariano published a more heavily illustrated translation of Vitruvius in 1521 (Como), which included the first illustration of the Basilica of Fano.[23] The use of illustrations in these editions, like Daniele Barbaro's, still functioned more as the further explication of a problem, as the occasional visual demonstration of textual description, than as an equal partner in the communication of Vitruvius' entire program. Images, however, were becoming a more essential part of the medium of the architectural book, assuming an independent status in carrying the message, as with Serlio's well-known publications and as would Palladio's *Four Books* in 1570. That Barbaro would automatically recognize the epistemological value of employing illustrations for his Vitruvius, however, was not necessarily a given based on earlier examples and scholarly traditions of textual commentary; it speaks for his growing engagement with architectural practice, one conditioned by his Paduan experience. This interest resembled the encompassing involvement of Trissino and Alvise Cornaro in the pursuit of the intellectual basis of architecture as a Liberal Art as well as in its creative production. While Venetian patricians regularly made decisions on the building programs they funded and supervised for the government, and as private patrons, Barbaro was unusual in his level of theoretical engagement. His desire to penetrate deeply into this realm makes it likely that he would have taken an interest in Palladio with his

11   Daniele Barbaro's edition of Marcus Pollio Vitruvius, *I dieci libri dell'architettura di M. Vitruvio, tradotti et commentate da Monsignor Barbaro eletto patriarca d'Aquileggia*, Venice, Per Francesco Marcolini, 1556, titlepage

12   Daniele Barbaro's edition of Marcus Pollio Vitruvius, *I dieci libri dell'architettura di M. Vitruvio, tradotti et commentate da Monsignor Barbaro eletto patriarca d'Aquileggia*, Venice, Per Francesco Marcolini, 1556, with Barbaro coat of arms (*verso* of titlepage, atributed to Giuseppe Salviati)

specialized training in architectural humanism, and lends credence to Douglas Lewis's argument for Barbaro's early knowledge of Trissino's protégé.

Barbaro's pursuit of Vitruvian studies can be documented to the period of his assignment at the Orto dei Semplici or Botanic Garden toward the end of his long Paduan experience, which had lasted more than a decade. His appointment as supervisor of the construction of the Botanic Garden in 1545 coincided with the date that he gave for beginning the gestation of his Vitruvius. He declared at the end of Book Ten that he had been working on it for nine years, which would have been about 1546–47. Manfredo Tafuri postulated that the presence in Padua in 1547 of the noted philologist and Vitruvian scholar Claudio Tolomei (1492–1555/57), founder of the Roman Accademia della Virtù, may have provided the inspiration for such an enterprise. Barbaro was made a *provved-*

itor del Comun in 1548, the same year that Palladio was first documented in Venice, then departed on his ambassadorship to England, returning in 1551 as patriarch-elect of Aquileia. Erik Forssman believed that it was at this time that Palladio and Barbaro began their close collaboration.[24] In Venice during this period Barbaro and Palladio intersected with the ambassador of Urbino, Count Giovanni Giacomo Leonardi, formerly a friend of Trissino and a familiar of his Murano villa, and another noble with specialized interests in architecture. Leonardi's particular expertise was recorded in his *Book of Fortifications* of 1553, which Barbaro would append to his first edition of Vitruvius.[25]

Barbaro's and Palladio's visit to Rome in 1554 provided an opportunity to experience on site the architect's Vitruvian methods of drawing, and its productive role in the observation, analysis, and reconstruction of ancient buildings. His commentary indicates how

valuable this was for increasing Barbaro's comprehension of visual interpretation and explication:

> And with regard to Vitruvius, the building of Theaters, Temples, Basilicas, and those things which have the most beautiful and most hidden reasons for their proportions [*compartimenti*], have all been explained and interpreted by him [Palladio], with ready skill of hand and mind; he it is who has selected the most beautiful styles of the ancients from all over Italy and has made measurements of their works in existence.[26]

The image conjured up by the description of a younger contemporary, Paolo Gualdo, suggests that Palladio and Barbaro engaged in an open-air seminar where ancient Rome was their object. Gualdo described Palladio's fifth trip with his "special friends" the "Venetian Gentlemen," saying that "again they devoted themselves to studying, measuring and discussing the beauty and grandeur of those marvelous buildings."[27]

An increase in the number of drawings in the second edition of Vitruvius of 1567 is evidence of Barbaro's even deeper understanding, which by then also included an intimate working knowledge of Palladio's building practices from the enterprise undertaken in conjunction with his brother Marc'Antonio: their magnificent villa at Maser (ca. 1554–58) in the Trevigiana.[28] Palladio, who was noted for his genial personality – in addition to Gualdo who was quoted at the beginning of this section, Vasari similarly said: "With his many great virtues he has conjoined such an amiable and gentle nature that it makes him beloved of everyone" – and who, after all, had been mentored by Trissino, was unusual in the degree of closeness to several of his patrons, among whom by this time could be counted Daniele Barbaro.[29]

The collaboration of Palladio with both brothers at Maser offered closer acquaintance with Marc'Antonio, whose career as a statesman was established by 1559, when he was elected to the Senate, and a year later as *savio di terraferma*. In the 1560s Palladio's presence on several occasions at the Barbaro family palace at San Vidal on the Grand Canal was noted (figs. 13 and 14).[30] Marc'Antonio was away on embassy to France as orator of the Republic between 1561 and 1564. On his return, he was elected as one of the *provveditori al sal*, signaling his engagement with the cultural affairs of the government, which would show his continued support for the principles of architecture of his brother and Palladio.

It is to just this time, around 1565–70, that Paolo Veronese's portrait of Daniele has been dated on stylistic grounds, after the painter had been engaged on the fresco cycle that decorated the villa at Maser (fig. 15).[31] The ecclesiastical dress that alluded to his patriarchal title differentiates the sitter from his earlier portraits: black silk *berretta* (cap) and velvet *mozzetta* (cape) over a fine pleated white tunic. Daniele's activities, however, had not really changed since his

13 (*above left*)   Palazzo Barbaro, Grand Canal at San Vidal, Venice

14 (*left*)   Renaissance portal, Palazzo Barbaro, Grand Canal at San Vidal, Venice

15 Paolo Veronese, *Daniele Barbaro*, Amsterdam, Rijksmuseum (2529 B 6)

16 Paolo Veronese or "Alberto d'Hollanda" (Lambert Sustris), *Marc'Antonio Barbaro*, Vienna, Kunsthistorisches Museum (PG 29)

university days in Padua; still a scholar, books again are the featured attributes of the composition. This time, the viewer is allowed a glimpse of their content, confirmed by the illustrations of the two open architectural treatises, one propped against a monumental column, the other held up on the table at which the patriarch-elect is seated, turned in his chair as if gravely listening to the discourse of an unseen friend on architectural principles. Given the portrayal of the subject and the style, the portrait may have been made to commemorate the second edition of Vitruvius of 1567.[32] Certainly, it captures the essence of Barbaro's activities. Daniele's removal from civil life had been lamented, "neither layman nor priest," and he was never to succeed to the patriarchy, since its incumbent, Giovanni Grimani, outlived him; thus his studies remained his primary vocation.[33] He and his brother Marc'Antonio, in a portrait dated 1572, attributed to Paolo Veronese or Lambert Sustris (Vienna, Kunsthistorisches Museum) are represented, then, at approximately the same age, about 54 years old (fig. 16). By contrast, however, Marc'Antonio's portrait shows a patrician in active service to the State – but this reflects a later chapter in both Marc'Antonio's and Palladio's careers after Daniele's death, as well as in the changing fortunes of Venice, to which we will return.[34] The wealthy Barbaro family was one of the *case nuove*, admired for a number of distinguished scholars in the fifteenth and sixteenth centuries, and con-

sidered to be *papalisti* due to their several associations with the patriarchy of Aquileia.[35] The aggrandizement of their property at Maser followed the pattern of *papalisti* investing in the *terraferma*, the growth of which contributed to their fortune, as did their interests in the salt trade (fig. 17). Cultural allusions to the court of Rome were incorporated into the program for the villa, which in addition to its practical Venetian functionalism, to its indebtedness to theories of ancient domestic architecture, demonstrates awareness of the sophisticated development of monumental landscape architecture in Rome since the time of Bramante. Palladio had been nurtured on Vitruvian theory that gave primacy to the choice of site, in which the villa was to be "planned elegantly and practically" (*Four Books*, Bk. 2, ch. 13, 46).[36] In Pirro Ligorio's contemporary work as architect to Cardinal d'Este (and later as papal architect in Bramante's Belvedere Courtyard), in Jacopo Vignola's and Bartolomeo Ammannati's *vigna* for Julius III, Palladio and Daniele Barbaro saw villa and landscape integrated through antique elements, such as nymphaea and grottoes, which inspired their interpretation at Maser.[37]

* * *

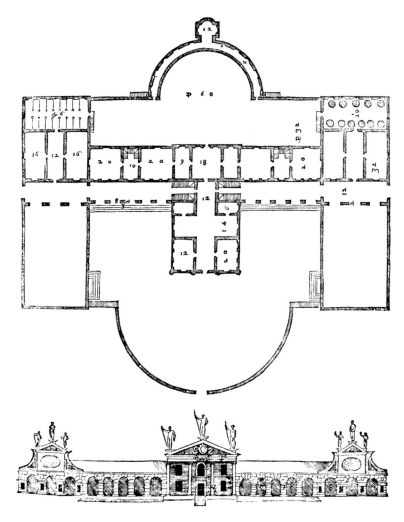

17   Andrea Palladio, Villa Barbaro at Maser, *I quattro libri dell'architettura*, Venice, Appresso Dominico de' Franceschi, 1570, lib. 2, cap. 14, 51

A Program for Architecture

In the crucial period of his first works in Venice, Palladio's association with Daniele Barbaro and the principles of Vitruvius established him as a Romanist. This was not only through patronage and its political implications, but intellectually through the reproposal of a Vitruvian language of architecture and its realization – a scientific approach to a project through drawing and its resultant program. Rudolf Wittkower emphasized the significance first of Trissino for the elevation of Palladio as an architectural humanist, then of Daniele Barbaro for the furthering of his scientific investigations, especially in mathematics, to which early biographers spoke for Palladio's affinity: "a young man of very spirited character and with a great aptitude for science and mathematics."[38] Barbaro's education in the faculty of arts and letters, which encompassed the disciplines of natural philosophy and dialectic, was strongly oriented in the Aristotelian bias of the University of Padua. In Wittkower's analysis of Barbaro's Vitruvius, it is Barbaro's method – logical and deductive – that reveals itself as Aristotelian, while the thought is often

derived from Platonic ideas, and a similar fusion is ascribed to Palladio. Manfredo Tafuri has, however, further differentiated Barbaro's Platonic ideas from the earlier mysticism of Neo-Pythagorean and Cabalist theorists due to his incorporation of a logical, scientific approach.[39] More recently, the particular Aristotelian logic of the philosophy professor Pietro Pomponazzi (1462–1525) and his influence on Vicentine and Paduan circles has been proposed; Barbaro was predisposed by his early schooling in Verona, where he had been a student of another notable Aristotelian, Benedetto Lampridio (died 1540), philologist and poet.

To some extent, the Averroist tendencies of the University of Padua, legitimizing a separation of philosophical enquiry from religious dogma, were enacted in the humanist researches of the patriarch-elect.[40] The independence of rational thought processes to examine the nature of things seems fundamental to Barbaro's empirical statements in his commentary. Also, he must have found in Palladio's archaeological methods an analogy between architecture and philology, with a shared insistence on going to the original sources. Even on drawings copied after other sources, Palladio would verify measurements through his own observations, as he said in the author's "Foreword to the Readers" in the *Four Books* (p. 5),

I elected as my master and guide Vitruvius, who is the only ancient writer on this art. I set myself the task of investigating the remains of the ancient buildings that have survived despite the ravages of time and the cruelty of the barbarians, and finding them much worthier of study than I had first thought, I began to measure all their parts minutely and with the greatest care . . .

Similar methods were being argued for an approach to history writing, and the tensions between tradition and critical historiography that resulted in the negative reception of Barbaro's efforts as historian of the Republic seem to provide a parallel to emerging distinctions between the status of *proto* (head builder) and architect.[41] The Vitruvian operations as described by Barbaro and practiced by Palladio were grounded in scientific procedure aimed at uncovering principles that allied architecture with other universal forms of knowledge, such as pure mathematics. Barbaro required that the architect "demonstrate [prove], design, distribute [arrange], order, and direct."[42] That such authority was based on a scientific procedure is affirmed by the continuation of Palladio's description discussed above,

I became so assiduous an investigator of such things that, being unable to find anything that was not made with fine judgment and beautiful proportions, I repeatedly visited various parts of Italy and abroad in order to understand the totality of buildings from their parts and commit them to drawings.[43]

The knowledge produced by this enquiry into the principles of ancient architecture would not lead to copies of set models, but rather to an equal ability on the part of the modern architect to explore the appropriate types and to produce a correct design congruent with the particular local requirements of the project. This faith in learned principles liberated the architect from mere reproduction because it provided a system in which the intellect was applied to a specific problem – experience provided examples to test – which resulted in original compositions. Palladio observed this toward the end of his "Foreword" (p. 6):

> while still remaining greatly indebted to those who, through their own ingenious inventions and the experience they gained, have bequeathed us the rules of this art, for they opened up an easier and more direct route to the study of new things, and (thanks to them) we know of many things that would perhaps have remained hidden.[44]

He then announced that for lack of examples of ancient palaces and villas he would include designs of his own fabrics. If we are attentive to what Palladio has just told us about his method, then we can recognize the revolutionary import such a statement had for established custom. His "investigatione di cose nuove" was a critical operation that threatened the primacy of the decision-making body in Venetian architecture, patricians, and re-placed it into the hands of specialists, architects.

In this sense, Barbaro's hopes to educate his fellow patricians to engage with the theoretical body of architecture, which Tafuri has characterized as perhaps the most original aspect of the commentary, embodied a contradiction and was fated to meet resistance.[45] If Venetian architectural language had managed to absorb the classicism of Sansovino and Sanmicheli under the terms of the Romanizing program of building (Doge Andrea Gritti's *renovatio*), it had also established a perception of that style as continuing to operate subject to the traditional system of *provveditori* and *proti*. Furthermore, once the presence of a classical style was superimposed on the Venetian urban landscape, framed as an identifiable alternative to the recognizable characteristics of Venetian tradition, then it presented an opportunity to engender opposition. Nor were the political circumstances of the late 1550s so receptive to the adoption of the imagery of the "first Rome" as had been the post-Cambrai period that had established it. As Tafuri described it, the "metastorical" dialect of Venetian architectural language was bound up with the unique identity construction of the city, whereas the "universalism" of ancient Roman architecture could all too easily be read as associated with the papal heirs to Rome, thus being bound up in the hardening factionalism of *giovani* versus *vecchi* (see pp. 36–40) Also, support for Sansovino and Sanmicheli – still active – may have precluded such wholesale adoption of Palladio and his rigorous approach to ancient and modern architecture from those who were inclined to Roman style. It is here, operating within class analysis, that a clearly defined factionalism seems to fail late in the mid-sixteenth century, but the very contradiction that Tafuri noticed in Barbaro may offer the possibility for further refinement of the categories of analysis. An implied critique of Sansovino in the words of the opening preface of Palladio's *Four Books* was preceded by the limited mentions in Barbaro's commentary.

The eventual success of Antonio da Ponte (*proto al sal* 1563–97), who had begun as a carpenter, was founded on the possibility of

18 Jacopo Bassano, *Antonio da Ponte*, Paris, Musée du Louvre

his offering an architecture sufficiently versed in the vocabulary of Sansovino and mid-sixteenth-century classicism, yet not averse to incorporating local architectural models as desired by his patrons. In his portrait, he is shown with the instrument that at once identified his craft, but also linked it to the science of mathematics – a compass – and the rich velvet of his clothing indicates his comfortable economic status (fig. 18).[46] As *proto*, da Ponte satisfied those who supported a classical style within the traditional framework of architectural practice, and effectively brought his experience into service.

For the second group of supporters of the classical style, however, a reliance on "models" and on experience was not adequately grounded in the scientific exploration of an architecture based on classical principles, or "types." When Vitruvius described the ideal education of the architect as grounded in both practice and theory, he provided the justification for scientific method:

> In all things, but especially in architecture, there are two inherent categories: the signified and the signifier. The signified is the proposed subject of discussion; it is signified by a reasoned demonstration carried out according to established principles of knowledge.[47]

It was this paradigm of approaching architecture as a science that would distinguish Palladio and Barbaro.[48]

The "program" is what Ackerman so perceptively framed as the social dynamic encompassed by brick and stone, marble and wood, terracotta and lead. It is more than expressive of values; it forms such values while being a product of them. The dimension of the program that is perhaps the most subversive aspect is the projectual, the projection of the architect's mode of intellectual and creative process. The program is structured around the discipline of the architect's thought, or method of thinking. Here we recognize that intersection of *techne* and *eidos* that Tafuri described, or of "mechanical" and "liberal" stages as Puppi stated.[49] The sixteenth century was a territory of new mental models: "Europe" grew out of the forced recognition of Christianity's multiple personalities; new identities were being forged, together with new processes for shaping the spaces these identities would occupy.[50] Whoever controlled the program shaped control over the terrain, which itself would shape human action. With the adoption of the scientific procedure enunciated by Barbaro, and practiced by Palladio, the engrained grooves of a known pattern would be indelibly rewritten. It was crucial that, with the loss of the familiar in pursuit of the ideal, recognizable identity be extracted from the old to forge a connection to new values. This, too, was the role of the program, to re-place memory, through erection and erasure. Nor was it insignificant that the most common mnemonic device was architectural images.[51] *Loci*, that is, "place," and *imagines*, "images," were supplied with form, content, and arrangement: a building imagined, objects chosen for their suggestive associations, the structure of the building and placement of the objects ordered so as to provide an unfolding mental experience of recall. Content governed distribution, as a building is compartmented according to its function and meaning. An architecture of memory was not only the province of rhetoric, but of history. In the "Prologue" of Leon Battista Alberti's *On the Art of Building in Ten Books*, a Thucydian notion of historical evidence is attributed to architecture:

> As to the imperial authority and fame that the Latins got from their building, I need only mention the various tombs and other ruins of past glory still visible all around, which have taught us to accept much of the historical tradition that may otherwise have seemed less convincing.[52]

Not only was contemporary identity at stake, but that of posterity, and the authority to determine that lay in the interpreter of the program. Among the several disciplines in the Liberal Arts that Vitruvius thought indispensable to the architect, from philosophy to music, medicine to geometry, he stated: "He should know a great deal of history because architects often include ornaments in their work, and ought to be able to supply anyone who asks with an explanation why they have introduced certain motifs" (*Ten Books*, Bk. 1, ch. 1, pts. 5–6). More than a knowledge of ancient forms, more than a strict expression of structure, the architectural elements were invested with an iconography that held historical content and purpose. The program of architecture thus had several functional

19 Andrea Palladio, with figures attributed to Giovanni Antonio Rusconi, *Caryatids*, in "L'Architettura, col commento di Daniele Barbaro in volgare," Venice, Biblioteca Nazionale Marciana, MS. It. IV, 152 (5106), 369

metaphors, from declaring its social activity (church, house, etc.), to structural role (column and support, etc.), to ideological message, as Vitruvius illustrated with the figures of the Caryatids and Persians (fig. 19). He moves from the obvious, that these are marble statues used to support a roof, to the historical lesson drawn from knowledge of their specific origins: the lesson in the case of the enslaved Caryatids was atonement for the sin of their state in siding with Greece's enemies, whereas the defeated Persians were to remind the Greeks to be ready to defend their independence.[53] In this way, an architect filled the building with typological content. Determination of the program first demanded consideration of type and function.

Howard Burns has found in the process of Palladio's work an analogy to the Albertian notion of the origination of ideas in the mind (echoed in Barbaro's Vitruvius). In the sheets with multiple abbreviated sketches for an individual project, such as those for a Venetian palace, Palladio studied alternative arrangements from his mental repertory of architectural forms appropriate to the current site and commission (figs. 20 and 21). Palladio recollected the repertory both through memory and drawn records, the fruit of his assiduous consideration of ancient and modern architecture and theory, of types in recombination subject to principles derived from his studies.[54] In this form of rapidly drawn alternatives, Palladio was not concerned with invention through graphic means. Rather, he was visualizing his research in the permutations of type that would yield the Vitruvian ideals: "durability, convenience, and beauty" (*utilitas, commoditas, venustas*).[55] In true Vitruvian architecture there was not one correct model, since no particular situation would be identical with another. Therefore the key was in the approach to the design. The place of drawing in the process functioned differently for Palladio, where, for example, it was a mental operation first, and the graphic forms were a demonstration of the intellectual work. For Michelangelo, by comparison, it produced an evolving sequence of organically developed designs.[56] Both Palladio and Michelangelo realized *disegno* differently, reproducing the "idea," a concept held in the imagination. This is guided by the *giudizio* of the architect, whose understanding of the principles and their application to the

circumstances form the rationale for the decision-making process, one that partakes both of the mind and the senses. Vasari described the qualities that distinguished the true architect:

> After all, however, good stones and well-tempered tools apart, the one thing essential is the art, the intelligence, and the judgment of those who use them, for there is the greatest difference between these artists, although they may all use the same method, as to the measure of grace and beauty they impart to the works which they execute. This enables us to discern and to recognize the perfection of work done by those who really understand, as opposed to that of others who know less.[57]

That difference, Vasari later attributed to an internal arbiter, the *giudizio dell'occhio*:

> All these things are best appreciated by a correct eye, which, if it have discrimination, can hold the true compasses and estimate exact measurements, because by it alone shall be awarded praise or blame.[58]

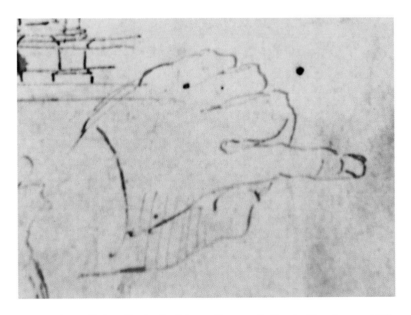

21　Andrea Palladio, *Sketches for Palazzo Communale, Brescia, Nymphaeum at Villa Maser, and Venetian Palaces*, London, Royal Institute of British Architects, X, 15, detail of Palladio's hand

20 (*left*)　Andrea Palladio, *Sketches for Palazzo Communale, Brescia, Nymphaeum at Villa Maser, and Venetian Palaces*, London, Royal Institute of British Architects, X, 15

Although Palladio said little directly concerning the process, the very format of his *Four Books*, with its emphasis on drawn and measured illustrations, reinforces the conclusions inferred from his drawn and built remains. He did allude to the value of visualization in the forewords to Book Three (p. 5) and Book Four (p. 3):

I have devoted, after long hours of immense effort, to organizing the remaining fragments of ancient buildings into a form that will (I hope) delight those interested in antiquities and which devotees of architecture will find extremely useful: in fact, one learns much more rapidly from well-chosen examples, when measuring and observing whole buildings and all their details on a sheet of paper, than one does from written descriptions, when reliable and precise information can only be extracted slowly and with a considerable mental effort by the reader from what he is reading and can only be put into practice with great difficulty.[59]

Drawing, then, has a cognitive effect, more directly and completely communicating information to the viewer than words to the reader, which require a process of assimilation and translation in the mind in order to reproduce an image. Palladio's labor and his long studies present to his audience the repertory of examples and discussions of the principles by which they were conceived so that they may have access to the type appropriate to their situation:

I intend therefore to illustrate in this book the form and ornaments of many ancient temples of which one can still see the ruins and which I have recorded in drawings, so that anyone can understand the form and ornaments with which churches must be built. And although one can see only portions of some of them standing above ground, I have nonetheless proceeded to deduce [*conietturando*] from them what they must have been like when they were complete, taking into consideration the foundations that could be observed as well. Vitruvius has helped me immensely in this because, by comparing what I have observed with what he teaches us, it has not proved too difficult for me to arrive at an understanding of their appearance [*aspetto*] and forms.[60]

Palladio's "conjecture," in the procedure of reconstruction, is a similar activity to the one that an architect must go through in creating a work, when "type" is processed for the solution to a particular problem.[61] It is the scientific sequence of "dimostra, dissegna, distribuisce, ordina e commanda." *Giudizio* is the active principle of the program, for it animates the assembly. The difference between what occurs when the architect has recourse to such a process as compared to one who depends on a model is epitomized by the originality with which Michelangelo was always credited; yet, as Vasari explained:

Michelangelo enjoyed so profound and retentive a memory that he could accurately recall the works of others after he had seen them and use them for his own purposes so skillfully that scarcely anyone ever remarked it. Nor has he ever repeated himself in his own work, because he remembered everything he did.[62]

Michelangelo goes beyond merely copying a model, for he sees through the particulars of all possible appropriate examples to arrive at what is the essential "for his own purpose." Such a transformation is executed through the judgment and *memory* of the architect. The incorporation of this intellectual and creative process is a requisite to truly powerful architecture, and what makes architects such as Palladio still relevant; it is not just the use of the Palladian and thermal windows, domes, and frontispieces. In helping to shape the epistemological changes of the later sixteenth century, there were different ramifications arising from both architects' methods. On the one hand, the reliance of Michelangelo on personal creative development worked out in the drawing itself placed an emphasis on innate genius. His followers, therefore, were reliant on Michelangelo as a model, since his method argued its own singularity. Palladio, on the other hand, was proposing a method based on something outside of his own authority, access to principles that could be learned and that would provide solutions specific to the program. The very process of experimentation would ally architecture with other developing modes of scientific investigation in the intellectual circles frequented by the commentator and illustrator of the Vitruvius of 1556.[63]

The Greatest Work of Art

Palladio's *I quattro libri dell'architettura* has been characterized as his greatest work of art, albeit a paradoxical success.[64] Like his other works, it has a relationship to other models, such as the architectural treatises of Leon Battista Alberti, Francesco di Giorgio, Sebastiano Serlio, the editions of Vitruvius by Fra Giocondo, Cesare Cesariano, Daniele Barbaro, and to the available repertory of modes of architectural drawing, such as perspective, orthogonal projection, and various illusionistic techniques.[65] Palladio was concerned to convey a maximum amount of information with a minimum of distortion, yet his predominant choice of orthogonal projection (*orthografia* or *orthographia*) over perspective (*scenografia* or *skiographia*), for example, would result in the sacrifice of some visibility of details and three-dimensionality to achieve the least distortion. In some drawings, a middle way might be used, and this could extend even to the pages of the *Four Books*, where the one technique of illusionism consistently employed was shading (figs. 22a, b and 23a, b).[66] Where a rendering in orthogonal projection was strictly followed, Palladio devised a way to present the missing information abstracted as a separate graphic. This rises out of traditional workshop practice for executing details of ornament: bases, capitals, cornices, and the like, as separate full-scale drawings to be used as templates by their executors in wood and stone. These detail drawings were called *sagome* by Palladio, or sometimes simply *profili* or *modelli*, and known as *modani* in central Italy.[67] Their purpose was to translate the three-dimensional into pure two-dimensional form, replete with all the signs that would communicate by a simple curve or straight edge the intricacies of a particular classical molding. There is little in such an image to help a viewer imaginatively to reconstruct the

22a Andrea Palladio, Temples of the Sun and Moon (Basilica of Maxentius), plan, section, and elevation, *I quattro libri dell'architettura*, Venice, Appresso Dominico de' Franceschi, 1570, lib. 4, cap. 10, 37

22b Andrea Palladio, Temples of the Sun and Moon (Basilica of Maxentius), section, profile, and details of soffit, *I quattro libri dell'architettura*, Venice, Appresso Dominico de' Franceschi, 1570, lib. 4, cap. 10, 38

three-dimensional object, but to a builder it provided a pattern easier to read and use than a drawing with illusionistic rendering. An element, such as the soffit of a cornice, could be shown in perspective, but would be invisible if presented straight-on in orthogonal projection, so it is extracted and a segment of the design is presented as though it, too, was drawn straight-on. These different views are often presented on the same page, whereas in the conceptual building the viewer would be forced to move from one ideal point of view, to look at the elevation, then move, so as to position oneself directly beneath the cornice looking up. The representation of the façade as a view divorced from the context supplied by perspective is thus granted a forceful independence. Palladio mediated this rupture through another convention of rendering, the section. This imaginary view through a plane of the

interior of a building might achieve its own independence,[68] or demand that the viewer simultaneously encompass multiple layers of a building, as with Bramante's Tempietto in Rome (fig. 24).

Here the silhouette forms a single image on the page, but an irregular line reveals the section of the interior on the left, and the elevation on the right. Strong incised parallel hatching throws forms into relief, so the left half becomes concave and the right convex, while the division is not a simple line, but rather is rendered in foreshortening to give the depth of the stone cladding. The rustic character of the line and its implied jagged surface give the impression of an ancient ruin, legitimizing the otherwise wholly conceptual rendering of multiple views, impossible to be simultaneously perceived in the world of space and time. Palladio thus posited specific places for the viewer of his buildings to inhabit,

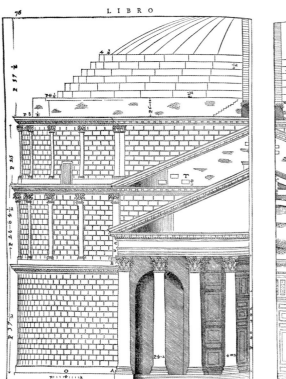

23a   Andrea Palladio, Pantheon, façade and façade under portico, *I quattro libri dell'architettura*, Venice, Appresso Dominico de' Franceschi, 1570, lib. 4, cap. 20, 76–77

23b   Andrea Palladio, Pantheon, ornaments of portico and elevation of interior, *I quattro libri dell'architettura*, Venice, Appresso Dominico de' Franceschi, 1570, lib. 4, cap. 20, 80–81

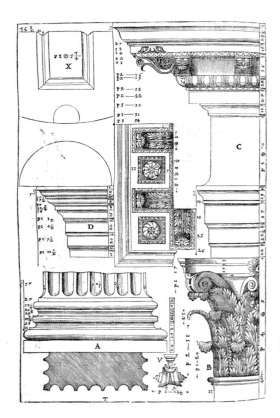

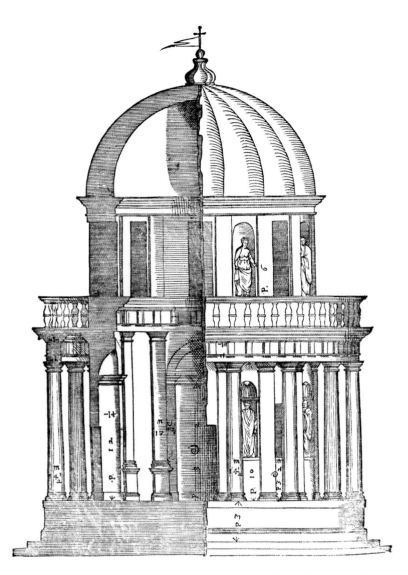

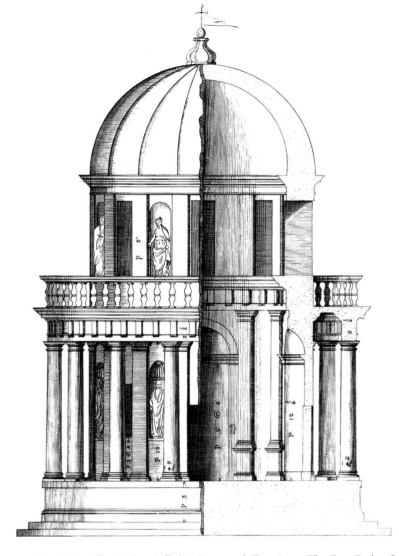

24 Andrea Palladio, Bramante's Tempietto, *I quattro libri dell'architettura*, Venice, Appresso Dominico de' Franceschi, 1570, lib. 4, cap. 17, 66

25 Isaac Ware after Andrea Palladio, Bramante's Tempietto, *The Four Books of Andrea Palladio's Architecture*, Bk. 4, ch. 20, London, 1738

directly in front of, or from the side. The same holds for the interior, for its assumed "transparency" would require movement from an initial position at a given moment in time to a new one, behind the façade or the side wall, or else before the final construction of the cladding or after exposure and age have stripped it to reveal structural layers. The plan unites these separate views. It represents the total essence of the building, for, in its drawn state, all is implied: the complete elevation, of exterior and interior simultaneously, the entire circumference without so defined a prejudice for one aspect, and space both without and within the building, as well as ornament and proportion. The ideal place for the viewing of the plan is in the mind's eye.

Did Palladio's own method of communication, then, contribute to a tension between façade and building, or can we rescue a notion of correspondence from other of his theoretical efforts or actual practice? The graphic transformation of the *Four Books* in subsequent editions and translations is well known; the two eighteenth-century English-language editions of Palladio that we have inherited from the efforts of the refined neo-Classical circle of Richard Boyle, 3rd Earl of Burlington (1695–1753), offer conflicting interpretations of his style. The first edition was produced by Giacomo Leoni in 1715, and its baroque style was criticized for its libertine departures from the original, so Isaac Ware was supported in reproducing a more "faithful" edition, which was issued in 1738. It is the cool, rationalized, and more precise engravings of the latter that have made their way onto the same bookshelves that hold Wittkower's *Architectural Principles*, since Ware's translation was reproduced in a Dover facsimile edition in 1965 and remains in print.[69] The very conceptual elements of Palladio's illustrations are rendered even more abstract in Ware's graphic representation (fig. 25). And it is not only the dissemination of a specific interpretive character in the graphic effects of the *Four Books*: it has frozen our perception of the architect a full decade before his death in 1580, and subsequent to his encounters with the actual design and execution of church façades. His projects for churches, let us remember, are represented only by a few brief mentions in the text, so this entire aspect of his production, the most significant in Venice, must be inferred by his discussions of Temples. Palladio both equated the ancient and the Christian temples as places of worship and understood the further history of the Christian temple to have incorporated the form of the ancient basilica.[70] This confluence demonstrates a significant characteristic of Palladio's thought about the past: his ability to encompass historical transience in his project of emulation, whether of the physical fabric or its function.

"The Cognizance of History"

After the *Four Books*, Palladio next published *I Commentari di C. Giulio Cesare ("The Commentaries of Julius Caesar")* (Appresso Pietro de' Franceschi, Venice, 1575), in which he included illustrations of the Roman camps, battle arrays, and city walls, made, he declared on the frontispiece, "to facilitate for the reader, the cognizance of history" (fig. 26).[71] Examining the purposes for which Palladio entered into publishing ventures, there is a general one ostensibly to communicate the state of knowledge about a subject and the method of its scientific investigation, from which principles and models would be derived, as he did in his own work as discussed above. The after-history of the *Four Books* demonstrates his overwhelming success in achieving that aim.[72] Then there are specific purposes, which here will be limited to concentrating on those aspects relevant to Palladio's development of patronage relationships, and their effect on the profession of architecture.

The first is that Palladio's publications, which book-end his Venetian career – beginning in 1554, with plans for further publications unrealized at his death – convey his status as a humanist.[73] Palladio had academic associations (with the Accademia Olimpica in Vicenza, and Accademia del Disegno in Florence) as discussed, but his book production transmitted literary as well as visual expression of his intellectual accomplishments, most importantly, of the classics as not only observed, but read. The dedications brought him associations with patrons of prestige, a common strategy of authors, such as the dedicatee of the *Caesar*, Jacopo (Giacomo) Boncampagni, General of the Church (1573).[74] His collaboration on the Vitruvius associated him with a highly regarded humanist, Daniele Barbaro. That he intended to confer such status in some measure to his sons is exemplified by the *Caesar*, which had originated with his eldest and third-born sons, Leonida and Orazio, who had both died untimely in 1572, leaving their father to bring it out in their memory, as his foreword declares. The education and apprenticeships of his sons are further indications of the professionalization of his family status, with Leonida an architect, his second-born Marc'Antonio a sculptor (working with Alessandro Vittoria in

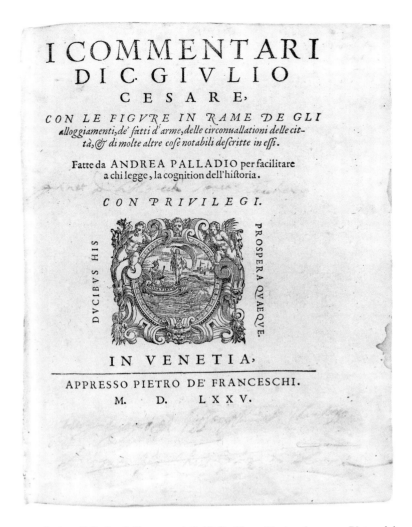

26 Andrea Palladio, *I Commentari di Giulio Cesare*, Venice, Appresso Pietro de' Franceschi, 1575, titlepage

Venice by 1560), Orazio having taken a degree in jurisprudence from Padua and working with his father, and the fourth son, Silla, a member of the Accademia Olimpica in Vicenza, and fulfilling bureaucratic offices for the academy, as well as acting as his father's literary executor.[75]

Second, they communicate his role as collaborator and educator. The former role is one of the transformative contributions of Palladio to the profession. It stems in part from the unusual circumstances of his specialized humanist education with Giangiorgio Trissino, still actively acknowledged many years after the Vicentine aristocrat's death in the foreword to the *Caesar*, whom Palladio credits with having introduced him to the study of ancient military discipline.[76] The relationship between an artist elevated in the *famiglia* of a patron in a court system would not be the same as what Palladio would find in the Republic. Yet the interactions between Venetian magistracies and local aristocracies in the Veneto, particularly in the cultural environments of patrician circles, academies, and the Studio of Padua, prepared him for success in developing strong personal relationships with several important patrons, notably Daniele and Marc'Antonio Barbaro and Jacopo Contarini, as fellow humanists. Palladio seems to have been able not only to invent and propose complex programs of his own to prospective clients, but to engage in active collaboration with so-inclined patrons, as his comments already cited convey.[77] His publications advertise this collaborative relationship, itself then serving as a role model to educate other practitioners and their clients to their roles. Gualdo remarked on this two-way process by which Palladio advanced his work: his already quoted statement, "Palladio was a most able and attractive conversationalist, so that he gave the most intense pleasure to the Gentlemen and Lords with whom he dealt," was completed by:

> The same is true of the workmen he used, whom he kept constantly cheerful, treating them with so many pleasant attentions that they all worked with the most exceptional good cheer. He eagerly and lovingly taught them the best principles of the art, in such a way that there was not a mason, stonecutter, or carpenter who did not understand the measurements, elements, and rules of true architecture.[78]

Palladio expressed his goal in the *Caesar*, "that the fruits of my labors since my youth to know and bring to light many of the most noble memories of antiquity, be not only for my own use, but to provide access to all those who have a similar desire for this knowledge."[79] His publications provided a mutual platform for a new patron–client relationship to emerge.

Third, his publications show different aspects of his business practices. In this period, there was a spectrum of possible relationships between author, printer, publisher, and bookseller, and Palladio's changed over time, showing his growing success in Venice. His early books, the "Description of the Churches of Rome" and the "Antiquities of Rome" probably had a ready pilgrim and tourist market, making such publications fairly safe ventures for the printers. For such works, authors were often paid only in copies of the book; printers could finance such runs themselves or obtain partial or whole financial backing from publishers, or from a sponsor such as

the Church. Such information is not always evident from the text, unless there are supporting documents.[80] One such source of information is the copyright, or privilege, the application for which may be found in government records, the evidence usually displayed on the frontispiece, and violations in legal records. Indeed, sometimes it was only the fines levied on the latter that would produce income for the privilege holder, particularly if the arrangement to cover the costs of producing the book did not return parts of the profits of book sales to an author. The scholar Giangiorgio Zorzi identified Palladio as having contributed costs towards the publication of the *Four Books*, although it was his printer who received the privilege; it is unknown whether Palladio was paid outright for his drawings and text, or was recompensed with some other arrangement.[81] Dedicatees were often financial backers, or publishers, or flattered in the hope of obtaining their sponsorship for a privilege.[82] Palladio himself applied for and received the privilege for the *Caesar*: it constituted a memorial for the loss of his two sons who had begun the work.

That Palladio had the means to act in part as publisher as well as author also indicates that his economic status was more secure, although it was never to the point that he disdained independent activities of a modest nature, although this defies the image of the architect as a heroic builder of great monuments. The *Caesar* would elevate Palladio to the status of other humanists, notably his patrons; it would indicate his expertise in ancient military technique and strategy – a necessary art for governance and the beginning of the development of the specialized professional in military engineering – and demonstrate again his invaluable ability to render the subject in both visual and literary terms, thus performing acts of collaboration and education. When the *Caesar* was published in 1575, Palladio's practice constituted a range of activities, from services such as providing expert opinion, to supplying the design for a capital, to co-designing the program and co-supervising the establishment of a major public building campaign; even at the apex of his career he continued his private enterprises.[83]

PART II

VENETIAN PATRONAGE

INTRODUCTION

PALLADIO ARRIVED ON THE VENETIAN SCENE in the 1550s. His earliest successes came in the second half of that decade, and they were for ecclesiastical projects. This would remain the trajectory of Palladio's career in Venice, despite the growing acknowledgment of his fame and stature as architect. A number of reasons have been offered by scholars to explain this pattern. At the core of all explanations lies the nexus of relationships – alliances and enmities – from cultural to political realms that governed decision-making. Overlapping contexts conditioned the field for Palladio's reception and the response of the architect to those conditions, both in the relations he established with specific patrons and in his development of an architectural enterprise. These conditions in turn affected the field, maybe more than could have been expected in terms of future architectural style. Yet, perhaps, it was this effect on the field that has more to commend our attention to it, for the process of Venetian identity creation (the so-called myth of Venice) is characterized by such strategies of assimilation, which we will explore.[1]

Palladio's Venetian Career

The three decades of Palladio's activity in Venice until his death in 1580 was a period that marked a shift in the dominance of the ruling families of the Venetian patriciate and in emphasis from colonial empire to city-state. There was an established cultural hegemony. It was expressed in a dominant architectural language whose voice was accepted in its interpretation of the classical past and Venetian tradition. As Palladio challenged himself in his own project to absorb the precepts of ancient architecture, so he challenged Venice:

I hope therefore that this manner of building will, to the benefit of all, soon achieve that level so desirable in all the arts, and which

almost seems to have been achieved in this part of Italy already: for it is not only in Venice, where all the fine arts flourish and which is the sole remaining exemplar of the grandeur and magnificence of the Romans, that one *begins* to see buildings of quality since master Giacomo Sansovino, the celebrated sculptor and architect, *first began* to make known the fine style [*la bella maniera*], as can be seen in the Procuratie Nuove (not to mention his many other beautiful works), which is perhaps the richest and most ornate building made since the ancients.[2]

This was Palladio's opening salvo in his "Foreword to the Readers," in Book One of his *Four Books* (p. 5). His next words continued to direct the Reader to a smaller and lesser known city, Vicenza, where he credits the architectural sagacity of his noble patrons with giving him the "opportunity to put into practice what I now publish."

Palladio's characterization of Venice and its architectural practice was the fruit of nearly twenty years of attempting to establish his work in the city. What is particularly significant is his identification of recent architecture there as heir to ancient Rome. But his wording also implies that Venice has not yet fully realized her heritage, and, by extension, that his own uncompromising efforts had been better comprehended by the Vicentine nobility. The date of publication for his *Four Books* was a crucial one for his mature career: 1570 was a year that brought important personal changes to Palladio's life, as it was one that began an era of upheaval and crisis for Venice. The last decade of Palladio's life coincided with a period in Venetian history that can be characterized, without resorting to hyperbole, as a major turning point, setting the course for its subsequent development in the modern era. In 1570 the same Jacopo Sansovino that Palladio speaks of in his preface died, so too did Palladio's great patron and collaborator, Daniele Barbaro, patriarch-elect of Aquileia, and Palladio himself transferred his family from Vicenza to Venice. While these events were significant to the architect, the fundamental relationship between Palladio and the Serenis-

ANDREAS PALLADIVS

ex eleganti antiqua tabella
apud March. Capra Patricios Vicetinos.

sima had been established in the 1550s. The story relating how the expressive content of Palladio's architectural language was disclosed in this environment is entwined with the story of the formation of the city's modern identity.

A somewhat heterogeneous collection of activities will be grouped in this chapter with the intention of demonstrating how Palladio operated as an architect in circumstances other than his major building commissions. Many were never realized beyond paper, but they demonstrate his ambitions in two areas of patronage not otherwise well represented in his Venetian œuvre: designs for palaces and commissions in parish churches. Another activity, perhaps undervalued, reaches into the broader aspect of architectural practice in the city – projects for which he was called in as an expert, outside of any formal capacity. The last category to be considered will be the patronage of one of the youth groups in Venice, a Compagnia della Calza (Company of the Hose), whose membership was drawn from the patriciate, some of whom had been private patrons of Palladio, and would form links to further patronage opportunities to be explored in later chapters.

CHAPTER TWO

THE STATE OF THE PATRICIATE

PALLADIO'S CAREER IN VENICE DID NOT MIRROR the pattern of patronage that he had experienced in Vicenza, where domestic projects for the local nobility prevailed. For private patrons from the Venetian patriciate his main efforts in domestic architecture remained outside the city, in the villas that he designed on the *terraferma* for the Pisani, Corner, Barbaro (fig. 27), Foscari, Mocenigo, Badoer, and Contarini. There would be no substantial practice in palace building in Venice. Despite this lack, the members of the Venetian patriciate with whom Palladio associated were crucial for his establishment in the capital and his success as in a new area for him of ecclesiastical projects. This was a period in which Venice experienced further structural transformation of the family and social estates, which affected the practice of patronage – and clientage – as did changes brought about by external political and economic forces. Palladio came to Venice already associated with some particular cultural, social, and political networks, and the implications of these connections will first be examined.

A growing concern over incipient factionalism throughout the sixteenth century has been regarded as a result of the myriad tensions straining the Venetian ideal of *unanimitas*, and can be seen in the new constructions of identity that emerge in the period. The role that culture played in both shaping and reflecting that identity is significant, and monumental architecture, above all, was at issue in defining the visual expression of the State.

"Refeudalization" of the Terraferma

In order to understand the circumstances of Palladio's entry into Venice, it is important to look at the character of Venetian society in the preceding period of the second quarter of the sixteenth century. At this time he was gaining stature as an architect in Vicenza and beginning to acquire Venetian patrons. The larger political and economic situation of the years in which the Veneto struggled to

recover in the aftermath of the War of the League of Cambrai (1508–17) and the Peace of Bologna in 1530 produced a sort of détente among what would otherwise seem to be irreconcilable groups. It was particularly those aristocratic cultures in the cities governed by La Dominante, as Venice was called, that sought to re-establish their hegemony, economic and political, circumscribed as it was by the ruling class of Venetians who were inserted into the local scenes as territorial overseers in the highest jurisdictional (rector and *podestà*), military (captain), and religious offices. To do so required cooperation with these Venetian authorities, and the ability to rebuild their capital, which, as various writers have observed, belonged to some of the same trends of "nascent capitalism" that could be found north of the Alps, where classic economic theory has traditionally been associated with the growth of Calvinism.[3] During this period of reconstruction, Venetian economic interests included increased land reclamation alongside mercantile endeavors founded on trade and shipping, carried on by the patrician class as well as by Venetian citizens (fig. 28).[4]

Concerns that landed interests would transform the Venetians' long-held maritime identity and encourage aristocratic pretensions fueled contemporary rhetoric that opposed these interests (although they had long been entwined in actual fact). The effects of land ownership were characterized by the traditionalist Girolamo Priuli in his *Diarii* in 1509:

How many citizens and nobles there were who could have put their money into land and other goods, but did not want to do so, to spare themselves the trouble of going to the mainland! Many too wanted to avoid the expenses of horses and carriages, for the mainland calls for luxuries, such as estates and great houses, with other expenditure, and much of the income is consumed in such pleasures. Some, again, were anxious not to turn their sons into country bumpkins, for ever attending to their estates, and to give them no such pretext they were reluctant to

ventures. The *cittadini* ran the bureaucracy of government and the professions and skilled trades, with further distinctions being made for those of native birth, *originari*, from whom the members of the chancery were drawn and who enjoyed tax privileges in trade similar to the patriciate. The *popolo* ranged from successful foreigners, desirous of acquiring the privilege of citizenship, to modest shopkeepers, artisans, and laborers, situated in guild structures, to the poor, sustained by the charity and justice of the organized relief programs of the upper estates – although estate was no sure definer of wealth or poverty. Pressures from the disruptions of war on the *terraferma* had enlarged the poor, since *contadini*, country peasants, had moved into the urban capital. The clergy had some distinct privileges, but Venice limited these, and it was not named as a separate order by contemporaries.[8]

The "closing" or *Serrata* of the patriciate had evolved through a series of laws beginning during the dogates of Pietro Gradenigo (1288–1311), Marino Zorzi (1311–12), and Giovanni Soranzo (1312–28), with the modern character of the patriciate assuming greater definition in the fifteenth century, which Stanley Chojnacki termed the "second *Serrata*." A profound indication that the long process of

28   Cesare Vecellio, "Merchant," *De gli habiti antichi, et moderni di diversi parti del mondo libri due*, Venice, 1610, woodcuts by Cristoforo Guerra [Christoph Chrieger], Biblioteca del Museo Correr, Stampe H 34/1, tav. 91

buy land and wanted their heirs to apply themselves to commerce and become merchants instead, following the most ancient custom of Venice.[5]

This reshaping of identity along an aristocratic model became increasingly obvious even to an outside observer; a century later, the English ambassador (1610–16), Sir Dudley Carleton, wrote:

> Theyr former course of life was marchandising, which is now quite left and they looke to landward buing house and lands, furnishing themselfs with coch and horses, and giving themselfs the goode time with more shew and gallantrie than was wont. . . . They now send them [theyr sonnes] to travaile and to learne more of the gentleman than the marchant.[6]

Although Priuli predicted cultural decline in the move away from the urban center, both writers, a century apart, saw that the move to the country resulted in gentrification – exemplified for both men by the adoption of the horse and carriage (fig. 29). The proud structure of the social contract that Venice boasted as the key to her longevity as a Republic was at stake, the balance of power that resulted from her "mixed constitution."[7]

Venetian society was divided into four "orders" or "estates": the legally recognized distinctions of the closed patriciate; the *cittadini*, or citizens; the *popolo*, or people; and, less officially, the clergy. Generally put, the patriciate governed the Republic and their business

29   Paolo Veronese, *Villa with Carriages*, Stanza di Bacco, Villa Barbaro, Maser

delimiting the patriciate had reached another defining moment was the creation of an official record, the *Libro d'oro*, or Golden Book, in 1506. Any fluidity that had allowed penetration into the governing class was now curtailed. The right to membership required stricter proofs, defined by paternal registration in the Great Council and legitimate patrician birth. As the makeup of the patriciate became more rigid, so too did defining categories of identity within it, whether by longevity of the family, size, or income, with the largest and wealthiest known as *i primi della terra*, the first of the land, playing the most influential roles in Venetian government.[9] The many parallels that had allowed for a certain harmony between the patrician-merchant class and the citizen-merchants would be strained by a further shift of major wealthy families in the patriciate to a landed, agrarian role that more closely simulated courtly models of nobility, already present in the "neo-feudal aristocracies" of the mainland.

The rapprochement of Venetian patricians and *terraferma* aristocrats seems to have had its cultural apotheosis in the villa *all'antica*, which was both a display of the accumulation of wealth and a statement of sovereignty in the rural landscape.[10] Palladio would be instrumental in shaping such an environment and he made his name in it. Through its adoption of the style of ancient architecture, the Veneto farm was elevated to the status of the urban *palazzo*, transferred to the country, and endowed with the functions of the classical *villegiatura*, or villa life. That these country estates were intended to produce capital through their intensive agricultural endeavors distinguished them and their owners from the pleasure villas built as suburban retreats or from those constructed elsewhere in Italy as seasonal country residences, such as contemporary villas being made for the cardinals of the papal court, for example. The chivalric pleasures of hunting (Palladio's patron Zorzon Corner is shown with one of the falcons his family imported for this purpose) and other entertainments formed a part of most owners' activities, as did classical study (fig. 30). The Venetians often claimed to model themselves on that earlier Republic to which they felt themselves true heirs, the Roman Republic of the *rei rusticae scriptores*, whose agricultural treatises were incorporated into the humanistic studies of the elite. In a dialogue set in 1553 between a Brescian nobleman and his guest, Cato the Censor's rejection of Rome for the country is cited as a virtue, and the speaker rhetorically questioned:

> What else can it be that persuaded so many Romans to give up their high state in order to live and die in their villas, if not the clear realization that only here can one find that treasure of liberty, plus all the delights that every sensible man in the world could enjoy?[11]

The appeal to liberty was not casual in this context, but would have been recognized as one of the crucial rhetorical concepts to bind the disparate estates of the Venetian territory, the *terra libera*, as it was often referred to. Indeed, one of the justifications that Venice had made in her annexation of its mainland cities was their *repatriation* into the Republic, which superseded in its Christian state the earlier province of Roman Venetia.[12] Like many other assertions

of statecraft, such themes reconciled less palatable realities and made coexistence profitable. Similarly, visual signs could suggest inclusion within a caste of privilege, yet disguise some of the real distinctions, or even erase them in perception. The classical language of the villa that "re"-colonized the Veneto thus could express the idea of Venice as the new Rome. It developed along with the growing "aristocratization" of the Venetian patriciate, especially in one segment that was already so predisposed, churchmen.

The granting of ecclesiastical titles approximated that of nobility. Incomes from accrued benefices were tantamount to fiefs, and some families clearly felt they had hereditary rights to certain offices.[13] Such expectations could lead to familial discord, as in the Grimani family when in 1550 Patriarch Giovanni Grimani bypassed his nephews to succeed him as patriarch of Aquileia, preferring instead that Daniele Barbaro be nominated to the right of succession. He responded sharply to his brother Vettor Grimani saying that they had gone over this "a thousand times" and he had had enough of cataloging the defects of Vettor's natural son, Antonio, the abbot of Sesto; moreover, he had to endure their sister Paola Querini's "tears over the villanies and injuries" done to the family interests in not choosing her son.[14] Certain families were consistently linked with the Church, as Doge Andrea Gritti cautioned in regard to the Corner, Pisani, and Grimani, "three houses in this city want all the bishoprics."[15]

The painting *Girolamo and Cardinal Marco [di Giorgio] Corner Investing Marco, Abbot of Carrara, with his Benefice*, attributed to Titian and his workshop (fig. 31), visually demonstrates such entitlement as a hereditary bequest, for the portrait of the cardinal, who predeceased his brother in 1524, is believed to be posthumous. The use of the convention of the profile portrait at this date not only betrays its origins from another source (in this case a medal), but provides contrast to the three-quarter- and *profil perdu*-views of Girolamo and the young abbot rendered *dal vivo*, from life. There are two areas of focus: the meaningful gazes of father and son intersecting with the fixed straight-ahead point of view of Cardinal Marco, and the play of gesture, with the title prominently transferred from the hand of the cardinal to his namesake, underscored with a rhetorical flourish of *demonstratio*. As such, the painting functions as a surrogate for the legal record, with Girolamo witness to the transaction.[16]

Both the Pisani and Grimani were critical to Palladio's early Venetian patronage in the Veneto; the Grimani would figure significantly in his career in Venice itself. The profile of the Venetian cardinalate in the first half of the sixteenth century confirms these families' ecclesiastical pre-eminence: of the eight red hats from Venice, three were Corners, two Grimanis, one Pisani, as well as a Contarini and a Bembo, all patrician families.[17] Nor were the grand ecclesiastical families consistently united among themselves in their policies and attitudes. Their competition for greater preferment was a keen wedge. The deaths of Doge Leonardo Loredan and the Medici pope Leo x in 1521 brought about a curious situation that illustrates the potential for political damage from such rivalry. In that year a father and son of the Grimani family were considered respectively *dogabile* and *papabile* (that is, electable), but it was not

30   Titian, *Giorgio [Zorzon] Corner with a Falcon*, Omaha (NE), Joslyn Art Museum (1942.3)

31 Titian and workshop, *Girolamo and Cardinal Marco Corner Investing Marco, Abbot of Carrara, with his Benefice*, Washington, National Gallery of Art, Timken Collection (1960.6.38)

to be that Venetians would simultaneously govern both states. Doge Antonio Grimani claimed that his victory over Giorgio (Zorzi) K.P. di Marco Corner of the wealthy and powerful della Regina branch had caused Corner to urge his son, the Cardinal Marco portrayed above, to campaign against the election of Grimani's son, Cardinal Domenico, and therefore "almost ruined this State."[18] Certainly, it is interesting to contemplate what the presence of a Venetian pope would have meant in these years, but in any event, soon – in 1523 – both dogal *corno* and papal tiara were again vacant.

* * *

"Cazzadì i papalisti":
Distrust of Factions among the Patriciate

Venice encompassed conflicting attitudes over her ecclesiastics. There was ample internal distrust of Church office holders: political, financial, and jurisdictional: political, because of potentially divided allegiances; financial, because wealth was drawn away from Venice's coffers, while enriching a limited circle of families and Rome; jurisdictional, even though the Republic had always asserted civil preeminence. Despite misgivings about Venetians becoming ecclesiastics, it was nevertheless more desirable than the alternative of these offices going to men of other nations, and other loyalties. So Venice fought with the papacy both to retain ecclesiastical offices and to reserve the right to their nomination, one of the main, ongoing causes for discord and diplomacy with the Church. Such insistence, however, could prove acute enough to cause open rupture. On the one hand, some patricians who accepted Church preferment without the imprimatur of the Venetian government found themselves exiled in Rome;[19] on the other, Venice's intransigence over nominations, a main target of the more militant popes, could affect the political advancement of their interests within the Curia. The Interdict of the Della Rovere pope Julius II that accompanied the League of Cambrai (1509–10) reversed earlier custom by stripping the right of nomination from all but the positions of the patriarchate of Venice and the archbishopric of Candia.[20] Only diplomacy and/or mutual benefit in the face of a third party, such as the emperor, reconciled Venice and Rome in this contest for control, as in the patriarchy of Aquileia, which was in contested Habsburg territory. Yet as the troubled history of Giovanni Grimani's long tenure (1546–93) dramatically demonstrates – from accusations of heresy to his failure to obtain the cardinalate – the sixteenth century was consistent only in its mutability.[21]

Rigid definitions of the patriciate were matched by other indications of increasing factionalism, and one group targeted by legislation from the later fifteenth century through to the sixteenth century was that related to holders of ecclesiastical offices, called *papalisti*. Legislation indicates particular concern over the transmission of information, so when any matters regarding Rome were brought up in the councils, they were expelled with the call *Cazzadì i papalisti!* Such concerns seem to have been justified, for one papal nuncio, a diplomatic representative, wrote that he had "discovered all these sentiments through conversations with these prelates, who because they have no part in the government of the state will venture to speak a trifle more freely than do the other noblemen . . . Priuli, the bishop of Vicenza, was the most open with me."[22] Actually, private speech with a nuncio was forbidden to office holders, but that was true for all other representatives of foreign powers as well. The laws that particularly infuriated the papacy, however, would also have significance for architectural programs; these were laws concerning ecclesiastical property. Restrictions increased over the alienation of property away from the State made through pious bequests to various Church foundations. The Church was already a large landholder in the *terraferma* through wealthy monasteries and benefices, which now drew a different kind of attention with the economic reorientation of Venice (in which they were the greatest stakeholders). A direct impingement on the aggrandizement of the physical church was the law requiring permission to erect new churches. New regulatory agencies were set up to oversee compliance.[23]

The greatest division that was remarked in the period was based on the criteria of genealogy, the relative antiquity of the families of the *Golden Book*. Those houses that were known as the *longhi* (long, in the sense of time, or "old") had been present in Venice before the year 800, whereas those called the *curti* (short, or "new") had come after that date. These divisions became known respectively as the *case vecchie* and *case nuove*. Even further subgroups were identified; for example, among the *longhi* there were twelve *case apostoliche*,

houses that had elected the first doge, and in the *curti* there were the *ducali*, who were most commonly elected to that office. Relative newcomers were the *case nuovissime* who had been admitted into the closed ranks of the patriciate with the War of Chioggia in the years 1378–81.[24] The effect of such identifying characteristics as factions in the Venetian political process has been debated, as has its incipient relation to modern party politics. What was unusual for Venice was the open acknowledgment at the end of the fifteenth century and the beginning of the sixteenth of such a division: of *partialità*. Discord surfaced primarily in dogal elections, as Marin Sanudo reported on the election of Agostino Barbarigo in 1486:

> There arose in the city a cursed discord between noblemen of the old and new families . . . people talked of nothing else but of these highly important matters, splitting the city into two parties: . . . it was said there had never been such hatred and party division [*partialità*] . . . And already the news was spread through the whole of Italy that there was a great party division between the nobles of the old and new families in Venice, as in many Italian cities.[25]

Thus such factionalism did have an actual outcome, for the dogeship was not held by a member of the *longhi* (or *case vecchie*) between 1382 and 1612. The division was also behind the defeat of Giorgio Corner's bid to become doge in 1521 discussed above; it was attributed to more than inter-family rivalry, to the fact of his being from an "old house." Real power as realized through the important offices of the Republic, however, was held by a hybrid mixture of *curti* and *longhi*, known as the *case grandi*, which was more a result of their size and wealth.[26] But if this division was largely genealogical, there was another first manifested as discord between generations, between ardent youth and prudent age, *giovani* (young) and *vecchi* (old). By about the mid-sixteenth century, however, these identities of *giovani* and *vecchi*, along with those of the old and new houses, had begun to take on an ideological cast.

Historians have found the *giovani* and the *vecchi* much more elusive to define as coherent groups. There are no sources, such as the *Golden Book*, that provide lists of criteria for membership; these were not structured groups, but more alliances of individuals with attitudes shared in varying degrees, what might be called "political clans," loosely operating as a "set" under particular circumstances.[27] Collective identities, however, can be discerned to have hardened beyond the clash of generations, particularly around the political events at either end of the sixteenth century, with an important difference, in that the second half of the century had progressively coalesced around certain issues and ceased to be a matter of youth or age. This generation largely began to come of political age in the 1550s, the period when Palladio was trying to establish himself in Venice. Differences continued to be fueled during the succeeding decades over the impact of: wars with the Turks in the years 1537–40 (when seaports in the Morea were ceded for peace) and the first years of the 1570s with the devastating loss of Cyprus; the consolidation of Habsburg power and the successions of Ferdinand I and Philip I in 1556; the Church emerging from the sessions of

32   Titian, *Doge Andrea Gritti*, Washington, National Gallery of Art, Samuel H. Kress Collection (1961.9.45)

the Council of Trent (1545–48, 1551–52, 1562–63), as seen in the institution of the Index of Forbidden Books (1559); substantial development in land reclamation (the institution of controlling magistracies included the Provveditori sopra i Beni Inculti formed in 1556, and later, in 1587, the Provveditori sopra i Feudi); and internal reorganization of the government, such as the repeal of the Zonta (additional members) of the Council of Ten in 1582.[28]

The formation of a more ideologically predisposed identification of *giovani* and *vecchi* had begun earlier in response to those who had come to power during the post-Cambrai period of reconstruction under Doge Gritti. One of the cautious policies that had inflamed the *giovani* around 1500 had led to the loss of the "two eyes of the Republic" (Modon and Coron) to the Turks, but contemporaries did not then characterize such disagreement as factions that threatened the vaunted homogeneity of the patriciate, so much as being between persons who could garner support for their more or less extreme positions.[29] Marin Sanudo described the bellicosity of the

"zoveni" (*giovani*), such as Giovanni Emo who had protested against pacification of the Turks, those young patricians who had exchanged the parti-colored hose and fashionable doublets of their youthful associations for the imposing, if sober, toga upon their entry into the Great Council. Such bellicose qualities would unquestionably be needed by *giovani* and *vecchi* alike once the League of Cambrai was enjoined against Venice, and a war footing may have blurred the age distinction leading to a more ideological alignment of these categories.

An embodiment of matured power can be seen in Titian's portrait of Andrea Gritti (fig. 32), a hero of the wars of Cambrai, from the assault to regain Padua, and as negotiator with the French, later doge (1523–38). No longer relying on zoomorphic semblances, Titian presents the natural authority of the aged doge's whitebearded yet still-strong features. Even more than the physiognomy, however, the treatment of the format contrives to express the swelling breadth of dogal power. The broadly painted *manto d'oro*

33   Nicolò Boldrini, woodcut after Titian's lost *Votive Painting of Doge Andrea Gritti*, Venice, Biblioteca del Museo Civico Correr, Varie coll. 69/4, tav. 303

and fur-lined toga occupy two-thirds of the composition. In the portrait, status is annotated through the costume appropriate to rank; it takes on a life of its own, but its expansion is checked by the hand of the doge that conspicuously controls its heavy folds, almost as though placed on the hilt of a sword. For the visually literate there is another reference, replete with further associations: the model for the hand has long been recognized as Michelangelo's *Moses*, known from a cast brought from Rome to Venice by Jacopo Sansovino. Through the incorporation of the commanding presence of this hand, Titian has played a subtle game, allowing the person of Gritti to usurp that of his former League opponent, Julius II, for whose tomb the *Moses* was designed and is thought to be portrayed. Equally, Titian has made a *paragone* to the art of Michelangelo, an artistic contest for the superiority of painting over sculpture, with this allusion, claiming the victory for *colore* in the lively tinted flesh over cold three-dimensional marble. Gravity is stressed both through expression and in the abstract volumes of the design.[30] The Gritti represented here is one of the *vecchi*, who had consolidated his reputation as hero, and through wealth and kinship alliances (notably with the Corner, Grimani, and Pisani) into the dogeship.

The mutual obligations and benefits of *i primi* to each other are said by Sanudo to be represented in Gritti's official votive painting for the Doge's Palace, which was destroyed by fire in 1574. The name saint of Alvise Pisani dal Banco, bankroller, procurator, and one of the influential Forty-One electors of the doge (the Quarant'uno), has been included with Sts. Marina and Bernardino, together with Venice's own St. Mark, who presents Gritti to the Virgin and Child; the figure of St. Louis of Toulouse with his distinctive miter and crosier can be seen at the right in the woodcut by Nicolò Boldrini (fig. 33) that records the lost painting (substituting a portrait of Doge Francesco Donà for Gritti).[31]

With the *giovani* who attempted to enter into the ruling oligarchy of their elders in the 1550s, the actual correlation to age dissolved as programmatic alignments began to be maintained even after the generation matured. Venice was a gerontocracy. Many studies have discussed the unusual longevity of Venetians in comparison to other populations in the sixteenth century; the doge, for example, had an average age at election of 72, compared to the pope's of 54 (and death at 64).[32] Increasingly, however, the *giovani* and the *vecchi* became associated with a set of ideological positions that arose in response to events, and to a conception of what Venice should be and had been. Had the patriciate continued to have shared mercantile-based fortunes, rather than interests becoming more diversified between the *stato da mar* and the *stato da terra*, it seems likely that the fracture within it would have remained cyclic and generation-bound.

Although there were more issues putting pressure on the social structure of Venice than her response to the Turks, together with other elements in play over the century that inexorably restricted the former volume of trade in the Levant, this constituted a real threat to the financial advancement of the significant group of less wealthy nobles. Land ownership and the ability to profit from it required an investment of capital unavailable to a group that had been able to participate in trade. Studies have shown how poorer nobles rarely held the influential offices of government, and expensive posts that were shortcuts to high office, such as ambassadorships, were beyond any but the wealthy. The Grimani were an example of the success that trade could bring, rising from a medium-sized family to become one of the *case ducali* as recently as the mid-fifteenth century.[33]

The redefinition of Venice was inevitable as the fortunes of Italy were reshaped in this period. Control over that intractable process

34 View of Piazzetta San Marco along the Molo, Venice

was at first in the hands of the *vecchi*, initiating what has been described as the *renovatio urbis romanae* of Venice guided by one of the heroes of the League of Cambrai, Doge Andrea Gritti, and by his councilors, who initiated the "Romanization" of the Piazza San Marco (fig. 34).[34] Gritti was a strong personality whose policy choices contributed to the developing oligarchical and aristocratic character of government in the first half of the sixteenth century. The generation that entered into political life in the post-reconstruction period confronted increased division between more exclusive executive councils, such as the Council of Ten and College, and the larger bodies, such as the Senate and Great Council. Like today's governmental policies that condone covert action, the principle of "national security" was invoked to divert business to the Ten, who were responsible for state security, creating an even more limited group, called the Zonta (*aggiunta*, meaning an additional body). The encroachment on the tradition of open debate was countered by the complex electoral procedures, but the War of the League of Cambrai had allowed an unusually homogenous ruling group to emerge and retain some of the "emergency" war powers.[35] If initially in the sixteenth century the *giovani* were regarded in traditional age-related terms, associated with the impetuosity and green-ness of youth, after mid-century, as these politicians aged, the cycle of experience that brought them to higher offices was no longer the guarantee of transformation to a *vecchi*. Also, as the identification became more ideologically based, more of a parallel can be seen between the *giovani* and the *case nuove*, with the more numerous but concomitant higher number of poor families, and therefore associated views on the value of tradition, the importance of trade, and thus a militant stance in regard to foreign powers. Equally the same can be said of the *vecchi* and parallels with the *case vecchie*, many of whom had turned to land,

were developing aristocratic habits, and valued the maintenance of security. *Papalisti* from the *case nuove* also found a natural alignment with these latter values, more generally held by *i primi della terra*. Sir Dudley Carleton's description of the Venetians grown "factious" makes some of these same links:

> Betwixt the old families and the new a perpetual faction. The new are for most in number, the old in welth and dignitie; the new by this meanes carrie away all principal offices in the government as the Duke is ever of late chosen among them but the old have the love of the people. The opinion of many is that this will one day be the ruin of theyr common wealth. It may be marvayled how at the death of a Duke the election of a new being to pass through all theyr nominations where everyone will advance in what he may his own familie it may notwithstanding be easely foreseene who shall be chosen: but it falls owt in this sort. First all the old families are excluded. Next all Papalini. Then such as have children: and unwillingly they chuse a maried man. They will have one that hath run through the principal offices of the commonwealth withowt any note of misgovernment, and with these circumstances the election is not great but within two or three and of those one for the potencie of his familie and frends is soon distinguished from the other. [marginal note:] There are case dogale such as have had Dukes and other poore families which have had none; the greater of these shall endeavor to keep downe the less.[36]

This report was written the very year that a member of the *case vecchie* finally returned to power after more than two centuries, which reflects the final loss of coherence of the *case* as factions. In part, these tendencies are more clearly expressed from the vantage point of hindsight, from the remarks of those who commented upon the current events around 1600, and sought their origins in the preceding years. There are enough contemporaries, though, who openly refer to these factions, and not always in terms that would be considered complimentary, and Venetian ambassadors had long been trained to size up such differences at the courts of foreign powers, to take them seriously, despite running contrary to the "myth" of Venetian homogeneity.[37]

The clearest division that would be attributed to the *giovani* and *vecchi* lay in their attitudes towards Rome, with the *vecchi* identified as pro-papal, and thus a natural alignment with *papalisti*, who were likewise excluded from certain government positions. As the century progressed, other allegiances were assumed to follow on this, such as the *giovani* anti-papal stance then implying anti-Spanish and pro-French positions. While the French became embroiled in the Wars of Religion (1562–98), the Habsburgs had strengthened their positions in Italy, the Treaty of Cateau-Cambrésis of 1559 confirming their possessions of Milan, Naples, Sicily, and Sardinia – a threat to the nervous balance of power that Spanish influence over the papacy only increased. The *giovani* also would strive to dismantle some of the structures of government that had increased its oligarchical character. The attitudes of the *giovani* on land ownership on the *terraferma* replacing maritime trade also seem implicitly negative in their association of land ownership with a high percentage of ecclesiastical families, the *papalisti*, but by this period many *giovani* too had investments in land, so the distinction between land and sea seems to be more rhetorical and symbolic. Even if this was the case, the rhetoric is revealing for its nostalgia for the heroic Venice of the late fourteenth century through to the fifteenth, a period of expansion between the wars of Chioggia and Cambrai. Acute pressures from foreign powers affected all these interconnected issues, and whether Venice would be better preserved through a more militant stance or conciliatory position divided policy-makers. This debate would be carried into the aesthetic realm as well, competing for the proper definition of *venezianità* – "Venetian-ness."

Oratorical structure has been one means by which scholars define the composition and interpret the motivations of these factions; this structure included the developing humanist historiography.[38] Another approach has been to attempt to match political realities with the rhetorical construction of identity through the prosopographical analysis of policy decisions. No source in the later sixteenth century compares to the acerbic political commentary recorded in the voluminous diaries of Marin Sanudo (entries from 1496–1533), so the historian is left to reconstruct the validity of such factions from the voting records of specific magistracies, the few terse records of debate, and the reports of observers and chroniclers.[39] The self-interest of the papal nuncios has been a particularly fruitful source in their confidential assessments of the favor or resistance of individuals regarding the Holy See; whereas the reverse can be found in Venetian ambassadors' reactions to papal policies.[40] Despite differences of interpretation, sources point to a shift in the power structure in the last quarter of the sixteenth century. By the beginning of the seventeenth century, one observer claimed that "Here they no longer speak of old and new houses but of *Papalini*

and *Republichisti*."[41] The election of a member of the *case vecchie*, Marcantonio Memo, to the dogeship in 1612, only a few years after this statement was made, confirms that new allegiances had replaced the one seemingly coherent voting block based on genealogical origins. By this time, however, the Republic had survived another papal interdict (1606–07), now with the *giovani* in power. Nevertheless, that dominance began to develop only in the 1570s: the *vecchi* were fully in place through the War of Cyprus (1570–71), as we shall see when we examine how this rivalry between *giovani* and *vecchi* would affect Palladio's career. The decade of the 1570s was a turning point, and shortly after Palladio's death in 1580, the *giovani* had come of age. The repeal of the Zonta of the Council of Ten in 1582 affected the decision-making structure of the government, empowering the *giovani* (although a number of *vecchi* continued to hold significant personal power).[42] The same dynamics were played out in the realm of cultural politics. Affiliations between persons and ideas affected choices about patronage. What was at stake was how the Republic would represent itself.

The Public Image of the State

No art asserted the visual presence of the State more definitively than architecture, since it rendered the image of the body politic in stone and marble. The justification for attributing *partialità* to cultural projects requires the establishment of an alignment between defined ideological positions of backers and an analysis of their style, whether in art, architecture, ritual, literature, music, or any other cultural practice, including personal display.[43]

Strategies have been employed by scholars to test notions of group adherence and the attendant development of cultural policies, such as determining patterns of preference within the patriciate and the expressive content of building "programs" (used in the modern sense of transaction between architect, client, function, and historical position), which James Ackerman has called "geopolitics."[44] Venetian magistracies have been studied, as another means than kinship relations, for their modes of influence on public architecture, especially the Procurators of San Marco and the Salt Office.[45] The work of Manfredo Tafuri has incorporated both the genealogical and the ideological in a broad purview of what he has called "the debate on the *imago urbis*," in his *Venice and the Renaissance*.[46] The debate is framed by the factionalism described above as a significant condition of public life in sixteenth-century Venice. Tafuri has laid the groundwork for the descriptive parameters necessary to translate motivations for political action into cultural policy by associating the rhetorical components of architectural style with their counterparts in the language of decision-making in the council hall. Such an approach can provide another means of testing the validity of group identities, such as the *giovani* and *vecchi*, by analyzing the expressive content of their production, Ackerman's "program." Tafuri has proposed such an identification for the support for a style of *severità repubblicana* by *giovani* and one of magnificence *alla romana* by *vecchi*.

tion for life, although in some cases a *proto* might be employed for a specific phase or for the duration of a single project. These positions were won through competition, as were commissions for a number of major building projects, and consequently there was a limited amount of mobility as architects changed posts. The influential patricians who became procurators of San Marco were the only officials, other than the doge, who were elected for life, and such offices were usually considered a prerequisite of achieving the *corno*. This relationship is demonstrated visually in the sworn oath of the future doge, whom we have already seen to have succeeded Doge Leonardo Loredan in 1521, Antonio Grimani (fig. 36).[47] The procurators of San Marco *de supra* were charged with the responsibility for the physical fabric of the ducal chapel, the Basilica of

36   *Commissione* of Antonio Grimani for procurator *de supra* in 1510 from Doge Leonardo Loredan, Venice, Biblioteca del Museo Civico Correr, MS Correr, Cl. 3, 906, f. 5r

35   Giovanni Battista Mariotti and Francesco Zucchi, engraving after Giovanni Battista Maganza, *Portrait of Andrea Palladio* (Vicenza, Valmarana Collection), in Giovanni Montenari, *Del Teatro Olimpico di Andrea Palladio in Vicenza*, Padua, 1749

Venezia "alla romana"

When Palladio arrived in the city in the 1550s, Jacopo Sansovino with his circle of supporters was firmly established in the cultural hegemony of the city. By the time of Sansovino's death in 1570, the historical situation had altered circumstances for Palladio (fig. 35), as it altered the political climate of his patrons, and the reception of his style, which in any case had been formed in a different context than had his predecessor's. Palladio acknowledged Sansovino's role in bringing the *bella maniera* to public architecture in Venice, both in the "Foreword" to Book One in the *Four Books*, and in the elements of the Basilica in Vicenza that suggest Sansovino's Library of San Marco. His remarks indicated, however, that he expected to succeed Sansovino in bringing the classical style to "perfection" in Venice. Yet Palladio would never operate from the official position that Sansovino had occupied, as *proto* of an important magistracy.

Many of the major magistracies in Venice required the permanent services of a supervising architect, called a *proto*, usually a posi-

37   Jacopo Tintoretto, *Jacopo Sansovino*, Florence, Galleria degli Uffizi

San Marco and property owned by it, such as the Procurators' Offices in the Piazza. Given the stability of the magistrates and their wealth, the effect on the public architecture of the civic center of the city, and the symbolic weight of the care of the chapel, the position of their *proto* was of great importance. Sansovino had arrived in Venice in 1527 after the Sack of Rome, and was recommended to do necessary work on the domes of San Marco. According to Vasari, Sansovino's Roman connections, including Cardinal Pietro Bembo (official historian to the Republic) with Cardinal Domenico and his nephew, Procurator (later patriarch and papal general) Marco di Gerolamo Grimani, introduced him into the circle of the doge, which included Procurators Vettor Grimani (brother of Marco), Giovanni di Michiel da Lezze, and Antonio di Giambattista Capello. On the death of its previous incumbent, Bartolomeo Bon, in 1529, Sansovino was elected as *proto della procuratoria di San Marco de supra* (fig. 37).[48]

To define the *proto* in this period during which the profession of architecture was emerging is not a simple task. The title of "architect" came to be applied with distinction; as Vincenzo Scamozzi described in his *L'idea della architettura universale* (Venice, 1615), the *proto* (or *capomaestro*) "occupy themselves with the execution,

because they would be able to have experience, but not the theory proper to the Architect trained in Science." To Scamozzi there was a clear hierarchy; while duties and qualifications could vary, even the *proto* of the Arsenale, whom he admitted had a high level of mastery, was still not to be considered an architect but rather by this criteria an artisan.[49] In the eighteenth century, Tommaso Temanza looked back at those who had been called *proto* and reasoned that "Everyone knows that the term *Proto* in our vernacular [Venetian] signifies Architect. So our Palladio was called, and so Sansovino." He explained the origins of the word as deriving from the Greek for *primo*, in use in Venice rather than Tuscan. Temanza cited Galileo Galilei's different evaluation of the *proto* of the Arsenale, as involved "in the causes of things," which, using Scamozzi's own standards, would raise the status of the *proto* to a practioner of science, buttressed by as unimpeachable an authority as could be imagined. For Scamozzi's comparison of *proto* to *capomaestro* and to the classical *Praefectus fabrorum*, as essentially meaning the head builder, Temanza rejoined with classical examples that would be indisputably considered architects and were so titled. He then made the additional point that *proto* could mean the "office," which also fitted the meaning of *Praefectus fabrorum*, whose incumbents could be architects. The last example he offered in this regard was the clincher: "Also Vitruvius was Prefect of the Military office; so such a President must be an Architect of the merit of Vitruvius."[50] Such disparity can be explained by the different periods in which these authors were writing: Temanza, from the point of the academically trained architect, took the status of the profession much more for granted, whereas Scamozzi was fighting to establish it, and differentiate it from the craft tradition.

Venice proved slower to emancipate artists and architects from the guild system to the level of a profession than other centers in Italy in the sixteenth century. The system of magistracies being run by elected patricians must have contributed to the need for control over professionalism, since the *proto* was expected to supply expertise, and even art, but the primary authority was vested in the patrons. The work of Tafuri has shown how crucial the conflict between an architecture of science and one of experience was in the decision-making of the period, another indicator of differing *mentalités*. There was no equivalent of the Florentine Accademia del Disegno, which some Venetian artists, including Palladio, petitioned Vasari to join in 1566.[51] Sansovino was able to negotiate the gap between architect and *proto*. Like most other architects in the first half of the sixteenth century, he came out of training in sculpture and/or painting, rather than the building trades, such as stonemasonry as Palladio would, and as would the one architect to rival Sansovino for prestigious private commissions in Venice, Michele Sanmicheli of Verona (fig. 38). Vasari's evaluation of architecture in north Italy gives them equal importance: "Michele Sanmicheli and Jacopo Sansovino brought the true style of architecture to north Italy after Falconetto showed the way."[52] Sanmicheli's travels as engineer for the Magistracy over *terraferma* fortifications and his work for Veronese patrons filled a successful career.[53] Between them, Sansovino and Sanmicheli brought the Roman Renaissance style to

38 Giorgio Vasari, "Michele Sanmicheli," *Le vite de' piu eccellenti pittori, scultori, et architettori*, Florence, Appresso i Giunti, 1568, 3:512

both *stato da terra* and *stato da mar*.[55] Venice was thus laden and circumscribed by a "foreign" architectural language, one that no longer incorporated her visual past without explanation and justification in an explicit program.

Such support was forthcoming from the patrons who had brought Sansovino to prominence in Venice, who would constitute a network that promoted the new style. It was a moment of radical historical change and one of opportunity. Under Doge Gritti, Venice had entered into a period of reconstruction: building had been curtailed during the War of the League of Cambrai, but in the first quarter of the sixteenth century the State sponsored a number of projects, especially of restoration, for important areas such as the Rialto market and bridge (from 1514), including the Palace of the Camerlenghi (1525–28), and as the Piazza San Marco, including the Zen chapel in the Basilica of San Marco (1504–21), work on various parts of the Doge's Palace, and the Old Procurators' Offices (1514–32) – which were then known as the Procuratie Nuove.[56] Ennio Concina has eloquently remarked of the Old Procurators' Offices, generally attributed to the *proto* of the Procurators of San Marco, Bartolomeo Bon,

> how a building of the first Cinquecento could reproduce with surprising fidelity the romanesque construction of the Procurators' Offices built under Doge Sebastiano Ziano (1172–1178) . . . excepting the addition of another story, this proto-Renaissance result is a true and proper transcription, an updating of the medieval model. In sum, this is also a case, culturally central, of that which we may define as a *renovatio more veneto*, revelatory

39 Jacopo Sansovino, Palazzo Dolfin, Grand Canal at Rialto, Venice

the Grand Canal, not surprisingly for some of the wealthiest, predominantly papalist, families in Venice: the Corner, the Grimani, the Dolfin (fig. 39). These examples represented the *summa* of Venetian palaces for Francesco Sansovino, Jacopo's son and author of *Venetia, città nobilissima et singolare*:

> It is enough to know that the most important of all the palaces on the Grand Canal, are four: (I speak in regards to architecture, for the artifice of their live stone, for mastery, for the size of the building, and of expense, because these cost just over 200 thousand ducats,) that is, the Loredan at San Marcuola, the Grimani at San Luca, the Dolfin at San Salvador, and the Cornaro at San Maurizio. These for the size of their circumference, for height, and for every other quality that is required by a harmonious ediface, were made in our times, and according to the doctrine of the ancient Vitruvius, from whose rules the best Architects are not permitted to depart.[54]

This encomium singles out the distinguishing factor, identifying Sansovino and Sanmicheli as practitioners of Vitruvian architecture. If Sansovino's main activity was carried out within the city, indeed transforming its political and mercantile centers *alla romana*, Sanmicheli's would mark the perimeters of La Dominante, securing of the by now accentuated sacralization of the forms of the past, of the declared immutability of the *species urbis*.[57]

In following their *proto* Bon with Sansovino, the procurators imported an architect whose training and style were indebted to Tuscany and Rome. The architectural quotations, paired columns or the use of engaged column with pier, would not come with references to the doges of the past, like Ziani, but with those to the emperors of the ancient *caput mundi* and the occupants of the See of St. Peter – Julius II, the Medici, Paul III Farnese.[58]

That Sansovino was able to have such a unique impact was due to the patronage of the procurators, which had a somewhat unusual composition in this period because of the number who had been admitted by payment in support of the war. These included Sansovino's greatest supporters, Antonio Capello and Vettor Grimani, who each gave 8,000 ducats at entry in 1522 and 1523 respectively. Although not without conflict, Sansovino continued to have wide support among the procurators, even after the death of Doge Gritti in 1538.[59] Patronage by those who decided on State building projects in the civic center, and his position as their *proto* in renovating that center, gave the language of Sansovino's architecture a significant place in establishing a new model: he continued the Old Procurators' Offices in the mode in which it was begun, but proposed building in the Roman Renaissance style for the new offices across from the Doge's Palace, which became the Library (begun 1537), for the Loggetta (begun 1537) at the foot of the Campanile, for the church of San Geminiano (begun 1557) opposite the Basilica in the Piazza, and for the new Mint (begun 1535, the "Zecca," under the control of the Salt Office). In each of these, the mode of the architectural style was attuned to the program of the building and communicated it to observers.[60]

Sansovino's Library demonstrates how an architectural motif can carry symbolic import. In the design of the repeated bay motif (fig. 40), Sansovino rearticulated a window type familiar to Lombardy and the Veneto, the *fenestra veneziana*, and re-presented it with Roman elocution. The complex piers demonstrate Sansovino's familiarity with arcaded Roman antiquities, such as the Julio-Claudian Theater of Marcellus in Rome, yet the rich *chiaroscuro* of the sculptured surface dominates the architectural form and played to Venetian taste. Of the masterful blend of classical and Venetian elements, Deborah Howard has said that "The degree to which Sansovino managed to assimilate the indigenous architectural tradition . . . is remarkable."[61] It is instructive to compare his handling of the motif to Palladio's, which is closer to the interpretation by such Roman "moderns" as Bramante, as in the ceremonial window of the Sala Regia (Royal Audience Hall, Vatican Palace, 1504), and to its dissemination by Sebastiano Serlio, a Bolognese architect and theorist who had been a student of Baldassare Peruzzi, who was exposed to the circle around the papal court (figs. 41 and 42).

Serlio had come to Venice in 1527. His impact on Venetian architecture was not, however, through built projects, but through his publications, and it was through their influence that this motif came to be known as a "Serliana." His *Fourth Book* or *General Rules of Architecture . . . On the Five Styles of Building* (*Regole generali di architettura sopra le cinque maniere de gli edifici*, or *Quarto libro*), on the classical orders, was published in Venice in 1537, contemporary with the Library, and his acknowledgment of Gritti in the dedication (p. III) underlines the force of the doge's cultural impact:

> In Venice I received every possible benefit, both spiritual and worldly. The Doge, master Andrea Gritti, a prince never sufficiently praised, has brought the following men to the service of his illustrious Republic, and they are making this city, with its noble and beautifully constructed buildings, as marvelous as God made it impressive by the nature of its site.[62]

A Romanized version of a locally popular vernacular motif was thus made available in the seductive format of the illustrated architectural book. When Serlio discusses the motif used as a repeating bay, he describes its adaptability to the Venetian situation, while sustaining the need to conform to classical architecture (XXXIV/153v):

> In Venice, this noblest of cities, building practice is very different from that in all the other cities in Italy because, as a result of the city being very densely populated, the site has to be narrow and must be compartitioned with great care. . . . With all this in mind, I would say that these façades could be built with even more openings, respecting the ancient way of building, in the manner shown here.

In a passage that chides Venetians for constructing unsupported loggias on their façades, he illustrates how a single motif may be used for the central bay (XXXIIIV/155v):

> I have shown above two ways in which house façades in the Venetian fashion can be built. However, in those façades the Venetians like to have several balconies, which in that city are called *pergoli*, projecting from the windows. They build these in order to enjoy more easily the waters of the canals and the coolness which can always be felt from them, since the houses for the most part have their façades over said canals. They also provide the perfect place for viewing the triumphs and naval celebrations which often take place in that most fortunate of cities, and represent great ornament for the buildings themselves.

The motif is thus given a ceremonial status, analogous to the upper bays of the Library during processions.[63]

Both motif and format found their way to Palladio and were transformed in his Basilica in Vicenza (fig. 43), which Serlio had consulted on, and later in the balance of text and image in the more

42 (*facing page bottom left*) Sebastiano Serlio, window for a Venetian palace, *Libro primo [-quinto] d'architettura, di Sebastiano Serlio bolognese* (*Regole generale d'architettura*, 1537), Venice, Appresso G.B. e M. Sessa fratelli, 1559, cap. 6, fol. 32

43 (*facing page bottom right*) Andrea Palladio, "On contemporary basilicas and the designs of the one in Vicenza," *I quattro libri dell'architettura*, Venice, Appresso Dominico de' Franceschi, 1570, lib. 3, cap. 20, 43

40 (*left*) Jacopo Sansovino, top story window bay,
Library of San Marco, Venice

41 (*below*) Donato Bramante, window of the Sala
Regia, Vatican Palace, Vatican City

LIBRO QVARTO.

TERZO.

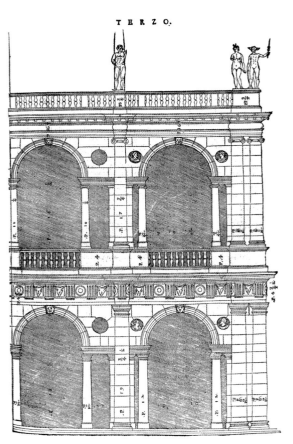

44 *View of the Capitoline Hill*, Rome, ca. 1554–1560, Paris, Musée du Louvre, Cabinet des Dessins (11028)

45 (*facing page*) Jacopo de' Barbari, detail of Piazza San Marco, *View of Venice*, 1500, Venice

influential *Four Books*, so much so that the motif is alternatively known as the Palladian window ("Palladiana"). Where Palladio had credited Sansovino with "beginning" to make known the "bella maniera," and praised the Library for its "richness" and "ornateness" (*Four Books*, Bk. 1, "Foreword," 5), he reserved unqualified praise for his own porticoed design: "I have no doubt at all that this building can be compared to antique structures and included amongst the greatest and most beautiful buildings built since antiquity, both for its size and its ornaments, as well as because of its materials" (*Four Books*, Bk. 3, ch. 20, 41, misprinted as 42). Palladio saw his own use of the repeating bay motif as the contemporary equivalent to the ancient classical style, but Sansovino's accommodation of local vernacular would enhance the reception of his Roman Renaissance style and give it a Venetian identity that would continue to resonate beyond the generation of his immediate supporters.

The history of Church–State relations is bound up in the reception and adoption of artistic language by various proponents. Its analysis remains a moving target, however, particularly in such a period of great change. In Italy following the Peace of Bologna in 1530, Venetians were not unaware of the consequences of foreign dominance on the peninsula, or of their uneasy relations with Rome.[64] In the transformation of their own civic center, Venetians were certainly conscious of developments in Rome, where imperial thematics would play out what was held in the balance in Europe with the triumph of Charles V in 1536. André Chastel has discussed how Pope Paul III turned the ruined city to his advantage, by taking the opportunity to impose projects of urban "renewal"; in a foretaste of the "Third Rome," buildings were demolished to highlight antiquities and urban spaces that the procession would pass.[65] Paul III had wanted to utilize the traditional site of the Capitoline Hill, the civic seat of Roman government,

but its condition made this impracticable; by the next year he had asked Michelangelo, despite his protests, to level a space in the center of the complex to accommodate the equestrian monument of Marcus Aurelius – the beginning of what became a grand design to remodel the site entirely and a reminder of the imperial past (fig. 44). Charles V's processional route had passed through the Forum to the Piazza San Marco (now Piazza Venezia), where a final triumphal arch was passed through before continuing on the via Papalis, an important site for Venetians resident in Rome since the Palazzo Venezia had been built by a Venetian pope and housed the Republic's senior cardinal.[66]

Certainly, one of the most fraught acts of urban intervention in a pre-existing fabric is the imposition of regularized thoroughfares. Such decisions impact the lives of the body politic in profound ways, from the immediate losses of shelter or livelihood as property lines are redrawn and zoning changed, to the sense of history of place, from the destruction of the visual record to the re-routing of familiar movement. In the imposed rationality of Vitruvian planning, there is an opportunity for architectural enterprise to realize a utopian ideal, but this was often in conflict with a desire to conserve the past, even a classical one, unless a program was framed explicitly as reviving that past, and so overlay this achievement upon its consequences.

Tafuri has traced architectural passages that align Vitruvian notions of rule and order with the political writers and humanists of the late fifteenth century who were formative for Gritti and his colleagues.[67] Possibly the most radical aspect of Sansovino's transformation of the Piazza San Marco lay even beyond the style of the buildings in their proposed relationships to each other, in the treatment of the public space. The clearest break with the past was in his realignment of the south side of the Piazza, by ending the Library and isolating the Campanile to create a more regular shape

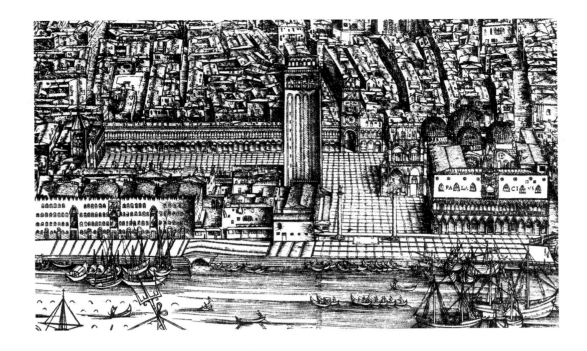

of the projected New Procurators' Offices facing the Old Procurators' Offices, a phase he did not live to realize. This brought the notion of the *foro marciano* into sharper focus than it had had in its medieval form (fig. 45), and produced a new mental order for the center, a perspective similar to those urged in Serlio's theatrical scenes or in the scenography of paintings by young artists such as Jacopo Tintoretto.[68] But the period of the Gritti *renovatio* was a rare interval when the city *imago urbis* could identify itself as the new Rome without the usual conflict that this allusion could induce.

Venice was able to claim unbroken continuity from the "first" Rome, one that had not been sundered by the Sack of 1527, but was inviolate in Venice. Gritti's policies and political support created opportunities for papal sympathizers to convert their taste for the courtly style of the Roman Renaissance to assert Venetian glory and uniqueness. The belief in the uniqueness of Venice always produced tension when compared to other centers, and to Rome above all, due to Rome's dual territorial and spiritual claims. In terms of imagery what did it mean to proclaim the Roman Renaissance style, developed at the Julian court – the enemy of Cambrai – under Bramante and Raphael, and continued under the Medici – whose Tusco-Roman and European ambitions had contributed to the events that led to the Sack? Or did the dispersion of the artists of the Roman court, of which Venice was such a notable beneficiary, realign the very meaning of the style (at least temporarily): a reminder of the origins of Venice, populated by refugees from the barbarian invasions of Attila the Hun, the same whom Leo I had repulsed from Rome?[69] This style was aided by new means of dissemination, as in the work of Serlio, itself transformed by the city of its production, as well as by the "diaspora" that took root where its seeds fell, that is, in Mantua (Giulio Romano), Venice (Sansovino, Serlio), and France (Serlio, Rosso Fiorentino, Francesco Pri-

maticcio). As the style became disassociated with Rome, it could be more easily assimilated.[70] As was also the case with Titian, Sansovino's very longevity contributed to his primacy, particularly given his position as *proto* to the procurators. Sansovino also absorbed the "culture" of the *proto*, and became "naturalized," so that his style came to be seen as Venetian – and thus for Palladio perhaps not sufficiently rigorous in its dialogue with antiquity.

"di andar . . . per servitio di alcuni Signori venetiani"[71]

In the 1540s, when Palladio began projects for his first Venetian patrons, and successfully initiated his Basilica in Vicenza, he had also further widened his experience, through travel and his growing connections. The fall of 1548, just as his final designs for the Basilica were being readied, coincided with the first notice documenting his presence in Venice.[72]

The growing reputation of Palladio, once the construction of the Basilica was underway in the spring of the following year, is demonstrated by his being consulted on the town hall of Brescia in 1550, and, according to his early biographer, on the new St. Peter's in Rome.[73] Venice must have seemed full of opportunity to the architect, with a number of the major building projects of Sansovino coming to fruition, including work in the Piazza on the Loggetta (architecture in 1542, sculpture in 1549), the Mint (1549), and the continuing work on the Library (suspended at sixteen bays in 1554), not to mention the palaces that would be praised in *Venetia, città nobilissima et singolare*, or charitable institutions (*scuole* and *ospedali*) and churches.[74]

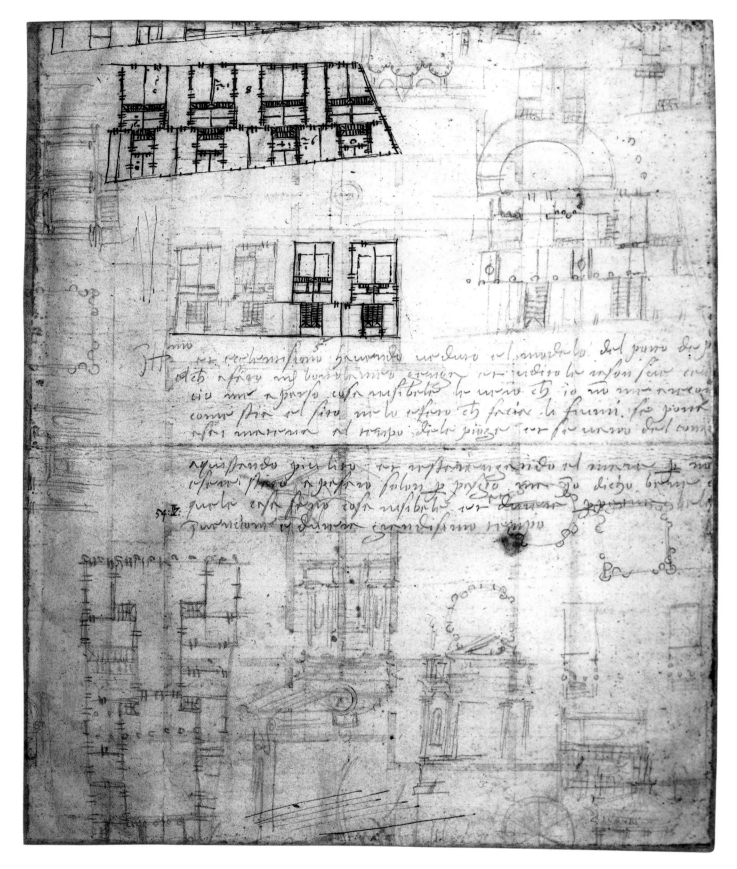

46   Andrea Palladio, *Studies for Ground Plans and Autograph Memorandum*, London, Royal Institute of British Architects, XVI, 9v

CHAPTER THREE

DOMESTIC, PUBLIC,
AND RELIGIOUS PROJECTS

ALTHOUGH THERE HAVE BEEN ATTRIBUTIONS of palaces to Palladio (including a collaboration with Daniele Barbaro on the Palazzo Trevisan, Murano), his early ambitions in this area were not met. That he retained hopes, however, may be seen through a discussion of a number of unrealized projects from grand water-front palaces to public housing schemes. Palladio designed no parish churches, but his superb skills as a stonemason and designer did result in some select parish and private commissions for altars and memorials in various churches. These projects were fruitful for the further contacts he would gain among Venetian clients.

Acknowledgment of Palladio's expertise was the foundation for his authority in both the public and private arena as a judge of proposed projects, executed works, and the development of programs in a wide variety of areas that would touch on all aspects of his practice. As we imagine his working life, it probably constituted more of the episodic requests to provide his expert opinion, interspersed with rounds to the major building sites he was accumulating, and of minor commissions to bolster his long-term, but not individually lucrative salaries.[75] The "quotidian" Palladio that is revealed by his presence to offer his opinion or advice will be examined both here and in other chapters as it occurs in relation to specific projects, the most prestigious being the Doge's Palace.

"I devised the following plan for a site in Venice"

Palladio's advice was highly sought in Venice; one such memorandum indicates that he gave his opinion on a model by Bartolomeo Genga for the seaport of Pesaro that had been sent to the ambassador of Urbino, Count Giovanni Giacomo Leonardi (fig. 46).[76] Although this could not have occurred prior to the summer of 1553, it placed Palladio in an environment that would link his most

important Vicentine and Venetian patrons: while Trissino had died in 1550, Leonardi had been close enough to witness his will in 1543, and Daniele Barbaro had returned to Venice in 1551 following his assignment as ambassador to England (in 1548), and had already accepted the title of patriarch-elect of Aquileia.[77] If the memorandum does date around 1553–54, it also provides us with another insight into Palladio's initial ideas about his Venetian career, since there are a number of preliminary sketches of palace designs on the sheet. Guglielmo De Angelis d'Ossat made a connection of one of these (London, RIBA, XVI, 9BV, "A") to an unexecuted "plan for a site in Venice," which was one of two published in the *Four Books* (Bk. 2, ch. 17, 71, "The site of this first project is triangular," and 72, "I devised the following plan for a site in Venice"), with the names of the patrons discreetly withheld (figs. 47 and 48).[78] To date, Palladio's work for Venetian patrons had been for villas, and given the pattern of his career in Vicenza, where most of his projects were domestic architecture, both palaces and villas, this drawing shows that he expected to entertain similar commissions in Venice; he even entertained ideas for housing projects, as the sketches for two blocks of four row houses along an angled frontage on the upper part of the Leonardi sheet and plans on the *recto* with indications for a Venetian destination testify (fig. 49).[79]

Several proposals have been made to link the two unexecuted projects in the *Four Books* with specific sites in Venice, most agreeing that the "triangular project" was also destined for the city due to the long, narrow, irregular site, tripartite arrangement, and water door. The elevation of three superimposed orders is similar to the "Venice plan," although the latter is more ornate, terminating with Composite over Corinthian and Ionic, and the plan has a coffered tetrastyle hall (on which, *Four Books*, Bk. 2, ch. 8, 36–37). Renato Cevese has offered a cogent analysis of the experimental sequence of spaces in the "triangular project," in which Palladio

DI ALCVNE INVENTIONI SECONDO DIVERSI SITI. Cap. XVII.

MIA INTENTIONE era parlar folo di quelle fabriche, le quali ouero foffero compiute, ouero cominciate, e ridotte à termine che prefto fe ne poteffe fperare il compimento: ma conofcendo il più delle volte auenire, che fia di bifogno accommodarfi à i fiti, perche non fempre fi fabrica in luoghi aperti; mi fono poi perfuafo non douer effer fuori del propofito noftro, lo aggiugnere à' difegni pofti di fopra alcune poche inuentioni fatte da me a requifitione di diuerfi Gentil'huomini, le quali effi non hanno poi efequito per quei rifpetti, che fogliono auenire. Percioche i difficili fiti loro, & il modo c'ho tenuto nell'accomodar in quelli le ftanze, & altri luoghi c'haueffero tra fe corrifpondenza, e proportione; faranno (come io credo) di non picciola vtilità.

Il fito di quefta prima inuentione è piramidale; la bafa della Piramide viene ad effer la facciata principale della cafa: la quale ha tre ordini di colonne, cioè il Dorico, il Ionico, e'l Corinthio: La entrata è quadra, & ha quattro colonne: le quali tolgono fufo il uolto, e proportionano la altezza alla larghezza: dall'vna, e l'altra parte ui fono due ftanze lunghe vn quadro, e due terzi; alte fecondo il primo modo dell'altezza de' uolti: appreffo ciafcuna ui è vn camerino, e fcala da falir ne i mezati: in capo dell'entrata io ui facea due ftanze lunghe vn quadro e mezo, & appreffo due camerini della medefima proportione, con le fcale, che portaffero ne i mezati: e più oltra la Sala lunga vn quadro e due terzi con colonne vguali à quelle dell'entrata: appreffo ui farebbe ftata vna loggia, ne i cui fianchi farebbono ftate le fcale di forma ouale, e più auanti la corte, à canto la quale farebbono ftate le cucine. Le feconde ftanze, cioè quelle del fecondo ordine haurebbono hauuto di altezza piedi uenti, e quelle del terzo xviij. Ma l'altezza dell'vna, e l'altra fala farebbe ftata fino fotto il coperto; e quefte fale haurebbono hauuto al pari del piano delle ftanze fuperiori alcuni poggiuoli, c'haurebbono feruito ad allogar perfone di rifpetto al tempo di fefte, banchetti, e fimili follazzi.

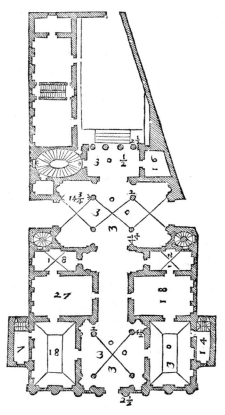

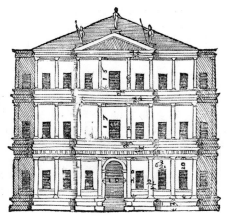

FECI

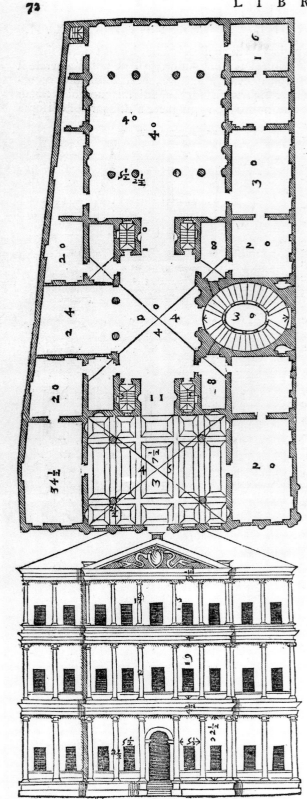

FECI per vn sito in Venetia la sottoposta inuentione: la faccia principale ha tre ordini di colonne, il primo è Ionico, il secondo Corinthio, & il terzo Composito. La entrata esce alquanto in fuori: ha quattro colonne vguali, e simili à quelle della facciata. Le stanze, che sono da i fianchi hanno i uolti alti secondo il primo modo dell'altezza de' volti: oltra queste ui sono altre stanze minori, e camerini, e le scale, che seruono a i mezati. Rincontro all'entrata ui è vn'andito, per il quale si entra in vn'altra Sala minore, la quale da vna parte ha vna corticella, dalla quale prende lume, e dall'altra la scala maggiore, e principale di forma ouata, e uacua nel mezo, con le colonne intorno, che tolgono suso i gradi: più oltre per vn'altro andito si entra in una loggia, le cui colonne sono Ioniche vguali a quelle dell'entrata. Hà questa loggia un'appartamento per banda, come quelli dell'entrata: ma quello, ch'è nella parte sinistra uiene alquanto diminuito per cagion del sito: appresso ui è vna corte con colonne intorno, che fanno corritore, il quale serue alle camere di dietro, oue starebbono le donne, e ui sarebbono le cucine. La parte di sopra è simile à quella di sotto, eccetto che la sala, che è sopra la entrata non ha colonna, e giugne con la sua altezza sino sotto il tetto, & ha vn corritore, ò poggiuolo al piano delle terze stanze, che seruirebbe ancho alle finestre di sopra: perche in questa Sala ue ne sarebbono due ordini. La Sala minore haurebbe la trauatura al pari de i volti delle seconde stanze, e sarebbono questi uolti alti uentitre piedi: le stanze del terzo ordine sarebbono in solaro di altezza di diceotto piedi. Tutte le porte, e finestre s'incontrerebbono, e sarebbono una sopra l'altra, e tutti i muri haurebbono la lor parte di carico: le Cantine, i luoghi da lauar i drappi, & gli altri magazini sarebbono stati accommodati sotto terra.

FECI

48   Andrea Palladio, "On Some Projects for Different Sites," *I quattro libri dell'architettura*, Venice, Appresso Dominico de' Franceschi, 1570, lib. 2, cap. 17, 72, "I devised the following plan for a site in Venice"

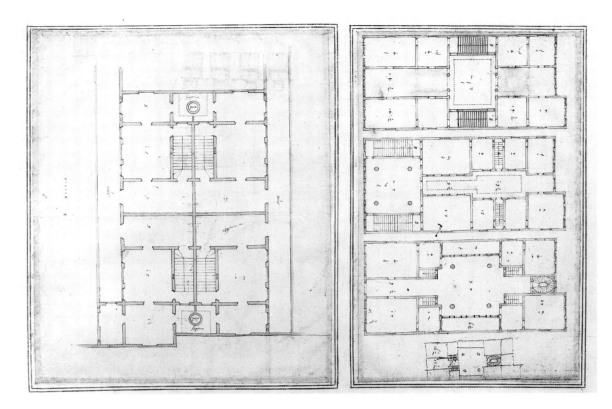

49   Andrea Palladio, *Studies for Ground Plan for Small Housing Development* (A) *and Four Ground Plans for Palace* (B), London, Royal Institute of British Architects, XVI, 9r

50   Ottavio Bertotti Scamozzi, "Reconstruction of a Section for the Triangular Project," *Le fabbriche e i disegni di Andrea Palladio*, Vicenza, 1796, lib. IV, tav. XXXIII

51 Mocenigo and Contarini dalle Figure Palaces, Grand Canal at San Samuele, Venice

52 Jacopo de' Barbari, *View of Venice*, Venice, 1500, detail of Mocenigo Palaces at San Samuele

arranges rooms of diverse orientation and size along an axis beginning with a four-columned single-bay cross-vaulted atrium at the waterfront, debouching into a large transverse four-columned triple-bay cross-vaulted salon with four arched openings, and terminating in a loggia.[80] The spatial effects are evocatively reconstructed in Ottavio Bertotti Scamozzi's drawn sections from Palladio's plans and elevations (fig. 50). The design, although retaining a traditional Byzantine tripartite organization, would have significantly reinterpreted the Venetian *portego*, the long hall that drew light into the core of Venetian palace interiors. De Angelis d'Ossat identified the site as that of the future Palazzo Grassi at San Samuele. Another site on the Grand Canal at San Samuele was later identified with the "triangular project," as that of the Mocenigo palaces, belonging to the future Doge Alvise Mocenigo (1570–77) and his brother Giovanni, since the "casa nuova" was undergoing construction in 1579 (figs. 51 and 52). A positive factor in favor of this hypothesis is that it strengthens the ties of patronage between Palladio and Alvise Mocenigo: Mocenigo frequented some of the same academic circles as Palladio's early supporters in Padua and Vicenza (he was *capitano* in the latter city from 1539 to 1541), and would be critical for Palladio's late entry into State patronage.[81]

The importance of the palimpsest of cultural and academic circles in Palladio's introduction to Venice cannot be overestimated. It seems likely that the frequency of Giangiorgio Trissino's stays in Venice during the 1540s offered Palladio an opportunity to join him there, for example, if he accompanied Trissino to Rome in 1541, it was from Padua via Murano. Trissino had enthused on the delights of his residence there at San Donato, and the gardens of Murano were noted for gatherings of intelligentsia. The will that Leonardi

had witnessed in 1543 even specified that Trissino would be buried at Santa Maria degli Angeli (although this was superseded). Interlocutors in the Paduan humanist Sperone Speroni's *Dialogues* link supporters from Trissino's circle to that of Daniele Barbaro, naming Leonardi, as well as the founder of the Accademia della Fama (also known as "della Veneziana"), Federico Badoer, and helping to clarify the network that brought Palladio into Barbaro's ambit in the 1550s, and turned his attention to success in the Serenissima.[82]

A tangible example of how the collaboration that would produce the villa at Maser and Vitruvius would be translated into Venice can be seen in two projects that originated with Barbaro. The first is a palace designed for Camillo di Bernardo Trevisan at San Donato in Murano (fig. 53), described as "undoubtedly the most important house of the Renaissance" on the island (Richard Goy), but "not a manifesto of the new architecture" (Manfredo Tafuri).[83] The earliest attribution assigns it to Daniele Barbaro, with the nineteenth-century author of a monograph on the Palazzo Trevisan describing him as "a follower of Palladio."[84] Later scholarship identified elements used elsewhere in Venice by Palladio (most notably at Santa Maria della Carità), such as the Doric frieze (fig. 54) and bi-apsidal spaces (fig. 55) typical of his plans and theories of the ancient house, such as the "Corinthian Hall." In this circumstance, the collaborative relationship might be imagined as similar to that of the production of the Vitruvius, with Barbaro as the author of the commentaries and Palladio contributing his direct knowledge from his study of ancient monuments and texts, as well as his design skills towards specific aspects of its realization. Trevisan had taken a degree in law at Padua and was the lawyer for the Accademia della Fama, as well as a host of notable gatherings at his palace, which was designed and built in 1556–57, with its decoration by Alessandro Vittoria and Paolo Veronese and his team through 1558, contemporary to the *équipe* for the Villa Barbaro at Maser.

Barbaro was also the agent in 1557 for the widow Giulia Ferretti, who commissioned a tomb monument in Santo Stefano in Venice for her husband, Giovanni Battista Ferretti (died 1556), a lawyer from Vicenza who had studied in Padua (fig. 56).[85] The innovations in this tomb represent a turning point in Venetian sculpture and tomb architecture, and even the conceptualization of the individual, since Alessandro Vittoria's bust of Ferretti is the first *all'antica* portrait bust to be introduced into Venice. It is placed on a sarcophagus, which Howard Burns has attributed to Palladio, based on comparisons to his work in Vicenza, where Vittoria had just been engaged in the decoration of the Palazzo Thiene.

The association of Palladio with a rigorously classical language and its impact when inserted into the fabric of the city has led scholars to hypothesize his two domestic projects for Venice in the *Four Books* as potentially being critiques of contemporary works by the reigning masters Sansovino and Sanmicheli, or at least as hopeful

53   Daniele Barbaro with Andrea Palladio, façade, Palazzo Trevisan, Murano

55 (*right*)   Daniele Barbaro with Andrea Palladio, plan of Palazzo Trevisan, Murano, in Francesco Muttoni, *Architettura di Andrea Palladio*, Venice, 1740–48, tav. 37, 35

54 (*below*)   Daniele Barbaro with Andrea Palladio, Doric frieze, Palazzo Trevisan, Murano

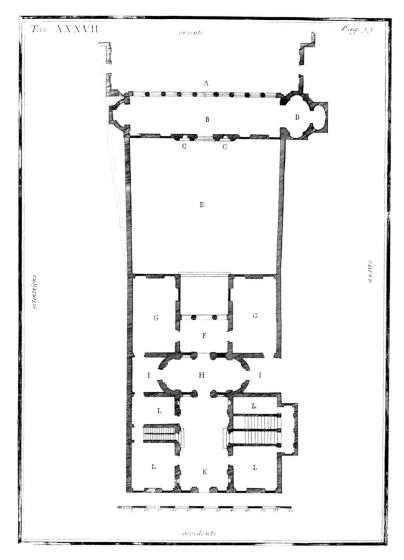

56 Alessandro Vittoria (copy substituted for original bust now in Paris, Musée du Louvre) and Andrea Palladio, tomb monument of Giovanni Battista Ferretti, Santo Stefano, Venice

IOAN. BAPT. FERRETTO.
VICENT. IVR. VTR. DOCT.
PRÆSTANTIS. ET. INTE
GER. VIRO. IVLIA. VXOR.
PIIS. ET. SIBI. POSVIT.

alternative proposals for two of the most imposing examples of palace building then underway: identifying the "triangular project" with Sanmicheli's palace at San Luca for Girolamo di Marino Grimani, and the "Venice plan" with Sansovino's palace for Giorgio ("Zorzetto") di Giacomo Corner della Regina (or specifically, "Cha Grande").[86] Yet, as Palladio's words in the *Four Books* indicate, these inventions for difficult situations remained on paper. This failure of Palladio's ambitions cannot be simply attributed to the alignment of factions, but must take into account the patterns of patronage that were identified with individual families. Papalist family patrons of Sansovino might find themselves in the company of a member of the *giovani* in voting to defend his work against the claims of a more radical classical style. A later case in point is the debate from 1582 to 1588 over the completion and proposed modification of Sansovino's Library by Vincenzo Scamozzi, a severe critic of the

classical style of his predecessors. If political alignments behind choices made by the Venetian government in matters of architectural style can be held to be valid, then the actions of Andrea di Giovanni (Zuane) Dolfin require some kind of justification, for this member of a strongly papalist *case vecchie* family is found to be voting with the conservative *giovani* who succeeded in blocking the intervention in Sansovino's design advocated by Marc'Antonio Barbaro, among others.[87] If we think of the supporters of a classical style as falling into different groups defined by generational alliances, however, this alignment becomes more meaningful in our exploration of Palladio's fortunes in the city, rather than invalidating the categories of analysis. One such group, the early adopters of the Roman High Renaissance style imported to Venice by Sansovino, Sanmicheli, and Serlio, remained adherents of that interpretation of ancient architecture, especially since their own family

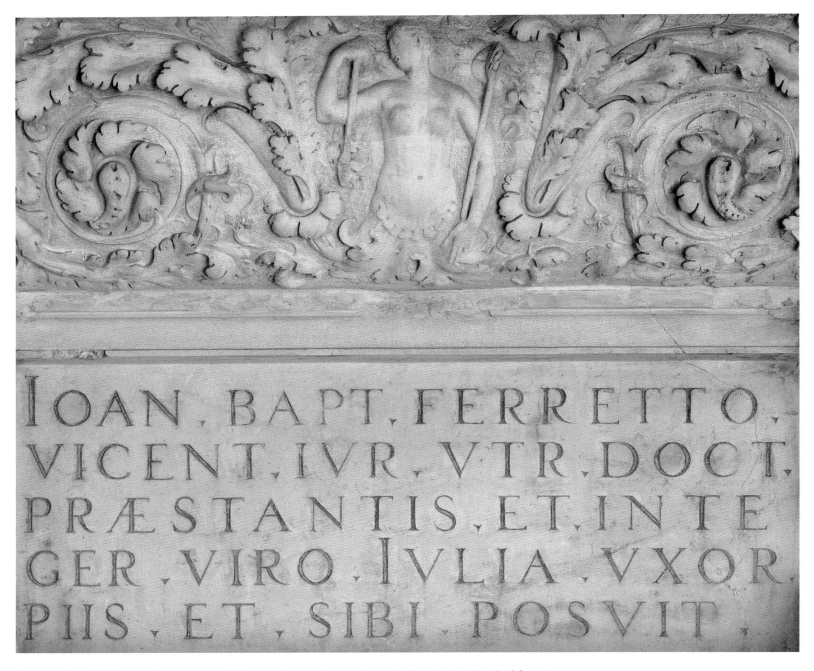

IOAN·BAPT·FERRETTO·
VICENT·IVR·VTR·DOCT·
PRÆSTANTIS·ET·INTE
GER·VIRO·IVLIA·VXOR
PIIS·ET·SIBI·POSVIT·

above   Andrea Palladio, tomb monument of Giovanni Battista Ferretti, Santo Stefano, Venice (detail of fig. 56)

identities had become bound up with it from the grand palaces praised in *Venetia, città nobilissima et singolare*, which, indeed, was the case with Dolfin. That a rapprochement with Sansovino's classical style later could be envisioned with upholders of a conservative *venezianità* can be understood as typifying Venetian strategies of assimilating her own past, illustrated by both patrons and *proti*.

One of the more outspoken partisans of the later Library debate was Leonardo Donà, a leader of the *giovani* and doge (1606–12), who would figure strongly in the history of Palladio's reception. In the instructions he left for building his own palace in an important zone of urban development of the Fondamenta Nuove, a delibe-

rate reference to earlier aesthetic values has been seen, specifically *mediocritas*, expressed in the fifteenth century as appropriately republican (fig. 57). A contemporary chronicler reported Donà's brother Nicolò as saying "that for all the money spent it would have bought the most beautiful palace in Venice, and one in the best site, which this *casa* [house] was not, nor had it the form of a *palazzo*."[88] While it is certainly true that the ornament of Donà's palace lacks the rich classical decoration of the Istrian cladding of the Corner, Pisani, and Dolfin palace façades, its vocabulary, nonetheless, is that of Rome. Its external decorum, in fact, is related to a number of other palaces whose classicizing stone ornament largely consists of the window surrounds, string courses and cornice, loggias, and portal; the combination of windows with round-headed arches topped by straight lintels, rectangular frames with straight lintels, and square-framed windows distinguished these Renaissance palaces from their Veneto-Gothic and -Byzantine forebears. The decoration of Donà's palace is not so far from the vocabulary of the earlier palace of Andrea Gritti near San Francesco della Vigna (fig. 58), where one would have expected a sharper contrast given their differing political philosophies, especially as concerned personal display. Donà was not rejecting the grammar, but the rhetorical style of its application. Moreover, what both palaces do have in common is their notably monumental scale.

Through the vocabulary of *mediocritas*, both the Donà and Gritti palaces convey territorial control through their massive occupation of Venetian real estate. A sense of power, not the luxury of magnificence, is the particular mode that is expressed. The Gritti Palace was actually two palaces joined by a garden, and was considered adequately impressive – yet discreetly located away from the center – to be bought by the Venetian government from Gritti's heirs in 1585 and given to the papal nuncio.[89] There is no doubt that the Republic felt it had to provide a sufficiently grand habitation for the legate, and it may be that the deciding element by that date was Palladio's embellishment of the façade of the facing church, where the luxurious marble cladding was employed in the service of religion. Since the papal nuncio might be called upon to house visiting Church dignitaries, the Gritti Palace had to be commodious enough to accommodate the ceremonial needs attendant upon princes of the Church. The exterior space then comprised the campo, and the façades of palace and church performed a liminal function in the city, one of the rare *loci* where foreign powers were ceded a presence, even though it too would be effectively inscribed into the State by ritual means. One such example can be seen in the dogal *andata* of 1598, on the occasion of the recognition of the visit of Cardinal Aldobrandini:

> Thus processed his Serenity [the doge], the most eccellent Collegio, and the usual Magistrates. The Cardinal [previously incognito during his visit to the city] came to meet them in the court of the *casa* so described, attired in the robes of a cardinal, accompanied by many prelates, and, with a joyous face, he received his Serenity. Walking and talking with him on the right hand, they ended up in a large upper room, where a baldacchino with two seats were prepared, and stationed themselves to be seated, with the Cardinal on the right hand. They passed diverse compliments between themselves, and then we returned below in the usual order, the Cardinal having wanted to accompany his Serenity up to and outside the portal of the Palace that gave onto the campo of San Francesco, processing for reasons of *acqua bassa* [low water] to enter the boats at Santa Giustina, accompanied by Signor Giovanni Battista dal Monte, General delle Fantiere, who one finds as a member of the court of the Cardinal.[90]

A tension between public and private in the typology of the palace existed where *magnificenza* could be upheld as a civic adorn-

57 Palazzo Donà, Fondamenta Nuove, Venice

58 Palazzo Gritti, San Francesco della Vigna, Venice

59   Andrea Palladio, *Façade Elevation for a Waterfront Palace*, Vicenza, Museo Civico, D 27

ment or seen as a monument to individual pride. Similar tension resonated in attitudes toward ecclesiastical architecture, between the purity of *simplicitas* and the desire (as here expressed by Palladio) to "consider the dignity and grandeur of God," which required "magnificent ornaments." Palladio's words are from his "Foreword to the Readers" for Book Four on temples (*Four Books*).[91] This same language could be applied to the impressive finished *Façade Elevation for a Waterfront Palace* (Vicenza, Museo Civico, D 27), which suggests how Palladio would have approached a prestigious palace commission in Venice, although its destination has been debated (fig. 59).[92] His exploration of the waterfront palace type can be seen in the two studies on the London sheet (RIBA, X, 15, "D" and "E") in figure 20, in which he develops the theme of the central triple light, but with orders on two storys, rather than the application of the

temple front that would become a hallmark of his domestic design.[93] The only compromise made with Venetian tradition in the Vicenza drawing is the tripartite palace typology with a water entrance, but the use of the monumental Corinthian order announces a façade solution that differed from those of Sansovino and Sanmicheli, as well as his own proposals in the "triangular project" and "Venice plan" in the *Four Books*, but which would only be realized in the temple fronts of his Venetian churches, and may indicate a later date. The design would have been a unique insertion into the fabric of the city, and signals Palladio's inventiveness, possibly at odds with the conservative nature of Venice. The interesting variation of the rustication of the lower podium story and two *piano nobile* storys, the differentiation between the storys of the fenestration with its lower Serliana, and the rhythms of the balconies bespeak an assured assimilation of the current masters, coupled with his now considerable experience of ancient Rome, that marks the culmination of his early period as he sought to establish himself in the city.

The generation of *proti* competing at the same time as Palladio to establish themselves in their careers in Venice represented a mix of backgrounds, some coming from a traditional guild training, others with increasingly specialized knowledge, particularly as engineers, reflecting the epistemological division between "experience" and "science."[94] Regardless of that fundamental difference, this generation had grown up with and absorbed examples of the new classical style of architecture, so the gap between their products and those of the humanist architect had become less apparent in their style. Palladio's lack of "compromise" has been seen as an explanation for his failure to attain significant domestic commissions in Venice, but the period of his later prominence saw few new major palaces begun during the War of Cyprus.

From the Hand and Mind of the Master

Palladio's two independent commissions for parish churches were both for liturgical furnishings, now lost, and bracket the beginning and end of his Venetian career. His first work to be executed in Venice was for the high altar of San Pantalon, possibly arranged through the offices of his imminent villa patrons Nicolò and Alvise Foscari of the San Pantalon branch (*ramo*) of the family. The last notice of Palladio in the city before his death was in 1579, when he was present at San Giorgio Maggiore, and also had been paid for the design of a *pergola* at San Zulian.[95] Both represent the value that would continue to reside in Palladio's knowledge of the stone-mason's trade, translated into his capabilities as an extraordinary designer of classical ornament, and whose opinion would be sought on the work of others.

The first work in stone that was produced by Palladio in Venice was a design for the high altar of San Pantalon (1555–58).[96] This was initiated by the priest, Monsignor Nicolò Moravio, who asked his parishioners to subscribe to a building fund. Among the patricians who either complied or later acted as a Church Works Committee (*procuratori*) were: Bernardo di Nicolò Giustinian, Alvise di Galeazzo Contarini, Alessandro di Faustino Barbo, Matteo di Alberto Marin, and Alvise di Federico Foscari. The last, together with his brother, would be some of Palladio's most fortunate patrons, since he designed for them the lovely Villa Foscari at Gambarare di Mira, known as "La Malcontenta," *circa* 1560 (fig. 60).[97] There is no visual record of the altar, but such a project reflects the kind of work that Palladio had long experience in, from his training in the Pedemuro workshop in Vicenza, to the level of detail that he brought to his building projects.

Another significant aspect of this commission, although one that remains divided between art and architectural historical literature, is the fulfillment of Palladio's design with an altarpiece by Paolo Veronese, his moving late work, the *Miracle of the Boy Bitten by a*

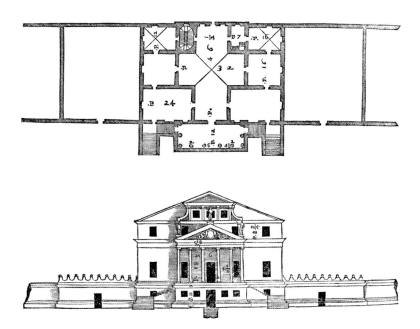

60   Andrea Palladio, Villa Foscari at Gambarare, *I quattro libri dell'architettura*, Venice, Appresso Dominico de' Franceschi, 1570, lib. 2, cap. 14, 50

Serpent and Resuscitated by San Pantalon (fig. 61).[98] This was ordered by the parish priest, Bartolomeo Borghi, in 1578, who was depicted in it as a witness to the miracle, and some connection to Palladio's patron, the patriarch Giovanni Grimani, is suggested by the inclusion of a famous antiquity, the "Grimani torso."[99] As with many of Palladio's monumental architectural projects, the decoration would take place after his death; yet the long association of his classical framework and the art of Veronese suggests a compatibility of intent. After the death of Paolo, the chapel was completed in 1599 with *laterali* by Palma il Giovane, showing the *Miracle of the Paralytic by San Pantalon in Front of Emperor Maximilian* and the *Martyrdom of San Pantalon*. The church was restructured and reoriented in the late seventeenth century, and the high altar dismantled, only the paintings were replaced in a chapel dedicated to the titular saint, with Palladio's altar lost.[100]

These limited parish commissions do not, however, match the larger aspirations for Palladio's architectural enterprise. These were to be achieved in the arena of religious architecture, a departure from his former practice in the Veneto, and for patrons from patriarchs to monastic orders to the State itself, the subjects of Parts III and IV. His ambitions for domestic architecture would be realized only in the convent of Santa Maria della Carità, where he recreated the house of the ancients. But Palladio's practice had a practical side to it as well, and as he established himself in the late 1550s and the 1560s, he was more and more frequently called upon for his expert opinion. Some of these came in the arena of private housing, such as the arbitration in late 1566 when he was called in as part of a panel that included Sansovino to judge the work at the Palazzo Grimani at San Luca (which he may have thought on

of the Doge's Palace after the fire of 1574, discussed in Part V. Increasingly in the 1570s, Palladio was involved in work for the State, during the dogate of Alvise Mocenigo (1570–77), and the period of the War of Cyprus. He was seen as an expert in all manner of stonework, including sculpture, as his judgment of the work by Domenico da Salò for a tomb monument of Giovanni dalla Vrana in San Giuseppe in Castello shows (fig. 62).[105] Dalla Vrana was the *armiraio* ("admiral") of Sebastian Venier at the Battle of Lepanto, and the tomb frontal depicts the Venetian galleys. In the 1570s the bulk of Palladio's opinions would be sought for the defense of the Republic, by the Arsenale, and magistrates for the fortresses, no doubt enhanced by his demonstration of erudition in military engineering and strategy with his publication of the *Caesar*.[106]

62 Domenico da Salò, tomb monument of Giovanni dalla Vrana, San Giuseppe in Castello, Venice

61 Paolo Veronese, *Miracle of the Boy Bitten by a Serpent and Resuscitated by San Pantalon*, San Pantalon, Venice

earlier in his study for a "triangular project" in the *Four Books*).[101] We also find Palladio with Giovanni Antonio Rusconi in 1572 requested by the patricians Marco di Benetto Marin and Piero di Gerolamo Malipiero to judge the subdivision of their palace at San Benedetto into separate habitations.[102] That both the hand and the mind of Palladio were increasingly valued is demonstrated by recommendations of State *proti* that he be consulted,[103] and by his role in the *vigna* (a large walled garden with casino) at "Quattro Cantoni" on the Lido for his first mainland Venetian patron, Vettor di Giovanni Pisani, and his brother Daniele between 1573 and 1575.[104] Palladio both provided his exemplary classical details with *sagome* (template drawings) for the capitals and structural expertise on the vaulting executed by Rusconi, while Antonio da Ponte was responsible for the walls of the garden; this was exactly the moment when the same team were involved in work of the restoration

Despite support from influential Venetian patricians, Palladio remained an outsider, in contrast to Jacopo Sansovino (1486–1570). His most significant opinion, on the restoration of the Doge's Palace after the second fire of 1577 was not followed, as we shall see. Yet as Palladio's architectural status rose, he was often called in as an expert to give his opinion on everything from altarpiece frames to fortifications. In a sense, this may be seen as a form of independent enterprise on the architect's part, since he did not hold the office of *proto* with any of the magistracies that routinely supplied experts. Palladio's practice represents a shift in the profession of the archi-

tect, from a traditional reliance on practical experience to a newly evolving scientific approach. The mentality that Palladio and his supporters represented had been shaped in the intellectual environments of the courtly households and academies of Vicenza, Padua, Rome, Venice, and Murano. As the next generation came of age and the last of the Compagnie della Calza were formed, some of these cultural links would also prove significant in establishing networks of patronage and shared tastes for the *usanza nuova* of Palladio's architectural language.

63   Giovanni Grevembroch, *Stemmi of the Compagni of the Compagnia della Calza degli Accesi*, Venice, Biblioteca del Museo Civico Correr, Cod. Gradenigo-Dolfin, 155, 1:4

CHAPTER FOUR

COMPAGNIA DELLA CALZA DEGLI ACCESI

Looking to the decade beyond Palladio's first executed commission in Venice at San Pantalon, we can see how this trajectory of patronal relationships continued to evolve and define his career. His lost "Half-theater of wood to serve as a Colosseum" for the Compagnia della Calza degli Accesi in 1565 linked the academic cultures of Venice with those of Vicenza.[107] By this date, Palladio had become thoroughly identified with a patronage base that notably included the Foscari, the Badoer, the Pisani, the Barbaro, and the Grimani, among others already mentioned. These patrons were particularly associated with broad changes taking place in Venetian society that saw the expanded development of the *terraferma*, objectified in their magnificent villa projects, and not incidentally were from houses that held important Church benefices. In relation to the incipient factionalism that was feared in response to these changes in the orientation of the patriciate, these patrons were associated with a set of ideological positions often accorded to the *vecchi*, especially pro-papalist affiliations and oligarchical tendencies. Additionally, their academic and cultural aspirations coincided in an expressed taste for Roman style. Palladio's entry into Venice from a patronage base of *terraferma* families would condition his opportunities in the capital. The tension between incipient factions in the patriciate affected the career of Palladio, since on the cultural front they concerned themselves with conflicting conceptions of the identity of Venice, what it had been and what it should be.

By controlling the image of the city, unofficial factions expressed the virtues they believed to be consistent with Venice in a struggle to impose *their* vision onto the idea of unity and concord that was so much a part of its mythopoeia.[108] The exploration of other cultural sub-sets, "social unities," can likewise reveal linkages; Tafuri formulated the notion of adherents to a specific style, i.e., *partita palladiana*, to describe shared taste for the architect's style and its promotion. Actual institutionalized groups provided the foundations for meaningful networks that were often reinforced through family alliances. The Compagnie della Calza, might be called "cultural clans," since these were patrician youth groups dedicated to self-display and entertainments previous to their coming of age and entering the Great Council (fig. 63). Equally formative for habits of mental thought, influencing social and religious beliefs, but enduring into maturity, were the academies, which could be seen as "intellectual clans." Both produced lasting and often intersecting networks of patronage.[109] Such social networks are fluid and multi-layered, and most telling when multiple points of contact can be shown, and a consistency of pattern is found when compared to the circumstances of career and production of the architect.

The location of Palladio's lost theater after the antique has been satisfactorily identified in the vicinity of San Simeon Piccolo, probably in the grounds of the Foscari Palace, since, in 1565, the prior of the Company of the Accesi was Gerolamo di Pietro Foscari (1562–65), of the San Simeon Piccolo *ramo* of the family (fig. 64).[110] His father, Pietro di Marco Foscari (1512–1581), may well have been the catalyst for the commission, since his support for such an endeavor on the grounds of the family palace would have been necessary, especially as he was keenly interested in building and classical culture (fig. 65). Pietro was of Palladio's and Daniele Barbaro's generation and had attended the Studio of Padua in 1529; as we have seen, his sister Paola Foscari had married Vettor Pisani of Bagnolo, Palladio's first Venetian patron on the *terraferma*, linking them all to the same intellectual climate of Padua. Pietro's father, Marco di Giovanni, and Palladio's mentor, Trissino, had moved in the same Medicean papal circles that included the cardinal bishop of Vicenza, Nicolò Ridolfi, and the Grimani family of Santa Maria Formosa, and Pietro would reinforce family ties when he married Elena, daughter of Marco Grimani – procurator, briefly patriarch of Aquileia, and papal general – and Bianca di Francesco K.P. Foscari. Pietro's mother, Orsa di Filippo Capello of the Santa Maria Mater Domini *ramo*, would relate him to the Barbaro family of San Vidal through her mother, Maria di Zaccaria K.P., Daniele Barbaro's pater-

64   Giovanni Grevembroch, *Gerolamo di Pietro Foscari as Priore of the Compagnia della Calza degli Accesi*, Venice, Biblioteca del Museo Civico Correr, Cod. Gradenigo-Dolfin, 155, 1:7

65 Dionisio Moretti, detail of Palazzo Foscari, Grand Canal at Rio Marin and San Simeon Piccolo, Venice, from Antonio Quadri, *Il Canal Grande di Venezia*, Venice, 1831, pl. 15

nal great-aunt.[111] Responsibility for the architectural renovations of the family palace on the Grand Canal and Rio Marin in Venice (little of the Gothic building remains incorporated in the present structure), and their "casa grande" at the Arena in Padua (destroyed in the early nineteenth century), has been attributed to Pietro, and the special nature of the latter site may have occasioned his study of the ancient theater.[112] Palladio was known not only to Gerolamo Foscari's father, but to the father of another of the company, Francesco Badoer, commissioner of the innovative villa at Fratta Polesine, whose son Marc'Antonio and his two cousins were also members of the Accesi and could have been additional supporters of this commission.[113] Pietro Foscari would later play a crucial role in the restoration of the Doge's Palace that involved Palladio, as would the Badoer, where their connections in the sphere of State patronage will be further explored.

Palladio's theater was built to debut a performance of *L'Antigono* on 28 February 1565, a tragedy written by the Vicentine Antonio Pigatti, Conte De Monte, and published a month later in Venice by Giovanni Battista Maganza, with a dedication to Francesco di Giovanni Pisani.[114] Maganza had accompanied Palladio and Trissino to Rome in 1545, and would share other patrons both in Vicenza (Capra, Thiene) and in Venice (Jacopo Contarini). The sponsorship of Pisani may have been to secure the publication privilege, or it may indicate the closer cultural involvement of Palladio's friend and patron at Montagnana and at his *vigna* on the Lido, indicating, in any case, the continued ties between academic circles from Padua to Vicenza to Venice. The theme of Antigone has been analyzed as an allegory of Venice as the New Jerusalem, and a defense of magnificence as compatible with love of country, one of the recurring tensions in government relations with the *Calza*.[115] The theater was decorated by twelve scenes (subjects unspecified) on canvases measuring 7½ feet painted by Federico Zuccaro. According to Vasari, Zuccaro had come to Venice as artist to the patriarch of Aquileia, Giovanni Grimani, the third of the Grimani brothers of Santa Maria Formosa to hold this title. Where his brother, Procurator Vettor, had patronized Sansovino, Giovanni would become a supporter of Palladio, as will be seen in Part III. Zuccaro and Palladio had probably just returned to Venice from a trip they took together to Cividale, one of the patriarchy's principal towns, suggesting their personal as well as artistic collaboration.[116]

The silence in later sources about Palladio's theater after the antique has led scholars to conclude that it was soon destroyed, attributable to its being erected on the property as an ephemeral wood and canvas outdoor structure. Its inheritance would be in Palladio's late project for the Teatro Olimpico in Vicenza, and in the links he would form through his associations with this cultural set.

PART III

THE PATRIARCHS

66a Giovanni Grevembroch, *Patriarch of Venice*, "Gli abiti de Veneziani," 1754, Venice, Biblioteca del Museo Civico Correr, Cod. Gradenigo, 49, 2:12

66b Giovanni Grevembroch, *Patriarch of Aquileia*, "Gli abiti de Veneziani," 1754, Venice, Biblioteca del Museo Civico Correr, Cod. Gradenigo, 49, 2:5

INTRODUCTION

PALLADIO SUCCEEDED IN OBTAINING HIS FIRST monumental project in Venice in 1558 – for the façade design of the church of San Pietro di Castello, which was the patriarchal and episcopal seat of the city, although it was not completed in his lifetime.[1] He was subsequently commissioned by the patriarch of Aquileia to execute the façade of the church of San Francesco della Vigna, the only church façade that he would see built. These façades have raised different issues regarding the circumstances of their commission and initiation, fidelity to the architect's design and its relation to contemporary architecture, and their respective programs and patrons. Palladio's designs were the public face of the two patriarchates, and the individual patricians who held those offices. The patriarch of Venice (fig. 66a) and the patriarch of Aquileia (fig. 66b) held telling roles in the complex and often uneasy relations of Church and State in Venice.

These two venerable patriarchates exerted supra-metropolitan control over the episcopates in their respective territories. By the sixteenth century, both had been displaced from their medieval seats, with the title of the patriarchy of Grado translated to the patriarchy of Venice, and the patriarchy of Aquileia removed from Habsburg threat in Aquileia to reside in Venetian-held Udine. The patriarchy of Venice was moved to the site of the bishopric of Olivolo, in the *sestiere*, or district, of Castello, at the eastern edge of Venice. The church of the patriarch was San Pietro di Castello, which was the cathedral of Venice until the fall of the Republic in 1797. As Venice had expanded her territories on the mainland in the fifteenth century, and again after the War of the League of Cambrai (1509–17), many of the dioceses belonging to the two patriarchates had come under her governance, which curtailed the temporal rule once the prerogative of the patriarchs. To ensure further political control, Venice insisted on the rights to the election of the patriarchs, which was contested by both Rome and the Habsburg empire. Although Venice managed to obtain agreement over the nomination of the patriarch of Venice, the case for the nomination of the patriarch of Aquileia was far more tenuous and was disputed for most of the century. Characteristic of the Republic's mistrust of the Church was a preference for selecting the patriarch of Venice from among those patricians who had fulfilled civic roles for the government rather than from churchmen. Uncertainty over the retention of the nomination of the patriarch of Aquileia led to another strategy, the addition of a patriarch-elect, who would automatically succeed in the event of the death of the incumbent.

That Palladio's first major commission in Venice was for a church façade signals a new direction in his career. The innovations that he would bring to church design reflect his ideas about the ancient temple, familiarity with modern solutions, and intelligent accommodation of patrons' needs in the public expression of their respective programs. Investigation of the circumstances of these commissions shows how Palladio moved from the *terraferma* to the capital having established a critical base of support, one that conditioned future alignments as well. The patronage of the patriarchs conferred a high status on the architect's services in the ecclesiastical community, leading to further important commissions.

CHAPTER FIVE

SAN PIETRO DI CASTELLO

T HE PATRICIAN VICENZO DI ALVISE DIEDO was patriarch of Venice (1556–59) when he ordered a marble façade for San Pietro di Castello from Palladio in early January 1558. Although we have only Palladio's contract to judge by, the six large columns and smaller square pilasters that it called for are consistent with his development of the application of the antique temple front to the façade of the Christian church.[2] His vision for the classically ornamented marble façade would have publicly communicated the high dignity of the patriarchate. Work on the façade halted with the death of the patriarch on 8 December 1559, and was not resumed during Palladio's lifetime. Unfortunately, all that may record that the façade was begun are drawings reportedly made by Antonio Visentini of some fragments of a doorway that were evidently preserved when the present façade was erected by Francesco Smeraldi.[3] The initial failure of execution cannot be adequately explained alone by the death of Diedo less than a year after the contract for the façade, and points to the growing division among the patriciate in the second half of the century. Patriarchal power was contested between Church and State, exemplified in the public debate over Diedo's finances, which he blamed on the expenses of living and building in the style appropriate to his position, as will be discussed below. Not until the election of Patriarch Lorenzo Priuli (1590–1600) was the façade executed by Francesco Smeraldi on Palladian models, and Priuli's elevation to cardinal is celebrated in his coat of arms on the patriarchal palace (figs. 67 and 68). It was completed in 1596, the year of Priuli's elevation to cardinal, and would reflect the associations of Palladio's legacy in the lagoon. The importance of this church reached beyond its position as the cathedral of Venice. As the church of the patriarch it assumed a status shared by an elite number of venerable institutions, not least its namesake in Rome, whose pastoral authority was wielded by the pope. The receipt of this commission illustrated the growing authority of Palladio and the influence of his connections.

That the Barbaro brothers, Daniele, patriarch-elect of Aquileia (1551–70), and the statesman Marc'Antonio, supplied the vital link in this context is supported by the primary evidence for the project, in which they are both named as witnesses to the contract executed between the Patriarch Diedo and the two stoneworkers (*tagliapietre*) – who undertook to carry out the work "according to the designs made by Palladio" ("secondo la forma delli disegni veduti et considerati da loro, fatti da mes. Andrea Palladio").[4] The Barbaros remained crucial members of Palladio's network of patrons who can be credited with bringing the architect to the patriarch's attention. Following the publication of the Vitruvius in 1556, Palladio

68   *Stemma* of Cardinal Patriarch Lorenzo Priuli, Patriarchal Palace, San Pietro di Castello, Venice

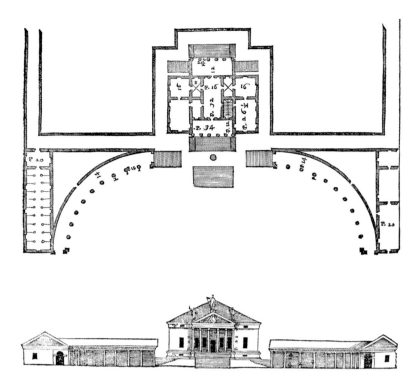

69   Andrea Palladio, Villa Badoer at Fratta Polesine, *I quattro libri dell'architettura*, Venice, Appresso Dominico de' Franceschi, 1570, lib. 2, cap. 14, 48

remained closely involved with Daniele Barbaro and his brother Marc'Antonio, while the center of their activities shifted to the building and ornamentation of their villa at Maser.

Palladio's circle of Venetian patrons on the mainland had continued to expand in the later 1550s, adding projects for Leonardo di Antonio Mocenigo, who had become his father's heir while on embassy (1556–58) to Ferdinand I Habsburg in Germany, and for Francesco di Pietro Badoer (fig. 69).[5] During this period the *cantiere* for the Basilica in Vicenza was quite active and Palladio trained a reliable team capable of operating there without his daily supervision.[6] He continued to fulfill commissions for his Vicentine clientele, as well as working on projects in various *terraferma* cities, including Udine, where he stayed for a time in 1556.[7] In this same period, from the summer of 1554, Vicenzo Diedo had been *capitano* of Padua, the position from which he was elected to the patriarchy late in December 1555, and he had twice previously been elected in 1552 as one of the *riformatore dello Studio di Padova* – often an indication of academic interests – although he did not serve, preferring instead power appointments as one of the *savi di terraferma* and *consigliere ducale*. The pattern of Diedo's appointments on the *terraferma* in the service of Venice leading to his elevation offered ample opportunity to interact with other of Palladio's patrons and to observe the architect's growing fame.[8]

When Vicenzo Diedo assumed the patriarchy of Venice, it had been in existence little more than a century, when the title had been transferred from the more ancient seat of Grado, to be first held by revered St. Lorenzo Giustiniani (1451–60) at the site of the bishopric of Olivolo. The seat is located at the eastern edge of the district of Castello, connected only by a long wood bridge, near the Arsenale and across from the mouth of the lagoon at the Lido (the "duo castelli" of Benedetto Bordon's map of 1528). It seems marginal in reference to the civic center developing around the Doge's Palace and chapel at San Marco, but was nevertheless loaded with significance for Venetian aspirations to render the past a power to serve present exigencies. The place resonated with the founding memories of the early city in Rivoalto, on the island of Torcello, at Olivolo Castello.

As a distinct metropolis was forged in Venice in the Middle Ages, the rivalries between the patriarchates of Grado and Aquileia reflected her position in the balance of power between eastern and western empires.[9] Central to this was the patriarchal supra-metropolitan authority, which granted control over episcopates in the territories of the upper Adriatic, including Venice herself. The ancient basis for asserting patriarchal rights, which extended beyond spiritual authority to include temporal rights as well, was the same that Venice had used to establish the privileges of the ducal chapel itself as predicated on apostolic foundation by St. Mark.[10] As Venice had expanded on the *terraferma* in the early fifteenth century, many of the dioceses belonging to and including Aquileia itself had come under her governance. In 1445 a treaty between Venice and the patriarchy of Aquileia formalized this political reality, with the domain of the patriarch limited in its temporal rule, and the remaining territory in Friuli put directly under a Venetian governor based in Udine.[11] Since the patriarch of Grado had always resided in Venice, the translation there of the patriarchal seat both reflected the actual orientation of sees to capital, and a concern to ensure continued control, the Republic having also requested that she be invested with the rights of election. In the nexus of Church and State relations in the sixteenth century, the patriarchates of Venice and Aquileia were diplomatic thorns in the sides of popes and emperors alike, producing irritation with Venice of the first order. Both patriarchates claimed ecclesiastical governance of territories under the military and political control of the Habsburgs. This was further exacerbated by the Austrian occupation of Aquileia in 1509, which was governed by the patriarch from the Venetian-held city of Udine.[12] Venice broadly insisted on the nomination of bishops in her lands in defiance of papal prerogatives. When negotiation and diplomacy over these perennial differences broke down as it did during the War of the League of Cambrai, Venetian interests were severely curtailed, although the right to the nomination of the patriarch of Venice was salvaged.[13] Not until 1552 would a similar, but less binding, agreement to Venice's right of nomination be reached for Aquileia; its more tenuous nature kept the Republic's ambassadors occupied with finding a more permanent solution at the court of Rome for nearly the remainder of the century.[14]

★   ★   ★

70 Marco Sebastiano Giampiccoli, *Ingresso del patriarca a San Pietro*, Venice, Biblioteca del Museo Civico Correr, Gherro II–I, 789

"By God and San Marco"

Venetian ambivalence about churchmen over the issue of divided loyalty often surfaced in the election of patriarchs from the ranks of those inculcated in civic duties rather than ecclesiastical. As the ceremony of investiture for the patriarch of Venice – seen here in an eighteenth-century engraving of a patriarchal *possesso* (fig. 70) – made abundantly clear, the office was subject to the State:

> When the patriarchal seat is vacant, the Senate promptly elects the successor, who may be (according to Stringa) ordained with the befitting conditions, and the usual ceremonies at the patriarch's; the doge with the Signoria ride on the chosen day in their boats of gold, go to take him with great ceremony from his house, conducting him up to the church of San Pietro di Castello with a following of a grand number of gondolas, and especially those from all the parochial churches, trimmed in cloths of silk and of gold with the insignia of their churches, and arms of the new prelate, where in each one of these gondolas the priest, and dignatories of the church that is represented is present. The doge then gives with great solemnity and festivity there in said patriarchal church the possession of the patriarchy. Then he [the new patriarch] is conducted to the upper story of the palace of his residence, the doge takes his leave of him and returns to his doge's palace.[15]

The election of the patriarch was accompanied by the pledge "By God and San Marco," with Venetian sovereignty established through Marcian allegiance.[16] The selection of Vicenzo Diedo followed this pattern of civilian experience rather than religious vocation, as his previous engagement in Padua and the *terraferma* attests (fig. 71a). He was celebrated in the inscription over the inner portal of the church of San Pietro di Castello: praised for his accomplishment as a magistrate, for his wisdom, integrity, and his prudence.[17] In order for that experience to be entrusted into this new sphere of activities, the Venetian Senate also tried to select men of the qualities attributed to Diedo by the author of the inscription. Some, it seems, would have strongly dissented from this assessment of the patriarch. A violent attack on Diedo's character in the conduct of his office surfaced as one of the early signs of strengthening *giovani* anticlericalism.[18] The complaint was made by Giovanni di Bernardo Donà (called "dalle renghe" for his haranguing oratory) in July 1559 that this rich and powerful prelate had evaded the payment of tithes (*decime statuali*), with the aid of two Roman cardinals who had procured the exoneration from Paul IV, and the acquiescence of the doge, Lorenzo Priuli (1556–59) – to whom he was related, a factor not noted in scholarship on this debate, but pertinent to patterns of Priuli patronage. Giovanni Donà's colorful oratory painted a picture of a hypocritical prelate "eating paternosters" in public, while indulging himself in private with his wealth. On the other hand, Diedo retained a positive opinion from papal supporters, including Girolamo di Marino Grimani (father of the future Doge Marino, 1595–1605, from the San Luca branch).[19] The clash between the wealth and privilege of ecclesiastics and the ascetic ideals of religious life had always been a theme of Venetian discourse, but it was increasingly articulated as a political tool.

It has been most frequently supposed by scholars that the failure of the façade of San Pietro was simply due to Diedo's death in December of the same year that his taxes were investigated. Yet it has not been seriously examined before that his debt of 2,000 ducats (and exorbitant expenditures on a banquet said to have run to 900 ducats – what a party!) might be connected with a work stoppage

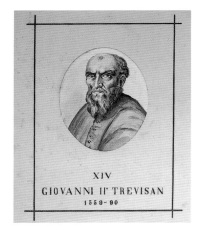

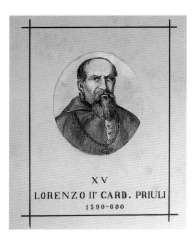

71a–c Portraits of Patriarchs
Vicenzo Diedo (*above left*),
Giovanni Trevisan (*above right*), and
Cardinal Lorenzo Priuli (*right*),
Venice, Biblioteca del Seminario
Patriarcale

impediments that affected the immediate progress of the work. It was not taken up again in Palladio's lifetime.

That the façade remained incomplete after the patriarch to succeed Diedo, the Benedictine Giovanni di Paolo Trevisan (1559–90), took office, lends some credence to a theory of lack of sufficient funds, as well as different interests, for in his previous tenure as abbot of Santi Cornelio e Cipriano, Murano, he had undertaken the renovation of the monastery, including the construction of a chapel attached to the church (fig. 71b).[22] Within a few years of his succession, however, Patriarch Trevisan had a different project to concern him. Following the directives of Trent, which he attended, his attention turned to the institution of a seminary, which he originally located in the parish of San Geremia, but transferred to San Cipriano on Murano (formalized in 1592).[23] In the later years of his tenure, rights of jurisdiction over the monastery of San Cipriano became an element of contention between Venice and Rome, with the pope conceding it to the patriarch. At San Pietro, Trevisan did not carry out major building projects, only his burial site at the foot of the altar dedicated to his patron saint, with an altarpiece confirming his allegiance to *Sts. John the Baptist, Peter, and Paul*, by Paolo Veronese and his studio, inscriptions on the side walls, and a portrait bust, an ensemble reorganized in subsequent rebuilding to become one of the side-aisle chapels.[24] Actually, it is tempting to speculate that the patriarch followed his own lead, when he authorized churches and monasteries under his jurisdiction to sell off columns to the *deputati sopra la fabbrica del Palazzo* in 1574, to restore the Doge's Palace after a disastrous fire (more about which in Part v). Trevisan commended the transactions to expedite the rebuilding of the fabric for the "honor" and "dignity" of the Republic.[25] Dispersion of the original materials collected for the façade would, of course, further retard its construction, any such action indicating that support for the project had lapsed.

Not until the following patriarch, Lorenzo di Zuanne Priuli (1590–1600), another distinguished governor and diplomat, ascended to the office would San Pietro di Castello finally receive its façade (fig. 71c). According to his contemporary, Giovanni Stringa, Priuli paid for it himself.[26] Lorenzo's branch of the Priuli (Da San Polo al Magazen) has been described as "living in relative poverty," but his impressive political career prior to attaining the patriarchy was an expensive one that included several embassies (Tuscany, Spain, France, Rome), which probably required financial assistance as well as influence (*broglio*) from relatives.[27] In analyzing the manner in which the Priuli operated politically, Martin Lowry found a "vaguer pattern" than the Barbaro, more difficult to prove that different branches collaborated, yet their parallel successes suggesting "family continuity." Paul Grendler has noted that Lorenzo's election as patriarch of Venice also carried a welcome increase in annual income, and this may have enabled his patronage of the new façade. Priuli was a contemporary of the younger generation of Palladio's patrons, such as members of the Compagnia della Calza degli Accesi, one of whom was married to his sister, and the rich branch of the Priuli "di Scarpon di San Felice" was especially interconnected with such

due to the financial difficulties incurred by this scandal, which probably meant that he left his successor no funds, preventing its immediate completion (especially since the next patriarch had his own building agenda). Lack of funding has left many a church bereft of its façade, the more important and magnificent, unfortunately, the more likely. The inscription honoring Diedo notes that he had sponsored work on the fabric of the church and patriarchal palace, which further supports its having been begun. In fact, Diedo had defended himself, stating that he had gone into debt because he had spent so much money ("molti danari") in the repair of the church and palace, nor could he satisfy it immediately (asking for eight years to pay it), if he was to "have the means as patriarch to live honorably, for the honor and reputation of the status which had been granted him by the doge and the Senate."[20] The particularly splendid façade envisioned by Palladio specified fine materials and quality workmanship. A monumental order of six engaged Corinthian half-columns and smaller order of six pilasters in Istrian stone, together with the other decorative stonework for doors and windows, architrave and cornices, would have required considerable expenditure. The contract stipulated that the stonemasons were to be paid 1,910 ducats for its assembly, and, typically, the money was to be disbursed as the work progressed.[21] Giovanni Donà may not have been wrong in castigating Diedo for illicitly evading taxation, but the inquest may have reflected financial

families as the Barbaro, Pisani, Grimani, Capello, and Mocenigo. Another possible factor may have been that the association of the project with Patriarch Diedo, whose mother was a Priuli, suggested a family obligation, and although it was a different branch it was the prestigious one to which the brother doges Lorenzo (1556–59) and Gerolamo (1559–67) had belonged.[28] The logic of completing the façade according to a design by Palladio seems congruent with family status and associations.

The façade was erected by Francesco Smeraldi in only two years, between 1594 and 1596 (fig. 72). Shortly before, in 1592, the patriarch had assisted at the consecration of the State's votive church of Il Redentore, designed by Palladio in 1576.[29] Although there is no visual record of Il Redentore before 1610, its façade was probably built by the date of its formal consecration in 1592. Il Redentore would have been the second of Palladio's façades to be seen in Venice, after the one façade project completed during his lifetime, for the patriarch of Aquileia at San Francesco della Vigna, to be discussed in the next chapter. The visibility of Il Redentore and its civic significance on the one hand, and the patronage of Palladio by a predecessor in the patriarchy of Venice and by the patriarch of Aquileia on the other, also may have determined Priuli to revive a Palladian project for San Pietro di Castello. The relationship of Smeraldi's façade to Palladio's original project of 1558 is problematic, but the composition is unmistakable in championing the new syntax of the church façade invented by Palladio.[30] The idea for a monumental temple-front façade first proposed in Venice for San

72   Andrea Palladio, modified and executed by Francesco Smeraldi, façade, San Pietro di Castello, Venice

Pietro di Castello now denoted consequence by its associations. Priuli was ambitious; the completion of the cathedral façade coincided with his elevation to the cardinalate in 1596.[31]

CHAPTER SIX

SAN FRANCESCO DELLA VIGNA

T HE POWERFUL PRELATE AND NOTED MAECENAS, Giovanni di Gerolamo Grimani, patriarch of Aquileia (1545–93),[32] provided Palladio with his only opportunity to realize the completion of a façade project within his lifetime – at the church of the Observant Franciscans at San Francesco della Vigna (figs. 73 and 74). The branch of the Grimani family at Santa Maria Formosa in Venice held a virtual monopoly on the patriarchate through most of the sixteenth century.[33] How Giovanni came to choose Palladio for the project over the still-living original architect of the church, Jacopo Sansovino, favorite of his brother, Procurator Vettor Grimani (died 1558), from whom he inherited the rights to the exterior and interior façades and the family chapel, is embroiled in the tumultuous life of the patriarch. On his return from the Council of Trent in 1563, Giovanni Grimani would take up the reins of family patronage in the palace at Santa Maria Formosa, and in the family chapel and façades at San Francesco. His personal experiences, from accusations of heresy to unrealized aspirations for a cardinal's hat, mirror larger changes in the religious and political climate in the sixteenth century, and would influence the cultural choices that he would make. So would his association with Daniele Barbaro, patriarch-elect of Aquileia, and whose interest in San Francesco della Vigna was strengthened by the presence of his family chapel there. Grimani's acceptance of the Vitruvian project that was being developed in theory and practice by Barbaro and Palladio suggests that it presented the decorum appropriate to his dignity. An interpretation of its program as a celebration of the patriarchate of Aquileia will highlight Palladio's innovative development of the monumental temple-front church façade.[34]

Certainly, the prestige of being awarded the earlier commission for the cathedral of the city, despite its abortive history, had brought Palladio to the attention of the ecclesiastical community of Venice by the early 1560s. Here, he would have the success in Venice that had until then eluded him, and it would bring him renown as an

73 Jacopo Tintoretto, *Giovanni Grimani*, Private Collection (formerly London, P. and D. Colnaghi, 1983)

74 (*facing page*) View from above of the zone of San Francesco della Vigna to San Pietro in Castello, Venice

architect in a field as yet relatively untried by him, but with which he would now be identified in the fabric of the city.[35]

Championing Palladio

Giovanni Grimani was no doubt aware of Palladio much earlier, well before even the commission for the façade of the Venetian patriarch at San Pietro di Castello. Giovanni may have learned early of Palladio through his elder brother and predecessor, Cardinal Patriarch Marino Grimani, who owed his red hat to the influence of Trissino, the architect's early mentor. Trissino had long-term relations both with Cardinal Marino and his famous uncle, Cardinal Patriarch Domenico, both assiduous collectors. Grateful letters from Marino to Trissino in the 1520s reveal that the latter had used his considerable influence with several popes to lobby for benefices and the cardinalate, and that the two exchanged hospitality between Padua, Venice, Murano, and Vicenza; they remained in contact to the year of the cardinal's death in 1546, during the formative years of Palladio with Trissino, and the early ecclesiastical career of Giovanni Grimani in the abbacy of Sesto.[36] Already by 1551, Giovanni Grimani showed his active interests in architectural matters, participating in the choice of an architect to renovate the choir of the cathedral of Padua.[37] In that same year Daniele Barbaro had received papal approval of his nomination as patriarch-elect of Aquileia, an appointment that Grimani favored, suggesting their prior as well as continuing association.

It seems likely, too, that Grimani would be well informed on Palladio's project during the 1550s in the transposed patriarchal seat of Udine: the handsome palace for the noble Floriano Antonini, who was his city's ambassador to the Serenissima and frequently in Venice, and whose family was host to Patriarch Grimani in one of their palaces.[38] Palladio's Palazzo Antonini, now the Banca d'Italia, on via Gemona, was only partly finished according to his designs, but it is the first palace to be described in the *Four Books* (Bk. 2, ch. 3, 4–5), following Palladio's encomium to the enlightened taste of his patrons (fig. 75):

> I am sure that those who look at the buildings included below and know how difficult it is to introduce a new approach [*usanza nuova*] – particularly in building, which is a profession everyone is convinced they know something about – will regard me as extremely fortunate to have found gentlemen of such noble and generous character and discriminating judgment that they have been convinced by my arguments and rejected the obsolete approach to building without grace or beauty.[39]

The inscription GENIO URBIS UTIN* ("to the embellishment of the city of Udine") on the façade of the Palazzo Antonini publicly attests to the general benefit conferred on the city through the patronage of such works, which Palladio says "are inherently beautiful and are both useful and a credit to the patrons" (*Four Books*, Bk. 2, ch. 17, 78 misnumbered as 66).[40] The suggestion has been made (by Antonio Foscari and Manfredo Tafuri) that Grimani may

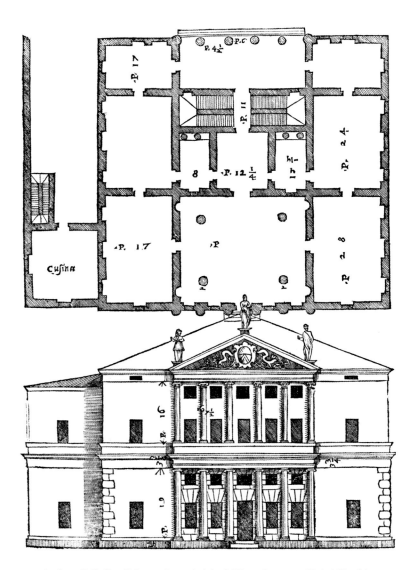

75   Andrea Palladio, Palazzo Antonini in Udine, *I quattro libri dell'architettura*, Venice, Appresso Dominico de' Franceschi, 1570, lib. 2, cap. 3, 5

have been instrumental in procuring such commissions in Udine for Palladio, but it does not seem likely at this early date, especially since Giovanni (Ricamatore) da Udine was active there as an architect in the 1550s (as Magrini noted) and already a Grimani familiar and potential source of information on local developments, such as conveying the rising reputation of Palladio.[41] Giovanni Grimani's older brother and predecessor in the patriarchy, Cardinal Marino, patronized Giovanni da Udine as an architect on patriarchal projects in the 1530s at Aquileia, Udine, and San Vito al Tagliamento.[42] On the other hand, by 1563, when patriarch and patriarch-elect were present together in Trent (Giovanni arrived on 18 June and stayed three months), there is a more compelling case for Palladio's active relationship to both, and for Grimani's influencing the selection of Palladio for the urban intervention at the Castello in Udine.

More widespread acknowledgment of Grimani's absorption in the new architecture in the early 1560s is testified to by the role he was given in Paolo Paruta's *Della perfettione della vita politica*

(Appresso Domenico Nicolini, Venice, 1579), a dialogue on the virtues of civil life that included both Grimani and Barbaro as interlocutors. Paruta gave Grimani the voice for introducing Barbaro's works, both the commentary and translation of the *Ten Books* and the treatise on perspective, which shows Grimani positioned in the thick of the Vitruvian debates engaging the interests of intellectual circles of the city.[43] The most distinguished feature of Giovanni Grimani's life would be his extraordinary patronage and collecting, a *mecenatismo* on a public scale that would ensure his enduring *fama*.

The origins of the new church at San Francesco della Vigna built by Jacopo Sansovino for the Observant Franciscans dated to the reign of Doge Andrea Gritti, commemorated in the foundation medal of 1534 (figs. 76a, 76b, and 77,). The medallist, Andrea

76a–b   Andrea Spinelli, bronze medal, 1534: obverse, *Portrait of Doge Andrea Gritti*; reverse, *Church of San Francesco della Vigna*, Washington, National Gallery of Art, Samuel H. Kress Collection (1957.14.1006.a–b)

Spinelli, presented the powerful profile visage of the doge on the obverse, and a perspective view of Sansovino's first design of the church on the reverse. Although the plan would be modified by the Franciscan supervisors of the church according to a list of recommendations (*relazione*) written by the neo-Platonist Fra Francesco Zorzi, the medal supplies an indication of the type of façade   that Sansovino had originally designed, and can be supplemented by an undated commemorative medal with a frontal view of the façade, which had been conceded to the Grimani family.[44] Both medals show that Sansovino had planned for a main story framed with four impressive columns on pedestals placed at regular intervals across the façade. This was topped by a truncated second story with two short columns that continued the vertical line of the central order flanking the portal, while volutes took the place of the outside bays, making a transition from the triangular pediment crowning the façade. Some differences between the medals appear in the treatment of the openings, which are probably less reliably portrayed. In the dated medal, tondi were placed over the portal and in the pediment, with niches in the outer bays and a double-light in the center of the second story. The undated frontal view medal instead shows tondi in the side bays over niches, with a Serliana in the truncated

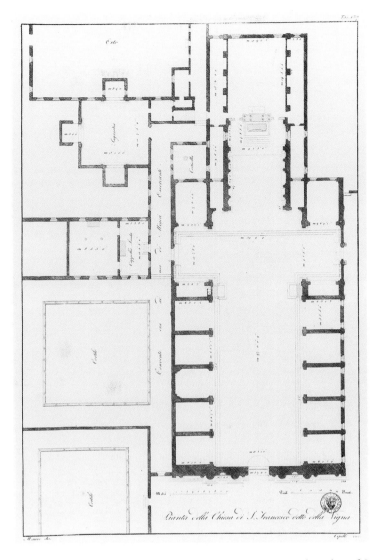

77   Leopoldo Cicognara, Antonio Diedo, and Gianantonio Selva, plan of San Francesco della Vigna, *Le fabbriche e i monumenti più cospicui di Venezia*, ed. F. Zanotto, Venice 1858, 2:137

second story. The basic composition reflected Sansovino's Tuscan background, and specifically projects for the Medici popes, including the temporary façade for the cathedral of Florence (built for Leo x's entry in 1515) and the competition for the façade of San Lorenzo (1516–17), although not employing here the paired columns with niches associated with his sources in Bramante and Raphael, and used in other of his projects in Venice.[45]

The body of San Francesco della Vigna was substantially complete by late 1554, when the choir was in use and final funds were granted, although it was not consecrated until 1582. The rights to family chapels had been issued since 1535, with the first going to the brother of the Superior, Francesco di Daniele Barbaro, Daniele's and Marc'Antonio's father. Other prominent supporters of Sansovino followed during the next few years, including, in 1536, Vettor di Gerolamo Grimani, and Vincenzo (the Younger) di Antonio

Grimani, as well as the reservation of the chancel for Doge Gritti.[46] Until his death in 1558, Vettor undertook the primary role in Grimani family patronage in the church. As early as 1542, Vettor and his brother Cardinal Marino were conceded the rights formerly granted to their uncle, the humanist and collector Cardinal Patriarch Domenico Grimani (died 1523), for the exterior façade of the new church; then a few months later, Vettor was granted the interior façade as well.[47] Nothing was accomplished, since their plans for transferring an exterior tomb memorial honoring Vettor's grandfather, Doge Antonio (1521–23, whom we met lamenting the lost tiara for Domenico), were contested by the Lateran Canons of Sant'Antonio di Castello, where the original legacy for the deposit of the doge had been left.[48] For a while, in 1544, it had looked as though the funds allotted to Sant'Antonio di Castello for the

UEDUTA DELLA CHIESA DI S. ANTONIO DI CASTELLO
canonici Regolari
Architettura di Giacomo Lanfrani

78 Luca Carlevariis, *Sant' Antonio di Castello*, Venice, Biblioteca del Museo Civico Correr, Gherro I–I, 185

project would be transferred to San Francesco della Vigna, but this was finally renounced later in that year. This coincided with the desire of the former patriarch of Aquileia, Marco Grimani (died 1544), who had received the *renuncia cun regressu* from his brother Marino in 1529, but returned it to him in 1533 (and predeceased his brother), to be buried in the cloister at Sant'Antonio di Castello.[49] Vettor (together with Vincenzo di Antonio) therefore redeployed Sansovino on the new exterior façade of Sant'Antonio di Castello.[50] Representations of its façade before the church was demolished in the nineteenth century show a pedimented two-story composition similar to that of the Spinelli medals for San Francesco della Vigna in the distribution of the columns and relation between storys, except that the columns are paired, which is typical of central Italian models, and both usages can be found in Sansovino's other built façades (fig. 78).[51]

★　　★　　★

The "Renewed" Aquileia

During the 1540s and 1550s, as San Francesco was being completed, Giovanni Grimani had been primarily preoccupied with his ecclesiastical career and ambitions for a cardinal's hat, but he also continued to be active in the family tradition of art patronage and collecting. He was particularly involved in the recuperation and aggrandizement of the collections of art and antiquities foreclosed upon his brother Marino's death, which included treasures possessed by their uncle Domenico. These were housed in the family palace at Santa Maria Formosa that he had shared since 1532 with his brother the Procurator Vettor, inhabiting the *piano nobile*, which still retains some of the decoration executed for them in the decade after their coming into exclusive possession of the property (figs. 79–81).[52]

Giovanni's overriding concern with his career, however, began from the time of his succession as patriarch, since he had to defend himself from accusations of heresy, which severely prejudiced his

79 Ramo Grimani land entrance, Grimani Palace, Santa Maria Formosa, Venice

80 (*above*) San Severo Canal water façade, Grimani Palace, Santa Maria Formosa, Venice

81 GENIO URBIS, Ramo Grimani land entrance, Grimani Palace, Santa Maria Formosa, Venice

hopes for a cardinalate and even for the patriarchal *pallium* (white stole) that represented pontifical authority. As to the tenor of the times, it should be remembered that the Venetian institution of the Tre Savi sopra la Eresia was created in 1547, as Peter Laven pointed out in his history of Grimani's vicissitudes. Even Daniele Barbaro did not escape the aspersions of heresy, although his rectitude – "la virtu et integrita et bona dottrina de'l Barbaro" – was such that both Venice and Rome would dismiss them as "calumny."[53] Twice it seemed that Grimani might attain the cardinalate. First, in 1554 the Del Monte pope Julius III (1550–55) promised Venice that he would reserve a future place for Grimani, but the pope's death intervened. There was little hope during the tenure of Paul IV Carafa (1555–59), a former Inquisitor, who believed that even suspicion of heresy was enough to taint any candidate for the purple, and who was not particularly well disposed towards Venice; he is shown here in Palma il Giovane's *Paul IV Receives the Venetian Ambassador* in the Oratorio dei Crociferi at the Gesuiti (fig. 82). A second moment came in 1561, when the Medici pope Pius IV (1559–65) agreed to the Venetian ambassador Marc'Antonio Da Mula's petition for a cardinalate reserved *in pectore* (in expectation), but the latter received the red hat instead (earning exile from an angry

Grimani be made in the accession of the number of cardinals." Grimani's satisfaction of the committee convened at the Council to review his heresy was cited, "the doctrine of the patriarch was made known to be holy and sincere and entirely free from all suspicion," and the College appealed to the "paternal charity" of the pope: "We ask for the publication as cardinal of a patriarch who is noble, good, of approved and justified doctrine, who was already promoted, already voted, and promised this by us."[55] Despite his success on appealing to the Council, which did absolve Grimani of heresy, if not conceded in the most complimentary terms towards his theological scholarship, Grimani still had not been promoted to a cardinalate when Pius IV died, and a brief foray to Rome, hoping to participate in the conclave, was forestalled by the election of the Ghislieri pope Pius V (1566–72). Grimani made a last concerted effort during the pontificate of Gregory XIII Boncompagni (1572–85), spending most of late 1580 to the spring of 1583 in Rome (where he was contesting Venetian sovereignty over a patriarchal feud).[56] But, unfortunately for his aspirations, the following pope, Sixtus V Peretti (1585–90), refused to allow Grimani ever to bring up the issue again.[57]

Ironically, it was that same year, 1585, that would be the only time that Grimani officially entered the seat of the patriarchy, thanks to the Venetian government's (not the papacy's) dispensation to undertake pontifical ceremonies in Udine without the *pallium*.[58] For the first twenty years of his patriarchy, Venice had actively supported his candidacy both for reasons of pragmatic political benefit, since the lack of the cardinalate made his authority – and the borders of the Republic against Austria – less secure, even to endangering control of the succession, but also for prestige, "for the honor and dignity of our Republic."[59] Despite their own concerns over securing the periphery of Italy, Rome did not want too strong a buffer state under Venetian sway; several popes would declare in so many words that "princes did not make cardinals."[60] Equally intransigent positions regarding jurisdiction came to be voiced in Venice, with Leonardo Donà querying the desirability that any Venetian should be exposed to such an obvious conflict of loyalty to the State – could any man serve two masters? – this in a debate between the *savi grandi* in 1588 over the advisability of recommending the creation of Venetian cardinals.[61] Donà's comment, "it was not in the public interest, that among our nobility too many concerns with the pope as a lay prince has not gone well," highlights his view of the papacy as a temporal power.[62] Mutual animosity was no doubt fueled by Donà's being ambassador to Rome in the years 1581–83, when Grimani appealed to the papal court against Venice's wishes over the jurisdiction of the feud of Taiedo. Such actions on Grimani's part reveal his conviction in the independent authority of the patriarch, heir to a grand, if curtailed, tradition of temporal and spiritual rule, to be defended against transgression.[63] Donà could see this only as personal ambition on the part of the patriarch, whom he called "more ambitious than Lucifer."[64] Venice had continued to instruct her ambassadors to negotiate for the cardinalate and the *pallium*, but as Donà's remarks would reveal, by the 1580s internally opposition was increasing, contributing to the

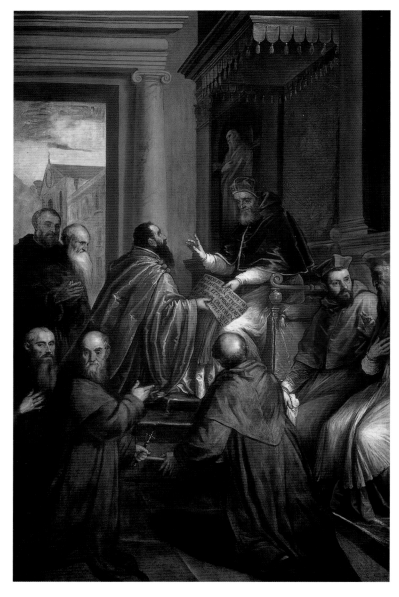

82   Jacopo Palma il Giovane, *Pope Paul IV Receives the Venetian Ambassador*, Oratorio dei Crociferi, Campo dei Gesuiti, Venice

Venetian government), while new accusations caused Grimani to flee Rome without taking leave of the pope, further blackening his name.[54] At this time, Grimani determined that he would lay his case before the third session of the Council of Trent (January 1562–December 1563), which was actually located in his see of the patriarchy of Aquileia, and less controlled by the cardinal inquisitors. Here he was described as well thought of, as a "personality of great valor and much good" ("quale sapevano essere personaggio di gran valore e molta bontà"), an opinion that even extended to Cardinal Carlo Borromeo. Venice too found the moment opportune to press for Grimani's elevation: the papal nuncio was to be summoned before the College and read a letter being directed to Rome that stated: "We have already for a long time, reverend monsignor, desired and voted that the most Reverend Patriarch of Aquileia

growing factionalism among the patriciate. The arc of the patriarch's career – although the initial accusations seemed to have been motivated by resentment of his assumption to what amounted to a familial inheritance that he then "willed" outside of the family, fueled by unfavorable interpretations of his religious views that had been formed in a pre-Tridentine climate – grew to mirror the difficult triangle of relations between Venice, Rome, and the Habsburg empire, vacillating over the course of the century. Just as new laws defined the Venetian patriciate more rigidly, so too the pronouncements on Church doctrine that were codified at Trent would change definitions of orthodoxy: conflict continued over the areas of jurisdiction that were at stake.[65] Grimani's acts as a patron resonated with his persona as patriarch, as public statements of his and his family's *virtù*: in this realm the palace inscription acknowledged his contribution, GENIO URBIS ("to the embellishment of the city").[66]

Genius of the City

Despite the date of 1562 that tradition has assigned to Palladio's façade of the church of San Francesco della Vigna, taking into account other activities of patron and architect, it seems far more likely to have been begun at least a year or two later. Giorgio Vasari reportedly saw the work underway in 1566, although he may have known of it somewhat earlier through his Venetian correspondents, and he was well enough informed to know the order:

> He [Palladio] also began the façade of the church of San Francesco della Vigna, which is made of Istrian stone at the very magnificent expense of the most reverend Grimani, patriarch of Aquileia. There are columns four palms wide and forty high of the Corinthian order, the entire basement already built from the lowest part of the column .[67]

The façade was completed before 1572, when it is referred to in a dedication to the patriarch: "Today in competition with the Emperors of antiquity he [Giovanni Grimani] spent a huge amount for

83 and 84   Grimani Chapel, San Francesco della Vigna, Venice, with (*left*) a view of the tomb slab

the marble to raise the entire grand machine of the façade, and inside, for the rich chapel in the church of San Francesco" (figs. 83 and 84).[68]

The 1560s was Palladio's first period of concerted production in Venice itself, recorded in the Barbaro palace at San Vidal, and the

85   Giovanni da Udine, *Council of Trent*, Loggia della Cosmografia, Vatican Palace, Vatican City

early years between 1561 and 1564 coincided with a suspension of work on the Basilica in Vicenza as well.[69] While Giovanni Grimani had inherited Vettor's rights to the family chapel in San Francesco della Vigna on his brother's death in 1558, it was not until 1560 that he had engaged Battista Franco to decorate the vault, but the patriarch's departure for Rome in March following the new accusations of heresy, his examination, exoneration, and promise of a cardinalate, had kept him there until his flight in September 1561, by which time Franco had died. The Romanized Venetian artist had worked for the Grimani previously, on Giovanni's floor in the family palace in the early to mid-1550s, as well as for Daniele Barbaro, for whom he had executed the altarpiece for the family chapel in San Francesco della Vigna in 1552, shortly after Daniele had received the *renuncia*.[70] The patriarch and patriarch-elect thus can be shown to

share ideas about artists and style, as well as concern over the decoration of the church; indeed, Barbaro was made protector of the Franciscans in January 1561 and his pious wishes for his burial there (requesting an unmarked grave in the "campo santo," and a stone instead of a pillow to be placed beneath his head) reflect his abiding concern for the spiritual requirements as well.[71]

Barbaro, together with the patriarch of Venice Giovanni Trevisan, was sent to the opening of the third and final convocation of the Council of Trent, and his participation through the closing sessions constituted his only sustained contribution to Church policy (fig. 85).[72] Here, in 1563, the vexed matter of the patriarch of Aquileia was finally taken up. Grimani himself appeared in Trent only from 18 June to the successful conclusion of the hearings on 17 September. His visit was a masterpiece of studied diplomacy: residing in a villa outside the city, it was quickly reported to Rome that after his arrival he was accompanied by a group of some twenty priests as he made the rounds of all the officials and cardinal legates of the Council – without speaking of the reason for his visit – but the Venetian ambassador to the papal court then said after the initial courtesy calls, Grimani "walked with no other than the [patriarch-]elect Barbaro . . . he wanted no other company."[73] Grimani's actions carefully preserved his status, as they would throughout his long career.

In the meantime, Grimani seems also to have pursued the completion of the chapel at San Francesco della Vigna and the hiring of a new artist. On his return to Venice, vindicated of suspicion of heresy, Grimani undertook to continue the interrupted decoration of the chapel as well as of a grand stairway in the family palace. It was an auspicious moment for the patriarch, who expected his cardinalate to be confirmed by Pius IV. The invitation to Federico Zuccaro to finish the chapel and execute the *scalone* not only followed his earlier pattern of selecting artists that reflected the latest manner in Rome, but could even be interpreted as a specific homage to the pope. Zuccaro was in Venice earlier than has been thought, by July 1563.[74] He had just executed the decoration of a Casino in the Vatican gardens, for which final payments were made in October 1563, a project overseen by Pius IV's artistic advisor, none other than the Venetian cardinal Marc'Antonio Da Mula.[75] By September 1564, Zuccaro had completed the chapel for Grimani and was employed at the palace at Santa Maria Formaosa.[76]

This interlude of positive expectation ended with the death of the pope in December 1565, which took Giovanni to Rome, where Daniele Barbaro also had been sent to add his persuasion to that of the ambassador's on Grimani's behalf, since the latter hoped to claim a place in the conclave on the strength of Pius IV's earlier promise. His vicar in Udine supportively wrote of his "great pleasure" in hearing of what the "learned doctors in Rome had said of his cardinalate and entry into the Conclave" and that this time he hoped the patriarch received "justice" for he had "right on his side." By the time of Grimani's arrival, however, Pius V had just been elected, in January 1566, and he soon cancelled the patriarch's hopes, who returned to Venice.[77] Pius V offered the *pallium* instead to Daniele Barbaro, whose noted integrity led him to refuse it, first in 1566 and again in 1569, despite the fact that this meant that neither would enjoy full rights as patriarch.[78]

The most opportune time for Grimani to have undertaken the step of commissioning a new façade for San Francesco della Vigna would have been between late 1563 and 1565, on his triumphal return from Trent, while completing the family chapel and embellishing the family palace.[79] As already mentioned, a closer relationship between Patriarch Giovanni Grimani and Palladio is indicated in other commissions in just this period: Palladio was in Udine, the patriarchal capital, during the Council of Trent in 1563, overseeing the restructuring of the city center (fig. 86); soon after, in 1564–65 he prepared a model of the Palazzo Pretorio for another of the patriarchy's principal towns, Cividale, when he was accompanied by Federico Zuccaro on a trip there. And, of course, it was in 1565

86   View from Udine city center to Castello with Arco Bollani by Andrea Palladio

that Palladio and Zuccaro were involved with the Compagnia della Calza degli Accesi, the mother of whose *priore*, Gerolamo di Pietro Foscari, was Elena, daughter of Giovanni Grimani's brother, Marco, former procurator, patriarch of Aquileia and finally papal general.[80]

These connections help to explain why it is not entirely surprising to find Giovanni choosing Palladio to design the façade, rather than Sansovino, the architect of the church and protégé of his deceased brother, Vettor. Moreover, Grimani may have first retained Palladio to design a family tomb monument, which would not necessarily be in the brief of a building's architect, but was often an independent charge.[81] Giovanni had gone his own way before, frustrating his brother and sister, as may be recalled, in selecting the patriarch-elect outside the Grimani family. But rather than interpreting the choice of Palladio as a betrayal of Vettor's faith in his brother to carry out the project, it seems instead consistent with an interest in promoting the family's *magnificenza* and *pietas* with the most powerful architectural statement that could be made. That this meant overlooking the architect of the church, Sansovino, rather implies that Giovanni shared with Barbaro, Palladio, and others in Venice a new conception of architecture than what was offered by the venerable *proto* who had embodied the vision of his brother and others during the Gritti *renovatio*, although one that conceivably could coexist with the central Italian style introduced in the body of the church, while updating it: the *bella maniera* begun by Sansovino taken to its logical conclusion in the *usanza nuova* of Palladio.[82]

Since Giovanni and Vettor had for so long shared the family palace at Santa Maria Formosa, it can be assumed that Vettor was well aware of his brother's independent tastes as they transformed the *casa de statio*, and he still freely designated Giovanni, together with his widow, as his executors, specifying that the family chapel in San Francesco della Vigna be completed as they directed.[83] In fact, although Vettor was recognized for his patronage of Sansovino, the renovation of the family palace shows that *both* brothers were deeply engaged with the contemporary architectural currents in the city. The campaign of restoration of the Grimani Palace at Santa Maria Formosa that was carried out in the 1990s by the Superintendents of Monuments has provided new insight on the archaeology of the construction and confirmed that it was rebuilt and added on in phases, as something of a laboratory of architecture and decoration over the forty or so years of its engendering.[84] The diversity of the classical language in the style of the renovations and additions has concerned its historians, who have predominantly followed Tommaso Temanza in his attribution of the architecture to Michele Sanmicheli with the help of others, and in seeing Giovanni as responsible for its direction. The restoration, together with a re-examination of documents, has emphasized, rather than suppressed, distinctions, not only between styles present in the palace, but construction techniques. This has led its examiners to propose the palace as a "collection" of the leading Romanist architects of the sixteenth century in Venice, including Jacopo Sansovino, Sebastiano Serlio, Michele Sanmicheli, and possibly Palladio as well, according to a recent attribution of an oval stairway. Sansovino's son, Francesco, described it as "the famous palace of Patriarch Grimani, adapted in the Roman style."[85] The appreciation of such a coexistence of styles over that of a single hand places the responsibility for homogeneity in the hands of the patron (or in this case, initially, patrons), who becomes the authorial voice; it lies with the patron to "collect" the most telling examples in order to enunciate his *concetto* ("concept of the whole"). The mentality of such *collezionismo* was deeply engrained in Giovanni and his brothers, and their uncle, Cardinal Domenico, and would constitute their most valuable contribution to the public good, first in the display of antiquities at the palace inscribed with this intention, GENIO URBIS, then in the donation of the collection with other precious objects to the Republic. The role of the architect here was probably to provide a design and any necessary structural expertise, a similar role to that which has been described for the Barbaro brothers' *cantiere* at Maser; the main difference at the Grimani Palace being that designs were not for the whole, but for parts, which probably explains why authorship was not claimed for individual architects.[86] If this was the guiding mentality of Giovanni Grimani, then rather than being bothered by the conjunction of different architects in the body and façade of San Francesco della Vigna, the succession could have been seen as a benefit: an exhibition of the two leading architects of their day.

A Patriarchal Temple

For the rehabilitation of his ecclesiastical reputation and family honor, the façade of San Francesco della Vigna would have to express the virtues appropriate to the patron's status. If early on in the 1540s under Vettor's direction the emphasis was intended to be dogal, alluding to dynastic history and his own expectations to ascend from the Procuracy, the return of Doge Antonio's tomb monument to Sant'Antonio di Castello had interrupted such designs.[87] Palladio's façade project of the 1560s was conceived in the moment that Giovanni was claiming his own noble rank, that of cardinal (in expectation) and patriarch. In Paolo Paruta's *Della perfettione*, the description of the "great works" (*opere grandi*) that impart *magnificenza*, which is a virtue of nobility, is put into the mouth of Daniele Barbaro:

> Magnificence, responded Barbaro, as a virtue of nobility, is itself worthy of not just any work: so that there is not often occasion to demonstrate it; but in those things where it is usually employed, which one does only on rare occasions; like banquets, weddings, buildings; where it becomes one to spend without consideration of expense, but only to the grandeur and beauty of the work: because there comes a time to spend things in order to make things. And under this, I would say more generally, it is possible to reduce it to other things as well, like feasts, public games, livery, the building of temples, of palaces, or of other private or public edifices: such things, if they have grandeur, and if they are made with noble devices, and with suitable decorum, they render the man truly worthy of the name of "magnifico." And although the moral virtue is not had in the making of such works, so much as in the arts that they belong to.[88]

Paruta's dialogue continues with a discussion of the attendant virtues of Magnificence, including Liberality, Hospitality, and Magnanimity, then the participants debate the lost Magnificence of ancient buildings and spectacles and whether modern buildings partake of such virtue, one of whom makes the interesting observation: "But in the grandeur and the ornament of temples, does not it appear to you all that the moderns have begun to want to contend with the ancients?"[89]

The context of Giovanni Grimani's larger enterprise, the ruling *concetto* for both San Francesco della Vigna and the Grimani Palace, was in the interests of creating a setting of titular church and palace of the magnificence appropriate to a cardinal patriarch.[90] Actually, the Grimani Palace operated as the patriarchal residence *de facto*, since Giovanni never resided in Udine and governed through a vicar; his family palace in Venice was thus the site of the "Renewed" Aquileia.[91] Whereas Marino Grimani in 1524 had proclaimed Udine to be the "Nuova Aquileia," the building program that he instituted there languished because of his successor's non-residence. It was not until the year before Giovanni's death that it would be continued, when the "torre Marino" with its "all'antica" grotesque decoration by native son and papal court artist, Giovanni da Udine, was conserved in the new patriarchal palace initiated by Co-adjutor Francesco Barbaro (fig. 87), mirroring Marino's contribution to the decoration of the family palace in Venice (fig. 88).[92] The setback that Grimani received in Rome in early 1566 did not dim his ambitions to have his cardinalate *in pectore* recognized; although without it or the *pallium* he could operate only from a distance, making Venice his capital. In the next few years, he embarked on the final phases of the transformation of the family palace (the remaining wing of the peristyle courtyard, Studio of Antiquities, and Salon of Doge Antonio) and the building of the façade of San Francesco della Vigna, as observed by Vasari in 1566. Neither project had precedent in scope and originality. Just as the presence in the campaign of decoration of the 1530s in the palace of a favorite artist of the cardinal patriarchs, Giovanni da Udine, linked Rome, Udine-Aquileia, and Venice in their programs, so too did the installation of the extraordinary collection of antiquities in their new *forma Romana* setting, "foremost, not only in Venice, but nearly of any other city . . . and exceptional to see."[93] And it was intended to be seen, as the inscription GENIO URBIS announced; not by accident was it listed under public collections by Sansovino in 1581 even before

87   Giovanni da Udine, ceiling, Palazzo Patriarcale, Udine

88   Giovanni da Udine and Francesco Salviati, ceiling, Sala di Apollo, Grimani Palace, Santa Maria Formosa, Venice

89   Andrea Palladio, drawing for a church façade, London, Royal Institute of British Architects, XIV, 10

its donation to the Republic by the patriarch, where it was seen by Thomas Coryat, for it had long attracted famous visitors as one of the sights of the city. Shared preferences for artistic style and antiquarian discernment identified Giovanni Grimani with the enterprises of his family *illustri*, both in the program of decoration and in the presence of antiquities that had been unearthed in Rome for Cardinal Domenico in the palace on the Quirinale, or in those whose provenance was in the patriarchal lands of Aquileia:

> I observed a little world of memorable antiquities made in Alabaster, and some few in stone, which were brought thither by Cardinall Grimannus Patriarch of Aquileia, being digged up as it is thought, partly from out of the ruines of the foresaid citie of Aquileia, after it was sacked by Attila King of the Hunnes; and partly from Rome and other places.[94]

With this grand donation of the collection to the Republic, Giovanni once again sacrificed his family's private benefit for the public glory that would instead accrue to the Grimani name; his fulfillment of the stature appropriate to the patriarch of Aquileia was no less than would be expected of a cardinal's, but, most of all, such a gesture was perfectly tuned to the requirements of a Republic where excessive personal magnificence was suspect, unless expressed in the service of the State.

The same standard of magnificence prevailed in Grimani's patronage of the façade of the church of San Francesco della Vigna,

as well as his support for the "new approach" to building introduced by Palladio. Any modern viewer of the façade will have some difficulty remembering just how innovative it was at the time, given the number of neo-Palladian churches that followed over the next centuries; while a classically ornamented façade had been anticipated by Sansovino, Palladio's monumental composition for San Francesco della Vigna had no built precedent, only the analogy to the unfinished design for the patriarchal church of Venice. Descriptions of the façade and church have agreed in contrasting the celebratory, triumphal character of Palladio's exterior to the pious restraint in the classical language of Sansovino's interior, finding in the latter the expression of the Franciscan values of *simplicitas* required by the original program.[95]

The magnificence of the façade, then, alluded to its patriarchal counterpart and to the status claimed by Grimani. In the two drawings by Palladio that are now most frequently associated with San Francesco della Vigna (London, RIBA, XIV, 10, and Vicenza, Museo Civico, D 17), there are clear references to such an iconography in the architect's extensive studies of ancient triumphal arches, such as the Arch of Trajan at Ancona (figs. 89 and 90).[96] On the executed exterior façade, the addition of half-pediments to each side and the removal of the attic from the design as shown in the drawing in London have suppressed overt references to the triumphal arch *type*, while the interior façade monument depicted in the Vicenza drawing would have retained its derivation had it ever been executed.

90   Andrea Palladio, with figures by Federico Zuccaro, drawing for a tomb monument, Vicenza, Museo Civico, D 17

91 Vincenzo Scamozzi, Francesco Smeraldi, Girolamo Campagna, and Sante Peranda, tomb monument of Doge Marino Grimani, San Giuseppe di Castello, Venice

92 Sebastiano Serlio, Arch of Trajan, *Libro primo [-quinto] d'architettura, di Sebastiano Serlio bolognese* (*Il terzo libro*, 1540), Venice, Appresso G.B. e M. Sessa fratelli, 1559, cap. 4, fol. 119

A tomb monument for the next Grimani to be elected doge, Marino (1595–1605, from the collateral branch of San Luca), in San Giuseppe di Castello (1599–1604), shows the strong dependence that Venetian sepulchral monuments had on the triumphal arch (fig. 91). The proximity in Castello of San Giuseppe and Sant'Antonio with their respective Grimani dogal monuments suggests a keen awareness of the impact such mutually reinforcing dynastic statements would make. The triumphal arch was both an effective formal solution for sites that often had to accommodate portals, and for the honor imputed to the dead by symbolic association; in this case, it has been suggested that its designer knew Palladio's Vicenza drawing and based the monument at San Giuseppe di Castello on it.[97]

Yet at San Francesco della Vigna, even without a direct reference to the arch *type*, a strong element of triumphal architecture remains in the façade design. It is expressed foremost in the classical language of the orders themselves, but also in the arrangement for its decoration. In the London drawing, Palladio has provided for two consoles, one above the other, in each of the bays formed by the

major order, whereas in the façade of San Francesco della Vigna there are framed panels for inscriptions over the framed niches containing sculptures, with framed panels in the bays of the wings. Provisions for such elements of decoration are more frequent in Palladio's drawings after ancient triumphal arches than in those for temple façades. For example, similar consoles can be found in the intercolumnar bays of the Arch of Trajan, to which the London drawing has been compared. In Serlio's rendition of the Arch of Trajan (fig. 92), he annotated these consoles with the letter "E," "Between the columns on the cornice marked E – from what is implied by the inscriptions in those places – there used to be some bronze statues" (*Third Book*, ch. 4, fol. CXXII/107v); a translation of 1611 gives the understanding that such consoles would have accommodated busts in particular: "The foure tables with the Cornices upon them, which stand betweene the Columnes, are thought to be placed there, for holding up of halfe Images" (*Third Book*, ch. 4, fol. 56v).[98] Where the attic story of the London drawing has been replaced in the façade by a temple pediment with a carved and

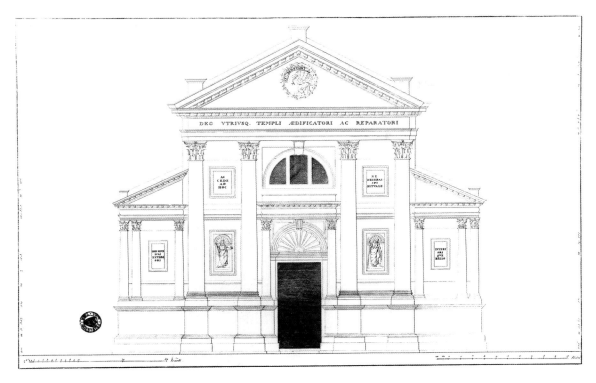

93   Leopoldo Cicognara, Antonio Diedo, and Gianantonio Selva, façade of San Francesco della Vigna, *Le fabbriche e i monumenti più cospicui di Venezia*, ed. F. Zanotto, Venice 1858, 2:133

inscribed roundel, a horizontal emphasis is retained in the strongly projecting architrave in which the frieze bears an inscription. For Palladio, the magnificence of a temple façade was justified by reference to the holy temple of Jerusalem: "One reads that this temple was the largest, most splendid, and most lavish in the city, and to tell the truth, its remains, ruined though they are, suggest such magnificence that one can imagine all too well what it was like when it was complete" (*Four Books*, Bk. 4, ch. 6, 11).[99] On a later occasion he defends the use of ornament, again citing this revered model, and further names the Corinthian order as most suitable for temples (*Lettera per la facciata di San Petronio a Bologna*, 11 January 1578):

> But I do not know where this German reasoning comes from, to note that festoons, foliage, and fruit detract from the gravity of the work, since these and other ornaments were made in the construction of the grand temple of Jerusalem, and the ancient Egyptians, Greeks, and Romans put ornament in every sort of fabric including sacred temples, as well as the richest order of these ornaments, that is the Corinthian, which they dedicated to temples.[100]

The Corinthian, well known to be the order that Vitruvius allowed for greater adornment, was recommended by Serlio for sacred temples dedicated to "all those Saints, male and female, who led a virginal life. Also monasteries, and convents which cloister maidens dedicated to divine worship," and, since "tombs are to be for people of upright and chaste lives, this type of ornament could be used to preserve decorum," as well as being favored by the Venetians.[101] Palladio shared a social theory of architecture in which the splendor of the orders must be matched both to the social status of the patron and to the function of the building. The principle of "decorum or conveniency" that guided his architecture found its apex of expression in the temple. For each of the patriarchal façades that he designed, the Corinthian, with its overtones of sacred magnificence, was employed in both the major and minor orders.[102]

Despite the magnificence that gives credit to its patron, the façade of San Francesco della Vigna does not obviously refer either to Giovanni Grimani personally, or to the glorification of his family: neither his nor their name nor their images are present in the inscriptions and sculptured figures (fig. 93). John Sparrow was the first to read the program of the main frieze inscription, DEO UTRIUSQUE TEMPLI AEDIFICATORI AC REPARATORI, as alluding to the restoration of both a physical church and a spiritual one. In this he followed the lead of Wittkower's exposition of the theories of Vitruvius and Daniele Barbaro, and of Fra Zorzi: "the human body was to be taken as a model in the construction of sacred buildings because it was itself a sacred Temple made after the likeness of the Deity."[103] Building further on Sparrow's interpretation, Foscari and Tafuri have proposed that the program represented even more specifically Grimani's celebration of the closing of the Council of Trent and the renewal of the Church through its reforms. The epigraphs in the left and right outer bays, SINE IUGE EXTERIORI and INTERIORQUE BELLO ("not without an unceasing external and inter-

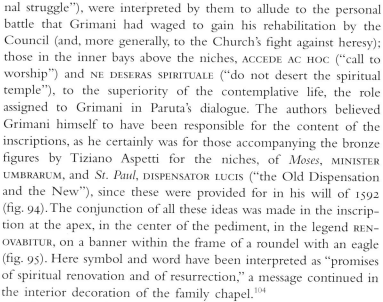

94 Andrea Palladio, façade, San Francesco della Vigna, Venice, with bronze figures of Moses and St. Paul by Tiziano Aspetti

95 Andrea Palladio, detail of façade, San Francesco della Vigna, Venice

nal struggle"), were interpreted by them to allude to the personal battle that Grimani had waged to gain his rehabilitation by the Council (and, more generally, to the Church's fight against heresy); those in the inner bays above the niches, ACCEDE AC HOC ("call to worship") and NE DESERAS SPIRITUALE ("do not desert the spiritual temple"), to the superiority of the contemplative life, the role assigned to Grimani in Paruta's dialogue. The authors believed Grimani himself to have been responsible for the content of the inscriptions, as he certainly was for those accompanying the bronze figures by Tiziano Aspetti for the niches, of *Moses*, MINISTER UMBRARUM, and *St. Paul*, DISPENSATOR LUCIS ("the Old Dispensation and the New"), since these were provided for in his will of 1592 (fig. 94). The conjunction of all these ideas was made in the inscription at the apex, in the center of the pediment, in the legend REN-OVABITUR, on a banner within the frame of a roundel with an eagle (fig. 95). Here symbol and word have been interpreted as "promises of spiritual renovation and of resurrection," a message continued in the interior decoration of the family chapel.[104]

This exegesis of the façade as assuming the character of an "ex voto and propitiatory work" is compelling, except for the assumption that Palladio and Grimani had intentions so far apart as to

exclude their mutual comprehension: that Palladio would not have identified with the "self-celebratory" motives of the patriarch, and that Grimani would not have understood the "self-sufficient universe" created by the architect. If Grimani's inscriptions could be viewed as a dialogic rather than a dialectic, then Palladio's design established a new semantics for the church façade in Venice.[105] Palladio's concern for the program went beyond the general function of the Christian temple to provide a controlling framework as a vehicle for the public expression of the patron. The transformation of elements associated with the triumphal arch, as shown in the London drawing, demonstrate Palladio's consciousness not only of the decorum of form but of the expressive function meant to be framed by it. Eliminating the consoles described by Serlio as supporting portrait busts, niches were introduced in their place in the built façade; niches meant to contain sculptures were, on the other hand, a ubiquitous motif in Palladio's studies of ancient temples. This suggests that Palladio was complicit with Grimani in designing an external façade with a different program than the dynastic celebration originally envisioned for it when the rights were first acquired, especially given the proposal advanced by Foscari and Tafuri that dates the Vicenza drawing for the unrealized interior earlier than the façade construction; with the funerary monuments transferred to the interior, where the triumphal arch form is fully retained, only a suggestion of its character is retained on the exterior, which is thus strengthened in its temple associations.

Pantheon of Patriarchs

The burial of Doge Antonio at the homonymic Sant'Antonio di Castello, alongside his son Pietro (died 1517), a knight of the Hierosolymitan Order, identifies it as the location where temporal rulers of the Grimani family were congregated in their burials, prompting Giovanni to inter his brother Procurator Vettor there. Ultimately Giovanni would claim the place for himself in the family chapel that Vettor had initiated at San Francesco della Vigna, but nothing has yet disclosed when the project for the interior façade

monument shown in Palladio's Vicenza drawing was abandoned (fig. 96). Giovanni may have continued to entertain plans for its eventual execution, which together with the chapel would give him two major sites for multiple burials, since he had excluded the most public with his exterior façade program.[106] The iconography of the Vicenza drawing for the interior façade, as well as the reported burials there, bears out an interpretation that San Francesco della Vigna had been reconceived as a "pantheon" of the patriarchs of Aquileia. There was already a precedent for the memorialization of a patriarch in the church. The brilliant humanist and poet laureate Ermolao Barbaro was eulogized in an epitaph on the wall of the Barbaro family chapel as patriarch of Aquileia (1491–92/93), a title the Venetian government had refused to recognize (fig. 97).[107] As already noted, the patriarch-elect Daniele Barbaro, adhering to his principles for the reform of sepulchral practices, would later be buried in the "campo santo" outside the church. When Giovanni

96 Jacopo Sansovino, interior façade with Grimani Chapel on right, San Francesco della Vigna, Venice

97 Barbaro Chapel, San Francesco della Vigna, Venice, with *stemma* of the Barbaro family

inherited the Grimani rights to the façades and chapel, he must also have assumed the familial responsibility of the disposition of his patriarchal brothers and uncle, which Vettor had earlier undertaken.

The Vicenza drawing leaves some questions open as to what was intended to be carried out, particularly in the figurative content, which is attributed to Federico Zuccaro (and therefore not before summer 1563 or after July 1565, since he did not return until 1582).[108] As is not untypical for Palladio, the drawing presents two architectural solutions, which have implications for the content. Both solutions provide for three sarcophagi, one in each of the side bays and one in the center of the attic. The left side uses the most highly decorated order, the Composite, and the sarcophagus at the top shows elaborate *all'antica* foliage curling around a lion's-claw footing; the right side is in the Corinthian order, with the top sarcophagus echoing the graceful profile of the other two in the bays below. The inter-columnar position of the sarcophagi in the bays and the dimensions of the higher portal in the left-hand solution allowed room for only one allegorical figure, seated on the top sarcophagus; the placement of the sarcophagi in the basement zone below the columns in the right-hand solution accommodated niches in the bays, and the smaller portal left space for a figure in the lunette above it. Federico Zuccaro then supplied the figural elements; these are drawn in ink over the architectural framework. The left side shows a bearded, reclining male figure on the sarcophagus within the bay, and a crowned, seated female personification on the sarcophagus in the attic; the right side likewise displays a bearded, reclining male on the sarcophagus below the niche, in which is a standing female figure, and another, this one crowned, placed over the portal. In addition, caryatids have been added to the attic order; between each pair is a scene meant to be in relief (as are the two victory figures in the spandrels over the portal, and the festoons between the capitals in each bay).

We cannot assume a perfect knowledge of Giovanni Grimani's intentions on the part of Federico Zuccaro, since, quite likely, this drawing was a means of proposing different possible programs to realize the monument, but there are several indications of the constants that were under consideration. The chief of these is the indication of at least three burials. Next, that in both solutions an identifying attribute was proposed for the two sarcophagi in the bays, because both reclining figures are shown to wear miters. Either one (left side) or three (right side) allegorical figures were projected. Two relief scenes could be included in either scheme. It is the presence of the reclining figures as mitered that connects the iconography of this drawing to Grimani's ambitions. There has been some confusion over this episcopal attribute, since as we have seen in Daniele Barbaro's portrait in Amsterdam, as well as a related drawing in Munich (fig. 98), the usual patriarchal headwear was the *berretta*. The miter, however, was part of the patriarchal costume when attired ceremonially, *a pontificale*, together with crosier and ring, evoking papal authority and pastoral care. At San Francesco della Vigna, even Daniele Barbaro's pious burial contributed to the foundation of a patriarchal pantheon, although this identity was carried only through memory and not by means of visual records carved

in stone, since he requested that he be buried in patriarchal costume with its regalia (miter, ring, and crozier), rather than the Franciscan habit requested by so many who wished to die well: "vestito alla Patriarchal con la mitria anello & crosetta al chollo."[109] Since no cardinal's hats have been represented, Zuccaro may have simply provided attributes coeval with his patron Giovanni's status as patriarch, and not further designated individual characteristics; the patriarchy was the element that the three brothers and their uncle held in common.[110]

If the two reclining figures are to be identified as patriarchs by this attribute, it remains first to examine the evidence for the disposition of the Grimani *illustri*, and then to see what other iconographic elements further suggest. Several reports provide the number and identity of the actual burials displayed on the inner façade, but it is not clear at what point this arrangement superseded plans for a different and more elaborate disposition than was ultimately realized. In 1581 Francesco Sansovino (who was loyally silent as to the merits of the exterior façade imposed on his father's building) said that upon

> entering the church in the interior façade over the grand portal, are reposing two Cardinals of the Grimani family, Domenico created by Pope Alexander VI, & Marino made by Clement VII. Equally there was Marco, Patriarch of Aquileia, who in the year 1537 was General of Paul III for the league that opposed the forces of Suleyman. From the left are five chapels: the first of which is of the same Grimani, & especially of Patriarch Giovanni.

Giovanni Stringa also saw them, for he added in his edition of 1604 that the "cassoni" were covered in scarlet.[111] Magrini named the same patriarchal members of the family on the interior façade, and later described Domenico and Marino as being placed in wood urns, suggesting a provisory arrangement, but mentioning Giovanni's burial and interment of their ashes in the chapel.[112] Foscari and Tafuri further suggested the possibility that Giovanni originally might have intended a place for himself on the façade as well. We also have to consider that Marco, like Daniele, had firmly stated his burial preferences, in case of his death outside Venice:

> that his bones would be taken to the monastery of Sant'Antonio, and there put in the cloister in a sepulcher of the value of 200 ducats, nor by any means do I want to be buried in church, because neither for me nor others is it appropriate to bury the bones of sinners, above all mine, in similar locations, nor do I wish them to be at altars nor façades, so that at no time is [Mass] celebrated where the bones of a sinner repose

(although Giovanni's record for respecting others' wishes when it came to the fulfillment of his own schemes was decidedly poor, or it may have been intended to be a cenotaph).[113] Marco's career veered between the secular and the Church: he had been a procurator of San Marco *de citra* (1522–28) before becoming patriarchelect, which he abdicated in turn (back to Marino), becoming papal general under Paul III, which also linked his activities to those of

98   Paolo Veronese,
Daniele Barbaro, Munich,
Staatliche Graphische
Sammlung (12893)

his brother Vettor, grandfather Antonio, and uncle Pietro, who were honored at Sant'Antonio di Castello (a favored site of his uncle, Cardinal Domenico, as well). It is also just possible that the design at one time accommodated four burials – all the Grimani patriarchs – since close examination of the Vicenza drawing reveals that Palladio's right-hand solution was extended with a light touch in black chalk: completing the outline of the smaller portal and showing the placement of a sarcophagus over the door, whose profile is traced in a couple of overlapping strokes, its top extending above the architrave into the lunette (in the position occupied by Zuccaro's standing allegorical figure). Four tombs on the interior could have replaced what had been intended to be commemorated with the four consoles on the London drawing as the new program for the exterior façade evolved.[114]

Regardless of his sepulchral presence, as its patron Giovanni would have been associated with the program of the interior façade,

especially with his assumption of the adjacent family chapel. The allegorical figures on the Vicenza drawing show disappointingly scant identifying attributes. The central figures for each of the solutions are crowned, and would have substituted for each other. Only the seated figure in the attic is holding an object aloft in her right hand (a jar with a flame?), the left resting on a support (a book?). She has been discussed as the personification of Faith, as a statement of the recently vindicated Patriarch Giovanni.[115] It would follow that the niche figures of the right-hand solution would be Hope and Charity, the other two theological virtues particularly cherished by St. Paul, who is important to the program of the exterior façade.[116] The two relief panels depicted are equally sketchy, but seem to show the conferring of dignities; on the left, an exterior scene is implied by the standing figure with a vaguely military cloak – possibly this alludes to Marco being named papal general by Paul III – on the right, then, it is probably the bestowal of a red

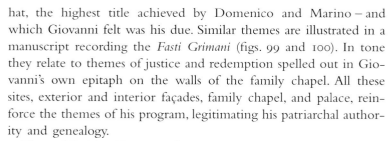

99 *Marco Grimani Receiving Command of the Papal Army*, "Origini dalla famiglia Grimana havuta dall' anno 666," 1627, Venice, Biblioteca del Museo Civico Correr, MS Morosini-Grimani 270, 59

100 *Domenico Grimani Receiving the Cardinal's Hat*, "Origini dalla famiglia Grimana havuta dall' anno 666," 1627, Venice, Biblioteca del Museo Civico Correr, MS. Morosini-Grimani 270, 48

hat, the highest title achieved by Domenico and Marino – and which Giovanni felt was his due. Similar themes are illustrated in a manuscript recording the *Fasti Grimani* (figs. 99 and 100). In tone they relate to themes of justice and redemption spelled out in Giovanni's own epitaph on the walls of the family chapel. All these sites, exterior and interior façades, family chapel, and palace, reinforce the themes of his program, legitimating his patriarchal authority and genealogy.

The public identification of San Francesco della Vigna as a patriarchal church, part of Giovanni Grimani's enterprise to recuperate his domain within Venice, can be even more securely attributed for Palladio's exterior façade. Such references do not replace, but enhance the typological language that could embrace several referents for a single symbol. Perhaps the most obvious omission from the façade iconography is the presence of the name saint of the church, St. Francis. One of the most readily recognized symbols of

the apostolic Church is in evidence, however, and is, of course the name saint of the patron: San Giovanni Evangelista, represented by the symbol of the eagle. This ties the exterior to interior, because St. John the Evangelist is also painted on the right-hand spandrel above the entrance to the chapel, reinforcing the identification between worldly and saintly patrons. For the exterior façade program, the emphasis on Giovanni would not necessarily preclude the inclusion of Francis, unless there was an overriding identity being proposed other than that of the order of the church, as seems to be the case here. For, in the evangelist symbol of the eagle in the pediment, denoting *renovatio vitae*, also lies the proclamation of the church as the "Renewed" Aquileia: the eagle, or *aquila*, was the seal of the ancient patriarchal city.[117] The *cathedra* of the patriarchs in the basilica of Aquileia bears the eagle in the center of the center step (fig. 101), and it could be seen on the *stemma* (coat of arms) of the city in views that continued through the period of occupation. Its use survives from early coins of the patriarchs inscribed AQU∗ILE∗ GEN∗SIS∗, AQUILEGIA∗ CIVITAS∗, or simply, AQUI∗LEGIA∗, in a legend around the figure of an eagle, and is also a reminder of the patriarchy's descent from Imperial power (fig. 102).[118]

In this context, turning back for a moment to the contemporary building and arrangement of the collections at the Grimani Palace, the privileging of the antique sculptural group of *Ganymede and the Eagle* that formed a centerpiece in the new Studio of Antiquities (seen in a drawing by Federico Zuccaro when it was populated by the collection [fig. 103], and as it has been restored [fig. 104]) may be another gesture to patriarchal iconography (now in the Museo Archaeologico, Venice, as a Grimani bequest [fig. 105]).[119] The Aquileian reference had deep roots at San Francesco della Vigna, since its foundation legend recorded a primitive church there dedicated to St. Mark, where, on his return from Aquileia, an angel had appeared to him with the portentous words: "Pax tibi Marce Evangelista meus" ("Peace be to you Mark my Evangelist"), as illustrated in the painting by Domenico Tintoretto of the *Dream of St. Mark:*

"*Pax tibi Marce*" for the Scuola of San Marco (now Venice, Accademia [fig. 106]), and adopted as the emblem of the Republic.[120]

Re-Inventing the Commemorative Façade

The references encoded in Palladio's architectural language display the magnificence appropriate to the patriarchal status that Giovanni Grimani wielded for almost half a century. Palladio's involvement in the iconography of the façade decoration would seem to be more complicit than allowed for in Foscari's and Tafuri's opposition of the architecture and of the figures and inscriptions, if less than the total authorship granted by Sparrow. He had to know enough of its proposed content to plan for the prominent framing of the epigraphs and to prepare the surface of the frieze. The antiquarian character of its presentation, what Sparrow has called "Palladian epigraphy," strongly suggests his agency in the presentation of the iconography. As Sparrow pointed out, the planned use of epigraphs

101   Patriarchal *cathedra*, Basilica Patriarcale, Aquileia

102   Gian Giuseppe Liruti, *Della moneta propria, e forastiera ch'ebbe corso nel ducato di Friuli*, Venice, 1749, tav. 3

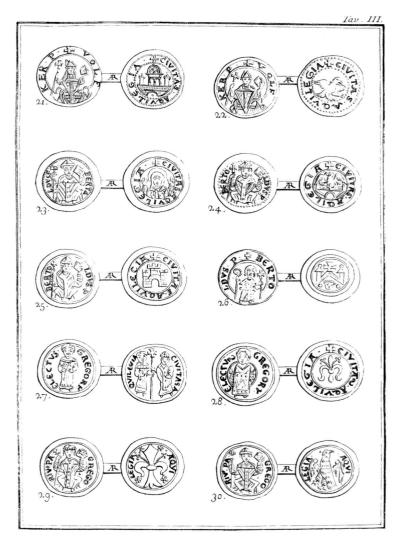

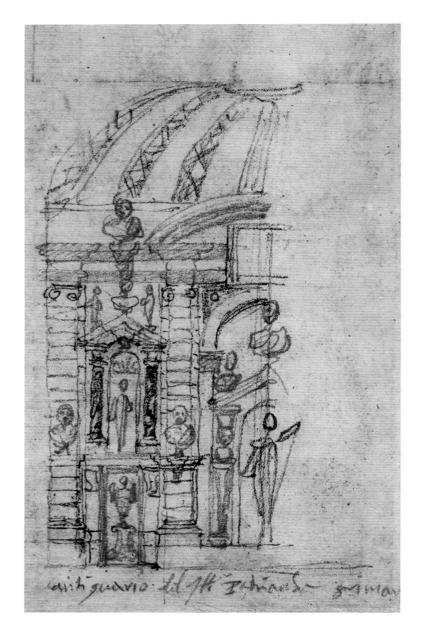

104   Studio of Antiquities, Grimani Palace, Santa Maria Formosa, Venice

103 (*left*)   Federico Zuccaro, "Antiquario del Ill.mo Patriarca Grimani" (detail of *verso* of drawing after Paolo Veronese's *Feast in the House of Simon*), London, British Museum

as a major design feature was a novelty in Venetian church façades before Palladio: most exterior inscriptions – in varying scripts – belonged to individual memorials, as on tombs, or were limited to the frieze, and often did not form part of a coherent program. At San Francesco della Vigna, Palladio began to forge a newly expressive type of commemorative façade through the display of epigraphs. Drawing upon his knowledge of classical architecture and the purposes of its decorative features, Palladio was at once heir to the investigations of Alberti and a contemporary of the research of Pirro Ligorio, in their penetration of this Romanizing element.[121] The historicizing purpose of inscriptions has been noted earlier as enhancing the program as visual evidence according to Alberti. Alberti has more to say on the subject of epigraphs, the most common purpose for temples being to announce their dedication, a practice that continued in churches:

Now I come to the subject of inscriptions. Their uses were many and varied among the ancients. They were employed not only in sepulchers, but also in sacred buildings and even private houses. The names of the gods to whom a temple was dedicated would be inscribed, according to Symmachus, on the pediment. It has been our custom to inscribe on our chapels details of their dedication and year of consecration. I approve of this strongly.[122]

A more ambitious programmatic function for epigraphs was recognized as well, in the chapter on "commemorative monuments" (aptly titled in the Giacomo Leoni translation of 1755, "Of Monuments raised for preserving the Memory of publick Actions and Events"):

They were also desirous of eternizing their Memory to Posterity, and of making even their Persons, as well as Virtues known

106 Domenico Tintoretto, *Dream of St. Mark: "Pax tibi Marce,"* Venice, Gallerie dell'Accademia

105 (*above left*) Roman late 2nd c. AD (after Greek, 4th c. BC), *Ganymede and the Eagle,* Venice, Museo Archeologico (inv. 145)

to future Ages. This produced Trophies, Spoils, Statues, Inscriptions, and the like Inventions for propagating the fame of great exploits.[123]

As a native son of Padua and an accomplished stonecutter, it would be more surprising to find that Palladio was *not* deeply steeped in appreciation for the classical epigraphy that had sparked humanist intellects there a century earlier.[124] Palladio was diligent in his recording of classical inscriptions as part of the architectural decoration, from triumphal arches to temples, as in the illustration of the frieze of the Temple of Concord (*Four Books*, Bk. 4, ch. 30, 124): "To judge by the inscription still visible in the frieze, the temple was destroyed by fire and then rebuilt by order of the Senate and Roman people" (fig. 107). In fact, the inscription served Palladio not only to identify the patron, but as a means of analyzing the history of the building, as his further comment on the Temple of Concord confirms, "which is why I allow myself to believe that it was not rebuilt to the same level of beauty and perfection as it was before."[125] His most impressive demonstration of this kind of reasoning is found in his analysis of the Pantheon, which he dated to two different phases from the evidence of the inscriptions on the friezes of the temple front.[126] In the façade of San Francesco della Vigna, the pediment roundel with the eagle bears the only inscription, RENOVABITUR, to be carved in stone, while the others, like the statues, are lettered in bronze, which provides a contrast for legibility. Palladio was concerned with the appropriate preparation of his surfaces to receive their ornament, as can be seen in the admiration he expressed for the technique used to cut the plane of the frieze for an inscription on the pediment of the Temple of Nerva:

There are some beautiful moldings in the architrave that divide one fascia from another, and these moldings and divisions occur only at the sides of the temple because on the façade the architrave and frieze were made to a plane so that they could place the inscription there easily; now one can see only these few letters, though they are broken and damaged by the passage of time.[127]

As noted here by Palladio, the intention of placing an inscription in the pediment predetermined the disposition of the architectural ornament. Of course in secular architecture where Palladio introduced the temple front, the ornament that he clearly expected to be placed there was one of personal identification, the *stemma*, or family coat of arms, in a *scudo* (escutcheon) in the center of the pediment – where the eagle roundel is placed at San Francesco della Vigna, often otherwise the position for an oculus. As we have already seen in the palaces of Giovanni Grimani in Venice and Floriano Antonini in Udine, inscriptions were used to address the public and identify its benefactors. This was also the case at the Villa Barbaro at Maser (fig. 108), where the brothers' patronage and hospitality is declared, and Marc'Antonio later commemorated his relationship to the architect in the latter's final work on the Tempietto there.[128]

Another aspect of the façade iconography at San Francesco della Vigna intimates that Palladio would have had cognizance of Giovanni Grimani's intentions in order to frame the program, and that it could well have been developed within the ambit of Daniele

107 Andrea Palladio, Temple of Concord, *I quattro libri dell'architettura*, Venice, Appresso Dominico de' Franceschi, 1570, lib. 4, cap. 30, 126

Barbaro. Ironically, it is also the aspect most removed in date from Palladio and Barbaro: Grimani's bequest of 1592 to Tiziano Aspetti for the figures of *Paul* and *Moses*. Yet the conjunction of inscriptions and figures seems teleological. Furthermore, it is too close to be a coincidence to find the same two church figures mentioned in the text of Fra Zorzi's *Memoriale* of 1535 for the church: first reference is made to Moses' building of the tabernacle in Exodus (25), then to Paul's Letters to the Corinthians, "Ye are the Temple of God" (First Letter 3: 16; 6: 19; and Second Letter 6: 16), and finally equating King Solomon's use of the form and proportions for his temple with the practice that should be followed at San Francesco della Vigna. Wittkower was the first to publish a translation of the *Memoriale* and he stated that, "It appears certain that Palladio, a generation later, knew Giorgi's memorandum and derived from it the mysterious 27 moduli which he applied to the width of the central portion of his façade."[129] It was a similar insight that led Lewis to apply a modular system (rather than the usual metric) to

Palladio's drawing in London (RIBA, XIV, 10), and to calculate its measurements to the built façade.[130] Sparrow took up Wittkower's assertion of Palladio's knowledge of Fra Zorzi's program, and expanded it to include the iconographic content of the inscriptions and statues of *Paul* and *Moses*.[131] Foscari and Tafuri agreed that Barbaro, Grimani, and Palladio would have known the *Memoriale*, but cautioned that while Fra Zorzi's philosophical works circulated in the academic circles to which they belonged, his harmonic theories of architecture had been superseded by a scientific rigorism. More problematic they thought, however, was the condemnation of Fra Zorzi's works and their eventual inclusion on the Index of prohibited books, heretical association with which Grimani would have been careful to avoid given his personal travails.[132] Yet it seems likely that for Grimani, as well as Barbaro and Palladio, the *Memoriale* was considered to be an important document associated with the program of the church, and one that still held some authority, allowing it to be reinterpreted in light of Grimani's enterprise.

Grimani's recent vindication at the Council of Trent had as its origin accusations made in 1560 based on a letter with his views on the subject of predestination, which were heavily influenced by the writings of St. Paul, and commentaries of Sts. Augustine and Thomas Aquinas. These were all revered Catholic sources, but Paul's thought had long inspired non-dogmatic interpretation. Grimani maintained his orthodoxy all along, but it must be remembered that the letter that was the basis for the new charges of heresy, particularly as it touched on the central issue of Justification, had been written in 1549, in a considerably different theological climate. The Venetian patriciate of the early sixteenth century has been remarked as having a Pauline bias, a theological position taken by a number of the important reformers of the Church. The extreme interpretation of Martin Luther, *solo Christo, solo gratia, sola fide* ("justification by Christ alone, grace alone, faith alone"), however, made more accommodating views on this doctrinal point increasingly suspect; one of the reasons Grimani was given to discourage him from taking his case before the Council was that the question of Justification, settled in 1547 during its first session, would be reopened. So it must be taken very seriously that Grimani continued with the iconography of St. Paul, as originally prescribed by the *Memoriale*.[133]

The inclusion of Moses as the other character on the stage of the façade highlights Paul's role as the agent for understanding the Old and New Law, in the context of the theme of enlightenment and rebirth. Like Giovanni Grimani, the patriarchy of Aquileia and the Church itself, Paul was seen as triumphant through many struggles and trials:

To save the Jews, Moses chose to be wiped out from the book of the living, and therefore offered himself to perish with the rest, but Paul offered himself *for* the rest. He wished to perish, not with those perishing; but in order that the others might be saved, he would give up eternal glory. And Moses resisted Pharoah, but Paul resisted the devil daily. Moses resisted for the sake of one people, Paul fought for the whole world, not by sweat but by blood.[134]

108   Andrea Palladio and Marc'Antonio Barbaro, tympanum, Villa Barbaro at Maser

In this reading from *The Golden Legend*, Paul is presented as the Redeemer, an *alterus Christus*, in whose sacrifice was salvation of the world.

The contrast of Paul and Moses recalls the positions on "justification by faith," over "justification by law," taken by reformers in the doctrinal debates preceding the Tridentine decree. The Augustinian general, Cardinal Girolamo Seripando (1492/93–1563), was one of the most prominent exponents of Pauline theology, but so was another of the special commission of cardinals that had been convened to deal with the issues to come before the Council who has greater direct resonance for the interpretation of the façade program; this was Cardinal Patriarch Marino Grimani, Giovanni's brother and Trissino's friend. Although he died a few months before the final decree on Justification, previously in 1542 Cardinal Marino had published a commentary on the *Letters of Paul to the Romans and to the Galatians* (*Commentarii in Epistolas Pauli, Ad Romanos, et ad Galatas*, Aldus, Venice), known also in a luxury manuscript version.[135] Marino's particular identification with Paul can be seen

in the title-page illumination by Giulio Clovio of the latter (*Commentarii in Epistolam Pauli, Ad Romanos*, London, Sir John Soane's Museum, vol. 143 [MS 11], fol. 8) kept in the Grimani palace at Santa Maria Formosa until the eighteenth century; his portrait in a border roundel is opposite that of Paul's set as a fictive intaglio (fig. 109). The commentary drew criticism that would surely have been more severe in the subsequent climate, in their expression of reform views on the nature of justification by faith. His exegesis included a range of phrases that could be compared to Luther's statements: for example, the people are released from Mosaic law, to live in the new, *in sola Christi gratia* ("by the sole grace of Christ"); on justification by faith, *sola fide Christi*.[136] Yet Grimani does not commit himself to faith without good works, which he explained as necessary but not causal. His scholarship was representative of early attempts in the Conciliar process to find a theological position that could diminish the rift in the Church, before a more intransigent attitude dominated. It is interesting to speculate on the appeal of Paul, as direct heir of Christ's evangelical

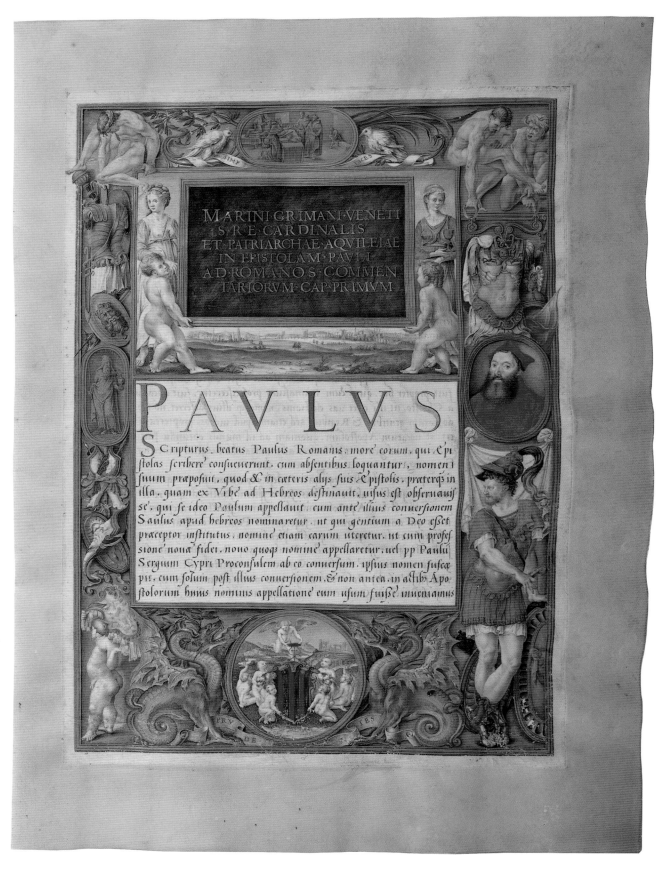

109 Giulio Clovio, titlepage with border roundel portrait of Cardinal Marino Grimani, *Commentarii in Epistolas Pauli, Ad Romanos, et ad Galatas*, London, Sir John Soane's Museum, vol. 143 (MS II), fol. 8

110 *Giovanni Grimani*, "Origini dalla famiglia Grimana havuta dall' anno 666," 1627, Venice, Biblioteca del Museo Civico Correr, MS Morosini-Grimani 270, 26

mission, among Venetian reformers and the patriciate. For the revelation vouchsafed to Paul even allowed him to contest the primacy of Peter, a sensitive issue in the Conciliar period to be negotiated by Grimani's exegesis, but also one embedded in the Venetian mythography of apostolic parity.

Giovanni Grimani was educated in this pre-Tridentine world. The themes of law and justice are as prominent as the messages of spiritual enlightenment and rebirth displayed both on the façade and in the family chapel. A contemporary identification of St. Mark as Moses the lawgiver reinforces the message of the Venetians as the chosen people under the law.[137] Giovanni's own *impresa* (motto) incorporated the scales of justice, the imagery of just rule finding its own parallel as one of the personifications of Venice (fig. 110).

In his statement of faith in the cross on the chapel walls, Giovanni echoed his brother Marino's affirmation: "One is crucified through the cross of Christ to the world" ("ut in sola cruce Iesu Christi cruce vivam", Galatians 6: 14).[138] It seems also a vindication, the imperfections of man's law, submitted to a higher judgment. In the organization of the visual and verbal exchange across the face of San Francesco della Vigna, Palladio has realized the patriarch of Aquileia's own final statement on the subject that was at the heart of Church reform in the sixteenth century.

With the execution of the façade of San Francesco della Vigna, Palladio literally succeeded Sansovino in the field of church architecture, the only building type acknowledged by the interlocutors of Paruta's dialogue as one where the "moderns" contended with the "ancients." The prestige of Palladio's two early patriarchal commissions, and of his particular patrician supporters and their ecclesiastical affiliations, had launched his Venetian career in a new direction in the 1560s. Over the last two decades of his life, Palladio would have the opportunity to continue his investigations of religious architecture in Venice, culminating in the prominent commissions for two churches *ex novo*, San Giorgio Maggiore and Il Redentore. These would be Palladio's St. Peter's, and would securely identify him with the sacred public image of the city. As at San Francesco della Vigna, Palladio would develop an innovative program whose meaning and function were intrinsic to each situation and whose most public expression was the façade. Just as the sixteenth century accepted the architectural frontispiece as a natural framework for the words of the text, so too would Palladio's façades provide a speaking visage. As with all forms of public presentation, Venice was intensely sensitive to such discourse, particularly as it defined the interests of the individual, family, or community, and the State. With his contribution to the development of the commemorative façade, Palladio introduced a historical dimension that extended beyond traditional dynastic and dedicatory proclamations and engaged with Venetian identity formation. The city's own past controlled appearance on all levels, from dress and customs, to other modes of personal and familial display, to public expression, regulated by decisions of patronage and funding. Such visual rhetoric was both transformed and transformative in a struggle to maintain the independent course of the Venetian state that was played out in embassies, the council hall, public processions, self-description. The figured façades of Venetian churches were a fundamental voice in the declaration of the relationship between Church and State, and it is this context in which Palladio operated that will be examined next.

PART IV

RELIGIOUS ORDERS

INTRODUCTION

FOLLOWING HIS PRESTIGIOUS COMMISSION for the patriarch of Venice, Palladio came to the attention of the religious orders in Venice. Monasticism is distinguished by adherence to a rule of community life, developed in the West by St. Benedict. A recent survey has identified some fifty monastic churches representing twenty-one different male and female orders by the mid-fifteenth century in the diocese of the patriarch of Venice alone: Francesco Sansovino counted fifty-nine monasteries, of which thirty-one were male religious and twenty-eight female.[1] This is less than a dozen fewer than the number of parish churches recorded at the time, and speaks to the density of the religious fabric within the city. Although the earliest years of Venice belong to episcopal and parish churches, and the founding of what became the chapel of the doge at San Marco, by the ninth and tenth centuries monastic communities were growing in the Realtine and lagoon islands. The first to be established were female and male Benedictine monasteries with close ties to the patriciate. The wealth, property, and aristocratic connections with which they were endowed became a part of their heritage, and that of Venice. The *sancta città* continued over the centuries to attract new orders in successive waves of reform, such as the Canons Regular, Cluniacs, and Cistercians in the eleventh and twelfth centuries, the great mendicant foundations of the Dominicans and Franciscans in the thirteenth and fourteenth centuries, and the Capuchins, Jesuits, and Theatines associated with the sixteenth-century "Counter-Reformation." The traditional orders were imbued equally with a spirit of renewal in the Renaissance, with Venetian patricians contributing to the formation of the Canons of San Giorgio in Alga and the Benedictine Congregation of Santa Giustina (later "Cassinese"). Variation in the conditions of the different orders, from economic status to devotional practices, naturally had an impact on the nature of artistic commissions.

Palladio's entry into ecclesiastical commissions in Venice was predominantly one of intervention rather than building *ex novo*, as witnessed by his patriarchal church façades. This was true of his first efforts for religious orders, including the Lateran Canons at Santa Maria della Carità and the Benedictine Cassinese Congregation at San Giorgio Maggiore, where he worked on monastic living spaces. His success at San Giorgio was rewarded with a commission to build their new church. He would be involved in this project for the rest of his life. Palladio's association with projects for the female religious houses, the Augustinians at Santa Lucia and Cistercians at La Celestia, will be treated in this section, for what can be learned of the way that building enterprises were carried out in such environments, and how he met the challenges of their particular requirements in the period following Tridentine reform.

CHAPTER SEVEN

SAN GIORGIO MAGGIORE

A BENEDICTINE MONASTERY WAS ESTABLISHED on the island of San Giorgio Maggiore in 982 (fig. 111). Traditional Benedictine monasticism is contemplative, "cloistered" from the world, and is focused on choral prayer. In the early fifteenth century, the Benedictines at San Giorgio Maggiore were among the founding houses of the Congregation of Santa Giustina, a union of formerly autonomous monasteries. It became the Congregation Cassinese in 1504 on the entry of the monastery of Monte Cassino, St. Benedict's burial place which illustrates the successful expansion of this new organization, and introducing a new model for emulation.

A program of physical renewal was embarked on throughout the Congregation, and had been underway at San Giorgio for more than a century when Palladio was commissioned in 1560 to execute a refectory, already partially begun twenty years before. Palladio's personal oversight of the project resulted in his achieving a level of quality and austere grandeur that clearly resonated with the new identity being established by Benedictine reform, for it was an architectural language that expressed the high status of the Order, while providing the spatial setting for their reformed observances. His success was confirmed when he received the commission for the new church in 1565.

The means by which Palladio managed large projects simultaneously, which can be discerned in the rich documentation for the church, provide insights into his design process and its implementation, as well as raising questions about how he incorporated change and accommodated patrons. The Benedictines had a strong tradition of direct involvement in architectural decisions and working practices. Palladio also had to provide for a patron deeply involved with issues of Church reform as well as for the Church's function as a site of patrician patronage and dogal ceremony. The majestic interior that Palladio created was a fitting site for these multiple activities, creating a sequence of spaces unified by the monumental order reflected on the exterior. Palladio's church plan was a creative adaptation of local models, Congregation requirements, and his study of the classical basilica form.

Benedictine Presence on the Island of San Giorgio Maggiore

The Benedictine presence on the island was formalized in 982, when the reigning doge of Venice, Tribuno Memo (979–circa 991), signed the act of donation recognizing the community under the leadership of Abbot Giovanni Morosini (982–1012).[2] This act of donation was to have resonances over the centuries, since the monks attempted to increase their control over property on the island and to maintain, simultaneously, maximum autonomy in jurisdiction over their own affairs and rights to protection directly under dogal authority.[3] According to Francesco Sansovino in 1581, a church, built by the Partecipazio family, had existed on the island as early as 790.[4] In the document of 982 conceding the property to the monastery, the titular saint of the church is designated as St. George the Martyr.[5] It was this edifice, presumably, that then was replaced with a new building by Morosini, in a complex that included a library, vineyard, woods, and mill.[6] In the thirteenth century, damage to Morosini's tenth-century church was sufficient to require rebuilding; it is not known to what extent. Sansovino's account indicates two separate events that damaged buildings of the monastery, though the church is specifically referred to only in association with the first incident, the destructive effects of a fire in 1205; he associates the patronage of Doge Pietro Ziani (1205–circa 1229) with the restoration of the monastery. The second event, which caused extensive destruction, was an earthquake Sansovino placed in 1229.[7] It was thus in a heavily restored form that Morosini's church survived until shortly before 1419, when the

112 Jacopo de' Barbari, *View of Venice*, Venice, 1500, detail of Isola San Giorgio Maggiore

abbot, Giovanni Michiel (1403–30), reconsecrated the church – a church that would not be replaced *ex novo* until the work of Andrea Palladio a century and a half later. The ruinous condition of the roofs, walls, and framing of the monastery's buildings had been deplored by a deputation of visitors in 1411 and reparation had been slated as part of Michiel's mandate for reform.[8] It is difficult to interpret Sansovino as to whether or not the church was amply reconstructed under Michiel, as other sources have alleged; he may have seen it as part of the rebuilding program that had spread over the preceding two centuries, the results of which can be seen in Jacopo de' Barbari's *View of Venice* of 1500 (fig. 112).[9] Soon after the consecration of 1419, under the rule of the same abbot, a momentous decision was taken to join the monastery of San Giorgio Maggiore to the newly formed Congregation of Santa Giustina.

The reformation of the Benedictine monastery of Santa Giustina in Padua was initiated by the election of Ludovico Barbo as abbot on 20 December 1408.[10] Barbo (1381–1443) came from a Venetian patrician family and had been involved previously in the foundation of the Congregation of the Secular Canons at San Giorgio in Alga in Venice.[11] The founders included other members of the Venetian nobility who had chosen the religious life, among them the future pope Eugenius IV, Gabriele Condulmer, then cardinal of Siena, and his cousin, the cardinal of Bologna, Antonio Correr, both nephews of Pope Gregory XII (Angelo Correr). Also present at San Giorgio in Alga was Lorenzo Giustinian, who would become the first patriarch of Venice and was later canonized. This phenomenon of advocacy for the religious reform of various houses was effected

largely through the creation of umbrella organizations, in the form of a "congregation" that drew together a number of previously independent houses under a newly Observant Rule.[12] The conditions of the much reduced community at Santa Giustina had led to the neglect of one of the most venerable properties of the Church in Padua, thus prompting Gregory XII (1406–09) to appoint Cardinal Correr as abbot *in commendam* of the monastery.[13] In May 1408, the monks of Santa Giustina, whose numbers had swelled with the addition of those embracing the reform of San Giorgio in Alga and students from the Studio in Padua, requested that they be designated a new community, to which Barbo was nominated abbot later that same year.[14] The Observant Congregation of Santa Giustina, then called "de Unitate," came into being with the bull of Martin V, "Ineffabilis summi providentia Patris," issued from Mantua on 1 January 1419.[15] This bull describes the Congregation as the union of four independent monasteries under the direction of Santa Giustina of Padua, including Santa Giustina, Santa Maria of Florence (the "Badia"), San Giorgio Maggiore of Venice, and Santi Felice e Fortunato of Aimone (in the diocese of Torcello).

If Ludovico Barbo can be said to be a "second Benedict" to the Order, then Eugenius IV (1431–47) can be called the "second *Pater*," after Barbo, to the Congregation of Santa Giustina.[16] The Venetian pope valued Barbo's counsel on contemporary ecclesiastical issues and granted numerous privileges to the young Congregation, perhaps none more important than that establishing its monasteries as directly subject to the Holy See, preventing the intervention of local ecclesiastical authorities.[17] This policy had both fiscal and political consequences for the independent actions of the Congregation.

Eugenius IV's active interest in promoting the Congregation, whose constitution was espoused by him as a model of (pre-Tridentine) reform, was not without its local effect on San Giorgio Maggiore. Upon Michiel's death, San Giorgio had passed into commendam, granted to Cardinal Gabriel Condulmer who was to be elevated to the papacy the following year.[18] As pope, Eugenius IV retained the commendam and nominated Barbo as governor on 18 November 1432, while continuing to urge San Giorgio's reunion with the Congregation.[19] Resistance to San Giorgio's participation in the Congregation had been expressed not only by a dissenting group of monks but by the Venetian government itself. Doge Francesco Foscari (1423–57) strongly opposed what was seen as the abrogation of the *jus patronato* of the ducal chapel of San Marco over San Giorgio, an objection founded on the document of donation of 982.[20] The Venetian Republic was increasingly jealous of its jurisdictional prerogatives over ecclesiastical holdings in its territories. The early Congregation's heavily Venetian character and the network of aristocratic support enjoyed by its founders, its papal sponsorship, and Barbo's personal eloquence in front of the doge and Senate served to secure State approval for San Giorgio's membership, without, however, surrendering the ducal rights of *jus patronato*. Doge Foscari's decree was given on 12 June 1442[21] and on 4 February 1443 (m.v. 1442) Eugenius IV issued the Bull "Ad exequendum debitum," sanctioning San Giorgio's affiliation.[22] The then prior of the monastery, Gregorio da Genova, became the first abbot of San Giorgio after the resumption of its membership in the Congregation. This reunion was enacted publicly in a ritual demonstrating the "repossession" of the island by the monks in the presence of the doge's son Giacomo Foscari, the new abbot opening and closing the portals of the church and beating his feet on the pavement to the sound of tolling bells.[23] The dissenting members of San Giorgio had been overruled, both because of the success of the Congregation, which had grown to include many prestigious Benedictine monasteries throughout Italy (such as San Benedetto Po in Mantua, 1419, and San Paolo fuori le Mura in Rome, 1430), and by the pressure exerted upon them by their tiaraed abbot.

Some of the immediate consequences of this great revival among these Benedictine monasteries were of a practical nature. Increased populations in a number of the houses of the Congregation had created pressing needs for more space. These physical requirements were responded to both by annexing other monastic properties, subordinating them to the major houses (such as San Giorgio and the Trevigian Santa Maria del Pero), and by building programs. These building programs that ensued were more than just physical restoration and expansion; they also satisfied ideological imperatives by providing the opportunity to express new ideals of reform and spirituality.

Fabric and Decoration under Palladio

When Palladio was given the commission for the refectory in 1560, walls already had been raised to the height of round-headed windows that he then endowed with straight cornices with powerful bracketed moldings (fig. 113).[24] For this relatively modest undertaking, he created a space with an intimation of the grand interiors of ancient Roman baths, through the use of a cross-vaulted ceiling, imposing classical moldings, and thermal windows on three walls (now blocked). His supervision over the execution of the work of wallmasons and stonecutters was realized by providing template designs for them to follow. This practice was equivalent to the architect's signature, even kept a trade secret by some, and enhanced the level of fidelity to the original design and Palladio's innovative language.[25] As with his domestic projects in Vicenza, Palladio composed a sequence of spaces inspired by both antique and contemporary examples, negotiating a change in the level from the cloister vestibule to the anterefectory and refectory proper. Palladio completed the commission in 1562, installing handsome red marble lavabos in the anteroom (fig. 114) as one of his collaborators, Paolo Veronese, began the monumental *Wedding Feast at Cana* (Paris, Musée du Louvre) for the end wall of the refectory (fig. 115). Attention to the whole of the architectural and decorative ensemble was integral to the patron's program.[26]

The choice of the subject of the "Istoria di la Cena del miracolo fatto da Cristo in Cana Galilea" as given in the contract between Veronese and the Benedictines was in the tradition of feast paintings' mimetic functioning in monastic refectories, the emphasis here being on the first public miracle performed by Christ when he transformed water into wine at the wedding feast at Cana (John 2:1–11) with its symbolic and Eucharistic overtones (fig. 116).[27] The painting and its commission to Veronese also demonstrate the patronage practices of the Benedictines and the impact of their mode of institutional organization in furthering their corporate identity, one that reflected their values of reform. Veronese's style was already associated with the Cassinese Congregation through previous commissions in Verona and Mantua, and he would continue to produce major works for them, including the high altar for Santa Giustina itself. Examination of the circumstances of these earlier commissions reveals that the artist was sponsored by important figures in the Benedictine hierarchy who would play key roles initiating and carrying out the new program of building and decoration at San Giorgio.[28] The lively portraits of clerics on Christ's left side of the feast suggest an homage to those Benedictines, such as Abbot Girolamo Scrochetto da Piacenza in his second term at San Giorgio (1559–64), and his successor, Abbot Andrea Pampura da Asola (1564–67), as well as their agents, the cellarers and procurators in charge of daily administration of labor at the monastery, some of whom, such as Benedetto Guidi, author of an ode on the painting, were well known in the academic and cultural circles of Venice. If the precise identification of many of these individuals remains open, the association of latecomer Andrea da Asola with the portrait of the Benedictine monk in the black habit that has been painted on paper and attached to the canvas has been cautiously accepted.[29] A small devotional painting by Veronese (now in Paris, Musée du Louvre) that shows the Virgin and Child between the protector saints of the monastery, St. George, and of the Congregation, St. Justine (fig. 117), seems to have been an earlier commission by one of these figures, for the kneeling Benedictine monk resembles the slightly older features of a monk garbed in dark blue in the *Feast at Cana*, and may have come from the abbot's quarters, a striking example of the personal devotional works that could be found in the living areas of the monastery.[30] It was also Andrea da Asola who continued his predecessor Scrochetto's patronage of Palladio at San Giorgio with his first grand church commission ex-novo in 1565.

In 1520 a Chapter General meeting at Santa Giustina had enunciated requirements for their new church in Padua that may be taken as a sort of general prescription for the Congregation. Describing a basilical plan generated from a North Italian Byzantinizing type, the Chapter called for: a three-aisled nave with side chapels, a crossing whose cupola was to form the module for the body of the church, a high altar to be located in the presbytery, "according to the custom of our congregation" ("prout est consuetudo congregationis nostrae"), pilasters sheathed with Istrian marble, and the length and breadth to be in proportions determined by the architect and the monks. A "master plan" for the ongoing renewal and building campaigns at San Giorgio Maggiore also was created at about this time. The church rendered in a plan of *circa* 1520 for the reform of the island monastery (attributed to Tullio Lombardo or Alessandro Leopardi) conforms to the Congregation

113 (*above left*) Andrea Palladio, refectory, Monastery of San Giorgio Maggiore, Venice

114 (*above right*) Andrea Palladio, anterefectory lavabo, Monastery of San Giorgio Maggiore, Venice

115 Reconstruction photo-montage of Paolo Veronese's *Wedding Feast at Cana* in its original site in the refectory, Monastery of San Giorgio Maggiore, Venice

116 (*above*) Paolo Veronese,
Wedding Feast at Cana, Paris,
Musée du Louvre (inv. 142)

117 Paolo Veronese, *Madonna and
Child with Saints George and Justine
and Benedictine Donor*, Paris, Musée
du Louvre (inv. 139)

paradigm, which suggests that the monks of San Giorgio envisioned a church plan close to that of the new plan for Santa Giustina (fig. 118).[31]

The importance of Palladio's church project to the monks was demonstrated by its being first commissioned in a wood model begun in late 1565, which took a year to build, and served to satisfy his patrons' initial requirements.[32] Construction on the site of the new church was begun in 1566 and the circumference of the nave elevation, the vaulting, and the dome over the crossing were reached in just under ten years, comprising Palladio's most extended and intense involvement in the successive campaigns that produced the church we see today (fig. 122). The fabric of the extended choir was finished between 1583–89, although it was probably conceived at the time that Palladio designed a new second cloister in 1579. Other work continued after Palladio's death in 1580, with altars diligently executed after his model, whereas the façade finally completed between 1607–10 has a more complex history and provenance. An unusually coherent campaign of decoration including the majority of altarpieces, high altar ensemble, and new set of historiated choirstalls was carried out primarily in the 1590s (fig. 119). The force of Palladio's conception of the church as a Christian basilica lends more of an appearance of unity than is reflected in the reality of its long building process and succession of abbots, protos, and incorporation of new ideas (figs. 120 and 121). The remarkable elements of San Giorgio – the extended retrochoir and solution for a three-dimensional high altar, enlarged transept and coordinated altar frames, temple-front façade with its tabernacle framed busts of the monastery founders – can best be understood not as a linear realization of an initial total design conception but as an ongoing response by patrons, architect, and builders to the exigencies of its function, and this included resistance to, as well as embracing of, a program of reform.

Choral prayer and the celebration of monastic offices was fundamental to Benedictine spirituality and, as a result, attention to the space of the choir – the place where the work of God, *opus dei*, was performed – became paramount in Congregation planning. The actual choir of Palladio's church, a virtually separate extended apsidal structure behind the area of the presbytery, outfitted with decorated choirstalls, was the third to be fabricated since San Giorgio had joined the Congregation of Santa Giustina (fig. 123), the former campaigns contributing to the substantial renovation of the church of 1419 that preceded Palladio's, according to Francesco Sansovino's description of the succession of church structures on the island.[33] In 1550, only fifteen years before Palladio began construction on the church of San Giorgio, a campaign to install a new choir had been undertaken, and it would be this choir that the monks used during construction of their new church, which would be situated further west as can be seen by comparison to the church of 1419 in Jacopo de' Barbari's *View of Venice* of 1500 (see fig. 112).[34] The 1550s choirstalls survive today in the night, or winter, choir, also called the "Cappella del Conclave" (since the election there of Pope Pius VII, 1799–1800), transferred there in 1593 (fig. 124).[35] The quadrangular seventy-two seat double-tier wood stalls do not possess either istoriated decoration or grotesques. The choir spaces of the old and new churches illustrate changing architectural solutions to reform, as a former position of privilege in front of the high altar in the nave would be transferred behind it, in what has come to be called a "retrochoir."

The choir of Palladio's church as finally realized is such a retrochoir, located in an apse extended behind and beyond the presbytery. It is separated from it both by a columnar screen and the lateral axis created by the crossing from the door to the corridor leading to the monastery and the door towards the sacristy. Further, while the presbytery is raised three steps up from the nave, the choir is another four steps up from the presbytery. The result is an apse elongated well beyond the areas demarcated by the arms of the transept and about equal to the squared area of the chancel, thus doubling it. From the exterior, both the extension and the separation are easy to read: the choir and chancel together are longer than the distance occupied by the crossing and the nave; and a drop in level from the roof of the presbytery to the choir is marked by a break in the cornice at the small turrets. The retrochoir ensured absolute visual and social (but not aural) separation of the monastic space from that of a lay audience, which provided both for reformed decorum of behavior appropriate to a religious community and for a new relation between a lay audience and the liturgy, in particular allowing access to the celebration of the Eucharist. These were particularly pressing issues for preaching Orders, and had been addressed by Observant Franciscans already in the fifteenth century, as well as for cathedral clergy, who became (often reluctant) participants in Tridentine reform; for an elite contemplative Order, such as the Benedictines, there were competing models, and initially less pressure for accommodating a lay population (itself often an elite audience for important ceremonial observances). Palladio would have been well aware of Sansovino's "seminal" example at San Francesco della Vigna in Venice, in which the retrochoir and presbytery are equal to the nave, with the high altar acting as a screen demarcating distinct spaces.[36]

Scholars now generally agree that the choir as finally realized by Palladio was not that of the first project and model of 1565, which included the area of the current quadrangular presbytery but without the extension in which the choir is now located. The fabrication of the entire circumference of the body of the church of San Giorgio had been completed in 1575 under Palladio's supervision and with the *proto*, wallmason Antonio Paleari da Marcò, who would be an important associate on other projects in Venice as well.[37] Christian Isermeyer dated the extension for the retrochoir to a revision of the project for the monastery made by Palladio before his death, in 1579–80,[38] when he added the new Cloister of the Cypresses (fig. 125).[39] It is to this date that Isermeyer assigns a drawing attributed to Palladio's studio (Archivio di Stato di Venezia, MM 857b), in agreement with Wladimir Timofiewitsch, who first discovered and published it. It shows a plan for the systematization of the monastery including the new church with an extended apse, the Buora dormitory and cloister, and Palladio's Cloister of the Cypresses (fig. 126).[40] One purpose of the drawing would have been to determine the relationship between the cloister and the choir, the new extension of the latter to be located in the space still occupied at that time by the remaining east end of the earlier church in which services continued until 1581.[41] The evidence provided by the drawing alone does not sufficiently buttress attribution of the design of the extended choir to Palladio. If MM 857b did come from Palladio's studio later in his life, the lack of articulation of the wall system in the drawing may indicate that the solution to the extended choir and choir screen was not fully worked out before his death (and not in the model), nor, of course would its construction have the benefit of his supervision. This would seem to be confirmed by Bortolo di Domenico's contribution of the design when construction began in 1583: to make the "internal façade of the new choir according to his drawing."[42] The design was probably intended to continue Palladio's scheme from the body of the church, but the stonecutter, though a long-time associate of Palladio in the San Giorgio *cantiere*, was not up to matching the master in complexity of articulation or subtlety of juncture between the fabrics. The new choir fabric was completed by 1589, and, exactly a decade later, it received the magnificently carved, eighty-seat choirstalls with forty-eight scenes from the life of St. Benedict.[43]

During construction, the 1550s choir must have been located in the old church in a position similar to that occupied by other traditional examples in the Congregation, in front of the altar, its increased size impossible to accommodate in the apse of the old church seen on the de' Barbari map.[44] A project for the nearby Congregation monastery of Santa Maria di Praglia, seen here in a drawing dating from the 1530s (fig. 127), shows the tenacious placement of the choir there in the new church consecrated in 1545.[45] By the time the 1550s stalls were transferred into the new church of San Giorgio in 1581, however, an arrangement like that at Praglia would have seemed terribly old-fashioned and not sufficiently private for the practice of choir offices.

Christian Isermeyer reasoned that for his original model, Palladio planned a choir configuration appropriate to his notion of the early Christian basilica, as, for example, in statements made in his *Four Books* of 1570.[46] Palladio describes San Giorgio in, "Of the Forms of Temples, and of the decorum to be observed in them" (Bk. 4, ch. 2, 7). He says:

> Particularly recommended too are churches that are made in the shape of a cross and have the entrance at what would be the foot of the cross opposite the high altar and choir, and two other entrances or two other altars in the branches extending on either side like arms, because being cross-shaped they represent, in the eyes of the onlookers, that wood from which our Salvation was hung. I made the church of S. Giorgio Maggiore in Venice this shape.[47]

The sequence of his description implies that the altar precedes the choir. Further insight as to the relation of the choir to the high altar is offered in "Of the Compartments of Temples" (Bk. 4, ch. 5, 10):

This form has not changed much, since they realized that the basilican plan turned out to be very convenient because the altar was placed imposingly where the tribunal was, the choir arranged neatly around the altar, and the rest was free for the people.[48]

Here, Palladio specifically advocates that the choir surround the high altar. This formation may have been what was originally planned for San Giorgio, since a contract of 1579 for one of the chapels on the south side of the presbytery, the Bollani chapel, identifies its position as "contiguous to the high altar, or choir" ("contigua capellae magnae seu Choro"), implying the extension of the choir in the planned presbytery and nave bay, surrounding the high altar.[49]

We also can compare Palladio's recommendations on choir projects contemporary to his *modello* of 1565 for San Giorgio, on the Pieve of Montagnana in 1564 and on the cathedral of Milan in 1570. Isermeyer notes of Montagnana that, although the choir was not completed according to Palladio's design, the placement of the choir today is as Palladio described it in a letter from Venice of 11 November 1564 to the *provveditori del duomo*: "this work abuts the wall" ("quest'opera andasse nel muro").[50] Palladio had been asked to provide a high chancel railing and monumental entry with a frontispiece and four columns, but proposed instead a new choir plan, which he pointed out would save half the labor and yet retain the majesty of the façade by attaching the stalls to the walls of the apse. Palladio's opinion of Pellegrino Tibaldi's plan for the choir of Milan Cathedral was solicited by the Milanese architect Martino Bassi, who received Palladio's reply written from Venice on 3 July 1570. Here, Palladio criticized Tibaldi's proposed extension of the choir from the apse into the crossing and the inhibited visibility of the high altar, and favored Bassi's solution for a choir and high altar under the *tribuna*: "because thus the divine offices would be possible to understand equally well from all parts of the church and the choir as principal and unique part would be in the middle."[51] Bassi's text mentions only the problems of visibility, but it also may be that his recommendations, agreed to by Palladio, were based on functional distinctions for canons' choirs, located centrally, not removed like monastic choirs, because lay participation was required. Both Tibaldi's and Bassi's choirs surrounded their respective high altars leaving an opening facing the nave; in Tibaldi's project, the high altar was placed toward the rear of the choir in the apse, such that its visibility would have been limited by the proposed extension of the sides, whereas Bassi put the high altar in the center crossing.

Isermeyer astutely opened another line of investigation in the interest of locating the decision to extend the choir within Palladio's lifetime: the background of the abbot of San Giorgio concurrent with its probable inception. He drew attention to the fact that Abbot Giuliano Careni (1575–79) was from Piacenza (he had been professed at Santa Giustina in 1532). The local Cassinese monastery in Piacenza was San Sisto, where, in 1576, the apse end of the church, begun by Alessio Tramello *circa* 1500, was destroyed in order to extend the choir behind the high altar on a quadran-

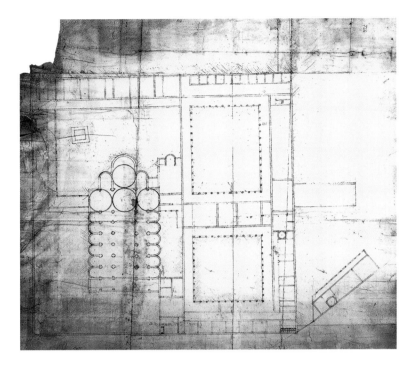

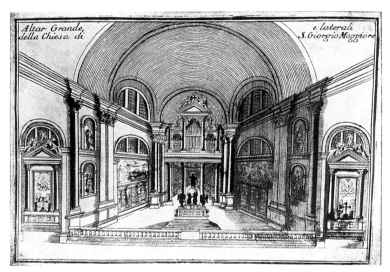

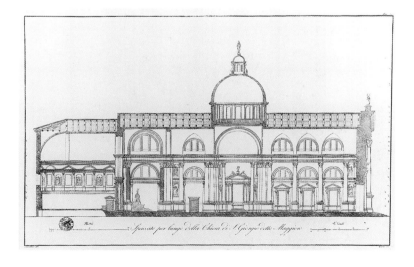

118 (*left*) Tullio Lombardo or Alessandro Leopardi, project for a new monastery complex at San Giorgio Maggiore, Venice, ca. 1520, Venice, Archivio di Stato, MM 744

121 (*below*) Leopoldo Cicognara, Antonio Diedo, and Gianantonio Selva, plan of San Giorgio Maggiore, *Le fabbriche e i monumenti più cospicui di Venezia*, ed. F. Zanotto, Venice 1858, 2:246

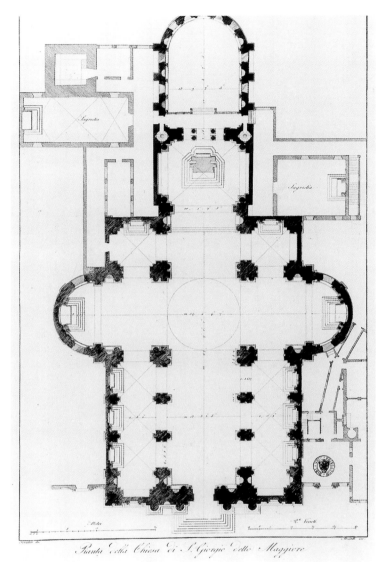

122 (*facing page*) Andrea Palladio, San Giorgio Maggiore, Venice, view from nave toward choir

119 (*above left*) Vincenzo Coronelli, engraved view of presbytery with high altar by Girolamo Campagna, *God the Father Standing on the Globe of the World Supported by the Four Evangelists*, and *laterali* by Jacopo Tintoretto with Domenico Tintoretto, of the *Communion of the Apostles* and *Miracle of the Manna*, San Giorgio Maggiore, Venice

120 (*left*) Leopoldo Cicognara, Antonio Diedo, and Gianantonio Selva, section of San Giorgio Maggiore, *Le fabbriche e i monumenti più cospicui di Venezia*, ed. F. Zanotto, Venice 1858, 2:242

124   Andrea Palladio, San Giorgio Maggiore, Venice, night or winter choir with choirstalls of the 1550s

gular plan.[52] The documentary sources for San Giorgio, however, credit Abbot Careni only with initiating the cloister, between the months of January and June 1579 when he was succeeded by Abbot Paolo Orio, a season during which the monk Fortunato Olmo in his fundamental history of the island monastery had said that not much construction could have been accomplished. It was Careni's successor, Abbot Orio (1579–84, 1588–died 1591), who was seen as having brought to completion the cloister and, during his second abbacy, the choir.[53] The choir, then, would have been begun under Orio in 1583, its construction principally carried out under the next

abbot, Celso Guglielmi da Verona (1584–88), and finished in 1589 under Orio.

Abbot Orio was a pivotal figure in the history of the monastery; it was under his reign that the transformation from its medieval to its modern character was recognized formally and publicly in the ceremony of 1581 when the venerable relics of St. Stephen were translated into the new church, then, according to Olmo, "almost finished" ("quasi finita").[54] Olmo's account also reveals the importance of Paolo Orio's nobility to San Giorgio's prestige, "But as the abbot was noble, so he built nobly" ("Ma come che l'Abbate fosse

123 (facing page)   Andrea Palladio, San Giorgio Maggiore, Venice, view from sanctuary through choir screen towards apse

nobile cosi fabbricò nobilmente").[55] The Orio family was identified with the origins of Venice, having come from Altino with eighty other families in 790 to settle on Torcello, and having produced a number of bishops. An ancestor, Joannes Aureo, had figured in the early history of San Giorgio as an underwriter of the concession of monastery and island to the Benedictines in 982.[56] Following a lengthy description of the translation of 1581, Olmo gives some insight into Abbot Orio's appearance and singular character, which he would have known at first hand, describing his resemblance to Pope Sixtus V – a famous builder – and his rigor in religion yet reciprocated love of his monks.[57]

In analyzing the contributions of the three abbots to the extended choir – whether carrying out a changed design by Palladio or initiating a departure from Palladio's model – one must consider that all of them would have had extensive experience in administering ongoing construction projects during their various abbacies. Previous to his tenure at San Giorgio, Careni had concluded the long litigation over the new choirstalls at Santa Giustina, where he was abbot from 1571 to 1574, and was noted for his reforms of the choral office.[58] He also had contracted for the pavement of the choir and presbytery at Santa Giustina in 1574 to Bortolo di Domenico da Venezia, who had been engaged as stonecutter at San Giorgio since the beginning of the construction of Palladio's church.[59] One should recall that the choir at Santa Giustina, while elongated, was still of the same type as its earlier choir, with the high altar *pala* at the back and the stalls wrapping around the presbytery, closed from the nave in front by a stone portal.

Celso da Verona was responsible for seeing through the major part of the actual construction of the choir at San Giorgio. His reputation at Santa Giustina, where in his first term (1580–84) he succeeded Careni and in his second term (1589–died 1591) Orio, was as an abbot who had accomplished more on the fabric in one term than had been done in twenty years. Upon his return to Santa Giustina, the description of his renovation of the small cloister there sounds as though his experience of Palladio's design for the Cloister of the Cypresses had profoundly influenced him as he tore down the inharmonious mixture of ancient colonettes "alla germana" (German, i.e., Gothic, style) and a "modern part in the new architecture designed by Donatello" to build in a unified style.[60]

Orio, between his terms at San Giorgio, followed Celso da Verona as abbot at Santa Giustina (1584–88), where the final phases of construction of the new church were taking place, and where he was also noted for his diplomatic skills and connections in the Venetian Senate.[61] During this same period, he had built a church dedicated to the Virgin at Torreglia in the Padovano.[62] What particularly stands out from Orio's previous experience, however, is his direct association with one of the earliest examples of a number of churches belonging to the Congregation that, in the 1570s, modified their apse ends in order to receive extended choirs. In 1571, as abbot of San Pietro in Gessate in Milan, Orio had the apse demolished in order to expand the quadrangular choir, which was described as "too narrow."[63] Other important examples of members of the Congregation following this trend in the 1570s were Praglia (1572), San

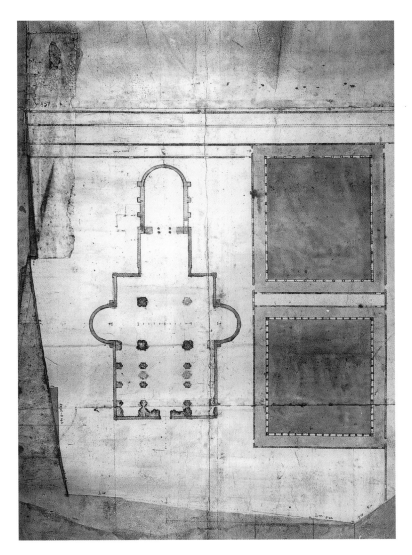

126 *Cantiere* of Palladio, plan of church, cloisters, and *fondamenta*, Monastery of San Giorgio Maggiore, Venice, Archivio di Stato, MM 857b

Sisto (1576), San Giovanni Evangelista in Parma (1587), San Pietro in Perugia (1591–92), San Pietro in Modena (1599), and Santa Giustina (1627),[64] though none is documented earlier than San Pietro in Gessate. Respect for Correggio's fresco in San Giovanni Evangelista in Parma did not prevent its destruction for the sake of the enlargement of the apse. The late date for the change of the choir at Santa Giustina demonstrates resistance to its removal from the presbytery and placement behind the high altar. This may explain why the examples of the 1530s, such as Monte Cassino (fig. 128), remained, until the 1570s, isolated attempts at the creation of a new reform type. Antonio da Sangallo the Younger's plan for the transformation of the apse of Monte Cassino (Florence, Uffizi, 181A) is a rare illustration of this transition, as it shows both the position of the old choir in the nave and the new retrochoir in the extended apse.[65]

In an analysis of a century of literature on the rapport between religious life and the visual arts, Paolo Prodi characterized the values of Catholic Reform as: the need to provide a foundation for the community of the faithful united in the Roman Church; the restoration of moral behavior; the promotion of the mission of the Church through pastoral function; and the expression of the new spirit of the purified Church.[66] Taken together with the various decrees that emanated from Trent, it is evident that the imperative to conscript the Christian populace at large, combined with the impetus of popular piety, led to corresponding changes in the architectural fabrics that housed these activities. Milton Lewine's influential analysis concluded that architects of Palladio's generation found their solution in the creation of sequential spaces and cautioned against viewing this from a post-Baroque perspective.[67] Even though engagement with a lay congregation did not comprise a major part of Benedictine spirituality, responding to – indeed, initiating – exhortations for the reform of religious discipline led to sympathetic transformations in the physical hierarchy of their churches. Thus, the removal of the choir from a position interceding between the actions of the Mass and its apprehension by exclusively defined lay groups to one no longer inhibiting a direct relationship was accompanied by a new prestige placed on the privacy achieved by the new placement of the choir, where the proper work of God could be carried out with decorum.

Private Patrons in the Church

Once outside the confines of the sanctuary, a new element entered into the decoration of the church: secular patronage. San Giorgio exhibits a unique combination of lay and religious patronage, one in which ultimate control was retained by the monastery. Only two altars, those adjacent to the sanctuary, are designated as family chapels, although several others in the nave were associated with lay patrons; these patrons were not allowed, however, to place their name or family *stemma* on these altars to designate them as family chapels, for the monastery held that it was inappropriate to allow lay "possession" of an altar.[68] As students of church decoration know, it is unusual to find such blanket retention of control since it devolves on providing independent means to finance the decoration. Such self-sufficiency was in marked contrast to the type of financing available to mendicant Orders, such as the Franciscans, who relied heavily on private contributions, and gave lay rights to chapel decoration. This is exemplified by the decoration of San Francesco della Vigna where, despite the unified architectural structure provided by Sansovino, the individual patronage of chapels resulted not only in widely differing decorative programs, but even in adaptation of the basic structural form (as in the compartmented stuccoed barrel vault of the Grimani chapel).[69] Circumstances, on the other hand, that demonstrate even more tightly controlled unity than at San Giorgio, where the situation was one of mixed patronage, may be found at Il Redentore, where building and decoration were financed by the State and the decorative program is a unified Christological narrative.[70] This renitence was not entirely due to the fact that San Giorgio is Benedictine; even within

the Cassinese Congregation there were differing patronage situations, according to the individual histories of each monastery and the traditional relations either to particular patrons or to local government. At San Benedetto Po, much of the patrimony had derived from the same Canossian source as that of the local ruling family, to which they retained strong ties, even after having entered the Congregation, which offered more independence than the vassalage of commendam.[71] The larger question, which can only be touched upon here, is that of the financial structure of the Benedictine Order as it had evolved in the new organization of the Cassinese Congregation.[72] The wealth that enabled a monastery such as San Giorgio to act independently derived largely from the revenues of long-held properties, and, as such, limited what could be realized without the liquidation of capital. Here, the Congregation could provide some leeway in distributing resources unavailable to the individual monastery, but this was usually an option reserved for the poorer monasteries, not one as rich in land-holdings as San Giorgio.[73] At San Giorgio, since the extensive rebuilding of the monastery had been going on for well over a century, it is obvious that a designated share of the revenue was directed to that purpose. We find, however, that when other calls upon the monastery's financial resources were made, most importantly those that required money rather than goods, the building and decoration suffered setbacks, indicating a limit to those resources.[74] Nonetheless, it is extraordinary to find a total decoration program undertaken and accomplished in such a relatively short time as that of San Giorgio – one undertaken, furthermore, in a period commonly identified as one of financial decline in Venice.[75] The dedication of Abbot Michele Alabardi in the 1590s towards the accomplishment of the decoration and intention to proceed with the façade was certainly a primary factor, and one credited to him by his monks. Equally, the inherent financial structure supported the achievement of the enterprise. But a more intangible element that contributed to the financial ability of the monastery were the perceived rewards for the spiritual benefits accrued from services performed by the monks on behalf of souls in their care. The status of San Giorgio Maggiore in this regard seems to have been relatively high, as attested to by the ability to attract patrons of great wealth and standing in the city of Venice, even those whose family connections were to other churches, and perhaps even more by the refusal of substantial endowments offered by prospective patrons when their demands seemed too onerous (offset by services willingly undertaken for deserving individuals of no particular family or wealth).[76] One compelling reason for this patrician support was the venerable history of the monastery, enriched over the years by the acquisition of relics, territorial possessions, and association with illustrious names from the Venetian past. The exclusivity of the lay patrons connected with the monastery was even more emphasized after the rebuilding of the church, when only a selected number of family chapels and tombs were refabricated and a selected number of individuals from contemporary Venetian public life were introduced.

Almost immediately upon the commencement of the fabric of the new church by Palladio, Abbot Andrea da Asola entered into an

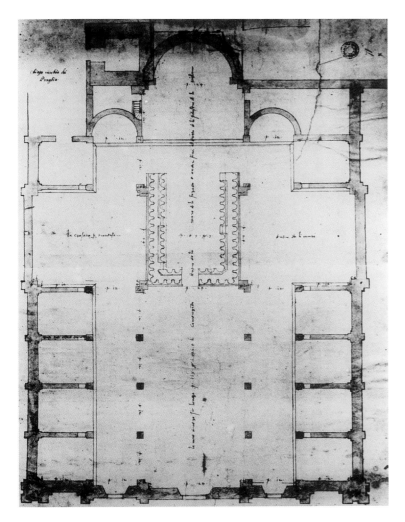

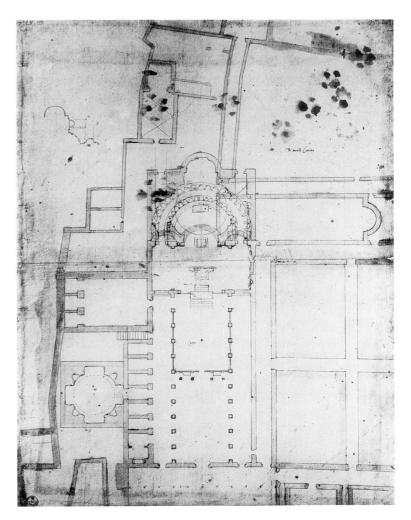

127 Andrea Moroni, plan of the earlier church of Santa Maria di Praglia, Padua, Biblioteca Civica, Raccolta iconografia e topografica padovana, XLVIII.4742, Praglia, Monastero, B.VIII, 744

128 Antonio da Sangallo the Younger, plan for the transformation of the apse of Monte Cassino, Florence, Galleria degli Uffizi, Gabinetto dei Disegni (181A)

agreement on 6 January 1566 m.v. (= 1567) with "the magnificent mister Marco Bollani" to remake the chapel of the *Casata* Bollani at the expense of the monastery "having been forced to ruin our church . . . with danger to persons, roof, wood, choir, altars, precious columns and the loss of every other ornament."[77] A condition given was that the work on the chapel would not begin until after the new church was finished. There is a threefold significance to this agreement and clause: first, that a family chapel was projected from the outset and very likely included in the architect's plans; second, that commencement of the chapel would not begin for some time, by which time circumstances would change – the individuals acting as the original parties to the agreement, for example; and third, that originally the financing of the decoration was the responsibility of the monastery, rather than the family. To anticipate the history of the Bollani chapel (fig. 129): it was never executed as planned, probably due to changes in the circumstances of the above-mentioned factors, prompting Olmo in his description to state the situation around 1619 as "On the other side outside the sanctuary there is

the altar of Sts. Peter and Paul of the illustrious house of Bollani, not, however, remarkable for its painting or fabric, being a picture of little merit, and the building all of Istrian stone."[78]

The desire for the completion and decoration of the chapel (to the right if facing the sanctuary) was represented to the Chapter of San Giorgio in 1579, on 26 March, by the most celebrated member of the Bollani family, Domenico Bollani (1514–79), bishop of Brescia, and his two nephews, Antonio (died 1587) and Vincenzo (died 1609), sons of his deceased brother, the senator Jacopo (died 1571).[79] From this *capitolo*, we learn of an earlier agreement, in the 10 July 1570 testament of Jacopo, the bishop's brother and manager of the family *fraterna* in Venice, in which the chapel was supposed to have been finished within three years from that time, that is, in 1573,[80] yet by 1579 the architecture of the chapel was still not finished.[81] As has been pointed out, the *basamento* of the circumference of the entire church was already in place, the transept vaulted and the cupola completed by 1575, so the clause allowing for a delay due to construction may refer to the sanctuary and choir.[82] Moreover, the agreement of 1579 called for the chapel to be executed on Palladio's design.[83] The architecture of the chapel, without decoration, was probably completed by 1583, when that of the matching chapel on the other side of the sanctuary was recorded as already finished.[84] Giovanni Giacomo di Pietro Comini was commissioned on 1 March 1592 to make the three altars on the south wall of the nave (that is, the right side if facing the high altar, and the same side as the Bollani chapel), which were to be modeled upon the Bollani altar.[85] Possibly the Bollani chapel disparagingly described by Olmo as being made only of Istrian stone was intended by Palladio as a model, or the armature for more luxurious decoration. The original intentions for the chapel were probably foiled first by the death of Domenico Bollani in 1579 (on 14 August) and then by the architect's death a year later in 1580 (on 19 August). Giangiorgio Zorzi hypothesized that Palladio had designed a sepulchral monument honoring Domenico Bollani (in the year following the bishop's death) for his two nephews, but that it had remained only in the project stage.[86] Domenico Bollani had been acquainted with Palladio at least since 1556, when, in his previous career as a secular statesman for Venice, Bollani as *luogotenente* for Friuli commissioned from him a commemorative arch in Udine in 1556, the Arco Bollani (see fig. 86).[87] The position of Bollani was a somewhat unusual one, parallel to that of Daniele Barbaro, for it was rare to find that the pope and the Curia could agree with the doge and the Senate on an individual in whom both sides felt they could place their trust.[88] Domenico had gained entry into the civil service upon undertaking an ambassadorship to Edward VI of England, who granted him knighthood in the Order of the Rose in 1547; after Bollani's return to Venice, he became a *savio della terraferma* in 1550. It was Bollani's success as *podestà* of Brescia, however, that made him a popular candidate on the vacancy of the bishopric in 1559. Bollani was active in prosecuting goals of Church reform in diocesan synods and at the Council of Trent in 1561 and in 1562–63, earning the personal esteem of Carlo Borromeo, who attended Domenico at his death and delivered his funeral oration. After accepting the bishopric, Bollani sought Palladio's advice in Brescia twice: the first time in 1562 on the Palazzo Pubblico; the second in 1567, for the rebuilding of the Brescia Cathedral.[89] The bishop's recommendation may well have been a channel through which Palladio was brought to the attention of the monks at San Giorgio Maggiore when they were considering an architect for their new church – the Bollani boasted long-time connections with the history of San Giorgio, including an abbot in the thirteenth century.[90]

Olmo's "picture of little merit" must have been substituted in lieu of the decoration hypothesized as originally intended by Palladio for this altar; nothing further is known about this altarpiece, which Olmo would have seen previous to 1619, the date of his history of the monastery, and which postdated Stringa's statement of 1604 that the altar was distinguished only by an inscription.[91] By the time that another monk and chronicler Marco Valle wrote his description in 1693, this first altarpiece had been substituted by another, which he tells us was executed by Federico Cervelli, an artist of

Milanese origin, around 1690,[92] the subject of which was St. Peter.[93] Nor does this painting survive in its place, for it was replaced by the altarpiece there today, Sebastiano Ricci's *Virgin and Child with Saints*, dated 1708.[94] Although beyond the bounds of the chronological scope of this study, it is worthwhile noting that Ricci's painting with its luminous, silvery tonality, a representative of a Veronese revival in the eighteenth century, provides a contrast to the other altarpieces in the church of San Giorgio, and is more reminiscent of the decoration carried out in the refectory during Palladio's lifetime.[95]

As evidenced by the inscription recorded on the altar table, SS* APOSTOLIS PETRO ET PAULO DICATUM, the altar was dedicated to the apostles Peter and Paul, whose major feast day is on 29 June.[96] The Bollani in 1579 had commissioned the monks of San Giorgio to say four Masses per week and one anniversary Mass, to be celebrated on the feast of the name saint of the bishop, St. Dominic (4 August), for the souls of the departed of the Ca' Bollani. For these services, the monks were to receive 900 ducats, 25 ducats to be paid annually by the heirs from the invested capital.[97] The monks received the remainder of the capital in 1622 (400 ducats), releasing the heirs from further financial obligations.[98] The memory of the Bollani, and that of Bishop Domenico in particular, was thus placed in the care of the monks of San Giorgio in perpetuity.

The matching chapel on the left side of the sanctuary (if facing the high altar) was more favorably reviewed by Olmo, who described it as one of the finest in the church and praised the Morosini. He noted that the fine maculated stone had various shapes that miraculously revealed the image of Christ on the Cross on one of the columns of the altar.[99] Olmo mentions nothing more about the decoration of the Morosini chapel, and this lacuna in the recitation of altarpieces executed under Abbot Alabardi in the 1590s encourages the hypothesis that it was the responsibility of the Morosini family and had been commissioned earlier, probably during one of the periods that Paolo Orio was abbot.[100]

The concession of the chapel to Vicenzo Morosini (1511–88), knight and procurator of San Marco, together with his son, Barbon (1545–1620), was made on 7 September 1583.[101] Vicenzo's motivation is clear; his other son, Andrea (born 1557), had died in 1582, and he wished to establish a family chapel and arrange suffrages for his soul.[102] The monks agreed with Vicenzo to celebrate an anniversary Mass on 3 November (during the octave of All Saints) and four masses per week, for which 25 ducats per annum were to be paid on the feast of St. George (the first payment was made on 23 April the following year), or the capital of 400 ducats could be paid at one time. The dedication of the altar was changed to St. Andrew. Burial rights restricting the use of personal names or *stemmi* were granted. The state of the chapel is described as finished but not ornamented ("finitam, sed nondum ornatam") to be furnished at the expense of Vicenzo ("fabricando, et ponendo ut supra expensis ipsius Clar.mi Procuratori"), and done within the space of three years, ("in una triennium Capelle perfectio facta").

It may well be that at least part of the intended decoration of the chapel was completed within this period. On 11 July 1585 the

monastery recorded the receipt of the entire 400-ducat capital.[103] This date would fit that usually assigned for the execution of the altarpiece for the chapel, Jacopo and Domenico Tintoretto's *Risen Christ with St. Andrew and Portraits of the Morosini Family* (fig. 130).[104] The inclusion of St. Andrew reflects the changed dedication of the altar, which was formerly San Pantaleone, although there remains unresolved confusion between whether the relics were actually those of the saint as inscribed on the altarstone, RELIQUIAE S. PANTALEONIS MART, or if they were instead those of another, San Platone.[105] Valle's conclusion was that there were both, citing the visual evidence of a stone relief sculpture to support the inclusion of San Pantaleone.[106] The sculpted figure of the saint, framed on either side by two slender columns, is one of the few remaining effigies to suggest what would have been typical of the decoration of the earlier church at San Giorgio.[107]

The composition of the Morosini painting is divided in half diagonally from the upper-left corner to the lower right: the light-filled right half shows Christ already ascended from the tomb, with two angels gesturing at the empty stone slabs while gazing in the direction of the donor portraits, and cherubim brandishing the martyr's palm and a white cloth canopy while bearing Christ aloft; a verdant low-hilled landscape appears in between the two halves; the left half is more soberly colored and occupies the foreground plane, with a bearded St. Andrew Apostle placed above the other figures flanking the base of the cross carried by the saint, who gazes across at the apparition of Christ. The members of the Morosini family portrayed include Andrea and Barbon (immediately below St. Andrew), Vicenzo (in front of his sons), and his wife Cecilia Pisani (by the side of her husband). The son on the right and Vicenzo stare resolutely outward, while the other son and his mother look piously towards the resurrected Christ.

Only the portrait of Vicenzo has a truly commanding presence; he is shown garbed in his red senatorial robes edged with ermine and holding the *stola d'oro*, which is worn over his right shoulder, badge of his procuratorial office and knighthood. This portrait was not modeled directly from the sitter, but probably based on a half-length portrait *Vicenzo Morosini* now in London, National Gallery.[108] The London painting must have been the "Ur"-portrait for subsequent representations of Vicenzo Morosini, such as the portrait in the Doge's Palace that bears the identifying inscription 1580/VINC*S MAUROC* EQUI, and therefore the London portrait probably should be dated slightly earlier, around 1578, the date of Morosini's election as procurator *de citra* of San Marco.[109] The coat of arms depicted below the inscription in the Doge's Palace portrait shows only those of the Morosini dalla Sbarra, the branch to which Vicenzo belonged, whereas during his ambassadorship to Gregory XIII in Rome in 1572 the pope had honored him with a knighthood and granted him insignia from the papal family's coat of arms, the Buoncampagni dragon, to be quartered on his *stemma*.[110] The Morosini-Buoncampagni *stemma*, despite all restrictions to the contrary, was placed at the top of the frame of the altarpiece at San Giorgio.[111] The relationship between Gregory XIII and the Morosini signals the family's ecclesiastical adherence, like

that of the Bollani family, who were also from the *case vecchie*.[112] Vicenzo Morosini's political career was also similar to Domenico Bollani's in its orientation towards *terraferma* appointments. Vicenzo's first major post was in 1555 as prefect of Bergamo; he became *savio della terraferma* in 1565, during the political alarms of 1571 when a Turkish invasion threatened Venice, was made *generale sopra i lidi*, and, in 1585, was balloted for doge.[113] Emmanuele Cicogna simply says, "He was one of the principal Senators of his time."[114] His immediate family had an unusual number of members prominent in public life. His brother Domenico (1508–57 m.v. [= 1558]) had also achieved a knighthood following several distinguished ambassadorships (in 1546 to Ferdinand; in 1552 to Emperor Charles V; in 1553 to Pope Julius III; 1555 to Paul IV), as well as holding important *terraferma* posts such as *podestà* in Verona (1546–47) and *riformatore dello Studio di Padova* (1552).[115] Domenico's excellent reputation and relatively early death probably contributed to his brother's rise in the Venetian government. Vicenzo's wife and the mother of his children, Cecilia, who is also portrayed in the *Resurrection*, was his second spouse, whom he had married in 1542; she was a Pisani dal Banco, granddaughter and daughter of procurators of San Marco, Alvise di Zuanne (Giovanni), elected 1516, and Zuanne (Giovanni) di Alvise, elected 1528, both distinguished ambassadors,[116] and the niece and sister of two cardinals, Francesco di Alvise (created 1517) and Alvise di Zuanne (Giovanni, created 1565), the latter two with ecclesiastical *terraferma* benefices as bishops of Padua.[117] Cecilia Morosini may have died as early as 1559, which could explain the somewhat primitive, wooden quality of her portrait.[118]

Vicenzo Morosini had a direct relationship with the architect, Palladio, possibly another avenue of introduction to San Giorgio Maggiore, and also with the artist, Jacopo Tintoretto. Ridolfi noted three paintings by Tintoretto in the collection of the Procurator Morosini.[119] Palladio is cited as being at the Morosini residence in Venice in a letter of 1572, but a more certain working relationship is documented in Venice in 1574 when Vicenzo was elected one of the three *provveditori sopra la fabbrica del Palazzo* when Palladio was asked to act as the main advisor on the work of reconstruction in the Doge's Palace, evidence of the expanding network of the architect's patrons, as discussed further in Part V.[120]

Most important, however, and possibly the most convincing explanation for the privileged position in which the Morosini were placed at San Giorgio, was that their ancestor Giovanni Morosini (died 1012) was the founding abbot of the monastery.[121] At the time of the concession of Vicenzo's family memorial there were still Morosini among the members of the San Giorgio community.[122] The desire to commemorate their past and simultaneously forge alliances with important contemporary figures in Venetian public life was a motivation for granting patronage, as it was for those seeking association with the new church.

The next phase of the decoration of the Morosini chapel is documented on 26 February 1587 m.v. (= 1588), the date recorded in Alessandro Vittoria's account-book of a payment to his nephew, the sculptor Vigilio Rubini, for the bust of Vicenzo Morosini (fig. 131).[123] Despite the signature, A. V. F., on the right shoulder, the bust

has recently been attributed to Vittoria's studio, probably Vigilio, working after a Vittoria prototype.[124] Vicenzo Morosini died less than a week after this payment was made. There is a pronounced resemblance between the bust and the painted portrait, which could have served as an additional model for the sculptor. The bust is placed on the wall to the left of the Morosini altar, over a doorway to the corridor leading to the sacristy and above the plain black stone set into the pavement marking the family tomb. It is set on a scrolled socle on top of a plinth that forms part of an elaborate dappled grey-purple marble frame surrounding Morosini's epitaph of black stone.[125] Both the choice of marbles and the elaborate reverse-curve of the scrolls on either side of the plinth match those of the altarpiece frame, which the monk and chronicler, Fortunato Olmo, had found so remarkable, and which, unlike any of the other altars, includes a reliquary urn that protrudes high enough above the frame to cover a portion of the painting. Vittoria must have designed both at this moment, thus unifying an otherwise ambiguous space into that of a chapel.[126]

Two more busts complete the decoration of the Morosini chapel. These busts are placed on independent marble consoles flanking the epitaph of Vicenzo. They represent, on the left, Barbon Morosini, and on the right, Domenico Morosini; both, on the basis of their style and the content of their inscriptions, probably date from the middle of the second decade of the seventeenth century. The style of the busts in the Vittoria mode has been described as "close to Paliari," a sculptor who was active at San Giorgio at that time.[127] Furthermore, the portrait of Barbon is as a much older man than either of the two sons portrayed in the Tintorettos' *Risen Christ*. The compelling reason, however, to date these busts around 1615 (and before his death in 1620) is that Barbon achieved the office of procurator *de supra* in that year, as commemorated in the inscription, BARBONVS MAVROCENVS/DIVI MAR. PROCVRATOR/VINCENTII FILIVS.[128] It seems logical that Barbon at this time would seek to emphasize further the family successes in attaining the most powerful offices in the Venetian government with the reminder that his uncle, Domenico, represented here in his bust as a still youthful-looking man (having died at only 49 with the already brilliant career outlined above), had acquired a knighthood, DOM∗ICVS MAVROCENVS/EQVES VINCENTII FRATER; of course, Vicenzo, founder of the chapel, had achieved both these titles.[129]

Monastic Patrons and Their Patron Saints

The significance for the monks at San Giorgio of the altars at either end of the transept arm is indicated by their position in the church and by the use of luxurious materials for their architectural framework. The paradigm set up in the cruciform analogy giving primacy to the "head" of the church, and thus instituting a descending hierarchy of importance from the high altar to those in the nave is here countered by the strong thrust of the perpendicular axis, the "arms" of the cross, created by the large and spacious transept, an innovation of Palladio's original plan to accommodate Benedictine liturgy

and State ceremonial practices. Olmo compares their scale and stonework of four beautiful columns and steps of marble to that of the high altar; the difference he notes is that "It has, however, a painted altarpiece."[130] The altar in the transept on the right as one faces the sanctuary was dedicated to St. Benedict, and was commissioned on 23 February 1593 (m.v. 1592) from Pietro di Comini and his son, Giovanni Giacomo, who were to supply white marble from Rovigno and fine-grained red marble from Verona, while the monastery provided the gray variegated marble for the four columns with their capitals and bases and for a *cassone* with a base of Verona marble (fig. 133).[131]

The dedication of the altar exalts the patron saint of the Order, whose life would be further celebrated in the 1590s decoration of the choir, and who in this altarpiece is made the visual focus of the transept. The monastery records show that Jacopo Tintoretto received 150 ducats in 1594 for the altarpiece of the *Coronation of the Virgin with Sts. Benedict, Gregory, Mauro, and Placido* (fig. 132).[132] Except for Carlo Ridolfi in 1648, most critics have agreed that the execution of the work is largely by Domenico Tintoretto.[133] The composition is designed on a principle similar to that employed by Jacopo Tintoretto for the *Paradise* in the Doge's Palace; a hierarchy of arrangement is imposed by concentric rings of figures screened from one level to another by clouds, rather than by naturalistic devices, such as perspective deployment in the landscape. The upper tier of figures includes the group of the Coronation supported by angels and cherubim: Christ, the Virgin Mary of the Crescent Moon, God the Father, and, at the very top center, the Dove of the Holy Spirit. The saints occupy the next level, with St. Benedict borne on a layer of clouds somewhat higher and in front of the cloud mass that supports St. Gregory flanked by Sts. Mauro and Placido.[134] On the terrestrial level there are two groups of figures, both shown with tonsured heads: on the left, three Benedictine monks, and on the right, two men in red senatorial robes.

The usual interpretation of this hierarchy is that the intermediate level occupied by the saints is indicative of their roles as intercessors; their body language conveys quite another message, one that would be especially pertinent to the Benedictine monks worshiping at the altar.[135] The act of transmission, rather than intercession, better explains the interrelationships of the figures. Benedict's direct perception of the heavenly event is indicated by his upturned gaze, one hand holding his Rule, the other stretched toward Gregory, his authority to transmit this vision symbolized by the crosier and abbatial miter. Gregory's enlightenment is shown by his gaze and gesture, as, looking at Benedict, he flings his arms wide open. A dove, the symbol of direct inspiration, hovers by his ear. The legitimacy of his *Life* of Benedict is thus established by its direct transmission. In turn, the two young disciples flanking Gregory look at him in awe: Mauro clasping his hands in devotion, while Placido clutches his martyr's palm to his breast in one hand, and, with the other, gestures down toward the figures below, who look piously upward, the ultimate beneficiaries and direct heirs of Benedict's wisdom as revealed through his and Gregory's writings.

131   Alessandro Vittoria, Morosini Chapel sculptural ensemble: Vigilio Rubini, bust of Vicenzo Morosini; Circle of Paliari, busts of Domenico and Barbon Morosini, Morosini Chapel, San Giorgio Maggiore, Venice

VINCENTIO MAVROCENO EQVITI S. MARCI PROCVRATORIS
GRADVM FACTIS CONSILIISQ PRECLARIS ADEPTO GRAVISSIMIS
REIP. TEMPORIBVS PROVISORIS GENERALIS MVNERE IN TVENDA
ORA MARITIMA FORTISSIME VSO ORATORIS DIGNITATE
APVD GREGORIV XIII ET AMPLISSIMIS ALIIS HONORIBVS
MAGNIFICENTISSIME FVNCTO PATERNA PIETATE LONGE
PRÆSTANTISSIMO ANDREAM. F. L. D. ET MIRIFICA INDOLIS
ADOLESCENTEM SVMMO CVM OMNIVM DOLORE PEREGRE
REDEVNDO BISANTIO MORTVVM EODEM HOC TVMVLO
CONDENDVM CVRAVIT PII IN PARENTEM FILII M. P.

VIXIT ANNOS LXXVII CAL MARTII
DECCESSIT ANNO M D LXXXVIII

133 Andrea Palladio, San Giorgio Maggiore, Venice, view of the transept with Jacopo and Domenico Tintoretto's *The Coronation of the Virgin with Sts. Benedict, Gregory, Mauro and Placido*

The two groups of figures below are described by Valle as, "portraits of monks and commissioners unknown to me" ("imagini Monachorum et Comessorum qui ignorantur"), and he also said that the first one in the middle was a portrait of Abbot Alabardi himself, with a cellarer on either side.[136] As attractive as this identification is of the abbot who would do the most to complete the decoration of the church, including the spectacular high altar ensemble, nave altarpieces, new choirstalls, and finish the architecture, including the Cappella dei Morti and night or winter choir, as well as commence the façade – and Olmo reports that Alabardi

had a special veneration for the Virgin – there are several reasons that mitigate against its being completely plausible.[137] The first is that the monks' physiognomies appear so generic as to make it difficult to agree that they are portraits of particularized individuals, although the monk nearest the center is taller than the others, as Alabardi was said to be.[138] The second reason is that this identification originated with Valle, and is not mentioned by Olmo who was a contemporary of Abbot Alabardi, and, moreover, an admirer, who surely would have made this claim himself. Even so, whether a tradition of identifying a portrait of the abbot had sprung up in

132 (*facing page*) Jacopo and Domenico Tintoretto, *The Coronation of the Virgin with Sts. Benedict, Gregory, Mauro and Placido*, San Giorgio Maggiore, Venice

the intervening time, or whether Valle himself during the composition of his history had acquired such respect for Alabardi as the moving force behind the 1590s campaign, the claim represents an equal interest for the reception history of this altarpiece commissioned exactly a century earlier.

In fact, what Olmo had to say about the *Coronation* was a lament that the saint whose relics were contained within the altar, St. Cosmas the Hermit, was not represented in the painting.[139] Of course, Olmo had a particular interest, being the author of a work published in Venice in 1612 on the life of the saint.[140] Multiple inscriptions attest to the presence of the relics of St. Cosmas in the altar.[141] The altar was consecrated under Abbot Alabardi on 8 March 1596.[142] The saint's relics had been brought to San Giorgio in 1058 and Venice's acknowledgment of this acquisition was reflected in a city-wide observance initiated in the eleventh century of the feast of St. Cosmas on 2 September, a celebration that appears neither in the general church calendar nor in that of Santa Giustina, again demonstrating the political import of relic possession, and the ties of monastery and State.[143]

Nowhere is the status endowed by the possession of a venerated relic more evident than in the history of the other transept altar, dedicated to St. Stephen Protomartyr. The arrival of the saint's body at the island monastery in 1110 was momentous enough to have occasioned the rededication of the church to include both Sts. George and Stephen.[144] The civic consequence of this acquisition was reflected in the institution of an annual dogal *andata con trionfi* to San Giorgio, both for the vigil and for the feast day of the saint, 25 and 26 December.[145] The ritual *andata* to San Giorgio was one of a limited number of official public appearances made by the doge, particularized furthermore by being one of the ten in which the doge was accompanied in procession by the triumphal insignia of the Republic.[146] Outside of the dogal basilica of San Marco, the *andata* to San Giorgio was unique in requiring two visits, in one of which the doge appeared publicly at night. Until its suppression in 1796, the nocturnal *andata* drew forth into the Bacino of San Marco a crowd of patricians (including noble women) and the populace celebrating the beginning of the Carnival season, providing a spectacle of lights that enraptured artists and chroniclers alike.[147] To describe briefly the components of the ritual: on 25 December, after attending Mass at the dogal chapel, the doge and his cortege bearing the *trionfi*, accompanied by the Signoria, foreign dignitaries, and the double choir of San Marco, embarked for San Giorgio, where the doge was formally greeted by the abbot before hearing Vespers. The doge with the same cortege returned the next day for Mass, after which he gave a repast for his cortege and the monks – a custom that lasted until 1562 when the monks requested that they be allowed to pay the cortege instead in order to avoid the great disturbance this collation caused in the cloister – after ceremonies at San Giorgio were concluded, the doge returned to the Doge's Palace, where he hosted a banquet for the forty-one electors. What Edward Muir has called "the Venetian liturgy" had developed into elaborate ceremonial protocol to govern the actions and appearance of the participants in the calendrical cycle of State

ritual.[148] Procedures were recorded in the official ceremonials of San Marco; these were often compilations of earlier protocols with additions or notations of events contemporary to the compiler.[149] Private diaries exist annotated by the doges themselves as personal "aides-memoires" for their responsibilities in ceremonial functions.[150] The extraordinary was not welcomed; in 1522 when Doge Antonio Grimani (1521–23) defied precedent in not taking his accustomed seat due to his extreme age and the cold, it was reported with great disapproval by Marin Sanudo.[151] Changes in precedent were debated as a governmental matter, such as the proper form to follow during an outbreak of plague or extreme weather conditions when the journey to San Giorgio over the water was considered too dangerous.

Giacomo Franco's engraving of 1614 of the "Giorno di Natale" (fig. 134) depicts the completed church of San Giorgio with its marble façade and one of the primary moments of the *andata*: the meeting between the disembarked doge and his cortege with the abbot and monks on the *campo* in front of the doors to the church.[152] Hierarchy and accoutrements were prominent. In terms of expressing sovereignty, the abbot's privilege to be attired *pontificale*, to wear a miter and cope and bear a crosier, was as significant as the *trionfi* to the doge. This mutual display was a visual acknowledgment of each other's status – a nod to a certain degree of *jus-patronato* of the dogal chapel of San Marco and an affirmation of traditional prerogatives enjoyed by San Giorgio. The ritual act denoted recognition of their relationship and public observation of privileged status. The liturgical nature of the ceremony within the political framework is revealing of the sacral nature of the State. For political motivations, inextricably enmeshed with religious ones, the ritual also served to reaffirm possession of the relic. Venice claimed an alternative apostolic succession to that of Petrine Rome via the State cult based on the possession of the body of St. Mark; this formed the basis of a "political theology" that justified Venetian ambitions independent of, or even in contradiction to, those of Rome, particularly in matters of jurisdiction and territory.[153] Sponsoring the cult and relics of the first Christian martyr St. Stephen served to reinforce the same ends, as revealed, for example, in an explanation of the origins of the ceremony based on the chronicle of Pietro Dolfin of 879, as the monastery was founded:

> For perpetual praise of God and defence of the Patria [homeland] and, because this church is under the patronage of San Marco and the ducal chapel, free from subjection to the Church [Patriarch of Venice], we intend to grant enjoyment of the same privileges.[154]

In fact, in Venice the custody of relics was governed by the State, and ecclesiastical institutions were subject to that control, which became increasingly rigorous in the sixteenth century.[155] Devotional and political aims were felt to be complementary, invoking divine intercession for the *patria* through means that extended from reliance on the apotropaic qualities of relics to more coded symbolic expressions of political alliances and enmities. Venice in the Middle Ages was perhaps more avid in its acquisition of relics than any other

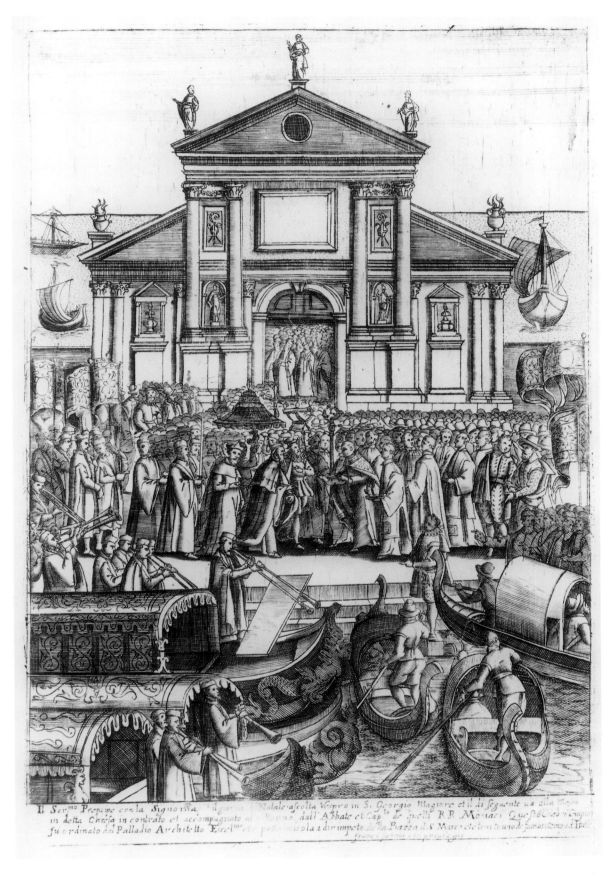

134 Giacomo Franco, "Giorno di Natale," *Habiti d'uomeni et donne venetiane con la processione della ser.ma signoria et altri particolari, cioè trionfi feste cerimonie publiche della nobilissima città di Venetia,* Venice, 1610, 1:35

city except Rome, and post-Tridentine piety witnessed a resurgence of interest in (and defense of) their cults.[156] Giovanni Botero famously claimed this in 1605, saying "in truth there is no city where one can find holy saints more important, more whole, and in greater number" ("Invero non è Città, ove Corpi Santi più insigni, più intieri, & in numero maggiore si trovino"), further explaining that the value of the relics for the Venetians lay in their ability to provide protection for the city ("come li Venetiani di Reliquie venerabili, con le quali la loro Patria santificassero, & molto meglio, che con profonde fosse, ò con grossi bastioni assicurassino").[157]

The authenticity of these relics was an uncomfortable issue.[158] There was a competing claim for the body of St. Stephen in Rome at the church of San Lorenzo fuori le Mura, also with a continuous literary tradition, one that furthermore seems to have ignored entirely a Venetian alternative.[159] Olmo was compelled to refute the persistent Roman hagiography, criticizing Jacobus de Voragine, for example, whose "mistake," Olmo contended, arose from a reliance on popular Roman sources in Latin and the *volgare* riddled with misinformation.[160] The iconography of the two-part altarpiece of St. Stephen in the old church of San Giorgio reflected an event that presented the only adequate defense that could be claimed for authenticity: the ability of the relic to perform miracles. In 1374 Abbot Bonincontro de' Boateri had commissioned from the painter *maestro* Caterino a gold-ground panel painting representing St. Stephen as a deacon, flanked on the right side by Sts. John, Mark, Cyprian, and Jerome, and on the left by George, Bartholomew, Benedict, and Lawrence, with a portrait of the supplicant abbot attired *pontificale*, and the inscription, BONINCONTRVS ABBA . . . H . . . CHRISTVS SIT . . . /MCCCLXXIIII NEL MEXE DI DECEMBRIO KATARINUS PINXIT HOC OPVS.[161] Atop the panel was a gilded wood-relief angel with a scroll reading, ATHLETA STEPHANVS IACET HIC IN PACE SEPVLTVS, or, alternatively recorded as, HIC IACET ATHLETA CHRISTI STEPHANVS IN PACE SEPVLTVS.[162] The sculpted angel and the inscription on the scroll commemorated the miracle that confirmed the true presence of the saint's bones, when in 1374 an angel appeared and spoke these words to a French soldier who had made a pilgrimage to San Giorgio to venerate St. Stephen. Both the painting and the relief sculpture were known to Olmo, by which time the objects had been separated and placed in different locations, to disappear by 1720.[163]

The first public act to take place in the new, almost finished ("quasi finita"), church of San Giorgio Maggiore was the ceremony on 15 August 1581 of the Feast of the Assumption of the translation of the body of St. Stephen from the high altar of the old church, which was about to be demolished.[164] Olmo described the ceremony, remarking upon the singular good fortune of Abbot Paolo Orio, who was privileged to view the saintly remains on only the second occasion that the *cassa* had been opened.[165]

One function of the ceremony was the public – and official – reaffirmation of the authenticity of the relic, executed with the authority of Pope Gregory XIII, as well as that of the patriarch of Venice, Giovanni Trevisan, as the papal representative, and the Doge Nicolò da Ponte and Venetian Senate, whose representatives were the procurators Marc'Antonio Barbaro and Andrea Dolfin. In honor of the significance of the occasion, a gold medal bearing the legend TRANSLATIO B∗ STEPHANI PROTOMARTYRIS AD ALIUM LOCUM HUJUS ECCLESIAE S∗ GEORGII, and on the reverse, NICOLAO DEPONTE DUCE VENETIARUM, & JO: TRIVISANO PATRIARCHA∗ MDLXXXI∗ XV∗ AUG∗, was struck and deposited in the new casket.[166]

The phenomenal recognition of the importance of the possession of the relic of St. Stephen embodied in the dogal *andata* had a profound effect on the form that the new church would take, if not providing the actual motivation for its undertaking. Bruce Boucher theorized that the removal of the relic from the high altar in order to satisfy the post-Tridentine preference for the Sacrament resulted in the enlargement of the transept space so as to accommodate the devotional needs attendant upon the altar of St. Stephen in its new location, a critical element of Palladio's plan.[167] Even more pressing had been the lack of space in the earlier sanctuary to accommodate the participants in the proper execution of the ceremony for the feast day of the saint. A rare description of the dogal *andata* from the monks' point of view reveals the state of the church around 1562, just previous to commissioning the new building from Andrea Palladio. An excerpt demonstrates their complaints:

> Where the singers should be while the abbot sings the oration: As it is improper to stand shoulder to shoulder with the abbot, the two singers should stand on the steps of the Sancta Sanctorum, a little lower. . . . When the singers in the choir accompany those at the altar: Finishing the commemoration of St. Stephen, the other singers in the choir go toward the altar and to their place on the steps of the Sancta Sanctorum, next to the others, to sing the Benedicamus, because there is no space in front of the lectern.[168]

Modifications required by the ritual would have included: the enlargement of the space in front of the church for the initial meeting of the doge and the abbot with their corteges; the extension of the sanctuary and choir to accommodate the double choir of San Marco that accompanied the doge and the Signoria; and creation of ambulatory space in the transept arm housing the new altar of St. Stephen for the procession of the doge and monks. In effect, the new transept was required to function as an alternate nave during the ceremony.

Abbot Alabardi presided over the consecration of the new altar on 15 March 1596.[169] The stonework had been commissioned from Giovanni Giacomo di Pietro Comini on 26 February 1593 m.v. (= 1594), together with that of the three altars on the same side of the nave, to be completed by Easter 1595 for a total sum of 1,400 ducats and to conform with the four completed altars opposite.[170] Further accounts show that the St. Stephen altar cost 600 ducats of that amount.[171] A lengthy inscription on gold ground adorns the pedestals on either side of the altar, extolling the history and translation of the saint.[172]

We have no information concerning the commission of the altarpiece of the *Martyrdom of St. Stephen*, other than Olmo's attribution of it, together with the *St. Benedict* altarpiece, to Jacopo Tintoretto.[173] Rodolfo Pallucchini and Paola Rossi assigned a *terminus post quem* of February 1594 based on the date of the construction of the altar, and presumed that the painting would have been finished the same year.[174] Given that the altar was to match the exact dimensions of the St. Benedict altar in the opposite side of the transept, however, it may have been commissioned at the same time as the *Coronation of the Virgin*, which was paid for in 1594, and thus would put the execution as much as a year earlier.[175] If there is a lack of documentary evidence for the genesis of the painting, there is visual evidence, one of Domenico Tintoretto's "hallmark" oil composition sketches, the *Martyrdom of St. Stephen*,[176] which corroborates an attribution to him, not only for the execution but for the design as well (fig. 135).[177]

In the altarpiece Domenico has portrayed St. Stephen's martyrdom by stoning (Acts 7: 54–60). As in the *Coronation of the Virgin* opposite, Domenico has structured the composition with a tripartite scheme. The upper, "celestial," tier is similar in conception to the *Coronation* since the figures are elevated by cherubim lit from below against a background aureole of clouds, cherubim, and angels. The central figure borne aloft is that of the Trinitarian God the Father (wearing a triangular halo); slightly below and on the right hand of God is the figure of Christ leaning in as if to focus on the scene below and encounter the direct gaze of Stephen, as does the figure of St. Michael Archangel on the left-hand side. The intercessors occupy the upper level with God, since the next two tiers lack the scrim of clouds of the *Coronation* that placed the figures in the frontal plane. Rather, the second level in the *Martyrdom of St. Stephen* is composed primarily of figures set in the far distance, creating the spatial effect of deep, box-like recession, against which a few larger figures are placed so that the action can be read clearly. Several of these figures occupy the same tilted ground plane of the lower tier where St. Stephen kneels, hands clasped in prayer and gazing upwards, framed by a bright halo. The intermediate figures are disposed somewhat symmetrically, with two bending over to pick up stones just behind the figure of the saint, two placed further back and poised in the act of hurling stones, and three smaller figures (the central may be intended as Saul receiving the garments of the persecutors) completing the almost circular arrangement in the forefront of the crowd in the rear. Stephen's swinging vestments and the counter-torsion of his body contribute to an upward spiraling movement that finds its culmination in the figure of God the Father. The basic elements of the composition are fleshed out in the oil sketch. The episode illustrates Stephen's vision and martyrdom, "But he, being full of the Holy Spirit, looked up to heaven and saw the glory of God, and Jesus standing at the right hand of God," after which he was cast out of the city and stoned while he prayed, "Lord Jesus, receive my spirit," and fell to his knees saying: "Lord, do not lay this sin against them." Besides Stephen's attributes of stones and the martyr's palm, there is an open book that lies on the ground beside the saint. Its pages curl thickly around the stones that seem to have been directed at it as well; the prominence of the book may reflect the importance placed upon direct

135 Domenico Tintoretto, *Martyrdom of St. Stephen*, preparatory oil sketch, Oxford, Christ Church (JBS 778, inv. 0365)

knowledge, the *lectio divina*, by the Benedictines,[178] yet it should be remembered that the open book was also a familiar and potent symbol for the city of Venice.[179]

Despite their later execution, Palladio had devised the parameters of a decorative scheme for the remaining nave altars. Of the six nave altars modeled on the Bollani chapel altar in Istrian stone, the first and third on each side contained painted altarpieces and the middle altars – with slightly richer marble decoration in their framing – sculptures, thus maintaining a symmetrical disposition of

136   Andrea Palladio, San Giorgio Maggiore, Venice, crossing pier

the elements of the architecture and decoration. Palladio's conception of the architectural framework for the altars both controlled the area to be occupied by the decoration and maintained correspondence with the architecture of the church. Since dividing walls are not present, chapels are defined by the framework of the altars and the corresponding spatial pocket in the nave aisles and entablature. The visual symmetry of the altars was enhanced by the choice of artists, with the pair of altars by the entrance given to the Bassano family, those in the middle occupied by sculptures, and the pair nearest the transept executed by the Tintoretto workshop. Both the stonework and the painting and sculpture were carried out during the tenancy of Abbot Alabardi in the 1590s, with two exceptions noted by Olmo, and contributed strongly to the development of coordinated altarpiece programs that would replace earlier church décor-by-accumulation or individual acts of patronage as an ideal.[180]

Throughout the church, altarpieces served as spiritual catalysts, their imagery attuned to the praxes of their various beholders. Nave and transept altars, for example, accommodated as diverse a range of function as they do audience. From the commemoration of lay patrons to the invocation of saintly intercessors, the imagery pro-

137　Andrea Palladio, modified and executed by Simone Sorella, Giovanni Giacomo Comini, and Giulio di Bortolo, San Giorgio Maggiore, Venice, exterior façade

vided direct access to inspiration, whether through the agency of affective meditation, requiring a developed spirituality, or by means of a devotion dependent on the didactic nature of images. The contemplation of altarpieces in a church involves an act in which image and audience are complicit.

Palladio orchestrated this relationship through his conception of order and ornament: the richness and preciousness of the colored altar marbles is a counterpoint to the grand scale of the interior Composite order on pedestals that supports the bold chiaroscuro of the projecting entablature around the perimeter of the vaulted nave ceiling and dome, and tied to it by the minor Corinthian order of the cross-vaulted aisles with their more subtle molding (fig. 136). The spatial experience is inseparable from the articulation of ornament, as he explains in the *Four Books* (Bk. 1, ch.1, 7), as are the roles of architect and patron in producing an organic whole:

> Beauty will derive from a graceful shape and the relationship of the whole to the parts, and of the parts among themselves and to the whole, because buildings must appear to be like complete

and well-defined bodies, of which one member [*membro*] matches another and all the members are necessary for what is required. Having weighed up these things by means of drawings and the model, one must carefully calculate the entire cost involved, making provision for the money in good time and preparing the materials that are likely to be needed, so that, when building, nothing is missing or hinders the completion of the work; for the patron [*aedificatore*] will get great credit.[181]

Church and City

The culmination of the building and decoration of the church of San Giorgio Maggiore was the completion of the façade in 1610 (fig. 137). This phase was the most public manifestation of the campaign that had been largely carried out in the 1590s but which continued well into the seventeenth century, including, for example, the tomb monuments on the interior and exterior façades of the

138   Andrea Palladio, San Giorgio Maggiore, Venice, interior façade

church. The façade has also excited the most controversy in relation to Palladio, whether "reading" the design, attributing the finished façade, measuring intention according to available evidence,
or describing the unstable process of architecture.[182] Despite Palladio's optimistic assessment of the role of the model in the passage
from the *Four Books* cited above, and the existence of such a model
at San Giorgio, it also was a starting point with limited flexibility
in reflecting evolution or level of detail, the latter usually supplied
during the building process.

For any substantial changes in the major concept of the project
set down by the artist in the *modello*, the abbot was supposed to
seek the approval of the Chapter General, or governing board of

the Congregation.[183] For San Giorgio, Palladio had duly designed
a *modello* in wood (no longer extant) in 1565–66, prior to construction of the church. A *modello* existed in at least a fragmentary
state up to the mid-eighteenth century, when Tommaso Temanza
saw it at San Giorgio. It is of interest that Temanza relates that this
modello, which he took to be Palladio's, included details such as the
niches on the façade, but "more simple, and harmonious" ("più sim-
plici, ed armoniosi") than those actually executed.[184] The utility of
such a *modello* from the point of view of the patrons was described
by Olmo in his history of the island monastery. Olmo notes that
in 1579 (during Palladio's lifetime) Abbot Paolo Orio left to his suc-
cessors "the prototype, or model, exceptional in inception" ("il tipo,

o modello, rarissimo in principio") so that the church could be built after he had left.[185]

It is worthwhile to reflect on the nature of administrative practices among the Benedictines at San Giorgio in order to assess the patron's means of control over a building project of this scale.[186] The Cassinese Congregation limited an abbot's term of rule to five years. Thus, though an individual monk was attached to a particular house, as abbot he would move among houses. The continuity of long-term projects was managed primarily by the daily involvement of other members of the local monastic hierarchy, such as the cellarer, who would serve as building coordinator, transmit details of projects to successive abbots, and who would often eventually succeed to the abbacy of his own house. This accumulated experience of building practice was in turn put to use in successive appointments, since a number of monasteries in the Congregation were constructing new edifices as part of their program of reform and renewal; the abbot who finally completed the façade in 1610, Domenico Perozzi da Cologna (1607–12), had gained his reputation as a practitioner of the science of architecture in this way: he was celebrated in chronicles of the Congregation as "lettered in Architecture and Geometry," an attribute that had enabled him to execute with uncommon success the fabrics of several churches, and crediting the "beautiful façade and prospect" ("bella facciata e prospettiva") of San Giorgio to his direction.[187]

When the circumference of the church was completed in 1575, the interior façade (fig. 138) received some of its ornament under Palladio's supervision, including the *ochio*, or round window (probably the filled-in area now containing a painted *tondo* by Tizianello),[188] and the pair of gray variegated marble columns after the Lateran Baptistry in Rome that frame the portal. The *terminus ante quem* of the columns is provided by their publication in the *Four Books* in 1570 (Bk. 4, ch. 16, 61 [misprinted as 53]-63): "I too made use of the design for the columns which I placed as ornaments at the door of S. Giorgio Maggiore in Venice; they were not as long as they ought to have been but are of such beautiful marble that they could not be excluded from the building."[189] Palladio made particular note that these ornaments demonstrated "the skill of the architect who realized how to use them so well without detracting from the beauty and dignity of the building." It is no accident that these were taken from what Palladio called the "Baptistry of Constantine," as he would have considered them apt quotations for the contemporary Christian basilica, since he stated he thought that it was "modern and made from the spoils of ancient buildings" although "everybody supposes that it is ancient." He resorts to his own earlier study (London, RIBA, XIV, 2) for the intricate carved moldings of the base and its singular motif of acanthus leaves that compensate for the problem of the length of the column shaft (fig. 139). Palladio thus provides an iconographical parallel, a history lesson, and a pattern for architects to emulate – as he has done.

Contemporary to Palladio's program were the sculptures placed in the upper two niches of the bays formed at the intersection of the interior façade and first nave aisle pier. These stucco figures of

139 Andrea Palladio, drawing after the columns of the Baptistry of San Giovanni Laterano in Rome, London, Royal Institute of British Architects, XIV, 2

the *Four Evangelists* were executed by long-time collaborator Alessandro Vittoria, the only sculptor represented up to this time in the church (fig. 140). Olmo singles them out for their excellence and says that the sculptor is not adequately praised, possibly a reference to the subsequent failure of Vittoria to receive the commission for the high altar (also with statues of the Four Evangelists) in the 1590s.[190] The elongated twisting figures activate their upper spatial zone of the interior façade, and are a reminder of Palladio's ideas about the classical partnership of sculpture and architecture.

Vittoria's influence seems to have extended to another sphere as well, in the introduction of a tomb format with the deceased represented by a bust "all'antica." The central overdoor and side bay tomb monuments of the interior façade belong to a later phase of

140 Alessandro Vittoria, *St. Matthew*, interior façade, San Giorgio Maggiore, Venice

ated with San Giorgio or generally with a Venetian project, and recently with a Florentine project in Santa Croce), the stepped slabs on top of the sarcophagus form a podium for the socle of the bust (probably in another hand), precluding the insertion of a reclining figure. The tabernacle is centered under a thermal window, and the flanking bays show statues in niches over doors with small reliefs and festoons above; the orders are raised on a high continuous socle. Palladio differentiated the architectural units using an applied temple front for the aedicules (as he does for altars), whereas the niches do not have this high degree of architectonic structure, but are treated more independently as voids carved into the wall surface with simpler moldings.

A drawing first identified by Rudolf Wittkower as a project for the exterior façade of San Giorgio (London, RIBA, XIV, 12 right side, now detached) also shows a pedimented aedicule with an urn raised on a pedestal, an indication that busts were planned in Palladio's conception of the program (fig. 142).[192] While their eventual realization occured in a later campaign of decoration, it is worth considering their significance as a part of the civic aspect of the church. In a recent study, Martin Gaier underscores the heavy restrictions placed by the Venetian State on the commemoration of individuals in the public space, particularly in regard to the politics of dogal representation, as well as the claims of ecclesiastical and civil rights in sepulchral custom, describing San Giorgio as "an unusual example of the interaction of state and private interests."[193] Palladio would continue his exploration of the framework of the commemorative façade at San Giorgio.

On the executed façade, portrait busts are placed in triangular pedimented aedicules like those of the London drawing, on small columns based on high pedestals, thus mirroring the monumental columns of the center block, in the outer left and right bays (figs. 143a–d). The architecture is designed with a strongly projecting central block, of a monumental Composite order on pedestals supporting a pediment that marks the nave, and a minor Corinthian order resting on the base supporting half-pediments that match the side-aisles.[194] In the left and right bays between the monumental columns are niches with signed statues of the co-titular saints of the church, Sts. Stephen and George, by Veronese artist Giulio del Moro, and in the story above them are the abbatial miter and crozier proclaiming the privileged status of the abbey, and in a center plaque, the epigraph announcing the foundation and completion of the church under Doge Leonardo Donà (1606–12).[195] The portrait busts represent two significant figures from Venetian history, personally allied with the monastery's past: Doge Tribuno Memo (979–91), sponsor of the original act of donation to the Benedictines in 982, and Doge Sebastiano Ziani (1172–78), a generous donor, who had been memorialized on the exterior of the old church. Both had followed a royal custom of the great medieval Benedictine houses having abdicated their ducal thrones and retired to monastic life before their deaths.

Memo is represented in the distinctive hood and mantle of the Benedictine habit, wearing an "all'antica" reversed ducal *corno*, and his association with the island seems to be confirmed by the

San Giorgio's construction, following the completion of the external façade, but although they do not belong to this discussion of the period under Palladio's supervision, they do reflect his ideas for their typology, as do the later altars discussed above. With his designs for the Grimani façades at San Francesco, the interior tomb type followed a long tradition of figures of the defunct reclining on sarcophagi in framed niches (Vicenza, Museo Civico, D 17; see above fig. 90), while the drawing associated with the exterior façade (London, RIBA, XIV, 10; see above fig. 89) suggested the intended placement of busts on consoles in the bays. On the interior façade at San Giorgio the deceased are represented in a bust-format on a socle placed on a sarcophagus and framed in a pedimented tabernacle, as in a drawing thought once to have been owned by Vasari, now in the State Museum in Budapest (fig. 141).[191] Although its destination and dating remain disputed (at one time it was associ-

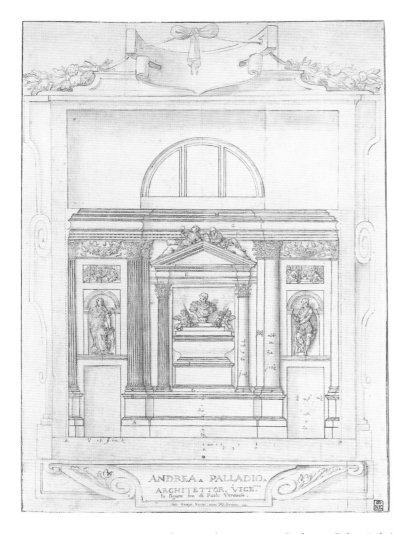

141　Andrea Palladio, drawing for a tomb monument, Budapest, Szépmüvésti Museum (1989)

142　Andrea Palladio, *Project for a Church Façade and Tomb Monument (?San Giorgio Maggiore)*, London, Royal Institute of British Architects, XIV, 12 right side (now detached)

inscription below, GLORIAM ABDICATO IMPERIO HANC INSULAM, yet more reliable sources record his retirement at San Zaccaria. No previous memorial to Memo is chronicled on the façade of the old church, so the portrait and inscription attest to the founding doge's presence like the possession of a disputed relic. The displacement of other figures that had rights on the old church façade may have been due to the sponsorship of Doge Marc'Antonio Memo (1612–15), whose tomb on the interior would mirror that of his illustrious ancestor, and send a message about the revival of the "case vecchie dogali" realized with his election, as well as to testify to his genuine piety.[196]

Ziani is shown as a Christian knight, in armour with a military cloak buttoned on one shoulder, and an antique ducal *corno*. His inscription, PACIS ARBITRUM, can only refer to the seminal event of the "myth of Venice," his role as negotiator of the Peace of 1177 between Pope Alexander III and Emperor Frederick Barbarossa – Rome and the Empire. It is telling to find such an assertion in the

context of the monastery with its associations of jurisdictional equality and privilege. As a multivalent concept, the monks were reminded that even this doge had renounced the world for the "peace" brought about by the contemplative life of monasticism, while new patrons, such as Leonardo Donà, doge during the stormy period of the Interdict of 1606–07, would have relished the parallel with the heroic defender of "public liberty," setting up a dialogue with the Doge's Palace across the Bacino of San Marco.[197]

Palladio may have intended an even closer reference to the earlier church of San Giorgio by incorporating these monuments in a porticoed façade, although one that reflected his classical notions of the temple that were evolving through the 1570s (as in the projects for San Petronio in Bologna and Il Redentore), rather than one like the medieval atrium seen on the Jacopo de' Barbari map. As he said of the public character of the temple (*Four Books*, Bk. 4, ch. 1, 5), "Temple fronts should be constructed overlooking the most impres-

143a   Andrea Palladio, modified and executed by Simone Sorella, Giovanni Giacomo Comini, and Giulio di Bortolo, San Giorgio Maggiore, Venice, exterior façade

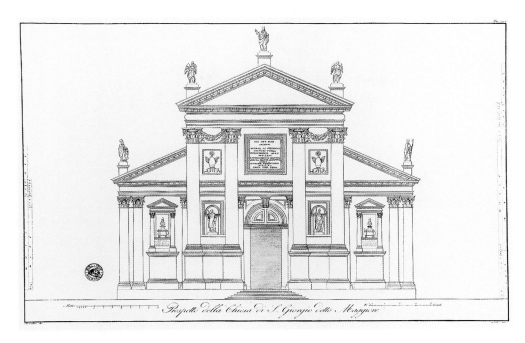

143b Leopoldo Cicognara, Antonio Diedo, and Gianantonio Selva, façade of San Giorgio Maggiore, *Le fabbriche e i monumenti più cospicui di Venezia*, ed. F. Zanotto, Venice 1858, 2:241

143c and d (*below*) San Giorgio Maggiore, Venice, exterior façade, details of bays and tabernacles with busts of Doge Tribuno Memo (*left*) and Doge Sebastiano Ziani (*right*) by Giulio del Moro

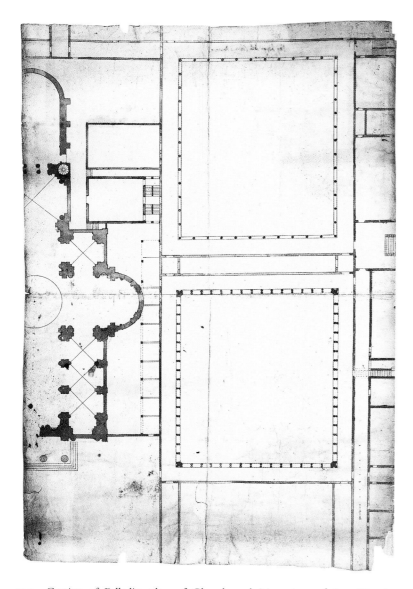

144 *Cantiere* of Palladio, plan of Church and Monastery of San Giorgio
Maggiore, Venice, Archivio di Stato, MM 857

sive part of the city so that it seems that religion has been placed
there like a guard and protector of the citizens."[198] An idea for such
a portico can be seen on a plan (fig. 144) discovered by Wladimir
Timofiewitsch in the Archivio di Stato in Venice (MM 857), that also
shows the retrochoir of the church and Cloister of the Cypresses
that Palladio designed in 1579.[199] The dating of the plan to Palladio's lifetime was questioned by Isermeyer since it includes the
Cappella dei Morti as well, which was begun in 1592.[200] The
drawing has been attributed most often to Palladio's *cantiere*, but also
to others, including Vincenzo Scamozzi, who would continue the
Romanist classical style in Venice and earn the support of Palladio's
former patrons.[201]

The momentousness of undertaking the new façade was underscored in the agreement of 1597 for the materials of the marble
façade of San Giorgio, when Procurator Leonardo Donà appeared

as co-witness; Istrian stone had begun to be collected late in the
second abbacy of Abbot Alabardi, during the same period when he
was commissioning the internal decoration of the new church.[202]
The commencement of the building project, however, was immediately hindered by a huge debt of 6,000 ducats, which the
monastery had incurred from its charitable activities during a severe
famine; it was not until 1599 that Jacopo Felice da Brescia
(1599–1604), then abbot of the monastery, initiated the actual
construction.[203]

Acting as *proto*, or supervisor of the works of the Procuratia de
Supra, in the 1590s was Simone Sorella della Porta, who was first
posited as a likely candidate for carrying out this role at San Giorgio
by Rodolfo Gallo.[204] Sorella was named in the contract measuring
stone for the façade, stone probably ordered in 1597 from Alessio
Cedin and his sons in Verona, which implies that the final form of
the façade had been determined by that time and did not include
a portico, possibly still due to financial constraints.[205] Sorella's death
in 1599, however, would preclude his involvement in the actual execution; for the final period of the erection of the façade between
1607–11, we have the names only of the stonemasons, who refer to
the model ("al modello fatto") they followed.[206] The masons, Giovanni Giacomo di Pietro Comini and Giulio di Bortolo, had
worked continuously for the monastery through the period of the
1590s and during the building of the façade.[207] The responsibility
for the final assembly and profile of the façade was theirs. The father
of Giulio, Bortolo di Domenico, had been employed as a stonecutter from the beginning of work on the new church under Palladio; he remained active in the 1590s as well, and was cited in 1593
as *proto*.[208] Originally under Palladio's supervision, the *cantiere* established at San Giorgio for the building of the church was able to
maintain continuity even under different managers, some of whose
personalities can be distinguished.[209] The inherent nature of a
monumental architectural commission required such an organization, parallels for which have been drawn in the administrative
structure of the monastery.

The façade was completed in 1610 under Abbot Domenico
Perozzi (1607–12).[210] The new church was then consecrated by the
patriarch of Venice, Francesco Vendramin, in the presence of Doge
Leonardo Donà, as recorded in the inscription by the high altar.[211]
Despite the degree of time between Palladio's death and the
completion of the façade, the inscription, honoring his CELEBRE
TEMPLUM ARCHETYPUM, stands witness that the monks themselves
saw Palladio as the primary architect of the entire church and that
his authorship conferred a degree of fame.

The relationship of Palladio's conception of the choir and façade
to the design as executed seems to be one of "translation." San
Giorgio has been seen as a crucial monument in the history of the
development of the Renaissance church, from Alberti to Vignola,
yet it was completed thirty years after the architect's death – and if
he had considered a porticoed design, which would have been a
remarkable contribution to the narrative of architectural history, it
was ultimately rejected. At the same time, Palladio had operated to
provide for the success and continuity of this important project,

establishing a *cantiere* that understood his new practices, and managing patrons that were accustomed to an active role in the process. By the time that the façade was being built, his other works would assert a paradigmatic authority as well: San Francesco della Vigna, San Pietro di Castello, and Il Redentore. It has been proposed that Francesco Smeraldi's completion of Palladio's project at San Pietro was based not only on the contractual material but relied on the model of San Giorgio, in which case San Giorgio may reflect its own conception at one remove if, in turn, its executors referred to the built example of San Pietro for guidance and inspiration. The pre-conditions for Palladianism, without the presence of its author, were established at San Giorgio.[212]

CHAPTER EIGHT

CONVENTO DELLA CARITÀ

In Venice [Palladio] has begun many buildings, but one above all that is marvelous and most notable, in imitation of the houses that the ancients were wont to make, in the monastery of the Carità.

Giorgio Vasari, *Le vite de' più eccellenti pittori scultori e architettori*,

Florence, 1568[213]

THE LATERAN CANONS OF THE CONVENTO DI Santa Maria della Carità were also members of a congregation born of fifteenth-century reforms of traditional Orders, in this case of the Canons Regular who followed the rule of St. Augustine.[214] While the Canons were a contemplative order, like the Benedictines, an important distinction may be found in their more public activity of preaching. With the impetus of reform, the Lateran Canons were eager to improve their situation, as they gained in wealth and patrician associations. It also has been hypothesized that the personal association of the Barbarigo family with the Carità was a factor in the selection of Palladio to expand the monastery; brother doges Marco (1485–86) and Agostino (1486–1501) were celebrated in a double tomb in the church, and the family continued to live in nearby San Trovaso.[215] Also sharing part of the complex was the adjacent Scuola Grande di Santa Maria della Carità, which, although one of the earliest of such foundations in Venice, was in somewhat of a financial decline in the sixteenth century, relative to the Canons and the expansion of their church and monastic buildings; this would be reversed in the next centuries affecting the building program.[216] The church had been rebuilt in the years 1441–45 (fig. 145), as the Canons gained in privileges and status under the Venetian pope Eugenius IV (1431–47).[217] Its Gothic flank can be seen at right angles to the Scuola in the painting by Carlo and Gabriele Caliari, "haeredes Pauli," from the Doge's Palace cycle of the *Peace of Venice of 1177* of 1584 in the Great Council Hall (fig. 146). The painting depicts Doge Sebastiano Ziani's recognition of Pope Alexander III, who had taken refuge as a monk in the Carità, staged in the *campo* in front of the entrance to the shared

146   Carlo and Gabriele Caliari, *Doge Sebastiano Ziani's Recognition of Pope Alexander III at the Monastery of the Carità*, Sala del Maggior Consiglio, Doge's Palace, Venice

147 Aerial view of Santa Maria della Carità and the Accademia Bridge, Venice

courtyard of the convent and confraternity that lay between the buildings (figs. 147 and 148). The significance of this narrative established the Carità within the cycle of civic ritual, which was celebrated in a dogal procession on 3 April, from a bridge of boats extended across the Grand Canal from Campo San Vidal, the present location of the Accademia bridge.[218] Subsequent history was not kind to Palladio's project inside the walls for the Canons: left incomplete; partially destroyed by fire in 1630; and finally, following the Napoleonic suppression, transformed in the nineteenth century into the State art academy and galleries, the Accademia di Belle Arti (fig. 149). Scholars, notably Elena Bassi, restored the contribution of Palladio to its rightful prominence in his œuvre. This recovery can be further extended to an understanding of his patrons and the importance of the site in the itinerary of the "myth of Venice," and in the civic and religious piety of the city.

★   ★   ★

Theater of Religion

One of the great preachers of the sixteenth century was Gabriele Fiamma (1537–1585), a Venetian *cittadino* who distinguished himself as abbot of the Carità, general of the Lateran Canons, and bishop of Chioggia (created 1584).[219] He gave the Canons a presence in the transformation of the religious life of the public through his prominence in this newly reinvigorated activity, rising to preach in the ducal basilica of San Marco and elsewhere in Venice and throughout Italy. Sermons were a crucial feature of many important occasions in addition to those of the liturgical calendar; another preacher records some 200 given over the course of three Lents at the Carità (*circa* 1524–27). Such religious oratory has been described as "*the* medium of communication" as much as the media of our own time – print, radio, television, film, and electronic – and equally significant in reflecting and forming cultural values, both popular and elite; it was performed not only in churches, but in *piazze*, in convents, in hospitals, in short, on all pious occasions and locations, drawing large crowds.[220] After the decree of the Council of Trent on the reform of preaching in 1546, "ecclesiastical rhetoric" had replaced the medieval tradition of the *Artes praedicandi* and was strongly influenced by the writings of Augustine.[221] It was no longer scholastic disputation or the "earthy," "forthright" sermons of fifteenth-century evangelists, but informed by classical and Christian rhetoric.[222] As Fiamma explained,

> The simple man sees in the mere letter and in the easy story many rare and precious things that marvelously delight him, but he cannot penetrate further. On the other hand, an elevated spirit, to whom God has given the grace of understanding and of penetrating the mysteries . . . can never be tired of reading and contemplating.[223]

Palladio's archaeological design for the Carità was the architectural equivalent of this new elevated sacred verbal discourse (*Four Books*, Bk. 2, ch. 6, 30, ideal plan and section [fig. 151]).[224] The often-noted theater-like character of the project with its terrace-rimmed open atrium and superimposed tiers of open loggias in the cloister possibly did have a functional and expressive relationship to these reformed activities of the Canons. Certainly, in terms of creating access between the living spaces of the monks, the rooms of the abbot, and the guest quarters to gain entry to the church and the areas of the choir and elevated *barco*, the new sacristy – Palladio's "tablinum" – and oval stair created elegant formal relationships between these areas on their respective levels, and added new ones, such as to and from the atrium and terrace above it.[225] A performative function seems to have invested the spaces of the new interior convent complex – atrium, terrace, and multi-level porticoed cloister – that display such close visual references to Roman theaters in the superimposed classical orders, as illustrated in Barbaro's Vitruvian commentary (fig. 150).[226] Contemporary Roman secular (i.e., Antonio da Sangallo the Younger's and Michelangelo's Farnese Palace) and sacred (i.e., Bramante's Belvedere Courtyard in the Vatican Palace) courtyard spaces often took on the function of a stage, as did public *piazze* in Italian cities, as for religious spectacles

148 View from above of former atrium and cloister, Santa Maria della Carità, Venice

in front of churches. Tommaso Temanza referred to a now-lost seventeenth-century inscription on a tablet over the door to the choir that referred to Palladio's "Theatrum Opus" in conjunction with the atrium destroyed by fire in 1630. Although Temanza's association of it with Palladio's theater for the Compagnia della Calza degli Accesi is no longer held to be tenable,[227] paintings such as Antonio Canaletto's imaginative reconstruction of the cloister (fig. 152) nonetheless reveal an impression of a stage-like quality to the spaces (terraced porticoes replace the missing atrium and refectory). If one supplies the missing atrium, as in Ottavio Bertotti Scamozzi's plate (which "completes" the cloister with its facing wing, never built), the impression is one of an outdoor pulpit created by the elevated balcony of the terrace (fig. 153). The eloquence of the architecture has become the built equivalent of ecclesiastical rhetoric. For this purpose, Palladio turned to classical forms that related, according to his reconstructions, a sequence of spaces and functions.

His model for this was his conception of the ancient house and the writings of Vitruvius, which Palladio explains in his opening chapter to his second book, "Del decoro, o' convenienza, che si deve osservar nelle fabriche private." Here, he discusses in social terms the "suitability" of the private house to the status of its inhabitants, particularly, as he says, "in a Republic."[228] In grand houses, there was a public dimension: the need for "loggias and spacious ornate halls" and "beautiful and ornate areas" in which clients could wait and walk about.

★   ★   ★

Theorizing the House of the Ancients

In his work for religious orders, Palladio found an outlet in Venice for his theories of domestic architecture, not otherwise able to be realized there. The impressive project described by Vasari is the only built Venetian project illustrated in Palladio's *Four Books* (Bk. 2, ch. 6, 29–32). Explicitly based on his studies of the ancient house, its forms and functions were translated at the Carità into designs for various living spaces within the monastery: "Corinthian" atrium, sacristy cum "tablinum," chapter house, oval stair, cloister and cells, and refectory with another cloister, garden, and dependencies.

Palladio was paid for a model in 1561 (also the date inscribed in the center of the Ionic frieze in the cloister), and a year later for his work as supervisor (covering a period from 1 June 1561 to 1 June 1562), but, except for his reappearance to correct some problems in 1569 and 1570,[229] the execution was handled by a wall-mason also closely associated with San Giorgio, Antonio Paleari da Marcò. Paleari began on the same date as Palladio's supervision, as we learn from the evaluation of his work in 1569, for which he was paid the following year, eight full years after the initial agreement.[230] Stonework in the monastery continued, since estimates made by the stonemasons Antonio da Bissone a San Vidal and Girolamo Testa-grossa indicate the work that had been accomplished by 1573. A year later, in 1574, Paleari, together with his brother, Giovanni Battista, signed a new contract to begin the walls of the refectory. Execution of the remaining Palladian project was hampered in its realization by the financial circumstances of the patrons, and there is little further documentation of this building phase. Our understanding of what was actually completed by this date (fig. 154) has been notably enhanced by Elena Bassi's comprehensive interpretation of the fragmentary evidence, physical and documentary, in its

149 (*above*) Andrea Palladio, Santa Maria della Carità, Venice, cloister elevation

150 Daniele Barbaro and Andrea Palladio, Roman theater, in Daniele Barbaro's edition of Marcus Pollio Vitruvius, *I dieci libri dell'architettura di M. Vitruvio, tradotti et commentate da Monsignor Barbaro eletto patriarca d'Aquileggia*, Venice, Per Francesco Marcolini, 1556, lib. v, 152–53

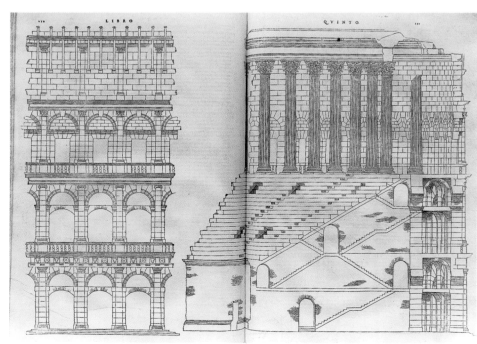

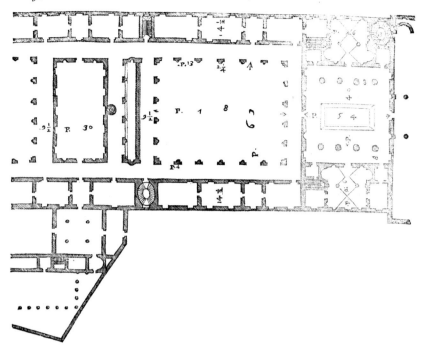

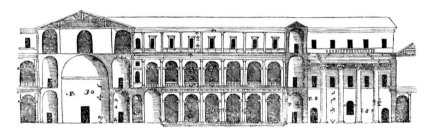

DE I DISEGNI che feguono, il primo è di parte di quefto Atrio in forma
maggiore, & il fecondo di parte dell'Inclauftro.

DELL'ATRIO

151 (*left*) Andrea Palladio, ideal
plan and section of Santa Maria
della Carità, *I quattro libri
dell'architettura*, Venice, Appresso
Dominico de' Franceschi, 1570,
lib. 2, cap. 6, 30

153 (*below right*) Ottavio Bertotti
Scamozzi, atrium, *Le fabbriche e i
disegni di Andrea Palladio*, Vicenza,
1796, lib. IV, tav. XXV

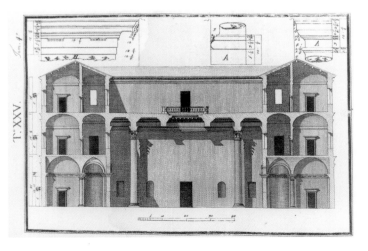

152 (*left*) Antonio Canaletto, *Caprice View of the Monastery of the
Lateran Canons*, Windsor, The Royal Collection (RCIN 406991)

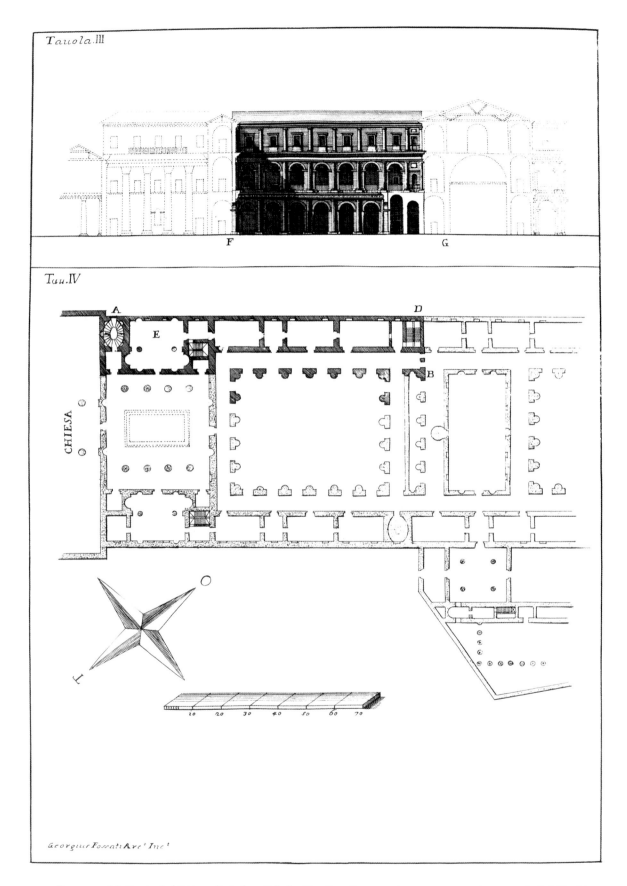

Tauola.III

F G

Tau.IV

A D

E

B

CHIESA

O

I

10 20 30 40 50 60 70

Georgius Fossati Arc.º Inc.

154   Francesco Muttoni, *Architettura di Andrea Palladio Vicentino di nuovo ristampata . . . con le osservazioni dell'architetto N. N.*, Venice, 1740–48, I–I: tav. III–IV, extant parts of section and plan demarcated on reversed version of design from Andrea Palladio, *I quattro libri dell'architettura*, Venice, Appresso Dominico de' Franceschi, 1570, lib. 2, cap. 6, 30

155   Andrea Palladio, elevation of the atrium of Santa Maria della Carità, *I quattro libri dell'architettura*, Venice, Appresso Dominico de' Franceschi, 1570, lib. 2, cap. 6, 31

above Andrea Palladio, Santa Maria della Carità, Venice, cloister elevation (detail of fig. 149)

156 Giovanni Antonio Moschini, "Atrium and Cloister of the Convento della Carità in 1828," in *Nuova Guida di Venezia*, Venice, 1847

reconstruction. She cites the surprising silence of earlier critics on this major project of Palladio, despite the grand conceptions in the ideal printed versions, a silence she attributes in large part to the devastating impact of its subsequent fortunes.

"The heart of the Palladian project, the Corinthian atrium, was burned and immediately forgotten."[231] With this single statement, Bassi has captured the dilemma of the Carità. For Palladio, the placement of the project in the *Four Books* was defined by this feature, since he followed his discussion of the private palaces with that of the atrium, which he considered to be the most important part of the ancient house – "notabilissima" – and which the Carità served to illustrate as the third of four types he would discuss: the "Corinthian atrium." He provides an enlarged plate of its elevation, and from that and his description of its measured parts, we learn that the center of the atrium was unroofed (forming an *impluvium*) and had two rows of four columns of the Composite order that formed side aisles covered over by open terraces at the level of the third story of the cloister elevation (fig. 155). Writers who saw the atrium before its destruction commented on its impressive columns, "beautiful, tall and large in diameter" ("belle, grosse e spesse"),

154

according to Francesco Sansovino in 1581;[232] or, in the words of English ambassador Henry Wotton in 1624, who described the *Atrium Graecum* and its columns of "meere Brick":

> Then which, mine Eye, hath never yet beheld any *Columnes*, more stately of Stone or Marble; for the Bricks having first been formed in a *Circular Moulde*, and then cut before their burning into foure quarters or more, the sides outward ioyne so closely and the points concenter so exactly, that the *Pillars* appeare one *entire Peece*; which short description I could not omit, that thereby may appeare, how in truth wee want rather *Arte* than stuffe, to satisfie our greatest *Fancies*.[233]

Palladio's use of monumental columns was unprecedented in this monastic context in Venice, although his designs for the colossal peristyle in the courtyard of the palace for Iseppo Porto in Vicenza (1542–52) have in common their archaeologizing approach to the ancient house (*Four Books*, Bk. 2, ch. 3, 8). The effect of the atrium would have been dramatically changed by the later addition of a roof, which Inigo Jones described in marginal notes to his copy of the *Four Books* and probably seen by him in 1597:

> The Atrio is finish'd, the Columns are of Bricks, with red Stucco, the Base and Capitals are of Stone, the Roof of the Gallery above the Entablature is of Timber, and was paved with Bricks, but by reason of the Rains passing thro' they have been obliged to make another Roof to the top of the Building, and supported by Pilasters, and covered with Tyles; so that about the Opening of the Atrio above is a covered Terrace to walk on.[234]

An anonymous ink-and-wash drawing in the Archivio di Stato in Venice was associated by Bassi with this transformation, probably done after Palladio's death, which was an attempt to solve the same problem of water leaking through the ceiling of the terraced atrium that Palladio had been called back for in 1569 and again in 1570 in replacing six coffers.[235] Both English authors were fascinated by the elegant use of brick with stone ornament, and Jones particularly mentions the coloristic effect that he believed was achieved by coating red stucco on the bricks. Recent conservation studies confirm the use of a red dressing through analogy to the surviving traces.[236] Little remained of the atrium after the fire that occurred at the Carità in 1630 in an already plague-stricken city, and some of these traces, such as the bases of the monumental Composite columns, were used in the erection of a modest two-sided "atria lapidea" (stone atrium), as seen by Giovanni Antonio Moschini in 1828 and reproduced in his *New Guide to Venice* of 1847 before it was roofed over in the early twentieth century which continued its conversion to the Academy as it is today (fig. 156).[237] Even some of Palladio's surviving architecture was removed as the complex was adapted, notably two return arches and end bays of the only completed wing of the cloister exterior; the changes visible in Moschini's illustration and documented in the accounts of the neo-Classical architects who made them in the initial phases, and in fragments of the atrium cornice uncovered in recent campaigns of conservation (fig. 157).[238]

157 Andrea Palladio, surviving element of atrium cornice, Santa Maria della Carità, Venice

Of the remaining elements, the single wing of the brick and stone cloister elevation is a lesson in the interpretation of the classical orders (figs. 158 and 159). The first and second stories of superimposed Doric and Ionic orders were originally open arcades, now glassed in and with a balcony added to the second story; the third story of Corinthian pilasters framed rectangular windows with straight lintels to the corridor and rooms behind, containing the cells of the monks (some of which still remain). The engaged columns of the arcade piers of the first two orders were made from fine molded curved bricks, as in the monumental columns of the

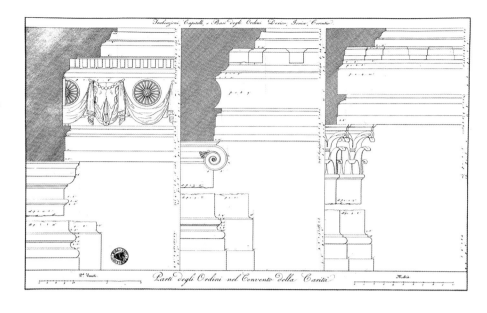

158 Leopoldo Cicognara, Antonio Diedo, and Gianantonio Selva, orders in the cloister of Santa Maria della Carità, *Le fabbriche e i monumenti più cospicui di Venezia*, ed. F. Zanotto, Venice 1858, 2:210

159 (*below*) Andrea Palladio, cloister of Santa Maria della Carità, Venice, *I quattro libri dell'architettura*, Venice, Appresso Dominico de' Franceschi, 1570, lib. 2, cap. 6, 32

atrium, and the frieze and soffits of the arcade orders were sculpted in terracotta. Only such features as pedestals, capitals, keystones, and window framing were made of white stone. Inigo Jones was told "that every Arch of the Perristilio would cost 1000 ducats."[239]

With these designs Palladio satisfied the functional requirements of the Lateran Canons in an architectural language so insistently classical that it expresses their ties to Rome. Scholars have long compared the superimposed arcades to both ancient and contemporary examples, even to the specific quotation from the Temple of Vesta at Tivoli in Palladio's otherwise uncanonical use of a Corinthian frieze with the Doric order.[240] Of particular interest are the comparisons to Bramante. In fact, Palladio, with his ambitious plans for the Lateran Canons, must have been cognizant of their seat in Rome at Santa Maria della Pace, whose cloister was designed by Bramante, the only modern master besides the author to be illustrated in the *Four Books* (Bk. 4, ch. 17, 64–66). Palladio honored Bramante as being "a supremely talented man and observer of ancient structures." Roberto Pane's analysis of the formal relationships at the Carità found that, despite allusions to ancient peristyle architecture, the cloister was closer to the courtyards of Bramante in its simple rectangular structure, correspondences between walls and supports, and succession of separate spaces. This idea was further elaborated by James Ackerman, who saw Palladio's use of classical "motives" as being "in a context that is much closer to Bramante – except that it has a warm brick colour – than to antiquity."[241] Bassi mentions the cloister of Santa Maria della Pace as an example of a contemporary classicizing solution to the traditional monastic complex, although without tying it specifically to the Canons, and she first theorized the Roman predisposition of the patrons to accept a "classicizing project" that was anomalous in Venice.[242] With the identification of Santa Maria della Pace as the seat of the Lateran Canons and home of their procurator general, granted to them by Pope Sixtus IV in 1483, this link can be even more firmly established, and is reflective not only of Palladio's emulation but of the patrons'.[243] The extreme proposal Palladio made in offering the

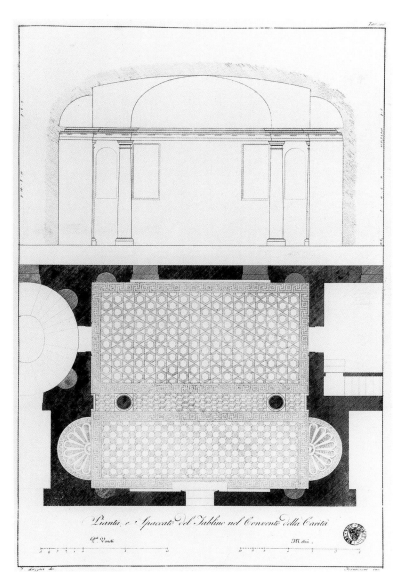

161 Andrea Palladio, tablinum (sacristy), Santa Maria della Carità, Venice

160 Leopoldo Cicognara, Antonio Diedo, and Gianantonio Selva, plan of a tablinum (sacristy) and chapterhouse for Santa Maria della Carità, *Le fabbriche e i monumenti più cospicui di Venezia*, ed. F. Zanotto, Venice 1858, 2:208

Canons the reconstruction of the ancient house would seem to require such cooperative understanding between architect and patrons, for his initial commission (and may explain later reservations).

The depth of Palladio's scientific enquiry into the forms of the ancient house is evident in his treatment of the "tablinum" or sacristy, which had been intended to have a counterpart in a chapter house across the atrium, which was never constructed except in the pages of the *Four Books* (Bk. 2, ch. 6, 30). The elegant harmony of the sacristy is derived from the juxtaposition of vaulted apsidal and rectangular geometrical forms (figs. 160 and 161). It reflects Palladio's understanding of Roman thermal spaces, as seen in the Baths of Caracalla, that had been explored in his Vitruvian researches on the ancient house with Daniele Barbaro, and realized in a domestic setting at the Palazzo Trevisan in Murano.[244] Palladio was attuned

to the appropriate succession of spaces and explains that (instead of its usual placement on axis between the atrium and peristyle courtyard) he had "found it convenient to position it to the side of the atrium," showing his practical approach to adaptation of classical forms in the context of his projects.[245] A Doric cornice in terracotta (possibly enhanced with a red wash) running around walls that looked like white marble, made of brick coated in *marmorino*, supported the vaulting (and was matched by the chromatic richness of the pavement).[246] Another practical consideration inspired one of the most lovely architectural passages in the complex, since he introduced two freestanding rose-colored marble columns at the point of transition between the apsidal space and the rectangular in order to support the internal walls of the cloister above. Palladio identified the function of the room: "This sacristy is used as a tablinum (that is what they called the room where they placed the images of their ancestors)."[247] The original orientation and decoration of the sacristy would have enhanced this meaning. Where the current entry is today was originally a window to the atrium.[248] The apsidal space was entered on the longitudinal axis, from an antesacristy that could be entered on each side: from the atrium, from the church, from the oval stair (which in turn gave onto the rectangular space of the sacristy, across from the door to the rooms off the cloister). This approach collected the traffic going into the apsidal space and directed it towards the altar that was originally in the apse opposite. Here was located the image of the ancestors to be revered, since a painting by Carlo Carliari was placed above the altar depicting *St. Augustine Giving the Rule to the Lateran Canons*

162   Carlo Carliari, *St. Augustine Giving the Rule to the Lateran Canons*, Venice, Gallerie dell'
Accademia, Quadreria

163 Frontispiece portrait of Gabriele Fiamma, to Giovanni Antonio Gradenigo, "Vita Gabriele Fiamma," in Gabriele Fiamma, *La rima*, Treviso, 1771

164 View of Rio Terra Sant'Agnese along the wall of Santa Maria della Carità, Venice

(Venice, Accademia, Quadreria), which includes lifelike portraits of what must be leading figures among the contemporary Canons (fig. 162). Although signed, the painting is not dated, and has been attributed on the basis of style and composition to around 1590, so it seems doubtful that Palladio's commissioners of the 1560s and early 1570s – the Reverend Don Paulo, Abbot Illuminato da Padova, or Abbot Francesco da Venezia – are depicted, but the aged St. Augustine may be a portrait of a particularly noteworthy canon, such as Gabriele Fiamma, who had just died as bishop of Chioggia in 1587 (fig. 163). In the background of the painting, a balustraded domed church and campanile can be seen, together with a pyramidal monument, an allusion to Rome.[249] In the sacristy, the niches on either side of the window walls toward the atrium and the Rio Sant'Agnese (fig. 164) were no doubt intended to house further images, as was common in Palladio's thinking throughout the *Four Books*.

The connection between the stories of the convent was made by a sinuous oval stair, which was an invention that Palladio credited to Marc'Antonio Barbaro, "a Venetian gentleman of great intellect." He praised this type of spiral stair *a chiocciola* (snail-shaped) with a void in the center for its abundant lighting from above and utility in restricted locations; the steps are cantilevered and supported by their insertion in the stairwell walls and appear to suspend themselves in the space (figs. 165 and 166).[250] Palladio could have attended the progress of the monastery when he lodged at the

Barbaro Palace at San Vidal across the Grand Canal from the Carità (1560, 1563), and discussed the plans with his closest patrons. Only the "elevated spirits" that Fiamma referred to would have fully understood the "mysteries" of the architectural language that lay within the walls, since their only exterior expression is the austere sequence of superimposed classical friezes without orders framing the view down the Rio Sant'Agnese (now Rio Terra Sant'Agnese), as can be seen in figure 164. Palladio's work at the Carità brings the intellectual collaboration he enjoyed with patricians such as the Barbaro brothers to fruition in a new context: the adaptation of his archaeological research and domestic building experiences as applied to the monastery of the Lateran Canons and their acceptance of his classicizing language.

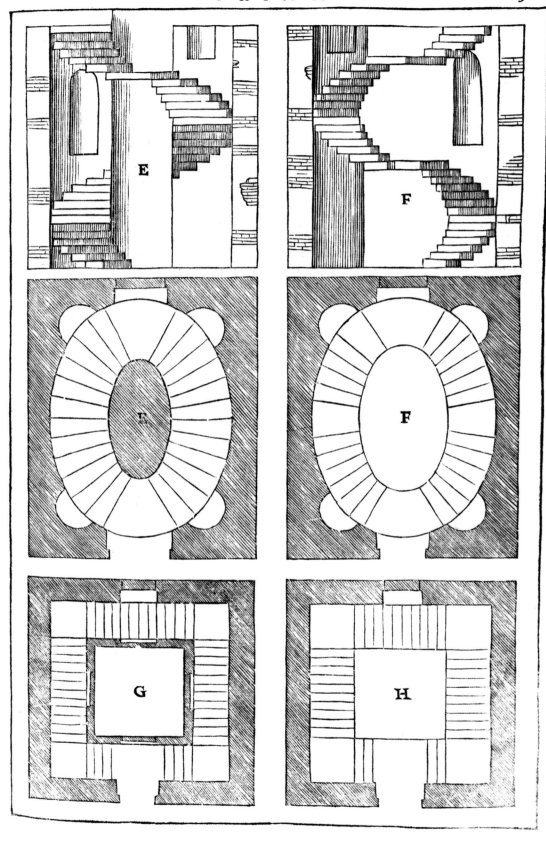

165 Andrea Palladio, stair "a chiocciola," *I quattro libri dell'architettura*, Venice, Appresso Dominico de' Franceschi, 1570, lib. 1, cap. 28, 63 "F"

166 (*facing page*)   Andrea Palladio, stair "a chiocciola," Santa Maria della Carità, Venice

CHAPTER NINE

SANTA LUCIA

Although Palladio's initial commission at Santa Lucia (Santa Maria Annunziata) was through the private patronage of the Venetian patrician Leonardo Mocenigo, the issues that the commission raised have a relevance for the discussion of his work for religious orders. Female religious were typically more sequestered, and frequently less in control of their wealth, than their male counterparts, so commissions were often transacted through intermediaries. Influential family connections of the governing abbess or prioress, as well as of the nuns and lay associates, could be leveraged in favor of a convent. Another important source of funding and influence was from families that had historical ties through their burial chapels, such as the origin of this bequest from Pellegrina Foscari Mocenigo (fig. 167). The Augustinian nuns at Santa Lucia operated in this manner, dependent in large part on outside contributions for major projects, both private and government-subsidized. The existing church had been given to a growing community of Augustinian nuns in 1476.[251] By the late sixteenth century, the convent had a sizeable population of about eighty nuns; it did not boast matching resources, so unlike wealthier institutions, it probably did not attract the better-endowed monachizations, as did the long-established Augustinian convents of Santa Maria degli Angeli di Murano and Santa Maria delle Vergini (respectively twelfth and thirteenth centuries).[252]

Reliable sources state that around 1565 Palladio was asked by his long-time patron Leonardo Mocenigo to design a new family chapel and high altar at Santa Lucia, an undertaking that was interrupted by Mocenigo's death in late 1575.[253] The Mocenigo chapel inaugurated the rebuilding of the church, which was claimed as being made according to a design by Palladio. The main construction and decoration of the remainder of the church, however, took place in phases from 1589 to its consecration in 1617, which makes the attribution to Palladio problematic; physical confirmation of Palladio's role is further impeded by the entire destruction of the fabric in the nineteenth century to make way for the train station in 1861 (figs. 168 and 169).[254] In support of a strictly qualified attribution of the larger church project, this study will relate Palladio's efforts to establish an iconography of architectural forms that would satisfy the needs of diverse patrons, often resulting in the meaningful reuse of inventions such as the "Corinthian" hall and *tablinum*.

Leonardo Mocenigo "dalle zogie" or "dalle perle"

A shared zeal for the realization of Palladio's vision of a new architecture may have virtually "bankrupted" one of the richer men in Venice, Leonardo di Antonio Mocenigo (1523–1575/76), knight and count palatine. In 1573 Leonardo owed the princely sum of 11,688 ducats to one of his two sons, Alvise, who received, in absolution of the debt, his father's house in the Santa Sofia (Sant' Euphemia) area of Padua, which had been remodeled to Palladio's design between 1557 and 1564.[255] The work on the Padua house was concurrent with another project that involved Palladio at a more fundamental level, the fabulous villa design for "un sito sopra la Brenta" at Dolo, immortalized in the *Four Books* (Bk. 2, ch. 17, 66 [misnumbered, =78]), made "at the request of the distinguished knight, Signor Leonardo Mocenigo." And the "villa sopra la Brenta" was not alone, but one of two villa designs by Palladio for this favored patron; another villa at Marocco (between Venice and Treviso), was also published in the *Four Books* (Bk. 2, ch. 14, 54) and would surely have impressed us more if we did not have evidence of the even grander vision at Dolo (figs. 170 and 171).[256] The building campaign under Palladio at the villa at Dolo ended at the same time as that on the Padua house, which was rented soon after.[257] The rental of the Padua house and the cessation of the building campaigns may have made funds available to start the new project for the Mocenigo family chapel at Santa Lucia around 1565, in confirmation of Antonio Magrini's dating.

168 Photograph of Santa Lucia, Venice, before demolition

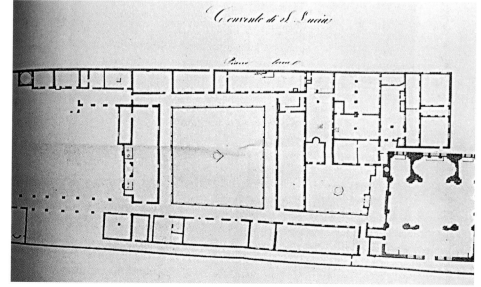

169 Cesare Fustinelli, plan of the Convent of Santa Lucia (oriented with the Calle delle Muneghe at bottom, Grand Canal at right), Venice, Biblioteca del Museo Civico Correr, MS P.D. C 857/3

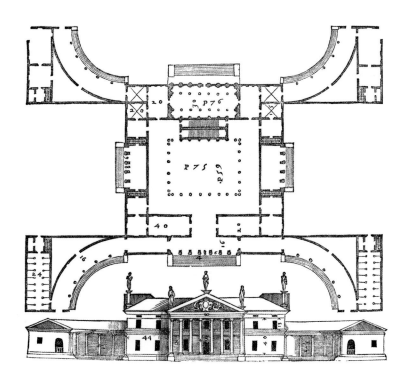

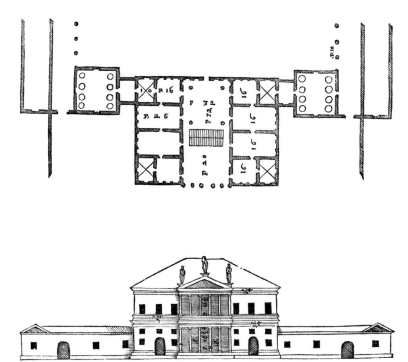

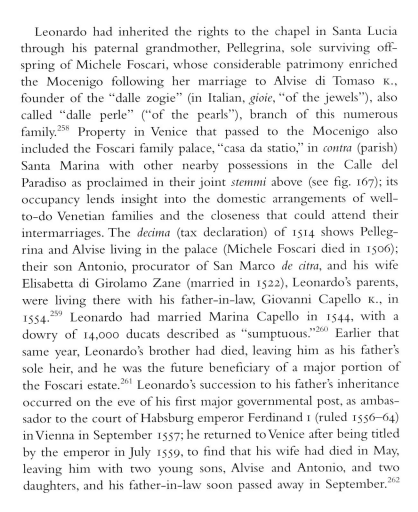

170 Andrea Palladio, Villa Mocenigo at Dolo, *I quattro libri dell'architettura*, Venice, Appresso Dominico de' Franceschi, 1570, lib. 2, cap. 17, 66 [misnumbered, = 78]

171 Andrea Palladio, Villa Mocenigo at Marocco, *I quattro libri dell'architettura*, Venice, Appresso Dominico de' Franceschi, 1570, lib. 2, cap. 14, 54

Leonardo had inherited the rights to the chapel in Santa Lucia through his paternal grandmother, Pellegrina, sole surviving offspring of Michele Foscari, whose considerable patrimony enriched the Mocenigo following her marriage to Alvise di Tomaso ᴋ., founder of the "dalle zogie" (in Italian, *gioie*, "of the jewels"), also called "dalle perle" ("of the pearls"), branch of this numerous family.[258] Property in Venice that passed to the Mocenigo also included the Foscari family palace, "casa da statio," in *contra* (parish) Santa Marina with other nearby possessions in the Calle del Paradiso as proclaimed in their joint *stemmi* above (see fig. 167); its occupancy lends insight into the domestic arrangements of well-to-do Venetian families and the closeness that could attend their intermarriages. The *decima* (tax declaration) of 1514 shows Pellegrina and Alvise living in the palace (Michele Foscari died in 1506); their son Antonio, procurator of San Marco *de citra*, and his wife Elisabetta di Girolamo Zane (married in 1522), Leonardo's parents, were living there with his father-in-law, Giovanni Capello ᴋ., in 1554.[259] Leonardo had married Marina Capello in 1544, with a dowry of 14,000 ducats described as "sumptuous."[260] Earlier that same year, Leonardo's brother had died, leaving him as his father's sole heir, and he was the future beneficiary of a major portion of the Foscari estate.[261] Leonardo's succession to his father's inheritance occurred on the eve of his first major governmental post, as ambassador to the court of Habsburg emperor Ferdinand I (ruled 1556–64) in Vienna in September 1557; he returned to Venice after being titled by the emperor in July 1559, to find that his wife had died in May, leaving him with two young sons, Alvise and Antonio, and two daughters, and his father-in-law soon passed away in September.[262]

He did not take up another ambassadorial post, a post that was often the prerogative of wealthier patricians on a faster track to the positions of power in Venetian government, but he did achieve them: senator, *savio grande* (also known as *savio del consiglio*, or "sage"), ducal councilor (*consigliere ducale*) – which the scholar Paul Grendler has described as working so closely with the doge that they might be described as a "collective personality."[263] A portrait of Leonardo's political generation has been lost to us with the fire of 1577 in the Great Council Hall in the Doge's Palace, since it had become common practice to insert living portraits in the replacements of the historical cycle. There is only a suggestion of the personalities in a pen study by Federico Zuccaro after Paolo Veronese's painting of 1562 of *Emperor Frederick Barbarossa Kissing the Ring of the Schismatic Pope Victor IV* (fig. 172), which Francesco Sansovino described as having been depicted therein:

Alvise Mocenigo (later doge), Agostino Barbarigo (who died on the day of Lepanto in 1571), Paolo Tiepolo, Knight and Procurator, Marc'Antonio Barbaro, Procurator, Marc'Antonio Grimani (father of Ottaviano), later Procurator, Nicolò Zeno (father of Caterino, himself son of another Caterino), Francesco Loredan (nephew of Doge Leonardo), Abbot of Vangadizza, Antonio Capello, Procurator, Giulio Contarini, Procurator, Lorenzo Giustiniano, Procurator, and his brother Antonio, Leonardo Mocenigo, Knight, and, on a parapet, Andrea Gradenigo (father of Alvise), in senatorial robes, Giovanni Battista Ramusio (father of Paolo), Secretary of the Council of Ten.[264]

Without making too much of the juxtapositions, this is still a sug-

172 Federico Zuccaro, Study after Paolo Veronese's destroyed 1562 painting of *Emperor Frederick Barbarossa Kissing the Ring of the Schismatic Pope Victor IV* in the Doge's Palace, Maggior Consiglio, New York, The Pierpont Morgan Library (1983.68)

gestive portrait of the company that Leonardo kept, a group with several names that are already familiar here.

Yet, as scholars have commented, despite holding such prestigious positions, no extraordinary "exploits" distinguish his political career, perhaps, it has been posited, because his "proper vocation" lay in his cultural endeavors: the collecting of antiquities, and the architectural endeavors he undertook with Palladio.[265] "Faithful admirer and patron" (Gallo), "an important rapport of esteem and reciprocal cordiality" (Puppi), "Palladio's most faithful and consistent patron" (Lewis) – these statements reflect serious conclusions, since they are made by knowing comparison with others of Palladio's patrons in mind – such as the Barbaro brothers and Jacopo Contarini.[266] The creative side of Leonardo is tantalizingly suggested in a surprisingly fresh and evocative pen portrait of a young man in an autograph account-book for the Dolo villa (fig. 173). Even here, while the sustained level of active patronage certainly implies a special relationship between this patron and Palladio, a more precise understanding of their rapport and of the intellectual character of Leonardo remains elusive; because no literary effects attest to his thoughts, we have only documents that record the implications of his actions. From such documents, however, some indication of the "privileged" position that Leonardo held as Palladio's patron may be found. For example, some degree of intimacy is implied in Palladio's having made an ebony cabinet (*scrigno*) that resembled the Arch of Constantine to house his patron's fine collection of silver medals, and after Leonardo's death its quality was attested to in the offer of it made by his son to the grand duke of Tuscany. Several such cabinets, together with a number of sculptures of classical subjects, Cupids, Bacchus, a hermaphrodite, Aesclepius, were described in the house in Padua when it changed hands from Leonardo to Alvise.[267]

From this, we know that Leonardo shared the interests in antiquity of Palladio and his closest patrons; from the buildings that Leonardo sponsored, we can deduce his support for enquiry into monumental classical form. The depth of Leonardo's engagement with a new scientific method of investigation may be more circumstantially judged through the context of mutual acquaintances, particularly in the Paduan environment. Lionello Puppi has advanced the attractive hypothesis that Leonardo could have been one of the "several Venetian Gentlemen" who went to Rome with Palladio in 1554, when the latter was engaged in the illustrations for Daniele Barbaro's Vitruvius, and which coincides with work for the Brenta property.[268] The rental of the Padua house remodeled by Palladio for the "erudite" Genoese Giovanni Vicenzo Pinelli (in Padua from 1558 until his death in 1601) has allowed scholars to link Leonardo to a circle that included among such stellar minds as Galileo, Jacopo Contarini (described as Daniele Barbaro's "cultural heir," an inheritance that included a close relationship with Palladio). Pinelli was interested in the proposals of Alvise Cornaro, whom Leonardo would have known through his wife's family, if not independently, and who formed part of Palladio's "early" education. And it is interesting that Pinelli cultivated Paolo Veronese, as Contarini did Francesco Bassano and Palma il Giovane, inviting a comparison to the *mecenatismo* of Cornaro with his household

173 Leonardo Mocenigo, pen sketch of a young man, Venice, Biblioteca del Museo Civico Correr, MS P. D. c 248, tomo 63, 9c

painter-turned-architect Falconetto.[269] Yet another connection to Palladio's Venetian patrons can now be made, since, in that same tax declaration of 1566, Leonardo declares his residence to be in the palace of the brothers Francesco, Jacopo, and Giovanni di Andrea Marcello.[270] Jacopo (Giacomo) Marcello (1530–1603) was one of the creators of the program in the Doge's Palace after the fire of 1577, together with Jacopo Contarini;[271] Sansovino described them as "Gentlemen [who were] connoisseurs of painting and of History." The Marcello (now Toffetti) Palace became famous for its external frescoes by Jacopo Tintoretto and for Jacopo's library (*degnissima –* worthy of regard), which further locates Leonardo among his political peers and in a particular cultural orbit.[272]

In turning to Palladio for the design of a new family chapel at Santa Lucia, Leonardo was honoring a long deferred wish to transform the family burial *archa* of the Foscari, and now Mocenigo, into a proper chapel. The final will of his grandmother Pellegrina in 1543 clearly expresses her motivation, to honor "the good memory of her father" ("la buona memoria de suo padre"), and by 1562 alms were being sought by procurators of the church to

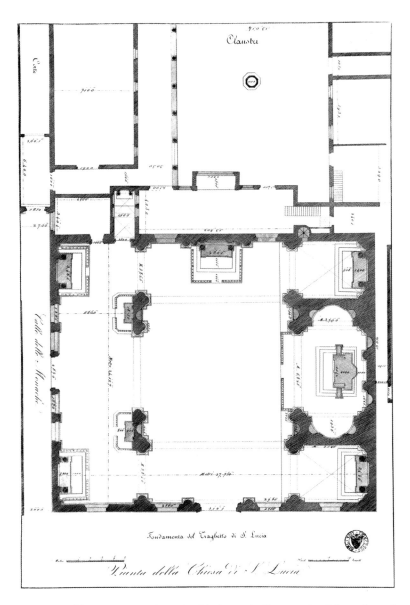

174 Leopoldo Cicognara, Antonio Diedo, and Gianantonio Selva, plan of Santa Lucia, *Le fabbriche e i monumenti più cospicui di Venezia*, ed. F. Zanotto, Venice 1858, 2:206

175 Andrea Palladio, Corinthian hall, *I quattro libri dell'architettura*, Venice, Appresso Dominico de' Franceschi, 1570, lib. 2, cap. 9, 39, "with columns that rose from the ground"

provide for its urgent repairs; thus, a need to provide an appropriate setting for his ancestors was acute for Leonardo by the mid-1560s.[273] It was at just this time that Palladio became engaged with major forays in ecclesiastical architecture in Venice: his first church design *ex-novo* for the Benedictines at San Giorgio Maggiore; his rising church façade for the patriarch of Aquileia; and mid-way through construction was his atrium-*tablinum*-cloister complex for the Lateran Canons. With this patron at Santa Lucia, Palladio was able to create an exercise in the iconography of architectural form on a compact scale (fig. 174). As both the contemporary transept of San Giorgio and the sacristy of the Carità illustrate, Palladio was concerned with the double-apse form that he would later publish in the context of his studies of the Tuscan and Corinthian atrium

in the form of the *tablinum* (*Four Books*, Bk. 2, chs. 4 and 6), as well as in the Corinthian hall (*Four Books*, Bk. 2, ch. 9, 39 [fig. 175]).[274] This was not solely a formal choice for the Mocenigo chapel, but one intended to convey meaning appropriate to its function in the context of a memorial site. The association of the *tablinum* fulfilled a deliberate program since, for Palladio, the classical use was for "the room where they placed the images of their ancestors" (*Four Books*, Bk. 2, ch. 6, 29) The purpose of the chapel was both sepulchral and, with the prestige (and income) conveyed to the convent by this important patronage, it also had the place of honor as the *cappella maggiore*, or high altar. Furthermore, images in the classical manner, that is, busts, were placed in the chapel, since Sansovino records his attribution to "Lionardo Mocenigo Cavaliere [Knight], [who] con-

176 Substitute for Alessandro Vittoria's lost *Bust of Leonardo Mocenigo: Bust of "Bernardo Mocenigo"* attributed to Giusto Le Court, Venice, Seminario Patriarcale

secrating the *cappella maggiore*, initiated [*diede principio à*] the beautiful and honored building, but [it was] interrupted by his death," to which Martinioni goes on to add: "The *cappella maggiore* founded by Cavaliere Mocenigo, is of oval form in the Composite order, with columns, cornices, and niches of Istrian stone, in which is the portrait of the founder, sensitively [*teneramente*] sculpted from life in marble by Alessandro Vittoria, celebrated sculptor, but singular among his portraits."[275] If Martinioni saw a life portrait of Leonardo by Alessandro Vittoria, unfortunately it cannot be identified with a late seventeenth-century bust in the Patriarchal Seminary that has a provenance from this chapel, which may have been substituted for the "portrait of the founder" that would date prior to his death in late 1575 (fig. 176).[276] The intention to include a classical portrait-bust type as a commemorative element had appeared in Venice only in the 1550s via the archaeologizing currents of nearby Padua, in the ambit of Palladio and his patrons, so its inclusion in the iconographical development of the design of the Mocenigo chapel would complement the architectural form of the "tablinum."[277]

When Sansovino in 1581 said that Leonardo had initiated the rebuilding of the church with his inauguration of the family chapel, he was writing from the distance of only a few years, but it still begs the question as to what was actually built by 1575 with the patron's death. The halt, given Palladio's ongoing presence in Venice, suggests that the loss of the patron terminated the financial means to finalize the chapel furnishings and move to the next phase of construction. Indirectly, this may be confirmed by the necessity of his son Alvise to sell the Padua house to pay his father's debts (although his brother Antonio was able to reacquire it at auction, only to have to sell it in turn to reimburse the dowry of Alvise's wife in 1619).[278] Only confused and fragmentary records from the convent remain, highlighting the difficulty of tracing female patronage during this period. Nevertheless, the chapel windows were paid for by Alvise in 1589, completing this part of the fabric under Prioress Chiara Ziliol.[279] The next year, in a motion brought before the Senate by Marc'Antonio Barbaro and Paolo Paruta, additional land was granted to the nuns and their procurators to proceed with a new chapel on the left side of the *cappella maggiore* to house their famous relic of St. Lucy.[280]

La "Nuntiata"

The new veneration of the Virgin as one consequence of the Council of Trent can be found in the devotional practices of the Augustinian nuns at Santa Lucia and reflected in the church and its decorative program. The convent received the revered body of St. Lucy in 1280.[281] It had arrived in Venice after the conquest of Constantinople in 1204 and had become a focal point of pilgrimages when first deposited at San Giorgio Maggiore, but the Senate had decreed its removal owing to the difficulty of getting to the island (and the capsizing of a group of pilgrims a year earlier on her feast day, 13 December, during a *burrasca*, or storm), as depicted in the Venetian edition of Jacobus de Voragine's *Golden Legend* (fig. 177). More than 300 years later, the monks of San Giorgio still mourned their loss (they retained an arm relic) in an altarpiece for the new church by Palladio, in which the unusual iconography, the *Miracle of the Immobility of St. Lucy*, by Leandro Bassano (1596), seems an ironic allusion to their former possession (fig. 178).[282] Prior to its dedication to St. Lucy, the church was dedicated to the Annunciation, La "Nuntiata," which remained a focal point of devotions. Some insight into their particular character at the convent is offered by Sansovino, who described the new devotions invented by the nuns' confessor for thirty-six years, Monsignor Giorgio Polacco; these included the *Novena*, that is the nine days before Christmas, in honor of the nine months that the Virgin bore Christ; the *Nunziale*, the day of the Annunciation to the Virgin; and special prayers for the supplication to Christ and Mary for a good death for the faithful.[283] The decorative program of the new church would reflect this iconography of Holy Family values.[284]

Palladio's undoubted sensitivity to liturgical spaces, his interest in their meaningful expression in architectural form, would seem to have found in Leonardo Mocenigo a patron of similar ambitions, and in Santa Lucia, a new charge: that of accommodating female spirituality. As in other convents in the city (and throughout Italy) the more rigorous sequestration of the nuns for performance of the divine offices, while allowing for their visual access to the high altar, another Tridentine phenomenon.

The solution taken at Santa Lucia was to place a conventional *barco*, as it was called in Venice, or *ponte*, a partial second-story floor raised on beams above the entrance to the nave, to form a choir

feno a lei el facramento del corpo del Signor : & che tutti quelli che li erão pfenti rifpondeffeno amé. Et i qllo medefimo loco fu fepelita & fabricata una belliffima chiefia martyrizata circa li anni del Signor trecéto & diece nel tempo di côftátio & Maximiano

Come fu tranfferito el corpo de fancta Lucia uirgine in Venetia. ca.ix.

El anno del Signor mille & diece Bafilio & conftátino ipatori:effendo la fycillia al loro fubiecta:comandarono che de fycillia fuffero transferiti li corpi de qfte beatiffime Lucia uirgine & fimilmente di fancta Agatha uirgine & martyre a conftantinopoli & fece li reponer ei uno honorato tépio:onde in pceffo de tépo effendo deuenuta la regia citta di conftátinopoli

177 Jacobus de Voragine, "The Translation of St. Lucy to San Giorgio Maggiore," *Legendario de Sanctis* (*Le legende de sancti*), Venice, Per Matheo di Codecha da Parma, 1494, 14

178 Leandro Bassano, *The Miracle of the Immobility of St. Lucy*, San Giorgio Maggiore, Venice

in the period of Tridentine reforms, greater control was exerted over formerly independent Augustinian sisterhoods, with jurisdiction moving to the diocesan bishop, on the part of the Church, and new lay magistracies, on the part of secular authorities.[285] This desire to control nuns manifested itself most prominently in stricter rules for *clausura*, which had previously been less regularized among individual convents, with reasonable latitude for performing convent business. Such changes had their effect on church architecture, since formerly, Augustinian nuns could recite the Holy Office in the presence of others, not necessarily separated by walls or screens; in fact, the earlier constitutions allowed lay persons for special reasons on certain holy days access to both choir and cloister. If Palladio was actually responsible for a new design stemming from the Mocenigo chapel for the entire church, which also had parochial functions, then a primary concern would have been to accomplish

opposite the high altar and *cappella maggiore*, and with its own private second-story entrance to the convent, depicted in an anonymous votive painting (fig. 179). For comparison there is the still extant *barco* in the church of the Augustinian convent of San Giuseppe in Castello, dating soon after its foundation in 1512 (fig. 180).[286] Such a traditional choice in and of itself would not provide an argument for Palladio's larger authorship of the church. The total spatial organization and reorientation of the church in relation to the convent does, however, argue that such a bold undertaking was proposed from the start of construction: that is, the Mocenigo chapel was the first step towards a new church. The fourteenth-century Gothic church of Santa Lucia that was replaced had its apse towards the Grand Canal, as can be seen in the detail of Jacopo de' Barbari's map of *circa* 1500 (fig. 181).[287] The orientation of the Mocenigo chapel rotated 90° counter-clockwise the location of the new *cappella maggiore*. Between 1609 and 1611 the remainder of the old structure was demolished and the new church built, which was said to be based on a model: "in a singular manner reduce [the church] to the design of the model according to which this building is to be done."[288] An inscription of 1611 commemorates the completion of the church under Prioress Eugenia Diedo and asserts its design by Palladio: "in splendidiorem hanc formam ex Palladii archetypo."[289] There are further questions about Palladio's original design raised by the area executed opposite the high altar and below the nuns' *barco*, since there are two eighteenth-century architects that record a variant solution to the long rectangular space with

179 *(above)* Anonymous votive painting, *Nuns Praying in Choir at Santa Lucia, Venice, after Lightning Strike, 17 April 1838*, Padua, Casa provincilizia delle suore canossiane

180 Entrance and nuns' choir, San Giuseppe in Castello, Venice

181 (*left*) Jacopo de' Barbari, *View of Venice*, 1500, Venice, detail of the convent of Santa Lucia (on the canal front to the right)

182 Francesco Muttoni, plan with elevation and section of Santa Lucia, Venice, Biblioteca del Museo Civico Correr, M.2658, tav. 23

183 (*left*) View of reconstruction of elements originally from Santa Lucia, including those from Mocenigo Chapel and the high altar, San Geremia, Venice

two supporting piers and two altars against the corner walls that was actually built.[290] Both Francesco Muttoni and Antonio Visentini show symmetrical designs for the church, which create a very different spatial effect than the built design, of a unity between the Corinthian apsidal chapels that counteracts the dominance of the entrance axis. In the notations Muttoni made on the plan with elevation and section of Santa Lucia preparatory to his planned publication, he cancelled out the apsidal walls under the *barco*, which suggests that he had first looked at another source than the church as built for his original plan before making corrections (fig. 182). Is this an indication that an original design by Palladio's was still available, although modified in execution (as at the Carità), or, instead, that his neo-Classical interpreters assumed a symmetry for which there was no evidence?

If there are problems with determining the extent of Palladio's involvement with the design for the church and subsequent fidelity to his model beyond the *cappella maggiore*, these still admit of a closer relationship to the architect than the Grand Canal façade. The latter shares identifiable Palladian motifs with other churches executed in the early seventeenth century, notably Le Zitelle, with its own attribution problems, and San Trovaso, with the thermal windows, and similarly, is a two-story design unlike any of the façades more

closely associated with him.[291] After the departure of Palladio, the lack of a guiding hand and then gaps in construction phases would not have promoted an ongoing *cantiere* at Santa Lucia; its execution was carried out through different sets of prioresses and procurators based on the executors' understanding of the "model." Even the most profound change introduced by Palladio's design for Leonardo Mocenigo's chapel, the reorientation of the church, was diluted by subsequent choices: around 1630 a new high altar was inaugurated directly across from the Grand Canal entry portal by the patriarch of Venice.[292] Only a faint memory of the original *cappella maggiore* can be gleaned from its partial reconstruction in the transept of the church of San Geremia after the demolition of Santa Lucia (fig. 183), a mixture of the relics of St. Lucy from the Baglione chapel and the former high altar from the Mocenigo chapel, which was described by Sansovino: "Above the altar is a rich and majestic tabernacle of the finest marbles with inlays of various colors divided into several orders, and ornamented with figures of bronze."[293] Its seventeenth-century tabernacle altar with a flanking group of the *Annunciation* may well have reflected Palladio's intention for a sculptural high altar, as realized at his churches of San Giorgio and Il Redentore, and congruent with the sepulchral character of the *tablinum* and "images of the ancestors" of the Mocenigo chapel.

CHAPTER TEN

LA CELESTIA

T HE CISTERCIAN NUNS AT THE CONVENT OF La Celestia also had intermediaries for the transaction of architectural commissions. Earlier in the sixteenth century concern over the scandalous behavior of the nuns had led to their being put under the direct oversight of the patriarch of Venice. In 1569 a fire in the nearby Arsenale severely damaged the convent. One of the procurators for the rebuilding of their cloister in 1570 was Giorgio Saler, a friend of Palladio. This situation, where it seems that Palladio provided only expert advice and drawings, provides an illuminating comparison to his other monastic projects.[294] The final form of the cloister (fig. 184) points to the limited degree of his involvement in the building, but this examination permits some insight into interaction among prestigious *cittadini* and patricians in their patronage. The convent was suppressed in 1810 and the church completed in 1611 by Vincenzo Scamozzi was destroyed, leaving only images of its splendid furnishings recorded for posterity (fig. 185); some of the external walls on the *campo* (figs. 186 and 187) and the internal cloister survive today, although transformed into other uses.[295]

"Celebrated for the Number and Quality of the Female Nuns, and for the Building, as well"

Francesco Sansovino recounted the thirteenth-century foundation of the Cistercians at the Celestia, as Santa Maria Assunta in Cielo (or Santa Maria Celeste) was popularly known, and its establishment as one favored by patricians, accepting many "gentlewomen."[296] This statement of the Celestia's prestige is confirmed by its comparative economic standing in the sixteenth century, which shows it to be the third wealthiest convent in Venice, after the Benedictine convents of San Zaccaria and San Lorenzo, of slightly under average size (a population in the fifties), and substantial per capita spending on the nuns, which no doubt reflected well on their lifestyle.[297] As with other elite convents, the Celestia had obtained

185 Giovanni Grevembroch, La Celestia overdoor with *Coronation of the Virgin*, "Monumenta veneta," 1759, Venice, Biblioteca del Museo Civico Correr, Cod. Gradenigo-Dolfin, 228, 3:83

184 *(facing page)*   Andrea Palladio, executed by Angelo da Corticelle, cloister, La Celestia, Venice

186 Andrea Palladio, executed by Angelo da Corticelle, exterior of cloister wall, La Celestia, Venice

187 (*right*) Andrea Palladio, executed by Angelo da Corticelle, bay of exterior cloister wall, La Celestia, Venice

numerous papal privileges over time and was directly subject to the pope, under the direction of a male Cistercian house of the Columba. There were typical conflicts in the convent between Observant nuns and conventuals, exacerbated, no doubt, by the rising rate of forced monachization beginning around 1450. According to a recent study of the phenomenon, patrician nuns "preferred Benedictine and Augustinian orders" and "the exclusively or predominantly aristocratic convents of early medieval foundations."[298] Here their lives, if not religious in vocation, might be closer to the life of traditional patrician women in its occupations, albeit in a female community with a restricted character. Both economically and politically a prestigious convent such as the Celestia operated with a measure of independence granted by its wealth, the nuns' ties to powerful families, and recourse away from local jurisdiction to Rome. Reports of the nuns' behavior by chroniclers such as Marin Sanudo reflect the worldly practices that made the Celestia one of the earlier convents to be targeted for reform in the sixteenth century: in 1509 he reported sixteen young patricians up before the Quarantia Criminal (appeals court) for too vigorously feasting the election of a new abbess with horns and pipes (*trombe* and *piffari*) and dancing through the night with the nuns against all laws for convents; in 1521 he noted that the patriarch had appeared before the Collegio denouncing the conventuals who had broken into the granary of the Observants; and finally, the proverbial straw, in 1525 he recounted how the patriarch together with a group of magistrates had gone to the Celestia and found the conventuals immodest in their attire and long hair (one of whom was person-

ally shorn by the patriarch), and on attempting to remove two of them found the door blocked by the others wailing.[299] There were protests over the ensuing government reforms and imposition of rigorous *clausura*, from formal appearances of the most prominent abbesses with their "entourage" of relatives before the Collegio, to rebellious flouting of rules by individual convents and nuns, but control of Venetian convents passed under the patriarch and, over the course of the sixteenth century, was successively more bureaucratized under State magistracies, including regulation of property and finances.[300] At the Celestia, reform was codified in the publication of a new Rule the next year, both in the vernacular, *Questa sia la regula del glorioso confessore miser Sancto Benedeto in vulgare ad instantia de le venerabile monache de la celestia observante nuovamente stampata* (Venice, Andrea de Rota de Leucho libraro nela contrada di santo Apollinaro, n.d. [1527]), and in Latin, *Ordo benedictionis sive consecrationis virginum secundum consuetudinem monialium sancte Marie de Celestibus ordinis sancti Bernardi per reverendum Beatum Laurentium*

Iustinianum venetiarum patriarcam (Venice, Andrea de Rota de Leucho libraro nela contrada di santo Apollinaro, 1527 [fig. 188]).[301]

Fire was one of the few allowable reasons for nuns to break *clausura* without recourse to written permission from the patriarch. The "horribile incendio" that occurred in the powder magazine of the Arsenale on 14 September 1569, a Tuesday, at 6:30 at night, was said to be an explosion felt throughout Venice and heard fifty miles away, destroying large parts of the Arsenal and its housing, fire extending into the nearby parishes and damaging the Trinità, San Francesco della Vigna, Santa Giustina, and, above all, the Celestia (fig. 189). Both the church and convent buildings of the Celestia were not only ruined by the fire, but by the explosion that weakened the structures, causing them to be unfit and in need of substantial reconstruction.[302] As was generally true in monastic environments, the first needs to be attended to were the urgent replacement of the housing. The Collegio met two weeks after the

188 *Ordo benedictionis sive consecrationis virginum secundum consuetudinem monialium sancte Marie de Celestibus ordinis sancti Bernardi per reverendum Beatum Laurentium Iustinianum venetiarum patriarcam*, Venice, Andrea de Rota de Leucho libraro nela contrada di santo Apollinaro, 1527, titlepage

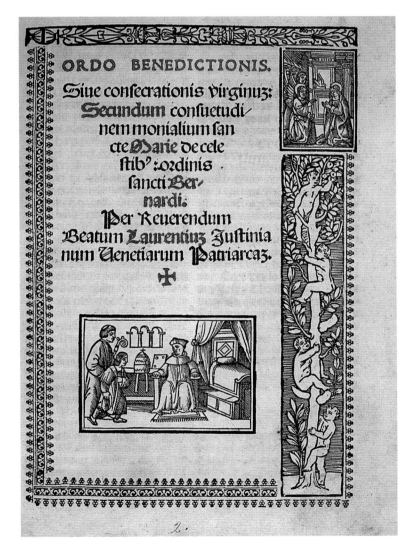

189 Ignatius Colombo, "Fire in the Arsenale," 1793, Venice, Biblioteca del Museo Civico Correr, Gherro I–I, 203

fire to decide what to do about it. Temporarily the nuns were placed at San Giacomo alla Giudecca (having been rounded up from their relatives' homes where they had first fled), unsatisfactory for the displaced Servite monks and for the government's strict sense of propriety, as well as inconvenient and incommodious for the sisters.[303] At the time, San Giacomo had a modest mid-fourteenth-century Gothic church and monastery with a single cloister.[304] This situation was expected to last only six months; it would be three years, five months, and three days before they returned to their rebuilt convent.[305]

The limitation on the nuns' active participation in the rebuilding process is illustrated by an incident that occurred one year after the fire. Patriarch Giovanni Trevisan expressed his outrage in 1570 on learning that some nuns had gone to visit the construction site at the Celestia, which he called "a thing of great scandal," both for their unauthorized disregard of *clausura* and for wearing lay attire to do it.[306] Instead, the nuns were constrained to act through male intermediaries under the jurisdiction of the procurators of San Marco *de supra* (fig. 190).[307]

Friendship and Patronage

The nuns under Abbess Angela Gradenigo had held a chapter meeting on 30 November 1569 to elect procurators to oversee the process of rebuilding their convent, and named Giorgio (Zorzi) Saler, Gerolamo Dolfin, and Giovanni Paolo Gradenigo.[308] From the ensuing history of the project, it appears that Giorgio Saler had taken a leading role, both in securing the services of Palladio and following through on the construction, and in meeting some of the financial burden that was incurred. Palladio is described as a "friend" (*amico*) of Saler in documents relating to a slightly later project for a *scuola piccola*, the Scuola dei Mercanti at the Madonna dell'Orto, which refer to Giorgio Saler's stewardship of the Celestia.[309]

Giorgio di Nicolò Saler was a member of a family of *cittadini originarii*, as was required of his position as *gastaldo ducale*, to which he had been elected in 1558 under Doge Lorenzo Priuli (1556–59) and confirmed by three *avogadori di comun* (state's advocates, or attorneys).[310] The *gastaldo ducale* was part of the judiciary, and one of the important roles was as custodian of the Cancelleria Inferiore (lower, or notarial chancery).[311] The Saler family seems to have been pursuing a rise in status from at least mid-century, when Giorgio's father, Nicolò di Giacomo (Jacopo), received recognition of their *cittadinanza originaria* in 1553 for himself (at age 70) and his five sons.[312] The family had originally come from Chioggia and were predominantly merchants, with some members rising to positions of worth in the state bureaucracy, as with Giorgio. They boasted a coat of arms bearing a black, half-length he-goat rampant on a field of yellow over three yellow roundels on a field of black. Wills and tax declarations indicate prosperity rather than wealth, largely in properties on the *terraferma*, and with a *casa* in *contra* Santa Marina in Venice, but substantial contributions of time and money may be inferred from the active roles played by Giorgio and his brothers in religious and charitable institutions in Venice, including the Celestia.[313] Giorgio, for example, was also procurator for San Giovanni Elemosinario and for the Scuola di Mercanti at Madonna dell'Orto (where he fulfilled various positions in its governance – as did his brothers – including the equivalent of *guardian grande*, called *governatore*, in 1567), and was a member of the Scuola Grande di Santa Maria della Carità.[314] Several sisters were nuns, including one at the Celestia. The Saler family was said to have a memorial in San Francesco della Vigna, but the family chapel in the new church of the Celestia would mark their most prominent achievement – now lost, except for records of its inscriptions. Giorgio Saler's association with Palladio for the rebuilding of the convent has, at least, restored notice of this citizen family.

Most scholars rightly disavow much in the way of direct design participation by Palladio, who was likely consulted for his expertise in assessing the structural situation and constrained to reuse and restore as much as possible, to minimize expenses and time in returning the nuns to their convent. This may explain why the cloister follows older monastic traditions of arcades carried on columns, although they are punctuated here with banded rusticated corner piers, a sixteenth-century touch (see fig. 184).[315] The procurators Saler and Dolfin entered into an agreement with a wall mason on 16 January 1570, six weeks after their election, which argues for a basic analysis already having been obtained from Palladio, who is named in the contract as having oversight for the trueness of the walls, the way in which the terracotta pilasters were to be made, "facendo le fasse, rigoloni et pilastri di terra cotta nel modo che gli sarà ordinato da messer Andrea Paladio," for the number of bricklayers to be hired, and for the final cost estimate with the procurators.[316] The wallmason was Angelo da Corticelle (Anzolo da Corteselle) di Matthio, who was not so obscure as some have declared, having competed for the opening for *proto al sal* in 1554.[317] Angelo da Corticelle may also have had a reputation as an expert in structural work, since he would also reappear to give his opinion a few years later after two disastrous fires in the Doge's Palace, where Palladio would again be consulted. A more extensive

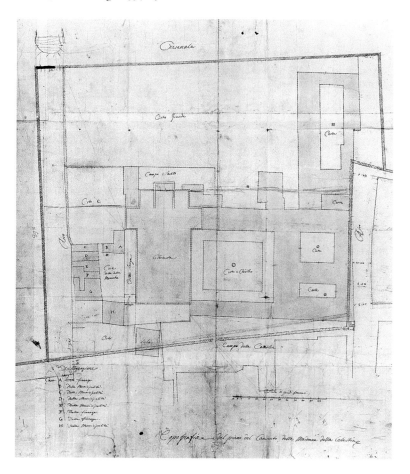

190 Giovanni Casoni, plan of La Celestia, Venice, Biblioteca del Museo Civico Correr, Cod. Cicogna 3341/3

intervention by Palladio might have been planned at the Celestia, but interrupted by Giorgio Saler's early death on 15 November 1571 at the age of 53, as was the timely completion of the cloister.[318]

On 9 December, one month after Saler's death, representatives from the Collegio reported on the progress that had been made at the Celestia.[319] Together with the *provveditori sopra i monasterii* they had visited in September, and found thirty to thirty-two rooms were habitable and safe, having been made quickly using the old walls restored after the fire. They agreed, however, that this was not enough to provide the necessary sequestered accommodations for the nuns, appropriate to their "honestà et dignità," particularly with the workers still present. Giorgio had assured them that all would be ready by Christmas, but his death put his design in jeopardy ("se la morte non havesse interrotto questo suo disegno"). On the previous Sunday, the same representatives had again gone to the site and met with those for the nuns, who requested a delay until the following Easter for their relocation, also citing a problem with the financing for a shorter period. There is an implication that more funding – perhaps an additional benefactor – needed to be found to complete Saler's plan ("ma restandosi hora dal lavoriero per mancamento de dinaro in modo che con difficoltà potranno fornir quella parte dissegnata dal Saler se non fanno altro provisione"). In fact, as we already know, the nuns did not return that Easter in 1572, but only the following spring. No further motions have come to light to show what measures were taken by the Collegio, but the lost inscriptions in the Saler chapel tell us that Giovanni Antonio (Zuan Antonio) Saler stepped in for his deceased brother to complete the rebuilding, thus keeping it in the family.[320] Was the conservative nature of the new cloister not, in fact, due to Angelo da Corticelle, but rather to Giorgio Saler, whose friendship with Palladio was in part due to an interest in architectural design? The Celestia may represent some insight into such a collaboration between the architect and his citizen friend in the particular environment of a female monastic institution in the sixteenth-century Venetian State.

PART V

THE VENETIAN STATE

facing page Palma il Giovane, *Arrival of Henri III at Palazzo Foscari* (detail of fig. 221)

INTRODUCTION

PALLADIO'S STATURE AS AN ARCHITECT, exemplified in the important ecclesiastical commissions he had gained from the mid-1560s, was recognized by the State, although he never received the type of public and domestic projects that had established Jacopo Sansovino. Nor did he succeed to the position of the *proto* for the Procurators of San Marco after Sansovino's death in 1570, whose charge of the Basilica and buildings in the Piazza had given Sansovino's career security and continuity. On the other hand, like Sansovino, Palladio competed for independent commissions under the control of the Salt Office (Ufficio del Sal), which had wide jurisdiction over State building in Venice, including the Doge's Palace. Generally, the Salt Office would propose the need for a building project; the Senate would nominate a small group of magistrates (*provveditori*) to make decisions for the specific project, which would then be funded out of the Salt Office, subject to the approval of the Council of Ten (Consiglio dei Dieci), who handled State security and finance. Because of the large numbers of buildings overseen by the Salt Office throughout the city, it had its own *proto* who bore varying degrees of responsibility for any given project. The rotation of the magistrates of the Salt Office meant that a designing architect's supporters might not see a project through, in contrast to the unique circumstances of procurators, who were elected for life. Also, since several government bodies were involved in the decision-making process, these groups might be composed of patricians with very different leanings, which could affect the project's progress.

Palladio's greatest successes in State patronage came during the 1570s while Alvise di Tomaso Mocenigo was doge (1570–77). This was a period in which Venice was undergoing a dramatic transformation, pressured by changes in Europe and the Levant – by the French wars of religion, revolt in the Netherlands, and Turkish control in the Mediterranean. Venice began the decade with the victory at the Battle of Lepanto in 1571 and the visit of the French king, Henri III, in 1574, but suffered fires in the Doge's Palace in both 1574 and 1577, and succumbed to the horrors of the plague of 1576, for deliverance from which the Senate vowed to build a church to the Redeemer. Palladio found architectural opportunities in both triumph and disaster, from interventions in the Doge's Palace (fig. 191) to his most significant commission from the State for this votive church, Il Redentore.

191   Andrea Palladio, column capital of portal to Anticollegio, Sala delle Quattro Porte, Doge's Palace, Venice

192   Andrea Palladio, *Early Project for the Rialto Bridge*, Vicenza, Museo Civico, D 25

CHAPTER ELEVEN

COMPETITIONS

IF PALLADIO HAD THOUGHT TO ESTABLISH HIMSELF under State patronage in Venice when he unsuccessfully ran for *proto* of the Salt Office in 1554, there is no record of his having attempted it again when it became vacant. The ambitions that initially drew him to Venice at this time may have been sparked by a competition sponsored by the Salt Office for a new bridge and market-stall complex in the commercial and financial heart of the city at the Rialto (fig. 192). Although the design was awarded to Sansovino, nothing came of his bridge. A year later, Palladio lost another project, again to Sansovino who was teamed with Michele Sanmicheli, for the Scala d'Oro in the Doge's Palace, which also came under the Salt Office's control. Another campaign to pursue the Rialto bridge took place around 1565, but again was not implemented.

Drawings reveal Palladio's conception for both phases of the bridge, and his later designs are presented in the *Four Books*. Palladio's projects for the State share an ideal vision of urban architecture executed on a grand scale. While his schemes were admired for these very qualities, the more pragmatic concerns of the Venetian magistrates predominated when it came to making choices. In the end, Palladio's paper project for the Rialto bridge took its place only in the imaginary cityscapes of Francesco Guardi and Antonio Canaletto in the eighteenth century.

Early Projects for the Rialto

The ambitions that drew Palladio to Venice encompassed public architecture as well as domestic. Palladio, though, despite the quality of his patrons, had no entrée comparable to that by which Sansovino had gained his position in the late 1520s as *proto* to the Procurators of San Marco – and which he still held. Other State enterprises required a supervising architect, however, and the Senate's decision to form a magistracy to oversee the renovation of

the Rialto complex attracted attention beyond the capital. This was indeed the case earlier in the century when in 1524, as major rebuilding undertaken in the aftermath of the great fire of 1514 was nearing completion, it was first proposed to draw up a commission to remake the wood bridge in stone; this demonstrated both a concern for the security of the sole bridge over the Grand Canal and for the prestige of the area.[1] The very origins of the city were connected to this location; its earliest church survived here, and the marketplace comprised not only the bustling stalls of vendors but banking, commerce, and trade.[2] Several State agencies were housed at Rialto, some recently refurbished, such as the palace of the Camerlenghi (State Treasurers), and others in need of it.

The care of these buildings fell under the competency of the Salt Office, which was responsible for most State construction projects in Venice, including the Mint (la Zecca) and the Doge's Palace. The large number of buildings that the *proto* of the Salt Office oversaw elevated the authority and importance of this position. What fluctuated much more for the *proto* of the Salt Office, in contrast to the *proto* of the Procurators, was the variability in the degree of involvement in any given project. The *proto al sal* might design a project and follow its execution even to the daily supervision of workers, or a competition might be held by the magistrates, *provveditori*,[3] of the project, which could be won by another architect, with the *proto* entrusted to execute it rather than its author, or it might be that the *proto* was called on to give his expert opinion, *perizia*, about the quality of the work, to propose a solution to a structural problem, or estimate the amount of money that it was worth. The *proto al sal* had expertise, but the Salt Office curtailed his authority, and with it the notion of authorship developing in the architectural profession in the sixteenth century. The position of the Salt Office *proto*, nonetheless, influenced architectural development in Venice because of its extensive responsibilities and its conservative nature. Like the *proto* of Vincenzo Scamozzi's description (*L'idea dell'architettura universale*, Venice, 1615), it functioned in the guild and

193 Antonio Canaletto,
*Capriccio with Palladian
Buildings*, Parma, Galleria
Nazionale

craft tradition, rather than in the academic and scientific. Vernacular style was more accessible to its practitioners, even as that style became more classical through the presence of works by architects such as Sansovino and Sanmicheli, who, although *proto* and *inzegnere* (engineer) themselves, had more humanist conceptions of the profession, which their magistracies were able to support.

The *provveditori sopra la fabbrica del Rialto* decided to hold a competition for the new bridge and market-stall complex soon after their election in 1551,[4] but it was not until three years later that any decisions were made. According to Marc'Antonio Barbaro (1518–1598), who would follow his elder brother Daniele as indispensable patron and friend of Palladio, plans and models had been sent by architects from all over Italy in 1554.[5] From this, and a later passage in Scamozzi's *L'idea*, several drawings by Palladio are thought to date to this early phase of the project (see fig. 192); whereas a second phase seems to date very shortly before the drawings' publication in the *Four Books* in 1570 (Bk. 3, ch. 13, 25–27), "the design of the following bridge is particularly beautiful and well suited to the site on which it was to be built; it was in the middle of the city which is one of the largest and most impressive in Italy and the mother city of many other cities; there is an enormous amount of traffic there from practically every corner of the globe."[6] Since we have no drawn evidence for Sansovino's projects, Palladio's invention has held particular sway in the imagination of an urban fabric, as visually demonstrated by its inclusion in several well-known fantastic reconstructions of Venetian and Vicentine scenes in the genre of the *capriccio*, as painted by Canaletto (fig. 193) and Guardi.[7] Sansovino's participation is suggested by the statement of his son, which blames the War of Cyprus for halting the project, based on Sansovino's winning model, therefore around 1570: "And in our times, it was decided to make it [Rialto bridge] of marble,

and therefore several models were composed, that of Sansovino prevailed over the others, as the most convenient, and beautiful for such a structure, but with the war with the Turks arising in the year 1570, the enterprise remained unfinished."[8] In 1553–54 the Rialto magistrates, however, moved forward only with the project for the new vendors' stalls, selecting the model of Sansovino, now known as the Fabbriche Nuove.[9] A number of Sansovino's strong supporters among the Procurators were active on other State building enterprises as well; these patricians remained intensely interested in the continued *renovatio urbis*, even after the death of Doge Gritti in 1538, and had accrued expertise and judgment that led to their being elected to such committees. Both procurators Vettor Grimani and Antonio Capello had served as *provveditori sopra la fabbrica del Palazzo*, for example, from 1550 to 1553 and 1553 to 1554 respectively, contemporary to their election to the Rialto magistracy, where they were crucial to Sansovino's initial success.[10] The history of the project, however, illustrates the tortuous process that constrained this magistracy, resulting in limitations on Sansovino's participation. Deborah Howard first discussed this as a symptom of a larger conflict between the procurators and the *provveditori di Zecca* in the mid-1550s, which had also manifested itself in the Piazza.[11]

Competition for the Proto al Sal

Another factor that may have caused a delay on decisions on the bridge in the years 1553–54 was the death of the *proto al sal*, Giovan Antonio Rossi, by 11 January 1554, when a competition was held to replace him.[12] Rossi's predecessor in the office, Antonio Abbondi, "lo Scarpagnino" (1517–49), had been *proto* for more than thirty years, and had achieved a high degree of authority and patrician patronage during that time, to a level exceeded only by Sansovino and Sanmicheli, and in some ways was even more ubiquitous in creating an architectural presence in the city. In his position as *proto al sal* Scarpagnino had been called to judge or execute Sansovino's work on various occasions, and the Salt Office depended on having their own expert with whom they were in agreement. Not until the 1560s would they find another architect of similar weight in Antonio da Ponte, who would gain his name and reputation from the bridge when finally erected (1588–91, with Antonio Contin), by then in competition with a new cast of characters, including Vincenzo Scamozzi (which lends his remarks in *L'idea* about the history of the project a special interest).[13] We learn from the *prova* of 1554 for the post of *proto al sal* that Antonio da Ponte, listed as *marangon* (carpenter), competed at that time, as did a number of other aspirants of varying trades, including one "maistro Andrea Palladio vensentin architetto." Neither were successful; when the decision was announced on 19 January, with the imprimatur of Giacomo (Jacopo) Pisani, one of the *provveditori del sal*, Piero Picolo (Piero de Guberni), formerly *proto alle acque*, had won.

Although Palladio's loss in this competition is, on the one hand symbolic of the general lack of success he would have in establishing himself in an official post for civic architecture in Venice, on the other there is a pragmatic explanation. The former rationale has been attributed to several reasons, among them that Palladio's relatively new-found stature in the Veneto had yet to translate into the capital; his patrons were not dominant in the crucial offices to promote him; and fundamentally his (and his patrons') idea of architecture ran contrary to the tradition of *proto* – not yet as evident as the first two factors, although it would later overtake them.[14] As to the latter explanation, given the prominence of the Rialto bridge project for the Salt Office at this time, the choice of the former *proto* for the Waterways Board would be logical, since this magistracy was also heavily involved in the reshaping of the area, contingent as it was on regulating both the water traffic and modifying the *riva* (street along the riverbank).

Competition for the Scala d'Oro

The next year, Palladio entered another State competition, and was again unsuccessful. Deliberations over the new stairway to be constructed in the Doge's Palace had begun in the fall of 1554, and four projects were chosen by the *provveditori sopra la fabbrica del Palazzo* to be presented to the Collegio.[15] Palladio's was one of the four, together with Sansovino who entered (presumably) with Michele Sanmicheli, Piero Picolo, now *proto al sal*, and a future colleague of Palladio, Giovanni Antonio Rusconi. This was a new group of *provveditori* who had replaced those mentioned earlier: Alvise Contarini, Alvise di Giovanni Mocenigo, and Benedetto Pesaro. Not surprisingly, Sansovino's and Sanmicheli's project for what would become known as the Scala d'Oro (Golden Stairway, after its rich gilded stucco decoration) won a majority of fifteen votes, but Palladio came in second with eight votes to Picolo's five and Rusconi's four. Of the little we know about Palladio's project, one thing seems typical of his practice: he did not shrink from requiring some structural modifications, which the others avoided.[16] Another factor to remember here is that even though Palladio did not get this commission, his work was brought to the attention of the select governing body of the Collegio: the doge, his councilors (*consiglieri ducali*, representatives for each of the six *sestieri*, or districts), and the three heads of the Council of Forty (*capi della Quarantia*) who comprised the Signoria, which together with the principal ministers (six *savi grandi* or *savi del Consiglio*, five *savi di terraferma* [Mainland], and five *savi ai ordini* [Marine]), made up the Full College (Pien Collegio). These officials presided over the business brought before the Senate (Consiglio dei Pregadi), which itself was elected from the Great Council (Maggior Consiglio), to which all eligible male patricians of age had the right to belong. One of the developments from the time of the League of Cambrai had been the strengthening of the powers of the Council of Ten and its Zonta (additional group of fifteen), which became associated with the growing oligarchic tendencies during the sixteenth century; decisions involving finance could be directed to the Ten, bypassing the Senate, which made its three heads (*capi del Consiglio dei Dieci*), together with the doge, ducal councilors, and *savi grandi*, the most powerful men in the government.[17] So, in addition to the private patrons and their networks, by 1555 Palladio had gained positive public notice among the decision-makers of the Republic. While this led to his being consulted by various State agencies for his expert opinion, he did not receive significant commissions until the 1570s, after the death of Sansovino and under the dogeship of Alvise Mocenigo.

CHAPTER TWELVE

TOMB OF DOGE ALVISE MOCENIGO

THE ATTRIBUTION TO PALLADIO OF the initial design of a tomb project for Doge Alvise Mocenigo (1570–77) in the Dominican church of Santi Giovanni e Paolo (San Zanipolo)[18] touches on issues of the sacrality of the State and of the preservation of that office through public ritual observances (figs. 194–96). No longer were dogal burials allowed in the State chapel of San Marco; consequently, the number of their tomb monuments located in Santi Giovanni e Paolo made it a "pantheon" of the doges.[19] Just as the doges used their private wealth to embellish the Doge's Palace, so they financed their own burial sites. The elevation of the family through its connection to dogal status is a theme that receives heightened expression in this composite homage to dynastic ambitions, and reflects contemporary tensions inherent in the conception of the doge in the Republic.[20] Moreover, the success that Palladio experienced in acquiring important commissions from the State during Mocenigo's tenure may be associated with his style as a bearer of such meaning, and equally account for the problematics of its adoption as an architectural language acceptable to those concerned with the preservation of a less overt oligarchy.

Alvise, knight and procurator *de ultra*, born in 1507 to Procurator Tomaso and grandson to another procurator, Lunardo Mocenigo, in direct descent from the line of two brother doges, was doge of Venice in a period that can be characterized as decisive for Venice's entry into the modern era.[21] His election, following on a severe famine, a damaging fire in the Arsenale, the loss of Nicosia, all in 1569, and increasingly pressing Turkish claims to Cyprus, was no doubt due to his resolution to combat this last threat, promising the people to "administer justice, and abundance with all his power, but this being a time of war, not to promise peace, and to persuade all to join in this war with the Turks for the conservation and defense of the State, and to increase the Christian faith," as well as to a perceived ability to manage the State in perilous times being a "man of great valor and experience in the management of the Republic."[22] The last quarter of the sixteenth century saw a shift in the fortunes of Venice, from triumph to crisis management, epitomized in the visual imagery associated with Doge Mocenigo. Expression ranged from celebration, with the victory over the seemingly invincible Ottoman navy at Lepanto, to propitiation, with raging plague leading to the doge's vow to build Andrea Palladio's church of Il Redentore. Disastrous fires in the Doge's Palace destroyed major works by Venetian artists; new works were created to honor the visiting French prince, Henri III, with all the pomp and splendor of this ritual-minded Republic. Mocenigo's dogate was the crucial period of Palladio's involvement with State patronage.

The culturally constructed identity of Alvise Mocenigo as doge and as princely representative of his house, or *casa*, was molded through a variety of representations. The chroniclers' tendency to compile a portrait of a doge as the sum of the events in his reign was not entirely superseded by the practice of humanist historiography in sixteenth-century Venice, and Mocenigo's was particularly turbulent: "there seemed to be no kind of ill luck or catastrophe that had failed to descend on our country under his ill-starred auspices. For it had suffered great losses of cities and whole kingdoms, fires, floods, famines, and at last the most terrible pestilence."[23] Certain roles were thrust upon him, while in other cases he was in control of the imagery by which he would be remembered; the contrast between the content of official votive portraits of the doge and those made to display his dynastic ambitions captures some of the ambiguity and tension that were never entirely reconciled in the rhetorical descriptions of the perfect and balanced society of the Republic. Mocenigo himself embodied the changes deepening in the patriciate in just this moment. His enormous wealth, and broad interests on the *terraferma*, confirmed his status as one of the *primi della terra*, "first in the land," indispensable to high office and associated with the increased aristocratization of the post-Cambrai polity, usually equated with the informal political set of the *vecchi*.[24] The verdant background of the votive painting seen by Carlo

195   Pietro Lombardo, tomb monument of Doge Pietro Mocenigo, interior façade, Santi Giovanni e Paolo, Venice

196   Attributed to Tullio Lombardo with Antonio Lombardo, tomb monument of Doge Giovanni Mocenigo, interior façade, Santi Giovanni e Paolo, Venice

Ridolfi in the Mocenigo Palace called the *casa vecchia* at San Samuele depicts the family landed patrimony and lines of dynastic inheritance established by the doge (*Doge Alvise Mocenigo and Family before the Madonna and Child*) through his brother Giovanni's sons (fig. 197).[25] His autocratic persona was said to have been founded on an abhorrence of trade and study of the lives of kings and princes, which contributed to his success as governor and ambassador: "he was feared on account of his great authority and eloquence. Indeed, he used this authority a trifle more severely than was appropriate to a commonwealth, and to a Republic more inclined to honour its Prince as a representative of itself than to obey him on account of his personal standing."[26] Yet he was thought to be no friend of the pope, a trait associated by scholars with the incipient development of the *giovani*. What Mocenigo and his successor but one as doge, Nicolò da Ponte (1578–85), may represent

is a transitional period, capable of entertaining diverse allegiances with the pragmatic goal of furthering Venetian interests in both the *stato da mar* and *da terra*.[27] Mocenigo's willingness to enter into the Holy League with the pope and king of Spain against the Turks in 1571 was offset by Venice's agreement to a separate peace with the Turks in 1573. If there was a cultural program expressed in the decisions made by those associated with this set, it was a cult of *venezianità alla romana*, a celebration of Venetian identity that continued to promote the image of empire, even as it was being curtailed in the East and turning west to a Europe dominated by the powers of France, Spain, and the Empire.[28] Viewed from this perspective, Mocenigo's acts of representation take on another resonance, as precursors to the subsequent constructions of self and dogal institution to meet an age of change that characterized Venice in the early modern period.

197   Jacopo Tintoretto with studio, *Doge Alvise Mocenigo and Family before the Madonna and Child*, Washington, National Gallery of Art, Samuel H. Kress Collection (1961.9.44)

The tomb monument of Doge Alvise Mocenigo and his wife, Loredana di Alvise di Zan Francesco Marcello, on the interior façade of the church is conceptually bold in its proclamation of dogal dynasty, since it is allied with the tombs on either side of two of the three members of the *casa* Mocenigo to precede him in that honor and be buried in Santi Giovanni e Paolo (fig. 198). The implication of unity through the architectural enframement supports Howard Burns's attribution to Palladio of elements of the design of the realized monument; only Palladio's own designs for other combined multiple tomb monuments match the power of this retrospective iconography. The silence of contemporary sources and its ultimate execution by others indicate, however, the strict limits of Palladio's direct involvement; it may have extended no further than a quick sketch, as in the idea for a double tomb similarly raised on pedestals with an attic story topped by a pediment that Burns has associated with another dogal project for the Priuli brothers, Doges Lorenzo (1556–59) and Gerolamo (1559–67), in San Salvador (fig. 200).[29]

Doge Mocenigo had acquired permission to erect a tomb in 1572, providing a *terminus post quem*, and his will of 1574 specified his desire that it be begun within his lifetime, or two years of his death, failing which, the money invested in the *zecca* (mint) for its execution would revert to charity.[30] Excluding completely the heavy central tabernacle of the top story, Burns found compelling analogies to Palladio's late style in the tomb types, with the treat-

ment of the orders whose pedestals form the basement, their profile moldings, and the use of antique motifs for the tabernacles between columns, such as studies of the Porta Aurea in Ravenna (Vicenza, Museo Civico, D 31r [fig. 199]).[31]

Execution of the work was begun, attributed to Girolamo Grapiglia (who later worked on the interior of San Pietro di Castello), but halted in 1580 when a lawsuit was brought by the Bragadin family protesting the engulfment of Bartolomeo Bragadin's tomb on the lower right side of the portal. The present monument was completed only in 1646, by Francesco Contin, following numerous complaints about the construction materials impeding the entrance area.[32] Francesco Sansovino's description of 1581 may indicate that the tombs at least were done by 1580, which dates them before Palladio's death: "Luigi Mocenigo Doge 84 elected in 1570 reposes over the major interior portal with Lauredana Marcello his consort. This lady of much valor predeceased her husband by some years." Such a minimal description contrasts with Giustiniano Martinioni's addition of 1663, which describes the recently completed inclusive monument of the "Casa Mocenigo" as "majestic and notable."[33]

The figurative program incorporates references to the personal achievements of Doge Alvise Mocenigo's reign, as well as to the Mocenigo as a *casa ducale*. The tomb adopts the iconographic innovation of the addition of a ducal *corno* to the family coat of arms, which is held by angels in a lunette over the central portal, and was

198 (?)Andrea Palladio, realized by Girolamo Grapiglia, and Francesco Contin, tomb monument of Alvise Mocenigo and Loredana Marcello, center of interior façade, Santi Giovanni e Paolo, Venice

199 (*below*) Andrea Palladio, *Drawing of the Porta Aurea, Ravenna,* Vicenza, Museo Civico, D 31, detail

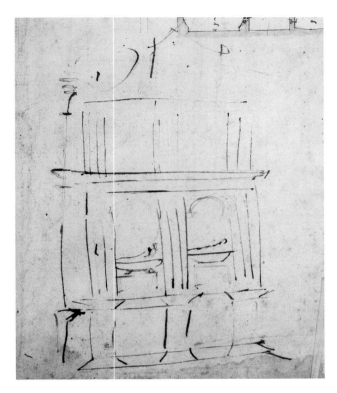

200 Andrea Palladio, sketch for a double tomb, London, Royal Institute of British Architects, IX, 14, detail

first used by Alvise's ancestor, Doge Tommaso Mocenigo (1414–23), for his tomb on the right nave wall.[34] Recumbent figures of Alvise and his wife, Loredana, mirror each other on sarcophagi in tabernacles in the outer bays of the upper story, both adorned with the ducal *corno*. Although the War of Cyprus had prevented Loredana's coronation as dogaressa, her funeral rituals in 1572 were described as being dogal in scale and grandeur (fig. 201); furthermore, Alvise's

201 *Funeral Bier of Loredana Marcello Mocenigo*, Venice, Archivio di Stato, Collegio, Cerimoniale I, 41v

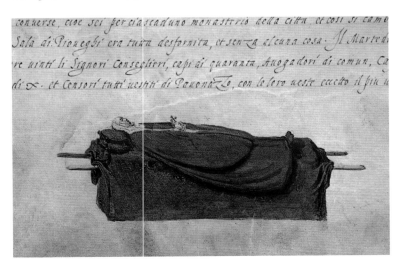

wills leave little doubt that they shared "no ordinary love, but rather one that was excessive and greatly extraordinary."[35] The deliberately planned proximity to the tomb monument of Doge Giovanni Mocenigo (1478–85) on the right and that of Doge Pietro Mocenigo (1474–76) on the left underscores Alvise's direct descent from the ducal line of the former of the brother doges.[36] The subsequent appropriation of two statues of saints, *Mark* and *George*, from Doge Pietro's tomb monument for the lower side bay niches between paired pilasters of Alvise's, further emphasizes the connection, which extends to the implication of a shared tradition of family glory in the defense of Venice in the Levant. The tomb monument of Doge Pietro Mocenigo introduced the concept of biographical representation of political events during the reign of the deceased to the ducal tomb type, with reliefs of *Pietro Mocenigo Restores the Kingdom of Karaman* and *Consigning the Keys of Famagusta to Queen Caterina Corner*.[37] The biographical elements in Alvise's tomb monument are more ambiguous in their reference to explicit events (deliberately, I would suggest), and present different aspects of his role as doge. The right-hand relief shows the *Doge Receiving Arnoldo Du Ferrier, Ambassador of the King of France*, which could refer both to the French negotiations toward the Peace of Cyprus and to the prestigious visit of Henri III in July 1574, and probably can be assigned subsequent to that date: the doge's diplomatic role as symbolic head of state is emphasized, as is Venice's special relation with France.[38] The left-hand relief of the *Doge Kneeling at Prayer with his Councilors* also refers to the doge in his public, ceremonial role as intercessor rather than his private devotional self, as evidenced by the inclusion of his councilors and his ducal *corno* on the pillow; the subject could as easily allude to his thanks on behalf of the Holy League in 1571 as to prayers for relief from the plague in 1576. Recently, the dogal figures and these two reliefs over the side tabernacles in the lower story have been attributed to Giulio del Moro (*circa* 1580), and the standing figures on the upper story, identified as Christ the Redeemer in the center tabernacle flanked by St. Peter and the Virgin on the extended column pedestals, as being by Francesco Cavrioli (*circa* 1646).[39] Taken together, these figures may represent the Holy League, with Peter symbolizing Rome, the Redeemer (to whom the fleet at Lepanto was dedicated under the banner of Captain Don Juan of Austria) Spain, and the Virgin Venice, and thus the victory that was the high point of Mocenigo's reign, and programmatically coherent with the dogal *virtùs* expressed in the reliefs.

The problem of making direct iconographical references from the figurative program to salient events in Mocenigo's dogate is, however, exemplified in the debate over the meaning of his votive painting in the Sala del Collegio in the Doge's Palace. The original meaning of the painting that was probably intended to be placed over the tribune alluded to the victory at Lepanto, as Staale Sinding-Larsen has shown in his analysis of the *modello*, specifically citing the presence of war galleys in the Bacino (fig. 202); by the time of its delayed execution due to the fire of 1574, however, both the subject and tribune location had been taken already for Mocenigo's successor, Doge Sebastian Venier (1577–78), who had

202 Jacopo Tintoretto, *modello* for the *Votive Painting of Doge Alvise Mocenigo Presented to the Redeemer*, New York, The Metropolitan Museum of Art, John Stewart Kennedy Fund, 1910. (10.206)

203 Jacopo Tintoretto and studio, *Votive Painting of Doge Alvise Mocenigo Presented to the Redeemer*, Sala del Collegio, Doge's Palace, Venice

been the Captain General of the Venetian forces at Lepanto.[40] The figures and background of the *Votive Painting of Doge Alvise Mocenigo Presented to the Redeemer* were adjusted, eliminating the galleys, but including an allegorical figure of Victory, St. Mark, Christ the Redeemer, and patron saints of the Mocenigo family (fig. 203).[41] The result is a more ambiguous reading, like the relief of the doge at prayer on the Mocenigo tomb, one that more generally signifies the doge's ceremonial role as intercessor for the Venetian State.[42] There is, however, another unmistakable message through an innovation in the iconography of the votive painting with the unusual representation of the doge's male relatives. Doge Alvise's two brothers, Giovanni (Zuanne) of San Samuele and Nicolò of San Stae, were both active in government, with the former "dogabile" in the elections of 1578, lending the votive painting subversive overtones of dogal dynasty that are shared in the program of the combined Mocenigo tomb.[43]

Lack of explicit documentation forces a cautious assessment of the direct patronage of Palladio by Alvise Mocenigo for projects intended for his private palace and family tomb monument. Alvise's position as doge presents a similar problem for his patronage of Palladio as a State artist. Dogal involvement in State projects was usually indirect, since they were carried out through magistracies, such as the Procurators of San Marco and the Salt Office, but explicit cases of patronage did occur: for example, Vasari praised Doge Andrea Gritti as "a great patron of genius" for his impact on the Doge's Palace.[44] There are indications, however, of the potential influence of Mocenigo and even direct intervention (extending to personal funding for a public project), as well as the symbolic link of the doge with works carried out during his reign.

CHAPTER THIRTEEN

PROJECTS FOR THE DOGE'S PALACE

FIRES IN VARIOUS AREAS OF THE DOGE'S PALACE in 1574 (beginning in the doge's apartments and moving up to the second *piano nobile*, including parts of the rooms of the Collegio, Anticollegio, Antipregadi – often known as the Sala delle Quattro Porte – and Pregadi – also called the Senato) and in 1577 (notably the Maggior Consiglio, Scrutinio, and Quarantia Civil Nova) destroyed centuries of important programs of civic decoration (fig. 204). The structural stability of the building was thought by Palladio to be seriously undermined by the second fire. The Salt Office was responsible for the maintenance of the Doge's Palace, and in each case followed the procedure of appointing magistrates to oversee the work, *provveditori sopra la fabbrica del Palazzo* (see Appendix II). Palladio's role in the restoration after the fire of 1574 included providing expert advice, in which he was joined by his sometime collaborator Giovanni Antonio Rusconi, an engineer, architect, and Vitruvian theorist. Palladio also provided drawings and models for classical moldings of some elements of the rooms. Palladio and Rusconi were directly responsible to the *provveditori*. The *proto* of the Salt Office, Antonio da Ponte, had oversight of the craftsmen who executed the work, and acted as supervising architect and paymaster, with some projects requiring Palladio and Rusconi as signatories as well. The more extreme nature of the fire of 1577 during the brief dogate of the Lepanto hero Sebastian Venier demanded a correspondingly greater canvassing of experts, whose evaluations of the damage and proposed repairs included reports by both the *proto* of the Salt Office and the *proto* of the Procurators of San Marco, among other *proti*, as well as Palladio. Palladio believed the root of the structural problem lay in its original design and construction. A chronicler's reaction to his solution suggests that his opinion, supported by Marc'Antonio Barbaro, was seen as not respecting the venerated building, and, by extension the Venetian political institutions it housed, and further, as being too expensive in the scope of its restructuring. Palladio was esteemed and his advice requested but not followed, a pattern consistent with his earliest attempts to gain State patronage.

The Fire of 1574

Chroniclers record their shock and distaste, when in 1574 (on 11 May), fire in the Doge's Palace in Venice forced the reigning doge, Alvise Mocenigo, to seek habitation elsewhere: this was *fuori consuetudine*, outside of custom. Most unusually, the doge took refuge in the family palace, or rather, in one of the Palazzi Mocenigo at San Samuele on the Grand Canal, the *casa vecchia*, residence of his brother Giovanni and nephew Thoma.[45] Mocenigo's departure from the dogal precinct violated the identification of the *person* of the doge with the *role* of the doge, which was achieved in part through a physical transference: the removal of the doge to the Doge's Palace for the remainder of his life following his election. Thus isolated from the association of family and place basic to a society centered in concepts of neighborhood, each new doge would join another order of dynastic succession than kinship, that of the State, with its mythic lineage. Yet the individual who became doge also transformed the office, bringing to it the charismatic elements of a personal history, so that it was never stable, but such was necessary for its animation. To lessen the endangerment of the State, the liminal was controlled through law and ceremony: for example, Francesco Sansovino, in his *Venetia, città nobilissima et singolare*, lists a few of the restrictions placed on the doge and his immediate family members, ending with the prohibition on leaving the Dogado without permission from the Great Council, "and, in sum, many other things that he is not able to do, which I will omit for the sake of brevity."[46]

Autonomy presented the clearest rupture with the ideal of the doge. An earlier parallel to Alvise Mocenigo's forced eviction from

204   Ludovico Toeput ("Pozzoserrato"), *Fire in the Doge's Palace*, Treviso, Museo Civico

the Doge's Palace came during the reign of Doge Agostino Barbarigo in 1483, when fire forced the doge and family members to move to the nearby Palazzo Duodo. The notion of establishing a separate residence was then debated but overruled. For those familiar with Venetian history, it will come as no surprise that this radical concept came up again fifty years later under Doge Andrea Gritti, whose reign (1523–38) has been identified with the increasing aristocratization of the patriciate.[47] The issue remained unresolved, and the apartments that Alvise Mocenigo occupied were those renovated under Barbarigo and the successive doges whose *stemmi* reinforce their aggregate nature. The chronicler Girolamo Savina annotated his account of the fire, "Dose scape del pallazzo."[48] There is a slightly accusing tone in recounting the cause of the fire, which resulted from an overheated chimney in the kitchens below the apartments, due, we are led to believe, to the extremely sumptuous banquet preparations. He then drew notice to "the doge, who, having gone out of the palace virtually alone, went to the house of Procurator Da Lezze in the Procuratia accompanied only by a few others; the doge then went to Signor Thomado in the house of Giovanni Mocenigo, Alvise's brother. That same night the ducal councilors determined that the doge must return to the palace, and he duly came back the next day, lodging where the fire damage was less severe." The liminal boundaries had been crossed; such extraordinary circumstances were all the more disruptive because they lacked the protection of ceremony.

Had the plans for the redecoration of the Collegio after the fire of 1574 been carried out as originally envisioned, the dogeship of Alvise Mocenigo would have been more overtly celebrated there, and his identity more prominently associated with one of the crucial rooms of government as commemorated in a contemporary engraving (figs. 205 and 206). Since the intended subject and central

205   Cesare Vecellio, *Tribune Wall in the Sala del Collegio Before the 1574 Fire*, engraved by Lodovico Ziletti, 2nd ed., 1575 (after 1570 ed.), New York, The Metropolitan Museum of Art, Joseph Pulitzer Bequest, 1917 (17.50.71)

206 *(facing page)*   View of Collegio with *banche* and dogal throne attributed to Andrea Palladio, Doge's Palace, Venice

position of Mocenigo's votive painting in the Collegio was taken by Venier, the doge who succeeded him while the work was still in progress, this modified the programmatic emphasis on the former's reign, without, however, sacrificing the content since the victory at Lepanto was included in the later *Votive Painting of Sebastian Venier* over the tribune.

In regard to the overall campaign of restoration following the fire, Lionello Puppi identified the question of "critical and historical importance" as being "what part Palladio may have played in the working out of the programme, which must have been prepared by the stewards [*provveditori*] in collaboration with their advisors, to whom we are not yet able to assign a name."[49] Surviving documents are not very revealing about the exact nature and extent

207a, b, c and d   Giovanni Battista Zelotti, *Allegory of "Aristocrazia,"* ceiling, Sala dell'Albero Genealogico, Castello "il Cataio," Battaglia Terme (near Padua) (*left*), with details showing (?)Pietro Foscari (*below left*), Doge Alvise Mocenigo (*below right*), and Vicenzo Morosini (*facing page left*)

208 Jacopo Tintoretto, *Vicenzo Morosini*, London, National Gallery, Presented by the National Art Collections Fund in commemoration of the Fund's coming of age and the National Gallery Centenary, 1924 (NG4004)

of Palladio's work at the Doge's Palace; the significance of his contribution may, however, as Puppi remarks, lie less in the attribution of specific architectural elements than in the role he had relative to the patricians in charge of its realization, for it suggests a further expansion of the varying degrees of creative relationship between patron and architect already demonstrated in individual cases with his villa clients. Under Doge Mocenigo, Palladio and his supporters would enjoy a favorable situation for State patronage (figs. 207a–d).

An account-book from 21 May 1574 to 26 July 1577 that exists for most of the overall campaign of architectural restoration for the series of rooms damaged by this fire shows some work still unfinished when the next disastrous fire in the palace occurred.[50] In a number of these documents, Palladio and Rusconi are present as *inzegneri* (although only Palladio is also styled *architetto*), who made a direct report to the *provveditori* and received their pay from the cashier of the Salt Office. This is indicative of their independent status and special relation to the *provveditori*, since they did not go through Antonio da Ponte, *proto* for the Salt Office, and by extension, the Palace, who was in charge of the weekly payments (*polizze*) to the various artisans and laborers carrying out the work.[51] Understandably, the first task undertaken was to secure temporary covering for the roof, doors, and window openings. It seems probable that the scope of reconstruction and need for dispatch demanded intense initial consultations on the plan and organization of the campaign between the *provveditori*, *proto del Palazzo*, and "engineers," since by August 1574 both Rusconi and Palladio were already in receipt of payment for their work and stone was arriving.

The overlapping, rather than consecutive, progress of the work in the various rooms argues for the general programs to have been laid out by this time, probably with the expectation that working out the specifics of the iconography would occur as the different elements, such as the cycles of ceiling paintings, were commissioned. A closer look at the individuals nominated as *provveditori* may make unnecessary the assumption of "advisors" other than the *provveditori* themselves for an initial general program for the restoration of 1574, and also suggests that Palladio was chosen for his ability to make a meaningful contribution based on their previous mutual experiences. Acting immediately after the fire, the Senate elected three *provveditori*: Vicenzo K. di Barbon Morosini (figs. 207d and

208), Pietro di Marco Foscari (fig. 207b), and Andrea к. di Pietro Badoer; a year later, in 1575, Marc'Antonio Barbaro replaced Badoer, who had been named ambassador to France.[52] It should be recognized that Barbaro, therefore, was not a part of this initial decisive phase, and it places more importance on Andrea Badoer; Barbaro's election in place of Badoer, however, as will be shown, provided a continuity of expertise sympathetic to the original group of *provveditori* aims, and this can best be supported by a closer look at these particular patricians.

Of the original three *provveditori*, only Pietro Foscari would be elected to the same role for the fire of 1577 while still engaged in completing the campaign from the earlier fire, an indication of his pivotal role in the eyes of his peers. Francesco Sansovino's limited biographical information confirms this, for there he is described as an art expert:

> About the Foscari palace at San Simeone [see fig. 65]: beautiful in appearance and with diverse ornaments. Pietro Foscari, Senator of remarkable spirit delighting himself with the beauty of sculpture and of painting, as a lover of foreign and domestic arts, not only decorated and restored the above palace, but made famous another of his palaces situated in the Arena in Padua, distinguished lodging of the king of France.[53]

Furthermore, it can be shown that Foscari was not only related in some way to all the other *provveditori*, including Barbaro, but to the doge as well, linking Mocenigo, himself an acknowledged intellectual, more closely to the program. Contemporaries often complained about the pernicious influence of family connections, "prevalent among us are bonds of friendship, obligation, and family, facilitating the few."[54] Many of the affinal ties linking Foscari to the other *provveditori* were through female members of their families and it has been shown that such "bilateral links" had become even more crucial in the so-called Third Serrata at the beginning of the sixteenth century as systems of reciprocal obligations.[55] These same ties also connect Palladio to Foscari through close patrons (see Appendix III).[56]

Pietro Foscari was related to the doge through his son Gerolamo's marriage into Alvise Mocenigo's immediate family (to Chiara, daughter of the childless doge's closest brother Giovanni). Pietro's career, while it did not display the diplomatic scope of his father Marco's, reflected a solid record of senatorial posts. Pietro Foscari's degree of contact with the doge is symbolically represented in the inclusion of both his and Alvise Mocenigo's portraits in the painting cycle by Giam Battista Zelotti commissioned by the *condottiere* Pio Enea degli Obizzi for his villa, Castello "il Cataio," at Battaglia Terme in the Paduan area of the Euganean Hills (fig. 206). This was probably occasioned by Foscari's support while *capitano* of Padua in 1571 and again while one of the doge's senior counselors, as *savi del Consiglio*, in 1576, when Obizzi was named *collaterale generale* of Venetian forces, a period during which Foscari remained fully engaged in the restoration of the Doge's Palace.[57]

Again through his son, Pietro Foscari's kinship relations also reveal close proximity to important patrons of Palladio, raising the likelihood of his cultural predisposition to favor the architect's intervention in the Doge's Palace – particularly as a connoisseur of the classical. His son Gerolamo was prior of the Compagnia della Calza degli Accesi (see fig. 64) when Palladio had designed the theater *all'antica* for them in 1565 (and the Accesi had commissioned Rusconi as well for a design for the performance of 1564 in honor of the Duke of Urbino).[58]

The important social and political ties formed by these youth groups have already been discussed, and Pietro's connections to another *provveditore*, Andrea Badoer, can be traced again through his son. Gerolamo's contemporaries in the Accesi, of the generation born *circa* 1540, included several offspring of three brothers of *provveditore* Andrea Badoer (his heirs, in fact): Alberto di Angelo,[59] and Marc'Antonio di Francesco, also officers of the Accesi (respectively *istitutore* and *camerlengo*), and Piero di Gian Alvise.[60] Some scholars have claimed that the Accesi was a continuation of the earlier Compagnia di Cortesi, whose noble members were said to be *di primi della terra* – first in the land). The Cortesi was founded by Francesco di Piero Badoer (Andrea's brother) with his brother-in-law, Giorgio di Gian Francesco Loredan; this connection also brought both Badoer brothers into the sphere of the Corner della Regina – along with the Grimani, premier commissioners of *alla romana* architecture in Venice and the Veneto – through marriage.[61] Even more to the point, Palladio had designed the graceful Villa Badoer at Fratta Polesine for Andrea's brother Francesco (died 1572), which makes Badoer another likely supporter for Palladio's architectural program (see fig. 69).

Pietro Foscari could similarly find such a direct link to Palladio and his patrons on the *terraferma* among his close relatives. As already pointed out in Part II, his brother-in-law was Vettor di Giovanni Pisani, who was the architect's first Venetian patron for his villa at Bagnolo di Lonedo, thought to have been commissioned on the occasion of his marriage to Paola di Marco Foscari in 1542 (see fig. 6).[62] Through his maternal grandmother, Maria di Zaccaria к.р. Barbaro (sister of the humanist Ermolao), who married Filippo р. di Giovanni Capello, Pietro also was related to Palladio's crucial Barbaro patrons (and fellow *provveditore*, Marc'Antonio). His marriage to Elena, daughter of Procurator Marco di Gerolamo Grimani, who had resigned the patriarchate of Aquileia in favor of his brother, further brought Pietro into the fold of the Barbaro-Grimani *consorteria*.[63]

The last fellow *provveditore* to be discussed in connection to Pietro, Vicenzo Morosini, turns out to be related by marriage, since Orsa Foscari married his son, Procurator Barbon, who would carry out the family chapel in Palladio's new church of San Giorgio Maggiore. Morosini, too, can be shown to have useful cultural connections[64] (his patronage of Tintoretto has been remarked in relation to that of Doge Mocenigo, Jacopo Contarini, Vettor Pisani[65] – all Palladio supporters – and one of his properties was rented to Paolo Veronese[66]); he already knew Palladio by 1572 when the architect was documented in his house,[67] possibly through his position as general in the defense of the Lido under Doge Mocenigo during the Lepanto crisis.[68] Morosini also knew Andrea Badoer, from their mission together as special ambassadors to congratulate the new pontiff Gregory XIII, Ugo Boncampagni (1572–85).

The choice of Marc'Antonio Barbaro as the successor to Badoer raises some further questions regarding the selection of this group at this time in overseeing the visual programs in architecture, sculpture, and painting that would constitute the expression of Venetian identity in these important rooms of government. Notwithstanding their credentials as art patrons – Marc'Antonio's being well known and Badoer's shown to be at the very least by association – there is also a critical political identification that relates to the doge as well. Both men were intimately involved in the secret negotiations for a separate peace with the Ottomans.[69] Barbaro had been resident in Constantinople from 1568 to 1574, where he was *bailò* (head of the Venetian consulate) for an unusually long period due to the War of Cyprus. In 1573 Badoer was sent out to join Barbaro in Constantinople along with the new *bailò*, couriering the treaty and signing for the peace, spending the next year there until they both returned in 1574. Badoer had been adamantly opposed to the Holy League because of his mistrust of Spain, and can be supposed, therefore, to have welcomed French participation in brokering the final agreement. It seems then that the mindset of 1574–75 was one in which some of the *vecchi, papalisti* among them, could take a pro-French position in support of peace and in opposition to Rome, although growing criticism of the terms would all too soon tarnish the doge and its adherents.

The iconographical programs immediately following the restoration after the fire of 1574 reflect a Venice that was redefining its position in the Mediterranean and at home on the *terraferma*, as well as asserting traditional values as defender of its empire, liberty, and religion, through both its power on sea and land and through peace. This message is clear in the Collegio ceiling, whose three main paintings placed along the center from the Anticollegio to the Tribune show *Mars and Neptune, Faith and Worship*, and *Justice and Peace before Venice Enthroned on the Globe*, the last directly above the doge's seat. These paintings appear to be the earliest ones commissioned as work on the several rooms was progressing, since Paolo Veronese received a payment installment on December 1575. The dating suggests that Barbaro was already working with Foscari and Morosini for this phase. The unusual presence of the arms of these same three *provveditori* in the central oval led one scholar to propose this as evidence of their responsibility for the invention of the program (fig. 209).[70]

There was precedent for patricians to act in this capacity in the Doge's Palace, for example, in the recently completed (1567) decoration by Giuseppe Salviati (della Porta) that had been destroyed in the fire of 1574 in the Sala delle Quattro Porte (or Antipregadi). The short-lived Accademia della Fama had been commissioned by the preceding doge and commissioners to invent a program and choose a painter for a subject that "should signify the power of the State, as it reigns in a virtuous Christian manner, in security and splendor."[71] Associated with the Accademia della Fama were Alvise Mocenigo and Daniele Barbaro; according to Francesco Sansovino, Daniele also had earlier invented the program for the room of the

209 Paolo Veronese, *Faith and Worship*, center ceiling oval, Sala del Collegio, Doge's Palace, Venice

Council of Ten, so it is not hard to imagine his brother Marc' Antonio and fellow *provveditori* in a similar role on the larger scale required by the restoration, or Mocenigo's interest and possible input while doge.[72]

The inclusion of Palladio and Rusconi by the *provveditori* equally seems a deliberate statement, more than simply augmenting the technical expertise of the *proto* da Ponte would account for, particularly since both were acknowledged Vitruvians.[73] This speaks to the collaboration between *provveditori* and architects who not only desired an iconography of subject matter, but of style, in which the classical framework of the architecture would provide a State setting of magnificence interpreted in a language of Roman grandeur. The charge to the *provveditori* was "to remake this Palace honorably and suitable to the public dignity."[74]

210 Doge's Palace, Venice, Sala delle Quattro Porte with ceiling compartments and portals by Andrea Palladio

For the most part, documents do not attribute specific elements of the designs for the refurbishing of the architectural structure and ornament to any of the three architects, so current scholarship is equally conservative, except where further support exists.[75] An exception is the general agreement that surviving evidence does support Palladio's direct involvement in part of the architectural decoration of the Collegio. There is a record of his having supplied a profile template, or *sagoma*, for a cornice believed to be for the elegant raised wood tribune with the dogal throne and the paneled *banche* (benches) along the side walls.[76] Despite the apparent unity of the *banche* and tribune in their materials and gilded decoration, there is a subtle differentiation of their status through their ornament: the more elaborate cornice with its pediment projecting over the dogal throne is framed by two fluted Composite columns, and carved festoons loop between the fluted Composite pilasters that separate the three rectangular panels with their gilded

moldings on either side of the tribune; in harmonious contrast, the *banche* along the wall rhythmically alternate larger and smaller rectangular panels with their gilded moldings framed by fluted Composite pilasters, matched below by alternating *cartelle* between the consoles supporting the bench. The impression is of richness and refinement, and of a grasp of classical detail in the varied modillions and moldings.[77]

Only in the Sala delle Quattro Porte (Antipregadi) is Palladio explicitly named by a contemporary source, Francesco Sansovino, as responsible for designing part of the decoration (fig. 210).[78] Since the author himself claimed responsibility for the *inventione* of the ceiling program, it gives credence to his assigning the *compartimenti* of the ceiling to Palladio, and his attribution of the stuccoes to Bombarda is supported by documentation.[79] Palladio's few statements in the *Four Books* (Bk. 1, ch. 22, 53) regarding ceiling decoration reveal a flexible attitude, born, no doubt, of the necessity to accommodate his patrons, and indicate his understanding that pictures would be placed in compartments of stucco or wood "according to various designs."[80] Mentally stripped of the rich stucco, the framework articulates the vaulted structure, outlining eight pairs of triangular encased lunettes and framing a large central rectangle with large circles at either end connected by pairs of smaller ovals on either side of the circles.[81] The most prominent features of the molding are the recessed rosettes alternating with acanthus-leaf modillions. The geometric shapes form a regular pattern and connect to the other dominating architectural feature of the room, the four portals (which have given it its name), through the alignment of allegorical statues later placed on the columns and cornice of the lintel of the rich marble door frames.

The importance of the decoration of this room is reflected in Foscari's, Morosini's, and Badoer's request to the Senate in September 1574 to allow the architects (proti nostri) to raid the warehouses of the Procuratia de Supra for columns and other marbles, which would be used for the portals of this room and of those connecting it and the Anticollegio, Collegio, and Senato: "for the restoration of our Palace, which, for the dignity of our State must be made even more ornate and noble."[82] The speedy acquisition and adaptation of costly precious colored marble for ten classically framed portals would have been both a logistical and a design challenge; the success by which it was met lends authority to their attribution to Palladio, as do comparisons to examples of his work. The patriarch of Venice, Giovanni Trevisan, was approached by the doge in October the same year to allow the provveditori to acquire columns and other stone needed for the palace from churches and monasteries under his jurisdiction, which he conceded to "expedite" the work with "honor" that was appropriate to the "dignity of the Dominio."[83] Stoneworkers inspected columns at various sites over the next two years, even buying one from Palladio's patron Leonardo Mocenigo κ., but the most difficult problem was no doubt finding the eight columns that needed to be paired in the Sala delle Quattro Porte, which were acquired from the priest at San Zulian (Giuliano) in August 1575.[84] As the columns were brought to the palace, specialists – stonecutters, sculptors, and polishers – worked to adapt their proportions, add bases, pedestals, capitals, and the ornate cornices that would adjust them in proportion to the height of the rooms (figs. 191, 211 and 213). The richness of the Composite capitals in the Sala delle Quattro Porte, and the beauty of the Corinthian capitals of the other rooms, with varying friezes, including a motif of Marcian lion's heads in the Anticollegio, are consistent with the profiles of touchstone buildings in Palladio's Four Books, notably the "Temple of Bacchus" (Santa Costanza, Bk. 4, ch. 21, 87 [fig. 212]) and the Pantheon (Bk. 4, ch. 20, 83 and 84), as well as his own works, such as the refectory vestibule at San Giorgio Maggiore (see fig. 114).[85] The architectural decoration in the Sala delle Quattro Porte was probably complete by the death of Doge Mocenigo, since his arms adorn the frieze; but before the other rooms were finished, another fire would ravage the palace.

★ ★ ★

The Fire of 1577

The relative consistency of the group of patricians serving as provveditori during the restoration of the Doge's Palace after the fire of 1574 was unusual, in that such officials usually were elected for renewable one-year terms, terms sometimes interrupted by election to other offices. This continuity facilitated the successful development of the initial program of 1574 for creating an impressive classical ambience in the rooms over the ducal apartments, and of managing overlapping phases in the execution of each of the room's individual decorative programs. Before the ceiling of the Senate was designed by Cristoforo Sorte, however, the occurrence of a fire in another area of the palace drastically intervened to change control of the situation, demonstrating the critical relation between cultural display and politics. The fire that started from two chimneys in the Magistrato dalle Acque (Waterways Office) located by the Basilica of San Marco and swept through to the Bacino side on the night of 20 December 1577 was of a different order of magnitude in its structural implications and symbolic import, for the room that perhaps best represented the Venetian patricians' republican ideal, the Sala del Maggior Consiglio (Great Council Hall), was largely destroyed, with severe damage to other rooms. Discussions over the fate of the palace and choices made about who would lead its renovation reveal fault lines in the patriciate and would embroil Palladio and his patrons in an unsuccessful bid for radical change in a State that identified its longevity with continuity.

A chronicler reported the widespread alarm of the public:

> The fire was first seen at 21 hours [9:00 pm], in the space of less than an hour it ran clear through the palace and out above the Ponte della Paglia and burned the room of the Great Council, the room of the Scrutinio, and penetrated the ceilings below where the offices of the Rason are; the fire lasted more than 7 hours into the night [marginal note: total 10 hours] without being able to extinguish it between all the assembled workers and laborers from the Arsenale; and other people from the city were out in great terror; armed nobles placed themselves at the mouths of the streets giving onto the Piazza to prevent any possible improprieties blocking the streets and not letting pass any citizens or nobles who were not there to put out the fire.[86]

According to this chronicler, only a miracle intervened to save the Basilica and other buildings when the strong wind that propelled the flames turned along the Piazzetta, where the new Library, for example, was in danger. The public character of the visual programs in the Doge's Palace is revealed by his lament for the lost paintings in the Maggior Consiglio, "by Zuanbellin, Pordenon, Tician, and other worthy painters of ancient histories in the time of Doge [Sebastiano] Ziani with Emperor Federico Barbarossa for the defense of Pope Alexander [III] and many other beautiful histories worthy of eternal memory; therefore all those consumed by the fire are to be restored." This desire to return the palace to its former state, "make it like it was before" ("com'era avanti"), would equally be felt in the decisions taken towards its architectural form.[87]

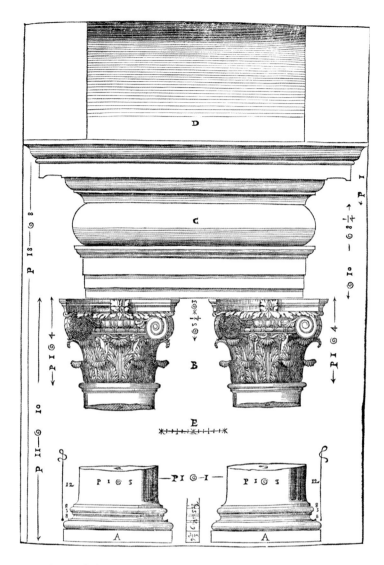

211 Andrea Palladio, column base of portal to Antecollegio, Sala delle Quattro Porte, Doge's Palace, Venice

212 Andrea Palladio, "Temple of Bacchus" (Santa Costanza), capitals, *I quattro libri dell'architettura*, Venice, Appresso Dominico de' Franceschi, 1570, lib. 4, cap. 21, 87

Three successive phases can be identified in the process of restoring the Doge's Palace, although Palladio can be securely identified only with the first two: first, to determine if it was possible to continue to meet in the palace, and, if not, to determine an alternative site; second, to evaluate the damage and propose a program for its restoration; third, to oversee and execute the selected program of building and provide for its decoration. The extraordinary wealth of descriptive testimony that accompanied the decision-making processes of the first and second phases provides insights into the status of architectural knowledge at this time, and into the relationship posited between style and structure by its practitioners. Investigation of the debates over location and the substance of form and rebuilding of the Doge's Palace also reveals, as Antonio Foscari has put it, "latent tensions" within the dominant group of the ruling oligarchy, in which one sector favored a strategy other than continuity in the architectural *renovatio* of the city.[88]

Palladio's patrons were again at the forefront in promoting the *usanza nuova*.

The disruption to the prime place of the business of government was the first to be addressed only three days after the fire by the election of three patrician officials, *deputati sopra l'informatione di luoghi*, deputies to evaluate alternative locations for the largest governing body, the Maggior Consiglio, for an adequate meeting space, with appropriate adjacencies for vote counting and other functions. Four experts were immediately called on to provide their advice within the week: Palladio, Antonio da Ponte, Simone Sorella, and Francesco da Fermo. Palladio held a leading position in the responses that were drafted, despite the fact that while he was simultaneously engaged in other State projects, he held no official office as did the others, respectively *proto al sal* (and *della fabbrica del Palazzo*), and *proti* to the procurators of San Marco *de supra* and *de citra*.[89] From a perceptive analysis of the proposals made and

213 *(facing page)* Andrea Palladio, portal to Antecollegio, Sala delle Quattro Porte, Doge's Palace, Venice

ANTI·COLLEGIO

votes taken regarding this immediate need, Antonio Foscari has interpreted the positions taken to reflect a larger, constitutional reordering implied in the unsuccessful proposals favored by Barbaro and his supporters, to remove the seat of the Maggior Consiglio to the government warehouses at the Terra Nova (by the customs house, or Dogana). Barbaro must have had this location already in mind since he tried to prevent the election of the officials to identify meeting locations with this prepared alternative, but he was decisively outvoted.[90]

Four days later, on 27 December, the three elected deputies presented the results of the written and drawn surveys by Palladio and the three *proti*, in which the measurements of the existing spaces were compared to other undamaged rooms within the palace and the courtyard; two deputies, Jacopo K.P. di Francesco Soranzo and Paolo K.P. di Stefano Tiepolo, presented a motion to the Senate for using the Canonica of San Marco, and the third deputy, Alvise di Benedetto Zorzi (later procurator), put forward the Basilica itself as a potential location, but the votes were inconclusive.[91] Sadly, none of the drawings mentioned in the reports survives, but some dissension does surface in the comments made as the other *proti* signed off on Palladio's report, taking exception to his negative statement about the Sala del Scrutinio: after mentioning that it would be difficult to get to it without going through the other burnt-out rooms, he wrote, "and other than this there is the weakness of the attenuated and dangerous walls," a precursor to his later critical attitude regarding the condition of the palace.[92]

All differences were put to rest on 29 December when the Senate was advised to abjure their differences, *non differir più*, in the presence of the doge, *consigliere* Vicenzo Morosini (concurrently *provveditore* with Barbaro and Foscari), the Heads of the Forty, Nicolò da Ponte, Dr. K.P. (and next doge), Francesco di Zuanne Andrea Venier, the *savi del Consiglio* (excepting Marc'Antonio Barbaro, and Alessandro [later procurator] di Alessandro Gritti), the *savi della Terraferma*, the *savi ai ordini* (excepting Maffeo Venier, and Procurator Girolamo di Antonio Priuli), and the three deputies: Zorzi, Soranzo, and Tiepolo. This was bringing in the institutional heavyweights. Tiepolo "too ardently" declared his concern for the lack of respect shown in housing the business of government in the "House of God," and his fear of the Terra Nova site – spacious and inexpensive to convert as it was – since it had been used as a prison. The deputies then submitted a new location for consideration, the Arsenale, which was championed by Vicenzo Morosini with a not-so-subtle dig at Barbaro:

> Here I am, Fathers! I have found the location for the Great Council to carry out its duties; I propose to you a site, in which there were never imprisoned Genoese, nor Turks, and is not a Temple of God, which won't serve you; I propose to you an amenable Garden, the delight of the Republic. Do you want that I should tell you of it? (At this point the entire Senate was watching Morosini in expectation of what he was about to say:) The location, I say, is your Arsenale; location more beautiful than all others, in which the dignity of the Republic is resplendent, location of adequate size, that in eight days, I promise you, can

be brought to accommodate all the Nobles, and who in the meantime may consult and restore the Hall of the Great Council.[93]

Morosini succeeded in a 121 yea vote, despite the repeated but now irrevocably doomed proposal by Barbaro and Venier for the Terra Nova site accompanied by the architects' report headed by Antonio da Ponte.[94] Barbaro's description of a site that would "honestamente" serve the government failed in the face of the "honorata" spaces of the Arsenale championed by Zorzi, since he was then in office as *provveditore al Arsenale*.[95]

The second phase commenced with proposing the election of three "nobles" to undertake the task of restoration, "di far restaurar esso Palazzo ruinato," which was finalized on 20 January 1578:[96] naming Alvise Zorzi (the recent *deputato sopra l'informatione di luoghi*); Pietro Foscari (concurrently *provveditore del Palazzo* for the fire of 1574, with Barbaro and Morosini); and Jacopo di Alvise Foscarini "ai Carmini" (one of the four ambassadors in the entry of King Henri III);[97] with Procurator Girolamo di Antonio Priuli replacing Zorzi later in the year.[98] With the exception of Zorzi, who had just successfully opposed Barbaro, the other new *provveditori* had strong ties to Barbaro, with Foscari probably acting as liaison between the two palace campaigns. Not only were Foscarini's and Marc'Antonio's children married to each other, but Foscarini could boast significant cultural credibility in his own right, with his palace and collections.[99] Priuli, father of future Doge Antonio (1618–23), and father-in-law to a nephew of the future Doge Alvise Mocenigo, was married to a Capello; his mother was a Pisani dal Banco; and one paternal great-aunt was married to the son of Doge Antonio Grimani and was mother of the reigning patriarch of Aquileia, Giovanni; another was Marc'Antonio Barbaro's paternal grandmother. Both Priuli's brother and son were bishops of Vicenza, and the Priuli villa at Treville has been considered an inspiration for the Barbaro villa at Maser (see fig. 17).[100] This was the authoritative group that would set the initial course of action, but thereafter there was a regular turnover of *provveditori* elected, with few serving out even their full year term, more typical of the patronage structure of the Salt Office and consequently aggregate nature of their decision-making.

Critical decisions now needed to be taken swiftly and the *provveditori* were required to give their opinion/s on "the relocation of the prisons and compartmentation of the first, second, and third floors of the 'old palace' for the accommodation of the magistracies, councils, and other governmental functions," and to determine a course of action within eight days, for which they sought further expertise.[101] Immediately following the decision of 29 December, an extraordinary group of thirteen experts ranging in the related building trades from hydraulics to cartography, from architecture to engineering, including Palladio, had been canvassed for their opinion of the condition of the palace and its restoration, to be presented to the Senate in ten days. The newly elected *provveditori* now asked a more elite group of six of the top experts, again including Palladio, to submit their evaluations regarding the integrity of the building and proposals for its restoration. The sworn testimony of the experts, who had submitted oral depositions on the first occasion and written statements for the latter (with the writer Francesco Sansovino adding his published opinion, based, as he says, on the precepts learned from his father), provides an intriguing commentary.[102] The confusing divergence between these experts' opinions reveals the fluid state of the profession of architecture and the different bases of knowledge from which their understanding of the principles of construction were derived – from a humanistic application of logic and rhetoric, to mechanics and mathematics – leading to diverse interpretations and solutions.[103] The rhetorical language describing the architectural remedies for the building is a thinly disguised prescription for the health of the State, revealing the charged atmosphere in which the patronage of this project would proceed (and during which Il Redentore was being built, as will be seen below).

The most extreme voice to assert that Palladio's opinion did not respect the venerated building, and that he was encouraged in this view by Marc'Antonio Barbaro, came from the same chronicler, Francesco da Molin, who had taken such a jaundiced view of Alvise Mocenigo's dogate:

> the opinions of all the best architects in the city were taken, and they all came to the conclusion, that the walls had remained sound . . . only Andrea Palladio the celebrated and famous architect concluded that there was nothing which was still structurally sound, and that the façade towards San Giorgio should be destroyed and demolished, and the whole building substantially renewed, and this opinion of his was fomented by Marc'Antonio Barbaro, Procurator of San Marco, a most able and prominent orator, to such an extent that although it appeared very extravagant to the whole Senate, all the same arguing with all his ability he kept the proposal alive for many days, and finally had a committee of three set up to consider the restoration of the Palace . . . who having for many days consulted with the architects . . . finally came before the Senate, and put the motion that the Palace should be restored neither more nor less than it was before.[104]

Palladio had, in fact, been consistent with the other experts in agreeing on the damage. The burning of the lead roof had made the Great Council Hall a smelting pot, burning tie beams and chains beneath the floor, turning marble to lime, all of which severely weakened the walls' adjoinment at the corner of the Piazzetta and the Bacino, the vaults of the story underneath the floor, and the columns supporting the loggias, particularly the large one by the Ponte della Paglia; the walls were perilously out of plumb, and fissures had appeared in the wall of the *Paradise*. Nor was his the most extreme opinion in cataloging the "defects" of the building, other *terraferma* experts, the Paduans Andrea dalla Valle and Paolo da Ponte – "barbarous manner of building" ("maniera barbara della fabbrica") – and the Veronese Cristoforo Sorte – "great danger in inhabiting a palace built on air" ("in tanto pericolo d'habitar un palazzo fabbricato in aria") – were even more openly critical. He did, however, judge the problems not to have come from the fire; rather, it was

seen as a precipitating agent in affecting the inherent structural defects, which departed from "ragione," "esperienza naturale," and the "esempio delle cose antiche": "I say to you in all sincerity and truth and all reverence that which, for reason and the experience of nature and for the example of the ways of the ancients, is my opinion." Palladio felt the statics of the palace were hopelessly compromised by violating these principles, "where all the parts of a building don't have a stable foundation, it's an easy thing for it to fail for any misfortune and more so for fire than for any other reason." He avoided setting the debate in stylistic terms through recourse to such structural references. Indeed, his statements do not explicitly recommend but only infer the radical step of proposing a new building: "for all these causes one may with good reason sooner fear the ruin of this palace than hope that it can be reconstructed by any architect whatsoever."[105]

Palladio's earliest biographer, Paolo Gualdo (1616), made a statement that furnishes further support that he had made drawings in preparation for a new palace "It [Teatro Olimpico] is not found illustrated in Palladio's treatise, because as we said he made it only in the last years of his life, as was also the case with his projects for the Ducal Palace of the Republic of Venice, the Rialto Bridge of the same city, and others that are among his noblest inventions."[106] The identification by Howard Burns of a "magnificent" presentation drawing now at Chatsworth for a "splendid palace" with a provenance from Palladio's ardent collector, Richard Boyle, Lord Burlington, as just such a project for the Doge's Palace has engendered some controversy over both its attribution and intention (fig. 214).[107] Despite the current lack of conclusive proofs, there are enough significant comparisons to Palladio's contemporary late works that the possibility that it represents an "ideal project" for the palace still deserves to be entertained.[108]

A contemporary project on which Palladio was engaged that has a relation both in style and function was for the restoration of the Palazzo Comunale (Town Hall) of Brescia, also as a result of fire. Palladio was first engaged there in January 1575 as a consultant with Rusconi at the time that the Doge's Palace campaign of 1574 was newly underway, but illness then kept Rusconi in Venice and Palladio was accompanied instead by the Bassanese architect Francesco Zamberlan (1529–after 1606) to work on the project that February.[109] Palladio had conceived the new Palazzo Comunale as an ornate three-story structure, thought to have been at the request "of the magnificent noblemen of the Council," as can be seen in drawings for its exterior and interior elevations by him and Zamberlan (figs. 215 and 216).[110] The drawing at Chatsworth also reflects the choice to use an *all'antica*-style superimposed order for a three-story palace façade, rather than a single monumental order.[111] Both exterior projects share the progressive articulation of the bays and diminution of the framed voids, as well as vertical continuity rising through the main orders. In the Chatsworth drawing, the ground-story arcade shows engaged Ionic columns without pedestals; the middle-story bays have engaged Corinthian columns with alternating triangular and segmental pedimented aedicules, whose column frames alternate straight and spiral fluting; and the

214   Andrea Palladio (attributed), *Elevation of a Public Palace* (for the Doge's Palace in Venice?), Chatsworth, The Devonshire Collection, SOS/B

215   Francesco Zamberlan, *Exterior Elevation of the Brescia Palazzo Comunale*, Brescia, Museo Civico, Pinacoteca Tosio-Martinengo (*recto*)

216   Francesco Zamberlan, *Interior Elevation of the Brescia Palazzo Comunale*, Brescia, Museo Civico, Pinacoteca Tosio-Martinengo (*verso*)

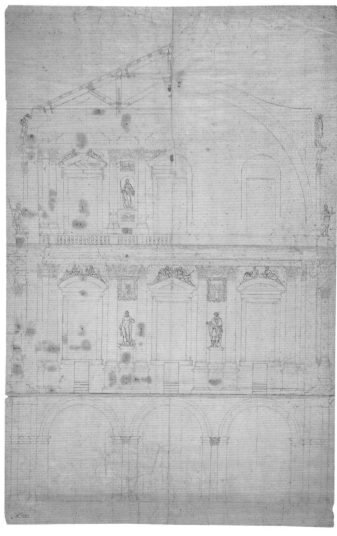

217   Andrea Vicentino, *Arrival of Henri III at the Lido in 1574*, Sala delle Quattro Porte, Doge's Palace, Venice

top-story bays have Composite pilasters with reversed alternating segmental and triangular pedimented aedicules with a simple molding. The subtly rhythmic composition of the eleven-bay façade as a whole is contained by a double order at the end bays, with a strong emphasis on the center bay as a triumphal arch motif created by a paired order framing niches with statues and reliefs and topped by a pediment with the Lion of St. Mark. The decorative character is further enhanced by the statues placed on freestanding columns at the ends of the ground story and framing the balconies of the top story and crowning pediment. A number of these same motifs occur in the Brescia drawings and the figurative draftsmanship of the Chatsworth drawing has also been attributed to Zamberlan.[112]

The decision taken on 21 February 1578 (m.v. 1577) to get on with all haste ("ogni prestezza") the work of restoration of the Doge's Palace signals the end to any debate over its replacement. The next day, the Council of Ten committed the substantial sum of 5,000 ducats towards this end, to be spent as the *provveditori* ordered.[113] Palladio's name appears no further, any ideal solution for "the finest great European palace façade between Michelangelo and Bernini" unrealized.[114] Yet he and his close patrons retained sufficient influence, sometimes directly through *provveditori*, or indirectly through Palladio's impact on associates, such as Zamberlan – often called his "disciple" – who is believed to have worked on the subsequent campaign of rebuilding, to suggest enough corollaries with the master's style in the architecture and furnishings of the room to lead to understandable, if unsupportable, attempts to attribute them to him.[115] A year later, the original *provveditori* from the fire of 1574 (Foscari, Barbaro, Morosini), and the first elected for the fire of 1577 (Foscari, Foscarini, Priuli) were replaced with a single

group, who, however, were in place for only six months;[116] the *provveditori* who replaced them in August 1579 were responsible for initiating the campaign for the redecoration, resorting, according to an early source, to the erudition of fellow patricians Jacopo di Pietro Contarini – Palladio's host when resident in Venice – and Jacopo di Andrea Marcello, and the Camaldolese monk Girolamo Bardi for the invention of a program.[117] In the ensuing campaign, the celebration of Mocenigo's *pax venetiana* in the Collegio would lead instead to promoting the triumph of Venice in the Maggior Consiglio, a signal of changed attitudes at the end of the decade.[118]

The two campaigns to repair the fire damage in the Doge's Palace reveal the different circumstances of State patronage encountered by Palladio during the dogate of Mocenigo and after. The expression of Alvise Mocenigo's dogal identity in the palace is now most prominent in the Sala delle Quattro Porte, due to the timing of its redecoration after the fire of 1574 and the shift of program in the Collegio. Above the cornice, gilded armorial shields with the Mocenigo *stemma* of per fess azure and argent a rose counterchanged reinforce the association. It is a room singularly well placed to remind palace habitués of this doge as they left and entered the other important State rooms to which it gives access, through portals whose rich marble surrounds have sustained agreement among scholars on Palladio's direct contribution to the 1574 campaign of restoration. The events of Mocenigo's reign as allied to Palladio's ideals for State architecture are present as well through the act of representation, in Andrea Vicentino's grand history painting on the wall between the doors of the Anticollegio and Senato, of the *Arrival of Henri III at the Lido in 1574*, whose focal point is the imposing triumphal arch designed by Palladio for the event (fig. 217).

HENRICO · UI · FRANCIA · ATQ
POLONIA · REI · CHRISTINAE
RELIGIONIS · ACERRIMO · PROPUG
NATORI · ADUENIENT · VENETORUM
RESP · AD · TERIS · BENVOLEN
TIÆ · ATQ · OBSERVANTIÆ
DECLARATIONEM

CHAPTER FOURTEEN

TRIUMPHAL ARCH
FOR THE ENTRY OF HENRI III

Renaissance cities were often transformed by ephemeral architecture, *apparati*, during the celebration of significant public events. There is something potent in the very transience of such elaborate efforts – both as an expression of the wealth and power that can command such resources and as an acknowledgment of a historical moment. Countering their obliteration, texts and images reproduced such efforts for further consumption. Palladio's commission for a triumphal arch for the ceremonial welcome of 1574 on the Lido for the new French king, Henri III (1574–89) was commemorated, together with a classicizing loggia, in an unusual number of descriptions, engravings, and paintings (fig. 218). The Senate elected the patricians Alvise Mocenigo and Jacopo Contarini to oversee the program. Together with Palladio, they conceived for the first time in Venetian civic pageantry an entry that was explicitly based on specific Roman Imperial models, with a direct reference to the Arch of Septimius Severus in Rome.

The Classical Triumph as a Contested Symbol

On 7 July 1574, the Florentine ambassador, Orazio Urbani, reported that "one finds the preparations made to date are far behind, and many architects, painters and other persons of similar professions are especially laboring on the arch that will be on the Lido."[119] The Venetians had been informed only on 24 June of the 23-year-old king's desire to visit the city on his hasty departure from his kingdom of Poland to take up the crown of France, and immediately set about organizing a fitting spectacle for this unprecedented entry of a reigning French monarch. The most critical element, among many delicate matters of diplomatic etiquette to be settled, was the moment of the king's formal reception to the city on Sunday, 18 July.[120] This was debated in the Senate, with Vicenzo

Morosini's successful proposal for Doge Alvise Mocenigo to pick up the king at his overnight lodging on Murano and accompany him in a galley to the formal ritual welcome at the Lido, issues of precedence being an indicator of the delicate balance between nations in a new political climate.[121] There he was to be met with the honor of a *baldacchino* (canopy) carried by six of the Republic's most distinguished procurators (including the next two doges, Sebastian Venier and Nicolò da Ponte), whose appointed speaker was Marc'Antonio Barbaro, selected for his personal cognizance of the king from his ambassadorship to France in the years 1561–64. The prominence of Barbaro is no doubt crucial to Palladio's involvement in the preparations for the entry, together with the identification of Jacopo di Pietro Contarini of *ramo* San Samuele (figs. 219 and 220) as responsible for the *apparati* of the Lido ceremony.[122] The choice of Palladio and his intimate friends ("suo intrinsichissimo amico") and patrons Barbaro and Contarini indicates a consensus among the decision-makers for classical form over tradition, although the other senator, homonymic of the doge, remains unidentified: "Henri III passed under a triumphal arch with three large portals, dedicated to his name, opposite the church of San Nicolò, and fabricated by Andrea Palladio, and by order of Iacomo Contarini and Luigi Mocenigo both elected by the Senate to oversee preparations on the Lido, and in imitation of the Arch of Septimius, made by the ancient Romans at the foot of the Campidoglio."[123] Although the choice of lodging for the king settled on the sumptuous Gothic-style Palazzo Foscari, with his retine at the adjacent Palazzi Giustinian, over Jacopo Sansovino's recently completed Palazzo Corner di Ca' Grande at San Maurizio, this was due to considerations of its splendid position "in volta di canal," at the bend in the Grand Canal, for the aquatic spectacles to be staged during the visit.[124] This was acknowledged by Jacopo Sansovino's son, Francesco, who had chosen four modern palaces

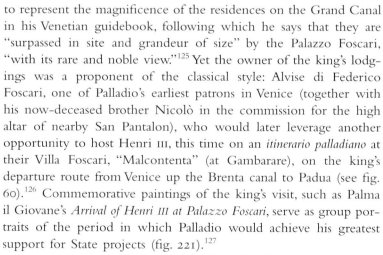

219 Giovanni Battista Moroni, (*?*)*Jacopo Contarini*, Budapest, Szépmüvésti Museum

220 Palazzo Contarini dalle Figure, Grand Canal at San Samuele, Venice

to represent the magnificence of the residences on the Grand Canal in his Venetian guidebook, following which he says that they are "surpassed in site and grandeur of size" by the Palazzo Foscari, "with its rare and noble view."[125] Yet the owner of the king's lodgings was a proponent of the classical style: Alvise di Federico Foscari, one of Palladio's earliest patrons in Venice (together with his now-deceased brother Nicolò in the commission for the high altar of nearby San Pantalon), who would later leverage another opportunity to host Henri III, this time on an *itinerario palladiano* at their Villa Foscari, "Malcontenta" (at Gambarare), on the king's departure route from Venice up the Brenta canal to Padua (see fig. 60).[126] Commemorative paintings of the king's visit, such as Palma il Giovane's *Arrival of Henri III at Palazzo Foscari*, serve as group portraits of the period in which Palladio would achieve his greatest support for State projects (fig. 221).[127]

The particular symbolic display of the lavish spectacle designed to welcome the young French monarch to Venice has been proposed as a corollary to the contemporary dominance of *vecchi* patronage, whose cultural style was embodied in the politically sensitive inclusion of a triumphal arch as one of the festival *apparati*, or architectural decorations. If elsewhere in Italy, indeed

in Europe, the triumphal arch had become a commonplace of ceremonial entries since the previous century, this was not so in Venice, where in fact it had been overtly rejected as smacking of "monarchy" as recently as the tenure of Doge Andrea Gritti.[128] The rigorously scripted actions of a formal visit from a reigning head of state were interpreted no less intently than its accompanying material effects, for their expressions of external relationships of one body politic to another, as well as serving the internal function of ritual self-affirmation.[129] In this context, the presence of a triumphal arch was more than an innocent selection from a repertoire of the motifs of classical humanism; it served to promote a State ideology based on Roman Imperial values through visual and ceremonial associations, just as the presence of a *baldacchino* connoted sovereignty.

The effective employment of the potent rhetorical device of the triumphal arch in the Renaissance was no better understood than by Emperor Charles V – or by the Italian states that were both the designers of his entries and the bodies upon which the current political reality of empire was being enacted. The metamorphic power of the Roman triumph imbued the coronation of Charles V in Bologna in 1530 with all the suggestive historical associations of the Holy Roman Emperor and the transformative elements of liturgical rites of medieval kingship.[130] Charles v's coronation was one event in a series of processions and entries through several Italian states in the years 1529–30, whose imagery was an eloquent display of the new *de facto* Habsburg sovereignty in the Italian peninsula in the guise of a peaceful union between Church and State. The emperor took a learned interest in the spectacles, which may have encouraged the surprisingly rare occurrence of the imitation of an actual classical monument, the column of Trajan, for his Mantuan reception by the Gonzaga court artist Giulio Romano.[131] Prior to this, few *apparati* were reported to demonstrate the archaeological intention ascribed to Palladio's production for Henri III.[132] More significant to this development may have been Charles v's victorious return to Rome in 1536 following his successful expedition to liberate Tunis from the Turks, described as "the finest triumphal progress of the century."[133] For the emperor's entry into Rome, Pope Paul III supported a team of eminent humanists in their urban reclamation of the ancient "via Triumphalis" (from the Porta San Sebastiano to the Arch of Constantine) and "via

Sacra" (through the Forum from the Arch of Titus to the Arch of Septimius Severus [fig. 222]); but the original route up to the Campidoglio (previously the location of the Temple of Jupiter) was avoided in favor of skirting around its foot to go to Piazza San Marco (now Piazza Venezia), then on to St. Peter's.[134] Charles v processed under all three ancient triumphal arches, which were decorated with inscriptions and allegories for the occasion by the leading artists and humanists of Rome, pausing to discuss the Arch of Septimius Severus before continuing past the Campidoglio. Reverberations of this event led to the initial move in the reconstruction of the Campidoglio by Michelangelo.[135]

There was, however, a still more topical model that relied on the same sacred geography of ancient Rome, that would have had the same appeal of such an archaeological approach, but with even greater thematic relevance for Palladio and his patrician advisors. This was the triumphal entry in 1571 of Marc'Antonio Colonna, general of the papal fleet, celebrating the victory of the Holy League – Rome, Spain, and Venice – over the Turks at Lepanto. It has been described as a "state occasion virtually unique in the

221   Palma il Giovane, *Arrival of Henri III at Palazzo Foscari*, Dresden, Staatliche Kunstsammlungen, Gemäldegalerie Altemeister (252B)

222　View of Roman Forum and Via Sacra from Arch of Septimius Severus to Arch of Titus

century – and in Renaissance Rome," closest to ancient *trionfi* and on a level with the reception of Charles v.[136] Although new inscriptions were again placed over the actual arches for the occasion, these drew the public's attention to contemporary analogies with "those ancient memorials of the subjugation of the east by the west," equating the Battle of Lepanto with that of the Milvian Bridge (Constantine's victory over Maxentius in 312), for example.[137] Commemorative materials of Colonna's triumph were not only available in Venice, but produced there, such as Domenico Tassoli's *livret*, or festival book, of 1571,[138] and probably more direct accounts were exchanged between patrons and artists, such as Vasari (in regard to his depiction of the battle in the papal Sala Regia), who certainly communicated with his Venetian agent, Cosimo Bartoli, in 1572.[139] The Lepanto victory remained a touchstone throughout Alvise Mocenigo's dogate, and reminders of Venice's role formed a promi-

nent theme in the program of Henri III's entry: his first formal act on arriving at the Lido was to knight the governor general of the triumph, Antonio Canal, for his valor in the Battle of Lepanto.[140]

An Archaeological Approach to Ephemeral Arts

Palladio must have played a crucial role with the commissioners in making a decision to employ a triumphal arch in the *apparati* on the Lido since he had been the first architect to introduce its use in the Veneto in the *possesso* of Cardinal Bishop Nicolò Ridolfi in Vicenza in 1543.[141] It had subsequently made rare appearances in Venice itself, but, as has been repeatedly noted, for celebrations of a very different import, the first being the procession in 1557 of Dogaressa Zilia Dandolo Priuli.[142] There was also a report of two

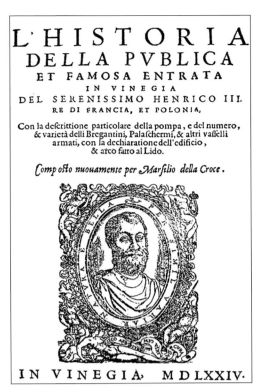

223 Rocco Benedetti, *Ragguaglio delle allegrezze, solennità, e feste fatte in Venetia per la felice vittoria*, Venice, Presso Gratioso Perchaccino, 1571, titlepage

224 Rocco Benedetti, *Le feste et trionfi fatti dalla Sereniss. Signoria di Venetia nella felice venuta di Henrico III. Christianiss. Re di Francia, et di Polonia*, Venice, Alla libreria della Stella, 1574, titlepage

225 Marsilio della Croce, *L'Historia della publica et famosa entrata in Vinegia del serinissimo Henrico III re di Francia, et Polonia, Con la descrittione particolare della pompa, e del numero, & varietà delli Bregantini, Palaschermi, & altri vasselli armati, con la dechiaratione dell'edificio, & arco fatto al Lido*, Venice, n.p., 1574, titlepage

"portone" erected at the Rialto during the celebrations that followed Lepanto, which would have added resonance of the victory to any subsequent employment of the triumphal arch (fig. 223); in that same year, the antiquarian Onofrio Panvinio's illustrated *De triumpho commentarius* was published in Venice, further validating the authority of the motif.[143] Palladio's early expertise in the arts of the imperial triumph came from his collaboration with Giangiorgio Trissino, who had personally participated in the emperor's coronation of 1530 in Bologna, and was an intimate of the Medici papal court that included Cardinal Ridolfi.[144] Only written accounts survive to describe Palladio's part in designing two Vicenza arches, one of them bi-frontal, but his participation in the larger planning of the processional route has been inferred from his close contact with Trissino at this time. Sources tell us that during their first brief trip to Rome in 1541, when they met Ridolfi at his villa at Bagnaia, the cardinal then conceived of visiting his see, where he would lodge with Trissino at Cricoli prior to the entry into Vicenza proper.[145] By the time of Palladio's later design for an arch for the Vicenza entry of Cardinal Bishop Matteo Priuli in 1565, he had acquired impressive first-hand knowledge of ancient triumphal arches, but his involvement in the later entry was limited, and once again there are no contemporary visual records known.[146]

By contrast, the entry of Henri III into Venice has left both engravings and paintings, as well as one of the largest collections of *livret*s produced for a single event (figs. 224 and 225). Bonner Mitchell has said of the view that *livret*s are untrustworthy and can be seen only as a literary genre, to the contrary, the expression of "intention" over "realization," is no less informative to the historian.[147] Doubts have been cast, for example, on the report of Henri III's supposed visit to the studio of Titian, yet this embellishment served to promote a favorite *topos*, that of Alexander and Apelles, at once a compliment to the king that appreciates art and to the city that produces worthy artists, and is thus a valuable barometer of contemporary mentalities.[148] The surviving visual evidence for the Lido *apparati* requires careful evaluation in conjunction with available texts in order to judge its import, whether in reconstructing Palladio's work, serving as a record of contemporary attitudes, or understanding its later reception and reuse. The temporary wood and painted stucco ensemble would have been dismantled shortly after the entry, so commemorative materials became substitutes for the original, executed, however, with varying degrees of architectural acuity.

Contemporary textual sources for the Lido *apparati* highlight Palladio's explicit citation of the Arch of Septimius Severus, including

226   Andrea Palladio, *Orthogonal frontal view and plan of the Arch of Septimius Severus*, Vicenza, Museo Civico, D 13v

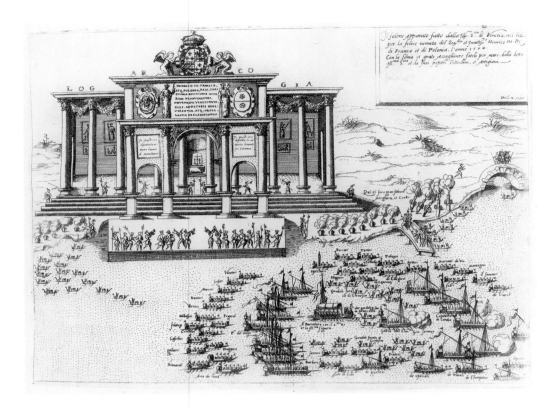

227   Domenico Zenoni, *Triumphal Arch for the Entry of Henri III*, Venice, Biblioteca del Museo Civico Correr, Stampe Molin, 2293

the two most often quoted *livrets*, those by Rocco Benedetti and Marsilio della Croce. Benedetti's account of 31 July preceded all others published that same year:

> His Majesty disembarked, and coming under the umbrella carried by six esteemed procurators of San Marco, that were Thomasso Contarini, Sebastiano Veniero, formerly general of the fleet of the time of the victory [Lepanto] and during the expectation of war, Nicolò da Ponte, Doctor and Knight, Marc'Antonio Barbaro, Ottavian Grimani, and Hieronimo Contarini, passed under a triumphal arch with three portals directed towards his Majesty by way of the church of S. Nicolò, fabricated by the most eccellent Architect, Paladio, similar to that of Septimius made by the ancient Romans at the foot of the Campidoglio.[149]

Marsilio della Croce's description followed some months later and expanded much further:

> Situated here on the edge of the Lagoon facing out to sea at the end of the bridge there was a four-sided building, 50 feet wide by 14 feet deep, and 44 feet 7½ inches high, which was suitable because it had three great openings or rather, as we wish to say, most beautiful triumphal arches, built according to the Roman custom in imitation of the Arch of Septimius Severus at the foot of the Campidoglio.[150]

Palladio's autograph drawings of the Arch of Septimius Severus show his extensive graphic study of the monument, as do his

knowledgeable comments on the arch from the *Antichità di Roma* (1554).[151] The presentation quality of the orthogonal frontal view and plan drawing in Vicenza indicate a likely role in the preparation of this example for his planned book on triumphal arches, a "Libro degli Archi" (fig. 226). Palladio announced these plans in the *Four Books* in his section on Piazze (Bk. 3, ch. 16, 31):

> Arches that are built at the ends of streets, that is, at the entrance to the square, are the greatest form of embellishment [*ornamento*] for squares; how they should be built, why the ancients made them, and why they were called triumphal will be explained at length in my book on arches, and I will present drawings of many of them which will be highly informative for those who might want to set up arches, now and in the future, for princes, kings, and emperors.[152]

The provenance of the Vicenza drawings, left by Palladio with Jacopo Contarini, once again reiterates their shared interests in antiquity and in a scientific approach to its recovery, as well as focusing our attention to the appropriateness of their collaboration on the Lido project. Palladio's drawings provide a more faithful record of his intentions for the arch than the prints and paintings produced in its wake and usually used for its reconstruction.

Contemporary visual sources are consistent in representing the analogy between Palladio's temporary arch for Henri III and the ancient Arch of Septimius Severus to which textual sources alluded. Judged to be closest in time to the event is an engraving (fig. 227) by Domenico Zenoni (active in Venice between 1560 and 1580). It depicts a rather schematic frontal view of a triumphal arch, yet it is identifiable as being derived from that of Septimius Severus by its syncopated triple-bay elevation. It shows a large central portal decorated by victory figures in the spandrels and two smaller side portals, over which legends identify painted subjects that were placed there. Four vaguely Corinthian columns on high pedestals supported the entablature of an attic story,[153] which was framed by pilaster strips on each end and allegorical figures flanking a central inscription, the arms of the Lion of St. Mark and of the Mocenigo family on either side of it, the whole surmounted by a crowned cartouche with the arms of France supported by angels, and labeled ARCO. Behind this another architectural element of the Lido ceremony was depicted, a loggia with an altar for the patriarchal *Te Deum* and benediction. This was a five-step platform with a single story of ten Corinthian columns strung with a festoon, on the closed rear interior wall of which were niches with figures having small scenes placed below, the side bays with open portals, and a small apsidal altar in the center on axis with the arch. In the first state of the print, the top entablature is shown flat, labeled LOGGIA; a later state shows an added triangular pediment and further inscriptions.[154] Zenoni's indecision regarding the loggia indicates his reliance on written descriptions, which were not particularly explicit about its entablature, such as Benedetti's:

Somewhat hidden behind the Arch there was a large and beautiful Loggia with ten large columns in the Corinthian order, and its pilasters bearing a well executed ceiling with beautiful compartments, and in the middle of the summit of the "Heaven" were depicted in a painting by an excellent painter, four winged victories with palms and crowns in their hands, that was placed in such a manner that it seemed as his Majesty was entering, that they wanted to crown him, alluding thus to the four victories attained by him in the field against his enemies. Around the interior of the Loggia were figures of all the Virtues. In the front was an altar behind a niche with a marvelous painting of the image of Our Lord Jesus Christ, in front of which the king kneeled to give thanks to his Divine Majesty for his safe arrival.

The writer noted only the major details of the architectural ensemble, and provided a direct attribution only for the arch by Palladio, not specifically associating him with the loggia, or describing its entablature. Nor does the later more elaborately detailed description of della Croce shed light on the inclusion of a pediment, since his description of the arch continues: "one passes through the arch to a loggia made facing behind the aforesaid [arch] erected by the honored and ingenious architect Palladio, under the care of Signori Luigi Mocenigo and Iacomo Contarini, honored gentlemen of great intellect and fine mind."[155] The description of the arch then goes on: "The middle arch is 14 feet wide and 26 feet high, and the two on either side are each 7 feet wide and 14 feet high, so that the four great pilasters which formed the openings were each 6 feet wide. A little above the central opening there was an architrave, frieze and cornice that ran all around said build-

ing, and was 8½ feet high but protected more at the back." The inscriptions and decorations on the arch follow; next, the loggia is described:

The loggia, as I have already said, was four-sided, 80 feet long by 40 wide, and the façade facing the arch was completely open with a colonnade made up of ten very beautiful columns imitating marble. . . . From the floor of the loggia there rose a flight of five steps, and above them hung garlands linked together from which was suspended the royal coat of arms. On each façade at the corner of the building there was a squared pilaster, and on each side of the loggia there was an opening 12 feet wide on the outside of which were two half columns flanking the opening, which was decorated with ten figures, and in the middle of the opening on the front façade there was a most beautiful altar in a niche,

and della Croce concludes with the decoration of the loggia.[156]

Wolfgang Wolters called attention to the often-made assumption that both arch and loggia were by Palladio, denying that the latter attribution was supported by the most reliable contemporary sources, such as Benedetti and Sansovino. Such doubts are reinforced by careful reading of Sansovino's description of 1581, which states that he was relying on his own first-hand experience along with the account of Benedetti, and directly names Palladio only as author of the arch.[157] Zenoni's engraving does not indicate any attribution for either of the *apparati* in the numerous identifying legends, and lacks the expert's level of observation of the architectural details of the temporary structures, limiting its usefulness for our purpose in understanding Palladio's contribution. Yet it became the fundamental visual point of reference for subsequent representations, just as della Croce's description would become the textual resource favored precisely for its expanded details. The pitfall is to mistake the rhetorical strategy of embellishment, *evidentia*, for documentary evidence rather than for what it was, a persuasive device to make an account of an event more vivid, to "bring it before the eyes."[158] Also necessary to take into consideration is the intended audience; such commemorative material was produced for various "addressees," some internal and others external, some for individual patrons and others for general appeal. Most of Zenoni's print is devoted to naming the boats of the *armata* of citizens and artisans arrayed in front of the Lido, as well as the State galleys and their illustrious naval commanders who accompanied the ceremonial dogal barge, the Bucintoro, with its royal passenger; the print market would be those who wanted to commemorate their participation, the Most Illustrious "Signoria, et da suoi popoli Cittadini, et Artegiani," of the legend inscribed at top right.

This image of the Lido *apparati* was converted to satisfy a different addressee in a painting now in Litomerice, produced as a memento of the king's stay in Palazzo Foscari, presumably for the Palladio's patron, Alvise (fig. 228).[159] The first state of Zenoni's engraving was used as the source for the frontal arrangement of arch and loggia, but there the resemblance ends, since the emphasis in the painting is on the figures in the foreground arrayed

Ten and the Sala dei Armi with its trophies from Lepanto; in the middle of the afternoon he was escorted to the private apartments of the doge and maybe was shown the reconstruction of some rooms in the Doge's Palace underway after the fire in May by one of its *provveditori*, Andrea Badoer.[175] All four ambassadors, together with Antonio Canal and Jacopo Soranzo, accompanied Henri III to the Arsenal on Saturday, 21 July, where he was impressed by the construction and arming of a *galea* in one hour (although he may have been even more amazed by the marvelous banquet all sculptured in sugar, even to the king's napkin, which crumbled as he tried to use it).[176] These military sites were typical components of State visits, as were other displays calculated to impress with the cohesiveness of the Venetian body politic. Jacopo Foscarini had the opportunity to play host to the king with his retinue and the Signoria at his palace across from the church of the Carmini, where the famous popular battle between the Nicolotti and Castellani was held – a symbolic statement of the readiness of the people in defense of the Republic.[177]

Zenoni's engraving visually expresses the idea of a strong and victorious Venice through the dominant position of Palladio's triumphal arch, bordered by small figures of soldiers with their armaments, presiding over a fleet of vessels in military formation

235 Domenico Tintoretto, *Jacopo Foscarini*, Venice, Museo Storico Navale (inv. 949)

236 Jacopo Palma il Giovane, *Votive Portrait of Jacopo Soranzo, Podestà of Padua (1569–70), and Giovanni Soranzo, Podestà of Padua (1589–91)*, Padua, Musei Civici, Pinacoteca Civica (inv. 680)

237 G. de Moustier, "Il nobilissimo e soperbo apparato fatto nel lido di Venetia dall'Ill.mo Si.ria alla venuta di Henrico III re di Francia, e di Polonia l'anno 1574," Venice, Biblioteca del Museo Civico Correr, MS P.D. 2416

reminiscent of the disposition seen in the many prints after the victory of Lepanto. The triumph being proclaimed here is that of Venice, not that of the visitor.

The circulation to France of festival *livret*s and images of the entry does show, however, that it also served Valois needs. Current French policy sought to check Spanish power, and the route via Venice was chosen in part to avoid contested Italian territories (i.e., Milan), as much as to demonstrate friendship with the Republic. Henri III's entire royal progress has been interpreted as a "triumph of faith": France's need to demonstrate loyalty to Rome in the wake of her refusal to publish the edicts of the Council of Trent (and lukewarm contribution to the muster of the Holy League forces) was served by the imagery of the king's victories over heresy, yet, as duke of Anjou, Henri III's abstention from the Massacre of St. Bartholomew promised his subjects reconciliation under the new monarchy.[178] The later reality of his reign, however, departed towards the "ultra-Catholic" faction led by the powerful Guise family.[179] Henri III's reign was cut short when he was assassinated in 1589, to be succeeded by the Protestant Henri of Navarre. Venice, in defiance of Rome's wishes, remained an ally of the French throne. Navarre's conversion to Catholicism and resumption of full diplo-

matic relations with Rome at the Treaty of Vervins of 1598 was the occasion yet again to celebrate the value of Venice's role as peacemaker among the European powers.

Retrospective representation of the Lido entry of Henri III appeared in Venice in the early 1590s, constituting both a tribute to the Catholic French king in response to the assassination and a subversive declaration of political support for Navarre, in defiance of papal policy. Palladio's arch was absorbed into Venetian mythology as Venice's welcome of the Catholic Henri III was reiterated in an engraving based on Zenoni's by the Paduan printer Francesco Bertelli and signed "G. D. M.," monogram of the engraver G. de Moustier, once recorded as bearing the date "1591" (fig. 237).[180] De Moustier rotated the architectural structures seen in Zenoni's print to place them in a three-quarters perspective, pushing them further into the background to allow for the greater detail of the various types of ships depicted, giving new emphasis to the naval aspect. He utilized the second state of Zenoni's print that showed the loggia with a pedimented roof. The impetus for Venice to reaffirm visibly its faith in the face of Rome's disapproval also may have spurred the fulfillment of the Council of Ten's long overdue commission from the studio of the deceased Titian for a votive painting of Doge Antonio Grimani, which was hung in the Sala delle Quattro Porte in 1589, the year Navarre succeeded to the throne. The painting, known as *La Fede*, also constituted the rehabilitation of the doge's inglorious naval career, presenting Grimani as *miles christianus*, and by extension valorizing Venice.[181] De Moustier's print version of the Lido *apparati* of 1591 was shortly followed in 1593 by the monumental painted representation of the *Arrival of Henri III at the Lido in 1574*, by Andrea Vicentino (see fig. 217), which was placed on the wall opposite *La Fede* in the Sala delle Quattro Porte, confirming the iconographical appropriation of the original event for allied contemporary purposes.[182]

The prominent location of Vicentino's painting ensured that it would replace earlier records as the primary visualization of the event. In the composition, Palladio's arch regained prominence lost in de Moustier's print, yet retained the angled orientation, becoming a manifestation of the architect's role in the construction of the image of the State. All later renditions show the arch as Corinthian, suggesting their origins in the vague visual records of Zenoni via de Moustier and della Croce's description of the loggia order. Vicentino places visual emphasis on the personages depicted at the moment of the king's approach to the arch, arraying them across the stage extending from the platform at its base. Yet, according to Canon Giovanni Stringa's updated description of Sansovino's *Venetia, città nobilissima et singolare*, the figures portrayed in Vicentino's painting reflect the politics of the 1590s rather than the participants in the original event named in the text.[183] The chief historical figures remain the same: Henri III is shown arriving with the Cardinal of San Sisto on his left and Doge Alvise Mocenigo on his right, being greeted by Patriarch Giovanni Trevisan. Of the three ambassadors named among the six carrying the *baldacchino*, however, only one can be identified as having carried out that specific role in 1574: Marc'Antonio Barbaro. Barbaro, aged 75 in 1593, was still a powerful force in the external affairs of the Republic, even in the changed climate that followed the reform of the Venetian constitutional structure formerly controlled by the *vecchi*.[184] The original inclusion of this supporter of Palladio in a pivotal role in 1574 would have sent a message appropriate to Venice's stance after the Peace of Cyprus, due to his importance as *bailò* to Constantinople during the period of the Holy League (1568–74) and subsequent peace treaty. Stringa places Barbaro between two other *vecchi* behind

the patriarch: Jacopo Soranzo, who had actually played a different role in the entry of 1574, as captain of the galley that brought the king to the Lido, and Paolo K.P. di Stefano Tiepolo, who was not named as a participant at all.[185] Instead, one of the only other figures named by Stringa, Jacopo Foscarini, is described as being behind the king at the head of the leading pairs of Venetian senators; originally he was one of the six bearers of the *baldacchino*. Stringa says that he is next to Antonio Canal, governor general of the entry. Liberties taken by Vicentino with the identity of the participants reinforce the contemporary message: Palladio's arch communicates that Venice has triumphed again. In 1593 European powers were paying new attention to both Barbaro's and Foscarini's activities, since they were empowered to erect the fortress of Palmanova at the limits of Venetian territory in the Friuli.[186] Other portraits of Barbaro at this time also retrospectively commemorated his election as procurator *de supra*, awarded for his success in managing the diplomatic feat of the Peace of Cyprus.[187] This was also a moment when both supported the insertion of an extreme classical architecture in the Piazza with Vincenzo Scamozzi's proposed alterations to Sansovino's Library and the Procurators' wing, backed up by experts from Palladio's former *cantiere*.[188]

Palladio's style – his language – may have been uncomfortably Roman for the faction that came into power in Venetian government in the last quarter of the sixteenth century, but that vocabulary could be harnessed to their motives of the State as well. The choice of Palladio to direct the decoration of the triumphal arch on the Lido to welcome Henri III in 1574 demonstrates the Republic's cognizance of the language of magnificence that was at the architect's command. The elevation of Palladio's arch into State mythology in Vicentino's Doge's Palace painting in the 1590s may have been a gesture towards the rehabilitation of Doge Alvise Mocenigo (and others associated with the Peace of Cyprus), whose reputation had suffered from the tribulations met during his tenure more than it had gained from reiterated association with the victory at Lepanto. Coincidentally, in 1592, Palladio's church of Il Redentore was completed, a monument to the response of Mocenigo and his contemporaries during a period of calamity that accompanied the plague that descended on the city with ferocious intensity a year after the king's visit.

CHAPTER FIFTEEN

IL REDENTORE

PERSONAL FINANCES COULD ALSO PLAY A ROLE in State commissions. When the Senate vowed in 1576 to erect a votive church to the Redeemer for delivery from the plague that raged in the city between 1575 and 1577, Doge Alvise Mocenigo stood and declared with great emotion that he would contribute 1,500 ducats towards its construction, as did the patriarch of Aquileia, Giovanni Grimani, for 1,000 ducats, and Senator Antonio Bragadin, for 500 ducats. The Senate voted a further 10,000 ducats and elected two *provveditori sopra la fabbrica*, Bragadin and Agostino Barbarigo. The patricians whose decisions shaped the location and design of the church also included Marc'Antonio Barbaro, Paolo Tiepolo, and the future doge, Leonardo Donà. The debates over the site of the church, its religious affiliation, and the form of its plan, whether circular or longitudinal, again reflect the developing political alignments of various networks within the patriciate at the beginning of the last quarter of the sixteenth century. A location on the Giudecca island was decided on and surveyed, and early in 1577 a longitudinal design for the church by "fedel nostro Palladio" was approved. The project would be supervised by the *proto* of the Salt Office, Antonio da Ponte. Within months of laying the first stone, Il Redentore was added to the dogal ritual calendar of annual visits on the third Sunday in July, even while still a construction site. Aside from continued requests for additional funds, however, there is little to follow the course of construction until the altars and pavement were installed in 1588 and 1590, and the church consecrated in 1592.[189]

The Capuchin Order was assigned as caretakers and constructed a new monastery adjacent to the church. Dedicated to vows of poverty, the Capuchins were founded on sixteenth-century ideals of Franciscan reform. Palladio, as at San Giorgio Maggiore, was required to accommodate multiple functions within Il Redentore: as a votive church and a site of State ceremony, and monastic activities.[190] In the plan Palladio continued his exploration of the typology of the Christian basilica. The solution of an apsidal extension was again employed in a separate monastic area for the choir. This satisfied general requirements for the reforms of liturgical functions. Palladio individualized the solution, however, through his architectural language. The choirs at San Giorgio Maggiore and Il Redentore may have a plan in common, but their respective elevations express the different ideals of the religious orders. Capuchin values of poverty and austerity are alluded to in the simplicity of the choir walls; these same ideals were in conflict, however, in the body of the church, in which the grandeur of the unified nave elevation celebrated the majesty of State ceremonial. The State and the Capuchin caretakers of the church came to agreement on one issue, not to allow private burials, thus preserving the *unanimitas* of the community seeking delivery from the plague.[191]

The conception of the monumental temple front distinguished Palladio's churches from others in Venice. Its visual impact transformed the Bacino into an extension of the city center, and indelibly associated Palladio with the expression of civic piety (fig. 238).[192]

Penitence and Victory:
King David and the Redeemer

Plague deaths had been rising at a frightening rate since its appearance in Venice in the fall of 1575, at its height at the rate of 400 souls a day, decimating the population.[193] "The Senate in consternation decreed a new round of prayers throughout the city to placate the ire of God"; meanwhile, nobles were trying to institute sanitary measures to halt its spread, "the great number of cadavers that one saw every day was the ultimate horror." Even the Doge's Palace was affected, and Doge Mocenigo was forbidden to go to the Senate and Collegio, since several deaths had occurred in the palace itself within the space of three days.[194] On 4 September 1576 a momentous vow was taken by the Senate in the doge's presence, to petition God in his mercy for clemency from the scourge through an act of public humiliation, supplication, and devotion. This would be enacted by the doge and Senate through a series of processions to San Marco for masses on the following Thursday, Friday, and Saturday, where, on the last day, the decision to build a votive church in his praise and glory dedicated to Christ the Redeemer was publicly declared. Further, it was promised that on the anniversary of the day that the city was liberated from the plague, a dogal procession to the new church would be initiated in perpetuity. An initial sum of 10,000 ducats for an appropriately modest devotional church ("not made of marble"), arrangements for the election of two *provveditori*, and an annual salary for two chaplains to be paid by the doge were voted. The next day in the Collegio, Antonio Bragadin and Giovanni Grimani, patriarch of Aquileia, declared their intention to contribute funds towards construction.[195]

The execution of the vow began with the series of dogal processions to the choir of San Marco: on the first day, the *savi di terraferma* carrying the Eucharist in triumph (under the dogal umbrella) surrounded by many lights, on the second, bearing a large Crucifix, and on the third day, the miraculous sacred image of the Virgin. Before Mass was celebrated on the final day, the doge rose and, "with *corno* in hand, and his usual gravity, and prudence," spoke of the following: "That God, afflicting the people for the sins committed by King David made a large number of the Israelite people die . . . and imitating the example of the aforesaid King David who took unto himself this scourge for expiation of his [God's] just wrath (the words of whom His Serene Highness deemed himself unworthy to utter), [the Doge] promised to erect by public decree a church titled with the name of the Redeemer."[196] This vow is commemorated in the fresco of 1619 on the interior façade of Il Redentore by the Capuchin artist Paolo Piazza (fig. 239), the grisaille relief-like image representing the doge and Signoria (including the two *provveditori* Barbarigo and Bragadin?) kneeling in front of the Redeemer, a prophylactic model of the city held up by two pages to the protector Sts. Francis, Mark, Roch, and Theodore, inscribed PROTEGAM URBEM ISTAM ET SALVABO EAM PROPTER ME (II Kings, 20: 6, spoken by the Lord God: "I will defend this citie for mine owne sake"). The biblical reference, which a viewer would have been expected to complete, continues, "and for my seruant Dauids sake," which is in the context of the Lord's deliverance of King Hezekiah of Jerusalem from a mortal sickness (cured by a fig placed on a boil), and therefore makes a direct allusion to the role assumed by the doge as well as to Venice as Jerusalem.[197]

Ten days later, Antonio (later procurator) di Andrea P. Bragadin of *ramo* Santa Marina – one of the wealthiest men in Venice, and whose election seems a logical outcome of the funds he had contributed towards the construction of the church – and Agostino (later procurator) di Lorenzo Barbarigo were elected as *provveditori*. This duty was not to supersede their other posts in the present or future, and, unusually for the State, it was a function they would both continue to serve until their deaths (at which time, in 1591, at Bragadin's death, the building was advanced enough for the *provveditori del Palazzo* to incorporate their duties).[198] They were commanded to inspect all appropriate sites in the city and make their report to the Collegio in three days, and once a decision on the site was taken, to get underway with its construction. The contentious decision on the site, however, would foreshadow the debates over the temporary housing of the Maggior Consiglio after the fire of 1577, and involve some of the same figures discussed earlier here in that context, notably Marc'Antonio Barbaro.

The selection of Bragadin and Barbarigo reflects their administrative experience, religious and charitable leanings, cultural links, and familial networks, and some of these in turn may explain what appears to be an uncontested choice of Palladio as the architect (despite controversial issues arising from the choice of site and plan). Bragadin (1511–1591) has been described as "a merchant in the best tradition of Venetian nobility," putting his mercantile skills to work in the public interests in various financial posts and gaining the great offices in the 1570s. He was known for his piety, and considered pro-Church and pro-Spain (although the latter comes in part from his position on reviving the Portuguese pepper trade in 1585, shared with Jacopo Foscarini, and against the successful Vicenzo Morosini, but which has alternatively been explained simply as pragmatically reflecting their respective mercantile interests). He was *capitano* in Brescia in 1568, the year following the Maggior Consiglio's and Bishop Domenico Bollani's request for Palladio's advice on its cathedral, and saw the city through a dire famine. Another reason that Bragadin may have been predisposed to Palladio was his early membership in the Compagnia della Calza dei Cortesi, begun by Francesco Badoer, patron of Palladio's villa at Fratta Polesine. His cultural and intellectual tastes may well have been influenced by his family, since his mother was Laura di Daniele Barbaro, Daniele's and Marc'Antonio's paternal aunt, and he was first married to a Corner della Regina (Maria di Giovanni [Zuane] di Giorgio [Zorzi] K.P., sister of Andrea Badoer's wife), then to a Mocenigo (his son by his second wife also marrying into the next generation of the Corner della Regina). Both Bragadin and Barbarigo were associated with the nearby site on the Giudecca of the female charitable institution known as Le Zitelle, which suggests a possible conduit for an apparent transmission of Palladian ideas from projects developed for Il Redentore.[199]

Barbarigo (1514–1587) was admired for his "vivacious intelligence," which he applied to administrative and judicial offices until the mid-1560s, when, unusually for a career confined to Venice, he began attaining higher offices. His brother, Francesco, served as *capitano* of Vicenza – the city of Palladio – in 1563, the same year that Agostino was elected to the Zonta of the Senate. His cultural experience with public monuments included election as *provveditore al sal* in 1572. Barbarigo was concerned with the health of the body politic as is reflected in his work as *provveditore alla sanità*, when a treatise on plague prevention was dedicated to him and a colleague (*Della provisione della pestilenza*, 1555), and in his participation on the board of governors for the newly instituted Le Zitelle (together with Giovanni Battista Contarini, brother of Jacopo and patron of Palladio). He has been described as pro-Jesuit for this and other associations. His mother was a Pisani, and his sisters married into prominent *vecchi* families: Querini, Dolfin, Bragadin, Venier. The

239 Paolo Piazza (Padre Cosmo da Castelfranco), *Ex-Voto for Venice*, interior façade overdoor, Il Redentore, Venice

continued stewardship of a project as expensive as Il Redentore indicates the respect of their peers for both *provveditori*, for which in 1585 Barbarigo was elected procurator *de ultra*, and Bragadin procurator *de citra*, both men having been *dogabile* in the elections of 1578 and 1585.[200]

News of their search for a location must have spread quickly, and the Franciscan Poor Clare nuns (Clarisse) at Santa Croce offered their site on the Grand Canal "with great charity and promptness" in the hopes of building "a temple much more beautiful and ample than that of Santa Maria Maggiore" (although they did suggest the dedication be changed from the Redeemer to the Holy Cross); Barbarigo and Bragadin had Rusconi (concurrently *inzegnere* for the *provveditori del Palazzo* with Palladio – who was in Vicenza at this time) survey the area and draw up a plan, which they jointly presented to the Senate on 17 November.[201] At this point, however,

votes were cast and failed to carry the Santa Croce site, upon which a new location was put forward, this time by *consigliere* Andrea Gradenigo, *capo della Quarantia* Gerolamo Zorzi, and one of the *provveditori*, Bragadin, for San Vidal (Vitale) on the Grand Canal, not far from the present Accademia bridge, to be officiated by the Jesuits and include a college, but, passing by such a slim margin, that the matter was taken up again a few days later on 22 November.[202] The reports of the speeches recorded by Cardinal Valier enable us to follow the course of the ensuing debates, amplified by the names of those who supported proposals and those who abstained or made counter-proposals, making it possible to follow developing alignments. This time only *provveditore* Barbarigo re-proposed the Santa Croce site; *provveditore* Bragadin, Gradenigo, and Zorzi again put forward the San Vidal site; while a new proposal supported by the doge and all the *consiglieri* (except Gradenigo and Zorzi) carried the

231

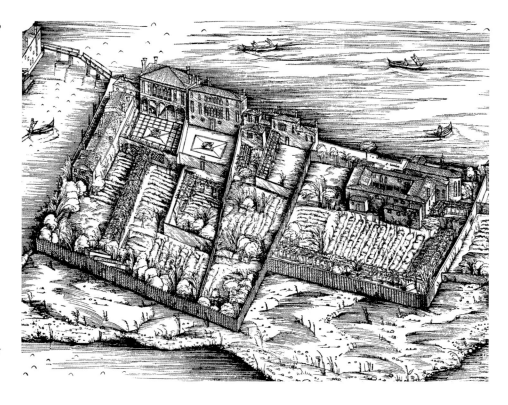

241 (*facing page*) Alessandro Varotari ("il Padovanino"), *Doge Alvise Mocenigo Kneeling Before a Model of Il Redentore*, Venice, Collection of Marchesa Olga da Cadaval

240 Jacopo de' Barbari, detail of Mocenigo property on the Giudecca, *View of Venice*, 1500, Venice

day for a location on the Giudecca officiated by the Capuchins.[203] Valier's history of the debate communicates a sense of the oratory of the great protagonists who spoke for the San Vidal and Giudecca sites, for the former, Procurator Paolo di Stefano P. Tiepolo, "a person of great authority" ("uomo di molto autorità"), for the latter, Leonardo Donà, future doge during the Interdict, both seen as quintessential examples of the respective developing factions of the *vecchi* and *giovani*.[204]

Valier, however, elides the debate over the site with that over the form of the church plan that the records of the Senate show actually took place a couple of months later, on 9 February 1577: the *savi del Consiglio* (with the exception of Barbaro), and *savio di terraferma* Federigo (Ferigo) Sanudo, successfully passed a vote to make the church "in *forma quadrangulare*, as in the best opinion of a majority of the Collegio and balloted by the *provveditori*"; over the counter-proposal of Barbaro and the *savi di terraferma* (with the exception of Sanudo) for a plan in *forma rotonda*; and over a compromise made by *savio di terraferma* Giorgio (Zorzi) Contarini, who proposed that there should be made "two models in relief, one in a circular plan and the other in longitudinal plan with all their adornments," and that the Collegio should view these models and compare their expenses.[205] A week later, the Collegio, with the authority of the Senate, issued a commission to Palladio on 17 February 1577 (= m.v. 1576), on the basis of a "design made by our faithful Andrea Palladio in *forma quadrangolare*" with measurements calculated by him and the *proto* Antonio da Ponte.[206] There is no record of any debate over the choice of Palladio, but scholars have associated him with the positions unsuccessfully advocated by his close patron Barbaro, which deserve another look;[207] the financial

contributions of Mocenigo, Grimani, and Bragadin may have translated into personal support for Palladio, who was, after all, then active in the Doge's Palace, with the additional backing of the *provveditori*, Barbaro, Foscari, and Morosini.

In Valier's compressed account of the above debates, Tiepolo spoke in favor of San Vidal, Barbaro proposed a circular-plan church and mildly supported the San Vidal site, followed by Donà's speech for the Giudecca site and a longitudinal plan, with Doge Mocenigo's words in support of Donà concluding the debate. Tiepolo's argument was less about the site and building than it was on the advantages of having the Jesuits officiate as well as educate Venetian youth. Barbaro's main aim was to persuade the Senate to accept a circular plan ("che queste Tempio fosse fatto in forma rotonda") and further, a point that is perhaps more significant than has been acknowledged (since Barbaro certainly succeeded in this), that the building "be magnificent and make resplendent the dignity of the Republic" ("essere magnifiche, e farvi risplendere la dignità della Repubblica"); his support of the San Vidal site, which he said "pleased" him, as it did others, seems motivated by its accommodation of a circular plan ("in nobile forma rotonda"). As given by Valier, Donà's speech replies to both: first he attacks the points made by Barbaro, "Who seeks the most magnificent buildings? One doesn't look for a Temple here, whether in a circular form, or not" ("Che cercate fabbriche magnificentissime? Non si cerca qui un Tempio, il quale sia di forma rotonda, o no"); he then more subtly undercuts those made by Tiepolo, "Who doesn't love the Jesuit Fathers? Who doesn't esteem them?" ("Chi non ama i Padri Gesuiti? Chi non gli stima?"), going on to catalog their virtues, but then denies that the Senate's brief included the expenses and

responsibility of establishing a college; instead, that it would be better served by the "sanctity of the Capuchins whose lives were devoted solely to the glory of God" ("eccellenti per la santità loro, mentre disprezzano tutte le cose umane, cercano la sola gloria di Dio"), noting that the property on the Giudecca could be acquired quickly and cheaply with a bridge built to facilitate the yearly dogal procession. Mocenigo then turned to him and said: "I don't seek, Leonardo, to confirm your views with further proofs. I am of the same opinion as you; and I so now propose it to the Senate" ("Non cercar, Leonardo, di confermare la tua opinione con altre ragioni. Io sono dello stesso tuo parere; io la propongo ora al Senato"). According to the records of the Senate, it was after the selection of the Giudecca site that the doge rose to his feet and made an emotional speech ("alcune parole con molto affetto") pledging 1,500 ducats, so Mocenigo's opinion of the plans is not actually known.[208] Mocenigo did have a particular attachment to the Giudecca because his residence there had been a favorite of his cherished deceased wife, since its gardens afforded her botanical studies, and it was where his electors to the dogeship had come to conduct him to the Doge's Palace (fig. 240).[209]

Mocenigo's generous pledge was retrospectively commemorated in a painting attributed to Alessandro Varotari ("il Padovanino"), *Doge Alvise Mocenigo Kneeling before a Model of Il Redentore* of *circa* 1630 (fig. 241). The kneeling doge gestures to present a page who holds a salver of gold ducats up to the Risen Christ over what has been called a "model" of Il Redentore, showing the Giudecca across the Bacino in the background. Behind the doge, whose heavy robe is held by another page, are several figures, possibly the later Mocenigo commissioners of the painting (rather than contempo-

raries of the vote).[210] Actually, whether a model for Il Redentore existed or not is a vexing question: contemporary practice, as has been often noted, for a project of this importance would say yes, but there is no evidence to indicate its existence, including this painting, since it was executed well after the church was completed and could itself have served as the "model." Certainly no three-dimensional model existed when Contarini's temporizing proposal for "doi modelli in relievo" was voted down on 9 February 1577, and the approval on 17 February of Palladio's quadrangular plan was based on a "dissegno."[211] It is difficult to know if an adequate wood model could have been prepared before the laying of the first stone on 3 May, given that there are no specifics recorded for the purposes of the sums allocated for construction by the *provveditori*, and there is a serious time factor if we consider that Palladio's wood model for San Giorgio Maggiore took one year to produce. Yet, could the *provveditori* and elusive *cantiere* established for Il Redentore have carried out Palladio's design with his drawings only? Contemporary practice suggests that masons and carpenters – as well as architects and sculptors – were fully capable of mental translation into three-dimensional form; it was the depth of design detail and problem-solving that would be missed if it was not already accounted for by Palladio's project drawings. Nor do any of these survive for the finished building in *forma quadrangulare*, presumably having been used up in the process,[212] but it may be that some idea of his unused project for a *forma rotonda* can be reconstructed from four drawings in London for centrally planned churches, the first three for a porticoed temple, the fourth for a cross-vaulted temple without a portico, and both types with apsidal choirs set off by column screens (figs. 242–45).[213]

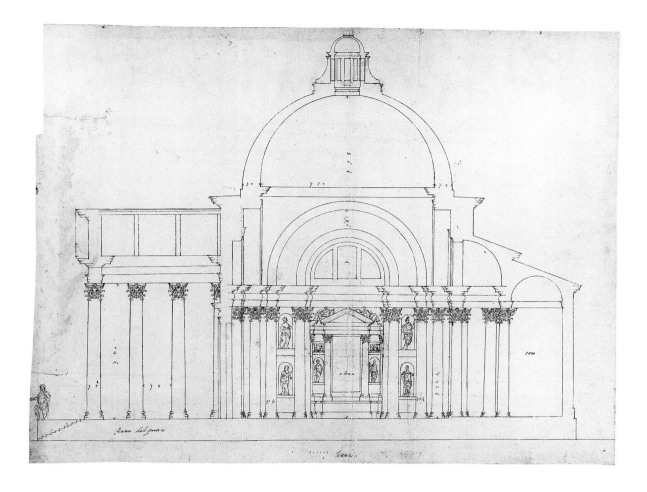

The measurements of the drawings for an 80-foot site help to narrow down the moment of their conception, since they match the land originally allotted on the Giudecca: dating them after the site vote on 22 November 1576 and before the plan vote on 9 February 1577. At the time of the site vote Palladio was still in Vicenza, where he had been since April, probably to avoid the plague; he had returned to Venice by 18 January 1577 (when he was paid for work in the Doge's Palace), which further confirms that he must have been focusing on the Giudecca site for these designs.[214] The quick turnaround of the commission on 17 February a week after the plan vote indicates that he had prepared both longitudinal and circular alternatives, in order to be able to present his finalized "dis-segno" "in forma quadrangolare" and projected construction costs for 12,000 ducats (woefully – if typically – under the actual costs of closer to 88,000 ducats) to the Collegio for acceptance.[215] Palladio's work in the Doge's Palace was under the auspices of the group of *provveditori* that included Barbaro, who may well have been in contact with the architect prior to his return and enabled his receipt of this prestigious commission.

But did Marc'Antonio Barbaro play a more fundamental role in the genesis of the designs as Deborah Howard has recently asked? These drawings have been seen as "points of departure" for the Pantheon-like Tempietto at the Villa Barbaro at Maser (its measurements scaled down by half), and for the more economical and simplified forms of Le Zitelle.[216] If the unsuccessful project ideas for a central planned "rotonda" type remained with Barbaro, as their provenance suggests, it may also indicate a high degree of input and collaboration between patron and architect: both interested in the theoretical and symbolic possibilities of architectural form. Howard makes a compelling argument that Barbaro's passion for the domed rotunda was further inspired by contemporary examples of Ottoman architecture that he had seen at first hand during his period as *bailò* in Constantinople, citing the "enthusiastic accounts" contained in his dispatches of the mosques of the Sultan's architect Sinan, as well as appreciation for the antique.[217] She further posits that some of the ideas that Barbaro brought back were translated into Il Redentore as it was built (fig. 246), including certain qualities such as the enhanced luminosity from the fenestration, centering of the dome over the crossing, small minaret-like bell towers, and the technology of external buttresses like those at Hagia Sophia in Constantinople.[218] In fact, Howard's analysis places some of the failure of Barbaro's project for a domed rotunda on the political associations raised both by these visual signs and by his personal history, having been the primary figure in the transaction of the by now discredited peace treaty with the Turks, as well as being one of the so far ineffectual magistrates to arrest the spread of the plague, itself commonly seen as a sign of God's displeasure with accommodating the infidel.[219] No one, however, was implicated to

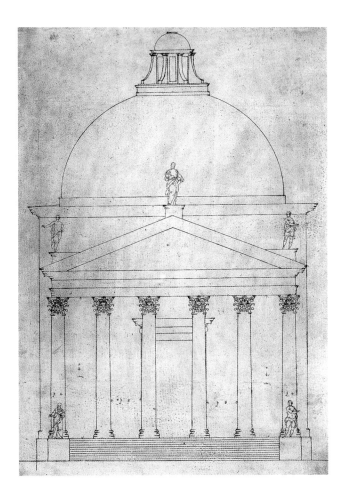

242 (*facing page*) Andrea Palladio, *Longitudinal Section for a Centrally Planned Church with Portico*, London, Royal Institute of British Architects, XIV, 14

243 (*left*) Andrea Palladio, *Façade Elevation for a Centrally Planned Church*, London, Royal Institute of British Architects, XIV, 15

244 (*below left*) Andrea Palladio, *Plan for a Centrally Planned Church with Portico and Extended Apse*, London, Royal Institute of British Architects, XIV, 13

245 (*below right*) Andrea Palladio, *Plan for a Centrally Planned Church with Extended Apse*, London, Royal Institute of British Architects, XIV, 16

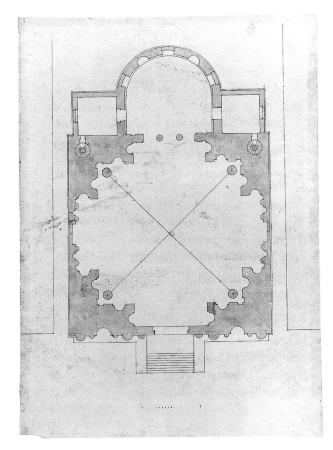

246 Andrea Palladio, Il Redentore, Isola della Giudecca, Venice

the Lord, and offered burnt offerings, and peace offerings: so the Lord was intreated for the land, and the plague was stayed from Israel."[221] Subsequently, annual processions in thanksgiving for the cessation of the plague bridged the Zattere to the Giudecca – as celebrated in the revived ceremonies today – processing from the palace to Santa Maria Zobenigo (del Giglio) across a pontoon bridge to San Gregorio to arrive there (fig. 247).[222] Venice constructed identity on a symbolic level: places were charged with typological parallels, and its people with a role in Christian allegory.

The allegorizing of the Bacino, like that of the city itself, responded to contemporary events, much as the exegetical approach to biblical prophecy derived significance from allusive interpretations.[223] The Venetian liturgy of the basilica of San Marco, known as the *patriarchino*, invested dogal ritual with meaning that conflated the history of the city with that of sacred events, expressed through cultural manifestations, from the temporary *apparati*, performances, and architectural structures that might accompany a singular procession to more permanent manifestations in painting cycles, published music, and monumental buildings, such as Il Redentore.[224] Allusive meanings were useful social and political tools precisely because they were unstable, multiple imageries that could be employed in confronting current situations in regard to the community, usually conveying the related messages of the triumph of the Chosen People (Venetians-Israelites) through the redemptive power of Christ or his typological precursors (Doge-David, or Moses, or Solomon). Venice was unusual in its rich deployment of Old Testament figures, as any look at its titular churches shows.[225] Its singular aquatic topography provided unique opportunities for allegory, such as aligning the Grand Canal with the River Jordan or the Bacino with the Red Sea. Titian's monumental woodcut of the *Drowning of Pharaoh in the Red Sea*, dating from 1549, was produced during the period of Venice's losses of Morea and seemingly unstoppable Turkish incursions in the Levant, the image becoming a prophylactic symbolic transference of victory through faith (fig. 248).[226]

In the case of the plague of 1575–77, the theme of deliverance was realized through Old Testament penitential imagery that alluded to the sacrifice of Christ required to save his people, and emerge in triumph, as the Redeemer. That such meaning was invested in the building of the new church of Il Redentore can be demonstrated not only by the speech and actions scripted in the vow and inaugural ceremony of Doge Mocenigo, but also by the contemporary production of imagery that expresses a similar mentality, as at the Scuola dedicated to the plague saint, San Rocco. Jacopo Tintoretto's *The Brazen Serpent* of 1575–76 depicts the moment when God's wrath, which had visited a plague on the Israelites, was tempered by his mercy in allowing Moses to set up a brazen serpent that miraculously saved the lives of the people (fig. 250). It was executed after a hiatus in the decoration, which ties it to the advent of the plague, and in a context of Old Testament Mosaic subjects on the ceiling and New Testament Christological subjects on the walls, directly flanked by the promise of the *Resurrection* and *Ascen-*

the same degree as the doge, whose vow to build this votive church sought to expiate the collective sins of Venice.

In his public speech at San Marco, Doge Alvise Mocenigo was paralleled to the Old Testament biblical figure of King David, and the populace of Venice stricken by the plague to the people of Israel. This was more than oratory, for, in addition to a commitment to build a votive church, Doge Mocenigo undertook to enact the penitential biblical role in public ceremony. Like other dogal *andate*, a direct link was made between sacred and civic geography through public ritual. On the occasion of the first votive procession to lay the foundation stone on 3 May 1577, the Marcian space was physically extended across the Bacino and Canale della Giudecca by means of a pontoon bridge.[220] The bridge originated at the Molo between the Columns of Justice in the Piazzetta, reinforcing the penitential role of the doge, who likened himself in his speech to King David erecting an altar as told to by the Prophet Gad, thereby hoping to assuage the wrath of God's just and terrible judgment by this pious undertaking. The analogy came from verses in the Bible in which 70,000 Israelites died of plague through the king's prideful actions: "And Dauid built there an Altar vnto

247   Giuseppe (Jakob) Heinz il Giovane, *Procession to Il Redentore*, Venice, Museo Civico Correr

sion, painted a few years later, and culminating with the monumental sacrificial scene of the *Crucifixion* on the wall of the Sala dell'Albergo painted a decade earlier.[227]

This kind of narrative strategy was based on concordances as found in the Biblia Pauperum, and shared a particular affinity with contemporary Capuchin piety. The popular diffusion of Fra Mattia Bellintani da Salò's spiritual exercises (*Pratica dell'orazione mentale*, Brescia, 1573) has been associated with the collaborative invention of the program by the artist and his patrons at San Rocco.[228] Bellintani's work would have been an apt reference for the iconography of Il Redentore, since he was *definitor generale* of the Capuchins from 1578 to 1581, and is documented as drawing up designs for enlarging the Giudecca monastery in 1592.[229]

The doge's vow shared with the spiritual exercises of the period the imagery of imitation and with biblical exegesis, the imagery of prefiguration, both in terms of the character of King David undertaken by Mocenigo, and in the dedication of the church to the Redeemer. David fulfills the role required for the plague as penitent, but also as victor. The choice of the particular iconographical character of David was evocative of its more fortunate earlier appearance in the Venetian narratives of history, when different circumstances prompted the adoption of imagery of the victorious David after the great naval victory of the Holy League at Lepanto

in 1571, such as the *rappresentazione* performed for Doge Mocenigo,[230] clearly a hopeful analogy to triumph against overwhelming forces through faith in Christ. In fact, the choice of the dedication of the votive church to the Redeemer also had its own echoes of Lepanto, since before the battle began the national flag was raised and lowered, and Don John of Austria raised the banner of the crucified Redeemer (blessed by the pope) on his galley; all others bearing crucifixes received indulgences.[231] That the significance was transferred to the new church is illustrated by the inclusion of the newly dedicated patron saint whose feast day celebrated the victory, Santa Giustina, together with the doge, kneeling before the Redeemer in one of the unique *oselle* (silver commemorative medals) struck for the vow to build the church (fig. 249).[232] Even the foundations of the new church, made from the wood of four galleys from the Arsenal, were a reminder of Venetian sovereignty in the *stato da mar*.[233] Yet this dual imagery of penitence and victory would not be enough to salvage Alvise Mocenigo's reputation in the compromised political climate after the Peace of Cyprus: he did not live long enough for the tide of blame to turn (he died on 4 June), "che col partirà di vita partì anco in quel tempo la peste della Città," with the joyful proclamation of the Senate officially announcing the cessation of the plague on 13 July 1577.[234] Instead the first procession honoring the vow was undertaken by Doge

237

248 Domenico dalle Greche after Titian, *Drowning of Pharoah in the Red Sea*, woodcut, 1549, Venice, Biblioteca del Museo Civico Correr, Stampe A. 15, c. 39, no. 48

249 Silver *Osella* of Doge Alvise Mocenigo, 1576: obverse, *Christ the Redeemer with Santa Giustina and Doge Mocenigo*, PARCE* POPVLO* TVO* 1576; reverse, *Hexastyle Porticoed Temple*, ALOYSII* MOCENI*CO PR* MVN REDEMP-TORI VOTVM, London, British Museum

250 Jacopo Tintoretto, *The Brazen Serpent*, center of ceiling, Sala Grande Superiore, Scuola Grande di San Rocco, Venice

Sebastian Venier on 20 July, who – as victor of Lepanto, and staunch opponent of the Peace of Cyprus – would receive the credit for lifting the city from its plight.[235]

The Form of Redemption

Palladio submitted his design for Il Redentore on 17 February 1577. The next day the Collegio authorized the *provveditori*'s request to purchase more land from the Lippomano family and enlarge the site of the church (to accommodate better the design that incorporated internal corridors connecting the sacristies to the chapels) to reach a total of 100 × 200 feet, as well as to negotiate for 170 × 440 feet of contiguous land on behalf of the Capuchins, whose small nearby hermitage of Santa Maria degli Angeli was inadequate to house the ninety-two friars needed as caretakers of the church. The representative assigned to the Capuchins was Paolo Tiepolo, who came to be looked on as their benefactor ("l'insegne

benefattore") – which must cause us to rethink his position solely as an advocate of the Jesuits – the negotiations taking place in the Maggior Consiglio over several months, and witnessed at his palace at Santa Maria Zobenigo.[236] Tiepolo, in addition to arguing on their behalf during critical votes, was probably instrumental in helping the Capuchins raise the funds for acquisition and construction, since most of it came from private gifts, rather than the State, which meant that it would occur more slowly and episodically in contrast to the church. Up to December, work on the sizeable church foundations was proceeding well – little else had been accomplished, according to the descriptions of the first procession celebrating liberation from the plague – and their impressive scale may have aroused the concerns raised by the Capuchins over aesthetic and functional issues that came to a head just as the new fire in the Doge's Palace caused attention to be refocused on its campaign of restoration.

The latter crisis probably accounts for some diversion from the campaign for the votive church and no new building expenditures for Il Redentore surface until 1579, indicating renewed progress (exceeding the original budget), in July and November – the final month that Palladio was in Venice before he returned to Vicenza.[237] This means that Palladio could have directly supervised little of the subsequent construction of the church before his death on 19 August 1580, given his age and the other major projects competing for his attention. Giangiorgio Zorzi insisted on this point in order to counter the persistent desire of historians who admire this work above Palladio's other churches and who want to see in it a correspondingly stronger element of his personal oversight.[238] Instead, it should be looked on as a magnificent example of the effectiveness of his design and management process, one that succeeds in communicating his ideas to be carried out by the local *cantiere* set up by him, through drawings and possibly a model. This was the same valuable ability that allowed him to collaborate with patrons and which produced the *Four Books*.[239] Timber from Cadore for the roof of the Doge's Palace was ceded to Il Redentore in February 1580, but only in 1582 was the wood armature used in the construction of the church promised to Le Zitelle, which suggests the elevation was in place, yet continuing expenditures indicate that the work progressed slowly but steadily, probably largely complete by the death of one of its *provveditori*, Barbarigo, on 31 March 1587.[240] It seems likely that the workforce was shared between the church and the monastery, with Zuan Maria di Pietro, *muraro* (wallmason) called "Monaro," identified as *proto* in accounts for the latter.[241]

It is, however, unlikely that the Capuchins, despite a tradition in building and active in the design and supervision of their new convent, could or would have assimilated the language of grandeur and magnificence so alien to their credo; rather, the project must have continued under the close guardianship of the *provveditori* over the *cantiere* (and with expert oversight provided when needed by Antonio da Ponte as *proto al sal* and Simone Sorella as *proto* of the procurators *de supra*). What Howard Burns ascribed to "the average Vicentine gentleman's habit of direct management of his estates and

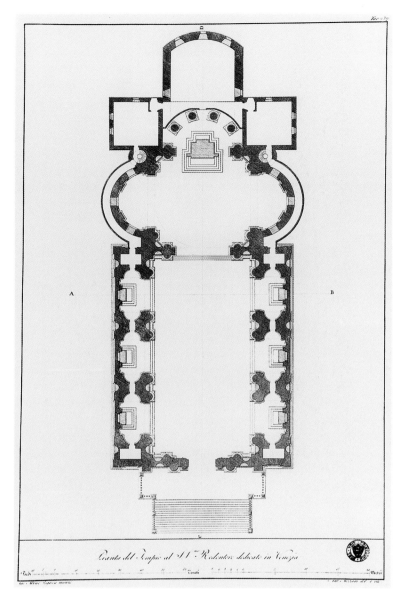

decorous housing of the monastic observances performed by its caretakers, the Capuchins, as well as enlarging the convent (figs. 251–54). The Capuchin Rule instituted in 1529 a strict reformed branch of the Franciscan Order, who wished to return to a primitive poverty and austerity even beyond that of the *osservanti*. The immensity and prestige of the undertaking so alarmed the Capuchins (still a small group of only about sixteen officiating in their church) that they appealed to the Senate, who referred the question to Pope Gregory XIII. Initially the pope sympathized with the Capuchins, suggesting that the Venetians create a special college of priests to officiate at the new church, but the Senate successfully instructed their ambassador to Rome, Antonio к. di Nicolò Tiepolo, to get his blessing, saying that their "scruples" over the "amplitude" of the church were because they were habituated to "buildings of little size and expense" and their current location was inadequate for services, whereas the new church and monastery would allow them to create a "studio" of preachers that would "result in the glory of God and saving of souls." The Capuchins did receive the important concession not to allow burials, "neither in the church or cloister, to Nobles or commoners," because it interfered with their Observant life.[244]

The Capuchin's concern over "magnificence" echoed the earlier opinion of Donà, who had attacked Barbaro on this point concerning the decorum that a votive church should express. Barbaro's conception of what was appropriate for dogal ceremony, however, succeeded in becoming the dominant expression through Palladio's powerful application of the classical language rejected by the Capuchins. Yet Palladio was able to harmonize both aesthetics in the church through his attention to materials and manipulation of

252 Fra Mattia Bellintani da Salò, Capuchin main cloister, Il Redentore, Venice

affairs, with all the personal accounting and supervision which this involved, [that] has simply been carried over into the field of building" can certainly be applied to the *provveditori* Bragadin and Barbarigo, both extremely experienced in managing the financial and material resources of the Republic.[242] It also was credited to the State by a Capuchin author disclaiming culpability: "I do not speak of the church being newly built in Venice, because it is a work of the Serene Dominion, which is made for their devotion and vow, and neither was instigated nor wanted by the Congregation, that they should not be blamed, even for the grandeur and magnificence of said church."[243]

When the Senate decided on the Giudecca site for their votive church, several purposes required accommodation, including the

253 Andrea Palladio, choir towards apse, Il Redentore, Venice

254 Andrea Palladio, choir towards high altar, Il Redentore, Venice

255   Andrea Palladio, nave towards presbytery, Il Redentore, Venice

architectural ornament. Palladio's advocacy of the use of brick and stucco, with stone to be used for the orders only to where it could be reached, was practical in the Venetian environment as well as economical.[245] Timofiewitsch has provided a detailed analysis of Palladio's modulated articulation of the spaces employed for the votive, ceremonial, and monastic functions inside the church (figs. 255 and 256).[246] The vaulted nave elevation is ornamented on each side by four pairs of monumental Corinthian half-columns framing three vaulted side chapels whose arch openings spring from a minor order of Corinthian pilasters. Between the paired columns are four intervening smaller bays with upper and lower niches. Thermal

windows above the altar in each chapel echo the larger thermal windows above the main entablature. The strong vertical rhythm of the orders is balanced by the horizontal continuity of a small meander frieze at the height of the base of the lower niches, and the entablature carried by the minor order forming the base of the upper niche: these continue "behind" the monumental order along the wall of the nave and into each chapel. A smaller flat band at the springing of the lower niche matches the modest entablature carried around the biapsidal niches of each chapel. The dominant entablature carried by the monumental Corinthian order is severe and imposing, continuing around the presbytery and supported by

256 *(facing page)*   Andrea Palladio, transept apse, Il Redentore, Venice

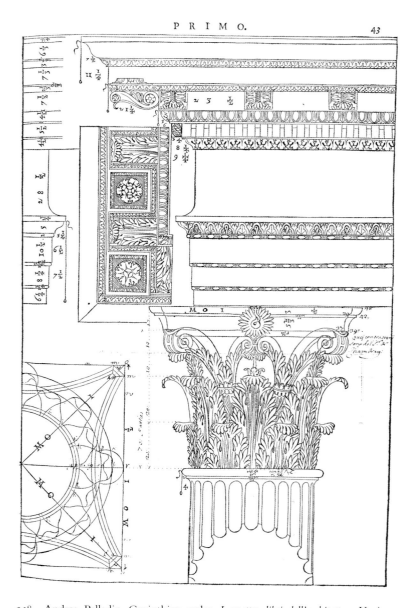

257 Andrea Palladio, Corinthian capital at crossing pier, Il Redentore, Venice

258 Andrea Palladio, Corinthian order, *I quattro libri dell'architettura*, Venice, Appresso Dominico de' Franceschi, 1570, lib. 1, cap. 17, 43

the freestanding columns, embracing both nave and presbytery while differentiating the choir, which has only a modest flat band at the springing of the vault. Continuing into the presbytery, the meander frieze also forms the base of the lower windows, while the entablature of the minor order continues from the bases of the upper niches to the bases of the upper windows. At the juncture of the nave with the interior façade and presbytery, an additional pair of orders with stacked niches turns the corner: with its high arched opening into the presbytery, the traditional triumphal arch reads more like a Palladian window, those columns forming part of the "four powerful beveled crossing piers." Chapels and presbytery are elevated from the nave by several steps. The windows in the apse ends of the transept are in two rows of three: the lower framed by alternating triangular and segmental pediments, the upper a rec-

tangular molding; only here does the monumental pair framing the central window become a flat pilaster. Pendentives provide the transition to the balustraded drum of the dome, which has flat pilasters alternating between a window and three niches, carrying an entablature around the springing of the dome, which has an oculus at its center. The Corinthian capitals that so enrich the interior are textbook Palladio (*Four Books*, Bk. 1, ch. 7, 24), the springy plastic acanthus leaves supporting the scrolls and interlocking where they intersect at the piers (figs. 257 and 258). The absence of the classical orders in the choir elevation plainly signals there is a different aesthetic at work there.

The kind of plain, undecorated wood stalls that were replaced at San Giorgio for more elaborately decorated ones was exactly in tune with the aesthetic of simplicity that the Capuchins espoused.

Wladimir Timofiewitsch, the author of the authoritative Corpus Palladianum volume on Il Redentore, remarked on Palladio's austere wall treatment in the choir as consistent with Capuchin ideals; we can say the same for its furnishings. The walls are devoid of the classical orders, the only ornament simple moldings for the five large windows and a flat band at the springing of the vault. Capuchin preference for an architecture that expressed their return to the primitive church, which generally eschewed classical ornament in favor of evoking the humble and rustic models of early hermitages, has been honored here. The luminous effects from the placement of windows and angles of light falling on largely unbroken white planar and curved surfaces both separate the space of the choir – as if it is a projector and the columns of the presbytery a screen – and connect it to the aesthetic purity of the dominant tonality of the entire church.[247]

Both architecture and decoration reflect the multiple interests at Il Redentore. The choir and cloister in their plain unadorned materials reflect the monastic vows of humility and poverty, whereas the façade and interior ornament proclaim the exalted status and grandeur of the State. Yet the devotional function of the votive purpose needed to be expressed in conjunction with the triumphal language of dogal ceremony. This was achieved in part by the adoption of what has been described as a Franciscan plan, and similarities to the organization of the sequential spatial units to San Francesco della Vigna have been identified.[248] Architectural requirements stemming from liturgical reforms in the Observant movement in the Franciscan Order during the fifteenth century were effectively transferred to other reform groups through the post-Tridentine period, influencing architects from Milan to Rome.[249] Capuchin liturgical use required access to side chapels without interruption of High Mass; here, as at San Francesco, the side chapels are carved out of the wall mass, and Palladio provided a connecting corridor between the chapels and sacristies on each side (creating concealed ambulatories around the transepts). As a result of this solution, the aisle-less nave forms a large unified space, both suitable for preaching and for the processional function of dogal ceremony. The biapsidal plan of the side chapels echoes on a smaller scale the perpendicular axis of the extended transept in the presbytery that provided the seating for the doge, Signoria, and important visiting dignitaries.[250] At Il Redentore the center of the crossing corresponds with the dome; this is unlike Sansovino's San Francesco, where the idea for a dome was discarded, or Palladio's own San Giorgio Maggiore, where the presbytery is placed behind the transept. The high altar situated at the head of the crossing, and behind it, the apsidal culmination of the nave created by a curved columnar screen, unifies the space with the transept by creating a tri-conch arrangement. Palladio neatly acknowledged the duality between monastic and State functions in his plan, without, however, losing any of the unity of the interior, since the arc of columns that creates a screen at the head of the presbytery acts as a semi-permeable membrane allowing the free passage of sound and light, while restricting visual access and distinctly differentiating the architectural vocabulary. The grace of this solution Palladio owed to his familiarity with diverse monuments, from the complexes of ancient Roman baths and temples, to the *tornacoro* favored by north Italian reformers such as Bishop Giberti in Verona, to the *schola cantorum* of early Christian churches in Rome and the Byzantine *iconostasis* of that most prominent model, San Marco in Venice.[251]

The foundation of Palladio's conception of the basilical form stemmed from his understanding of antique prototypes. As Timofiewitsch has discussed in relation to Il Redentore, Palladio's use of a colonnade to define the main apse from the retrochoir can be seen as a deliberate employment of motifs from ancient as well as modern structures that bore particular significance for his concept of the religious edifice. First, the colonnade functions as a diaphragm, marking the spatial sequences as found in Roman thermal structures; second, his equivalence of the basilica and the temple with the portico pulled into the interior find expression with the colonnade around the perimeter (Palladio, *Four Books*, Bk. 3, ch. 19, 38–40, and Bk. 4, ch. 5, 8–11); third, the semicircular colonnade suggests the ideal form of the circular temple in the center of which is the high altar.[252] In addition to the study of classical forms, in placing the choir behind the high altar Palladio responded to concerns for matching liturgical needs with ideal form. In both the *schola cantorum* and the Byzantine *iconostasis*, the sacred space was delimited by a colonnade entered by a triumphal arch. Palladio's use of a column screen marking the apse of the presbytery held deliberate overtones of Catholic Reform – in its reference to the return to a purified early church form and to those Renaissance models that adopted the columnar motif. As a telling model for the adaptation of the antique for Christian purposes, Michelangelo had converted the great hall of the Baths of Diocletian for Pius IV, who consecrated it in 1561 as Santa Maria degli Angeli (fig. 259). Palladio's drawings illustrate his deep knowledge of the thermal complexes of Rome, often cited as major influences on aspects of Il Redentore, from the thermal windows, to the sequences of spatial functions, to the column screen, and he surely would have known of plans for the transformation of the Baths of Diocletian (being considered as early as 1550), which he had studied well (fig. 260). Michelangelo had utilized columns to form a screened-off chancel for the strictly Observant Carthusian Order then assigned to the church (later modified when it became a titular church).[253]

Palladio's use of the extended retrochoir with a column screen seems to represent his thinking at the end of the 1570s, contemporary with the proposed date of change in the plan of San Giorgio. At San Giorgio, the primacy of the choir offices and dominant patronage by the Benedictines of their own church dictated that areas of the presbytery and choir are essentially equal, allowing each function its own importance. At Il Redentore, a low wall behind the columns with a single central opening further delimits the space and the functions of the friars from the remainder of the church and to guard their privacy as required by their observant practices. The employment of a column screen in a church built by the State and visited in conjunction with services at San Marco would necessarily evoke a connection to Venetian liturgy. The retrochoir with

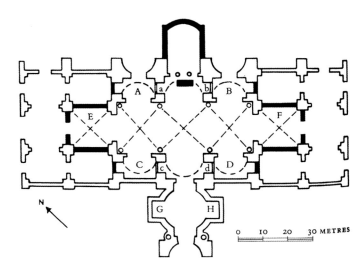

259 James Ackerman, reconstruction of "Michelangelo's Additions to the baths of Diocletian" (Santa Maria degli Angeli, Rome), from Ackerman 1986, fig. 137

260 Andrea Palladio, *Baths of Diocletian*, London, Royal Institute of British Architects, v, 8

its reform associations became absorbed into the Republic's vocabulary of civic piety.

Correspondence of Interior and Exterior: From Basilica to Temple

The façade's being the public face of the vow made by the State announces this in the formal terms of Palladio's classical vocabulary, rich materials of Istrian stone, and appropriately raised on a podium (figs. 261 and 262). The most salient feature is a monumental Composite order of two pilaster and column pairs, each forming a bay with a segmental-pedimented niche between. In the center they frame a portal with a triangular pediment supported by a smaller Corinthian order at the same height as the order on the recessed body of the façade, at the chapel height of the nave, which extends on either side of the central motif with the end segments of triangular pediments – Wittkower's "intersecting temple fronts."[254] The monumental order supports a triangular pediment that rises into an attic, itself telescoping back to reveal another layer of the façade extending to cover the upper clerestory of the nave and, above that, the dome, flanked by two small bell towers. The lantern of the dome and bell towers as well as the flanks of the church are painted stucco, punctuated by classical moldings around the thermal windows and pilaster pairs framing niches between them on the lower story and extending up to form buttresses in the clerestory. A strong *chiaroscuro* effect of the modillions in the various entablatures ties the more complex and simpler elements together, and also increases the plastic effect of the architecture from a distance.

261 (*right*) Leopoldo Cicognara, Antonio Diedo, and Gianantonio Selva, façade of Il Redentore, *Le fabbriche e i monumenti più cospicui di Venezia*, ed. F. Zanotto, Venice 1858, 2:230

262   Andrea Palladio, exterior façade, Il Redentore, Venice

The desire for correspondence between exterior and interior, not only on Palladio's part, but as a principle shared by Renaissance architects, drove the need to deform the classical temple prototype, so that it could fit a building that had a similar function of sacrality, but which had developed from a different typology altogether, one that gave the church its higher nave and lower side aisles, in turn resulting in the problem of the application of the temple front. This second type was the ancient basilica. Palladio himself acknowledged the derivation, and deftly used his explanation to account for another discrepancy from the ancient temple, the lack of exterior porticoes on contemporary churches: "We, however, having abandoned porticoes surrounding temples, build churches that closely resemble basilicas, in which, as I said, porticoes were built inside, just as we do now in churches" (*Four Books*, Bk. 4, ch. 5, 10).[255] The reason that Palladio gave for this usage was that early Christians met for worship in basilicas in private houses for fear of persecution. The discussion occurs in his chapter "On the Planning [*Compartimento*] of Temples," where the opening statement confirms a Vitruvian principle of correspondence to be even more important in temples, "that in all buildings their parts match each other and are so related proportionally that there would be none from which the dimensions of the whole and of all the remaining parts as well could not be determined." Further on, Palladio describes the adjustment that must be made "because the walls of the cella have to match up with the columns on the outside and be in line with them" (*Four Books*, Bk. 4, ch. 5, 9–10).[256] Timofiewitsch believes the "organic quality of the entire structure [of Il Redentore] derives from a strict unity between interior and exterior," which he finds to be in direct contrast to Wittkower's famous reading of the façade as intersecting temple fronts.[257] To take only two examples of the many eloquent descriptions of Palladio's intentions: Lionello Puppi writes: "through the interpenetration of two front sections, a close dialogue could be expressed with the internal pattern of nave and side aisles";[258] and Howard Burns expresses a correspondence extending to the treatment of the orders: "The solution adopted by Palladio (and here one must disagree with Wittkower) was obviously closer because it reproduces the system of the interior."[259] The common assumption here is that the essential Palladio required a close correspondence between interior and exterior, but the isolating nature of the reading as a double temple front threatens to destabilize the relationship in its isolation of the members, as "façade-ism." But is this uncertainty only the product of interpretation, or can it also be explained by Palladio's attitudes towards not only the architectural body, but the means he devised to present them to their audiences?

Palladio both equated the ancient and the Christian temples as places of worship and, further, understood the history of the Christian temple to have incorporated the form of the ancient basilica: "from the Basilica Portia . . . and which is now the church of San Cosmo e Damiano" (*Four Books*, Bk. 3, ch. 19, 38).[260] This confluence demonstrates a significant characteristic of Palladio's thought about the past: his ability to encompass historical transience in his project of emulation. The paradox that he presents to us takes two different forms, on the one hand his statements and drawings of ancient temples, and, on the other, the written, rendered, and actual presences of his building projects. The key is the element of the portico. The ancient temples depicted in the *Four Books* were all porticoed (and the orthogonal projection of the Pantheon provides a precedent for the double column), for, as Palladio explained, there were no extant examples of the classical types without: the temples "in Antis," "Prostilos," and "Amphiprostilos" (Bk. 4, ch. 3, 7).[261] Yet none of Palladio's façade designs as executed bears a portico, despite their all having been planned within about five years before (San Pietro in Castello, San Francesco della Vigna, San Giorgio Maggiore) and after (Il Redentore) the publication of his treatise in 1570. It would seem, then, that the projects preceding the *Four Books* were originally conceived as basilica-temples. Such a conception would tie the façade back into the interior; the notion of correspondence expresses what both Puppi and Burns had theorized, the expression of the interior onto the exterior. Palladio's contemporary advice (*Lettera per il Duomo Nuovo di Brescia*, 7 May 1567) on another architect's model for the new cathedral of Brescia displayed similar concerns:

As to the façade of said church, the exterior facing the piazza seems to me beautiful enough, but whoever would add columns or pilasters that extend all the way to the upper cornice that is at the top of the church, would please me much more, and it would have a more beautiful appearance, and there would be four of these pilasters, which would sufficiently ornament the façade of the church that matches the central nave, and the faces of the side aisles would have some pilasters smaller in proportion than the model, and extend to the upper cornices of the side aisles and make a half-frontispiece on each side, and thus it would seem to me to go very well when the design is made in this way.[262]

Twelve years later, in 1579, discussing designs that he had submitted for a façade for San Petronio in Bologna, he confirmed that not only were there no ancient temples without porticoes to be seen, although neither was "the portico in our times put into use," but he also continued with a proposal advocating the adoption of a portico as being all the more marvelous precisely because of that.[263] Palladio thus valued the challenge of bringing ancient forms to life, and just as porticoes had not been employed in contemporary churches, it seems that he similarly planned to reconstruct those examples of the aspects of temples no longer found in his time. The first place that the temples in antis, prostilos, and amphiprostilos were recreated was in Palladio's illustrations of Daniele Barbaro's translation of Vitruvius (fig. 263).[264] The rendering of the plan and façade of the temple types is even more emphatically detached than in the *Four Books*, described with a minimum of graphic information. Barbaro's Vitruvius commentary on the temple in antis characterized it as having pilasters at the corners and columns in the middle with a frontispiece above. In the plan it can be seen that the column bases are engaged with the façade wall, although the shaft is virtually in the round. The frontispiece in the elevation seems to have the indication of an attic behind it, and is contained within the larger gable of the roof. The triangular pediments incline at similar angles, and form a repeated motif. The projection of the central frontispiece is minimally indicated. In fact, any criticism on this score was anticipated by the authors (and here the voice must be Palladio's): "we leave the shadows, and filling in the drawing of figures, and little details, and the easy things, not affecting the quantity and subtlety of figures by hiding them in foreshortening or perspective, because our intention is to show the details, and not teach [the reader] how to paint."[265]

Palladio indicated that he had come to a positive opinion of the application of the portico to the church façade only gradually. It revealed a fundamental change, furthermore, in his notion of the correspondence of the façade. For what the portico related to is from the façade outward, to the piazza. Ancient porticoes, he said, extended not only in front, but usually all around the building.[266] The discussions both for and against the idea of a portico for San Petronio stress the effect on the surrounding urban space, for example, a supporter, Camillo Paleotti, says that "a consequence would be to render great majesty not only to the church of San Petronio and to the piazza, but also to the entire city."[267] Palladio

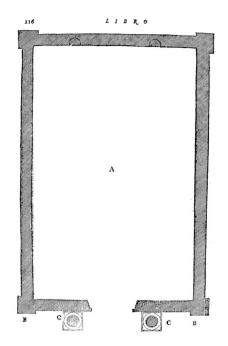

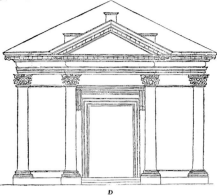

263   Daniele Barbaro and Andrea Palladio, Vitruvius' temple in antis, plan, and elevation, in Daniele Barbaro's edition of Marcus Pollio Vitruvius, *I dieci libri dell'architettura di M. Vitruvio, tradotti et commentati da Mons. Daniele Barbaro eletto Patriarca d'Aquileia, da lui rivedi et ampliati; & hora in piu commoda forma ridotta*, Venice, Francesco de' Franceschi Senese & Giovanni Chrieger Alemano Compagni, 1567, lib. 3, cap. 1, 116–17

clearly differentiated between the façade and the portico front, "o si voglia il portico o la facciata." In 1579 one of the detractors of the proposed portico for San Petronio asserted that Palladio did not make porticoes for his Venetian buildings.[268] It seems problematic, then, to describe Palladio's built façades that date before this change of conception as "porticoes in relief," even if he came to rethink their designs during their execution as his notion of the temple evolved.[269] This would be applying anachronistic criteria of a façade ideal in our judgment of Palladio's "intentions," since he was himself implicated in the formulation of new standards based on the antique that went beyond composition to the underlying relationship of the members, of face to body. It may be that the positive critical reception of Il Redentore's façade solution is due to its design being conceived in the period when Palladio's ideas were undergoing this transition to a new paradigm for the façade-exterior relationship, and with his actually having projected a porticoed temple for the rejected centralized-plan design. Only in the Tempietto of the Villa Barbaro at Maser in the last year of his life would he realize such a porticoed temple type.[270] With the exception of San Francesco della Vigna, all of Palladio's churches received their façades after his death, first Il Redentore by 1592, then San Pietro in Castello in 1595–96, and San Giorgio Maggiore between 1607 and 1611, but he had left drawings, contract descriptions, models, and details, depending on the project and the stage it had reached.[271] Just as modern perceptions of these façades have encompassed Palladio's later ideas into the viewing of his earlier projects, so could his have also had an influence at the time, extending to their later execution – and perhaps contributing to a subtle disjunction between the projects as originally conceived temple-basilicas and as executed temple-porticoes. The project of correspondence shifted, too, from a dominance of interiority, to one that embraces the environment. The seeds for such a perspective may be attributed to a powerful sense of urbanism, of architecture as a social function, with the church as the foundation of a civil society.[272]

Palladio's "Remote Control": Framing the Decorative Program

Just as Palladio claimed that the visage of the church must be publicly seen as religion employed in defense of the people, so too were the images that comprised its decoration. The doge and Senate had consolidated their vow to liberate Venice from the terrible plague in the succession of processions to the ducal chapel of San Marco. The doge's supplication made an analogy to King David, who erected an altar on behalf of his people, and to the sacrificial role of Christ, who redeemed humankind through the Cross. The dedication of Il Redentore was reiterated in its altarpieces, whose narrative was animated by the ducal *andata* instituted annually on the third Sunday of July, and comprised a *via triumphalis*.[273]

The first and only notices for the nave altars and altarpieces date from 1588, one being a payment granted by the Senate: "solely for the adornment of the altars of this church" ("per guarnimento solamente delli altari di essa chiesa").[274] Campaigns of decoration in both the churches of San Giorgio and Il Redentore were largely carried out in the later 1580s and 1590s, after the death of Palladio. So the question must be asked, can the programs of decoration evident at these two churches represent the ideas/intentions of the architect? And, if that can be answered with some degree of affirmation, how can some knowledge of what those ideas were about be arrived at? Testing the premise that Palladio exerted decisive influence over certain aspects of the decoration, we can begin by comparing later work to those parts of the decoration that were executed contemporary to the architect's presence, principally that

NELLA Prima ui è in forma picciola tutta la pianta, e tutto il diritto di quanto si uede di questo edificio così nella parte di fuori, come in quella di dentro.

Nella Seconda u'è il diritto del fianco del portico, e della cella.

Nella Terza ui è il diritto di meza la facciata, con parte delle mura, che sono da i lati del Tempio.

Nella Quarta u'è il diritto della parte di dentro del portico, & della cella, con gli ornamenti, ch'io ui ho aggiunti.

Nella Quinta ui sono gli ornamenti del portico.
   G, E il Capitello.
   H, L'Architraue, il Fregio, & la Cornice.
   I, I Lacunari del portico, cioè i Soppalchi.

Nella Sesta è disegnato il Soffitto del portico, & come uolta nelle anti, ò pilastri dell'antitempio.
   M, Il soffitto dell'Architraue tra le colonne.

Nella Settima ui sono gli altri membri.
   A, E la basa delle colonne del portico, la quale continoua ancho nel muro intorno al tempio.
   B, E la Cauriola, dalla quale cominciano, le diuisioni de i quadri fatti per ornamento nel muro sotto i portici.
   C, E la pianta delle colonne poste per ornamento de i tabernacoli nella cella.
   D, E la sua Basa.
   E, E il Capitello.
I quali ornamenti di dentro sono stati aggiunti da me, presi da alcuni fragmenti antichi trouati uicino a questo tempio.
   F, E la Cornice che si uede nelle ale delle mura, che fanno piazza da i lati del Tempio.

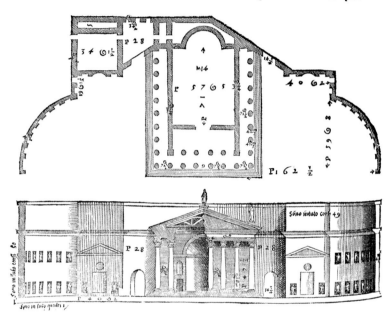

264 Andrea Palladio, Temple of Mars the Avenger, *I quattro libri dell'architettura*, Venice, Appresso Dominico de' Franceschi, 1570, lib. 4, cap. 7, 16

of the refectory of San Giorgio, and the design of the Bollani chapel that became a model for the nave altars there. Palladio's comments concerning the rapport between architecture and decoration also lend insight: discussing the Temple of Mars the Avenger (*Four Books*, Bk. 4, ch. 7, 15), "One can tell from the surviving remains that this was a very ornate and remarkable structure." He then describes the paintings placed there by Augustus, including works by Apelles; next he archaeologically identifies an exterior wall as belonging to the complex, "because of the numerous places for statues in it." He then turns to the *cella*, of which nothing remained (not even the wall), "even keys [*morsa*] in the walls that would allow one to say with certainty that there were ornaments or tabernacles," so he "devised some of [his] own" (fig. 264).[275] Then there is an analogy to Palladio's architecture by "remote control," practices developed

to manage absences necessitated by multiple projects, which could also guide future developments. Thus we may characterize a first phase of decoration as encompassing Palladio's presence, as well as those elements over which he extended control, even after his death. The second decisive phase includes those campaigns executed after the architect's death, particularly in regard to contemporary notions of decoration, their rapport in regard to Palladio's architecture, and to their original contributions.

In Palladio's writings, it is evident that he places more emphasis on sculptural decoration than on painting, although his mentions of the latter, if brief, are complimentary. It is easily explained by his training as a stonemason, one whose talents were suited to the finer task of stone carving. Indeed, even as Palladio followed the principle that harmony results from the disposition of parts to the whole, "through the form, the ornaments, and the materials we honor the Divinity as much as possible," he elaborates on the decorum to be observed in the appropriate choice of ornament (*Four Books*, Bk. 4, ch. 2, 7).[276] Palladio associated meaning with the employment of architectural ornament, using a Vitruvian grammar; it was this iconography that lent such power to his architectural language, both in terms of ornament and in plan and spatial conception. That the abundant niches in the elevation were intended to be populated with sculptures was also evident to the Capuchins, who felt that without filling the thirty-two double order of niches in the nave and crossing piers, and the further twelve in the drum of the dome, that the Senate had left the church incomplete.[277] In 1618 the contemporary *vicario* was also a Venetian patrician, Padre Girolamo da Venezia of the Vitturi family. He approached a Capuchin friar, born in Castelfranco and trained in Venice, who had just returned from an extended and productive period in Rome working for Pope Paul V and his nephew Cardinal Scipione Borghese. This was Paolo Piazza, now Padre Cosmo da Castelfranco, who agreed to make a series of monochrome grisaille figures, with the *Prophets* and *Sibyls* (upper and lower nave), *Four Evangelists* and *Latin Doctors of the Church* (upper and lower piers), carrying out the typological theme of predestination. The Senate agreed to pay for the materials and labor of the *chiaroscuri*, evidently agreeing with the economical and timely solution proposed by substituting for statues the illusionistic *sagome* in oil on canvas laid on wood templates (fig. 265). These, together with the lunette-shaped *Ex-voto for Venice* over the portal of the interior façade, were to be put in place for the procession by Doge Antonio Priuli (1618–23) in 1619; he was so impressed with the effect that he invited Piazza to execute work in the Doge's Palace.[278] Additional figures of the *Twelve Apostles* were added in the drum of the dome by another friar, Padre Massimo da Verona, in 1640. Palladio's treatment of the wall had engendered the necessity for its adornment.

Palladio's enframement also structured the grammar of the series of altarpieces in Il Redentore and San Giorgio; their syntax achieved a remarkable conformity with an emerging style of State through a series of events and timing.[279] The two natural disasters had played their part: from the raging plague that led to the Senate's vow in 1576 to construct the votive church of Il Redentore; to the fires of 1574 and 1577 in the Doge's Palace that bracketed it, the latter, as we have seen, culminating in the rebuilding of the major government and audience chambers, including notably the rooms of the Senato, Collegio, Quattro Porte, Scrutinio, and Maggior Consiglio. Already, a coherent pictorial language was being employed in a number of projects sponsored by the Venetian government around the civic center; for example, the multiple talents in painting and sculpture employed in decorating the Biblioteca Marciana. This claim to coherence is not meant to submerge the importance or distinctiveness of individual style, but rather to explore the collective phenomenon that occurred as a result of a number of projects of unusual scale that were executed for corporate patrons of will and means. In his important study of *soffitti veneziani*, Juergen Schulz was the first to draw attention to what he called "collaborative efforts" with the imperatives of State undertakings that involved all major artists' workshops active in Venice at the end of the sixteenth century.[280] Three ingredients contributed to an unusual degree of collaboration within a limited time frame: desire for speedy completion; tradition as a common model; and complexity of form and program that subordinated individual contributions and enhanced decorative unity. Since architectural projects were by nature collective enterprises, one might look for the application of the operating principles of the *cantiere* if the architect were the dominant figure, as was often the case in government projects being directed by the *proto* of the Procurators of San Marco. Since Palladio was consulted on the restoration of the Doge's Palace, and, according to Sansovino as discussed above, responsible for the designs of the enframement of the new ceiling in the Sala delle Quattro Porte, their stylistic mode of elaborate compartmentation was appropriate for a secular vocabulary. It has proved difficult for critics to admire the individual results of such collective enterprises, often parceled out to a wide range of hands in a master's *bottega*, particularly as we have been used to exalt the originality and greatness of the individual artist above a standard of general achievement. A useful comparison to Venice in the last quarter of the sixteenth century is the Rome of Sixtus v.[281] A negative reception has generally been accorded to the caliber of artists' styles collaborating on the various projects executed under this pope. Yet he and his architect-engineer Domenico Fontana are lauded for their extraordinary accomplishments in the transformation of early modern Rome, all in the five years of Sixtus's short reign. The Sistine program shares the above requisites described for collaborative efforts in Venice, above all, the determination of the State to express its identity as the leading feature of any enterprise, and to use artists as means to that end.

It is clear that, at Il Redentore, State prerogatives for its embellishment outweighed the concerns of its monastic caretakers for a more austere decor. Nevertheless, imperatives of speedy completion and cost containment no doubt drove the commissioners to those artists' studios already at work for the State, together with a strong – even unremitting – commitment to what was by now identified as Venetian tradition in style. The altarpieces constituted a straightforward Christological cycle, in consonance with the dedication of

265 Andrea Palladio, view of the interior of Il Redentore, Venice, before 1950 with works *in situ* by Paolo Piazza (Padre Cosmo da Castelfranco), chiaroscuro *sagome* of *Prophets, Sibyls, Four Evangelists and Latin Doctors of the Church* (nave and crossing), and by Padre Massimo da Verona, chiaroscuro *sagome* of the *Twelve Apostles* (now dispersed)

the church. We have already remarked on the symmetry and order of the altars under Palladio's design control. The disposition of the subjects of the altarpieces suggests that they were meant to be experienced in a particular processional order, as proposed by Wladimir Timofiewitsch.[282] Furthermore, the significance of this order can be measured in its deviation from the usual patterns of narrative placement. Beginning on the right side of the nave by the entrance and moving counter-clockwise towards the high altar are the altarpieces of the *Adoration of the Shepherds, Baptism of Christ*, and *Flagellation*, next the high altar (now dismembered), whose main sculptural

266 Francesco Bassano, *Adoration of the Shepherds* (*"Nativity"*), Il Redentore, Venice

267 Paolo Veronese and heirs, *Baptism of Christ*, Il Redentore, Venice

figures included a *Christ on the Cross*, flanked by *Sts. Mark and Francis*, then the left side nave altarpieces of the *Entombment, Resurrection*, and *Ascension* continue in narrative sequence moving from the high altar towards the door (where the model of Venice is held aloft, like a heavenly Jerusalem). Traditionally, pictorial cycles began at the apse end by the high altar (e.g., Vasari's program of the *Passion* cycle for his renovated altars of Santa Croce in Florence demonstrates what Marilyn Lavin has called a "wraparound" pattern, the most common and associated with early Christian church decoration and renewed in Counter-Reformation cycles in Central Italy).[283] Even when conforming to regularizing Tridentine impulses, Venetian decoration asserts its independence from Roman tradition. The signed *Adoration of the Shepherds* (frequently called the *Nativity*) by Francesco Bassano signals the ceremonial character of the sequence with its prominent candle and small boy playing a long horn (*pifaro*), both featured props in the dogal procession, which included the accompaniment of the famous double choir of San Marco (fig. 266).[284]

Along with the only payment document for the nave altarpieces in 1588 is another reference to that same date by Carlo Ridolfi (*Maraviglie*, 1624), who said that Paolo Veronese began the *Baptism* before his death that year (fig. 267).[285] The painting was finished and signed by his heirs, brother Benedetto and sons Carlo and Gabriele: "heredes Pauli Caliari vero. fecerunt." The other signed paintings include another by Francesco Bassano, the *Resurrection*, and Palma il Giovane's *Entombment*. The *Flagellation* and *Ascension* (which seems to have a donor portrait) are attributed to the school of Jacopo Tintoretto. As in the Doge's Palace, the language of these workshop products are conservative by definition, since what was desirable was a visible continuity of a master's identifiable style. The altarpieces on the right side of the nave display common, but selective, episodes from Christ's life, ending with an incident chosen from the Passion showing Christ's flagellation (fig. 268). This choice was not casual. Frequent references to the scourge of the plague as a flagellation of humanity can be found in the Senate's deliberations over the building of the church and in the votive masses

268   Domenico Tintoretto and workshop, *Flagellation*, Il Redentore, Venice

votive procession to Il Redentore in July 1577, which Palladio may have known and even prepared.[289] This had been erected at the site of the new church where the foundations had been laid; processing through a temporary decorated portal onto a fine carpet down to a large choir, or *teatro*, with a dogal *sedia* and benches for the Signoria, reverence was made to an *altare eminente* raised up many steps in the middle of the space, which was surmounted with a masterful *imagine* of the Redeemer, decorated with precious materials (cloths). The procession continued on to the *altra parte* of the altar and through a second portal raised for the occasion.[290]

The altar that we see today was transformed in 1680, retaining original elements of the marble architecture such as the altar table and the three splendid bronze figures of the *Christ on the Cross*, *St. Mark*, and *St. Francis* (fig. 269). One of the rare documents that specifies what work is being paid for dates from 1590: 4,000 ducats for "finishing the pavement" (a striking geometric marble design in the presbytery and apses, and red and white marble squares in the nave); and "for two figures of bronze that go on the high altar." Their designer, the sculptor Girolamo Campagna, claimed them as his work, and the figures are signed by the founder, Francesco Mazol.[291] It may be that Campagna received this important commission through his close friendship with Francesco Bassano, who had painted two of the nave altarpieces; also, both were close to Jacopo Contarini, probably through him involved in the redecoration of the Doge's Palace after the fire of 1577, and therefore likely to come to the attention of the *provveditori* as artists associated with State projects, as were the Tintoretto and Caliari (Veronese) studios.[292] Trained in Verona by a pupil of Sansovino, the fluid and sinuous style of the figures drew upon the same contemporary stylistic currents of late Renaissance Venice as discussed for the painters of the *imprese* of the Doge's Palace, and complimented their work in three-dimensional media. Originally, the high altar was in the form of a gilded and ornamented wood tabernacle with inset paintings and raised aloft by figures of angels, flanked by the two saints, and topped by the Redeemer (fig. 270).[293] The tabernacle-type altar grew in popularity in response to the Counter-Reformation. Not only did it exalt the Eucharist as the Tridentine decrees required, but it solved the problem of the double-sided altar needed for the new choir arrangements in reformed churches, and could be seen from Milan to Rome, as the drawing of *circa* 1564 by Pellegrino Tibaldi for an early phase of the design for two angels supporting the tabernacle-type high altar of Milan cathedral illustrates (fig. 271).[294] Campagna would confront this problem again shortly at San Giorgio Maggiore. In both contexts, he proved himself adept at fashioning a dynamic that responded to the spatial and ceremonial functions, with figural style and pyramidal composition acting as a pivot under the dome, as participants returned to the nave as they began to make their exit. The first altarpiece on the right side of the nave would be a symbolic reminder of the sacrifice enacted at the Mass, Palma il Giovane's *Entombment*, which provides an instructive comparison with its treatment by Jacopo Tintoretto in the Cappella dei Morti at San Giorgio (figs. 272 and 273).[295]

attended by the doge and Signoria. The plight of the city is recalled in a private work probably commissioned by members of the Mocenigo family in retrospective commemoration of the doge's role on the occasion of the completion of the church, Palma il Giovane's *Doge and Signoria Implore the Redeemer for Liberation from the Plague* in Verona.[286] In the Tintoretto studio *Flagellation*, the body of Christ at the column is displayed like the classical plague icon St. Sebastian, thus invoking the notion of protection as well as sacrifice.[287] The returning procession would have been gladdened as the iconography of the left side altarpieces was taken from the afterlife of Christ, the culmination of the promise of redemption stemming from his sacrifice on the Cross featured on the high altar.

Palladio might well have predicted that the high altar would be dominated by a sculptural group; the plan of the church with a screened retrochoir necessitated some type of two-sided altar. The form that this had taken in Vasari's churches was that of the two-sided painted altarpiece set in an elaborate architectural framework for the altar.[288] A temporary altar had been employed for the first

269 Andrea Palladio, nave with view of high altar, bronze figures of *Christ on the Cross, Sts. Mark and Francis* by Girolamo Campagna, Il Redentore, Venice

270 Wladimir Timofiewitsch, reconstruction of original high altar by Girolamo Campagna, Il Redentore, Venice, from Timofiewitsch 1972, fig. 45

A generally more "affective" style of devotional painting can be seen as an instrument of Church reform. Elements of what Federico Zeri called "arte senza tempo" that developed in the circles around Cardinal Farnese in Rome can be seen in other centers, as artists responded to the same currents that influenced their patrons. In Venice, the circumstances that had produced a demand to fulfill State patronage had strengthened workshops of major artists, some still headed by their masters in the last decade of the century. To some extent, Venetian technique and style contributed to bringing about the new style in Rome, notably the use of dark grounds, rapid painterly brushwork, the flicker of light and shadow on elongated forms. Even patrons as erudite as the Benedictines accepted the representation of popular devotional subjects by painters as a means of attaining a heightened religious state. Subjects that stressed the mystery of the Eucharist, the suffering of Christ and his Passion, and martyrdoms of saints not only reflected Tridentine icono-

271 (*right*) Pellegrino Tibaldi, drawing for the Tabernacle of Pius IV, Milan, Duomo, in Milan, Biblioteca Ambrosiana, Cod. F 245 Inf., 78

272 Jacopo Palma il Giovane, *Entombment*, Il Redentore, Venice

273   Jacopo Tintoretto, *Entombment*, Cappella dei Morti, San Giorgio Maggiore, Venice

graphy, but increased an affective relationship between beholder and image. Particularly moving was Venetian artists' treatment of the subject of the Entombment. The choice of this subject proves its special appeal. Both Palma il Giovane's Il Redentore altarpiece and Jacopo Tintoretto's for San Giorgio reach out to attract the viewer's empathetic reaction with the swooning body of the Virgin, which expressively captures a mother's sorrow for her son. This is strictly a device from popular legend, and its wide distribution for diverse patrons illustrates its attraction in the face of theological inaccuracy. In Palma's version, the direction of the movement of the body towards the tomb reorients the usual downward dynamic, since it is lifted up diagonally to the tomb at the right: reinforcing its compositional relation to the high altar – a reminder of Christ's sacrifice upon the Cross is dimly visible in the hill of Golgotha in the background of the painting – the figure of the Virgin becoming the dominant link to the contemplation of the Eucharistic mystery on the altar table below. This subtle shift in emphasis on the intercessory role of Mary in the context of a church devoted to the iconography of Christ the Redeemer, in fact, often interpreted as symbolizing the Holy Sepulcher in its form, is an indication of the future Mariological trend in spirituality, as reflected in the dedication of the State's next response to a similar crisis in the 1630s. Apparently Il Redentore successfully fulfilled its votive function: the "new Palladio," Baldassare Longhena, would design a church, Santa Maria della Salute, that would become another link in the chain of spiritual "forts" protecting the city.[296]

274 Giacomo Franco, "Venetian Procurator with Il Redentore," *Habiti d'uomeni et donne venetiane con la processione della ser.ma signoria et altri particolari, cioè trionfi feste cerimonie publiche della nobilissima città di Venetia*, Venice, 1610, 1:9

Urbanism and Sacrality

Within a decade, Palladio had established himself as the premier architect for ecclesiastical buildings, a genre he had not been particularly strongly identified with previous to Venice, although his architectural expertise had always been in demand. This had finally led to a State commission when the Senate took the unusual step of deciding to build a votive church for intercession from the terrible plague of 1575–77 and awarded the project to Palladio. Their choice of a location on the Giudecca, visible from the Piazza and across the canal from the Zattere, matched Palladio's stated position on the public role of churches: "Temple fronts [*fronte*] should be constructed overlooking the most impressive part of a city so that it seems that religion has been placed there like a guard and protector of the citizens" (*Four Books*, Bk. 4, ch. 1, 5).[297] When dogal decree freed the view of Palladio's San Giorgio façade on its adjacent island (in 1610, contemporary to the first engraving of *Il Redentore* with its façade and only the sculpture of *Christ the Redeemer* on the dome[298]), it was ensured that Palladio's design language established a syntactical relationship between these churches and the civic center (fig. 274). Such visual rhetoric was brought to life in the annual processions to these churches led by the doge and his councilors, accompanied by representatives of the State church of San Marco, as well as foreign dignitaries, notably ambassadors, in which were displayed the *trionfi*, insignia of Venice's claim to sovereign status. Thus, conformity of State and religion is proclaimed through the grammar of Palladio's contributions, mediating real tensions between the political entities of Church and State.

Giovanni Stringa's new edition in 1604 of Francesco Sansovino's *Venetia, città nobilissima et singolare* of 1581 revealed the imprint of Palladio amplifying the civic core, not through secular public buildings, but with these churches in the Bacino, describing Il Redentore:

> How very beautiful, rich, and noble this church is a difficult thing to explain; save that for architecture, and for its other noble qualities it is not a whit inferior to that of San Giorgio Maggiore. It was made, as I said, on the model of Palladio, architect of great fame in our time; a model truly worthy of high praise, because it brings to viewers no little desire or longing [*vaghezza*], and such that it entices the souls of each one of us to gaze on such a well thought-out composition. It can be only 500 good steps further from the Piazza S. Marco, which makes little less than half a nautical mile: as one stands in the Piazza looking at its façade [*Frontispicio*], which looks just toward the sunset, it is totally graceful [*vaga*] in form fabricated in Istrian free-stone [*pietra viva*].[299]

The language of desire, the longing of the soul, enunciated by the canon of San Marco, traversed the fluid space, bringing Palladio's churches into the orbit of the Basilica and Doge's Palace, the sacred civic center of the lagoon city.

PART VI

CHARITABLE INSTITUTIONS

INTRODUCTION

AMONG THE MORE REMARKABLE INSTITUTIONS in Venetian society were hospitals, and lay confraternities, called *scuole*. Palladio would face the issue of aligning his ideas about classical architectural form with a strongly established building tradition. These institutions provided charity and succor to the poor and endangered, such as orphans, young women, the ancient, and the infirm.[1] Francesco Sansovino likened these religious congregations to "Academies or Public Schools where one learned and exercised Christian works to the benefit of the souls of the members, in death, as in life, and of great benefit for the impoverished to the greater glory of God."[2]

The *scuole* were under the oversight of the Council of Ten, and each had its own set of rules, called *mariegole*. Two aspects of these lay confraternities are noted as particular to Venice: their autonomy from ecclesiastical authority and their role in perpetuating the "myth of Venice."[3] The *scuole* were of two distinct sorts, the *scuole grandi* and *scuole piccole*, which shared in the exclusion of clergy and patrician members from their governing boards. These institutions were hailed as a natural political outlet for citizens and merchants otherwise disenfranchised from civil offices, other than in the doge's chancery. Their dual ecclesiastical/civil nature was recognized by Sansovino as he described their being "copiously furnished with silver, vestments, sacred relics, and other things pertaining to religious rites, representing also a certain mode of civic government, in which the citizens, almost as if in a Republic of their own, have ranks and honors according to their merit and quality."[4] By Palladio's time, there were six *scuole grandi*, whose large all-male memberships, in addition to their charitable responsibilities, were important participants in civic ritual in Venice. The membership of the more than two hundred *scuole piccole* were more varied, could include women, and might be affiliated with a specific group, such as trade or nationality.[5] The wealthier *scuole grandi* and some of the *scuole piccole* displayed their pride and devotion in the construction and decoration of their meeting places and were a source of an important and distinctive type of patronage.[6]

Hospitals were another source of commissions. Their associations were more diverse, some run by *scuole*, others by lay patrons, religious, or State institutions. Terms used to describe these institutions were often interchangeable, the most universal being *ospedale* (*ospitale, hospitale*), applied to hospice as well as care-giving functions. There was a sharp growth in their number in response to Tridentine reforms; twenty-eight new institutions were founded in the sixteenth century alone.[7] The resources of their patrons and the requirements of their building varied greatly according to their populations and functions.[8]

Palladio was engaged in these spheres of patronage to a varying degree, mostly as an expert and designer of fine stonework, which documents for the Scuola dei Mercanti and l'Ospedaletto attest to, and, in the case of Le Zitelle, as a paradigm for its architectural form. A crucial aspect of these institutions was their strong devotional practices, present even in a lay environment. Their recourse to Palladio confirms his reputation in the fabrication of the religious architecture of the city.

facing page Andrea Palladio, drawing of the unfinished façade of Jacopo Sansovino's Scuola Grande della Misericordia (detail of fig. 289)

275 Mariegola of the Scuola dei Mercanti, *St. Christopher and Confraternity Members*, Venice, Archivio di Stato, Scuole piccole e suffrage, B. 403, frontispiece

CHAPTER SIXTEEN

SCUOLA DEI MERCANTI

Palladio was involved with a new building for one of the *scuole piccole*, the Scuola dei Mercanti (Mercatanti, Mercadanti), or merchants, which was attached to the church of the Madonna dell'Orto, whose original dedication to St. Christopher had earlier given its name to the Scuola, as the Scuola di Santa Maria e San Cristoforo dei Mercanti, in 1377 (figs. 275 and 276).[9] The year 1570 was an important one for the Scuola, as they prepared to welcome the Scuola Santa Maria della Misericordia e San Francesco dei Mercanti e Naviganti to unite with them and join their site at the Madonna dell'Orto. This was a prestigious decision for the Scuola dei Mercanti, because the Scuola della Misericordia, originating in 1261, was one of the oldest and most venerable of the *scuole piccole* in Venice. From the middle of the sixteenth century, the members of the Scuola Santa Maria della Misericordia e San Francesco had been unhappy with their quarters at the Frari, a situation that became acute in 1570 when they were unable to perform their rituals and were insulted by the brothers.[10] The Scuola dei Mercanti officers were eager for a merger, and this inspired their building campaign on the foundations of the old Scuola di San Cristoforo.

Palladio's friendship with Giorgio Saler, with whom he was working at La Celestia, was fundamental to his involvement with advice and designs for the building of the Scuola from late 1570 through to 1571.[11] Saler was an important member of the Scuola dei Mercanti, having been on its *zonta* (an expanded governing board) in 1566 and 1570, governor in 1567, and, most critically, one of the procurators overseeing the new fabric in 1571.[12] The death of Giorgio Saler that November terminated the favorable relationship of the architect and Scuola, as is apparent from the suit for non-payment brought by Palladio the following spring. The extent of Palladio's contribution to the building was limited, and consequently put into question. Yet it is worth examining the degree of his involvement for the insight it provides into an otherwise little-known aspect of his career in Venice in the realm of *cittadini* patronage.

The consequences of *scuole* patronage for the architectural projects that they sponsored bear strong resemblance to that of the Salt Office, particularly in the revolving leadership of the officers. The transitory character of governance fostered a conservative tradition in taste that could come into conflict with another aspect of their patronage: their competitiveness with each other as expressed in the buildings that they commissioned and decorated. The results of such competition among the *scuole grandi* are poignantly illustrated in the

276   Andrea Palladio (advice and designs), Scuola dei Mercanti at Madonna dell'Orto, Venice

types present in the city. The dominance of the tradition over the architect has been interpreted by Manfredo Tafuri as "reducing" the status of the architect to that of *proto*.[17]

A distinct building type had evolved in Venice to suit the needs of the *scuole*.[18] A large ground-floor hall accommodated charitable activities, typically with a flat, beamed ceiling supported by columns raised on high pedestals, called the *androne* (fig. 278). On the *piano nobile* story above, a large hall, called the *salone*, was used for meetings of the chapter of dues-paying members, or *capitolo*. A smaller room opening off this, called the *albergo*, where the board of sixteen governing officers, or *banca*, met, was usually eliminated in *scuole piccole*. The officers of the *scuole* held yearly terms, and were headed by a *guardian grande*, although more typically called *gastaldo* or simply *vardian* in the *piccole*. The Guardian was aided by a deputy, the *vicario*, and other officers. For special projects, procurators would be elected

278 Plan of Scuola dei Mercanti at Madonna dell'Orto, Venice, after Rodolfo Gallo 1955, fig. 14

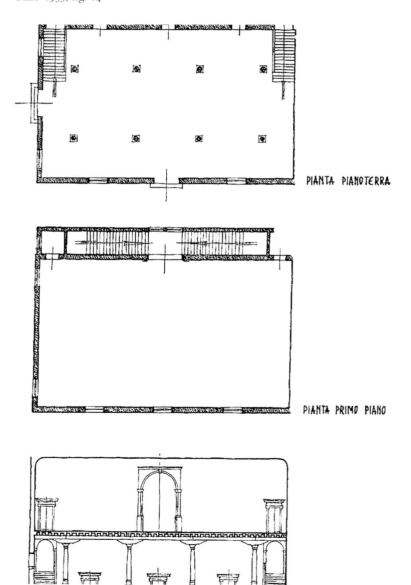

PIANTA PIANOTERRA

PIANTA PRIMO PIANO

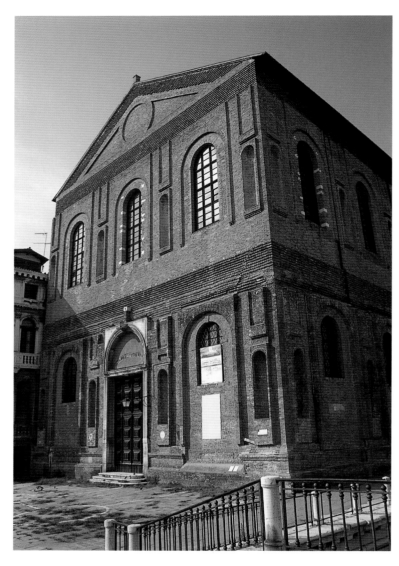

277 Jacopo Sansovino, Scuola Grande Santa Maria della Misericordia, Venice

magnificent derelict of Jacopo Sansovino's new meeting house for the Scuola Grande Santa Maria della Misericordia o della Valverde (fig. 277). The travails of its building history have been documented by Deborah Howard, showing that, from its inception, the grandeur of the scheme was at odds with the financial means of the Scuola.[13] The Scuola Grande della Misericordia's ambitions for their project are revealed in their selection of Sansovino, recently elected *proto* to the Procurators of San Marco, whose model was chosen in 1531.[14] If this choice argues for an innovative appreciation of the central Italian language of the Roman High Renaissance by the voting members, decisions made the following year would seem to contradict such a supposition, when the architect was constrained to remove the free-standing columns planned for the waterfront façade from his design.[15] Adherence to the typology of the *scuola* form also led to the rejection of vaulting proposed by Sansovino in his subsequent revised model of 1535,[16] and reinforces its importance in asserting identity within the larger repertoire of building

279 Jacopo de' Barbari, detail of the Scuola dei Mercanti at Madonna dell'Orto, *View of Venice*, 1500, Venice

280 Exterior view of side chapels of Madonna dell'Orto adjoining back of Scuola dei Mercanti, Venice

to oversee the progress and report to the *banca*, to which an additional elected body of twelve, the *zonta*, would be added for decisions.

Did the same conditions of patronage apply to *scuole piccole* as to the *scuole grandi*? The answer is as diverse as the institutions themselves, but among the more prosperous similar ambitions did apply: "Quasi à imitatione di queste grandi," as Francesco Sansovino noted of the Scuola della Passione.[19] In the case of the Scuola dei Mercanti, the desire to align with the proud Scuola della Misericordia unhappy at the Frari was long-standing, dating back to 1556; the acceptance of the proposal for unification in 1570 indicates that their resources were sufficiently attractive.[20] The building and decoration campaign that followed would distinguish the unified Scuola dei Mercanti (now corporately dedicated to Mary, Francis, and Christopher) from among the other *scuole piccole* in the city during the later sixteenth century. The promise of increased membership necessarily prompted investigations into renewing and expanding their building, "Immitando le Vestigie delle scole grande."[21] The addition of a "small *albergo*" (variously referred to as the "albergheto" and "albergo pizzolo") would reinforce their image of prestige in relation to the other *scuole* of Venice. Even their terminology for the *guardian grande*, which they called *governatore*, reflects a heightened sense of status.[22]

The first governor of the new Scuola, the lawyer and notary Domenico Bonamor, negotiated with the prior of the Madonna dell'Orto, Giovanni Trevisan, to provide more space for the newly aggrandized membership. The church willingly leased adjacent territory behind the Scuola, somewhat larger than what was presently occupied by a storehouse recently built by the prior's brother, to be used for the small *albergo*, which would be built above – and

share in practical facilities such as the latrine (figs. 279 and 280). One of the practical concerns of the church fathers was that the expansion of the Scuola would not cut off the light from the adjacent chapel of San Vicenzo, although the agreement of the Valier family, whose family chapel it was, was not sought until the project was nearly completed in 1573.[23] The foundations of the old Scuola di San Cristoforo were first surveyed by Gian Giacomo de' Grigi. When Palladio was subsequently consulted, he agreed with de' Grigi's estimation of the adequate strength of the old perimeter walls.[24] With the Mercanti's decision to select Palladio to help refurbish their site, they chose an architect who had gained a reputation close to equaling the recently deceased Sansovino's. His current church and monastic projects showed him adept at an expressive architectural formulation of the devotional programs of his patrons.

In 1573 the governor, Valentin Cesaro, celebrated the completion of the *albergo* of the Scuola dei Mercanti with a gilded inscription placed over the inside portal.[25] Also in July of that year, Palladio concluded his litigation with the confraternity begun in May 1572, in which he was awarded payment of 15 ducats; this was less than the 25 ducats he had sued for, but more than the gift of his services that the Scuola had claimed he promised them.[26] From this, it can be concluded that some limited responsibility for the architectural design and construction should be given to Palladio. As a comparison, Jacopo Sansovino was paid a monthly salary of 5 ducats by the Scuola Grande della Misericordia for on-site supervision of work as required.[27] Palladio stated that he had made the designs of the Scuola ("fatto li dessegni nella fabricha") and acted as the supervising architect ("architeto al servicio") for eleven months without compensation.[28] By comparison with the number of years that

281 Andrea Palladio (advice and designs), ground floor interior ("androne"), Scuola dei Mercanti at Madonna dell'Orto, Venice

282 Jacopo Sansovino, ground floor interior ("androne"), Scuola Grande della Misericordia, Venice

several *scuole grandi* took, this in itself indicates a modest building program.

Indirect evidence provided by some unpublished documents allows further refinement on the contribution made by Palladio. The procurators had acted with alacrity and hired wall masons within a month of the agreement with the prior of the Madonna dell'Orto, on 9 January 1571. Some kind of design, however basic, had to exist since the masons were instructed to place stone where the windows, doors, and stairway would be, and to prepare for the "pilastrelli" of the façade.[29] Even more revealing is the contract signed by stonecutters on 12 February. Masters Salvador de Vettor and Zorzi "q[uondam] Vicenzo taiapiera a S. Moritio e compagni" undertook to work the Istrian stone, *piera de rovigno*, and specifically to follow the profile given to them ("segondo la sagoma che li e sia data") to make the portal to the campo with its adornment, cornices, and frieze, whereas the portal to the *fondamenta* was to be made after their design ("juxta la forma del dessegno suo a noi dato"), as were the windows. The eight columns were to be as large as those in Santa Sofia, not specifying the origin of a design for them, or for the large portal for the stairway ("come nel desegno").[30] Beyond a basic program, then, it would seem that Palladio could have provided a template for the main portal on the campo, whereas the stonemasons produced the rest to their own designs.

This assumption is borne out in examination of the surviving Scuola building. The conformation was predetermined by the decision to use the old Scuola di San Cristoforo as the foundation. Most revealing is that the interior plan is eminently typical of *scuola* architecture: there is no introduction of vaulting or of solutions outside this typology that would identify Palladio as providing a more original design – the conservative nature of the *scuole* predominating. In the ground-floor meeting room, the space is divided into three aisles by the eight Tuscan columns on high pedestals that support the traditional carved wood beams of the ceiling (fig. 281). The interior ornament seems stark in contrast to Sansovino's at the Scuola Grande della Misericordia with its twelve pairs of Corinthian columns, continuous architrave, and wall niches flanked by columns in the *androne* (fig. 282). The stone enframements of the doors and windows of the two-story Scuola dei Mercanti punctuate otherwise unassuming brick walls. The motif of round-headed tabernacle frame with straight lintel, or triangular pedimented lintel (as in the *fondamenta* portal), had entered into the vernacular by this date. A comparison to Palladio's substantial intervention at the already initiated refectory at San Giorgio Maggiore, in the fenestration and cornice, for example, shows the higher level of quality that could be expected with a greater degree of involvement by the architect (in, admittedly, a much wealthier institution). The complaint of the confraternity about re-doing the portal, on the other hand, because it was "disgraceful, deformed, irregular, and without design" ("vergognosa, diforme, bislonga, et senza disegno"), seems almost gratuitously insulting, but, conversely, provides confirmation that they considered it to be Palladio's work.[31] By spring 1571 a commemorative inscription honoring the first governor of the

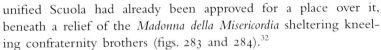

283 Giovanni Grevembroch, pen and ink drawing of overdoor relief and inscription of the Scuola dei Mercanti at Madonna dell'Orto, Venice, "Monumenta Veneta," 1759, Venice, Biblioteca del Museo Civico Correr, Cod. Gradenigo-Dolfin, 228, 3:59

284 Andrea Palladio, executed by Salvador di Vettor and Zorzi di Vicenzo, campo portal, Scuola dei Mercanti at Madonna dell'Orto, Venice

unified Scuola had already been approved for a place over it, beneath a relief of the *Madonna della Misericordia* sheltering kneeling confraternity brothers (figs. 283 and 284).[32]

The expectations of the Scuola to have Palladio's services gratis illustrate the interdependency of personal and professional obligations. Palladio claimed that he undertook the work in good faith ("bona fede").[33] At Giorgio Saler's request he had gone to the site of the Scuola to initiate the work and provide his counsel, and he went there from day to day for three months without pay. He then described how he was persuaded to continue for another eight months only by the repeated visits of Saler and also of the other building deputies. This was an important distinction, because the confraternity had argued that their refusal to compensate Palladio was due in part to his having taken the project on out of friend-

ship with Saler, whom he had come to know through the work at La Celestia.[34] But there may have been more complex family dynamics at play too, for the very figure who opposed Palladio's claims in such harsh language was none other than Vicenzo Saler, Giorgio's brother, *vicario* of the Scuola in 1572, and presumably in a position to know about the architect's arrangement. He also would be on the *zonta* the next year, which held the unanimous vote finally to authorize resolution of the dispute with Palladio.[35]

Vicenzo became governor in 1575 and declared his intention to take up the adornment of the now completed Scuola "con qualche bella pittura," by personally paying for an *Assumption of the Virgin* (identified as a lost work by Jacopo Tintoretto) for the *albergo* together with his *vicario* and the *banca*, in the hope of inspiring future governors to do the same. In this, it seems he was success-

285 Paolo Veronese, *Annunciation*, overdoor from the Scuola dei Mercanti at Madonna dell'Orto, Venice, Gallerie dell'Accademia

ful, since the "many portraits from life" in the *Assumption* recorded the visages of the officers of 1575 and bound them into the permanent representational devotional narrative of the Scuola.[36] In 1575–76 a grand soffit was ordered; in 1577 an altarpiece of the *Nativity of the Virgin* (Venice, Palazzo Farsetti, on deposit from the Accademia), attributed to Benedetto Caliari – "a stupendous work with many figures," probably including portraits – was sponsored by the current governor and his colleagues; new benches of walnut were commissioned in 1580.[37] In painted form Palladian architecture also entered the Scuola, as in the presence of the temple façade in Paolo Veronese's over-door of the *Annunciation* with the arms of the Mercanti and its commissioners displayed, with the "most majestic architecture" (fig. 285).[38] By 1581 there were said to be so many paintings that the inscription honoring Governor Valentin Cesaro had to be moved so that it could be seen. The Scuola dei Mercanti would go on in the 1590s to execute a decorative cycle that would further rival those of the *scuole grandi*, making it unique among the *scuole piccole* in the late sixteenth century.[39]

Domenico Tintoretto's vivid group portraits of the brotherhood in 1591 offer a telling glimpse into the shift in their ambitions begun with Giorgio Saler's solicitation of Palladio and the union with the Scuola della Misericordia in the early 1570s. There is little to distinguish their representation from that of the portraits painted of magistrates in the various government offices, either by dress, pose, or formal composition, which has been said to be unique in *scuole* portraits before this date.[40] The two canvases that depict thirty-six

members of the Mercanti originally flanked the altarpiece of the *Nativity of the Virgin*, attributed to Jacopo Tintoretto and studio, in the upper-story *sala del capitolo* dedicated to the Madonna della Misericordia (figs. 286–88).[41] The ducal vestments with long fur-trimmed sleeves of three of the kneeling members of the *banca* in the left and right front rows, with the *stola* identifying the guardian or governor (at the time, Bortolomio Moro) and *vicario* or vice-governor (Mario Finitti), were usually granted to the most illustrious of the *scuole grandi*, yet appear here in the context of a *scuola piccola*.[42] The governor of the Mercanti in 1590, Francesco di Gasparo di Jacopo Dardani, of an old *cittadino* family, was described as similarly robed with his sons in a painting once located by the altar dedicated to St. Christopher on the ground story, and embodied such a rise in status; he was also a long-time *confratello* of the nearby Scuola Grande della Misericordia, even *guardian grande* in 1572 and 1586, thus enhancing by this connection the *scuola piccola*.[43] The elevation of the *scuole* group-portrait type by Domenico Tintoretto may also reflect his own identification not only as a member of the Mercanti (as was his father Jacopo) and inhabitant of a nearby parish to the Madonna dell'Orto, but as a member of the *banca* himself.[44] Vicenzo Saler, too, looks out at us somewhere from among one of the more elderly faces of the *zonta* of 1591. The carefully observed and observing confraternity brothers bespeak the artist's familiarity, and recall the republican *pietas* that Sansovino had characterized as the dual nature, civil/ecclesiastical, of the *scuole*.

In relation to Jacopo Sansovino's work at the Scuola Grande della Misericordia, Tafuri raised the question as to whether the particular patronage of the *scuole* subscribed to a "civic taste," distinctive to the citizenry, as opposed to the state or patriciate. If so, what would this mean to the employment of Palladio in this environment? Tafuri concluded that such a taste would operate to the detriment of the architect's ability to carry out his design in the face of conservative tradition, hence privileging the *proto*. Howard's account of the Scuola Grande della Misericordia confirms the problematic course of *scuola* patronage. It would follow that Palladio's rigorous classical independence from local traditions would not find a ready acceptance in this context, although the prestige of his work would be a desirable quality, contributing to competitive display. There is also a pragmatic level to Palladio's architectural practice that dealt in more utilitarian projects, from renovations to advice, and this seems more to have been what the Scuola dei Mercanti sought. Yet the handling of any classical elements could be implicated in a conflict over the values expressed in the architecture. Palladio's claim had been at least partially vindicated by the judgment of the experts called in to adjudicate in 1573, including Giovanni Antonio Rusconi, himself accounted a Vitruvian. The Scuola, however, had recourse to the free services offered by one Master Salvador, a follower of Sansovino, who now stood for tradition. Ultimately, however, in the corporate mentality of the *scuole*, the success there of Palladio, like Sansovino, would rest on the few individual supporters who could persuade their brethren of its decorum – and worth. And, unfortunately, not only the change of officers, but the death of his primary advocate, Giorgio Saler, would leave his architectural contribution open to criticism.

The expression of a civic identity in *scuole* architecture seems strongest in the internal typology, and was not confronted by Palladio at the Mercanti, which retained the flat beamed ceilings and functional plan. In their exteriors, composition and typological references made in *scuole* façades place them between palace and church architecture: a visible allusion to their dual nature.[45] The Mercanti fenestration is equally ambiguous, with the exception of the triangular pedimented waterfront portal, which echoes the roofline with its oculus framed by a flat molding that continues the perimeter of the pediment, suggestive of a nave elevation. Another work may show us Palladio's formulation of a theory on this building type, an impressive, if problematic, drawing in Vicenza (fig. 289).[46]

Honoring a scuola *Exemplar in the New Style*

The articulation of the Vicenza drawing elevation is close enough in detail and proportion to that of the unfinished façade of Sansovino's Scuola Grande della Misericordia to cause scholars to question the attribution to Palladio and the drawing's purpose, further complicated by the presence of two hands in the figural decoration. The provenance of the drawing in the group donated by Gaetano Pinalli to Vicenza has reinforced the reliability of

Antonio Magrini's identification: "There is no doubt," he wrote in his monograph on Palladio of 1845, "that the drawing that I now describe is after this religious building." Magrini speculated that the drawing must have been done after Sansovino's death, and remarked on the rarity of Palladio's use of the two-story orders.[47] Palladio probably had Sansovino's model of 1533–35 to follow and would have studied it with special interest, as the most important contemporary example of confraternity architecture at this date. But to what end? This type of presentation drawing was used to explain visually the appearance of a building project, demonstrate alternative solutions for ornament, and subsequently might serve as a guide for construction drawings and elements of decoration, and/or for reproduction in other media, including books. For the most part, then, the intended audience was the patron. Could Palladio have expected the Scuola Grande della Misericordia to turn to him after the death of Sansovino in 1570? There is no evidence that they did so. Or was it intended to demonstrate to the Scuola dei Mercanti what a *scuola grande* aspired to in their building campaign as a suggestion for their own – particularly since Palladio had countenanced the external expression of the two-story elevation of the *scuola* plan at the Mercanti, although in a considerably less elevated and decorative language than the Misericordia drawing?[48] The most compelling explanation remains that the drawing was intended for similar purposes to others of the provenance of the Vicenza group.

Lionello Puppi's astute reconstruction of the provenance led him to conclude that the drawings in the group that represented monuments of antiquity had been part of a collection taken to Venice by Palladio in order to prepare them for intended publication, but at his death left to his patron Jacopo Contarini, and eventually ending up in Vicenza. Puppi exempts the "modern" Venetian projects from the purpose of publication, however, as "demonstration" drawings of unrealized works for patrons, and a record of his "difficult relationship" with the city.[49] The content of this group, including a waterfront palace (D 27r) and the Rialto bridge (D 25r, D 25v, D 19r, D 20r) already discussed in earlier chapters, and the Scuola façade, does lend itself to an interpretation of these drawings in the context of such a *paragone*. Yet, in my view, this makes the argument for their intended publication more, not less, forceful. Nor does the use of these drawings as presentation tools for clients seem incompatible with such an eventual function, for Palladio's intensive re-employment of drawings in his architectural practice – his graphic research – has been eloquently described by modern historians. But Puppi is right that this group is distinct from the Vicenza drawings of antiquities in that they were not records or reconstructions of monuments that already existed, but, potentially, buildings that could be executed that represented his authorship. The analogy to the treatment of modern works in the *Four Books*, and its discreet references without explicit identification of the Rialto bridge, further supports a hypothesis that the Vicenza drawings had multiple messages to "demonstrate," one that in published form could reach a significant audience. Here, though, another distinction remains to be made in terms of asserting authorship: the drawing of the Scuola Grande della Misericordia façade has more

286 (*above left*)   Domenico Tintoretto, *Group Portrait of the Governors of the Scuola dei Mercanti* (left side), Venice, Gallerie dell'Accademia, Quadreria

287 (*above right*)   Jacopo and Domenico Tintoretto, *Nativity of the Virgin*, Venice, Gallerie dell'Accademia

in common with Palladio's drawing of Bramante's Tempietto (D 26v), also in the Vicenza group (but included by Puppi with those intended for publication), as projects by modern masters.[50] Furthermore, with the death of Sansovino in 1570, the Misericordia project necessarily changed status, because it would not be executed by him; either this freed Palladio to acknowledge his work visually in a future publication, or even to appropriate it, the authorship of the realized paper project being Palladio's. That Palladio's draftsmanship had such power of representation is testified to by the endurance of his Rialto bridge images.

Palladio had spoken of future books that contained "public architecture"; his son Silla had planned to republish the *Four Books*, "extending them to include other modern and ancient buildings."[51]

289   Andrea Palladio (figures attributed to Bernardino India, drawing of the unfinished façade of Jacopo Sansovino's Scuola Grande della Misericordia, Vicenza, Museo Civico, D 18

288 (*left*)   Domenico Tintoretto, *Group Portrait of the Governors of the Scuola dei Mercanti* (right side), Venice, Gallerie dell'Accademia, Quadreria

The *scuola* type had not been illustrated in Palladio's publication of 1570, although he had no doubt studied the new buildings of the Scuola Grande di San Rocco (Bartolomeo Bon, Antonio Scarpagnino, Gian Giacomo de' Grigi, 1515–60) and, as Vicenza D 18r shows, the Scuola Grande della Misericordia with close atten-

tion. The opportunity to investigate this particularly Venetian civic typology was given impetus by Palladio's work for the Scuola dei Mercanti, but remained elusive in its further realization either built or in print.

CHAPTER SEVENTEEN

L'OSPEDALETTO

THE COMPLEX OF THE OSPEDALE DI Santa Maria dei Derelitti ai Santi Giovanni e Paolo, more familiarly known since the seventeenth century as "L'Ospedaletto," was founded by a lay congregation in 1528 for the care of orphans, the derelict, and the elderly. The early years showed close links to the reform movements of the Compagnia del Divino Amor and the Somaschi. The chapel and oratory gained in importance as the orphans were trained in musical recitation, among other skills. The discovery of Palladio's association with the Ospedaletto allows his interaction with charitable organizations and their role in the social structure of Venice to be yet more deeply explored (fig. 290).[52]

The growth of the institution required the building of a new infirmary between 1571 and 1574, which was carried out by the *proto al sal*, Antonio da Ponte (fig. 291). This freed up space to begin a new church more in keeping with the growth of the institution and ideals of reform, which became the focus of building activities between 1574 and 1580. The governor and deputy director of the building fabric of the Ospedaletto at the time that attention was shifted to the church was the patrician Giovanni Battista di Pietro Contarini (1538–1599), the brother of one of Palladio's closest patrons, Jacopo Contarini of San Samuele. Palladio was commissioned in 1575 to provide designs for a high altar, which was dismantled in subsequent seventeenth- and eighteenth-century reconstructions of the church, notably during the work of Baldassare Longhena (died 1682) on the interior and exterior (fig. 292).[53] Its altarpiece, the *Coronation of the Virgin* by a Titian pupil, Damiano Mazza (died 1576), was adjusted to its new enframement and remains *in situ*.[54] The commission of the high altar represents on Palladio's part a commitment to his Venetian patrons, and, on their part, a recognition of his innovative approach to ecclesiastical furnishings.

The decision to produce a new high altar was probably in part an opportunistic bid to gain eligibility as one of the four churches designated for the Jubilee year of 1575, thus trying to ensure financial support for the rebuilding of the church through almsgiving.

Although the governors were unsuccessful in this attempt, they were allowed to place collection boxes in the four churches that had been nominated, and they also voted to use other funds, including offerings from the processions of the children and half of the money from the singing of the girls.[55] Like the *scuole*, *ospedali* had to balance their concern with providing for their needy populations with that of their desire to institute building campaigns, although housing and caring for their inmates necessarily initiated physical growth. Financing the endeavors of these relatively recent institutions rested heavily on the resources of their governing boards, as special bequests for the fabric of the church illustrate.

Spiritual health was the ultimate goal. With a sense of civic responsibility, the network of lay patrons both male and female – patricians, citizens, merchants, well-to-do artisans – helped to formulate these institutions targeted to specific groups, as the relief efforts of the Counter-Reformation period became increasingly organized into what the historian Brian Pullan has called "the new philanthropy." The "Spedale di S. Giovanni, e Paolo" was recognized in this arena of lay Catholic charity, as Francesco Sansovino describes:

> Which [the "Spedale"] grew over time both in building fabric as in exercise of piety, becoming a famous place, and celebrated among others in the city, with the help of its Catholic brethren, administrating for the love of God with all their power, sustaining thus religious and Christian actions.[56]

The inspiration and direction of the "new philanthropy" in Venice is encapsulated in the story of the Ospedaletto. From its early sixteenth-century origins in the currents of Catholic reform, with charismatic figures such as Girolamo Miani and Guillaume Postel, to an enterprise more regulated by prescriptions from Trent and controls legislated by the State, the Ospedaletto, and other institutions like it, became sites for the intersection of the estates of Venetian society. Giuseppe Ellero has described the period as a

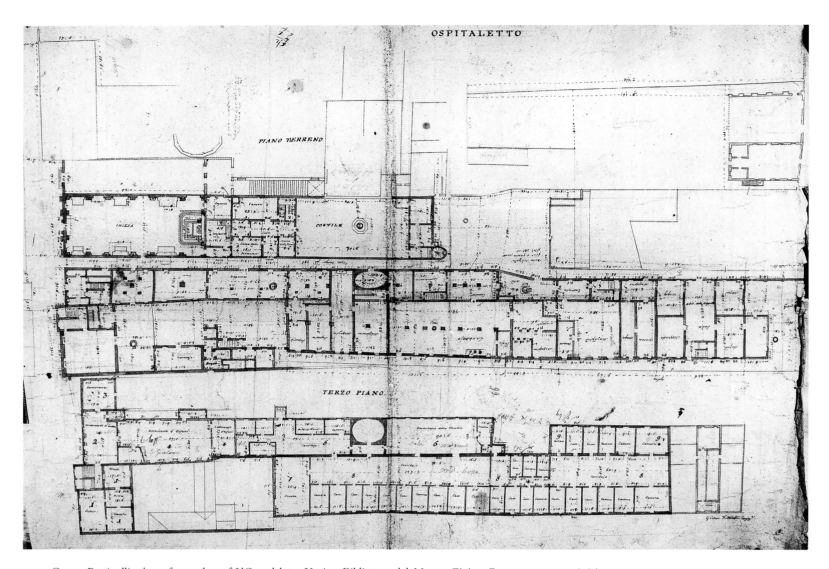

291 Cesare Fustinelli, plan of complex of L'Ospedaletto, Venice, Biblioteca del Museo Civico Correr, MS P. D. c 818/17, 1–2

"rinascità cattolica" ("Catholic Renaissance"), an idea that may offer another way to conceptualize a continuity in reform aims without reference to a model of opposition as contained in the notion of the "Counter"-Reformation.[57]

Piety and public service were combined in the role of governance at the *ospedali*, which, unlike the *scuole*, had patrician participation. It has been surmised that Giovanni Battista Contarini's position as governor, or *presidente* in 1573, and election to supervise the building program as *deputato sopra la fabbrica* in 1574, and his repeated presence on the board of governors thereafter, were crucial to Palladio's involvement in the new church.[58] As noted in earlier chapters, during the dogate of Alvise Mocenigo (1570–77), his brother Jacopo Contarini and Palladio were active together in several prestigious projects, and tradition has it that Palladio resided at the family palace at San Samuele when in Venice. Giovanni Battista's relationship to the patriarch of Venice, Giovanni Trevisan, whom he accompanied to the Council of Trent, has been remarked

upon in terms of his pious activities with religious leaders of the city: later Giovanni Battista and the Somaschi were active in helping Trevisan to establish a patriarchal seminary amid some resistance, and may have attempted such educational and vocational reforms at the Ospedaletto in 1578.[59] Through this connection, however, an even earlier link can be made between the spheres in which the patrician and the architect moved, since the visit to Trent had also included one of Palladio's closest supporters, Daniele Barbaro. It will be recalled, of course, that Palladio counted both the patriarchs of Venice and Aquileia among his first major patrons in Venice. Scientific and academic interests, as well as a profound interest in architecture, were elements held in common between the Barbaro and Contarini brothers, who were instrumental in forging the shape of Palladio's career through the particular relations developed in their patronage – and collaboration.

The actual high altar designed by Palladio for the Ospedaletto was lost in the subsequent rebuilding of the church, although the

292　Baldassare Longhena (design), façade, L'Ospedaletto, Venice

altarpiece remains in the magnificent Baroque setting provided for the ever increasing fame of the young *figlie di coro* (girl choir), as do two large plinths now supporting statues. It is described in the contract.[60] The stonemasons Pasqualin and Marchio were contracted to provide the altar designed by Palladio with its stone ornament ("iusta il dissegno fatta da esso misier Andrea Palladio"), who also would provide their templates ("et iusta le sagome che da esso misier Andrea li saranno date"). An alteration was then made to the existing design, difficult to interpret with certainty, although providing a tantalizing further description of its elements: it substituted the four columns that were to go in the middle of the altar ("eccettuando però le quattro colonne che vano in mezo di esso altare, le quali con i suoi capi[telli] et basse siano fatte far per detto Hospitale"), and the cornice beneath the vault that was in the center of the altarpiece ("et la corn[nice] sotto il volto che va in mezo della Pala").[61] Instead, the "colonne grandi" of the intended design were to be fluted piers ("la qual non vi [è] intendendo che quelle colonne grandi che sono dissegnate si intendano pilastri canellati"). There were to be five steps whose bases were to be made according to templates provided by Palladio as well ("iusta la sagoma ordinaria del sopradito misier Andrea Palladio"). The whole was to be made of beautiful stone ("bellissima pietra"), according to the design ("iusta il sopradito dissegno"), and the contract included the stipulation that the altar table was to be of a single piece of stone ("la pietra dell'altar come il parapetto siano tutti di un pezzo"), for which work, carried out with due diligence, the stonemasons would receive 225 ducats. Six months later an amendment recognized that the original contract for the improvements of the altar ("li miglioramenti dell'altar") had not included the small piers around the church walls ("pilastri piccoli"), to be executed by the same stonemasons for an additional 208 ducats.

There have been various attempts to reconstruct the design from the information contained in the contract with the stonemasons and its amendment, from the architectural elements left from the earlier church and the altarpiece itself, and from comparison to Palladio's own repertory. There are rather large variations between the conceptions of Palladio's altar, not entirely surprising, because the evidence is fragmentary and inconclusive. What they do agree on, however, is that Palladio was seeking an appropriate form for the altar of a hospital church, in this case with the specific needs related to its choir function: the physical seclusion of the choristers and their auditory accessibility.

The contribution of Palladio to the manifestation of "Catholic Renaissance" ideals regarding the decorous relation of choir to altar to liturgical practice in his architectural programs had significant currency as demonstrated by requests for his advice, such as the cathedrals of Montagnana (1564) and Milan (1570), in addition to his own projects in Venice.[62] For the Ospedaletto, the traditional placement of women's choirs would have been a primary consideration in the design as well. These might be separated from the congregation by being raised a story above it, in a *barco*, also called a *ponte* or *pontile*, or hanging choir, that could be located over the entrance (as originally at Santa Lucia), or in a space that gave access

to the service through grilles in upper-story walls to the side or behind the altar, as eventually here. Notices show that some kind of choir had existed since 1566 and may have been taken into account in the new church.[63] In addition to the choir, requirements surrounding the space allotted to the high altar included room for the celebrants, among which were the most promising orphans in training by the Somaschi for a life in the Church, and the governors who were privileged to experience the services seated in the presbytery.[64] The position of the high altar with its altarpiece in relation to these different groups of participants in the liturgical ritual must have posed a stimulating problem to the architect.

The architectural historian Elena Bassi was the first to suggest a link to Palladio's earlier essay in designing an altar, which took the form of a ciborium, for a hospital church at Santo Spirito in Sassia in Rome during his trip there in 1546–47 (fig. 293).[65] An altar in this form solved a problem of visibility for patients confined to their beds in hospitals; the importance of making the action of the Mass visually accessible would lead to the broadly instituted type of the tabernacle altar for similar reasons. That such an altar also could serve as a centerpiece for a choir screen can be imagined by comparison with Girolamo Campagna's high altar for the former Benedictine convent at San Lorenzo (fig. 294).[66] A different reconstruction was posed by Giuseppe Pilo in his monograph on the Ospedaletto, in which the altar was framed by two giant Ionic piers on tall plinths, the altarpiece in a central larger bay, flanked by niches with four fluted columns, and an arch over the cornice of the central bay. The piers would have formed part of the altar wall, behind which was the choir (at the present level of the sacristy; it was subsequently moved above as a hanging choir). The plinths are identified with those now supporting the statues of Sts. Francis and Sebastian (figs. 295 and 296). Pilo utilized Antonio Sardi's contract of 1659 to extract further details about the existing high altar, and to hypothesize that the Palladio altar was not completed, although some elements were taken over in Sardi's design for a new one.[67] Bernard Aikema and Dulcia Meijers propose that Sardi's intervention was not based on any assumption that the altar was incomplete or in the wrong style, but, rather, that it was an outcome of the continuing development of the musical activities that necessitated structural changes for the choir, choir wall, and organ. This particularly affected the area of the "volto" and "cornise," and probably the supporting elements of the orders also became inadequate for the eventual institution of open *cantorie*, singers' balconies, above the high altar. In their reading, the altar assumed the traditional Renaissance form of a pediment ("frontespizio o frontone") supported by the four columns.[68]

Was Palladio responsible for a larger program for the Ospedaletto? This question was initially advanced in the affirmative by Bassi, who pointed to similarities in the church to Santa Maria Nova in Vicenza (1585–89), also executed after Palladio's death, and to other projects conceived at the Ospedaletto during Giovanni Battista Contarini's tenure (such as the *casa delle donne*), and to the impressive oval stairway *a chiocciola* or *alla lumacha* (spiral, or snail-shaped) actually built by Antonio Sardi's son, Giuseppe, in the years

293 Saulnier, engraving of interior of Santo Spirito in Sassia, Rome, with altar by Andrea Palladio

294 Simone Sorella, interior of San Lorenzo, Venice, high altar and choir grills by Girolamo Campagna

1662–66.[69] Yet Antonio da Ponte's presence at the Ospedaletto preceded that of Palladio and just as likely included responsibility for the church as well as the areas of the hospital where his involvement is documented. Even the stonemasons Marchio and Pasqualin, usually cited in support of a connection to Palladio, had equally close associations with da Ponte, and so cannot be said to work for either architect exclusively.[70] The stairway raises a crucial issue for the evaluation of Palladio's contribution: there can be little doubt that its fundamental inspiration was Palladio's celebrated and well-published stairway for the Convento della Carità. In principle, then, his "authorship," with its attendant implications of authority, lies behind the "modelli et piante" (models – which could be two-dimensional renderings as well as sculptural – and plans) that the talented Sardi employed for what he, however, considered to be his own "Nova scala a lumacha."[71] A more cautious view of Palladio's direct involvement is warranted, while acknowledging that by the mid-1570s his architectural presence had become more pervasive. This was achieved by the particular type of relationships that Palladio had forged with his patrons, stretching the traditional constraints of their disparate social status in shared intellectual and academic enquiry, resulting in a new role for the architect as distinct from the *proto*, above all in the process of designing the program. Even when not acted upon, Palladio's ideas were valued as the demands on him for advising and evaluating show, and as the influence of his writing and built works prove – a Renaissance Rem Koolhaas – stimulating his patrons' thinking about their projects.

The hospital as a civic form approximated the social structure of Venice, as its priority of seating in the choir would proclaim, but despite patrician predominance, there were not the same inflexible castes in roles of governance. Patricians and citizens alike might share the roles of president. If this work on behalf of society's good opened up an arena for interaction between them, it also introduced another group into a public realm otherwise limited in access: patrician women. The board of male governors at the Ospedaletto was matched by a board of female governors, and the direct administration of the hospital devolved on a prioress. The focus on the life and livelihood of the inmates found a natural parallel to the family, the predominant place for a female sphere of influence. Charitable organizations such as these were an acceptable means for wealthy patrician women, often widows, to take a more

295 Baldassare Longhena, renovation of interior altars, with high altar by Tommaso Ruer, L'Ospedaletto, Venice

worldly "public" role,[72] a lay alternative to the cloister that also provided an opportunity for exercising governance and *de facto* decision-making. If the *de jure* signatures and minutes of the male governors exclude direct knowledge of the possible interaction of architect and female community, it can at least be supposed that there was a consultative potential between Palladio and the women concerned about the function of the institution. Shared spiritual and social concerns become a window on a less accessible segment of Venetian society, which can be seen to have a network that inter-sected with others of Palladio's patrons. As Palladio strove to shape

a syntax for female space within the architectural grammar that he was defining for the choir, how did the tradition of female exclusion and separation affect his thought? Was the experience at the Ospedaletto one that would influence his final designs for Il Redentore, about to be commissioned as the plague of 1575–76 ravaged the city, or for San Giorgio Maggiore, extending the principles of his earlier design to a new degree of removal of the choir in his last years there? One of the prominent governesses at the time of Palladio's intervention at the Ospedaletto reaffirms the notion of several of its historians to describe this as the

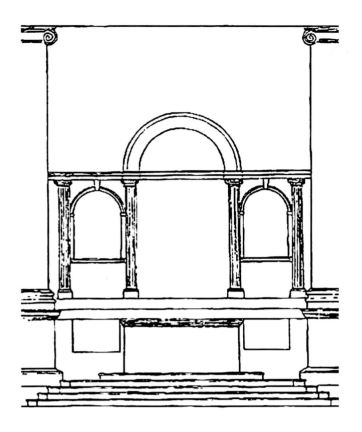

"Contarinian period." This was Andriana Contarini di Sebastiano Bernardo, widow of Vincenzo di Alvise Contarini of the *ramo* of Madonna dell'Orto. Andriana's husband was the brother of the renowned cardinal Gasparo Contarini, leader of Catholic reform and philosopher of the ideal of the Venetian State.[73] Her efforts merited the praise of another figure, Cardinal Agostino Valier, who dedicated to her, as an exemplar of pious behavior and educational reform efforts, a book of instructions to virgins, widows, and married women.[74] That the impulses for reform were transmitted by women in the city can be followed through what correspondence exists, through their testamentary dispositions, and through their efforts in establishing institutions that would realize an active Christian life not only as a matter of personal salvation, but as a public good. Looking at the disadvantaged of their gender and children above all, these women were instrumental in the "new philanthropy," and in creating a demand for its new buildings by Palladio and other architects.

296 (*left*) Giuseppe Pilo, reconstruction of Andrea Palladio's high altar, L'Ospedaletto, Venice, from Pilo 1985, fig. 7

CHAPTER EIGHTEEN

LE ZITELLE

A N INSTITUTION TO HOUSE YOUNG WOMEN in danger of entering a life of prostitution was founded in Venice by the Jesuit Benedetto Palmio in 1558 and, in 1561, was located on the Giudecca, "un loco bonissimo e bellissimo" – a wholesome and beautiful place. The Conservatorio delle Zitelle, now Santa Maria delle Presentazione (fig. 297), was distinguished by its formative patronage by Venetian patrician women, one of whose early leaders was Andriana Contarini née Bernardo. Both the location and the occupational training in lace making, of *punto in aria*, contributed to the isolation of the young women, seen as necessary to their salvation.[75]

The first expansion of the complex came in the mid-1570s to satisfy a need for adequate housing. Only in the 1580s was a new church constructed, which from the early seventeenth century was associated with the name of Palladio, who had died the year before it was begun (fig. 298).[76] The two-story church façade with its upper thermal window facing the Piazza emerges from the center of flanking hospice wings topped by a low dome with a lantern and framed by twin towers. The angled corners of the centralized plan modify the interior from a square into an octagonal shape, with a shallow atrium and raised presbytery, articulated by flat Corinthian pilasters with a pronounced cornice. Thermal windows over the two lateral chapels provided private access to church services for the girls, *le zitelle* (fig. 299).

The attribution to Palladio, above all, captures the beginning of an important phenomenon in Venetian, and later, world architecture: Palladianism. It has often been maintained, however, that a closer connection than simple emulation of Palladio exists, even to the use of his designs.[77] This has been tied to Zitelle patronage. Many of the same patricians, male and female, were involved in poor relief throughout the city.[78] One protector, or trustee, Giovanni Battista Contarini, has just been discussed as instrumental to Palladio's patronage at the Ospedaletto, and may help to

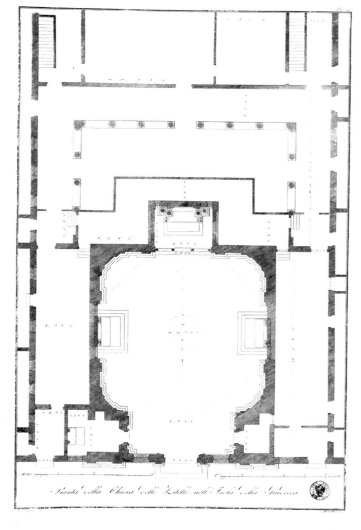

298 Leopoldo Cicognara, Antonio Diedo, and Gianantonio Selva, plan of Le Zitelle, *Le fabbriche e i monumenti più cospicui di Venezia*, ed. F. Zanotto, Venice 1858, 2:240

297 *(facing page)*   Le Zitelle, Isola della Giudecca, Venice

299 Thermal windows with grills above side altar, Le Zitelle, Venice

explain the employment of one of the same stonemasons at the Zitelle. Yet another was Agostino Barbarigo, one of the *provveditori* of the nearby Il Redentore, who may have operated as a conduit for unused designs by Palladio. But is it necessary to see the direct hand of Palladio at the Zitelle to acknowledge the force and influence of his re-conception of religious architecture? It remains meaningful to explore its adoption in the context of the reform efforts being undertaken at the Zitelle, and how this was managed, as a manifestation of his didactic success in communicating his ideas to his patrons, and to those who followed.

It now seems clear, from exhaustive research in the archives by scholars looking for evidence of Palladio's presence and an earlier date for the inception of the church, that Nicolò Doglioni's account of the laying of the first stone in 1581 must be respected. Despite the typically uncertain finances of this type of charitable institution – the governess, Andriana Contarini, just in this year paid off the debt for acquiring the property twenty years previously – it was an event of great prestige: present were the heads of both State and Church (to put them in Venetian order), with the attendance of the doge (Nicolò da Ponte), patriarch of Venice (Giovanni Trevisan), the Signoria, and crowds of people.[79] The church was executed in a relatively brisk campaign. Materials had been laid by from the first phase of work on the housing; some financial aid and surplus timbers from the Redentore building site were granted by the Senate in 1582; more were financed through some bequests; and significant progress was already noted by 1583.[80] A date of 1586 recorded in the presbytery marks the first phase of the interior decoration, with the altar and burial site commissioned by the Bergamese merchant Bartolomeo Marchesi in his will of 1583.[81] Its altarpiece by Francesco Bassano reflects the dedication of the church, showing the *Presentation of the Virgin in the Temple*, a subject that reflected both the charity enacted by the benefactors of the institution, represented in perpetuity, as well as speaking to its

inhabitants as a model of virtue (fig. 300). The church was consecrated in 1588 by the co-adjutor to the patriarch of Aquileia, Francesco Barbaro, son of Palladio's patron Marc'Antonio Barbaro, who would become a notable reformer upon succeeding Giovanni Grimani a few years later.[82]

A persistent trend to make Palladio its author, if not executor, was begun in the literature on the Zitelle as early as Giovanni Stringa's statement in 1604 that "this church was made on the model of Palladio, but executed by Bozetto."[83] This proposal regarding Palladio's contribution has also been expanded to include the program for the complex as a whole, begun during Palladio's lifetime, when he was engaged with other projects, such as the Ospedaletto, linked to patrons of the Zitelle.[84] It has been equally recognized that economic conditions may not have favored either an elaborate type of model or its global realization. Rather, of necessity, work would be conducted in phases when financially possible, since this was an expensive undertaking that needed to be balanced against other demands on the growing institution, such as dowries for the young women. The phased nature of the construction process has been used as an explanation both for the delay in execution and level of fidelity to Palladio's style. Yet Stringa's use of the word *modello* also should be approached cautiously, for its meaning in the Renaissance encompassed a range of possibilities, from a three-dimensional built model, to drawings, to style or example.[85] The executor named by Stringa as "Bozetto" has been identified with Jacopo (Giacomo Bozzetto), who had worked in the Doge's Palace after the fire of 1577, and died in 1583. This provides only a tenuous connection to Palladio.[86] But, no more direct evidence has been found to support Stringa's assertion.

Perhaps the problem can be approached from another perspective by asking the question differently: was it possible, by the time of Palladio's death, for local practitioners, *proti* and stonemasons, as well as patrons, to have grasped and internalized to this degree the lineaments of his architectural language to create such a building as the church of the Zitelle without his actual participation? Or, did the architect's death release his work from its exclusive associations to become available, at least in quotations, such as thermal windows and dome, treatment of orders and spatial arrangements, or even in ideas of proportions and types, in a similar way as for Jacopo Sansovino a decade earlier? Since his collaboration with Daniele Barbaro on Vitruvius in the 1550s, to his own publication of the *Four Books of Architecture* in 1570, Palladio had made his principles accessible through theory and models. That patrons and *proti* would continue the debate over the insertion of classical architecture as represented by Palladio into the urban fabric resonant with issues constructing Venetian identity is readily demonstrated in the opposition met by later architects (such as Scamozzi) when they conflicted with tradition.

It is the nexus of patrons that has provided the most compelling argument for the reception of Palladio and his architectural language at the Zitelle. Female governance played an even more prominent role at the Zitelle than the Ospedaletto, and, if religious in orientation, it was a secular institution, unlike the cloistered communities of Augustinians and Cistercians at Santa Lucia and the Celestia. The governess Andriana Contarini was praised by Cardinal Valier as an exemplary widow, one of the "imitators of that holy Martha" ("imitatrici di quella santa Marta"), whose tireless efforts created a haven within the walls of Venice in the hospice. Andriana was one of the founders of the institution, as her letter regarding the search for an appropriate site has already revealed. Her sister, Marina Bernardo, also a fellow governess of the Ospedaletto, would become *madonna*, or prioress (also called *madre*) of the Zitelle, in charge of the daily administration, holding this position for more than forty years, admired for her "resolute spirit" ("animo risoluto"). As the director of the Zitelle, Marina Bernardo was in charge of maintaining relations between the two congregations of male and female boards of governors, and its internal administration, as well as the conduct and physical life of the institution. Her "Libro di madonna" is one of the few surviving documents to testify to the early period of construction, 1575–76, when the *casa da statio* was amplified and substantial building materials were accumulated. Another of the Zitelle founders was Lucrezia Priuli di Pietro Contarini, sister of Jacopo and Giovanni Battista Contarini, the latter already noted above as a trustee (protector). Moreover, their household factor from San Samuele, Gerolamo Presagno, acted in that capacity at the Zitelle, while his son was factor at the Ospedaletto. One of Giovanni Battista Contarini's colleagues at the Ospedaletto, Gerolamo Andrusian, was his fellow *deputato sopra la fabbrica* in 1574, and subsequently elected as *cassiere*, or treasurer, a position he held also at the Zitelle, where he would have handled accounts for construction as well, in conjunction with Madonna Marina.

The contemporary experience of the Ospedaletto building program, in which the *proto al sal* Antonio da Ponte and Palladio were both present, must have been a crucial reference for the Zitelle patrons, especially those involved with both locations. It is tempting to hypothesize a more specific connection from the limited evidence of Marina Bernardo's "Libro di madonna," in which the name of Marchio *tajapiera*, one of the stonemasons of the Ospedaletto high altar, appears in 1575. As noted above, however, there is not the exclusive rapport with Palladio and a *cantiere* to confirm more than the opportunity. One name does stand out as having more continuity, albeit in a modest capacity, Stefano Paliaga di Antonio, who is listed several times in the "Libro di madonna" among other providers of materials, such as sand, lime, and stone, as well as in one of the only notices from the period of the church in 1582; his son Zuanmaria then appears as a supplier of bricks in documents from 1589 through to 1597, when other buildings were added to the complex. Only in the latter phase is there a master at the level of a *proto* named; this was Bortolo, who has been identified as the *proto* of the Scuola Grande di San Rocco. The absence of documentation for the period when the church was under construction limits the conclusions that can be drawn from this fragmentary information. But there is another small inference that can be drawn to connect the Zitelle building program with another site in which Palladio was architect and the supervisor of the work was

300 Apse with high altar and Francesco Bassano's *Presentation of the Virgin in the Temple*, Le Zitelle, Venice

the *proto* Antonio da Ponte: Il Redentore. The name of Stefano Paliaga appears there in an estimate from 1586, although for materials for the new Capuchin cloister, rather than the church itself, about which there is little information for the artisans. Although unlikely to have any formative role, the employment of some of the same workers may indicate communication at other levels for the practical operations of these building sites. There has been some speculation that this may have occurred at the highest level of patronage as well.

The group of drawings (London, RIBA, XIV, 13–14–15–16; see figs. 242–45) that have been attributed to Palladio's proposal for a central planned "rotunda" type for the Redentore voted down in 1577 (9 February 1576 m.v.) have been seen as a possible point of departure for the Zitelle.[87] This hypothesis necessitates a re-examination of the possible chronology of some kind of involvement, either by Palladio, or indirectly through his patrons, making the probability of his early contribution to a global planning effort less

301 Frontispiece portrait of Andrea Palladio in Lord Burlington's publication of Baths, edition of Ottavio Bertotti Scamozzi, *Le terme dei Romani, disegnate da Andrea Palladio, e rippublicate con la giunta di alcini osservazioni da Ottavio Bertotti Scamozzi, giusta l'esemplare del lord co, di Burlingthon impresso in Londra l'anno 1732*, Vicenza, Per Francesco Modena, 1785

likely (although not invalidating the idea that a full-scale project was intended from the start). The drawings may have provided a vehicle – or *modello* – for the consideration of a centralized plan, uncommon in Venice, although a type that suggested itself for a church dedicated to the Virgin, as even in a revered example, Santa Maria della Rotunda – the Pantheon – in Rome. Three of the drawings depict the plan, section, and façade of a porticoed circular-plan temple (RIBA, XIV, 13–14–15), while the fourth lacks a portico, and an interior cross-vault is indicated with variant articulation of columns and niches (RIBA, XIV, 16).[88] Both versions show consideration of a restricted site (with *calle* indicated on either side as at the Redentore) and different solutions for an anterior

choir space that removes it from the main body of the church through a columnar screen, elements of concern at the Zitelle. The differences, however, between these drawings that represent alternative projects for the Redentore "in forma rotonda" and the Zitelle as executed seem greater than a simple scaling down for a more modest public presence would explain: the translation of the circular to quadrangular plan, eradication of the niches and columns to be replaced by flat pilasters, the two-story façade. Yet, the idea of a domed central-planned church was given currency by the prominence of the Redentore and nearby San Giorgio projects. The translation as a composite work also dependent on other available examples, such as Palladio's Santa Lucia, makes better sense if the work was directed more by its patrons than by the guiding mind of an architect of the caliber of Palladio, since such a process still allows for his influence to be seen.

There are several possible ways that the Zitelle governors could have had access to Palladio's alternate designs for the Redentore,

302 San Trovaso, Venice

because one of them, Agostino Barbarigo, was elected as one of the two *provveditori sopra la fabbrica* of the Redentore, and his colleague, Antonio Bragadin, can also be found at the Zitelle.[89] We have already seen that the Senate would vote to help the Zitelle with its project by granting timber from the Redentore construction in 1582, so it may be that the *provveditori* were instrumental in this connection as well. Another means suggests itself upon examination of the provenance of the drawings, again relying on Lionello Puppi's investigations: even more directly, Giovanni Battista Contarini may have been privy to the drawings through his brother Jacopo (unless he had been made aware of them even earlier by Palladio himself). The particular route that these drawings took to London was via Lord Burlington's purchase of drawings in 1719, which Puppi has traced from Bernardo Trevisan back to Vincenzo Scamozzi, who inherited them from Jacopo Contarini, left to him by Palladio in the studio at the Contarini palace at San Samuele. Burlington's acquisition is usually discussed in relation to his subsequent publication of Palladio's drawings after Roman baths, which it has been supposed Palladio had with him in Venice with intention to proceed in publishing further books of architecture (fig. 301).[90] The versatility of Palladio's approach to design is articulated by Howard Burns (on RIBA, XIV, 13–14–15–16): "The group of drawings illustrates Palladio's normal working procedure: the deliberate and systematic evolution of alternatives, which even if they were not chosen as they stood, could still be drawn upon in subsequent designs."[91] Presumably Palladio expected his close patrons and collaborators to understand this didactic process and benefit from it in their building enterprises. That he was successful in developing a strategic design process and associated grammar of ornament and typology is reflected in the recognizable syntax of such examples as Le Zitelle and San Trovaso (fig. 302). The Venetian patricians who founded the Zitelle brought formidable resources and experiences to their enterprise, and the agency demonstrated both by women and men in this common enterprise of reform is expressed in their utilization of a Palladian language.

CONCLUSION

With his many virtues he has conjoined such an amiable and gentle nature that it makes him beloved of everyone.

Vasari, *Lives of the Artists*, 1568[1]

THE OUTCOME OF PALLADIO'S CAREER IN VENICE led to his being addressed as "architectus Illustrissimi Dominii Veneti" (Architect of the Most Illustrious Dominion of the Venetians), indelibly connected to the architectural fabric and cultural prestige of the Republic (fig. 303).[2] His critical importance to the profession of architecture stems from this period in the capital. He developed particular relationships with patrons that were a happy confluence of his esteemed personality, and his unusual training and early experience as an architect who collaborated with his patrons in the discovery of ancient architecture and developing the principles of a new way – the *usanza nuova* – of architecture. He put into production an immensely effective tool to communicate his theory and practice both to builders and to their patrons in the *Four Books*. Finally there is the legacy of the buildings themselves. Palladio's built works in Venice presented his program for architecture on a monumental scale and altered the civic landscape.

The individual circumstances of each building provided opportunities for Palladio to apply his ideals and practical knowledge of architecture. He was noted for educating his patrons and for educating his workforce in these. His practice was affected by the network of patrons that he developed and the historical circumstances of a changing society. As a result, he became deeply engaged in the genre of ecclesiastical architecture. His commissions reflect issues of Church and State that troubled the early modern period, and substantiate the claims that architectural style was associated with particular affiliations in this debate, but these alignments were not yet the more developed factions of the early seventeenth century. The buildings and cultural projects associated with them reflect more complex sets of overlapping associations that reveal intersections between familial, social, economic, and political networks. Confluences between power and patronage were most favorable for Palladio in the 1570s. Palladio's interventions in the city fabric began to attract attention as *cose notabili da vedere* ("notable things to see"), in the language of the visitors' guidebooks, such as Sansovino's, and in the new genre of artists' lives, such as Vasari's.

The King's Palladian Itinerary

When King Henri III came to Venice in 1574, the most monumental symbol of this singular visit of state was the ephemeral architectural *apparati* designed by Palladio and his patrons, Jacopo Contarini and Alvise Mocenigo. This may have been enough to pique the interest of the youthful king in this architect's work. Henri III displayed an aesthetic for cultural display that seemed to have included the usual tastes of a cultivated gentleman in collections of antiquities, contemporary masters of painting, curiosities, and current architecture – even to the extent of going to building sites. He was credited with asking to see several rooms in the Doge's Palace, including the private apartments of Doge Mocenigo, and the *provveditori* for the restoration after the fire only a few months previously may well have acquainted him with their plans for an even more splendid rebuilding during their official attendance on the king. Palladio's patrons were in a position of dominance at this time as their roles in the king's visit indicates, especially since the French were among the few powers to support the Peace of Cyprus, with which the doge, Marc'Antonio Barbaro, Andrea Badoer, the Soranzos and Tiepolos, and others would be associated. Henri III was notorious for his unofficial nocturnal forays into the city; on one night he visited the patriarch of Aquileia, Giovanni Grimani, at his palace at Santa Maria Formosa to see the famous collections, view the celebrated palace, and watch thirty *gentildonne* dancing the galliard. It seems likely that he was shown the new façade of Grimani's church at San Francesco della Vigna. On his visit to San Giorgio Maggiore, where he conversed with the abbot, the king would have been able to see the breathtaking complex of Palladio's refectory with its decoration by Veronese and almost completed circumference of the new church, vaulting, and cupola. Less reliable is the report of his going to Le Zitelle, but the institution housing girls of dangerous beauty was probably as much an attraction as the plans for a new complex that were being forwarded by the brother of Jacopo Contarini, whom the king favored for his role in the programming of the *apparati* for his visit. Although the king and his retinue were lodged in the Gothic-style Palazzo Foscari, its *padrone*, Alvise Foscari, was an early supporter of Palladio in Venice, and his taste for the new architecture would be made evident on the departure of Henri III when he traveled up the Brenta canal, stopping for *pranzo* (luncheon) at the Villa Foscari at Malcontenta (Gambarare). Henri III's host in Padua was Pietro Foscari, whose palace at the Arena boasted an intimate connection with classical architecture, literally emplaced in the Roman ruins of the ancient theatre, and who was another of the *provveditori* engaged in the restoration of the Doge's Palace. Thus the king's visit to Venice and his ceremonial leave-taking to Padua comprised a kind of Palladian itinerary.[3]

Yet Palladio's career in Venice did not take the expected form of predominantly domestic and secular public architecture as would have been predicted from the commissions that had made him famous in Vicenza and the Veneto and brought him to the attention of his Venetian patrons. Instead, his major contribution to monumental architecture in Venice allowed him to develop the typology of the church and its furnishings, for a variety of religious and charitable institutions, and even for the State. Palladio's largest-scale domestic efforts in Venice were the cloisters of the monastery of the Carità. Understanding of Palladio's work in Venice is also affected by the publication date of the *Four Books*, in 1570, when so many of his great works were still to be realized. His place in the history of a development of an architectural form is expressive of the complex nature of his accomplishments in the genre of ecclesiastical architecture. In attempts to establish a new church plan in response to the demands of his reform-minded patrons, his solutions found similar responses in contemporaries such as Galeazzo Alessi in Milan and Jacopo Vignola in Rome; the unified nave with extended choir found widespread application. On the other hand, one of the most admired elements of Palladio's churches, the monumental temple-front façades, found little immediate resonance outside of Venice. Yet Palladio's churches with their scenographic façades transformed the Venetian urban appearance, and have become inescapably associated with the image of the city. Palladio's workshop practices and patronage network led to immediate emulation, in the churches of Le Zitelle and San Trovaso. Even more profoundly, Palladio's major church commissions were themselves the epitome of a design process, one in which the architect's own evolutionary ideas would introduce change and modification of the original model into the site, as would the working conditions over time, and especially after his death as building continued.[4] The work of Vincenzo Scamozzi and Baldassare Longhena in Venice would take up his challenge, not only in terms of design but also architectural practice. The intellectual authority that was the basis of Palladio's creative process was fundamental to the establishment of the modern profession of the architect and a new dynamic in patronage, for when Gentlemen began to practice architecture, Architects could become gentlemen.

APPENDICES

APPENDIX I

CHRONOLOGY OF PALLADIO'S WORKS
ACCORDING TO PATRONS

Year	Part I Foundations	Part II Patronage	Part III Patriarchs	Part IV Religious Orders	Part V The State	Part VI Charitable Institutions
1548	First documented in Venice					
1549						
1550	Death of Giangiorgio Trissino					
1551						
1552						
1553		(circa) Memorandum to Leonardi				
1554	L'antichità di Roma; Descritione delle chiese				Competitions: Proto al Sal; Scala d'Oro	
1555		Altar of San Pantalon; designs for Venetian palaces			Rialto Bridge complex (I)	
1556	Daniele Barbaro's Vitruvius	Daniele Barbaro, Palazzo Trevisan, Murano				
1557		Tomb of G. B. Ferretti				
1558			Design for San Pietro di Castello			
1559						
1560				San Giorgio Maggiore refectory		
1561				Model of Santa Maria della Carità		

Year	Part I Foundations	Part II Patronage	Part III Patriarchs	Part IV Religious Orders	Part V The State	Part VI Charitable Institutions
1562						
1563			(circa) Façade of San Francesco della Vigna			
1564						
1565		Theater for the Accesi		San Giorgio Maggiore model of church		
1566				S. Giorgio Maggiore construction; design of Santa Lucia	(circa) Rialto Bridge complex (II)	
1567	Daniele Barbaro's *Vitruvius*, 2nd edn.					
1568						
1569				Repairs at the Carità		
1570	Death of Daniele Barbaro, Jacopo Sansovino; *I quattro libri d'architettura*			Repairs at the Carità; Cloister of La Celestia		Scuola dei Mercanti
1571						
1572					Tomb of Doge Alvise Mocenigo	
1573		Pisani *vigna* on the Lido		La Carità refectory	Arch for Henri III's entry	
1574					Doge's Palace fire (I)	
1575	*I Commentari di C. Giulio Cesare*					Altar of L'Ospedaletto
1576				San Giorgio Maggiore circumference completed, dome	Il Redentore	
1577					Doge's Palace fire (II)	
1578						
1579				San Giorgio Maggiore extended choir, Cloister of the Cypresses		
1580	Death of Andrea Palladio					
1581						Le Zitelle

APPENDIX II

PROVVEDITORI FOR THE DOGE'S PALACE
1533–1600

After Giambattista Lorenzi, *Monumenti per servire alla storia del Palazzo Ducale in Venezia, pt. 1, Dal 1253 al 1600*, Venice, 1868, 599–600.
Appendix 32, "Serie dei Provveditore sopra la fabbrica del Palazzo."
ASV, Secretario alle Voci, Elezioni del Senato, Reg. 1–6, Senato, Deliberazioni, 1532 27 March–6 December 1600.

Date of Election	Name	Fondo
13 May 1533	Tommaso Mocenigo Paulo Trevisan Giacomo Soranzo P.	Reg. 1, c. 58v, Delib. Sen., 27 March 1532 (Doc. 428)
28 May 1534	Leonardo Emo	
19 June 1546	Lorenzo Giustinian	
March 1550	Gabriel Vendramin Vettor Grimani P.	
19 August 1553	Giulio Contarini Antonio Capello Francesco Venier	
7 October 1553	Maffio Venier	
2 October 1554	Alvise Contarini Alvise Mocenigo K. Benedetto Pesaro	Reg. 2, c. 52v, ibid.
30 May 1555	Antonio Giustinian	
12 August 1555	Maffio Venier	
15 October 1555	Federico Morosini Paolo Contarini	
24 October 1555	Alvise Foscarini	
10 October 1556	Bernardo Venier Alvise Contarini Lodovico Gradenigo	

Date of Election	Name	Fondo
21 June 1557	Alvise Foscarini	
15 October 1557	Alvise da Mula Girolamo da Ca Taiapiera Giovanni da Leze	
15 October 1558	Giacomo Soranzo K. Ferigo Morosini Antonio Calbo	
13 October 1559	Antonio Zorzi Andrea Barbarigo Nicolò da Ponte, Dr. K.	
4 February 1560	Polo Contarini Andrea Bernardo	Reg. 3, c. 48, ibid.
17 October 1560	Giovanni Mocenigo Francesco Badoer Giovanni Bondumier	
12 May 1574	Andrea Badoer K. Vicenzo Morosini Pietro Foscari	Reg. 4, c. 74, Delib. Sen., 12 May 1574 (Doc. 786)
9 May 1575	Marc'Antonio Barbaro P.	
20 January 1578	Alvise Zorzi Pietro Foscari Giacomo Foscarini K.	Reg. 5, c. 130v, Delib. Sen., 16 January 1578 (Doc. 849)
22 November 1578	Girolamo Priuli	
21 February 1579	Giorgio Corner Giovanni Mocenigo Antonio Bragadin	Reg. 5, c. 31, Delib. Sen., 7 February 1579 (Doc. 885)
10 August 1579	Francesco Bernardo Giacomo Soranzo K. P. Paolo Tron	

Date of Election	Name	Fondo
15 January 1580	Giovanni Mocenigo	
12 April 1580	Girolamo Priuli	
12 July 1580	Giorgio Corner q. ser Gia.	
22 October 1580	Antonio Tiepolo Alvise Zustinian Marco Corner	Reg. 5, c. 141, Delib. Sen., 8 October 1580 (Doc. 916)
20 October 1581	Alvise Grimani Daniel Priuli Andrea Bernardo	
22 July 1582	Domenico Duodo	
27 November 1582	Lorenzo Donado Giorgio Zorzi Giacomo Contarini	
18 April 1584	Francesco Donado Giacomo Salomon Vicenzo Molin	Reg. 5, c. 141v, ibid.

Date of Election	Name	Fondo
10 November 1584	Giacomo Contarini	
27 July 1585	Tommaso Morosini Paolo Paruta Francesco Foscari	
7 December 1585	Giovanni Moro к.	
3 February 1587	Pietro Capello Giovanni da Molin Luca Michiel	
12 April 1588	Gio.Battista Foscarini Nicolò Gussoni Vicenzo Molin	Reg. 5, c. 183v, ibid.
11 December 1600	Vicenzo Capello Lorenzo Loredan Girolamo da Mula	Reg. 6, c. 71, Delib. Sen., 6 December 1600 (Doc. 1116)

GENEALOGY OF PATRONAGE:
PALLADIO, THE DOGE, AND THE DOGE'S PALACE 1574

A Note about this Table

ORGANIZATION: The structure focuses on bilateral connections rather than on the complete descendent or antecedent relations typical of single-family genealogies. Not all parents or siblings are included, only those individuals necessary to plot the framing of a group identity of patronage for the Ducal Palace fire of 1574 (indicated in italics) and their links to other Palladio projects. Females are listed under their natal family, therefore siblings are presented vertically, and marriage between houses horizontally. Generations (indicated in color and also by bullet points) reflect marriage alliances and offspring rather than being organized by individuals chronologically distributed by birth dates.

SOURCES: Genealogical information, particularly for females, is often fragmentary and contradictory, so the reader is advised to refer to the text and notes for details of primary and secondary sources on individual cases, which future research may better clarify or correct. Basic sources consulted include the versions of Marco Barbaro's patrician genealogies (ASV, BCV, BMV), those of Girolamo Alessandro Cappellari Vivaro (BMV) which include "filia," and Giuseppe Giomo, Avogaria di Comun, 107/2, "Cronaca Matrimoni dei nobili veneti," Libro d'oro, Nascite, and Provveditori alla Sanità, Necrologi (ASV) marriages of patrician women, as well as records of births, marriages, deaths, and wills (ASV), when necessary and where available.

This table is intended to be exemplary rather than definitive. It is hoped that the reader will use it as a springboard for making further connections with the patrons of other commissions in Palladio's Venice, such as the Contarini, Priuli, Foscari of San Pantaleon, Barbarigo, Bragadin, and others.

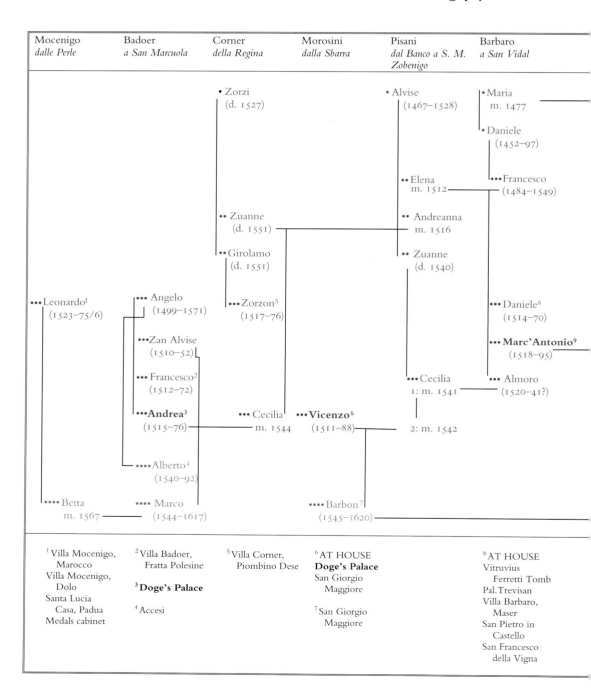

Mocenigo *dalle Perle*	Badoer *a San Marcuola*	Corner *della Regina*	Morosini *dalla Sbarra*	Pisani *dal Banco a S. M. Zobenigo*	Barbaro *a San Vidal*
		• Zorzi (d. 1527)	• Alvise (1467–1528)		• Maria m. 1477
					• Daniele (1452–97)
			•• Elena m. 1512		••• Francesco (1484–1549)
			•• Andreanna m. 1516		
		•• Zuanne (d. 1551)	•• Zuanne (d. 1540)		
		•• Girolamo (d. 1551)			
••• Leonardo¹ (1523–75/6)	••• Angelo (1499–1571)	••• Zorzon⁵ (1517–76)			••• Daniele⁸ (1514–70)
	••• Zan Alvise (1510–52)				••• **Marc'Antonio⁹** (1518–95)
	••• Francesco² (1512–72)		••• Cecilia 1: m. 1541		••• Almoro (1520–41?)
	••• **Andrea³** (1515–76)	••• Cecilia m. 1544	••• **Vicenzo⁶** (1511–88)	2: m. 1542	
	•••• Alberto⁴ (1540–92)				
•••• Betta m. 1567	•••• Marco (1544–1617)		•••• Barbon⁷ (1545–1620)		

¹ Villa Mocenigo, Marocco Villa Mocenigo, Dolo Santa Lucia Casa, Padua Medals cabinet	² Villa Badoer, Fratta Polesine

³ **Doge's Palace**

⁴ Accesi | ⁵ Villa Corner, Piombino Dese | ⁶ AT HOUSE **Doge's Palace** San Giorgio Maggiore

⁷ San Giorgio Maggiore | | ⁸ AT HOUSE Vitruvius Ferretti Tomb Pal. Trevisan Villa Barbaro, Maser San Pietro in Castello San Francesco della Vigna |

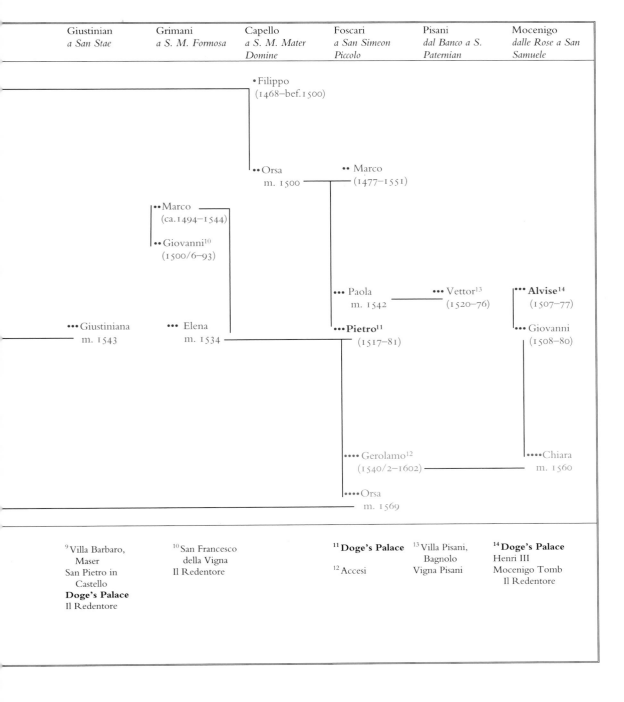

Giustinian *a San Stae*	Grimani *a S. M. Formosa*	Capello *a S. M. Mater Domine*	Foscari *a San Simeon Piccolo*	Pisani *dal Banco a S. Paternian*	Mocenigo *dalle Rose a San Samuele*

• Filippo
(1468–bef.1500)

•• Orsa
m. 1500

•• Marco
(1477–1551)

•• Marco
(ca.1494–1544)

•• Giovanni[10]
(1500/6–93)

••• Paola
m. 1542

••• Vettor[13]
(1520–76)

••• **Alvise**[14]
(1507–77)

••• Giustiniana
m. 1543

••• Elena
m. 1534

••• **Pietro**[11]
(1517–81)

••• Giovanni
(1508–80)

•••• Gerolamo[12]
(1540/2–1602)

••••Chiara
m. 1560

••••Orsa
m. 1569

[9] Villa Barbaro,
Maser
San Pietro in
Castello
Doge's Palace
Il Redentore

[10] San Francesco
della Vigna
Il Redentore

[11] **Doge's Palace**

[12] Accesi

[13] Villa Pisani,
Bagnolo
Vigna Pisani

[14] **Doge's Palace**
Henri III
Mocenigo Tomb
Il Redentore

NOTES

m.v. = more veneto (for dates in the Venetian style in which the year begins on 1 March)

PART I

1 Gualdo 2000, 12.

2 For Palladio's life and career, from the many excellent studies on the architect (with English-language editions cited here if available): the intelligent recent monograph by Boucher 1998; the indispensable catalogue raisonné by Puppi 1986; the insightful volume by Ackerman 1977b (orig. pub. 1966). The chronology of this period is largely based on the early biography of Paolo Gualdo (BMV, MS It. x, 73 [7097], 156–57), later published as "Vita di Andrea Palladio," edited by G. Zorzi (Gualdo 1958–59), 93–104, and translated in Lewis 2000, 11–12; the reliable research of Magrini 1845; the archival work of Dalla Pozza 1943; and assembled with further documentary research and study of drawings and letters in four indispensable volumes by G. Zorzi 1959, 1965, 1967, and 1969. More specific studies of Palladio's Vicentine patrons include: Zaupa 1990; G. Barbieri 1983; Battilotti 1980b.

3 For Trissino the fundamental biography is Morsolin 1984 (originally published in 1878); F. Barbieri 1980; Puppi 1973; Piovene 1963. The likeness of Palladio is elusive, a contemporary portrait mentioned by Vasari is lost (by Orlando Flacco, in Vasari 1878–85, 5: 299). For a comprehensive assessment, see Piva 1980: notably, Lionello Puppi proposed El Greco's *Portrait of a Man* in Copenhagen, Statens Museum for Kunst, an identification recently supported by Hadjinicolaou 1995; and Puppi also identified as Palladio the *Portrait of a Man* in Vicenza, Museo Civico, which he attributed to Francesco Bassano, *circa* 1580, but the current attribution is given to Leandro Bassano, *circa* 1600, and therefore a less likely

candidate, as in Attardi 2003 (see here fig. 3); most secure is a portrait in the Valmarana collection in Vicenza with an identifying inscription and date of "1576," attributed to Giambattista Maganza, and the source for many later images of the architect (see here figs. 35 and 301).

4 Gualdo 2000, 12.

5 On the Basilica, see the authoritative Corpus Palladianum volume (2) by F. Barbieri 1970, esp. ch. 3. Also G. Zorzi 1965, 43–74, 303–46; Puppi 1986, 110–16; Boucher 1998, ch. 4, 93–110.

6 The first notice of Palladio's presence in Venice is from 1548, in connection with a close Vicentine patron, Count Giacomo Angarano; see G. Zorzi 1969, 78; Puppi 1986, 116–17; Battilotti 1982, 175. In addition to the references on the Basilica above, for a summary of the dates when Palladio was in Vicenza to supervise construction, its most active period was between 1549 and 1561, see Burns 1991.

7 Puppi 1986, 12, and the entirety of "Palladio's Cultural Background," for example, on how the Vicentine ruling class came to adopt the insertion of the classical language of architecture into the city under "the aegis of an aristocratic movement which granted the prerogative of culture and power only to nobility of blood, founded on wealth; the glorification of this class had to be expressed with suitable pomp and later, because of an awareness of a lack of continuity with the immediate past, it had to be adapted also to the 'new usage'" (10–11); see also Burns 1991, 214–16.

8 Morsolin 1984, for examples in the pontificate of Paul III, ch. 19 (1541–43) and ch. 21 (1545–47); Gualdo 2000, 11–12; in Puppi 1986, 13 and 25 n. 47, 16 and 26 n. 76, 21 and 28 nn. 116–17, for a critical evaluation of the evidence for various trips; Boucher 1998, 16–23.

9 On the Villa Pisani: G. Zorzi 1969, 52–60; Puppi 1986, 98–101; Boucher 1998, 76–80. G. Zorzi (1969, 53 n. 7) wrongly gives Vettor's birth date as 1528; Douglas Lewis (1972b) first documented it as 1520 in a paper, delivered to the Washington Renaissance Colloquium, in typescript in the Library of the National Gallery of Art, Washington, D.C. He was the elder of three brothers: "Vetor Pisani et fratelli," his brothers Marco, born 1524, and Daniele, born 1525. On the Pisani dal Banco at Bagnolo, see: Gullino 1984, esp. 45–51 (further Pisani patronage in Venice is discussed below); for the Santa Maria Zobenigo and Santo Stefano branches: R. Gallo 1944; and for the San Polo branch: Kolb 1984, esp. 238–39; as San Paternian, Mason 1996, 72. Vettor's wife Paola Foscari came from a prominent branch of the Foscari at San Simeon Piccolo: her great-grandfather, Procurator Marco (died 1467), was brother to Doge Francesco Foscari (1423–57); her grandmother was Paola Gritti di Triadano; her father, Marco di Giovanni, described as captain of the faction of the "Ottinati" (BMV, Cappellari Vivaro, vol. 2, s.v. "Foscari"), sponsor of pro-oligarchical legislation (see Ventura 1980, followed by Tafuri 1989, 112–13; for a complete biography, see Gullino 1997b; and Gullino 2000, 139–40, who speculates on Marco's possible role in bringing Palladio to Vettor's attention, but see further here in Part II); one of her brothers was Girolamo, bishop of Torcello (died 1564); and another, Pietro, became a senator in 1550. He was *capitano* in Padua in 1571, and *consigliere ducale* in 1574, when he was host to Henry III of France in his palace in Padua, one of the highlights of sumptuous celebration of the decade, and significantly was one of the *provveditore sopra la fabbrica del Palazzo ducale* in 1574 during Palladio's involvement (on which, see more below in Part V and Appendix III).

10 Puppi 1980a, 10–16; Azzi Visentini 1984, 165, notes that while there is no direct documentation of Cornaro as a member of the Infiammati, his only daughter Chiara was married to one of the members, Giovanni Corner della Piscopia.

11 Howard 1987, 135, provides a useful family tree of this branch of the Corner at San Maurizio (sometimes called the "della Regina" after Zorzi's sister, Caterina, Queen of Cyprus); see further below. For an overview of the Corner branches, see Lewis 1996, 861–63. As already noted, one of Elena Pisani Barbaro's sisters was married to the brother of Girolamo Corner, demonstrating the significant interrelations formed by Procurator Alvise di Giovanni (Zuanne) Pisani dal Banco's daughters through their marriages; thus, for example, Daniele Barbaro's maternal relative, Andreanna Pisani, was married to Zorzon Corner's paternal uncle, Giovanni Corner; the importance of the Corner's ties to other of Palladio's early patrons was recognized by Lewis 1972a; Lewis 1981, esp. 370–80; but also see Tafuri 1989, 7–8 and 202 n. 33, who notes a "traditional" hostility between Doge Gritti and the Corner (based on the personal enmity between the doge and Cardinal Francesco remarked on by the imperial ambassador to Rome, and cited from Finlay 1984, 109 n. 64), a reminder that not all such interrelationships were productive. On the Villa Corner: G. Zorzi 1969, 192–98; Puppi 1986, 134–38; Boucher 1998, 117–21; Douglas Lewis is engaged with the forthcoming Corpus Palladianum volume.

12 Maylender 1929, 3: 266–70; Azzi Visentini 1984, 158–78, gives a full account of the cultivated "salons" in Padua and their connection to the university and notable humanists to provide a context that links Cornaro-Trissino-Barbaro.

13 "Che vogli esser contento di allevar li figlioli con il timor di Dio con buoni costumi et con buone lettere per che eesendo tali saranno grati alla Maesta de Dio et buoni in servicio della patria," trans. from Kolb 1984, 230 and 237 n. 39, from ASV, Notarile, Testamenti, Marco Graziabona, b. 1187, pezzo 24, fol. 3. Francesco was born in 1509 and had married Marietta di Vincenzo Molin in 1534. On Palladio's stay, see G. Zorzi 1965, 220, document of 7 October 1553, in ASV, Notarile, Testamenti, Giovanni Maria Coradine, 60. For further on the villa: Puppi 1986, 131–33; Boucher 1998, 112–17.

14 Elena Pisani Barbaro's will names her as daughter of Procurator Alvise Pisani, the wealthy banker and political force (ASV, Notarile, Testamenti, Cesare Ziliol, b. 1257.282, 1 October 1552, proved 30 December 1568), therefore her mother would be Cecilia di Benetto Giustinian, her brothers were Procurator Giovanni (Zuanne), who married a granddaughter of Doge Andrea Gritti (Benedetta di Francesco), and Cardinal Francesco, and she had four sisters (note that ASV, Avog-

aria del Comun, 107/2, "Cronaca Matrimoni," 16, gives Elena as daughter of Alvise di Marin Pisani, but this is a later compiled source; R. Gallo 1944, "Ramo di Santa Maria Zobenigo," does not list a Barbaro among Alvise's daughters' husbands, but see Gullino 1996b, esp. 71; Alberigo 1964, 89; ASV, Giomo, vol. 2, s.v. "Pisani"); see ASV, Barbaro, "Albori," VI; 27, 123, "F," for the Santa Maria Zobenigo (later San Stefano) ramo of Alvise P., 129, "L," for the Bagnolo branch of Vettor (also Alvise di Marin) and 113, "D," for the Montagnana branch of Francesco (on whom, see Kolb 1984, esp. 227, 238–39).

15 Stella 1976; re-examined by Olivieri 1992.

16 For Venice as a "new Rome" and other analogies, see Chambers 1970, esp. 20–30; Howard 1987, 2–3; Marx 1978; Muir 1979, 23 (also Muir 1981, 24); Puppi 1982; Tafuri 1982; Tafuri 1984a, 32–35; Concina 1984b; Wolters 1987, esp. 256–59; P. Brown 1991, 527; Pincus 1992; Casini 1996, esp. 41, 150, 174, 309. Also see Sinding-Larsen 1974, 230–32, 238; Chastel 1969.

17 Most recently, Azzi Visentini 1996, with references to her earlier works, such as Azzi Visentini 1984, 149–51. Tafuri 1989, 125 and 249 n. 120, highlights the significance of the architect Andrea Moroni's association with Barbaro at the Botanic Garden. Barbaro's colleague was the medical professor Piero da Noale.

18 Gualdo 2000, 11.

19 Puppi, ed. 1988, 3–9, on the tradition of the *Mirabilia urbis Romae* in relation to Palladio's guides.

20 In addition to note 19 above, Chastel 1983, 240 n. 18, 252 n. 1.

21 "Ho potuto, da molti fidelissimi autori antichi e moderni che di ciò hanno diffusamente scritto, come da Dionisio Alicarnaseo . . . e molti altri. Né mi son contentato di questo solo, che anco ho voluto vedere, e con le mie proprie mani misurare il tutto," Palladio 1988a, 11.

22 Trans. from Wittkower 1962, 65 (a variant can be compared from Puppi 1986, 20). "Nei disegni delle figure importanti io ho usato l'opere di M. Andrea Palladio Vicentino," from Barbaro 1556, Bk. 1, ch. 6, 40. An amplified edition was issued in 1567, by Francesco de' Franceschi Senese and Giovanni Chrieger Alemano Compagni, and published in a modern edition with studies by Tafuri 1987, xi–xl, and Morresi 1987, xli. Barbaro's preparatory manuscripts are in BMV, MS It. IV, 152 (5106) and 37 (5133). Part of Barbaro's commentary has been published by Caye 1995. For its relation to contemporary archi-tectural theory, see Morresi 1998b, 274–76; Puppi 1981, 134–86; Kruft 1986, 95–97. A resumé of the bibliography on Daniele Barbaro may be found in Tafuri 1989, 245 n. 92, updated in Tafuri 1987, xxxiii n. 2; to which add Ackerman 2002. See esp. Alberigo 1964, for a thorough biography; and on the relationship between Palladio and Barbaro, see esp.

Forssman 1966, and esp. 68–69, for the above quotation; Fontana 1985. For a comparison of themes on Venice in the two Italian editions and the Latin edition of 1567, see D'Evelyn 1996.

23 Marcucci 1978; Schlosser 1977, 251–57. An earlier illustrated translation by Marco Fabio Calvo remained in manuscript. An edition whose Aristotelian commentary was influential for Barbaro's thought was that of Giovanni Battista Caporali published in Perugia 1536 (also including the Basilica of Fano); see Wittkower 1962, 68 n. 1, 92; Puppi 1986, 28 n. III. See also the summary in Morresi 1998b.

24 "L'opera . . . di nove anni apunto," Barbaro 1987, 274. Tafuri 1987, xiii, formulates Barbaro's possible inspiration as a competitive response, "una civile competizione della cultura veneziana con quella romana," and xxxiv n. 5, warns against overestimating Barbaro's competence in architectural matters prior to 1545. Forssman 1966, 68–99, where distinctions are made between those illustrations attributed to Palladio and to others for which see now Cellauro 1998. There are discrepancies on the date of his departure for England: Alberigo 1964, 91, recounts that he was chosen as ambassador on 12 October 1548, scheduled to leave after 8 February 1549, yet the official appointment was granted only on 25 April 1549, with the first dispatches arriving in July; Tafuri 1987, xii, gives the date of departure as 12 September 1548, which seems too early. Lewis 1982, 349–51, lays out his reasoning for Padua, with the university, and particularly Alvise Cornaro, as providing a center for the generation including Trissino, and Girolamo Corner, to share their mutual interests in architecture, which in turn attracted the younger generation, such as the Pisani, Corner, and Barbaro, who became Palladio's patrons.

25 *Libro delle fortificazioni*; see Tafuri 1987, xxii and xxxviii n. 51, for modern editions; Concina 1983, 15 ff., on Gritti, 55 ff., on links between the books by Barbaro, Leonardi, and Palladio.

26 Trans. from Wittkower 1962, 65. "Et quanto appartiene a Vitruvio, l'artificio dei Theatri, dei tempii, delle Basiliche, & de quelle cose, che hanno più belle e più secrete ragioni di compartimenti, tutte sono state da quello [cioè dal Palladio], con prontezza d'animo, & di mano esplicate, & seco consigliate, come quello che di tutta Italia ha scielto le più belle maniere degli antichi," Barbaro 1556, Bk. 1, ch. 6, 40, discussed in Forssman 1966, 70. In addition to the previous chapter on drawing procedures, add C. Frommel 1994, on the development of orthography, Bramante's correspondence between plan-elevation-section, and Raphael's dependence on Bramante's methodology, also on the use of pictorial shading with orthography (Bramante, 111, Michelangelo, 119). Here, too, the Vitruvian practice of "measuring and drawing . . . governed not by chance or mere practical experience, by true princi-

ples" is recounted in Raphael's "Letter to Leo x" (trans. from Jones & Penny 1983, 201; Golzio 1936, 78), and similarly described in Barbaro, see 1987, 69; and Tafuri 1987, xv and xxxv n. 21.

27 Most of what is known about this trip is by inference from intertextual references, for example, the dedication of Barbaro's Vitruvius translation to Cardinal d'Este, and the dating from Paolo Gualdo's biographical sketch of Palladio just quoted, which continues: "At the same time he published a little guidebook to the city's antiquities [*L'antichità di Roma*, 1554], which is commonly sold together with the book called *The Wonders of Rome* [*Descritione delle chiese . . . in la Città di Roma*, 1554]," Gualdo 2000, 11, with a history of its publication; Italian text in Gualdo 1958–59, 91–104, from BMV, Gualdo, 156–57.

28 Lewis 1973; Lewis 2000, 203–04, identifies a rapid sketch on London, RIBA, XVI, 5v as a first design for Maser *circa* 1548–49 (dated by the sketch for Count Giacomo Angarano's villa on the same sheet) and evidence for a pre-England relationship; but cf. Battilotti 1985c, 36 and 42, noting Howard Burns's caveat against regarding this type of sketch as a *primo pensiero* (see further below, and Burns 1982, 80), and 44, where she provides building documentation for the nymphaeum by September 1554; on the latter, Kolb 1997; and Lewis 1997, with a review of the literature. On Maser generally, see G. Zorzi 1969, 172–73; Puppi 1986, 156–59; Boucher 1998, 131–36.

29 Gualdo 2000, 12; Vasari 1878–85, 7: 531.

30 On Palladio at San Vidal: 25 February 1560 and 9 January 1563, in ASV, Notarile, Testamenti, Vettor Maffei, prot. 8120, 281–82, and prot. 8132, 292–93 and 301–03 respectively, see Battilotti 1982, 182, 187–88; but note as Gullino 1996b, 74, documented that the palace was transferred to another branch of the family by this time, hypothesizing that Daniele had maintained an apartment there. Boucher 1979, 280 and 282, on Barbaro's bequest to Palladio as "our beloved architect" ("architetto nostro amorevole"), from ASV, Notarile, Testamenti, Vettor Maffei, B. 657, no. 270.

31 On Veronese's portrait: Pignatti 1976, cat. 143, 78, 129; P. Rossi 1980, 242–43; R. Pallucchini 1984, cat. 100, 90, 177; Rearick 1988b, cat. 60, 99, with fuller bibliography; the patriarchal *berretta* and costume are wrongly identified as a cardinal's in the otherwise useful context in Severin 1992, 215. For a portrait drawing in Munich (Staatliche Graphische Sammlungen, 12893, see below in Part III, fig. 98), previously identified as a preparatory study (Fiocco 1928, 142), see Rearick 1988b, cat. 8, 54–55, who argues that this may be for an earlier portrait *circa* 1561 (now lost), once in the collection of Consul Smith, where Barbaro was described as holding a drawing by Palladio for the villa at Maser (Cocke 1984, cat. 193, 361, attributed the drawing instead to Paris Bordon). The arguments for Veronese's presence at Maser

between 1561 and 1562 are given in Lewis 1997, 36, with a summary of the recent literature; and for dates in 1559–60 and 1562, see Battilotti 1985c, 46.

32 For a comparison of the two editions, see Morresi 1987; Cellauro 2000. Forssman 1966, 69–70, describes the drawings added, some of which were also used in Palladio's *Four Books*, including an additional drawing in Barbaro's Latin edition published contemporaneously to the second translation, and some of which were re-employed in Barbaro's *La pratica della perspettiva* (Venice, 1569). P. Rossi 1980, 242–43, on Veronese's fidelity of form and detail in the representation of Palladio's illustrations in the portrait.

33 From a discussion in the Council of Ten, 20 October 1550, ". . . aggiondendosi la mala satisffattione de'l Barbaro, che si dice che veneria a restare ne clerico, ne laico, senza poter far deliberatione alcuna della sua vita," ASV, Consiglio dei Dieci, Secreta, Sesto, in P. Laven 1967, 189–90 n. 36. See also Paschini 1962.

34 For Marc'Antonio, see Yriarte 1874; Gaeta 1964; Howard 1996a, 203. Marc'Antonio Barbaro was made *savio alla terraferma* again in 1564 as well as six more times in the succeeding decades. During the period when this portrait was made, Barbaro had been made *bailò* (head of the Venetian consulate) in Constantinople (1568), and later, after the Battle of Lepanto in 1571, undertook the delicate mission of treating for peace with the Turks (1573), on which see Part V. On Sustris's portrait: Marchesi 1993.

35 On the Barbaro family: for humanists, including the patriarch of Aquileia, Ermolao (1491–92/94), see King 1986, 320–27; aa.vv. in *I Barbaro*, esp. Gullino 1996b, 67–77, for the *ramo* Santa Maria Mater Domini; Grendler 1979, 293–94, notes their exclusion from office as papalists together with the Grimani of Santa Maria Formosa, the Trevisan, and Corner della Ca' Grande; Grendler 1990, 71–72, for Marc'Antonio.

36 Palladio 1997, 123.

37 On the sources of the garden architecture at Maser, see Kolb 1997, 15–17; and in addition on Maser: the now prevailing views of Huse 1974; and Burns with Fairbairn & Boucher 1975, 196; are ably summarized in Boucher 1998, 131–36, that "Palladio's role here was one of coordinator," for patrons who actively participated in the conception of building and decoration.

38 Gualdo (2000, 11) continued: "Trissino encouraged his natural abilities by training him in the precepts of Vitruvius, and even took him three times as far as Rome itself. There Palladio measured and made drawings of many of those sublime and beautiful buildings which are the revered relics of Roman antiquity"; also see Wittkower 1962, 61.

39 Wittkower 1962, 67–68; recent scholarship has tended to de-emphasize Platonic influence, including Wittkower 1992, on Grasso; however,

see Tafuri 1987, xvi, who contrasts Barbaro's ideas about mathematics to Fra Francesco Zorzi, author of *De harmonia mundi* (Venice, 1534) and the architectural program of 1535 of Jacopo Sansovino's San Francesco della Vigna; for which, see Foscari & Tafuri 1983, pt. 1; also Howard 1987, 66–67, who revised ideas about the relationship between Sansovino and Zorzi; Morresi 2000, 475–78. On Palladio and Platonism, see now Mitrović 2004, 167–70.

40 Zaupa 1990, 9–18 and esp. 15 n. 1, documented the Pomponazzi family presence in Vicenza and its importance for the intellectual ambiance of Palladio and his patrons; for his training in Padua and writings, see further in Alberigo 1964, 89. On the orientation of the University of Padua, see Nardi 1958. Tafuri 1987, xvi, xviii, followed P. Laven 1957, 1: 122 ff., in describing Barbaro's simplified Aristotelianism as influenced by Bonaventure. John Martin intends a study of the humanist visual culture of this period and I should like to thank him for discussing his plans with me.

41 Cozzi 1963–64, esp. 231–34, 237–38, 547 n. 64. Vasoli 1991 contrasts the philosophical aims of the academic circles with those of the political institutions of the state in regards to historical investigation.

42 "Dimostra, dissegna, distribuisce, ordina, e commanda" (Vitruvius 1987, Bk. 1, "Proemio," 7); for a fuller discussion, see Tafuri 1987, xvii. Rowland and Howe intro. in Vitruvius 1999, 17, comment: "Vitruvius is aware of the importance of experimental methods and direct observation in the cumulative growth of science," giving examples and contemporary sources, and contend that he developed a "critical method," similar to that of rhetorical training.

43 Palladio 1997, 5.

44 Palladio 1997, 6.

45 Tafuri 1987, xx–xxi. Williams 1997, 4–6, has described a new principle of culture in which "Art comes to be understood as a *superintendency* of knowledge," with implications for power as mediated through representation, and 14–16, for the position of architecture (and architects) within such a system.

46 Arslan 1960, 1: 361; Ballarin 1971; Severin 1992, 217, with further bibliography.

47 Vitruvius 1999, 22, in Bk. 1, ch. 1, pt. 3; Morgan in Vitruvius Pollio 1960, 5, translates the last phrase as "a demonstration on scientific principles."

48 Puppi 1986, 16 and 26 n. 69, 23 and 28 n. 104, for the background of Quatremère de Quincy's notion of "type," applied to Palladio's methods; Tafuri 1987, xix–xxi, xxiv–xxvii; Tafuri 1989, 127–28; for further on the concept, see Calquhoun 1981, 195 and 207 n. 46, and on "Typology"; S. Lavin 1992, ch. 2, "The Transformation of Type," esp. 90–91.

49 Ackerman 1991c; Tafuri 1989, 125–26; Puppi 1986, 21. On *techne*, see Williams 1997, 11–12, 22–23, 34–36; Roochnik 1998.

50 "Christendom," as Hale (1994, 4–5) has ob-

served, "had, until now, always been a flexible concept"; this in contrast to "the increasingly concrete one of Europe," which once was defined as the Christian west, see pt. 1, "The Discovery of Europe."

51 See the indispensable Yates 1966, esp. 2–4 on the principles of mnemonic place systems; also, on how architectural configurations preserve a set of cultural meanings, Calquhoun 1981, 191–93.

52 Alberti 1988, 5 (no folio number for the *editio princips* is given for the prologue, between fols. 1 and 4); for the Giacomo Leoni translation of 1755: "How much Authority accrued to the Roman Name and Empire from their Buildings, I shall dwell on no further, than that the Sepulchres and other Remains of the ancient Magnificence, every where to be found, are a great Inducement and Argument with us for believing many Things related by Historians, which might otherwise have seemed incredible," Alberti 1986, n.p.

53 Vitruvius 1999, 22 (in Bk. 1, ch. 1, 5–6). D'Evelyn 1998–99, esp. 159–60 and 164–67 on the porticoes as architectural histories, elaborating on Barbaro's distinctions between political, natural, and architectural history (163).

54 In such a procedure, drawings act as "mediation," see Burns 1982, 80, who cautions that these sketches do not necessarily represent the initial stages of a project.

55 Vitruvius 1999, 26 (in Bk. 1, ch. 3, 2). "The physical reality of the monuments had to be considered, not so much in order to explain the difficult wording of the text [Vitruvius], as to define a typological mechanism of very wide application and to place it in the present situation and linguistic context," Puppi 1986, 21.

56 Burns 1982, 77, 79, contrasts Palladio and Michelangelo; Summers 1981, pt. 1, ch. 4, 60–70 and esp. 478 n. 34, on *furia*, the Platonic notion of inspired invention, attributed by Vasari to Michelangelo's practice of rapid sketches (Vasari 1878–85, 1: 174, "E perchè dal furor dello artifice sono in poco tempo con penna o con altro disegnatio o carbone espressi, solo per tentare l'animo di quel che gli sovviene, perciò si chiamano schizzi"); for the importance of Leonardo in revolutionizing the drawing process, see Gombrich 1966, 59.

57 Vasari 1960, 61–62, Introduction to "On Architecture," ch. 1, pt. 18.

58 Vasari 1960, 98, Introduction to "On Architecture," ch. 7, pt. 35. Palladio speaks of the discretionary judgment ("giudicio") that should be exercised by the architect in the *Four Books*, Bk. 1, ch. 23, 54 (Palladio 1997, 59), regarding vaults. See the extended discussion in Summers 1981, 3, 332–46, 352–79, on Michelangelo and *giudizio*, and 519 n. 49, on Vasari's Aristotelian-influenced theories of the *concetto* and *disegno*; also see Williams 1997, ch. 1 on Vasari's *disegno*, esp. 33–35, 45–48, for *giudizio*; Klein 1979, esp. 165, on Venetian theorists and *giudizio*; Klein 1970, 85, on Vasari.

59 Palladio 1997, 163.

60 Palladio 1997, 213.

61 Palladio depends more on the Aristotelian notion of imitation than the Neo-Platonic, although as Lee 1967, 13–15, remarked, it was not until Gian Pietro Bellori's lecture on the "Idea" in 1664 (published in his *Vite de' pittori, scultori et architetti moderni*, Rome, 1672) that a definitively Aristotelian theoretical basis was articulated for the arts, "he thought of the Idea not primarily as an archetype of beauty existing *a priori* in metaphysical independence, but as derived *a posteriori* by a selective process from the artist's actual experience of nature." Lee further noted that the Venetian theorist Lodovico Dolce had anticipated, albeit with some inconsistencies, this Aristotelian philosophy of imitation (*Dialogo della pittura intitolato l'Aretino*, Venice, 1557), so it was current in Palladio's ambiance. The empirical method of forming a composite mental image was made famous in art theory through the story of Zeuxis painting the ideal beauty of Helen (influentially formulated in Erwin Panofsky's *Idea* [1968, orig. pub. Leipzig, 1924], who discussed its many instances in Renaissance theorists). Puppi 1986, 20, among others, credited Palladio's *ars combinatoria* with "the transformation of the original symbolic meanings into the modern forms of a new stylistic context"; and Tafuri 1989, 127, on the *ars combinatoria* as a "typological laboratory" (Puppi 1986, 158, also has recourse to this notion), a "field of variables," in which there is a productive tension between "type" and "invention."

62 Vasari 1987, 425, *Life of Michelangelo Buonarroti* (for the Italian, see Vasari 1878–85, 7: 227); also Panofsky 1972, 171; for Michelangelo's position on the classical theory of imitation, see Summers 1981, 193 and 511 n. 17.

63 In Vicenza in 1556, it is worthy to note Palladio among the founders of the Accademia degli Olimpici; see Boucher 1998, 248–53; Puppi 1986, 277–82; G. Zorzi 1969, 257–63, on the Accademia Olimpica, 282–327, on the Teatro Olimpico.

64 Lewis 2000, 15, describes the "exceedingly famous" *Four Books* as "heavily prejudicial to an accurate study of Palladio's own work"; Howard 1980, 226, for an account of the impact of this "most influential of all architectural books."

65 Oechslin 1987, on architectural drawing techniques.

66 Palladio 1997, 36–38, Temple of the Sun and the Moon, 73–83, Pantheon. For a salient description of the former, see Rykwert 1980 (properly identified as the Basilica of Maxentius with its double gable). Sometimes there is a mixed effect, e.g., a column profile presented and where cut-off shifted to a perspective rendering (i.e., Temple of Vesta, Palladio 1570, Bk. 4, ch. 14, 53), and certain plans in the edition of 1570 were given rudimentary indications of ground (i.e., Temple of Giove, Palladio 1570, Bk. 4, ch. 12, 42), in Palladio 1997, 265, 254,

respectively. Palladio's role in relation to the woodcutter's is not clear in all cases, but some of these embellishments seem likely to have been added in the process of reproduction.

67 Cooper 1994b; Carpo 2001, 171–73 n. 82, who interestingly relates graphic processes to typographic technologies. Note surviving drawings include those after ancient ornament. Palladio also presents cross-sections of columns, as seen from straight-on from an over-head viewpoint.

68 See Lotz 1981a, 11–19, for Bramante's use of the Albertian convention of "transparency," and the development of other strategies from multiple perspectives to orthogonal projection, including the "imaginary glimpse inside a ruin."

69 Its editor, Adolf Placzek, noted that Leoni's edition had a wider circulation previously (Palladio 1965, vi).

70 See Palladio 1570, Bk. 3, ch. 19, 39, for the ancient basilica (Palladio 1997, 200–201).

71 *I Commentari di C. Giulio Cesare, con le figure in rame de gli' Allogiamenti, de' fatti d' arme, delle circonvallatione delle città, & di molte altre cose notabili scritte in essi. Fatte da Andrea Palladio per facilitare a chi legge, la cognition dell' historia*, in Puppi, ed. 1988, 173–94, with commentary and full bibliography, and Palladio's intended preface to a related classical text known only in fragments, *Proemio ai "Discorsi" di Polybio* (1579), 195–96.

72 Palladio 1997, xxi–xxiii, ed. Tavernor and Schofield, provide a history of editions; Howard 1980 on influence; i.e., Lewis 2000, 13–15, "such a phenomenal, global, and enduring success that its deleterious effects on Palladio himself has been almost entirely overlooked."

73 Puppi 1986, 123 n. 28, makes this point succinctly; also Puppi, ed. 1988, 180. A similar case can be made for Palladio's contemporary, Giovanni Antonio Rusconi, as Cellauro's (2001) discovery of his extensive library inventory reveals (Rusconi owned Barbaro's Vitruvius *Commentaries* and *Treatise on Perspective*, as well as Palladio's *Antiquities of Rome*, *Four Books*, and *Commentary on Caesar*).

74 "Dedica," Puppi, ed. 1988, 187–88.

75 G. Zorzi 1965, 304–09, discusses his family; the memorial in the "Proemio," Puppi, ed. 1988, 189.

76 The tribute to Trissino as "gentiluomo dottissimo" in the "Proemio," Puppi, ed. 1988, 189.

77 Puppi, ed. 1988, 176–85, in relation to the military disciplines; on patronage relations in Venice more generally, see Logan 1972, esp. 170–76; Hochmann 1992, 95–96, on the role of *literati*, 171–77, on the competence of amateurs (regarding painting, but applicable to architecture); for contrast see Warnke 1993; in discussing Giulio Romano, Talvacchia 1996, 190, describes how expertise changed the status of the court artist; for further bibliography, see Cooper 1996b.

78 Gualdo 2000, 12.

79 "Dedica," in Puppi, ed. 1988, 187.

80 Important new work in book history has been coming out, and I would like to thank Stephen Parkin for his expertise on this topic. See the substantial sections on Venice in Richardson 1999 and Richardson 1994; also Gerulitas 1976; useful insights for this period in Grendler 1977, esp. 3–24.

81 G. Zorzi 1965, 312, as well as evidence derived from Silla's actions as literary executor; these are discussed by Puppi, ed. 1988, 61, and 59 n. 3, for previous transcriptions of the privilege; excerpted in Tiepolo et al. 1980, 71, cat. 190, 21 April 1570, in ASV, Senato, Terra, reg. 48, 20, concession (and an undated insert of the printer's application in idem, filza 55). Richardson 1999, 69–76, on the functions of the privilege.

82 Puppi, ed. 1988, 175–76 n. 7, transcribes the privilege (with earlier copies noted) and notes some complications in the relative dating for the *Caesar* between the privileges applied for in Savoy in 1574 (26 January [1575 if *m.v.*], in BCV, MS Cicogna 3617) and those in Venice in 1575; note that the intended dedicatee of the *Polybius* was the Grand Duke of Tuscany, Francesco de' Medici; also see the privilege in Tiepolo et al. 1980, 71, cat. 191, undated insert in minutes of 2 March 1575, in ASV, Senato, Terra, filza 66, of Palladio's application, and the Senate's concession of a fifteen-year privilege (with Tiepolo et al. 1980, 72, cat. 192, 14 December 1574, in ASV, Capi del Consiglio dei Dieci, Notatorio, filza 9, the approval of the Riformatori dello Studio di Padova, including Marc'Antonio Barbaro). Richardson 1999, 49–57, on the functions of the dedication; it is likely that the earlier dedication of Books III–IV to Emmanuele Filiberto of Savoy helped to secure favorable conditions for his application there.

83 G. Zorzi 1965, 312, sees Palladio's financial situation somewhat ameliorated later in the 1560s, but notes that the modest salaries he received required him to continue acquiring commissions, with outlays such as the 400-ducat dowry for his daughter Zenobia in 1564.

PART II

1 In essence, Venetians drew on beliefs and presumed historical events to proclaim that her good government brought the Republic liberty, justice, and peace; as Muir 1981, 23, described the operation in his perceptive analysis: "the myth represents the world view of a particularly cohesive community, an index of cultural symbols from which can be read the peculiarly Venetian mentality." For further historiographical constructions of this concept, see Angelo Ventura 1984, and Gaeta 1981; and recently Crouzet-Pavan 1996. The seductive effect of the myth extends to its historians, as recognized by Grubb 1986. The manifestation of the "myth" in the visual arts

has been productive, beginning with Padoan Urban 1968; and recent examples include Rosand 2001; Bettagno, ed. 1997; P. Brown 1996; although the most sustained efforts have been made in regard to the decoration of the Doge's Palace, especially for its representation of the "Peace of Venice of 1177": as in Sinding-Larsen 1974; Wolters 1983; P. Brown 1988b; Cooper 2001.

2 Palladio 1997, 5 (emphasis mine), who then names his principal Vicentine patrons, beginning with Giangiorgio Trissino. Sansovino's building, referred to in the quotation as the "Procuratia Nova," has been generally considered to refer to the Library of San Marco in the Piazzetta, whereas the later wing of the Procurators' building in the Piazza took on this name, succeeding the building it faced, which then became known as the Old Procurators' building (Procuratie vecchie). On these buildings, see M. Zorzi 1987; *Le Procuratie vecchie* 1994; *Le Procuratie nuove* 1994.

3 For Palladio and his patrons, see Zaupa 1990, III–VI, 12–13, 21, 26–27, on the "repubblica internazionale del denaro," relying on the theories of Max Weber; Olivieri 1981 (but cf. the remarks in Tafuri 1989, 252 n. 138; and Foscari & Tafuri 1983, 167 n. 39); Olivieri 1985.

4 Crouzet-Pavan 2002, 115–16, "men and families made use of the sea and land, drawing profits from both," captures well the long-term interdependence between Venice and both the mainland and the Mediterranean; for classic studies of *terraferma* economics (see the following note for patricians and villa life): Luzzato 1961, 250–62, "ma fosse anche vero che la maggior parte dei vecchi patrizi-mercanti avessero già preferito di trasformarsi in *rentiers*"; Luzzato 1938, esp. 75 ff.; Beltrami 1956; Stella 1956; Woolf 1968; Pullan 1973; Braudel 1958; Braudel 1982, 284–87; Knapton 1992, esp. ch. 1.

5 Trans. from Chambers & Pullan, eds. 1992, 161 (from Priuli 1938), although this passage is in response to bank failure, Priuli supported shipping and trade as the traditional occupation. For more of Priuli on this issue, see Ackerman 1990, 92–93; and Tenenti 1973.

6 On the relation between the Venetian patriciate and the *terraferma*: Carleton's undated report of *circa* 1612, London, Public Record Office, State Papers 99, file 8, is quoted from Cozzi 1958, 15 n. 2; a fuller excerpt also in Chambers & Pullan, eds. 1992, 26–31. There is a recent focus on *terraferma* studies, see the characterization of Crouzet-Pavan 2002, 132–37; for Vicenza, see Grubb 1988; more generally, see Grubb 1986, 72–82; Knapton 1992, esp. ch. 4; Cozzi 1984; the fundamental work remains Ventura 1964b; on which see Knapton 1998; Crouzet-Pavan 2002, 134.

7 On the constitution: Maranini 1931; and now Gullino 1996a; also see the analysis by F. Gilbert 1968; and on the shift, see Gaeta 1984. On the concept in relation to the "myth of Venice" (for which see n. 1 above): Gilmore

1973; Bouwsma 1968, 58–64, 148–49; Logan 1972, 1–19; Finlay 1980, 32–33; Muir 2000.

8 On the concept of the orders (*ordo*) or estates (*status*), see Burke 1992. For Venice, see the magisterial work by Pullan 1971; and specifically Pullan 1999; on the division of "estates," and keeping in mind that there were poor patricians and wealthy citizens, honorary grants of nobility to foreign nobles, total disenfranchisement of slaves and the "vile," Queller 1986, 30, went so far as to say: "The patrician government was, in a very important sense, a welfare scheme for poorer members of the nobility"; Cowan 1982; Romano 1987; Romano 1996; see also F. Gilbert 1973, esp. 281.

9 The *Libri d'oro*, or "Golden Books," were overseen by the *avogadori di comun*, or state attorneys (the registers are in ASV, Avogaria di Comun). On the makeup of the patriciate in the Renaissance (with background and references on what has been called the *Serrata* of 1297), see Gullino 1996c; Rösch 2000; S. Chojnacki 1973, 71; S. Chojnacki 1994, 356; S. Chojnacki 2000a; and S. Chojnacki 2000b, 53–75; Grendler 1990, 51–57; Finlay 1980, ch. 2, esp. 45; the classic article by Cecchetti 1872. As a republic, the patriciate was not technically nobility, although designations such as N. H. (*nobil huomo*) were increasingly applied. Limited patents of nobility were able to be granted with the agreement of the Imperial representative, with the Prague concession of 1437 naming the doge as duke of the mainland territory. In 1516 Emperor Maximilian granted independent rights to transfer of feudal titles, which would be regulated by a newly created magistracy later in the century. A patrician could accept ennobling from other princes, such as knighthoods granted by the emperor, and admittance into chivalric orders; and the increased desirability of titles formed the same impulse that enhanced the prestige of ecclesiastical titles; it was even found in the academy, i.e., the title of Dr.! Also on feudal rights as affected villa ownership, see below. Note that a similar process occurred with the citizen class, who instituted the *Libri d'argento*, or "Silver Books"; for example, registration as *cittadini originari*, requiring legitimate second-generation native birth. For current research on these parallel trends, see Grubb 2000, 339–64. For the conflicts and ambiguity revolving around the visual display of nobility, see now P. Brown 2004, ch. 1, 1–22, predominantly addressing the urban elite.

10 On the development of the Venetian villa type: for pre-existing villa typologies, see Kubelik 1977; for the effect on villa culture and Palladio, see Ackerman 1990, esp. ch. 4, with earlier literature on this subject; especially pertinent is Ackerman 1991c, with updated notes and references; in addition, see the translation of Bentmann and Müller 1992 (reviewed by Cooper 1994a); Cosgrove 1993;

Goldthwaite 1993; Gullino 1994; Battilotti 1995; for a comparison of Venetian and Roman *villegiatura* respectively, see Holberton 1990; and Coffin 1979, including Trissino's visit to Bagnaia, near Viterbo (35).

11 Trans. in Ackerman 1990, 130, from A. Gallo 1566, Day VIII. I thank Janet Farber, associate curator at the Joslyn Art Museum, Omaha, Neb., who confirmed Douglas Lewis's identification of the sitter based on an inscription.

12 Grubb 1988, 15–19, on Vicenza. On general notions of Venice as *terra libera* and its relation to myth, Crouzet-Pavan 2002, 127–28; Finlay 1980, 32–35.

13 Pullan 1965, 125–34; Pullan 1973; Prodi 1973, 417. Further, see Prodi 1977; cited in Goldthwaite 1993, 126–27, on the so-called refeudalization of the Italian countryside by urban elites; and for the Veneto, see Gullino 1980; Muraro 1986, 79–82, was interested in this as it related to villa culture, with references to the *more nobilium*; for the Pisani feuds and investiture of titles, see Kolb 1984, 228, 235 n. 13, in which she describes Palladio's villa at Montagnana in its "role as *rappresentazione* of its proprietor's status within the feudal system of land ownership"; see also Ackerman 1990, 104.

14 "Se mille volte io con voi et voi con me mi ho doluto et discontentato della natura dell'abate et del suo prociedir, et adesso non accade racontar questi cathalogi, et quando mi ricordo sentir li lamenti de mia cugnata, per vederla lacrimar delle vilanie et ingiurie dittole per questo vostro, non scio se debbo dir fiol, non posso contenirmi ch'io non l'habbia santamente in odio." Letter of 19 April 1550, ASV, Capi del Consiglio dei Dieci, Ambasciatori, Roma, B. 24, n. 27, quoted in Paschini 1948, 62; also see Carcereri 1907, 7–8; P. Laven 1967, 188.

15 Reported by Sanudo (*I diarii*, 1879–1903, 58: 465), trans. from Finlay 1980, 85; see also in Liberali 1971b, 106 (for a useful review of Liberali's multi-volume series, Cairns 1980); on the Pisani, see R. Gallo 1944; on the Corner, see Liberali 1971a; Arbel 1988. Another version of this saying is reported by the papal nuncio Gerolamo Aleandro, "Tre case, Cornara, Grimana, Pisana . . . vogliono abbracciare tutto l'ecclesiastico del loro Dominio," in a letter to Ambrogio Ricalati, 23 November 1534, cited by Foscari & Tafuri 1983, 134, from the *Nunziature di Venezia*, Gaeta, ed. 1958, 1: 301. The Corner family members descending from Marco K. will be referred to here under the broader heading of the Corner della Regina, so-called due to his daughter Queen Caterina, sister of Giorgio (Zorzi) K.P. rather than the next generation differentiation in which descendents inheriting property at San Maurizio become known as the Corner della Cha (Ca') Grande.

16 Shapley 1979, 1: 497–98, an identifying link to a portrait medal in the Kress Collection (Washington, D.C., National Gallery of Art) was made by Douglas Lewis.

17 Domenico Grimani (1493–1523), Marco Corner (1500–24), Francesco Pisani (1517–70), Marino Grimani (1527–46), Francesco Corner (1527–43), Gasparo Contarini (1535–42), Pietro Bembo (1538–47), Andrea Corner (1544–51); the information taken from the analysis by Hallman 1985, tables 1.2, 1.3. Palladio would also count the Contarini among his patrons; for the problem of a villa of 1546 for Francesco and Paolo Contarini at Piazzola sul Brenta (near Padua), see G. Zorzi 1969, 62–66; Puppi 1986, 108–09. Cardinal Pietro Bembo was an important conduit for the introduction of the Roman Renaissance style of the circle of Bramante and Raphael to North Italy, and his association with the architectural patron and theorist Alvise Cornaro in Padua brought him into the ambit of Trissino and the young Palladio.

18 The pope elected was Adrian VI, Florensz of Utrecht (1522–23). For an account of the papal election, see Pastor 1969, 5: *s.d.*; and of the dogal election, Finlay 1980, 155, who reports Grimani's accusation based on Sanudo (*I diarii*, 1879–1903, 32: 433). For the Grimani and their patronage: Law & Lewis 1996.

19 Ippolito 1987.

20 Seneca 1962, 144–46, for the terms of capitulation.

21 In addition to the works already noted on the career of Patriarch Giovanni Grimani, see Benzoni 1961, 121, 125; Paschini 1957, pt. 3; De Leva 1880–81.

22 Report of 18 April 1589 from Raffaele de' Medici to Grand Duke Ferdinand of Tuscany, trans. in Chambers & Pullan, eds. 1992, 83–84; quoted from Fulin 1865, 15. *Cazzadì* is the Venetian form, from the verb *cacciare*, to send away; according to Mutinelli 1978, 154–55, the "Espulsi," or "discacciati," were those who had to leave the Council when matters were discussed or voted on that were of direct benefit to themselves and their relatives, legislature that began on the election of the ambassador to Rome on 25 September 1302 in the Great Council, with *papalisti* mentioned from 7 November 1459 in the Council of Ten (288, *papalisti*, are defined as patricians who have relations with the court of Rome); for sources of the deliberations, see Queller 1986, 184, 188, 222 (the law of 1459 is in ASV, Consiglio dei Dieci, Misti, XXIII, 118 [148]). For some of the most important legislature regarding Church and State relations in Venice, see: Sagredo 1865, 102; Cecchetti 1874, e.g., 2: 51, "Expulsis papalistis et affinibus"; Battistella 1898; Stella 1964; Bouwsma 1968; summary in Franzoi & Di Stefano 1976b, xx–xxvi; Cozzi 1990; Cozzi 1987; Cairns 1980, 82, 97, introduces a cautionary note as he reminds us of the political role of the Venetian ecclesiastic; Crouzet-Pavan 2002, 218, with further references.

23 On Church property, see the following: testamentary dispositions *ad pias causas* were scrutinized by magistrates, and *provveditori* were elected to regulate *beni inculti* on the *terraferma* and for more oversight over "Monasteri e Conventi, Ospedali e Luoghi Pii"; Cipolla 1947; Stella 1958a. In Grendler's typically cogent analysis, he notes that such laws were passed with the support of noted *papalisti* (1977, 203–05, esp. n. 10, which is informed by Lowry 1970–71, chs. 4–5); yet those were the members of the Venetian patriciate allied with expansion on the *terraferma* (including Marc' Antonio Barbaro, Alberto Badoer, Jacopo Foscarini), thus linking their interests with the Republic rather than the Church. The legislation alienating ecclesiastical property was an important factor in precipitating the Interdict on Venice of 1606, as, for example, Malatesta, BMV, IV, said, it was unfavorable to the "libertà di Religione"; and is fully published in Cornet 1859, 265 (in ASV, Senato, Terra, reg. 75, 19, 26 March 1605, from earlier laws of 1536, on the alienation of property), 268 (in ASV, Senato, Terra, reg. 73, 151, 10 January 1603 *m.v.* [= 1604], from earlier laws of 1561, prohibiting construction), 269 (in ASV, Senato, Terra, reg. 72, 49, 23 May 1602, regarding emphyteusis).

24 The most stable group of names are the twenty-four families considered *longhi*, or *case vecchie*. The term *evangelisti* was applied to the four *case vecchie* who signed the foundation agreement for the monastery of San Giorgio Maggiore in 725: the Bembo, Bragadin, Corner, and Giustinian. There were a very few exceptions admitted between 1381 and 1646, mostly foreign nobility, *ad honorem*, which became increasingly a gesture as prohibition of their participation in the Great Council – the definitive attribute of the patrician male – was debated in the late fifteenth century. There were later openings after the Wars of Crete (1645–69) and the Morea (1684–1718), and in the later eighteenth century. See Morando di Custoza 1979, 10–12, for the classification of noble families. In addition to the earlier literature on the Venetian patriciate, add Lane 1973, 427–31, "The Apex of Oligarchy"; J. Davis 1962.

25 Trans. in Chambers & Pullan, eds. 1992, 72–73, from BMV, Sanudo, 271r–273r, September 1486, "a far caxar," here means to arrange the exclusion.

26 For the political makeup of the patriciate, see above, and in addition: see the analysis of political careerism by Grendler 1990, 35–59; Finlay 1980, 196–226, for electioneering; Queller 1986, esp. chs. 3 and 4, on the Broglio; Cozzi 1958, 5, on the larger proportion of wealth in *case vecchie*, with *case nuove* split between *ducali* and a large group of poor nobles; Pullan 1971, passim.

27 Casini 1995 uses the term "political clans," in reference to the Calze; Braudel 1982, titles ch. 5, "Society: 'A Set of Sets,'" or "ensemble des ensembles," which he uses as an explanatory device to describe the interrelationships of different segments of society while maintain-

ing a tangible sense of the fluidity of any categories.

28 A contributing factor to the breakdown between "youth" and "age" was the admission for money of younger men into the powerful procuracies after 1516; see Chambers 1997, 38–43, which his analysis shows to have been most powerful between 1516 and 1538, and 1571 and 1573.

29 Seneca 1962, 34–42, on the lack of a coherent "program" of political factions *circa* 1500.

30 See D. Brown's entry with previous literature (1990), determined by style to be executed posthumously, *circa* 1540; on the cast, see Suida [1933], 145 n. 43; it has been proposed by Tietze-Conrat 1946, 81 n. 44, that the doge has picked up his mantle to stride forward in procession, and this view has been adopted by subsequent writers. An overview of Gritti's patronage is in Howard 1996b.

31 "I saw a new painting in the Collegio, which included the likeness of the doge [Andrea Gritti], kneeling before Our Lady with Babe in arms, and with St. Mark presenting him. Behind Our Lady are three saints, Bernardino, Alvise, and Marina. The explanation circulating is that they have argued as to which of them elected the doge. Bernardino says, 'He was elected on my day.' St. Marina says, 'He was elected for having recaptured Padua on my day, July 17.' And St. Alvise says, 'I have the name of the procurator, Alvise Pisani, his in-law, who was in the Forty-one and who was cause of his election to doge.' So St. Mark, seeing this argument among the three saints, decided to present them to Our Lady and the Son to determine which of them was behind the election of His Serenity to the dogeship." Finlay 1980, 158, for this translation from Sanudo (*I diarii*, 1879–1903, 55: 19). For a summary of the previous literature on this work, see Romanelli 1990, 36–38.

32 For the political consequences of the gerontocracy, see Finlay 1980, 124–41; C. Gilbert 1967.

33 For the implications of wealth and size of family on political power, see esp. the conclusions of Chojnacki 1973, 58–71.

34 See the various contributions to Tafuri, ed. 1984; and for the account of his election in Finlay 1980, 155–61; also as art patron, Howard 1996b; and Olivieri 1998.

35 See above, Finlay 1980, 181–96; F. Gilbert 1973, 290; Cozzi 1973, 334–35.

36 Quoted from Chambers & Pullan, eds. 1992, 26; also Cozzi 1958, 15; from Carleton's undated report of *circa* 1612, in London, Public Records Office, State Papers 99. file 8.

37 Cozzi 1958, 4, noted that *case vecchie–case nuove* rivalry was still present in the elections of Doges Nicolò da Ponte and Pasquale Cicogna; the extent of da Ponte's identification with the *giovani* has been argued; cf. W. Brown 1974, 139–42. On the end of significant factionalism between *case vecchie* and *case nuove*, see Finlay 1980, 283–84, who notes the decline dating from the elections of 1605.

38 Bouwsma 1968 exemplifies this approach at its best; also see the influential analysis by Cozzi 1963–64 of the role played by public sponsorship of history writing.

39 Finlay 1980, 1–13, discusses the problems of the sources in general; the prosopographical analysis is typified by the work of Grendler 1990; and Grendler 1979; as well as Cozzi 1973; note that these authors differ in their emphasis on interpretation, which is analyzed with a sharp eye for the limits of such categories of "exemplarity," by Grubb 1986, 53–59.

40 Discussed by Benzoni 1987; Pizzati 1997.

41 Report of the Mantuan ambassador, 1609, trans. from Finlay 1980, 284 (from Luzio 1917, 96). Lane 1973, 405, sees these as "embryonic parties," the failure of which in the mid-seventeenth century signified "stagnation": "Parties were to prove vital instruments of change in the nineteenth century's democratic development of republican institutions"; Chabod 1958; for the seventeenth century, see Cozzi 1958, *passim*.

42 See the comments of the French ambassador, Huralt de Maisse, to King Henri III, 8 May 1583 (in Paris, BN, Fonds Français 10736, 301–02), trans. in Chambers & Pullan, eds. 1992, 81–82, "Behold, Sire, how this crisis has now been resolved, with the older members of the Republic very angry that the young have forced such changes upon it, and the young, on the other hand, very happy, being liberated (so they say) from the tyranny of the Council of Ten, against which there remains [after the abolishment of the Zonta] amongst them much secret hostility."

43 On the notion of "Style," see Ackerman 1991d: "Style is not discovered but created by abstracting certain features from works of art for the purpose of assisting historical and critical activity . . . style is a means of establishing relationships" (4).

44 For proposals on such methods, see esp. Ackerman 1991c, 453–54, on "Geopolitics"; Lewis 1981, on "Patterns of Preference"; on the study of patronage, and the distinctions of *mecenatismo* and *clientelismo*, see Cooper 1996b.

45 Howard 1987, a pioneering monograph in its organization around diverse patronage groups, discusses the differences between magistracies and their practices of patronage; for the Procurators of San Marco as patrons, in addition see Boucher 1986; now expanded in Boucher 1994, esp. 609–35, with references to recent studies on the individual buildings in the Piazza San Marco built for the Procurators; on the Salt Office, see Calabi & Morachiello 1987, pt. 2; on the Arsenal, Concina 1984a. For Vicenza, see Burns 1991, 194–205. For the description of the various magistracies, guilds (*arti*), and organization of the building trade in Venice, see Caniato & Dal Borgo, eds. 1990.

46 Tafuri 1989; Tafuri 2001. Concina 1995 has applied similar criteria to the following centuries; and see also Concina 1993.

47 Actually this was his second chance at a

procuratorship, since he was stripped of the first for the losses of the Venetian fleet at Zonchio in 1494, then exiled, living for a time in Rome with his son, Cardinal Domenico. Despite the asperity of his comments at the time of his election as doge, chroniclers bemoaned his senility at his death at the age of 90; for his political career, see Finlay 1980, 136, 147–55; Chambers 1997, 34–37, which includes his *Commissione* of 1494 (Venice, BCV, MS Correr, Cl. 3, 158), and dogal *Promissione* (London, BL, MS Add. 18000).

48 In addition to the previous note for Sansovino, see: Tafuri 1972; Boucher 1991, *passim*, and I: 37–44; for the Scala d'Oro competition, Morresi 2000, 308–10, cat. 56. On the Procurators of San Marco: Chambers 1997; Mueller 1971 on function and fiduciary duties; Molmenti 1888. For a list of *proti*, see Cecchetti 1886, xiv.

49 Scamozzi 1964: "Essi si occupino della esecuzione perchè possono aver pratica ma non teoretica propria degli Architetti Scientati" (ch. 26, 82); "posiachè i proti sono anche nelle più vili arte ed esercitij della Città" (ch. 29, 87); discussed in Fontana 1989.

50 Temanza 1778, 305, "Sa ognuno che la voce *Proto* nel nosto vernacolo significa Architetto. Così appellossi il nostro Palladio, così il Sansovino," 260–61, "Per altro Proto è voce significante anche uffizio, come fu quella di *Praefectus fabrorum*; ma di uffizio, che impiegar debbe un uomo, che sia Architetto. Anche Vitruvio fu Prefetto delle macchine militari; ma un tal Presidente dovea essere un Architetto del merito di Vitruvio," Galileo is cited from his *Discorsi e dimostrazioni matematiche intorno a due nuove scienze* (Leiden, 1638), 1, "le conferenza dei quali mi ha più volte ajutato nell'investigazione della ragione di effetti non solo meravigliosi, ma reconditi ancora."

51 Rosand 1970a, 34 (the letter is reproduced in H.-W. Frey, ed. 1940, 215), who notes that the reborn Accademia Veneziana Seconda (1593) admitted a few artists; Rosand 1997, 184 n. 61; Hochmann 1992, 58; also some artists were members of the Venetian Accademia Pellegrina, see Tafuri 1989, 248 n. 103; Aquilecchia 1980, 95; Maylender 1926–30, 5: 444–46, 4: 244–48, respectively. On the profession of the architect: Ackerman 1991a; Kostof, ed. 1977. For guilds and building trades in Venice: Sagredo 1857; Monticolo & Besta, eds. 1905–14. Also see *Cultura, scienze e techniche* 1987; and the introduction to Concina 1988, 7–30.

52 Vasari 1878–85, 5: 324, although, in the *Life* of Sansovino, Vasari gives Jacopo sole credit (7: 502–03).

53 Sanmicheli became *ingegnere alla Serenissima*: in 1535 the Council of Ten bestowed the double positions of *ingegnere alle fortezze* and *ingegnere ai lidi*; for the general situation, see Concina 1995, 210; but also Howard 1987, 38, notes his work from 1535 to 1542 for the Waterways Board (Magistrato alle Acque), then for the

provveditori alle fortezze. For recent literature, see Burns, Frommel & Puppi, eds. 1995. A welcome forthcoming monograph by David Hemsoll and Paul Davies will join the earlier work by Puppi 1971.

54 Sansovino 1968, 1: 387, "E per tanto da sapere che i principalissimi di tutti i Palazzi del Canal grande, sono quattro. (parlo per architettura, per artificio di pietre vive, per magistero, per grandezza del corpo, & di spesa, percioche questi soli costano oltre à 200. mila ducati,) cioè il Loredano à San Marcuola, il Grimano à San Luca, il Delfino à San Salvadore, & il Cornaro à San Mauritio. Questi larghi per circuito, per altezza, & per ogni altra qualità che si richiede à bene intesi edificij, furono fatti ne tempi nostri, & secondo la dottrina dell'antico Vitruvio, dalle cui regole à gli ottimi Architettori, non è lecito di partirsi." He then describes each one, the Palazzo Loredan being earlier than the others, the Palazzo Grimani being by Sanmicheli, and the Dolfin and Corner palaces built "on the model of Sansovino."

55 See particularly the work of Concina 1995, an overview on 210–11, 226–29; and earlier, Concina 1991; Concina 1984a; Concina 1983; also Marchesi 1984; Marchesi 1978; Morachiello 1991.

56 Concina 1995, 345–50, for recent bibliography on these structures; and as well see the overview in Boucher 1994, with additional references; and Howard 2002, 166–69.

57 "In effetti la circostanza di maggior rilievo sta nel fatto che l'edificio del primo Cinquecento riprende con sorprendente fedeltà la costruzione romanica delle Procuratie, edificate da Sebastiano Ziani (1172–1178) . . . Se si eccettua la differenza di un piano, aggiunto nella riedificazione, quella protorinascimentale risulta una vera e propria transcrizione, un aggiornamento del modello medievale. Insomma, è questo ancora un caso culturalmente centrale di quella che possiamo definire una *renovatio more veneto,* rivelatore dell'ormai accentuata sacralizzazione delle forme del passato, della dichiarata immutabilità della *species urbis,*" Concina 1995, *Storia,* 156–57. Deborah Howard has kindly alerted me to the current issue regarding the reidentification of Bartolomeo Bon as Pietro Bon, which has gained some recent acceptance, and merits further attention; see also Howard 2002, 151, who notes the significance of the original model of the Procuratie Vecchie being supplied by a Tuscan called "il Celestro."

58 Lotz 1981b on Roman Renaissance elements of architectural style, such as the double column and pier with engaged column.

59 That not all supported Sansovino, i.e., for the opposition of Pietro Grimani, see Howard 1987, 21. For analysis of the admission to procuracies by money, see Chambers 1977, 38–49, esp. 47–48, for Sansovino's supporters; Boucher (1986, 61–62; 1991, 1: 40) has proposed that the new impetus for public building came from the economically advantaged group of procurators thus elected.

60 See generally in Howard 1987, chs. 2 and 3; as well as the telling aftermath, in Tafuri 1989, 161–79; Cooper 1995; and Morresi 1998a.

61 Howard 1987, 27. As Deborah Howard has generously pointed out in a personal communication, Sansovino uses a contracted form of the motif, with some similarity to such local application of minor orders framing arches as the Torre dell'Orologio in the Piazza.

62 Trans. in Serlio 1996, 251 (also in Chastel 1983, 276 n. 77). "In Venetia ricetto di tutto il ben humano e divino, Il Sereniss, et non mai apieno lodato Principe, messer Andrea Gritti, ha condotto al servigio de la sua inclita Republica questi singular huomeni, che cosi fanno stupendo questa Città di nobili, ed artificiosi edifici come la fece Dio mirabile di natura e di sito," Serlio 1537, Bk. 4, 111. For the attribution to Serlio of the Grimani Palace at Santa Maria Formosa, see now Bristot & Piana 1997, 45–47, 51. See Onians 1988, esp. chs. 19 and 20, on Serlio and Venice; also S. Frommel 2003, esp. 16–26, 56–76, on the Serliana and the Library, see 67, 70–72; only the *Fourth Book,* on the orders, and the *Third Book* (*Il Tèrzo libro,* 1540), on antiquities, were published in Venice before Serlio departed for France. On the Serliana, see Wilinski 1965, 115–25; Wilinski 1969; and for subsequent discussions, see De Jonge 1989, who further refines an analysis of a Venetian window type that provided the basis for this motif in Lombardy and the Veneto, the "campata alternata." Serlio claimed to have been present at the excavations of the Theater of Marcellus; for his Roman period, see C. Frommel 1989.

63 Serlio 1996, 310–15. Howard 1987, 165 nn. 72 and 82, documented the bays of the Library rented out for Giovedì Grasso (Fat Thursday). Palladio 1997, 5, on the Library, 203, on the Basilica.

64 Gleason 2000 has shifted the focus from the War of Cambrai to the Peace of Bologna as the defining event of the period.

65 Chastel 1983, 207–15. Further see, Buddenseig 1969; Madonna 1979, 63; Ackerman 1986, see ch. 6 and catalog for history; Stinger 1990, esp. 139–40, on the transition of the Campidoglio from civic to imperial identity; and in subsequent years, Nussdorfer 1992, 3–16. I would like to express my appreciation to Alfred Moir for my introduction to the "Third Rome."

66 Palazzo Venezia (also called San Marco) was begun in 1455 by Pope Paul II Barbo (1464–71) while still a cardinal and used frequently by him as a residence, and by senior Venetian cardinals thereafter, including Cardinal Domenico Grimani, who embellished the palace with his antiquities; see Paschini 1927. For the use of the palace, see the description in Coffin 1979, 27–31, who describes Paul III's marked enjoyment of the palace; he would formally cede it to the Venetian cardinals, who disputed the grant of the Medici pope Pius IV

(1559–65) to the Republic in 1564, see Pastor 1969, 16: 343–44; Dengel 1909, 103.

67 See Tafuri 1989, 104–08, 238 n. 1, on Domenico Morosini's *De bene instituta re publica* (begun 1497), indebted to Gaetano Cozzi's identification of Gritti as a model prince, pro-agriculture, pro-urban splendor, pro-oligarchy, and a similarity between the tenets of Morosini to those of Francesco Patrizi da Siena, and in opposition to those expressed by Lauro Querini and Nicolò Zen.

68 Howard 1987, 11 fig. i, stresses the effect of the new alignment, as well as the new social order imposed despite the opposition of shopkeepers and particularly butchers (typically the most powerful stallholder in the market throughout history, according to the research of Helen Tangires, whom I would like to thank for this observation).

69 Chastel 1983, 222; Chambers 1970, 30, 68, 170.

70 The phenomenon that Chastel 1983, 178, described was called a "translatio" by Tafuri 1989, 108–12, which captures the sense of a transfer of the center; see now P. Brown 1996b, passim, for a broader discussion of this Venetian tactic.

71 G. Zorzi 1965, 332, Palladio was in Vicenza on 5 March 1555.

72 See above, Part I.

73 Gualdo 2000, 11–12; summarized in Puppi 1986, 120, St. Peter's, 129, Town Hall of Brescia (documents in G. Zorzi 1965, 90–91).

74 Howard 1987, 6, who notes, however, that worsening inflation in the mid-sixteenth century impacted on building negatively. Camerlengo & Piva 1980 provide a useful chronology of building activity.

75 G. Zorzi 1965, 308–12, for figures.

76 Inscribed on the sheet in London, RIBA, XVI, 9v (the enumeration of the sketches on the sheet will follow Fairbairn [1981–], 1–15, a hand list accompanying microfilms of "The Palladio Drawings," esp. 13, with the upper and lower halves of the sheet designated as A and B; note that the current matting reverses r–v); see a summary in Puppi 1986, 133–34, Leonardi was in Venice from 1551 to 1558.

77 Barbaro's first post had been *provveditore di comun* in 1548, one of the limited number of civil posts that he would hold; the ambassadorial post required substantial funds, but it was a fast-track to influential government positions, and Daniele was quickly earning a reputation as a trusted statesman. See the biography by Alberigo 1964; and an overview of family patronage by Howard 1996a; as well as Part I, above.

78 Palladio 1997, 149–51, who said that they were not built: "because of those difficulties that can arise." Puppi 1986, 133–34, provides a history of the identification (after De Angelis d'Ossat 1956, 158), and further says, "it should be stressed that no private building was constructed by Palladio in Venice"; this despite Ridolfi 1965, 1: 310, and his early attribution of the Palazzo Erizzo Morosini Valmarana at

San Canciano; even less tenable attributions have been attached to later prints of Venetian buildings, e.g., the Luca Carlevariis inscription for Palazzo Tiepolo-Coccina at Sant'Apollinaire by Gian Giacomo de' Grigis.

79 Following Fairbairn [1981–], 13, and her A–B designation of the pasted sheets, which reverses G. Zorzi 1954, 117, fig. 20; which was followed by Burns with Fairbairn & Boucher 1975, 152, cat. 270 (B), although the RIBA number is incorrectly given as XVI, 16; and Puppi 1986, 32 (A). Another drawing for a Venetian project is discussed on a contemporary sheet by G. Zorzi 1954, 114, fig. 16, London, RIBA, XVI, 8r, "A," plan for a housing project in Venice, with a variant on the *verso* (Fairbairn [1981–], 13). See the inclusion of Palladio in a discussion of Venetian sixteenth-century urbanism in Huse & Wolters 1993, 16–20 (the Leonardi sheet *verso* row houses); and Concina 1995, 199–200 (on Sansovino), whose survey project promises to provide a large-scale scientific basis for future studies (see Concina 1981); in which pioneering work was begun by Trincanato 1984; Gianighian & Pavanini 1984; a broad view in Maretto 1992.

80 Cevese 2002, 167–70, remarks on the influence of Bramante in the "Venice plan" spaces, and finds the façade designs for the two projects more conventional than their plans, and with unresolved contradictions (tripartite arrangement of nine-bay three-story superimposed orders with a pediment and reinforced orders for the central five-bay section).

81 Summarized in Foscari 1980b; supported by Burns with Fairbairn & Boucher 1975, 154, cat. 274, for whose proposal on the Mocenigo tomb, see below, Part V, where his identification with the Accademia della Fama (or "della Veneziana") will be discussed. Bassi 1987, 131–37, cat. 23–24 (Casa Vecchia), 25–26 (Casa Nuova); the Casa Vecchia was reconstructed by Francesco Contin in the years 1623–25, and the two were linked by a lower "palazzetto" to form a grand frontage.

82 Sperone Speroni, *Dialoghi*, 2, La Fortuna, Padua, 1790, in Morsolin 1984, 263–42; Azzi Visentini 1984, ch. 4, 149–241, who posits Daniele Barbaro's association with Palladio as possibly from July 1545, when he was required to produce a wood model of the garden; Puppi 1980a.

83 Tafuri 1989, 122; Goy 1989, 216–27, with earlier bibliography; Bassi 1987, 528–43, cat. 83–86; on the decoration by Alessandro Vittoria and Paolo Veronese and team, see Martin 1998, 49–51; Wolters 2000, esp. 140–47, on Barbaro and the theory of grotesques after Vitruvius.

84 Urbani de Gheltof 1890, 35, "Andrea Palladio . . . fece scuola, ma ebbe a dir vero seguaci poco felici nelle loro invenzioni. Fra i migliori di questi però fu Daniele Barbaro, patrizio veneto," 37 (on the paternity of the palace) "il Barbaro applicò i concetti palladiani all'edificio," and he makes comparisons to the Carità.

and the building and decoration project at Maser; trans. from Goy 1989, 217; Bassi 1987, 528–43, made the most cogent and influential analogies to the Carità.

85 Burns 1987, 180 (and from my notes at the talk); Martin 1998, 42–46, describes the ensemble as the "transfer of the Paduan sepulchral mode to the Serenissima," with a full discussion of the implications, this also was Vittoria's first documented bust; a copy has been installed in the reconstructed ensemble now mounted on the right wall of the left apsidal chapel, but originally on the left nave aisle wall between the second and third altars (the original bust now in Paris, Louvre); Chiari Moretto Wiel, Gallo, & Merkel 1996.

86 Huse 1979; and Bellavitis 1980; Bellavitis 1982; all the hypotheses compared in Battilotti 1985a, cat. 1.10–1.11.

87 For a discussion of the debate over the Library, see Tafuri 1989, 161–79; Cooper 1995; for the background, see Morresi 1998a.

88 For the concept of *mediocritas* articulated in the writings of Nicolò Zen, see now P. Brown 2004, ch. 2, 23–52; and the fundamental article of Concina 1984b, 276–80; also in Tafuri 1989, 1–13, on Domenico Morosini's ideas and the Gritti *renovatio*, 104–08, and for a comparison of the Donà and Gritti Palaces, esp. 4–5, 184–91; Donà's will is excerpted in Cicogna 1969, 4: 420–21, from ASV, Notarile, Testamenti, Giulio Ziliol, B. 1245, 493, 28 May 1612. BMV, Sivos, 3: 182–83, "con quei danari spesi havrebbe comprato il più bel Palazzo di Venezia, et nel più bel sito che non era quella casa, quale non havea forma di Palazzo." See now Ceriani Sebregondi 2002.

89 BMV, Savina, 364, describes the vote to buy the palace, "In questo tempo fu per deliberation del senato comprada la casa grande a s. Francesco soleva esser del Dose Gritti per ducati 26 mille delli denari del publico per donada al papa laqual a fatta habitatione del suo legato," for which there was clearly a political motivation at this time as nephews of Pope Sixtus V, Cardinal Montalto and Don Michiel Peseto, were inducted into the Venetian patriciate.

90 "Così andata sua Ser.ta, et l'Ecc.mo Collegio, et Magistrati soliti, venne il Cardinale fino à mira la corte della casa sudetta in habito di Cardinale accompagnato da moltiss.i Prelati, et con allegra faccia ricevuta sua Ser.ta caminando egli alla man dritta si conclusse ragionando di sopra in un Camerone, ove era preparato un Baldacchino con due sedie, et postisi à sedere, stando pur il Cardinale alla man dritta, passarne insieme diversi complimenti, et noi col med.mo ordini riternorono à basso, havendo voluto il Cardinale accompagnar Sua Ser.ta fino fuori della porta del Palazzo, che sul campo di S. Francesco si licentio, andando per l'acqua bassa à montar nei piatti à S.ta Giustina, accompagnata dal Sig.or Gio. Battista dal Monte General delle Fantiere, che si trovava à far corte al Cardi-

nale"; from ASV, Collegio, Cerimoniale 1, cxli–cxlii.

91 Palladio 1997, 213. Quoted more fully below, "alla dignità, & alla grandezza di chi hà da esserVi invocato, & adorato devono riguardare," and "maggiori ornamenti," Palladio 1976, "Proemio a i Lettori."

92 First noted by Magrini 1845, 301; recent summary in Lewis 2000, 222–24, cat. 101; see also Puppi 1990, 100, cat. 48; both scholars tend towards assigning it to a Venetian situation in the mid-1550s, but acknowledge the comparisons made to Vicentine commissions, from the Palazzi Da Porto, Barbaran, and Piovene all'Isola, ranging in date from the early 1550s to the late 1560s (Burns with Fairbairn & Boucher 1975, 212–13, cat. 379, favored a later date in the 1560s). According to Puppi (1990, 100), a strong argument towards a Venice site is its provenance from the collection of Palladio's important patron, Jacopo Contarini, although this requires an explanation for why it was not published with other unrealized projects in the *Four Books*, such as continuing expectations of a patron or intentions for its inclusion in a future publication, both of which the quality of the drawing supports.

93 Lewis 2000, 224, figs. 151–52, tellingly compares magnified details "D" and "E" (after G. Zorzi 1954, "Progetti giovanili," 10) of RIBA, X, 15 (he uses the sketch for the Maser nymphaeum to date the sheet to 1554, another support for a mid-1550s dating for the Vicenza drawing). Close observation of the actual sheet shows that "E" has incised lines that indicate a triangular profile similar to one rendered in the Vicenza drawing, and just visible in the detail reproduced by Lewis. I would like to thank RIBA Assistant Curator Neil Bingham for his extraordinary courtesy in making it possible for me to view the drawings during the difficult period when the collection was closed for their move to the Victoria and Albert Museum.

94 Particularly acute in the specialization of military architecture, as in Concina 1984a, passim; Tafuri 1989, 122–38; and see above on Leonardi.

95 Niero 1982, discovered in the notes of Tommaso Temanza in the Seminario Patriarcale.

96 Foscari 1980a; Foscari 1982, discusses the lack of information with which to attempt a reconstruction.

97 On Villa Foscari: G. Zorzi 1969, 151–56; Puppi 1986, 169–71; Forssman 1973; Boucher 1998, 145–49, the dating has been debated, but accepted as largely done by the death of Nicolò on 7 September 1560. Nicolò and Alvise were in the direct line of descent from Doge Francesco Foscari, also known as the San Pantalon branch (Cà Foscari); see BMV, Cappellari Vivaro, vol. 2, s.v. "Foscari." For Alvise, see Gullino 1997a.

98 A rare exception is Foscari 1982, 92 n. 5.

99 For Veronese, see Rearick 1991, 248–50, who believes that the *Coronation of the Virgin* by Giovanni d'Alemagna and Antonio Vivarini may have been above the high altar previously; Rearick 1988a, 197–200, cat. 103 and 102, a drawing for the altarpiece (Paris, Louvre, RF 38.928), and note the original entrance from the south porch meant the composition would be viewed diagonally from the right; Cocke 2001, 207.

100 Da Villa Urbani & Mason 1994, for a history of the church and its decoration, and earlier literature; Foscari 1982, 94, fig. 80; and Foscari 1980a, 256, cat. 415, includes a plan of the old church. For the paintings by Palma, see Mason Rinaldi 1984, 131, cat. 468–69.

101 Tiepolo et al. 1980, 66–67, cat. 171–72, in ASV, Notarile, Testamenti, Marc'Antonio Cavanis, prot. 3278, 886v, and prot. 3279, 25v–26, 23 December 1566 and 9 January 1567.

102 Sambò 1990, in ASV, Notarile, Testamenti, Vettor Maffei, B. 8169, 101r–v, 26 August 1572.

103 In 1573 Guglielmo de' Grandi, *sottoproto alle acque*, recommended that Palladio be consulted on the Ponte San Giobbe, in Tiepolo et al. 1980, 77, cat. 210, ASV, Savi ed esecutori alle Acque, filza 119, 291–92.

104 G. Zorzi 1965, 139, "Libro di pagamento," 5 September and 23 October 1573, after Temanza 1778, 517; see now the full documentation in Chiappini di Sorio 1988.

105 I would like to thank Vittorio Mandelli for his generous indication of this unpublished document in ASV, Notarile, Testamenti, Vettor Maffei, B. 8171, 419v–420, 1573 (which will be part of a forthcoming article on the monument). Johanes Vrana was from Dalmatia (now Croatia), and I would like to thank Nadja Aksanija for her help in locating his origins.

106 These opinions and Palladio's government associations will be discussed in Part V below. For an opinion linking Palladio to work at the Frari in 1577, see Battilotti 1999, 508 cat. 161.

107 Vasari-Milanesi 1878, 7: 100, *Life* of Taddeo Zuccaro, provides the most information for the form of the theater: "Palladio had made for the Company of the Hose a half-theater of wood in the form of a coliseum." On the Accesi, 1564–65 (Puppi 1986, 199–201; G. Zorzi 1969, 277–82; see in addition: Casini 1996, 300–01, 303–04, 307; Casini 1995, 37–38, who stresses Foscari, Grimani, and Mocenigo patronage as a symptom of the strength of the *vecchi* and displayed through such public rituals; Foscari 1979, for the most detailed study; Olivato 1982, updating her earlier work; the documents are transcribed by Padoan Urban 1980, esp. 147–50, including the "Pergamena Foscari"; another copy is in BCV, Cod. Cicogna 2991; further documentation is provided in Venturi 1983, 12–13 (statutes), 30–33 (costumes), 112–17 (events), 129–34 (statutes), 140–41 (membership).

108 Tafuri 1989, passim, as this is a governing theme throughout. Cf. Grubb 1986, 53–59, who cautions against an uncritical acceptance of such categories of exemplarity. The strategy followed here is to focus on the cultural, political, and familial links that can be associated with such identifications.

109 Casini 1996, esp. ch. 7, is also currently working on a study of the Calza. Gullino 2000, 150, describes the *Calza* as "piccole corti," little courts. Emphasis on noble identity can be seen in the rich costumes and markers such as *stemmi*, as in Padoan Urban 1980, 150–51, who identifies the Accesi motto ("Et duriora") and coats of arms contemporary to the 1562 priorate of Giulio Contarini (I have added identifying numbers running in columns from top down then left to right for the *Compagni stemmi*; the larger central *stemma* is that of the Accesi): Giulio Contarini del Zaffo (1), Andrea Dolfin q. Giovanni (2), Santo Venier (3), Giovanni Bragadin (4), Marc' Antonio Badoer di Francesco (5), Vincenzo Pisani (6), Benedetto Dolfin d'Andrea (9), Gerolamo Foscari di Pietro (12), Giorgio Contarini di Lorenzo (13), Giovanni Francesco Grimani q. Zaccaria (14), Alberto Badoer (15), Francesco Faeta "nobile cremasco abate" (16), Pietro Badoer (7), Mattia Donà q. Alvise (10), Nicolò Michiel (8), Giovanni Malipiero di Nicolò (11); on Andrea Dolfin, see Mancini 1999. For the emblematic content of the *stemmi*, Pilo 1991, 140–41.

110 Olivato 1982, resolved the location. On the San Simeone Piccolo branch of the family (as distinct from the San Pantalon branch represented by Nicolò and Alvise Foscari): Foscari 1979; Gullino 2000, whose focus is the recuperation of the impressive political career of Marco Foscari (1477–1551), and who blames Gerolamo for the eventual financial decline of the family, which was once considered to be second in Venice only to that of Doge Andrea Gritti (to whom they were related through his paternal great-grandmother, Paola di Triadano Gritti, aunt of Andrea), and see the family tree on 14 (more here in Parts I and V).

111 See Part I on Paola Foscari Pisani and on the Barbaro of San Vidal (and Maser), and Part III on the Grimani of Santa Maria Formosa; also Gullino 2000, for useful family trees with Foscari connections to the Capello family of Santa Maria Mater Domini (36), and Grimani (39, 115); Elena Grimani Foscari was Doge Antonio Grimani's great-granddaughter, and it was the original negotiations over her proposed marriage to Alemanno di Jacopo Salviati, nephew of Leo X de' Medici and uncle of Cosimo I de' Medici (94) that connected Marco Foscari and the then-Procurator Marco Grimani, Trissino, and the patriarch of Aquileia, Marino Grimani, 93–97, 114–26; also see ASV, Giomo, I: s.v. "Grimani."

112 See Part V for Pietro di Marco Foscari, for both the restoration of the Doge's Palace and under the visit of Henri III; as well refer to Gullino 2000, 107, who attributes the building projects to Pietro, 16–17, where he summarizes sources for the Foscari Palace at the Arena in Padua (destroyed 1827), 125–26, noting Elena Grimani Foscari brought nearby property both at the Arena and at San Simeon Piccolo (ASV, Archivio Gradenigo, B. 175 bis/1 and B. 186/8, respectively) to her marriage of 1534 as part of her "exceptional" dowry of 18,000 ducats.

113 These were the Badoer of the San Marcuola branch: ASV, Barbaro, s.v. "Badoer," I.1, 67, "F"; on Villa Badoer, see Puppi 1975; for further discussion of the family patronage of Palladio in connection with the Doge's Palace, see Part V.

114 The dating is provided by letter from Palladio in Venice to Conte Vicenzo Arnaldi in Vicenza, 23 February 1565, which says that he "undertook to make this blessed theater for which I am doing penance for all my sins now and in the future"; the privilege from 14 March 1565, ASV, Senato, Terra, reg. 45, 107; and dedication, all in G. Zorzi 1969, 281, docs. 1–3 respectively, and 277–81, for a discussion of the figures involved; see further in Puppi 1986, 199–201; on Maganza, see Ridolfi 1965, 2: 224–26.

115 See esp. Foscari 1979, 79–81; Casini 1996, 307.

116 For Palladio in Udine 1563, see in Part III; on the Cividale model, 1564–65, where according to Vasari (1878–85, 4: 274–75) he was accompanied by Zuccaro (Puppi 1986, 201–02; G. Zorzi 1965, 85–86).

PART III

1 Regarding the relative chronology of Palladio's projects, the order followed here assumes San Pietro di Castello's precedence over arguments for the earlier dating of the convent of Santa Maria della Carità: in her important monograph, Bassi 1973, 23 and 26, proposed a date for the Carità of 1555, associating Palladio's absence of 1555 from Vicenza on business in Venice with a document for stone ordered for the monastery (140, doc. 1, 30 January 1555 [or = m.v. 1556?], in ASV, SMC; however, the other documents cited in support, including designs attributed to Palladio (141, doc. 4, "Documenti relativi a lavori," in idem, B. 2)] are undated, therefore I see no compelling reason to date it so much earlier than the first document that names Palladio at the Carità, when he is paid for the model and as overseer for the year ending June 1562 (141, doc. 5, in ASV, Sala diplomatica Regina Margherita, no. 13-LXXIV, raccolta autografi); furthermore Puppi 1986, 177, does not accept the drawings that form the basis of her proof as autograph; nor does Boucher 1998, 152. See the summary of the literature on San Pietro di Castello and San Francesco della Vigna, respectively, in Puppi 1986, 162–63 and 189–91; and updated in Battilotti 1999, 483 and 493; Beltramini & Padoan, eds. 2000, 221 and 231.

2 Contract with Maestro Domenico de Menin da Venezia, his son Baldissera, and nephew Alessandro dated 7 January and published 9

January; G. Zorzi 1967, 30, cited from Magrini 1845, Annot. 37, XVII–XIX, said to be in the church archive; on which see Timofiewitsch 1980, 245 n. 24.

3　On the fragments by Antonio Visentini, San Pietro di Castello, Portal (London, British Museum, King's Library, lxxviii, 85, vol. 2, fol. 124, and vol. 3, fol. 159), which I was unable to trace, but for whose help I would like to thank Stephen Parkin, Curator of Early Printed Materials at the British Library: see G. Zorzi 1967, 30; and Puppi 1986, 163, also mentioning London, RIBA, F 6/4, 195, compares the designs to the Porta Almerico in Vicenza Cathedral of 1563–65. On Visentini (1688–1782) and the collection of drawings known as the *Admiranda urbis venetae*: Bassi 1997, esp. 3–11.

4　G. Zorzi 1967, 28, agrees with Magrini (1845, 46 and Annot. 37, XVII) that the contract supersedes Paoletti's assertion (1839) that traces of one of eight lost models had been followed by the architects completing the façade; rather, it seems that the contract was made on a drawing that would be supplemented by further specifications as judged necessary by the architect ("quanto sarà giudicato esser bisogno dal soprascritto Palladio"); see a full account in Timofiewitsch 1980, 245 n. 24; also Puppi 1986, 162–63, who reframed the issue noting the importance of the Barbaros.

5　Palazzo Mocenigo, Padua (Puppi 1986, 161–62); project for Villa Mocenigo, Marocco (Puppi 1986, 171; G. Zorzi 1969, 186–87); Villa Badoer, Fratta Polesine (Boucher 1998, 123–29; Puppi 1986, 149–51; Puppi 1975, 27; G. Zorzi 1969, 94–100). Both of these individuals figure in other projects: Badoer's son has been discussed already as a member of the Compagnia della Calza degli Accesi, and for his brother see Part V; see Part IV for Leonardo Mocenigo, whose father had rented their Paduan house to Trissino.

6　Burns 1991, 204–05; Boucher 1998, 93–109, esp. 104–05; Puppi 1986, 110–16; Barbieri 1970, 79–80; G. Zorzi 1965, 43–75, 303–46.

7　Puppi mentions plague in Venice in the years 1556–57 and Udine in early 1556, as inducement for Palladio and his clients to be "in villa." On Udine, Palazzo Antonini: Asquini & Asquini 1997; Boucher 1998, 121–22, 217; Puppi 1986, 148–49; G. Zorzi 1965, 224–27; Arco Bollani (Puppi 1986, 147–48, and 193, for the incorporation of 1563 into a route to the Castello, relevant below; G. Zorzi 1965, 81–82); work on public palaces attributed to Palladio in Udine, door and staircase (Puppi 1986, 147, skeptical of the attribution, citing Magrini 1845, 246–47, who noted that Giovanni Ricamatore, called "da Udine," was working for the city in the 1550s, which made him a more likely candidate); and Feltre, loggia (Puppi 1986, 154–56; G. Zorzi 1965, 75–81).

8　Diedo had a typical *cursus honorum*, with his only ambassadorial post early on (Poland, 1537), he was *podestà* in Bergamo (1540–42)

and Verona (1545–46), *luogotenente* in Friuli (1549–51), and *savio di terraferma* thrice (1547, 1549, 1551), then *consigliere ducale* for San Polo (1553), see Gullino 1991, who describes the family as rich and prestigious, and Vicenzo as ambitious and highly intelligent; probably inaccurately, BCV, Barbaro, "Genealogie," 3: "A," also lists him as a *capitano* for Vicenza, but I have found no independent confirmation. His mother was Elisabetta ("Betta") di Girolamo di Nicolò Priuli, see BMV, Cappellari Vivaro, 3: 252, "L," her first cousins were the brother doges, Lorenzo (contemporary reign, 1556–59) and Gerolamo di Alvise di Nicolò Priuli (1559–67), whose fraternal succession shows the importance of this branch of the family. For Diedo's career as patriarch of Venice, see Niero 1961, 89–92.

9　On the origins of urban Venice: see particularly Carile & Fedalto 1978; Dorigo 1983; Crouzet-Pavan 1992; and for a recent account of its architectural development, Concina 1995, with a topical bibliography; and Howard 2002. For an overview and recent summary of literature on the patriarchy of Venice, see Tramontin, ed. 1991; as well as Niero 1961; V. Piva 1938–60. On the transfer of authority, see Tramontin 1989; Tramontin 1991a, 33, on the Bull of Nicholas V, "Regis aeterni," 8 October 1451, authorizing the translation.

10　See esp. Tramontin 1970; Tramontin 1987; Niero, ed. 1996. In addition, see Part II, note 1 above on the Marcian legend and the "myth of Venice"; further in Tramontin 1991a, a bibliography on 44–45; and Fedalto 1991, 63–65, on St. Mark as guarantor of ecclesiastical independence. On the rivalry between Venice/Grado and Aquileia, see Dale 1997, esp. ch. 1, 7–11, expressed in their programs of building and decoration.

11　The situation is well summarized in P. Laven 1967, for the treaty of 1445, 185; for sources, see further in De Renaldis 1888, 122–23. Venetian dominance is typically expressed symbolically, as in the *View of the City of Aquileia* (Udine, Museo Diocesano), commissioned by the Metropolitan Chapter of Udine and donated by Patriarch Giovanni Dolfin, whose family *stemma* is shown at the top; see the catalog entry in *Poppone* 1997, 331.

12　Although Charles V granted a return of Aquileia under the terms of the treaty of 1445, it was retaken in 1542 as a reprisal for Venice's acquisition of Marano, and remained under Austrian temporal control; De Renaldis 1888, 204–47; P. Laven 1967, 186; for the resulting fate of the patriarchy, see also Paschini 1933, 34–35; a general history of the region in Paschini 1936, 3: 155–98, on the end of the patriarchal state, 199–222, for Venice's loss of Aquileia, 253–57, for Patriarch Giovanni Grimani.

13　See the earlier discussion of the War of the League of Cambrai above, and esp. for the agreement of 1513 given in Cecchetti 1874, 1: 399; also see P. Laven 1967, 186–87.

14　Various sections of the correspondence are reproduced in: Paschini 1948, 70–72, for the secret brief of Julius III Del Monte of 24 September 1552, given in Predelli, ed. 1876–1914, 6: bk. 26, no. 18, and for Ambassador Nicolò da Ponte's notification of 29 September, in ASV, Capi del Consiglio dei Dieci, Ambasciatori, Roma, B. 23, 177; also see Cecchetti 1874, 1: 422; De Renaldis 1888, 273; and a summary in P. Laven 1967, 190–91 n. 42, with later concessions.

15　"Quando vaca questa Sede Patriarcale, il Senato elegge tosto il Successore, che poscia (come dice il Stringa) ordinato con le convenienti conditioni, & con le solite ceremonie in Patriarca; il Doge con la Signoria montato in certo giorno determinato ne i Piati d'oro, và à levar con molto pompa alla casa sua, conducendolo fino alla Chiesa di S. Pietro di Castello col seguito di una gran quantità di Gondole, & specialmente di quelle di tutte le Chiese Parochiali, guarnite di panni di seta, e d'oro con l'insegne delle lor Chiese, & Armi di nuovo Prelato, dove in ciascheduna di esse Gondole interviene il Piovano, e Titolati della Chiesa, che rappresenta. Il Doge poi li da con molto solennità, & festa in detta Chiesa Patriarcale il possesso del Patriarcato. Dipoi condottolo di sopra nel Palazzo della sua residenza, si licentia da lui, e se ne torna al suo Ducal Palazzo." Sansovino 1968, 19. Generally see Padoan Urban 1998, 219–24.

16　Franzoi & Di Stefano 1976b, xxiv, note the challenge mounted by Clement VIII Aldobrandini (1592–1605) when he required the patriarch to go to Rome to be invested; see Niero 1961, 16, on the *conferma pontificia*.

17　VINCENTIUS DIEDUS AMPLISSIMUS MAGISTRATIBUS, DOMI, FORISQ AD/LVI* AETATIS ANNUM ADMIRABILI SAPENTIA, ATQ* INTEGRITATE/PERFUNCTUS, EX PRAEFECTURA PATAVINA, AD HUIUS CIVITATIS/PATRIARCHATUM ELECTUS, CUM TEMPLI, ÆDIUMQ* ADIACENTIUM/REPARTIONEM, & CLERI INSTITUTIONEM OPERAM, ATQ* IMPENSAM/PER QUADRIENNIUM NON FRUSTRA CONTULISSET; MULTIS RELIGIONIS,/ET PRUDENTIAE PRAECLARISSIMIS EXEMPLIS EDITIS, MAGNO TOTIUS/CIVITATIS MOERORE SEXAGENARIUS IBIIT* ANNO SAL*/M*D*LIX* SEX IDUS DECEMB; in Sansovino 1968, 7.

18　BCV, Lippomano, 464–79, in Cozzi 1958, 29, who noted that the ideal of poverty was held as a widespread traditional value for clergy; also Gullino 1991, 283–84.

19　BCV, Michiel, 12 March 1586, in Cozzi 1958, 28 n. 2; Grendler 1979, 308–09 n. 38, on Grimani, 319–21 n. 55, on Donà (of the San Polo branch). Bassi 1973, 23, noted connections between Palladio and the doge's cousin Gian Francesco (G. Zorzi 1965, 305), and Daniele Barbaro (Magrini 1845, 70).

20　BCV, Lippomano, 465, "molti danari spesi nel riparamento della Chiesa et Palazzo erano state causa, che lui non haveva satisfatto a questo debito, et che era ano conveniente farlo per dar modo ad esso Patriarca di poter vivere honoratamente per honore et riputatione di quel grado, che li era stato donato da S. S.ta e dall'Ill.mo Senato"; excerpts also in Gullino 1991, 783–84.

21 Compare, for example, the accord for 4,800 ducats to stoneworkers for final working and assembling of the Istrian stone façade of Palladio's San Giorgio Maggiore; ASV, SGM, B. 21, proc. 10a, "Libro," 45v, 30 June 1607, in G. Zorzi 1967, doc. 46.

22 Niero 1961, 92–98.

23 Tramontin 1967; Tramontin 1968; Tramontin 1991b, 117–24, for a summary.

24 Sansovino 1604, 102v, describes the original ensemble; compare the edition of 1663 (Sansovino 1968, 9–11), where Girolamo (Giovanni) Grapiglia's interior of 1621 is also described.

25 "Il che havemo conceduto, et concedemo acciò detti Cl.mi Sig.e habbino modo di espedir d[ett]a fabrica con quella honorificentia che si conviene alla dignità di questo Ser.mo Dominio," BCV, Cod. Cicogna 2583, "Variorum ad Venet. Eccles. atque ipsius Ven. Cleri. spectantia," pt. I, 104, 28 October 1574, "Pro fabrica palatii Ducalis" (see below, Part V, on the Doge's Palace fire of 1574).

26 Sansovino 1604, 103v.

27 Lowry 1970–71, 191–92 (after BMV, Barbaro, "Genealogie," 4: 16); Grendler 1977, 267–72, notes his conciliatory attitude towards Rome even in his civil career, and his interests in Church reform as patriarch; Grendler 1990, 84, on Lorenzo's brother, Procurator Alvise (*papabile* in 1606), 76, on his sister Chiara, married to Alberto di Angelo Badoer; see further in Part V.

28 BMV, Cappellari Vivaro, 3: 248, branch "C" shows their mutual origins with a single ancestor in Procurator Constantino di Lorenzo "del Banco," with great-granddaughter Elisabetta ("L," 252) the mother of Diedo, and Patriarch Lorenzo as a four-times great-grand-son ("E," 249, "da San Polo al Magazen"). Priuli's sister was abbess at San Lorenzo during construction of the church by *proto* Simone Sorella; see Guerra 2002, 294 n. 73, 295 n. 78, after Cozzi 1958, 124.

29 See Part V below for Il Redentore.

30 I am still largely in agreement with Timofiewitsch 1980, who provides a thorough comparison of the executed façade with the original contract, which accounts for the different number of columns and other discrepancies (but modified as in Tafuri 2001, 431, fig. 32), and sees Palladio's design as the basis for the executed façade; also that Smeraldi's probable references to other façade projects by Palladio, notably the model for the as yet unfinished San Giorgio Maggiore, were exaggerated by the later addition of elements, including the attic, as the result of changes made in the seventeenth-century rebuilding of the body of San Pietro. Guerra 2002, 278–80, believes the San Giorgio model to have included a portico and so stresses the importance of Smeraldi's San Pietro façade for the

executed design at San Giorgio; I agree that it is very likely that Palladio's built works were helpful references for the executors of his later projects. For elements that may have existed from the first campaign, see G. Zorzi 1967, 30; and Puppi 1986, 162–63, on the Vitruvian motif of the double pediment from the Basilica at Fano in Barbaro, and who also notes that the speed of execution may indicate a reliance on the earlier project, although evincing greater reservations over discrepancies, also 195, on the portal design compared to the Porta Almerico (side door) of Vicenza cathedral; Boucher 1998, 151–52.

31 Niero 1961, 105, and for more on his activities as patriarch.

32 Giovanni Grimani (born 1500/01), commendatory abbot of Santa Maria di Sesto and bishop of Ceneda, was named to the patriarchy in *renuncia cum regressu*, so he succeeded to the title only on the death of its incumbent, his brother, Cardinal Patriarch Marino, in September 1546. For an overview, see P. Laven 1967. The patriarchal succession has often been confused in accounts of the Grimani family, the main source followed here is Ughelli 1720, 5: 131–34.

33 The Grimani family, and especially the branches of Santa Maria Formosa and San Luca, have been well studied as patrons; see generally Logan 1972, 308–11; Hochmann 1992, 229–42; see more below.

34 A shorter version of this chapter was presented at the Annual Meeting of the Renaissance Society of America, Chicago, 2001, as "Venice and Aquileia: Cultural Strategies of a Dispossessed Patriarchy," and I would like to thank Patricia Fortini Brown, Sarah Blake McHam, Debra Pincus, Dennis Romano, and Patricia LaBalme for their helpful comments.

35 Two other important patrons probably antedated Grimani's employment of Palladio: the Benedictines of San Giorgio Maggiore and the Lateran Canons of Santa Maria della Carità, between 1560 and 1562. In both cases, Palladio was appointed with the reformation of different areas of their monasteries, which in planning and intentions bear closer resemblance to his domestic practice and will be discussed here in Part IV; the former assignment, for the monks at San Giorgio Maggiore, would result in Palladio's first commission for an entire church *ex-novo*, and was already being considered by 1564. On the mainland, he was engaged contemporarily on the dome of Vicenza Cathedral, see Puppi 1986, 165–66; G. Zorzi 1967, 15.

36 For the correspondence, see Grimani 1880. On Marino, see Paschini 1958.

37 De Tolnay 1965; updated in Bresciani Alvarez 1977; and further in Foscari & Tafuri 1983, 165 n. 25, who see Grimani's vote against Sansovino as coherent with his choice at San Francesco della Vigna.

38 For Floriano Antonini, see Asquini & Asquini 1997, esp. pt. 3, 25–40; Biasutti 1958, 8–9, gives

Giovanni's residence in Udine as Casa Antonini, now Palazzo del Torso, Piazza Garibaldi, and Cardinal Marino's residence as Casa Valentino, Via Manin (near the Palazzo Patriarcale), now Palazzo d'Oro; whereas Bartolini, Bergamini, & Sereni 1983, 310, instead name Giovanni's residence as the Casa Antonini in Borgo San Bortolomio, Via Manin, now Palazzo d'Oro.

39 Palladio 1997, 78–79, illustrated on 80. "Io mi rendo sicuro, che apresso coloro, che vederanno le sotto poste fabriche, e conoscono quanto sia difficil cosa lo introdurre *una usanza nuova*, massimamente di fabricare, della qual professione ciascuno si persuade saperne la parte sua; io sarò tenuto molto aventurato, havendo ritrovato gentil'huomini di cosi nobile, e generoso animo, & eccellente giudicio, c'habbiano creduto alle mie ragioni, e si siano partiti da quella invecchiata usanza di fabricare senza gratia, e senza bellezza alcuna" [emphasis mine], *Quattro libri*, Bk. 2, ch. 3, 4. On the construction of the palace according to Palladio's design: Asquini & Asquini 1997, esp. pt. 4a, 41–98; Bartolini, Bergamini, & Sereni 1983, 250–59; also G. Zorzi 1924.

40 Palladio 1997, 157. GENIO URBIS UTIN* FAMILAEQUE ANTONINORUM FLORIANUS ANDREAE FILIUS DICAVIT, Puppi 1986, 149.

41 Foscari & Tafuri 1983, 165 n. 25. Magrini 1845, 27, Palazzo Antonini, 245.

42 Paschini 1958, 2: 86–88.

43 "Tra queste parole tramettendosi Monsignor Grimano: Questo stesso e molto più ne dirà il mondo, veggendo i suoi libri della Perspettiva che tosto usciranno alla luce; né quali con tal diligenza ha trattato di questa scienza, per se nobilissima e a diverse arti necessaria, che pare che gli studi di lui le abbiano recato l'ultimo accrescimento e la compiuta perfezione," Paruta 1599, 41. P. Laven 1967, 205 n. 170, notes the misconceptions about such academic gatherings as somehow decadent and leading to the consequent denouncement of Grimani's participation; also in Paschini 1951, 64; Paschini 1962, 104–05, on the genesis of the dialog (written between 1572 and 1579) in Paruta's visit to Trent on return from his embassy to Emperor Maxmilian in summer 1563; Benzoni 1997, 23–25, on Grimani's role as exponent of the contemplative life (which Logan 1984, 277, had characterized as problematic); Tafuri 1987, xi and xxxiii n. 1, noted that Barbaro had figured as the proponent of both the active and contemplative life in diverse authors.

44 The supervisors included the Superior, Fra Giovanni (Zuanne) Barbaro, uncle of Daniele, and the procurator of the fabric, Fra Girolamo (Hieronimo) Contarini; for the *relazione* of Fra Zorzi, and a history of the building under Sansovino, see Howard 1987, 64–74 and nn.; Foscari & Tafuri 1983, pt. I, esp. chs. 5–6, 36–70, which supersedes Tafuri 1972; Morresi 2000, 134–52, cat. 23. Both medals are also reproduced in Puppi 1986, 198.

45 Also employed by Giuliano da Sangallo, as can be seen in designs for the same competition; for a history of the San Lorenzo façade and Michelangelo's winning design, never built (the surviving wood model shows the ultimate transformation of this façade type, before he turned his energies to his Roman projects for the Capitoline and St. Peter's and re-thought his use of the orders), see Millon 1988, 4–6; updated in Millon 1994a; cf. Elam 1992. For Sansovino, in addition to the above, see Lotz 1981b, 140–43; Shearman 1975; Howard 1987, 34; Tafuri 1992, 150–55, on a later engraving identified with the Sansovino project (also Tafuri 1984b); Bruschi 1994, 164.

46 See Howard 1987, 159 appx. 2, for a full chronology of chapel concessions with archival references, notes the purchase of the third chapel on the left by Vincenzo Grimani in 1537 and 1538, but also cautions that the document might read Gratiani not Grimani; the same chapel was later purchased by the Bassi in 1548 (the date when Vincenzo di Antonio returned his interest to Sant'Antonio in Castello, see below); Foscari & Tafuri 1983, further on Gritti, 205, doc. 9, on 28 December 1554 (in ASV, Senato, Terra, reg. 39, 199r–200v), and 131–32, for Daniele Barbaro's altarpiece commission from Battista Franco circa 1552. Vincenzo di Antonio Grimani (1524–1582), sometimes called "Spago," also known as "the younger," to distinguish him from his grandfather Vincenzo (died 1535), son of Doge Antonio; his mother was Elisabetta di Alvise Pisani p. dal Banco, see ASV, Giomo, s.v. "Pisani."

47 For the history and documents of Vettor's efforts, see Foscari & Tafuri 1983, 135–36, 163 n. 15, 186–89, docs. 5 and 6; Boucher 1991, I: 187–88, docs. 76 and 77; Gaier 2002a, 471–72, docs. 5.1 and 5.2; on 20 April and 9 June 1542, in ASV, SFV, B. 2, pt. I, 437–40 and 440–43 respectively.

48 Gaier 2002a, 149–78, and 455–64, for the most complete account of the commission.

49 Foscari & Tafuri 1983, 135–36, 200–03, docs. 7 and 8; Boucher 1991, I: 188–89, docs. 79 and 78; Gaier 2002a, 472–76, docs. 5.3 and 5.4: on 28 March and 6 December 1544, in ASV, SAC, T. X, 62–64, and 58–61 respectively; also discussed in Foscari & Tafuri 1982, 107 ff., where this is also characterized as a struggle between the heirs of the sons of the doge, Gerolamo and Vincenzo the elder; also Howard 1987, 69–70; Gaier 2002a, 149–78, re-examines the history in relation to the original legacy of their brother Piero, for a monument to Antonio as a sea admiral, and sees some of the ensuing problems stemming from laws forbidding commemoration of doges on external façades in inscriptions or sculpture.

50 Foscari & Tafuri 1982, III: Boucher 1991, I: 189, doc. 80; Morresi 2000, 278–82, cat. 46; Gaier 2002a, 463–64, doc. 2.13: on 29 June 1548 in ASV, SAC, T. II, 215.

51 For comparisons, see Howard 1977; at Sant'Antonio an oculus is placed in the second story.

52 The importance of the Grimani collections has received recent acknowledgement, as in the exhibition of 2002 Venezia! Kunst (my thanks to Matteo Casini for bringing this to my attention), with contributions by Ravagnan, Soccal, De Paoli, and Newerow; and its recent predecessor in Favaretto & Ravagnan, eds. 1997; these essays owe a particular debt to the ground-breaking work of Paschini 1956, one of a series of his studies on the members of the Grimani family; and Perry 1972, the first of her several studies on the collections; see also Logan 1972, 155–61, 175–80, 308–11, on the family patronage; and Logan 1984, 272–79; M. Zorzi, ed. 1988, 25–40, with profiles of the family, esp. 30–32, on Giovanni; Hochmann 1992, 229–42; and Hochmann 2002, 87. On the renovation of the existing Grimani casa di statio, see Bristot 2001; Bristot & Piana 1997; Wolters 2000, 137–40, 170–71, 250–52. On the living arrangements of the Grimani brothers prior to this time, see Foscari & Tafuri 1981b, 70; also Foscari & Tafuri 1981a, 75.

53 For Grimani's problems with heresy, see particularly P. Laven 1967, on the "Causa Grimani," 195 n. 76 (and for Barbaro, 191–92, quoted from ASV, Capi del Consiglio dei Dieci, Secreta, Sesto, 23 August 1550, to the orator in Rome; Paschini 1948; Paschini 1951, passim; Paschini 1957, 133–96; Carcereri 1907; De Leva 1880–81, 407–54; Pastor 1969, 12: 510, 16: 319–26. In the context of Grimani's patronage at San Francesco della Vigna, see Foscari & Tafuri 1983, 146–59. On the tre savi sopra eresia, see Grendler 1977, 40 and n. 40, with translation and secondary sources (also Grendler 1979, 283–84) for the decree of 22 April 1547, in ASV, Compilazione Leggi, B. 24, E, 442.

54 For Da Mula's efforts and elevation, see the report of Girolamo Soranzo, "Relazione di Roma, letta in Senato 14 Giugno 1563," in Soranzo 1857, 10: 96–100; but since Da Mula was exiled without making his own report, see his letters during the negotiations, in Paschini 1957, 153–66, from BAV, Cod. Barb. Lat. 5751, 122v, 31 August 1560, 172v, 26 October 1560, 194, 9 November 1560, 303, 21 February 1561; De Leva 1880–81, 435–54, from BCV, Cod. Cicogna 890, 1 May 1561 to Girolamo Seripando in Trent, reply 16 May 1561, summary of February 1561 (if m.v. = 1562?) negotiations, and from BUP, MS 2213–2214, in which Da Mula declares to have given him the right to be eternally downcast ("per le qual haverei cagione di dolermi eternamente," 437); also Pastor 1969, 16: 321–22; and Gullino 1986. Grimani's conviction that he was created cardinal in pectore in February 1561, pending proof of innocence (attained at Trent), was apparently enough to have his portrait painted by Tintoretto in the robes of a cardinal, specifically the mozzetta (see fig. 74 above), according to R. Pallucchini 1983, 186 (based on Paschini 1957), noting also his intention to participate in the conclave of December 1565 (on which see further below).

55 For the correspondence, see Cecchetti 1874, 2: 25–67, esp. 33–38, 49–61, for the opinion of the Venetian ambassadors, Nicolò da Ponte and Matteo Dandolo, in ASV, Capi del Consiglio dei Dieci, Concilio di Trento, 9 March 1563 (idem, 33), regarding Grimani's absence; for the letter to be read to the nuncio and sent to Rome, undated but between 22 October and 3 November 1563, in ASV, Consiglio dei Dieci, Secreta, Concilio di Trento, Reg. 7, 134v (idem, 56–58), "Habbiamo già molto tempo, rev.mo mons., desiderato e procurato che il Rev.mo Patriarca di Aquileia Grimano fosse assunto nel numero dei cardinali . . . con universale consenso di tutti quei santissimi e dottissimi padri principali di tutte le nazioni, che tutti, come miraculosamente, son divenuti in questa sentenza è stata conosciuta la dottrina del patriarca, santa et sincera et del tutto aliena da ogni suspicione . . . alla paterna carità verso di noi . . . Domandiamo la publicatione in cardinale di un patriarca nobile, buono, di dottrina approbata et giustificata, già promosso, già votato e a noi promesso." The sentiments voiced, or strategy being employed in the latter appeal, were even then not universally approved since the first round of votes was eleven sì, six nò, five non sinceri, and a rephrasing did not produce a unanimous result, being fourteen sì, four nò, four non sinceri. For Borromeo's opinion: "Monsigr. Patriarca era conosciuto per buono e di buona vita"; see Paschini 1957, 154, from BAV, Cod. Barb. Lat. 5751, 172v.

56 Grimani was allied with the pope over the matter of the feud of Taiedo, which Venice cleverly resolved so as not to concede jurisdiction by declaring it a grant to the patriarch. The matter infuriated anti-papalists who scorned Giovanni's efforts to plead his good intentions in front of the Senate in 1585. Summarized in Romanin 1857, 361–64; Paschini 1952–53.

57 On 24 October 1585 in a congregation of the Holy Office, see De Renaldis 1888, 346; De Leva 1880–81, 434; Carcereri 1907, 85–87; Pastor 1969, 16: 326.

58 On 11 November 1585, see De Renaldis 1888, 348; Paschini 1936, 255; P. Laven 1967, 204. Just previously, on 7 October 1585, Francesco Barbaro, Marc'Antonio's son, had become coadjutor, which, unlike the position of patriarch-elect in renuncia cum regressu (which his uncle Daniele had held), carried with it the right to govern conjointly; see the authoritative biography of this example of Tridentine episcopal ideals, by Trebbi 1984, esp. 53–64; Trebbi 1996.

59 This was a protest to Pius IV that he had injured Venice by his refusal to publish Grimani's promised cardinalate: "disconvenienti a Noi, all'honor et alla dignità nostra pub-

blica," in De Leva 1880–81, 432–33, from ASV, Senato, Secreta, Ambasciatori, Roma, vol. 8, 32, 16 March 1565.

60 "Se faremo cardinali, non pensamo di fare a richiesta di Principi, ma in vero non habbiamo determinato," reported of Julius III by Domenico Morosini on 17 November 1554, in ASV, Capi del Consiglio dei Dieci, Ambasciatori, Roma, B. 23, 189; in Paschini 1957, 147; Carcereri 1907, 10; "siamo risoluti di non voler fare cardinali ad instanza di principi, nè per prieghi o raccomandazioni d'alcuno," reported of Paul IV by Bernardo Navagero on 29 November 1555, in ASV, Capi del Consiglio dei Dieci, Ambasciatori, Roma, B. 21, in De Leva 1880–81, 413–14 n. 2; discussed by P. Laven 1967, 193–94 n. 66, 195 n. 79, 204–05.

61 BMV, MS It. VII, 1279 (8886), "Avisi notabili del Mondo, et deliberazioni più importanti di Pregadi, dal 4 marzo 1588 al 25 febbraio 1588 (*m.v.* = 1589), 120v–124v, 7 December 1588, Leonardo Donà, Gabriel Corner, Alvise Zorzi di Benedetto; see Grendler 1977, 30–32; Grendler 1979, 322 n. 56; and Cozzi 1958, 38.

62 Cozzi 1958, 38, from BCV, Michiel, 10 December 1588, "che non era utile al publico, che nella nostra nobiltà tanti interessi col papa come principe laico non stava bene." Michiel's is a detailed account of the debate, in which Donà not only protested against the territorial ambitions of the pope and cardinals as "lay princes," but against the loss of experienced politicians, as they became "foreigners," and stated that he "did not want to see a Venetian pope for anything, it would be the ruin of the Republic," citing the Medici and fall of Florence. Gabriel Corner and Alvise Zorzi responded, noting the diplomatic role of numerous cardinals to the benefit of Venice, and that it was better to have Venetians, rather than foreigners, such as only French or Spanish, exercising their spiritual governance over Venice, and, furthermore, the pope was no temporal prince since his lands were the "patrimony of Christ." The latter enjoyed a hollow victory, for, in the event, no Venetian cardinals were created at this time. See Grendler 1977, 25–35, who relates this to the problematic nature of the territorial church within the Venetian state.

63 See De Renaldis 1888, 326 ff.; Paschini 1936, 254 and 272 n. 1; Pashini 1952–53; Trebbi 1984, 53–63.

64 "Più ambizioso che non fu Lucifero," see in Seneca 1959, esp. 129, 137, 142, 145, 152–60; the correspondence in Brunetti 1933, 1: 138. See also the opinions recorded in BCV, Lippomano, 468v.

65 P. Laven 1967, 205, described Grimani as the "unfortunate pawn of a complex of struggles"; Martin 1993, passim, presents the changing definitions over the course of the sixteenth century in the Venetian Inquisitions of orthodoxy and heresy; also on which see Grendler 1977, 286–93, "The Impact of Index and Inquisition on Italian Intellectual Life." Schutte 1989; and Grubb 1986, esp. 57, provide a useful historiographical perspective on the pluralism of Catholic orthodoxy.

66 This is taken from the inscription over the entry portal to the courtyard of the Grimani Palace, in the Ramo Grimani off the Ruga Giuffa: GENIO* VRBIS* AVG* VSVIQ* AMICO* RVM, which Perry 1981, phrased as a dedication of his palace "to the embellishment of the city and the use of his friends" (221). The inscription would reverberate with the Palladian example on the Udine palace of the noble ambassador and Grimani familiar, Floriano Antonini (described above), as well as in Venice, with the prominent display on the Grand Canal façade of Ca' Dario at San Gregorio (to which I was first introduced by Peter Meller, who promised a study of the concept), GENIO URBIS IOANNES DARIUS.

67 Vasari 1966, 6, no. 1: 197; Vasari 1878–85, 7: 529. Tassini 1863, 285, is the source for a date of 1562; among scholars who previously regarded this date as too early are: Sparrow 1969, 41–42, although he mistakenly gives Vasari's visit as 1568, the date of the actual publication of his second edition of the *Vite*; Wilinski 1972, 329; Lewis 2000, 241 cat. 110; Foscari & Tafuri 1983, 171 n. 52, who make a strong case for a date *circa* 1564, after Grimani's return from Trent; Law & Lewis 1996, 13: 659, as 1565. Charles Hope has proposed that Vasari's correspondent in Venice, Cosimo Bartoli, who arrived there in June 1563, provided much of the information for the *Life* of Jacopo Sansovino prior to Vasari's five-day visit in 1566 (generously communicated to me in advance of his forthcoming publication on Titian documents; for Bartoli as a source on Titian, see Hope 1993, 175–76; Hope 1995; for Bartoli's correspondence, see in Frey & Frey, eds. 1923–30; and K. Frey, ed. 1941.

68 The quote follows a description of the "virtù hereditaria dell'Illustre Casa Grimana" (although the identities of Marino and Marco are switched), and includes praise of the palace and collection as well: "la quale hora a concorrenza de gli antichi Imperatori ha fatto con eccessiva spesa di marmori fin da i fondamenti inalzare la gran machina della facciata, & entrovia la ricca Capella nella chiesa di San Francesco. & ha edificato un Palazzo di tanto eccelso & ricco artificio, che ogniuno gratamente ricevutovi resta attorito delle meraviglie nelle statue di marmori antiche & moderne, delle preciose pitture e ricchi ornamenti in ogni luogo, della dotta religiosa & cortessima famiglia, imagine dell'illustrissimo Signore che vi regna, amatore & benefattore di ogni sorte de virtuosi tanto nelle liberali quanto in ogni altra arte," Contarini 1572, n.p., the work also situates Grimani with other figures linked to the War of Cyprus and victory at Lepanto, on which see more in Part V (esp. Marc' Antonio Barbaro); also partially cited by Gaier 2002a, 172, who uses Vasari and Contarini to date the façade between *circa* 1566 and *circa* 1570.

69 Palladio continued to work on other projects in Vicenza and the *terraferma*, including a model for the cathedral of Bergamo (Puppi, 1986, 183, dates after 1561; G. Zorzi 1967, 89–91), and on the Sanctuary of Monte Berico, outside Vicenza (Puppi 1986, 188–89, as from 1558).

70 There is still some debate over who introduced whom to the Michelangelesque painter Battista Franco, "il Semolei"; see Foscari & Tafuri 1983, 131–33, 148, and the bibliography in 160 n. 1, for the Cappella Barbaro *Baptism* and the Cappella Grimani vault frescoes of *Virtues and Angels*, altar wall lunette with the *Resurrection*, flanked by the *Calling of the Apostles* and *Massacre of the Innocents*, and the Grimani Palace; also a full discussion of the ensemble is in Rearick 1959; in addition, Wolters 1968b, 23–24, on the Roman compartmented vault type; Schulz 1968, 142–43, cat. 93; Merkel 1981, 202; R. Pallucchini 1981, 44–46. See Perry 1981, 217–18, "Sala di Apollo," *Coriolanus* lunette, arrayed like a fictive tapestry in the manner employed by both Michelangelo and Raphael and their followers; Wolters 2000, 138, 250. Puppi 1986, 169, sees Franco as the link between Palladio's commissions at San Francesco della Vigna and the Villa Foscari (in Venice, Franco rented from Girolamo and Pietro Foscari, relations of the brothers Nicolò and Alvise Foscari of the San Pantalon branch, patrons of Malcontenta).

71 Boucher 1979, 279, 281, on Daniele Barbaro's opinions on the decorum of burials in cemeteries outside rather than inside churches (expressed in his commentary to Vitruvius' *Dieci libri*, Bk. 4, ch. 8), and personal piety.

72 Barbaro left the Council only for about two weeks, in the second half of June 1562, to go to Maser. Paschini 1962, 90–95, also notes that his only recorded sacerdotal and episcopal act took place on his return from Trent, celebrating solemn Mass in Verona (after Valier 1719, 89).

73 "Non cammina con altri che con l'Eletto Barbaro; e che sebbene al principio per due o tre giorni, nell'andare alle debite ed ordinarie visite delli legati e ambasciatori fu accompagnato da qualche prelato amico, suffraganeo e parente, mai più poi ha voluto compagnia," in Paschini 1957, 186 (after Baluze 1762, 3: 457).

74 ASV, Notarile, Atti, Giovanni Figolin, B. 5598, 5, 8 July 1563, Federico in Venice requested his brother Taddeo in Rome to secure payment owing from the pope. I would like to thank Charles Hope for bringing this document to my attention.

75 Despite the cardinal's preferences, for, according to Zuccaro, Da Mula was reported to favor especially the Venetianized Romanist painter Giuseppe Porta, known as "Salviati" after his mentor, the Florentine Francesco Salviati (died November 1563), whose assistant he was

in Venice in 1539, when Francesco executed two of the ceiling paintings at the Grimani Palace; Vasari 1878–85, 7: "Life of Francesco detto de' Salviati," 46, on Porta and Da Mula, "Life of Taddeo Zucchero," 91, on the Casino, 95–96, on the Grimani chapel and palace. For Federico Zuccaro and Cardinal Da Mula, see Smith 1977, 6–7; and Grimani: see Foscari & Tafuri 1983, 144–49, who had argued that the artist was too occupied with papal commissions between 1561 and October 1563 to have come earlier (in agreement were Bristot & Piana 1997, 52), but the newly discovered documentation places him in Venice four months prior to their *terminus post quem*, although their general conclusions may still be supported. On Francesco Salviati, see Perry 1981, 217, "Stanza di Apollo" (1539–40), lost *Homage to Psyche* (Schulz 1968, 142–43, notes his use of the Roman system of *quadro riportato*; and as after ancient models, Wolters 1968b, 29–31; Wolters 2000, 136–39, 251–52); Cheney 1963; Hirst 1963. On Giuseppe Porta, see McTavish 1981.

76 Foscari & Tafuri 1983, 147–48, based on a letter from Cosimo Bartoli to Vasari (in K. Frey, ed. 1941, 201, 19 August 1564), the chapel paintings comprised lateral frescoes of the *Resurrection of Lazarus, Conversion of Mary Magdalene* (destroyed), and the *Adoration of the Magi* in oil on marble; these subjects seem to have been assigned earlier to Battista Franco; for his preparatory studies, and their relation to Zuccaro's compositions, see Rearick 1959; Gaston 1977. On the program of the *scalone*, see Perry 1981, 218, who interpreted the allegories as "Distributive justice, the defense of religion [the Four Cardinal Virtues defending the Three Theological Virtues], constancy to supreme things," which she sees as appropriate both to Giovanni's aspirations and his tribulations; Bristot & Piana 1997, 49, discuss the vertical connections between floors as part of the restructuring of the older areas of the palace by Giovanni and Vettor Grimani.

77 The consistory reservation of a cardinalate *in pectore* of 26 February 1561 (see above). This ambassador was Girolamo Soranzo, who would also report on Trent. "Ho inteso con mio gran piacere la sostanza de ciò che hanno detto i dottori in Roma intorno al suo cardinalato et all'entrare in Conclave. Iddio benedetto Le dica chi Le faccia giustitia, poichè da quelli anco ritruova il medesimo che ha havuto di qua, ciò è che la ragione è dalla sua banda," in Paschini 1957, 194–95, from BAU, Carteggio Maracco, 78, 28 February 1566 (this was Vicar Jacopo Maracco, 1557–77); P. Laven 1967, 198, 203–04, where, however, Pius v's election is incorrectly given as December 1565.

78 P. Laven 1967, 204 nn. 159 and 160; Paschini 1957, 195; Paschini 1951, 136; De Leva 1880–81, 433, from BUP, MS 2213–14, and BCV, Cod. Cicogna 890.

79 Foscari & Tafuri 1983, 171 n. 52, have persua-

sively argued for a date *circa* 1564 after his return from Trent (in part based on the belief that Zuccaro was not available); see above for other scholars' dating; Bristot & Piana 1997, 52, extend this reasoning to the dating of the palace campaign that "redelineated and enriched his public image."

80 For Palladio in Udine in 1563, for the incorporation of the Arco Bollani into a route to the Castello (Puppi 1986, 193; G. Zorzi 1965, 81–82); on the Cividale model, 1564–65, where according to Vasari (1878–85, 4: 274–75) he was accompanied by Zuccaro (Puppi 1986, 201–02; G. Zorzi 1965, 85–86). On the Accesi wood theater after the antique, see Part II.

81 Foscari & Tafuri 1983, 144, argue the precedence of the Vicenza drawing (Museo Civico, D 17) for the interior over the built façade; see further below (and fig. 90).

82 For Palladio on Sansovino's *bella maniera*, see Part I; and his own *usanza nuova* in reference to Palazzo Antonini, as above. Typical of the interpretive tradition casting Palladio in the role of Sansovino's betrayer, see Foscari & Tafuri 1983, 164 n. 24, who describe it as "una fiducia che verrà tradita." Howard 1987, 74, noted the columnar scheme would have seemed out of date; as did Boucher, in Burns with Fairbairn & Boucher 1975, 135.

83 Vettor's widow was Isabetta di Girolamo p. di Antonio Giustinian (for a partial family tree, see Humfrey 1994, and fig. 4; For Vettor, see Law & Lewis 1996, 658. Vettor was ultimately buried next to Doge Antonio at Sant' Antonio di Castello (Lewis 2000, 242 cat. 111, described the "modest" burial as an "outrage" committed by Giovanni, who usurped the chapel at San Francesco della Vigna); Gaier 2002a, 148–78, recounts Vettor's handling of the remains of his grandfather Doge Antonio during the years of wrangling over his tomb monument (these included provisional interment in the Pisani tomb in the presbytery to that family's dismay), which seems no less disrespectful. Some of the provisions of Vettor's will of 30 January 1554 (*m.v.* = 1555) were contested by his brother Giovanni; for Vettor's proved will of 27 September 1558, see ASV, Notarile, Testamenti, Antonio Marsilio, B. 1214, no. 1026; partially quoted in Lewis 1972b, 29 and 36 n. 49; Foscari & Tafuri 1983, 164 n. 24. The inventory of Vettor's possessions in ASV, Notarile, Testamenti, prot., Vettor Maffei, B. 8119, 364, 26 October 1558, referred to by Howard 1987, 70 and 173 n. 45, with mention of the two models by Sansovino for the *fabrica* of San Francesco della Vigna. The private archives of the Grimani also have extracts of family wills from 1516 to 1638, now available in ASV, Archivio privati Grimani di S. Maria Formosa, B. 1, no. 6, for Vettor, 9r–v, and for the *decime* (tax) of 31 January 1553 (*m.v.* = 1554) on fam-ily properties, 10–14v, including, "In contra de Santa Maria Formosa mi attrovo una casa de statio, nella qual habito insieme con R.mo Patriarcha mio fratello, le quale è

allo decime per ducato 100, et diese ne mai è stata affittata; mà sempre è stata per habitation della fameglia nostro . . . 110 d.," the total *decima* came to 1,307 ducats, in which for comparison, the largest single sum (313 ducats) was for rental property at San Samuele, with a separately taxed *casa* on the Canal Grande (30 ducats), where a poor widow was housed to oversee their warehouses (128 ducats).

84 From *circa* 1532, when the second *piano nobile* was acquired (from Antonio di Vicenzo's widow, Elisabetta Pisani), to the completion in the 1570s of the courtyard logge, Bristot & Piana 1997; Marilyn Perry's work of 1981 on the Grimani collections was instrumental in bringing attention to the sad plight that had befallen the neglected palace, now receiving its long-awaited conservation; to this end an important conference was held there in 1985, "Il Palazzo e le Collezioni Grimani a S. Maria Formosa," some of the conclusions of which are incorporated in Bristot & Piana 1997, 47 n. 11; Bristot 2001. For awareness of this monument and others, see Wolters 2000.

85 Sansovino 1968, 1: 385, "il famoso Palazzo di Patriarca Grimani, ridotti alla forma Romana." Bristot & Piana 1997, 47, attribute the "scala ovata" in the palace to Palladio, contemporary to his work on the church, after his invention for the convent of the Carità (see Part IV below), published in the *Four Books*, Bk. 1, ch. 28, "F."), although no further corroborating evidence has yet been uncovered. Tafuri 1989, 9, described the palace as a "collector's item."

86 Just as Palladio finessed his discussion of the nymphaeum at Maser; see Lewis 1997, 38.

87 Gaier 2002a, 149–78, and 470–76 on San Francesco della Vigna (see above on Sant'Antonio), makes the point that it would have been difficult to justify an external tomb monument for the doge due to the laws passed immediately on Doge Antonio's death, and that this affected the planning at the two churches.

88 "La Magnificenza, rispose il Barbaro, come è nobile virtù, cosi non fa di se degna qualunque operatione: ond'elle non ha occasione di spesso dimostrarsi; ma in quelle cose solamente si adopera, lequali rare volte si fanno; come sono i conviti, le nozze, le fabriche; ove conviensi spendere senza havere consideratione alla spesa, ma solamente alla grandezza, & alla bellezza dell'opra: peroche di vado ci viene occasione di spendere in cosi fatte cose. E sotto à quello, ch'io dissi più generali, ponno ridursi tutte l'altre anchora, come feste, giuochi publici, livree, edificationi de' tempi, de' palazzi, ò d'altri edificii privati, ò publici: le quali cose, se hanno del grande conveniente, rendono l'huomo veramente degno del nome di magnifico. Et quantunque la virtù morale non habbia à far essa quelle opere, che all'arte s'appartengono." Paruta 1599, 282–86. Note that the dedication in 1557 of Daniele Barbaro's dialogue *Della Eloquenza* by Girolamo Ruscelli to the Accademia Costanti

89 in Vicenza identified him as defining the attributes of nobility. On "living nobly," see now P. Brown 2004.

89 "Ma nella grandezza, & ne gli ornamenti de' tempi, non vi pare, che i moderni comincian à voler contendere con gli antichi?" Paruta 1599, 284–86, the last speaker is Francesco Foglietta, at Trent with the Venetian legate Matteo Dandolo.

90 Logan 1984, 278, ties the aristocratic comportment of Grimani's patronage to that of the Roman court, as illustrated, for example, in the description of a cardinal's residence in Paolo Cortese's *De Cardinalatu* (1510), as model. For a thorough discussion of the legitimacy of spending to promote the *cultus externus* and justification of the magnificence of the physical church, see Schofield 2003.

91 For more on the patriarchal vicars and the business of governing the patriarchy, see the letters of Paolo Bisanti, *vicario generale del patriarca di Aquileia* (1577–87), in Salimbeni, ed. 1977; on apostolic visits in the diocese of Aquileia 1584–85, see Socol 1986; and more references can be found in Trebbi 1984, 57.

92 On Marino's statement of the "Nuova Aquileia" ("New Aquileia"), see De Renaldis 1888, 217; and for the patriarchal residence, see esp. Biasutti 1958, 8–14 (Marino's intention for the Casa di Sant'Antonio are recorded in the *Annali* del Comune on 18 June 1524; Francesco Barbaro's "Parte di dar la casa dell'Hospitale," in AAU, Epistolario del cancellaria patriarcale Giovanni Bottana, 26 October 1592); also Rizzi 1983, 94–95; Bartolini, Bergamini, & Sereni 1983, 310; Tentori 1988, 134. Giovanni da Udine is best known for his work as painter and decorator in the Raphael workshop on such projects as the Loggia di Psyche in the Villa Farnesina for the papal banker Agostino Chigi, that set the standard for antiquarian taste in contemporary Roman patronage, as reflected in Cortese's *De Cardinalatu*; he was known to several generations of the Grimanis, from Doge Antonio, to Cardinal Domenico, to Cardinal Marino, to Procurator Vettor, and Patriarch Giovanni. See in Dacos & Furlan 1987: 163–73, the "alla grott-esca" vault frescoes in the "torre Marino" are undocumented but probably *circa* 1532–38/39.

93 Sansovino 1968, 1: 372, "fra i quali è principaliss. non pur di Venetia, ma quasi di ogni altra città, quello di Giovanni Grimani Patriarca d'Aquilea. nel quale, istituto prima da i Cardinali suoi antecessori con statue & medaglie havute da Roma, d'Athene, da Constantinopoli, & di tutta la Grecia, ha fabricato un luogo celebre & ripieno di bellezze antiche & singolari per quantità & qualità. Percioche vi si veggono in diverse stanze ch'entrano l'una nell'altra, figure intere & spezzate, tosi, & teste in tanta abbondanza che nulla più, & tutte elette & di pregio. Oltre à ciò lo studio appartato delle medaglie d'oro, d'argento, & di rame, con altre cose di gioie, di marmi, &

di bronzo, è rarissimo da vedere. Alfonso Duca di Ferrara & Henrico Terzo Rè di Francia l'anno 1574. vi stettero tutto un giorno à considerarlo, tratti dalla novità delle materie & dal diletto, che hebbero in luogo così segnalato" (and see 1: 153, for the funeral of Tiberio Tinelli, painter to King Louis XIII, held there). For an idea of the earlier state of the palace, see Favoretto 1984; Stefani Mantovanelli 1984. In the Grimani palace ceiling decorations, Giovanni da Udine worked as a stuccoist; see Dacos & Furlan 1987: 165–73, "Camera di Diana" (1537–39) with stuccoes of the nymph Callisto, "Stanza di Apollo" (1539–40, frescoes by Francesco Salviati); Perry 1981, 217–18; Marpillero 1937; Wolters 2000, 136, 138, 248, 250–53; Bristot 2001.

94 Coryat 1905, 1:321. On the collection and its display, see now Ravagnan 2002; Soccal 2002, 130; De Paoli 2002; Newerow 2002. Coryat saw the collection in 1608 after it had passed to the Republic and was housed in the Marciana Library; see Buffa 1997, 310. Favaretto 1997b, 38–41; Ghedini 1997, 98, 103, with references to the large number of objects from Aquileia. For more on the Quirinale, see R. Gallo 1952. Concina 1995, 231, made an astute observation regarding Scamozzi's architecture for the Statuario in the Library, interpreting its use of particular elements as suggested by Grimani (i.e., alternation of Corinthian pilasters and Ionic framed "nicchie 'alla greca' ") to express a *renovatio aquileiensis*. This kind of grandiloquent act is in keeping with the humanist building of reputation, or *fama*, see the essays in Fenster & Smail, eds. 2003.

95 Examples posing such a contrast include, Foscari & Tafuri 1983, 145; Howard 1987, 74; and some authors find Palladio susceptible of an intentional dialectic, Inglott 1980, esp. 153–54, 159. See Onians 1988, 310–12, on the expression of status through the use of the Corinthian order, dominating over choices made for less extravagant orders on the grounds of morality.

96 The histories for both drawings are summarized in Boucher 1998 (respectively 157 and 287 n. 12, and 288 n. 17); and in Lewis 2000, 240–43 cat. 110–11; also for Vicenza, see Puppi 1990, 101; also see n. 110 below; for London, RIBA, see Foscari & Tafuri 1983, 152; Gaier 2002a, 171–72.

97 For San Giuseppe di Castello: Timofiewitsch 1972, 268–73; Timofiewitsch 1963–65, who discovered Smeraldi's more prominent role in the design previously given to Scamozzi; and now Lewis 2000, 243; R. Pellegrini 2003. Scamozzi's involvement may have been connected to his acquisition of Palladio's drawings from Jacopo Contarini's bequest (Puppi 1990, 16–20, for the provenance). Smeraldi had erected the façade of San Pietro di Castello between 1592 and 1594, presumably with access to any surviving design materials.

98 Serlio 1996, 212, and on 344 (Bk. 4, XLIXv/171r), he says: "Amongst all the ancient exam-

ples of Corinthian work which can be seen in Italy, it seems to me that the Pantheon in Rome and the triumphal arch above the port in Ancona [Trajan] are the most beautiful and best conceived," giving the use of the order a special pedigree; and Serlio 1982, Bk. 3, ch. 4, 56v, "Halfe-Images" means bust figures; Serlio also describes a copper equestrian monument of the emperor on top of the arch. Lewis 2000, 243, had also proposed that the consoles of the London drawing may have indicated Giovanni's initial intention to place four commemorative busts on the exterior; Gaier 2002a, 171–72, speculates that two bronze busts known of Doge Antonio and Cardinal Domenico may have been intended for use in such a program (although this would have clashed with prohibitions against representing the doge externally). For Palladio's drawing "close" to the Arch of Trajan (RIBA, XIII, 13), Lewis 2000, 241; G. Zorzi 1959, 168, 135–36).

99 Palladio 1997, 221; he is describing the vestigia seen on the Temple of Peace carried in Vespasian's triumph on his return from Judea.

100 "Ma non so ove cavano questa sua ragione tedesca aponto che gli festoni, fogliami e fruti togliano la gravità all'opera, poichè nella costruzion del tempio grandissimo di Hierusalem furono fatti fogliami, frutii et altri ornamenti, e gli antichi Egipzi, Greci e Romani in niuna sorte di fabriche metevano tanti ornamenti di fogliami quanto nelli tempii sacri, anzi il più rico ordine di questi ornamenti, che è il corinzio, lo dedicarono a tempii," Palladio 1988a, doc. 3, 133; G. Zorzi 1967, 109, doc. 14.

101 Serlio 1996, 340 (Bk. 4, XLVIIv/169r), and 354 (LVv/177r), "Since Venetians in their buildings take great delight in their Corinthian work." I would also particularly like to thank Deborah Howard for her observations in regard to the use and symbolism of this order in relation to Renaissance theorists.

102 "Li capitelli vanno corinthi secondo il disegno fatto da detto Palladio, et così le sagome delle gornise," Magrini 1845, xviiii; G. Zorzi 1967, 30. Although, it should be noted that San Pietro di Castello was changed by Smeraldi to include the Composite for the major order, closer to the façades of Palladio's later churches. The derivation of Smeraldi's façade from the model of San Giorgio Maggiore is discussed here in the previous chapter. Foscari & Tafuri 1983, 154, note that Palladio uses, however, a Composite module of ten for the monumental order at San Francesco della Vigna. Onians 1988, 242–43, notes that Bramante's Corinthian interior for New St. Peter's would have been seen as the "greater glory of the new Church," and 312, describes the use at San Francesco della Vigna "to articulate the building's status to the outside world, since this was far and away the most important function of the orders in ecclesiastical buildings."

103 Sparrow 1969, 41–47, on San Francesco della Vigna, 45, for the quotation, 47 n. 1, for previous explanations of the program, often given as alluding to controversies surrounding the construction of the church, 46–47, for the following paraphrases in English of the inscriptions.

104 Foscari & Tafuri 1983, 145 and 158–59 (who follow Sparrow 1969, 43), and for the will, 177 n. 104; the will is also discussed in G. Zorzi 1967, 32; and a recent transcription is Schiavon 2001: from ASV, Notarile, Testamenti, Vettor Maffei, B. 658, no. 396, 29 August 1592 (with four codicils of which the following is the second, from 28 November 1592), "Di più ordiniamo che per il detto Titian siano fabricate di metallo secondo l'arte sua due altre figure una di S. Mosè, con iscritione nel piede sii intagliato lettere che dicano dispensatore lucis, al quale Titiano si dia ducati 500 per tale operazione e sue spese et altri ducati cinquanta di elargizione in segno di benevolentia." Grimani's will indicated that the two bronze statues in the chapel altar wall niches, of *Justice* and *Temperance* (inscribed DUCE IUDICIO and COMITI BELLO), had already been begun, see in Foscari & Tafuri 1983, 177 n. 104; Sansovino 1968, 52, in the "Additione," names their sculptor instead as Camillo Bozzetti, then also describes two additional epigraphs in bronze letters (missing) in stone tablets on the lateral walls: IOANN* GRIMANUS PAT* AQUIL* EX HIERO-NYMO PATRE ANT* PRINC* FILIO, IN SPEM CERTAM SIBI POSUIT HANC DOMUM QUIETIS, USQUE AD DIEM MUNDI ULTIMUM, and SI CHRISTUS DELETO CHIROGRAPHO IN LIGNO CRUCIS AFFIXO, QUOD ERAT CONTRARIUM NOBIS, RESURREXIT: NOS CON-VIVIFICATI IN ILLO, IN AETERNAM IUSTITIAM, & PACEM RESURGEMUS. On Aspetti, see Kryza-Gersch 1999, esp. 422–25.

105 Foscari & Tafuri 1983, 157; after Sparrow, who speaks of the inscription as "animating" the façade, but who assigns this role to Palladio. The notion of *architecture parlante* was articulated by French eighteenth-century theorists; on the migration of literary theory to architecture, see S. Lavin 1992, 115–16; Palme 1959; and for a stimulating discussion of which I would like to thank Alan Calquhoun, see also Calquhoun 1981, 195. Petrucci 1993, 24, notes that, in Venice, monumental public writing was largely found on tomb floor slabs rather than façades well into the sixteenth century, although civic examples could be seen in the Veneto, such as the city gates of Padua (1528–30) and Verona (1557) by Falconetto and Sanmicheli respectively.

106 For summaries, see Puppi 1990, 101; Foscari & Tafuri 1983, 143–45; Foscari & Tafuri 1982, 107–12, who characterized San Francesco della Vigna as celebrating the Grimani participation in the Gritti *renovatio*, and Sant'Antonio as a memorial to their doge and uncle; Gaier 2002a, 172, sees Palladio's project for San Francesco as the moment in which effort for a public (i.e., external) monument dedicated

to Admiral and Doge Antonio was definitively ended.

107 Sansovino 1968, 1: 51. For a bibliographical summary on Ermolao, see King 1986, 322–23; Bigi 1964; and for his unfortunate patriarchate which resulted in his exile on grounds similar to Cardinal Da Mula's, see Paschini 1957, 11–43, esp. chs. 3–4; Banfi 1956.

108 The now widely accepted attribution of the figures to Zuccaro was proposed by McTavish, in Burns with Fairbairn & Boucher 1975, 135–36. David Ekserdjian kindly indicated to me his emphatic agreement.

109 The phrase is missing from the copies in the ASV, transcribed in Boucher 1979, 281–82; but is cited from a missing version seen in the archives of San Francesco della Vigna by Corner 1749, 8: 51–52; Foscari & Tafuri 1983, 142–43.

110 G. Zorzi 1963, 99, associated the bishop's miter with Domenico Bollani, whose chapel at San Giorgio Maggiore was designed by Palladio (restated in G. Zorzi 1967, 54); Puppi 1986, 268, first retained the connection to the bishop, but proposed instead it was for Bollani's tomb in Brescia Cathedral (in the 1973 edn.), later, however, accepting it in the current context (Puppi 1990, 101); Foscari & Tafuri 1983, 144, suppose the miter to serve as a generic symbol of religion. Both the Corner and Pisani families, for example, among Palladio's patrons boasted several bishops, but none of their tomb projects seems to correspond as well to the proposed iconography, attribution, dating, and measurement of the drawing; cf. Gaier 2002b, which came to my attention too late to incorporate.

111 "Percioche entrandosi in Chiesa nella facciata di dentro sopra la porta grande, si riposano due Cardinali della famiglia Grimana, Domenico creato da Papa Alessandro VI. & Marino fatto da Clemente VII. Vi è parimente Marco Patriarca d'Aquileia, che l'anno 1537. fù Generale di Papa Paolo III. per la lega, che si fece contra le forze di Solimano. Dalla sinistra sono cinque cappelle: la prima delle quali è de' medesimi Grimani, & specialmente del Patriarca Giovanni," Sansovino 1968, 48. Palladio received his due in the later description added to the edition of 1581 by Martinioni in 1663, 52, "Ha questo Tempio il suo Aspetto tutto di pietra Istriana disegnato, & ordinato dal Famoso Architetto Andrea Palladio di ordine Latino, detto communemente Composito, mirabilmente compartito con misura, e proportione"; for Sansovino 1604, 115r–v, "tre cassoni, coperti di panno scarlato due Cardinali & un Patriarca della famiglia Grimani."

112 Magrini 1845, 65, "I Grimani aveano pertanto in S. Francesco della Vigna i sepolcri, in cui giaceano, altempo di cui parliamo, i due cardinali Domenico e Marino, l'uno fratello, l'altro zio di Giovanni, oltre Marco, fratello pur esso, tutti i tre Patriarchi di Aquileia: le loro urne stavano a ridosso della parete interna del prospetto"; 303, following his description

of the "Mausoleo" (Vicenza D 17), in which he identified the two episcopal figures with the patriarchs Marino and Domenico, "i quali aveano lor urne di legno a ridosso della vecchia facciata interiore: nè mancava l'onor del principato nello zio Antonio: quindi in quel loco il magnifico mausoleo. Colla nuova costruzione del loro successore Giovanni quelle ceneri di là rimosse ebbero umile loco nella cappella vicina, in cui Giovanni stesso volle composte le proprie." Lewis 2000, 243, refers to the provisory nature of the urns as indicated by their material and notes that there is a cassone painted with the Grimani arms in Kraków at Wawel Castle.

113 "Et farle condurre al monasterio di S.to Antonio, et sia li fatto in uno de claustri del ditto luogo uno deposito di valuta de Ducati dugento, né per via nessuna voglio esser sepulto in chiesa, perché né a me, né ad altri si conviene seppellire l'ossa de peccatori et massime le lie in luoghi simili, né voglio gli sia altare né si ne facci, acciò non si celebrasse in alcun tempo dove riposassero l'ossa d'un peccatore," in Foscari & Tafuri 1982, 120, from Marco Grimani's will, 1538/1543, in ASV, SAC, v. 10, 133; also in Cicogna 1969, 6–2: 787–88. On his activities as procurator, see now Chambers 1997, 42–43, 50–52.

114 See Lewis 2000, 243, on the repatriation of the bodies of Domenico, Marino, and Marco during Vettor's lifetime (after Paschini 1943, 116, 120; Paschini 1958, 64; Lotto 1962, 48); updated in regard to the burial of Doge Antonio at Sant' Antonio di Castello, in Foscari & Tafuri 1983, 170 n. 49, who also comment on the faint drawing of another tomb, which they suggest may be an alternative to the one in the attic; Foscari & Tafuri 1982, 108 ff. (Puppi 1990, 101, mis-records Doge Antonio's burial place as San Domenico in Castello). Tafuri 1985, 30–31, recasts slightly the earlier interpretation and places more emphasis on the possible inclusion of Giovanni himself in the monument.

115 Foscari & Tafuri 1983, 143–44 refute the figural identifications made by G. Zorzi (1963, 100), as Brescia (for a monument to Domenico Bollani), and by Lewis as Venice (in the 1981 edition of Lewis 2000, 243, who no longer claims this); followed by Puppi 1990, 101.

116 In Paul's statement in 1 Corinthians 13, 13, Charity is most important for grace. The Seven Virtues also featured prominently in the Grimani Palace *scalone* decoration, see Perry 1981, 218. Calvillo 2000 argues that Giulio Clovio's independent miniature of the *Theological Virtues* (Paris, Louvre, RF 3978) had special significance for its patron, Cardinal Marino, and that it was meant for his Pauline commentary, on which see below. Note that the four caryatid figures in Palladio's drawing could be enlisted in a program for the full complement of the Virtues.

117 Also recognized by Concina 1995, 221, "Se

infatti l'inscrizione e l'emblema alludano certamente al richiamo al rinnovamento del salmo 103 e l'aquila è simbolo del Cristo e della divina sapienza, quest'ultima è anche emblema tanto dell'evangelista Giovanni – patrono del cardinale [sic] committente – quanto della sede patriarcale di Aquileia di cui era titolare." Although he does not expand on this further in relation to the façade, Concina's characterization of the Grimani donation in support of a "renovatio aquiliensis" (231) further supports this reading.

118 Examples are from the engravings in Liruti 1749, nos. 22, 24, and 30; the latter is illustrated in *Poppone* 1997, 320, as is the patriarchal *cathedra*, 226; other examples include the legend on a fifteenth-century *denaro* (reverse) of Patriarch Antonio II Panciera (1402–11), the eagle is shown with wings spread, facing left, in Candussio 1992, 381–83; also see in Saccocci 1992, esp. figs. 4, 6, and 8, two *denari* and a *grosso* from the twelfth–thirteenth centuries, which show variations in the appearance of the eagle, whether both wings are spread, and which direction it faces. Tiepolo 1996, 148–52, concerned with the imperial double-headed eagle granted to Francesco Barbaro in 1433, and 152–53, distinguishes it from that of Aquileia, following del Torso 1978; and on its feudalities, 225–29, 243–65; also Mor 1978.

119 Bristot & Piana 1997, 47, arrangement for decorative apparatus attributed to Alessandro Vittoria after a design by Vasari (following Manfredo Tafuri's suggestion made at the conference of 1985). See Soccal 2002, 130, and De Paoli 2002, 133, for a reconstruction of the "Tribuna" with its collection in place. On the sculpture, Soccal 2002, 135 cat. 60, identifies the *Ganymede* as Roman late second century AD after a Greek fourth-century BC original; and the collection, see Favaretto 1997a, 54; Ghedini 1997, 98; Buffa 1997, 311–12; M. Zorzi, ed. 1988, pl. 16, where it is identified as Greek first century BC., red chalk drawing after *Ganymede and the Eagle* by Anton Maria the Elder and Anton Maria the Younger Zanetti, for *Delle antiche statue greche e romane, che nell'Antisala della Libreria di San Marco*, Venice, [n.p.], 1740–43, in BMV, Zanetti, 209. The drawing of the Tribuna by Federico Zuccaro has been dated to his trip to Venice in 1582, since it is on the *verso* of a copy after Paolo Veronese's *Feast in the House of Simon*, from 1570 to 1573, and does not yet show the Grimani collection as it would be installed in the Statuario Pubblico of the Library after Giovanni's death in 1593 and by the time of his next visit in 1603–04, in Ongpin 2004, cat. 10; it can be more securely identified by comparison with the restored Tribuna in the Palazzo Grimani as being the famous Studio of Antiquities, and as the inscription reads: "antiquario dell Ill.o patriarcha grimani."

120 Howard 1987, 64; based on numerous sources, including Corner 1749, 8: 13–14. On Mark's Aquileian mission, see the recent discussion in Dale 1997, esp. ch. 5. See variants in Muir 1981, 79, as "Pax tibi, Marce. Hic requiescet corpus tuum," from Andrea Dandolo's fourteenth-century "Chronicum venetum" (in *Rerum italicarum scriptores*, Bologna, 1938, 12: 10); also in Tramontin 1970, 45–46.

121 Note Sparrow's (1969, 39) comparison with Alberti's Holy Sepulcher (Florence, San Pancrazio, Rucellai chapel); also the previously mentioned Casino of Pius IV on which Federico Zuccaro had been at work has been described as "pages out of a picture-book . . . covered with reliefs, inscriptions, escutcheons, statuary, aedicules, and festoons," Lotz 1995, 108. The latter would qualify as "allusive, book-oriented display writing," contrasted with another for "conspicuous monumental plaques," in Petrucci 1993, 25–27, who notes the late sixteenth-century shift from clear examples of pure classicizing epigraphy to one that incorporated emblematic components, "initiating a much more complex relationship between word and image" – and this would extend to the architectural language as part of the same classical system of knowledge.

122 Alberti 1988, 255–56, in Bk. 8, ch. 4, 142v–143v.

123 Alberti 1986, 158, for the Leoni edn.; Alberti 1988, 239, in Bk. 7, ch. 16, 133–35.

124 For an insightful discussion of the importance of classical epigraphy to Venetian humanists and visual culture, see P. Brown 1996b, passim; Petrucci 1993, 16–28, for the humanist revival of monumental public epigraphy.

125 Palladio 1997, 336.

126 Palladio 1997, 285, "According to some it was built by M. Agrippa around the fourteenth year of our Lord; but I think that the body of the building was made at the time of the Republic and that M. Agrippa added only the portico, which one can deduce from the two tympanums [*frontispicio*] on the façade." *Four Books*, Bk. 4, ch. 20, 73; This is followed up by a comment on the inscription noting its restoration under Septimius Severus and Marcus Aurelius.

127 Palladio 1997, 233, in Bk. 4, ch. 8, 23.

128 Inscriptions over the villa's ground-floor windows in the frieze of the segmental pediment read: (left) HOSPES NON HOSPES and (right) NON SOLUM DOMINIS; over the *piano nobile* windows in the frieze of the triangular pediment: (left) NIL* TECTI* SUB* TECTO and (right) OMNIA* TUTA* BONIS; and the frieze beneath the façade pediment reads, DAN* BARBARUS* – PAT* AQUIL* ET* MARCUS* ANT* FR* FRANC* F* ("Daniel Barbarus Patriarca Aquileiensis et Marcus Antonius Frater Francisci Filii," in G. Zorzi 1969, 177 n. 48, who notes the prominence given to Daniele). On the attribution of the pediment program to Marc' Antonio Barbaro, *circa* 1557–58, see Lewis 1997, 37 (but cf. Puppi 1986, 158, for earlier arguments dating the pediment to the 1570s); Tiepolo 1996, 149–51, notes that the crowned double-headed eagle behind the central *scudo*

with the Barbaro arms is imperial, and the *triregno* (tiara) above is papal, neither are patriarchal, and further comments on the heraldic impropriety of the latter usage. In fact, one wonders whether Marc'Antonio had conceived a grander allegorical scheme than a strictly heraldic reading accounts for, but in any case a single-headed eagle is also featured in the pediment decoration, so there may still be a reference to the patriarchy; there is an eagle, one on each side for symmetry's sake, placed on festoons, at either side of a console at the top of the window that interrupts the cornice and inscription, and above the *stemmi* honoring their mother (Elena Pisani) and Marc'Antonio's wife (Giustiniana Giustinian). The allegorical program of the villa sculptures is enhanced by verse epigraphs, for which see Kolb 1997. The Tempietto inscription moves around the frieze of the porch: ANDREAS PALADIUS VICENTINO INVENTOR (left), MARCUS* ANTONIUS* BARBARUS* PROCURATOR* FRANC* FILIUS (center), ANNO DOMINI NOSTRI JESU CHRISTI MDLXXX (right).

129 Wittkower 1962, 106, translations of the *Memoriale* are taken from his appendix 1, 155–57; the use of the module had been earlier observed by Cicognara, Diedo, & Selva 1858, 2: 17.

130 Lewis 2000, 240–41; but cf. Burns with Fairbairn & Boucher 1975, 135, who later maintained their doubts in a personal communication to Foscari & Tafuri 1983, 152. On the history of its association, see Puppi 1986, 162–63, 191; Boucher 1998, 157 and 288 n. 17.

131 Sparrow 1969, 45–46 (who did not seem to know Grimani's testament, for he gave the statues a date of *circa* 1590, see 42 n. 4).

132 Another concept phrased by Fra Zorzi in his *Memoriale* (Wittkower 1962, appendix 1, 155) is also found in Palladio, who described the temple as a little version of the "bella machina del Mondo" (*Quattro libri*, Bk. 4, 3, "Proemio a i Lettori"); Palladio 1997, 213, "In the case of churches, they must above all consider the dignity and grandeur of God, who must be prayed and worshiped since He is the ultimate good and perfection; it is supremely appropriate that everything dedicated to Him should be made to the highest level of perfection of which we are capable. Indeed, if we consider what a wonderful creation [*machina*] the world is, the marvelous embellishments with which it is filled, and how the heavens change the seasons by their continuous revolutions according to the demands of nature and how they maintain themselves by the sweetest harmony of their measured movements; we cannot doubt that, since these small temples which we build must be similar to this vast one, which He, with boundless generosity, perfected with but a word of command; we are bound to include in them all the embellishments we can, and build them in such a way, and with such proportions that together all the parts convey to the eyes of

onlookers a sweet harmony and each church fulfills properly the use for which it is intended" (*Four Books*, Bk. 4, "Foreword to the Readers," 3). Foscari & Tafuri 1983, 150, where, it should be noted, Zorzi's works were not formally condemned until 1575 (although criticized earlier), and so would not yet have been decisively tainted, 158–59, contrasting Zorzi's mysticism, and 134, for the protagonists' connections to the Accademia della Fama (or Veneziana), closed in 1561.

133   On the letter, see P. Laven 1967, 197–202, including 198 n. 97, for a reference to a seventeenth-century English translation; Paschini 1957, 141, partial transcription, and 182, for the pope's protest "e si potrebbe anche in un certo modo metter in compromesso il decreto della giustificazione, il che in nessun modo si deve fare." On Pauline currents among the Venetian patriciate and in Church reform, see Cessi 1957; Logan 1972, 67–78; Jedin 1972, 141; Collett 1985, *passim*, where it is extensively discussed. There was a connection made between Grimani and the Benedictines, since one of the accusations that was rebutted in 1561 was that a heretical monk of Santa Giustina had been his preceptor in Padua, which he denied; see Paschini, idem, 133; De Leva 1880–81, 452, for the text. For general questions of orthodoxy and the patriarchy in this period, see Cavazza 1996.

134   Quoted from de Voragine 1993, 2: 358 "St. Paul, Apostle."

135   For Seripando, see the classic study by Jedin 1947. On Marino Grimani's Pauline theology, the following is indebted to Anderson 1969, 26–33, when Grimani was legate in Emilia. The date of the Sir John Soane *Commentarii*, executed by Giulio Clovio for his patron, the cardinal, was during or after the period when he was legate in Perugia, 1537–38, and the illustrations are replete with allusions to Grimani collections; for a history of the manuscript, see Alexander, ed. 1994, cat. 133; and Calvillo 2000, who also notes an important link between Erasmus and Cardinal Marino, as well as his uncle Cardinal Domenico.

136   From Grimani's *Commentarii* on Galatians, 132r and 144r, respectively, nn. 46 and 50, trans. in Anderson 1969, 31–32.

137   Marion Kuntz has explored this in connection with Guillaume Postel's follower Dionisio, see Kunst 1999.

138   Grimani, *Commentarii*, 172r, trans. in Anderson 1969, 33.

PART IV

1   Sansovino 1968, 1: 3, also noting there were seventy parish churches, one for each of the *contrade* (parishes); Tramontin 1989, 55–90, app. 86–90.

2   A number of copies of varying degrees of antiquity exist of the "Concessio monasterii s. Georgii Maioris" of 982. Cicogna 1969, 4: 284

n. 13, identifies the recension closest to the original as ASV, SGM, в. 1; also in Lanfranchi, ed. 1968, 15–26, doc. 1.

3   The most complete accounts of the subsequent history of the monastery on the island may be found in Corner 1749, G. Rossi 1969, Cicogna 1969, vol.4, and Damerini 1956, though the text of the last lacks footnote citations, which limits its usefulness. These are based largely on the manuscript histories of Olmo and Valle (see in BCV, BMV, BUP, SPV), both monks at San Giorgio, in the early and the late seventeenth century respectively, and on archival sources, which for this early period can be found in Lanfranchi, ed. 1968. I would like to thank Gabriele Mazzucco for making available to me his manuscript on the early period of the island.

4   Sansovino, 1581, "Cronico Veneto," 8, "Chiesa di San Giorgio Maggiore, & di San Giovanni Evangelista, edificate dalla famiglia Participatia, o Patriciaca, detta poi Badoara." This would be during the dogates of Maurizio Galbaio (764–*circa* 787) and his son Giovanni (787–*circa* 804). G. Rossi 1969, 242, argues that under the Partecipazio the church was probably officiated by priests, though there are no notices prior to 982. Previous to the dedication of a church on the island, it was known as the Isola Memmia or Cipressi; see Damerini 1956, 4–5 (where he also casts some doubts on Sansovino's information). The appellation "Maggiore" distinguished the island from that of San Giorgio in Alga.

5   "Hoc est ecclesiam beati Georgii martyris," Cicogna 1969, 4: 284–85 n. 13. Later, with the acquisition of the important relic of St. Stephen's body, the church was rededicated to include both, as in the consecration of 12 June 1419, "Sanctorum Stephani Prothomartyris & Georgii Martyris." BUP, Olmo, bk. 3, 316; Corner 1749, 168–69; G. Rossi 1969, 257; Cicogna 1969, 4: 312 n. 138. The earliest use of the double title appears to be 1114, see BMV, Olmo, bk. 3, 254–55; G. Rossi 1969, 248; Cicogna 1969, 4: 294 nn. 47–49.

6   Sansovino 1581, 81v, "All'incontro del Palazzo Ducale e situata l'Isola di San Giorgio Maggiore habitata da monaci dell'ordine di San Benedetto. Fu altre volte sottoposta alla Chiesa di San Marco, ma l'anno 982. ritornato di Guascogna Giovanni Morosino, dove era stato molti anni in vita romitica con Pietro Orseolo Doge 22. gia suo suocero, ottenne in dono l'Isola con la Chiesa che vi era, da Tribuno Memo Doge 24. & vi messe i predetti Monaci, facendovi una nuova Badia. Et vi era allora una libreria, con diversi altri ornamenti & richezze per commodo della Chiesa & nella Isoletta era presso alla Chiesa una vigna & un bosco, & un molino con due rote, che serviva al Palazzo Ducale, si come nella distesa della detta donatione si contiene, sotto dì 20. di Dicembre, sottoscritto da 136. testimoni."

7   Sansovino 1581, 81v, continues: "Avvenne poi per quanto si dice, che l'anno 1205. essendo

stato sbranato da alcuni cani del luogo, un figliuolo del Doge Pietro Ziani, mosso dall'ira & dall estremo dolore, arse il luogo con parte de i monaci, ma ritornato in se stesso & pentito per l'ammonitione del Papa, non solamente rifece il monastero, ma gli concesse diverse gratie, & lo honorò molto, percioche egli vi haveva un suo Palagio, con molini & altre cose ch'erano pervenute nella famiglia Ziana. Rifabricata vi adunque la Chiesa vecchia dal Doge in bella forma, l'Isola fu ridotta a cultura con dilicati giardini & con horti delitiosi, essendo del tutto divenuta libera del monistero. & ancora che l'anno 1229. andasse per terra gran parte del luogo per un terremoto che fece gran danno a tutta la città, tuttavia restaurato continouò fino a questi tempi." The legend of the monastery's dogs devouring the doge's son was current even in the seventeenth century; see BCV, Valle, ch. 50, 232. G. Rossi 1969, 248–49, and Cicogna 1969, 4: 294 n. 55, 537 ins. 20, favor a reading of Pietro Ziani's contribution as a consequence of the earthquake, which other sources date as early as 1223, whereas Sansovino's dating places it during the reign of Jacopo Tiepolo (1229–49).

8   Sambin 1970, appendix 1, 526–30, reproduces the visitation of 23 July 1411, from ASV, SGM, в. 13, proc. 4. See also below.

9   Sansovino, 1581, 81v, as given previously; the quotation then continues (81v–82r), "Ne quali essendosi molto invecchiato, parve a governatori de monaci di rifar la Chiesa su la forma d'un modello fatto altre volte & havendone data la cura ad Andrea Palladio Architetto di molto nome, fu ridotta in pochi anni al suo fine." Corner 1749, 168–69, casts doubts on the source associating the consecration of 1419 with the rebuilding of the church, "Ex ea scheda corrigendus est error in Petri Marcelli Historia, dum veterem Divi Georgii Ecclesiam afferit tempore Francisci Foscari Ducis aedificari coeptam, cujus consecratio electionem Foscari Ducis anno Mcccxxiii. peractam quator annis praecessit." G. Rossi 1969, 257, accepts the rebuilding of the church; Cicogna 1969, 4: 312 nn. 138–39, gives Olmo's Latin account; BMV, Olmo, 343r–v, before noting the contradictions in Marcello's dating and describing the more secure accomplishments attributed to Abbot Michiel, including the building of a cloister and infirmary, states: "E poi l'anno seguente 1419. consecro insieme anco la Chiesa in onore de'Santi Stefano e Giorgio la quale se fosse allora dal Michieli fabbricata, noi non ritroviamo nelle pergamene." Damerini 1956, 51, sees this as the fourth church, arising out of extensive restoration of the existing complex.

10   For an excellent critical bibliographical study of Ludovico Barbo and the Congregation of Santa Giustina, see Trolese 1983; some updates in Trolese, ed. 1984. The standard biographies of Barbo are Tassi 1952 and Pesce 1969; good concise studies can be found in Pratesi 1964

and Pantoni 1974. Barbo professed under the Benedictine Rule on 3 February 1409.

11 For bibliography, see Tramontin 1975, 154–58.

12 Hoppenbrouwers 1980, 679–83, gives the etymology of *observantia*. Fois 1980, discusses the application of *osservanza* to an Order, congregation, or group of religious as the active pursuit of a virtuous life lived according to the ancient, rigorous norms of the Rule; as regards Santa Giustina, see Fois 1980, 1041–44. See Fois 1979 on *osservanza* as an expression of the *Ecclesia semper renovanda*.

13 Commendam is the holding in trust and receipt of revenues from vacant ecclesiastical benefices. Cross and Livingstone, eds. 1983, 319. See Picasso 1975 for a summary of the practice; Penco 1961, 324–27, as a motivation for reform. The absenteeism inherent in the practice had led to enfeebled administrations in the case of many monasteries who were to join the Congregation or other reformed organizations, although this did not ensure the removal of the grant of commendam, as in the celebrated cases of the abbeys of Subiaco and Farfa. Enlightened jurisdiction was not unknown; besides Barbo and Antonio Correr, Carlo Borromeo, later canonized, held a number of benefices. As Leccisotti 1962 points out in regard to land holdings in Tuscany, wealth was restored directly to the monasteries since privileges were returned to them that had been granted to the holder of the commendam.

14 While abbot, Correr had desired an affiliation with the Olivetan Congregation (formed in the mid-fourteenth century), but this was protested by the few remaining original monks of Santa Giustina, because they wanted to remain "black monks" of the Benedictine Order; Correr thus resigned the commendam which was reassigned to Barbo. See Pepi 1970, 361; Sbriziolo 1973–74.

15 Margarini 1650–70, I:45–47.

16 Tassi 1952, 49, 71.

17 Margarini 1650–70, I:58–66, "Et si ex debito," Florence, 23 February 1435.

18 G. Rossi 1969, 259–60; Cicogna 1969, 4: 314 n. 145; Tassi 1951, 104.

19 Tassi 1952, 73. Barbo became bishop of Treviso in 1437, but maintained a strong presence in the Congregation. The jurisdictional structure of the Congregation was defined shortly thereafter in Eugene IV's bull on 23 November 1432, "Et si ex solicitudinis," in Margarini 1650–70, I: 50–54; the administrative structure formalized in its constitution, Leccisotti 1939, with the acts of the Chapter General meetings (on which see Cooper 1990b, 21).

20 ASV, SGM, B. I, in Cicogna 1969, 4: 284–85 n. 13, "Hoc est ecclesiam beati Georgii martyris que semper fuit capella beati Marci titulis ius scilicet nostri palacii.... Verum quia ecclesia fuerat pertinens ad dominium bassilice beati Marci que est capella nostri et libera a servitute sancte matris ecclesie. Volumus ut eadem libertate semper consistat, ut nullus episcopus servitutis usum requirere." Also specified was freedom from episcopal interference.

21 BCV, Cod. Donà delle Rose 132, "Primicerio di S. Marco e Dogado," pt. 4, contains the material related to San Giorgio, including: 136, "Ex.m Decretum Francisci Fuscari Ducis Venetiarum quod Congregatio possit eligere Abbate in Monasterio S. Georgii, prout fit in S. Justina"; of especial note: "Cum hoc quod reserventur nobis, ut predicamus juspatronatus et preeminente nostre." From observation it seems likely that the copyist's hand is that of Fortunato Olmo.

22 As noted by Tassi 1951, 104 n. 37. The bull is not in Margarini; instead, see Leccisotti 1939, xli n. 1. Barbo died at the monastery of San Giorgio later that same year on 19 September; his remains were transferred to Santa Giustina.

23 G. Rossi 1969, 259–60; SPV, Olmo, 348v, "E questi avuto insieme il consenso Francesco Foscari Doge pigliò l'intiero possesso dell'Isola nella presenza di Giacomo Foscari figlio del Principe con solenne entrata; imperciocche a nome della Congregazione apri, e serrò le porte della Chiesa facendo suonare la campana, e battendo de' piedi sopra il pavimento di[?] segno di vero dominio della Chiesa e Monastero." Muir 1975, 30, notes that "rituals reflecting ideological precepts were more akin to legal sanctions."

24 Cooper 1991, 272 n. 2 for documentary sources and the contract of 3 July 1560, in ASV, SGM, B. 26, proc. 13B-1; also in Puppi 1986, 179–82; Zorzi 1967, 36–41, 59, doc. 1; Cicogna 1969, 4: 264, 328–29 n. 205.

25 Examples include the doors to the refectory and anterefectory in 1561 by Nicolò Tagliapietra and the lavabos by Apollonio and Giacomo da Verona, see Puppi 1986, 180; G. Zorzi 1967, 61, docs. 9 and 7 respectively; Cicogna 1969, 4: 329 n. 205; on Palladio and template drawings, see Cooper 1994b, 500; Burns with Fairbairn & Boucher 1975, 253–54.

26 See Boucher 1998, 162–63, for a telling comparison of Palladio's *ricetto* (as it was described by Vasari) to that of Michelangelo's Laurentian Library.

27 Cooper 1991, 273 n. 4, the contract of 6 June 1562 and closing of the account on 6 October 1563, in ASV, SGM, B. 21, proc. 10; see now Habert et al. 1992, 43–44; Cocke 2001, 168–71, 191–92 cat. 13, with earlier literature.

28 Cooper 1991, where this is discussed in detail, including the administrative itineraries of the abbots and their agents.

29 Cooper 1991, 283–90; Habert et al. 1992, 48, only accepts this figure in the correct black habit as a Benedictine; Cocke 2001, 171, seems to allow for poetic licence with some of the other figures garbed in dark colored habits being identified with contemporary members of the monastery.

30 Habert et al. 1992, 327, propose a tentative identification of the kneeling donor with Abbot Girolamo Scrochetto; Cocke 2001, 138 and 171, suggests Benedetto Guidi, as a younger man, also portrayed in the *Feast at Cana* in the dark blue habit, in which case, another older figure in a dark green habit might be identified with Abbot Scrochetto.

31 "Item quod dicta ecclesia habeat tres naves et deinde alias duos pro capellis; et quod habeat crucem sive titulum et cubam in medio pulchram et correspondentem reliquo corpori ecclesiae; item quod altare maius statuatur in capite capellae maioris, prout est consuetudo congregationis nostrae, item quod pillastri dictae ecclesiae vestiantur sive incrustantur istriano lapide et similiter in ceteris locis quibus convenire videbitur. Longitudo vero et latitudo ecclesiae prout architectis et patribus monasterii expedire videbitur et proportio exegerit explicentur." Bresciani Alvarez 1970, 133–34 and 141 nn. 7–8, in ASP, SG, B. 491, 21. First cited in Baldoria 1891, 188; and in relation to liturgical function in the churches of Palladio by Isermeyer 1968, 45 and 56 n. 19; also in Ackerman 1977a, 153; Ackerman 1980, 300; and see now Beltramini 1991, 81 (on Tullio Lombardo and the drawing in ASV, MM 744); 1995, 73, on the "venezianità" of the neo-Byzantine type and Santa Giustina. San Giorgio was host to important reformers in the 1530s especially under Abbot Gregorio Cortese (1532–37), an intimate of Cardinal Gasparo Contarini, on whom see now Gleason 1993; for San Giorgio, Cooper 1990b, 76–87; and for reform thought in the Congregation at this time, Collett 1985, chs. 4–7.

32 The model was commissioned on 25 November 1565 and payments for it were made through to 12 March 1566, with the laying of the first stone the next day as recorded in the founding inscription; Cicogna 1969, 4: 265, 330–32 n. 214–15 (who includes excerpts of a majority of the documents relating to the building and decoration). For the transcription of the model contract generally considered to be the most reliable, see Magrini 1845, Annot. xxii, n. 41; also published as in ASV, SGM, B. 26, by G. Zorzi 1967, 44, 64, doc.18, who has the most complete documentary transcription of sources. Models could supply guidance in the absence of the architect but if the design conception changed as the building process moved forward a model may have not reflected matured ideas about the project, nor have been fully capable of solving problems that occurred in the course of construction that required more specifics. On models: Millon 1994b, 22, models could function to inform patrons, guide workmen, or serve in the design process, and were considered intellectual property, so "Brunelleschi's models were intentionally incomplete" to prevent design theft; Carpo 2001, 171–73, on the indeterminency of the design and building process in the Renaissance (note as is true of the linguistic terms "modello" and "disegno").

33 Sansovino 1581, 81v–82r. On Benedictine spirituality in relation to San Giorgio and

the earlier church, see Cooper 1996a, 82–83; Cooper 1990b, 27–45, with earlier literature, and for the "coro vecchio" of 1484 under Venetian patrician Abbot Antonio Moro (1479–84).

34 ASV, SGM, B. 22, proc. 13A–II, fasc. 7, loose documents and a bound account-book of the "Conto dela Fabriche del Choro della Chiesia," dating from 9 November 1550 to 5 April 1551. Cicogna 1969, 4: 327 n. 202; Isermeyer 1968, 47, 55 n. 10, 57 n. 34; Isermeyer 1980, 265 and 267–68 nn. 32–33.

35 Cooper 1990b, 62–63, from ASV, SGM, B. 22, proc. 13A–II, fasc. 7, "Coro nuovo dal 1550, e coro," 1593 *accordo* with Maestro Zanuto for the transfer of the stalls from the lower choir (where they had served in the Palladian church until the new choirstalls were ready) to the upper night choir: "Choro notte. E piu per condurre il choro da basso nel choro di sopra per la notte, cioè tutte le sedie, e lettorino, et agiongergli quello vi mancherà, che incomincia dal'entrare della porta grande verso il corridore insin' al segno segnato dal padre Don Giorgio, e lui Dandoli tutta la materia a' tutte sue spese. E doi scabelli grandi d'Albeo soaza di larese. Et la porta grande che s'apri da due bande del'arese soazada dentro e di fuori. Et la porta picciola che risponde alla lumaga a' tutte sue spese _d. E piu l'armario nella d.ta cappella dove è il sfondro, et li banche a scartori da una e l'altra parte che gionga dal muro alle sedie _d. E piu l'oratorio nel'andito. Et soarare la porta fatta, che risponde al corridoro, et farla correre _d. _s._ E nota che 'l'mon.rio non si obbligo di far spese a nissuno, salvoche a m.ro Gianetto, al quale continuarà el vino et albergo come sta di presente. Ma non di altri." Cicogna 1969, 4: 227 n. 202, 319 n. 178; Isermeyer 1968, 55 n. 10; Isermeyer 1980, 265, 267 n. 32, 268 nn. 33–34. Neither author gives the source for this document. I would like to thank the hospice master of San Giorgio, padre don Bernardo, for allowing me to visit the upper choir and examine the choir books.

36 Howard 1987, 72–73, goes into depth on San Francesco and observant examples in Venice and elsewhere, citing Bramante at Santa Maria del Popolo as an important precursor (for which she credits Bruce Boucher); also Foscari & Tafuri 1983, 117–18; precedents further discussed in Cooper 1990b, 85–102, particularly indebted to the work of Isermeyer 1968, on Congregation efforts, and Hall 1979, for Vasari's role in translating liturgical reform.

37 ASV, SGM, B.21, proc.13, loose. Transcribed in Cicogna 1969, 4: 331–32 n. 214; G. Zorzi 1967, 67–70, docs. 29–32. See Isermeyer 1980, 263 and 267 nn. 19–20. On Paleari, see Cooper 1995, 116; Guerra 2001, 107 n. 17, who provides evidence that the presbytery was not yet constructed although it formed part of the original plan.

38 Isermeyer 1968, 47; Isermeyer 1972, 112–14; Isermeyer 1980, 264 and fig. 121, laid out a

cogent argument (with earlier literature); amplfied in Cooper 1990b, 63–64; revised and updated in Guerra 2001, 95–98. Palladio's last documented appearance in Venice was made on 29 November 1579 to San Giorgio to consult on the translation; first in Timofiewitsch 1962, 163 n. 14; discovery discussed in Niero 1982, 136–37.

39 "Giuliano Careni Piacentino, che fu Abate l'anno 1576 fino al 1579. Pare che questi desse principio al nuovo Chiostro." SPV, Olmo, 379. "Novum claustrum et forestariae et infermaria sunt ex architectura ejusdem Palladii . . . Claustrum praedictum novum anno 1579 initiatum lego sub Juliano Carrerio [*sic*] Placentino abate, cui successit Paulus Orius an. 1579 a quo pars ejusdem claustri quae apud foresterias veteres et Camerae abbatiales perfectae." BCV, Valle, ch. 37, 159. See Cicogna 1969, 4: 332 n. 219; Isermeyer 1972, 114; Isermeyer 1980, 264–65 and 267 n. 27.

40 Timofiewitsch 1963, 335 and 337 n. 25, 339; Isermeyer 1980, 265–66 and 268 nn. 36–37 (disagreeing with the interpretation of C. Frommel 1977, 114–18 and 124 n. 10, where the drawing is numbered following Puppi [1973], 2: 366, fig. 505 as "857a," although the text reference is to 857b as here and in Isermeyer). Isermeyer 1972, 114, noted that 857b must have preceded the construction of the cloister, as it showed only seventeen bays instead of the eighteen actually built; furthermore, it does not show other later structures such as the night choir above the Cappella dei Morti, built between 1592–94 (on which see Cooper 1990b, 193–94; the "Libro delli accordi" with Bortolo di Domenico on 26 June–24 October 1592, in ASV, SGM, B. 22, proc. 13A–II, fasc. 7 and 9; other sources in Cicogna 1969, 341 n. 232, 353–54 n. 270; the overdoor date "MCCCCLXXXXIIII."). Guerra 2001, 99, dates the drawing (his 857/3) to the mid-1560s and cautiously attributes it to Paleari.

41 Another drawing unpublished until Cooper 1990b, fig. 22, ASV, MM 857f, is directly connected to the purpose of 857b (both are similarly color-coded in red, yellow, and green wash, with pencil and ink); 857f shows an enlarged view with measurements (composed of several sheets joined together) of the *fondamenta* along where the Porto Franco is now located, but then known as the *canton*, on the side facing the Riva degli Schiavoni. The schematic nature of the church and cloister plans in 857b may be explained by their purpose in establishing a relationship not only to each other, but to the new *canton*. If so, we may have evidence that the removal of structures from the *canton* formed a part of Palladio's overall plan for the monastery. The Magistrato alle Acque granted permission for construction of the new *fondamenta* in 1612. ASV, SGM, B. 22, proc. 13A–II, fasc. 10, "Canton della cavana." Wolters, in Huse & Wolters 1990, 7, relates this to a 1589 require-

ment to build an embankment; Guerra 2001, 98, discusses 857f (his 857/7) as having a topographical function and dates it near 857b.

42 The contract, 10 June 1583, in ASV, SGM, B. 22, proc. 13A–II, fasc. 7, loose, for the "fassa interno [for] il coro novo secondo il disegno dato da lui cioè quello del groppo ugnolo di sua manifatura." Cicogna 1969, 4: 334 n. 222; G. Zorzi 1967, 70, doc.33 (as B. 21, fasc. 13, loose). Bortolo also provided designs for the two portals of the choir. The alternating segmental and triangular pedimented niches of the retrochoir walls after the Temple of Jupiter on the Quirnal Hill testify to Palladio's contribution to the design concept, as often remarked; recently Guerra 2001, 98; also see Boucher 1998, 165–66, for a succinct discussion of classical influences at San Giorgio.

43 27 November 1589, from ASV, SGM, B. 21, proc. 10A "Libro," f. 6v, and in proc. 13, loose. Cicogna 1969, 4: 334 n. 222; G. Zorzi 1967, 71, doc.36 (as proc. 13, "fabbrica"). For a detailed account of the troubled history of the choirstalls (1593–99), see Cooper 1990b, 122–77; and briefly in Cooper 1996a.

44 Isermeyer 1980, 264–65 (reconstructed in his fig. 121), suggested the following sequence: the choirstalls of 1550 were taken from the old church before its demolition in 1581 (Cicogna 1969, 4: 333–34 n. 221) and placed into the new chancel, identified as that of Palladio's first project (according to Guerra 2001, 97–98, reconstructed in his fig. 8, this initially occupied only the restricted area of the last bay); the choir of 1550 was in use there during the construction of the extended apse in the years 1583–89 to house the new choir according to Palladio's second project (Cicogna 1969, 4: 334 n. 222 and G. Zorzi 1967, 70–71, docs. 33, 34, 36); after the night, or winter, choir was built between 1592 and 1594 (Cicogna 1969, 4: 341 n. 232), the stalls of 1550 were transferred to be used there until the new stalls and retrochoir were ready in 1598 (Cicogna 1969, 4: 335 n. 226 and 345–46 n. 246). For a study of the retrochoir, see Cooper 1990b, 27–120.

45 Beltramini 1991, 75–78, on Praglia, who attributes the drawing to Andrea Moroni (previously thought to belong to the earlier design phase under Tullio Lombardo), and confirms the removal of the choir behind the high altar in 1573. Another of Isermeyer's examples would seem to support the view that the choir would be placed in the traditional place in front of the altar in the old church of San Giorgio; the contemporary new choir at San Benedetto Po near Mantua, probably designed by Giulio Romano and executed in the 1550s, was not, as Isermeyer thought (1968, 46 and 57 n. 28; and was followed by others, such as Hall 1979, 4), placed behind the high choir (a parallel to Monte Cassino's new choir) but transferred there later. Previous writers on San Benedetto Po, in ascribing the design to Giulio Romano, also dated the placement of the choir to the same period (as implied in

Bellodi 1974, 90) but later scholarship has shown through the readings of various descriptions that: "Gli stalli del coro dovevano allora situarsi nell'*antica* collocazione, cioè davanti all'altare (l'uso attuale invalse all'incirca dopo il Concilio di Trento)." P. Piva & Pavesi 1975, 74–75. P. Piva & Pavesi propose two hypotheses: the first is that the transfer took place shortly after the systematization of the presbytery and sacristy in 1552; the second is that, as at Santa Giustina in Padua, there was resistance to "subverting the ancient order," and the altar and stalls changed position only around 1600 (the only *terminus ante quem* is much later, in 1678). See also P. Piva, ed. 1981, 1: 236. However, Giulio Romano's renovation of the Mantua Cathedral for Cardinal Ercole Gonzaga began in 1545 with the demolition of the choir and its extension into the apse. D'Arco 1842, xxxiii (appendix); quoted in Hartt 1958, 1: 244. In addition, see Marani and Perina 1965, 212–14. Most recently, on the date of Santa Giustina's retrochoir as 1627, see Beltramini 1995, 78–79.

46 Isermeyer, 1968, 47 and 57 n. 34.

47 Palladio 1997, 216. Magagnato & Marini, eds. 1980, 516–17 for commentary.

48 Palladio 1997, 220. Magagnato & Marini, eds., 1980, 518 for commentary.

49 Pointed out by Isermeyer 1972, 113 and 134 n. 16; Isermeyer 1980, 263 and 267 n. 21; Guerra 2001, 97, persuasively locates the choir in the adjacent nave bay to the Bollani chapel, as the quadrangular area of the presbytery identified by Isermeyer was not yet built, although intended as part of the original plan. For the Bollani chapel, see below.

50 Isermeyer 1972, 108–09, 112–13 and 133 nn. 6–8; Isermeyer 1980, 267 n. 23, feels that this project is closest to the original plan for the choir at San Giorgio. Isermeyer criticizes G. Zorzi's transcription of the document in Montagnana, Archivio della Chiesa arcipretale (77–84, doc.1), and advises instead the use of Magrini's (1845, 59–62, appendix 2, 9–10, Annot. 38–39, xix–xxi).

51 "Perciochè così i divini ufficii si potrebbero benissimo intendere ugualmente da tutta la Chiesa ed il coro come parte unica e principale sarebbe nel mezzo," Isermeyer 1968, 50–53 and 58 nn. 58–67, noting the possible influence on Palladio's placement of the high altar in Il Redentore as compared to San Giorgio (53); Isermeyer 1972, 116–18 and 134 nn. 21–22. The documents are republished in Magrini 1845, 103–05, appendix 7, 17–19, Annot. 59, xliv; G. Zorzi, 91–95 docs. 1–2. See Voelker 1977, 127–42, on the debate between Tibaldi and Bassi, with further literature. I am indebted for this interpretation to Richard Schofield.

52 Isermeyer 1980, 264–65 and 267 nn. 27–28. On Abbot Careni, Bossi da Modena 1983, 72. For further literature on San Sisto, see Ceschi Lavagetto, ed. 1985, esp. the article by Adorni 1985.

53 SPV, Olmo, 379v–80, "Ma Paolo Orio che fu mandato Abate l'anno stesso [1579] senza dubbio vi mise tutto lo spirito [the cloister]. E si deve veramente dire, che quella parte attacata alle foresterie vecchie insieme con le camere dell'Abate sia in tutto opere sua. Imperciochè il Careni cominciò allo 15 di gennaro, ma da gennaro fino a guigno, che viene l'Orio, dirà ognuno, che poco si potesse fare . . . Durò Abate l'Orio nel tempo in cui tali cose occorsero fino all'anno 1584, e D. Celso di Verona lo stesso anno gli successe, nel cui tempo si attese principalmente alla fabbrica del coro, che fu poi finito da D. Paolo Orio, che vi ritornò la seconda volta l'anno 1588 dopo il Veronese." BCV, Valle, "Chronichon," 88v, "1589. Paulus Orio iterum abas: quo anni chori structura perficetur." See Cicogna 1969, 4: 334 n. 222.

54 SPV, Olmo, 379v, "e l'occasione fu che essendosi quasi finita la Chiesa nuova l'anno 1581, pareva necessario il romper l'altar vecchio del Protomartire, e trasferire le ossa predette nella Chiesa nuova."

55 SPV, Olmo, 379v.

56 BCV, Barbaro, "Genealogie," 5: 299, 301r–v.

57 SPV, Olmo, 380r–v, "Fu l'Orio uomo singolare, che nella faccia rassomiglianza Sisto v. sapeva col tacere farsi temere, ed essendo in se stesso rigoroso oltra modo, ma benigno nelli soggetti Monaci, è incredibile, quanto dai medesimi era amato. Si dimostrò però sempre nelle cose importanti della Religione severissimo, e sapeva nel tempo ch'era Presidente (che vi fu più volte) riprendere, e correggere ancora gli Abati senza rispetto mondano. Ma avendo sempre il timor di Dio, e l'onore della Religione avanti agli occhi il tutto gli riusciva con ottimi eventi. Nè meno lo amavano i Prelati, che si gloriavano di avere nella Religione si grande, e singolar Prelato. Morì Presidente l'anno 1591, e fu sepolto in S. Giorgio con solenniss.a pompa funebre, che la più rara furono le lacrime de' Monaci tutti, e di amici non volgari nobili, ed anche Senatori, che se ne dolsero della perdita di tanto uomo fino a' giorni presenti"; Cicogna 1969, 4: 334 n. 226. BUP, Potenza, 35v (41v), praised Orio for his wisdom in governing and his skill in negotiation when abbot of Santa Giustina in 1584 and said of him: "In esso chi desidera saperle et vederle un ritratto de perfetto prelato."

58 BUP, Potenza, 33v (39)–35 (41). During his first abbacy at Santa Giustina he also furnished the altarpiece and frame for the high altar (the *Martyrdom of Santa Giustina* by Paolo Veronese). In his second abbacy (1579–80), he finished the building of the *infermeria* and *spetiaria*, and he died there in 1594 as titular abbot. He became abbot at Piacenza (1583–84), where he was renowned for his charitable works during the plague of 1583. Careni was president of the Congregation in 1573 while in his first term at Santa Giustina, and in 1576 while abbot of San Giorgio. Bossi da Modena 1983, 24, 72.

59 Bresciani Alvarez 1970, 164 n. 32; and Sartori 1970, 448, from ASP, SG, B. 493, 60.

60 BUP, Potenza, 35 (41), 36 (42), "essendo antiquissimo à colonette base alla germana benche fosse fatta una parte alla moderna de nova architettura de bianchi marmi desegnato del Donatello non di meno Il R.P.D. Celso volse buttare ognicosa per terra." Celso da Verona was president of the Congregation in 1581 as abbot of Santa Giustina, and in 1585 as abbot of San Giorgio. Bossi da Modena 1983, 24, 72.

61 BUP, Potenza, 35v (41v). At Santa Giustina Orio supervised the vaulting of the nave and the remainder of the church, as well as the removal of the barrier that had separated the new construction, and the erection of the large pilasters on the wall of the façade. He had professed at Praglia on 6 December 1540, and was president of the Congregation in 1579 and 1591 while abbot of San Giorgio, and in 1582 and 1587 while abbot of Santa Giustina. Bossi da Modena 1983, 24, 319.

62 BCV, Barbaro, "Genealogie," 5: 301v; BUP, Potenza, 38v (44v).

63 Bossi 1953, 3. The church has been restored following extensive destruction from bombing to a pre-Baroque state closer to its "original" conception as "una chiesa antica" (5); donations made between 1450–90 financed its construction but no documents survive to name its architect, who has been hypothesized to be Michelozzo (for the presbytery) or the ducal architect, Guiniforte Solari (2). Frattini 1983, 27 n. 1, narrows the period of construction to between 1460–76.

64 Isermeyer 1968, 46–47 and 56–75 nn. 22, 23, 25, 28 and 29; Beltramini 1995, 78–79, revised the date for Santa Giustina. I owe John Shearman for drawing my attention to an earlier re-siting of the choir at San Sisto, when in 1544 the relics of Sixtus were replaced in the high altar. See Ganz 1968, 29.

65 For more on Monte Cassino in this context, see Cooper 1996a, 84–86; Cooper 1990b, 35–37, noting that Palladio's first patron at San Giorgio and the commissioner of the choirstalls of the 1550s, Abbot Girolamo Scrochetto, had realized Sangallo's choir there while abbot (1541–46); also the Medicean patronage of Monte Cassino meant that Bramante's choir at Santa Maria del Popolo in Rome remained a critical model.

66 Prodi 1965, 129, with reference to Hubert Jedin's formulation.

67 Lewine 1960, I: 46–47, 73, 83.

68 The most salient illustration of this point is the monastery's decision to risk losing an endowment of 3,000 ducats for a chapel if their conditions were not agreed to; this was in the case of the testament of Maria Grimani, daughter of Doge Marino (1595–1605). She desired to leave 3,000 ducats to San Giorgio: 2,000 for the celebration of two daily Masses at the altar of the Crucifix (the second on the right side of the nave), one for herself and one for her

husband Lorenzo Giustinian; 1,000 "perche mi concedino l'Altare suddetto: et che nel frontispicio di esso si possino metter l'Arme di Cha Giustigniano et Grimani," and to erect a vaulted *arca* for their tombs between the two pilasters in front of the altar with an inscription; and for "la Crocetta d'Oro che donò il Sommo Pontefice al Ser.mo mio Padre" to be placed upon the altar. ASV, Notarile, Testamenti, Giulio Ziliol, B. 1245, 544, 6 November 1620. Presumably the will took some time through probate (the source of her sizeable wealth was her mother's dowry of 25,000 ducats), but two years later we find the monks presenting their terms to her commissioners in a meeting of the Chapter. Her primary consideration was that the Masses be celebrated, to which the monks agreed for the sum of 2,000 ducats, not however to restrictions on the use of the altar, "dare esecuzione alla pia dispositione predetta particolarmente nella celebrazione delle messe per lei ordinate non però nel particolare concernente l'Altare del quale et del Crocifisso antichissimo della loro Chiesa non intendono voler, ne poter disponere in conto alcuno." The monks, however, renounced the 1,000 ducats to retain *juspatronato*, "Restando però sempre l'Altare predetto et la Patromia, et Dominio di esso con il Santissimo Croceffisso proprio, e libero di essa Chiesa, e Monasterio, come sempre è stato; sopra il qual Altare ne meno nel Frontispicio, ò in ogni altra parte di esso non potrà mai posta Arma alcuna ne signo di Padromia [*sic*], ne per conto di essa Commissaria, ne per di altri." Instead, they agreed to grant burial rights and an inscription (reserving editorial rights) on the pilasters in front of the altar of their free will, albeit at the commissioners' expense, and to keep the gold crucifix on the same altar as Maria Grimani had desired. These conditions were agreeable to the executors of her will. ASV, SGM, B. 41, proc. 26, 9 and 11 July 1622.

69 Howard 1987, 67–69, is particularly interested in this aspect of patronage at San Francesco della Vigna. See also, Foscari & Tafuri 1983, 82–90, 131 ff. For a comparative study of the problem, see Humfrey 1990, which he was kind enough to share with me in manuscript originally.

70 Timofiewitsch 1971, appendix 1, 53–55.

71 For San Benedetto Po's medieval origins, see Bellodi 1974, esp. ch.1; also P. Piva 1980, esp. ch.1.

72 The crucial condition in relation to Church and State was a certain amount of autonomy, which protected the Congregation to some extent since taxes were levied by both and restrictions on the ownership of ecclesiastical property were increased. Stella 1958a describes the economic position of the Congregation. One of the most influential principles was established in the Bull of Eugenius IV, "Et si ex debito," of 23 February 1435 (Florence), when the Congregation was placed directly subject to the Holy See. Ramifications of this in a later, changed climate, can be seen when excused by Pius V in a brief, "Ad futuram rei memoriam," of 7 June 1571, from a tax levied on benefices in the Venetian domain after the conquest of Cyprus. See further in Predelli, ed. 1876–1914, 6: 324, no. 143, 7: 5, no. 5, 7, no. 14, 58, no. 60, 123, no. 19. The Cassinese levy to the Holy See was the highest paid by any congregation.

73 See Lanfranchi, ed. 1968, for the complete documentary history of the monastery from the tenth century to the twelfth, a period in which much of the property holdings were accrued. These are also listed in the *catastici* in ASV, SGM, B. 1.

74 Perhaps the most graphic illustration of this was when Abbot Alabardi was prevented from securing sufficient Istrian marble for the façade of the new church of San Giorgio due to a deficit of 6,000 ducats (possibly resulting from the charitable outlay of that amount during a terrible plague in 1591, see SPV, Olmo, 380v). SPV, Olmo, 383, on Alabardi's return from Milan for his second tenure: "e seguendo nelle incominciate imprese preparò abbondante materia di marmi, per farne la facciata della chiesa, e ne furono condotti tanti dall' Istria a Venezia, ch' empirono tutta la piazza vecchia. Ed avendo aggregata moltitudine di mattoni, era per non mancare a qualsivoglia accrescimento di fabbrica. Ma lo ritardò che cominciarono a mancar danari, che non facesse quanto voleva, sebbene fatto un debito di sei milla ducati, cominciò quando potè."

75 Knapton 1986, summarizes the political and economic condition of Venice between 1571–1644 and its historiography. For a corrective view of "dramatic millenarianism," see Elliott 1985.

76 The burden of daily and anniversary Masses was somewhat curtailed by the rebuilding of the church at San Giorgio, which must have occasioned something of a house cleaning, but the count continued to increase up until 1726 when the Church reduced the obligations of the monasteries; a situation reviewed in "Nota dell' obblighi di Messe ha il Monast.o di S. Giorgio di Venetia," revealing that the 2,288 Masses per year previously celebrated at San Giorgio were now reduced to 810 per year. ASV, SGM, B. 42, proc. 45A, loose.

77 ASV, SGM, B. 22, proc. 13A–II, fasc. 9 (in two copies) and B. 41, proc. 23, 1, "essendo forzati di ruinare la chiesa nostra qual ella si minacciava manifesta ruina, con pericolo delle persone, del coperto, legnami, coro, altari, collone assai preziose et perdita d'ogni altro ornamento"; transcribed in part in Cicogna 1969, 4: 351 n. 256; given in full by G. Zorzi 1967, 76, doc. 48. The relationship of Marco Bollani, designated as a patrician, to the members of the Bollani family later concerned with the chapel, the branch of Bishop Domenico, previously has not been made clear (ASV, Barbaro, "Albori," 2: 40, "C"; BMV, Capellari Vivaro, 1: "A"); there was a Marco di Bernardo Bollani, *podestà* of Padua, who was elected procurator *de supra* of San Marco in 1513, who was Bishop Domenico's second cousin (Cairns 1976, 11), but he died in 1517. I have identified as commissioner his grandson, Marco di Alvise (ASV, Barbaro, "Albori," 2: 40, "D"; BMV, Capellari Vivaro, 1: "B"), born on 29 December 1503 and died on 19 January 1587, a senator and twice one of the forty-one electors of the doge (in 1567 and 1570). It is also interesting to note in relation to the patronage of the matching altar that both Marcos, grandfather and grandson, married Morosinis.

78 SPV, Olmo, 375v, "Dall'altra parte pur fuori del santuario vi è l'altare de' SS. Pietro e Paolo fabbricato dagl' Ill.mi Bollani, non però riguardevole o di pittura, o di fabbrica, essendo la pittura di poco stima, e la fabbrica tutta di pietra istriana." See further below for the decoration.

79 ASV, Notarile, Testamenti, Antonio Callegarini, B. 3111, 136–38; copy in ASV, SGM, B. 41, proc. 23, 1; transcribed in part in Cicogna 1969, 4: 351 n. 256; given in full in G. Zorzi 1967, 76–77, doc. 49.

80 ASV, Notarile, Atti, Cesare Ziliol, B. 1258, 451, excerpted in the *capitolo* of 1579 by the notary Callegarini, "Teneantur prout ipse Rev. D. Ep.pi tam nomine suo proprio quam uti commissarius pro maiori parte ex testamento predicti Clar.mi fratris sui de quo rogatus fuit Specr.lis D. Cesar Ziliolus aulae Ser.mi Principis Venetiarum cancellarius sub *anno de 1570* die 10 mensis Iulii in publicam formam redacto ibidem per me notarium infr.tum viso et lecto promisit propiis impensis *intra triennium* proxime futurum sacellum sive capella predicta iuxta eandem formam perfici et ornari facere cum suis decentibus ornamentis, et si dominationi Suae Rev. vel nepotibus aut posteris suis predictis placuerit lapidem unam tantummodo in muro eiusdem capellae immittere id facere libere possint in illo inscribendo quicquid melius visum fuerit ad sui nepotum posterorumque suorum memoriam"; the transcription from G. Zorzi 1967, 77, doc. 49. The Cesare Ziliol *busta* containing the testament of 1570 of Jacopo Bollani was missing from its location in the notarial archive, so I have been unable to consult it. It may be that a number of the stipulations in the agreement of 1579 were restated from the earlier document of 1570, such as the assignment of the chapel design to Palladio. For the epitaph, see Cicogna 1969, 4: 451–57 inscr. 10.

81 G. Zorzi 1967, 77, doc. 49, "adhuc non plene perfectae."

82 Isermeyer 1980, 263 and 267 nn. 19–20.

83 "Sui iuxta formam circumspecti viri Domini Andreae Paladii ipsius ecclesiae architecti perficiendam et sibi benevisam ac ab ipso venerando capitulo approbatam." G. Zorzi 1967, 77, doc. 49.

84 See under the Morosini chapel below, ASV, Notarile, Testamenti, Antonio Callegarini, B. 3111; copy in ASV, SGM, B. 41, proc. 24; cited in part in Cicogna 1969, 4: 350 n. 253; G. Zorzi 1967, 49.

85 ASV, SGM, B. 21, proc. 10a "Libro," 7v, "li quali tre altari siano fatti di quella grandezza misura et forma come è aponto quello in detta chiesa fatto fare per il quondam Rev.mo Bollani vescovo di Brescia, il quale gli sii per esemplare et modello overo disegno dell'opera predetta et iuxta la ragion di quello sia tenuto"; Cicogna 1969, 4: 352 n. 259a; G. Zorzi 1967, 71, doc. 37 (as fasc. 13, 8).

86 G. Zorzi (1963) association of the drawing in Vicenza (Museo Civico, D 17) as well as a group of sculptures by Alessandro Vittoria, the figures of the *Risen Christ*, *Faith* and *Charity* (Brescia, Museo Civico dell' Età Cristiana Medioevale), with the project is not accepted since its almost universal association with a project for the Grimani family tomb in San Francesco della Vigna (Burns with Fairbairn & Boucher 1975, 135–36 cat. 245; Lewis 2000, 242–43 cat. 111) and the sculptures (dated 1577–78) were almost certainly destined from the start to adorn the tomb of Domenico Bollani located in the cathedral of the seat of his bishopric, as described by Temanza 1778, 491, from which they were removed after the partial destruction of the church. A drawing in Budapest (Szépmüvészeti Múzeum, 1989) for a funerary chapel was also identified as possibly destined for San Giorgio, due to its similarity to the executed chapels, but it has also been associated with a Florentine project for the Niccolini chapel in Santa Croce, see Lewis 2000, 245–46 cat. 112; Battilotti 1999, 489–91 cat. 97*; Morrogh 1985, 105–09; Burns 1980b, 166–67 cat. VII, 7. (See further below fig. 141.).

87 Cicogna 1969, 4: 452; G. Zorzi 1965, 81–82; see above in Part II on the Accesi, and Part III on the patriarch of Aquileia Giovanni Grimani.

88 The Bollani were one of the *case vecchie*, and considered one of the ecclesiastical families of Venice. For the politics of Domenico's position, his biography and career, see Cairns 1976, 231–39; also Cicogna 1969, 4: 452–57 inscr. 10 (not currently visible, rather gold-ground inscriptions in English [left] and Magyar [right] were added to the pilasters on either side of the chapel commemorating Hungarian Bishop Alexander Dessewffy and St. Gerardo Sagredo on 1900 September 25); Pillinini 1969.

89 On the Brescia Palazzo Pubblico, see here Part v, under the Doge's Palace; and G. Zorzi 1965, 92; on the Brescia Cathedral, G. Zorzi 1967, 54, 87–88, docs. 1–2.

90 Abbot Marco Bollani left a bequest of books in 1265 and was still remembered in the eighteenth century. ASV, SGM, B. 1, "catastico 982–1469," and B. 43, proc. 46A, 1276. Members of other branches of the Bollani continued to request burial in the *arca* of the Ca' Bollani at San Giorgio, for example, in Padua in 1628, Zuanne di Augustin Bollani. ASV, Notarile, Testamenti, Pietro Perazzo, B. 1221, 152. The line of Bishop Domenico ("C") extended from the San Felice branch ("B") and that of Zuanne ("G") from the San Fantin ("E"). ASV, Barbaro, "Albori," 2: 44.

91 Sansovino 1604, 168, "Di quello a corrispondenza del predetto del Morosino m'è parso solo por l'infrascritto epitafio fatto fare da chi fu eretto." For the designs associated with Palladio, see above.

92 "Pala Ludovici Cervelli Mediolanensis anno *1690*." BCV, Valle, ch. 8, 110v–111. Cicogna 1969, 4: 351 n. 256, notes that Cervelli was not yet born when Olmo wrote about the first altarpiece, excluding his participation.

93 "S.o Pietro il Cervelli di Milano." BCV, MS P.D. 745 C; the Correr inventory is datable to before 1708 by the identification of the painter as Cervelli.

94 406 × 208 cm. Daniels 1976, 129–30 cat. 453, with further literature, identified the saints as: Peter, Gerardo Sagredo (whom he gives as the titular saint of the altar, but at that time the dedication was to Peter and Paul), Scholastica, Catherine of Alexandria, Benedict, Jerome, and Paul; 1 cat. 2, a *bozzetto* for the altarpiece is noted as in Algiers, Musée National des Beaux-Arts (2834). In an exhibition catalogue by Rizzi 1989, 108–11, the *Guida didattica* (Goi 1989, cat. 28) identifies as certain the identities of: Peter, Gerardo Sagredo, and Jerome; as less certain: Catherine of Siena (instead of Scholastica), Catherine of Alexandria, Domenico (in any case, not Benedict), and, not previously named, James the Apostle or Rocco, and John. Ricci was the pupil of Cervelli.

95 For the Veronese revival, see Cocke 1980, 102–03; for Ricci's critics identifying the painting in this vein, see Daniels 1976, 129 cat. 453. I have always been tempted to think that if Paolo Veronese had had the longevity of Tintoretto, that he would have been the choice of the monks at San Giorgio to execute the painted decoration in the church as well, since Paolo also had the high altar of Santa Giustina in Padua to his credit. Ricci also executed work at Santa Giustina, an altarpiece commissioned in 1700 by Abbot Giovanni Barpi, from Ricci's hometown of Belluno, which may have brought him to the notice of the monks at San Giorgio. Daniels 1976, 84–85 cat. 287.

96 Cicogna 1969, 4: 351 n. 256.

97 Not in G. Zorzi 1967, 76–77, doc. 49; I have used the copy in ASV, SGM, B. 41, proc. 23, 3v. BCV, Valle, ch. 8, 110v, also notes that 25 ducats were paid in 1604.

98 A document of *circa* 1701 detailing the "Oblighi di Messe alle quali e tenute il Monastero di S. Georgio Maggiori" (an inventory compiled in anticipation of the reduction of Masses) notes the full payment of capital completing the monetary obligations. ASV, SGM, B. 42, proc. 45A. The last male heir to the Bollani of Bishop Domenico's line died in 1609; the brother of Vincenzo and Antonio, Domenico, bishop of Crete died in 1613, so the patrimony devolved to Jacopo's unmarried daughter, Cecilia. In Cecilia Bollani's will, made on 8 April 1624, she requests burial at San Domenico in Castello in the *arca* of the Ca' Bollani, and where her father was buried (Cicogna 1969, 1: 133–34 inscr. 51), and for her heirs to provide money for two torches for a yearly vigil at San Giorgio.

99 SPV, Olmo, 375v, "Ma gli altri [following the description of the high altar] non sono ne anco sennon [sic] bella fabbrica eccetto alcuni, che dovranno poi esser fatti di finissime pietre. Tra tanto, non ci può certo nella Chiesa occorrere il più bello di quello di S. Andrea, nel quale riposano le ossa di S. Platone, che posto tra il braccio, ed il Santuario alla parte di quelli che entrano; Fu con somma religione fabbricato dagl' Ill.mi Morosini. La bellezza delle cui pietre consiste che variando di diverse macchie, si vedono in esse alcune figurine di uccelli biscie, et altro. E quello che fa maravigliare tutti l'immagine di un Cristo N. S. Crocifisso, che si vede in una delle colonne di detto altare, qual è la prima cosa, che si mostri à forastieri in si degna Chiesa." "Sennon" is an insertion above the line. Cicogna 1969, 4: 350 n. 254, confirmed that the righthand marble column bore the appearance of the image of Christ, adding that he owned a sonnet written in the seventeenth century in praise of this miraculous natural manifestation of faith. I have found a sonnet on this subject with opening and closing lines different from those given by Cicogna; however, the manuscript came from his collection to the Correr, so it may be the same one: In "Sonnetti sopra Venetia," sonnetto 283, "Ad un Crocefisso spicca dalle macchie d'una Colonna di Marmo in S. Giorgio Maggiore di Venezia," BCV, Cod. Cicogna 1195. I have not been able to discern this image, which seems to be a romantic conceit.

100 SPV, Olmo, 381.

101 ASV, Notarile, Testamenti, Antonio Callegarini, B. 3111; copy in ASV, SGM, B. 41, proc. 24; cited in part in Cicogna 1969, 4: 350 n. 253; G. Zorzi 1967, 49. For Vicenzo and Barbon Morosini, see ASV, Barbaro, "Albori," 5: 324, "A"; BCV, Barbaro, "Genealogie," 5: 206–10; Cicogna 1969, 4: 457–59 inscr. 11.

102 ASV, Barbaro, "Albori," 5: 324, "A"; BCV, Barbaro, "Genealogie," 5: 206–10, for the Morosini family. See Cicogna 1969, 4: 458 inscr. 11, for Andrea, *Legum doctorem*, born in 1557 to Vicenzo and his second wife, Cecilia Pisani (herself the daughter of a procurator, Giovanni), and died while returning from Constantinople.

103 ASV, SGM, B. 42, proc. 45A. Cicogna 1969, 4:

350 n. 253, also refers to ASV, Notarile, Testamenti, Antonio Callegarini, 7 November 1585, al-though I found nothing regarding this matter in the *busta* for that date.

104 Pallucchini & Rossi 1982, I: 227 cat. 445, the attribution follows Stringa's (Sansovino 1604, 167), "cominciata dal Tentoretto e finita dal Giovine, se ben si crede, che non fosse da lui finita," and the date is given as between 1583–86 (based on the stipulation in the concession). P. Rossi 1975a, 26, following earlier scholars, associates a black chalk drawing of a striding male figure (Florence, Uffizi, 12952f–v) with the figure of Christ, but attributes it to Domenico, rather than Jacopo, an argument she finds to be reinforced by the attribution of the painting predominantly to Domenico; but, as with many Tintoretto drawings, there seems to me to be only a superficial resemblance to the figure of Christ in the painting, whose left leg is forward, rather than the right leg as in the drawing, and whose torsion as the figure leans to the left has a very different effect as a result. The practice in the Tintoretto workshop, particularly under Jacopo's direction, seems to have been to recombine various studies to supply the appropriate attitude and modeling for the figure, for example, the black chalk study of an angel in Darmstadt (Landesmuseum, Print Room, A.E. 1437) is closer to the Morosini *Christ* in the position of the legs and body than the Uffizi drawing, but lacks a correspondence in the arms (Hadeln 1922, pl. 33).

105 SPV, Olmo, 308; BCV, Valle, ch. 19, 134r–v; Corner 1749, 124; Cicogna 1969, 4: 350 n. 253. The relics were translated under Abbot Michele Alabardi on 6 April 1593. Corner 1749, 199.

106 BCV, Valle, ch. 7, 109, also ch. 19, 134, "et Imagine Lapidea sculpta in illa de S. Pantaleone, more antiquo cum hoc nomine expresso, S. Pantaleonis; quae Tabella, et Immago extat in Capella apud Portam huius Monasterii." Recorded in Pietro Gradenigo's *Monumenta veneta* in a watercolor by Giovanni Grevembroch, with the legend: "Tra i rari e vetusti monumenti della vecchia demolita Chiesa riserbati dalla consueta bell' indole de' Monaci di S. Giorgio Maggiore, ecco quella santa Imagine, che ivi ebbe culto, perchè rappresenta Pantaleone Medico, e Martire di eterna Gloria." BCV, Grevembroch 1759, 2: pl. 43, as ex-San Giorgio Maggiore; Cicogna 1969, 4: 350 n. 253.

107 Another example is the stone relief of Abbot Bonincontro de' Boaterii, which, after the erection of the new church, was set upright into the wall of the corridor to the Cappella dei Morti. Also depicted in BCV, Grevembroch 1759, I: pl. 43. Cicogna 1969, 4: 524–27 inscr. 19.

108 For which see in Part v on the Doge's Palace (fig. 208). MacColl 1924, 266–71, first published the London portrait, after its purchase in 1922 on the advice of Roger Fry. See P.

Rossi 1974, 109; P. Rossi 1994, 34–35; and now Mozzetti & Santi 1997. The London painting has undergone extensive examination by conservators and scientists, who came to the conclusion that it was an authentic work of Jacopo Tintoretto; Plesters 1979, 8; Plesters 1980, 41, 45; Plesters 1984, 30–31.

109 MacColl 1924, 270, "c," reproduces the Doge's Palace portrait, and describes it as "an inferior version in reverse" (271); P. Rossi 1974, 109, as "replica di bottega." Gould 1975, 262 cat. 4004, first noted in his catalog of 1959 another replica (location unknown), in which the sitter is oriented the same direction as the London and San Giorgio portraits (Plesters 1979, 24 n. 2, notes that Gould's entry on the London portrait was written before its restoration); see in Riccoboni 1947, pl. 54, xiii and xviii n. 5, xxvi cat. 75, II cat. 75. For a survey of Morosini's painted portraits, see now Mozzetti & Santi 1997.

110 ASV, Barbaro, "Albori," 5: 324–25, "A" and "B"; BCV, Barbaro, "Genealogie," 5: 208v–10; the other branch of the Morosini were the dalla Tressa; Vicenzo originated from the Morosini dalla Sbarra in S. Anzolo, and established the *ramo* called "in Canonica." Cicogna 1969, 4: 457–58 inscr. 11.

111 The scrolled strapwork frame of the coat of arms seems Sansovinesque and may be contemporary with the decoration of the altar.

112 My thanks to Howard Burns, who first mentioned this similarity to me. Crollalanza 1886–90, 2: 180, notes that Sixtus v created Gianfrancesco Morosini cardinal on 15 July 1588.

113 ASV, Barbaro, "Albori," 5: 324, "A"; BCV, Barbaro, "Genealogie," 5: 208v–10; Cicogna 1969, 4: 457–58 inscr. 11.

114 Cicogna 1969, 4: 458 inscr. 11, "Egli fu uno de' principali Senatori del suo tempo."

115 BCV, Barbaro, "Genealogie," 5: 208v–09; Cicogna 1969, 4: 459 inscr. 11. Domenico and Vicenzo had two brothers, at least one of whom, Lorenzo (born 1516), was active in the Senate (one of the twelve electors of Doge Priuli). Their father, Barbon Morosini (died 1515?), had married in 1505 Betta di Lorenzo Giustinian (died 1530), granddaughter of Bernardo K.P. Barbon's brother, Andrea (1499–1530), had been taken prisoner by the French during the War of the League of Cambrai together with their father, Zustinian (1468–1529), who had a notable *terraferma* military career (that is, Vicenzo and Domenico Morosini's uncle and grandfather).

116 Vicenzo's first marriage was to the daughter of Agostino di Marco Venier, in 1536. BCV, Barbaro, "Genealogie," 5: 209v–10; Cicogna 1969, 4: 457 inscr. 11.

117 ASV, Barbaro, "Albori," 6: 123, "F" (although female offspring are not identified). Cecilia was the widow of Almorò Barbaro, and also related through her father to Elena Pisani Barbaro of San Vidal, mother of Palladio's patrons.

118 I have examined her will of 27 January 1558 (if *m.v.* = 1559), which remains unpublished. ASV, Notarile, Testamenti, chiusi, Angelo Canal, B. 209–11, no. 339 rosso. From my observation of the surface of the painting, there appears to be a raised outline roughly triangular in shape surrounding her portrait to bust length and bounded by her sleeve below and Vicenzo's *stola* above. It is possible that a piece of canvas (maybe an earlier portrait or a copy made from one) was applied and blended into the composition. This was not looked for in the restoration of 1985 and so I have not been able to get technical confirmation, but there is precedent in the Tintoretto workshop practice for portrait faces to be on separate pieces of material, for example, *Doge Alvise Mocenigo and Family before the Madonna and Child* (Washington, D.C., National Gallery of Art; see Shapley 1979, I: 473–74 cat. 1406; and here in Part v, fig. 196); also refer above for Veronese's similar application in the *Wedding Feast at Cana*.

119 Ridolfi 1965, 2: 52; under lost works in Pallucchini & Rossi 1982, I: 265 (cross-reference 230 cat. 456), and, less certainly, 261, from the 1663 Martinioni edition of Sansovino (1968, 376).

120 Discussed in Part v, on the Doge's Palace.

121 G. Rossi 1969, 245; Cicogna 1969, 4: 284–88 n. 13, in the concession of 982 three members of the Morosini family are represented as signers, 289 n. 28, notes early biographers of Abbot Giovanni Morosini.

122 Bartholomio Maurocini *quondam* Benetto in his will of 1 June 1600 left 500 ducats to his son Lazaro, now don Fulgentio, a novitiate at San Giorgio. ASV, Notarile, Testamenti, Marin Rhenio, B. 843, 262.

123 T. Martin 1998, 144–45 cat. 42; T. Martin 1988, 266–67 cat. 37, I would like to thank the author for discussions of the work *in situ*.

124 T. Martin 1998, 144–45 cat. 42; T. Martin 1988, 266–67 cat. 37.

125 Cicogna 1969, 4: 457 inscr. 11.

126 Compare, for example, Vittoria's design for the reliquary urn of the altar of St. Saba at Sant'Antonino in Venice, which employs an equally decorative marble and similar reverse-curve scrolls. Thomas Martin has communicated to me his opinion that the frame of the Morosini epitaph was designed by Vittoria. For Vittoria's work in the context of painted, sculpted, and architectural ensembles, see T. Martin 1998. It is surprisingly rare to find Vittoria's and Tintoretto's portraits of *Vicenzo Morosini* mentioned together in the respective discussions of either.

127 T. Martin, who does not include these busts in his Vittoria catalogue, has expressed this opinion to me. Stringa in Sansovino 1604, 167, records only the inscription to Vicenzo, not those of Barbon and Domenico, which also suggests their later date, although Martinioni in his 1663 edn. of Sansovino (1968, 222), does not record them either.

128 Cicogna 1969, 4: 457 inscr. 11.

129 Barbon was one of the forty-one electors of Doge Marino Grimani (1595), whose wife was Dogaressa Marina Morosini and whose daughter, Maria Giustinian, had left a bequest for the altar of the Crucifix. Barbon's son, Andrea (born 1583, married 1600 to Laura di Michele Priuli P., died 1652), carried on the male line of the Morosini dalla Sbarra in Canonica. Barbon's great-great-great-grandson Michiel di Barbon, a knight of San Marco and ambassador to Leopold I in Vienna, was buried at San Giorgio in 1722, and was survived by his son, Barbon Vicenzo, showing the longevity of the sixteenth-century Morosinis' reputation and their continued attachment to San Giorgio. ASV, Barbaro, "Albori," 5: 324–25, "A" and "B"; BCV, Barbaro, "Genealogie," 5: 209v–10.

130 "Hanno l'uno, e l'altro quattro colonne bellissime di marmo greco, e la scalinata di cinque gradi della stessa pietra e grandezza che sono quelli dell'altar maggiore, hanno pero la palla, o icona dipinta." SPV, Olmo, 375v–76.

131 ASV, SGM, B. 21, proc. 10A "Libro," 7v, with an affidavit from the notary Marin Rhenio that the stonecutters had signed the document in chancery on 3 March 1593 and a promise by Abbot Alabardi that if the work was completed by *Quaresima* (Lent) 1594 they would receive four *bigonzi* of wine. Given in part by Cicogna 1969, 4: 352 n. 259; and in full by G. Zorzi 1967, 72, doc. 38 (as fasc. 13, fol. 9). According to BCV, Valle, ch. 8, 111, the altar cost 600 ducats, other than the stone supplied by the monastery (see also in BUP, Valle, 50). Note that the curvature of the apse is subtly reflected in the frames, although not in the stretched canvases of the altarpieces.

132 BCV, Valle, ch. 8, 111, "Pale ibi Jacobi Tentoretti, Comp. *1564*: pretio Duc. 100: precisè pro Pala D. Benedicti Giorn: *1594*." The *Giornale* entry Valle refers to seems to have been noted by him in BUP, Valle, 51, under "Pitture," "d.o [1594] Palla di S. Benedetto scudi 100./ Giac.o Tent.o d.ti 150." For the general campaign of decoration under Abbot Alabardi in the 1590s, including the historiated choirstalls, see Cooper 1990b.

133 Ridolfi 1965, 2: 59. Pallucchini & Rossi 1982, 1: 253 cat. A 110. P. Rossi 1975a, 16–17, associates a drawing in Cambridge (Fitzwilliam Museum, 2253r) of a seated male nude with the figure of Christ, but the relationship seems too generic to sustain.

134 The two groups of the Coronation and the saints are depicted in a hitherto unpublished black chalk drawing in the Uffizi (13032F), which is inscribed "Tintoretto" and cataloged as such (formerly under "il giovane," that is, Domenico). The drawing *scheda* notes a relationship to San Giorgio Maggiore. The drawing seems to me to be after the painting, rather than a preparatory compositional study – which were rare in Jacopo's work, and in Domenico's were more characteristically oil

sketches (see the altar of St. Stephen below) – nor is the study marked for transfer and the figures show little deviation from the finished painting.

135 Jameson 1890, for an overview of Benedictine iconography in the general context of monastic orders as represented in art; Jameson 1864, 13–17, on the Coronation of the Virgin.

136 BCV, Valle, ch. 8, 111, apparently Valle could find no record of lay commissioners (who, with their shorn heads, may have been connected to the monastery as *conversi*), and for Alabardi: 111v, "Verosimile tam quod primus ille pictii in medio est ipse Alabardus: et alii Cellerarii," and ch. 47, 219v (in Alabardi's biography), "Ipsius Imago, verissimile est quod sit illa prima ex Monachis in Icona Altaris S. Benedicti cum fuerit sub ipsa affermata." Mentioned by Cicogna 1969, 4: 352 n. 259.

137 SPV, Olmo, 382. The reported role of Abbot Alabardi (1591–95, 1596–died 1598) in the conception of the high altar ensemble as it was realized in the 1590s is discussed more fully in Cooper 1990b, 226–77, but lies outside the focus here on Palladio's contributions (for which see further below).

138 SPV, Olmo, 381v, "Era uomo di grande statura, e piegava più al magro, che ad altro."

139 SPV, Olmo, 376, "Ma ci duole, che manchi tra questi la pittura ed imagine del santo Eremita cosma." Olmo refers to St. Cosmas as the co-dedicatee with St. Benedict.

140 *Vita s. Cosmae eremitae cujus corpus Venetiis in Templo s. Georgii majoris quiescit*, Venice, 1612. See Cicogna 1969, 4: 356 n. 228, for a list of Olmo's writings.

141 Cicogna 1969, 4: 351–52 n. 258, also records several that were no longer extant by his day. In addition, the base of each of the four columns is inscribed (from left to right): ALTARE QUOTIDIE, PRO DEFUNCTIS, PRIVILEGIATUM, IN PERPETUUM; and in an oval in the center of the base of the stone frame, CORPVS S. COSMAE EREMITAE.

142 Corner 1749, 201.

143 For the eleventh-century translation of the saint, see also BMV, Olmo, 84–87; BCV, Valle, ch. 11, 119r–v; Corner 1749, 88–91; G. Rossi 1969, 246; Cicogna 1969, 4: 351–52 n. 258. On the date of observance at San Giorgio, see ASV, SGM, B. 22, proc. 13A, fasc. 8.

144 The relic of St. Stephen, together with those of Sts. James the Less and Pantaleone and a piece of the True Cross, were brought from Constantinople by a monk of San Giorgio named Peter (honored in an inscription saved from the old church, see Cicogna 1969, 4: 523–24 inscr. 18) under Abbot Tribuno Memo (1105–39, namesake of the doge who granted the foundation of the monastery), during the reign of Doge Ordelaffo Falier (1102–18). Considered testimony to the relic's authenticity was the survival of the ship through a violent three-day storm at sea, a common element in relic histories. SPV, Olmo,

285v–289 (and the entire bk. 2 of the Latin history, BMV, Olmo, 119–252, "Historia translationis corporis sancti Stephani protomartyris Constantinopoli Venetias anno MCX ad suburbanam insulam s. Georgii cognomento maioris," which ends with verses for the feast of St. Stephen at nocturnes, lauds and vespers); Sansovino 1968, 223; BCV, Valle, ch. 12, 120–25v; Corner 1749, 94–119; G. Rossi 1969, 247–50; Cicogna 1969, 4: 293 n. 43, and 485 inscr. 12–13.

145 The origins of the festival are somewhat confused; for example, see Sansovino 1604, 330v–331.

146 Sansovino 1604, 330v–331, including two *andate* instituted only in 1571 (for a description of the *andata* to San Giorgio, 341v–342 and 346v–347); by the time of Martinioni's 1663 edn. (Sansovino 1968, 504–05), the total number was twelve (two added in 1631 and 1656). On the consignment of the *trionfi*, see Pertusi 1977; Pertusi 1965.

147 Renier Michiel 1829, 2: 33–34, for one of the most complete descriptions of the *andata* for St. Stephen (30–37): "Allora il Doge montava ne' suoi magnifici peatoni accompagnato da' suoi consiglieri, dai capi delle quarantie, dai savi dell'una e l'altro mano, e dai quarant'uno che furono i suoi elettori. Veniva egli preceduto da certe barche co' lumi, appositamente dal Governo destinate, e seguito da innumerabili barchette di ogni maniera, fornite anch'esse di fanali, che tutte insieme coprivano lo spazio che avvi fra S. Marco e l'Isola di S. Giorgio Maggiore. Illuminavano questo spazio a dritta e a manca certi fuochi piantati sull'acqua, chiamati LUDRI, composti dicorda bene impecciata, che mandavano anche da lunghi un vivacissimo splendore, il quale riflettuto nell'acqua produceva un effetto magico." Concentrating more on the intersection between the official ceremonial of religious feast days and the popular celebrations such as the Carnival period preceding Lent, see Muir 1981, 156–81; Muir 1975, 101–03, for St. Stephen; Tamassia Mazzarotto 1980, 103–15; Musolino 1972, 205; Musolino 1965, 212–18. For the ceremonial in use at San Giorgio prior to the rebuilding by Palladio, see Cooper 1996a.

148 Muir 1975, 82.

149 For references to sources of Venetian ceremonials, see Sinding-Larsen 1974, 157 n. 3; Muir 1975, 143 n. 42 and 293.

150 The official dogal ceremonial in use during the period when the altars at San Giorgio were under commission was that of Doge Pasquale Cicogna (1585–95), for example, ASV, Collegio, Cerimoniale I (written beginning in 1593 and completed in 1599), itself probably a revision of Doge Gerolamo Priuli's (1559–67), for example, BMV, Lat. III 172 (2276), and also in Rio 1840, which would have been operative during the conception of the church.

151 Sanudo 1879–1903, 33: 551–53 (1522), "Et compito la predicha, iusta il consueto si andò a vespero a San Zorzi per esser la vizilia de

San Stephano, il cui corpo dicono esser lì a San Zorzi mazore in l'altar grande. Et il consueto a preparar a San Zorzi, di sora dove senta su la so cariega il Doxe con li oratori et Signoria, il resto da basso; ma per esser vechio et per paura dil fredo non volse esso Doxe andar di suso, ma stete da basso in choro; cossa mai più fata da niun altro Doxe lì a San Zorzi"; Musolino 1972, 205, who discusses the incident but does not cite Sanudo as his source, interprets "da basso in choro" to mean the nave, but it would have been within the choir enclosure (as still can be experienced in the Frari). For other problems encountered during the ceremonial in the earlier church, see Cooper 1996a.

152 G. Franco 1614, pt. 1: 35, with the legend "Il Ser.mo Prencipe con la Signoria il giorno di Natale ascolta Vespro in S. Georgio Magiore et il di seguente va alla Messa/in detta Chiesa in contrato et accompagnato al rittorno dall' Abbate et Cap.lo de quelli RR Monaci Questo Celebre Tempio/fù ordinato dal Palladio Architetto Eccel.mo etè posto in isola a dirimpeto della Piazza di S. Marco et è tenuto uno de famosi tempij d'Italia."

153 Demus 1960, 96–98, proposed that claims to apostolic heritage were realized by the use of the form of the Byzantine *apostoleion* appropriated for San Marco. Sinding-Larsen 1965b, 252, interpreted the new St. Peter's as usurping Venetian form and thus depriving it of its uniqueness as a symbol; Sinding-Larsen 1974, 182–85, on the state theology of San Marco, and 208–17, on the architectural implications of state ceremonies; carried forward in Howard 1993; For Venice generally, see Muir 1981. Deborah Howard has observed in a personal communication to me the prestige derived from long Benedictine association with ceremonies of kingship, such as Westminster Abbey in London, or St. Denis near Paris; for its translation in medieval Venice and dogal association with San Giorgio, see Cooper 1990a.

154 From BMV, Pace, "Cerimoniale," 62 (December), "Giovanni Morosini Monaco dimandò questa Chiesa di S. Giorgio, et S. Stefano, la quale fù sempre titular Capella di S. Marco, et ius perpetuo del Palazzo Ducale: onde Tribon Memo Doge di Venetia, che la fece fabricar, acconsentendo anche Vitale Patriarcha, et tutti li Vescovi, et Primati del Popolo di Venetia comessero opresso la medesima Chiesa potersi far Monasterio perpetuo à Laude di Dio, et diffesa della Patria, e perche questa Chiesa è della Patronia di S. Marco, et è Capella del nostro Palazzo libera dalla Servitù di S.ta Madre Chiesa. Intendiamo godi lo stesso Privileggio."

155 For example, the decree of 29 June 1588 (ASV, Procuratoria de Supra, SM, B. 83, fasc. 2, "intorno alla buona et sicura custodia delle Reliquie, et Corpi Santi di questa Città et Dogado"), requiring an inventory of all relics in the city and their safekeeping under locks to which three separate keys were held by the procurators *de supra*, the *procuratore delle chiese* and by the priest. R. Gallo 1934, 189–91 and 211, doc. 2; Niero 1965, 183 and 188. One of the few occasions that the *cassa* of St. Stephen was allowed to be opened demonstrated its status, when the Senate, in a rare instance, ceded a fragment of the relic to the emperor and archduke of Austria in 1399, in order to "conservare amicos." Corner 1749, 265.

156 Niero 1965, 184, gives a history of the veneration of relics in Venice, distinguishing various phases.

157 I have used Botero 1640, pt. 7, 797 (in the 1605 ed., bk. 2, 98–109v).

158 For the viewpoint of a modern Catholic scholar on a problem termed by him "irresolvable," see Niero 1965, 183, on the nature of the problem in general, and 197, on the body of St. Stephen.

159 From the popular account of de Voragine 1993, 45–50 (differently organized in the earlier trans. by G. Ryan and H. Ripperger 1969, 54–58 "December," on the invention, and 408–12, on the translation) to the *Acta Sanctorum* 1940, n.v.: 602, "Decembris," Venice's claim to possess the body of the protomartyr is rarely mentioned in Rome-based hagiographical sources. See for a summary of the opposing claims, F. Pellegrini 1880, 47.

160 SPV, Olmo, 294–95, declared: "Se poteva il demonio esser autore di cosi segnalato traslazione fatta a Roma."

161 SPV, Olmo, 289v, 340v; BCV, Valle, 108r–v; Cicogna 1969, 4: 611 inscr. 30. On *maestro* Caterino, see Testi 1909–15, 1: 237, 239, 243–45.

162 SPV, Olmo, 289v; Cicogna 1969, 4: 610 inscr. 30.

163 SPV, Olmo, 289v, remarked upon their separation. BCV, Valle, 108r–v, though relying on Olmo, seems to have thought that the earlier St. Stephen altarpiece was the miracle of the angel commissioned by Bonincontro, and that another altarpiece depicting St. Stephen with the above-named saints and dated 1374 had been commissioned on the occasion of the translation of the relic. Corner 1749, 122–23, recorded their absence. Cicogna 1969, 4: 610–11 inscr. 30, gave the inscription that had accompanied the angel relief in its last known location. See A. Zorzi 1972, 2: 600 and 603 n. 32, on lost works in Venice.

164 The last documentation we have for Palladio in Venice is his presence as a witness, together with the *proto* Antonio da Marcò, in front of Patriarch Giovanni Trevisan at San Giorgio on 26 November 1579, for the recognition of the relic in an *arca* in the altar of the old choir, which would have to be destroyed in order to lay the foundation of the new choir (it was deemed safest to remove the relic and replace it in a new container). This was in response to the papal commission of 15 October 1579 granting authority to the patriarch. The documents concerning the translation are published in Corner 1749, 276–84. Niero 1982, 133, 136–37, 138 nn. 34–38, noted the date (although as 29 November) in manuscript annotations made by Tommaso Temanza and called attention to the significance of placing Palladio in Venice so short a time before his death, but was evidently unaware of the previous publication of the documents; Timofiewitsch 1962, 163 n. 14.

165 SPV, Olmo, 294r–v, "Ma per non lasciare Paolo Orio, ebbe egli ne' suoi giorni favor singolare dalla bontà Divina, perchè essendo state sino a suoi tempi rinchiuse le Santissime ossa del Protomartire Stefano fino dal giorno ch'erano state portate a Venezia l'anno 1110. sennonchè una sola volta erano state aperte ad istanza dei Duchi d'Austria, furono nei tempi dell'Orio lasciete vedere la seconda volta, e l'occasione fu che essendosi quasi finita la Chiesa nuova l'anno 1581. pareva necessario il romper l'altar vecchio del Protomartire, e trasferire le ossa predette nella Chiesa nuova. Onde fu scritto a Roma a Papa Gregorio XIII. il quale avendo delegata la cosa al Patriarca di Venezia, allora Giovanni Trivisano, e concorrendovi il consenso del Senato, che di cosi segnalate reliquie v'era sempre stato gelosissimo, fu fatta una solennissima traslazione nel giorno dell'Assunzione della B. Vergine nel mese d'Agosto, e vi furono de' più rari personaggi presenti che si potessero allora trovare, perchè oltre il Serenissimo Principe, e Ill.mo Patriarca l'uno e l'altro Dottori di Legge, quello Principe, e questo Prelato di santissima vita, vi furono ancora Principi esteri, e non vi mancò il concorso della Sereniss.a Signoria tutta degl' Ill.mi Padri porporati, ed altri non porporati ancora, aggiunta la gran multitudine degli altri cittadini, e popolo, che mai vi fu tanta, e si nobil gente nell'isola. Quello, che nell'aprir l'arca si trovò è stato da me scritto nel secondo libro di questa istoria, che in vero bastò a confermare li presenti, e lontani ancora della verità dell'esistenza reale, e non fittizia confirmata da lettere Ebraiche, antichissime Latine, e del sangue del Protomartire, la polvere, li sassi, le ossa ed altre cose, che diedero piena sodisfazione alli più curiosi. Ed a chi non bastassero tanti manifesti testimoni quanti furono allora veduti, pare a noi di aver forse sodisfatto con altre ragioni cavate dalle cose esterne nel secondo libro, dove abbiamo scritto e provata questa traslazione, quanto si può da curioso spirito desiderare. Ma basta a noi che quelli, che si trovarono presenti restarono più che certi di tale verità! E refultò tutto ad onor di Dio Bened.o e del Protomartire ed a continezza del Sereniss.o Principe Niccolo da Ponte, Patriarca, Senatori, Abbate Monaci, e Popolo tutto."

166 Corner 1749, 281 (and reproduced in the frontmatter of his vol. 5); Cicogna 1969, 4: 486 inscr. 13. Recently, on the importance of Marc'Antonio Barbaro's presence, see esp. Guerra 2001, 103.

167 I would like to thank Bruce Boucher for this

observation, which he said had arisen from his work on the collaborative effort of Burns with Fairbairn & Boucher 1975. Earlier, Murray 1966, 603, had voiced the opinion that the presence of the double choir of San Marco for the feast would have necessitated a larger space, which he envisioned as the transept (reserving the apsidal choir for the monks). See Cooper 1996a for a confirmation of the ceremonial imperatives, cautioning about the confusion between "choir" as space and "choir" as vocal group, with the separation of voices ("double-choir") not necessarily spatially distinct, with earlier literature on this question and its implications for San Marco; Guerra 2001, 102–03.

168 ASV, SGM, B. 44, proc. 50, parchment, "Dove debe stare i Cantori quando lo Abbate canta la oratione. I do Cantori per che non è conveniente cossa i stiano aspala aspala cum lo Abbate: i stiano sopra el scali de Sancta Sanctorum: un pocha piu bassi," or "Quando i cantori che sono in choro se accompagna a quelli che sono al altare. Finita la commemoratione de S. Stephano gli altri Cantori che sono in choro vano verso laltare & ascedendo ancora loro sopra quel grado de Sancta Sanctorum apresso ali altri li sopra quel grado i cantono el Benedicamus: perche non e spacio davanti al letorino." I am basing the date on associated documents of 19 December 1562, supplications made by the monks to the Senate to substitute payment in lieu of the customary feast offered for the feast of St. Stephen. For the entire document, see Cooper 1996a.

169 Corner 1749, 201.

170 ASV, SGM, B. 21, proc. 10A "Libro," 15v; Cicogna 1969, 4: 352 n. 259a (not specified as *more veneto*); G. Zorzi 1967, 72–73, doc. 39 (as Libro, fasc. 13, 15, for 1,500 ducats). See above for the nave and south transept altars.

171 ASV, SGM, B. 21, proc. 13, loose, "Controscritto d'havere per accordii fatti et lavori aggionti come qui sotto distintamente appare," possibly 1596 (from a dated account on the other side), for itemized work totaling 4,709 ducats, 2 lire, and 12 soldi, in which the Benedict and Stephen altars are listed as 600 ducats each (Cicogna 1969, 4: 352 n. 259, following an imprecise statement by Valle, thought that the two altars together cost 600 ducats) and the three north transept altars together cost 800 ducats. Also related in the same *processo* is the "Conto longo" of Giovanni Giacomo, dating from 15 February through to 31 May 1596, for work done since 1 February 1592 through to 31 May 1596. See in G. Zorzi 1967, 50 n. 95.

172 Cicogna 1969, 4: 485–87 inscrs. 12–13.

173 SPV, Olmo, 376v, "sono opera del Tintoretto vecchio Giacomo"; BCV, Valle, 111, simply paraphrases Olmo's account, "Pale ibi Jacobi Tintoretti, Comp.*1564.*" Their opinion seems to be shared by the first published notice in Ridolfi 1965, 2: 59.

174 Pallucchini & Rossi 1982, 1: 253–54 cat. A 111.

175 A later date would make the execution, and possibly the commission, of the painting after Jacopo's death in May 1594 more likely. This was pointed out by von Hadeln (Ridolfi 1965, 2: 59 n. 4) when he noted that Cicogna had not put the date of the construction of the altar into *more veneto*.

176 Measuring 345 × 187mm., in monochrome oils on blue paper, squared for transfer. Byam Shaw 1976, 1: 209 cat. 778, with previous literature, connects the sketch to the British Museum group. Other drawings are attributed to Domenico and associated with the painting in Tietze & Tietze-Conrat 1944, 283 cat. 1634: Florence, Uffizi, 13006f, a black chalk drawing of a male bending over (again the pose seems too generic to relate it specifically to the *Martyrdom of St. Stephen*); Uffizi, 12947f, a black chalk drawing of a male bending over and advancing (P. Rossi 1975a, 25, as Jacopo, no connection to San Giorgio is mentioned); Cambridge, Fitzwilliam, 2252v, black chalk with white highlighting on light brown paper, a composition sketch squared for transfer (in the opinion of the Keeper, Mr. D.F. Scrase, more probably related to the *Battle of the Adige* in the Doge's Palace).

177 Pallucchini & Rossi 1982, 1: 253–54 cat. A 111, note that literature subsequent to Ridolfi (1648) gave the painting to Domenico, which they felt was confirmed by the sketch. On Domenico's graphic style, see P. Rossi 1975b (pt. 1), 205–11 (for San Giorgio, 209–10 and 211 n. 36); P. Rossi 1984, 57–81. It is interesting to note the genesis of another Congregation commission in 1597 to Domenico that has been documented graphically, the *Consignment of the Keys to St. Peter* (Modena, Galleria Estense) for Santi Pietro e Paolo in Reggio Emilia, for which there is also a contract of 1601 naming Domenico as the artist. The multiple sketches are discussed by Bauer 1978, 55–56, and also on San Giorgio, 54 and n. 60; Bauer 1975, 157–58 and n. 125, for San Giorgio.

178 Stockdale 1980, 62–81.

179 The Marcian lion places one paw upon the pages of the Gospel – open in times of peace and closed in times of war. Selmi 1973 discusses the political implications of the book in Venice.

180 SPV, Olmo, 381. For the term "coordinated altarpieces," see Humfrey 1990.

181 Palladio 1997, 7. The height of the pedestals also find their justification in Palladio's words; in speaking of the Composite order he defines the pedestal as one-third the height of the column, but continues saying that the ancients did not make it a rule to have pedestals "larger for one order than another" so he discusses the various proportions of pedestals in different examples from ancient buildings (Bk. 1, ch. 19, 51), Palladio 1997, 55. Bertotti Scamozzi 1968, 17–18), bk. 4, states that the exterior pedestals of San Giorgio also conform to these rules of

proportion, "Il maestoso Prospetto è decorato da un Ordine Composito co' Piedistalli sostenuti da un Zocco alto piedi 3, nell'altezza del quale sono contenuti sette gradini che giungono sino al piano del Tempio. Quattro sono le Colonne che fregiano il corpo principale di questa Facciata co' loro sopraornati, oltre i quali trovasi un gran Frontone con Acroterj e Statue. Il Piedistallo è alto quasi un terzo delle Colonne; ed esse sono poco meno di 10 diametri." For literature on precedents in the use of high pedestals on exterior façades, see Boucher 1998, 170–71.

182 The most recent extended analysis is Guerra 2002; see also Battilotti 1999, 495–96 cat. 116*; Boucher 1998, 166–70; Cooper 1990a.

183 Leccisotti 1939, 65 (18 April 1440); cited in Isermeyer 1968, 45 and 56 n. 18. This occurred, for example, at Santa Giustina, when the Chapter General had recourse to a model in their deliberations over the form of the new church in 1498. This stricture was repeated, such as in the *Regula* of the Cassinese Congregation published in Venice in 1580, "Nullas verò Praelatorum audeat mutare ipsos Modellos, aut fabricas, per alios inceptas, nisi Capituli Generalis, vel saltem Visitatorum, addito etiam peritorum consilio" (10).

184 Temanza 1966, 379–80, "Custodivasi intatto il di lui modello (di cui negli anni passati c'era ancor qualche avanzo), che servì poi di norma a chi in apresso fu destinato a soprantendervi." For the records of the model from 25 November 1565 to 12 March 1566, see Cicogna 1969, 4: 331 n. 214; Magrini 1845, Annot. 41, xxii; G. Zorzi 1967, 64, doc. 18. Guerra 2002, 294 n. 67, proposes that the model Temanza saw was a later one by Sorella.

185 SPV, Olmo, 379v, "lasciando ai suoi successori la loro parte, avendo dato a questi il tipo, o modello, rarissimo nel principio, che vi restò fabbricato dopo la sua partenza."

186 Carpo 2001, 171 n. 82, on the processual nature of Renaissance building; amply demonstrated in the arguments presented by Guerra 2001, 93–110; Guerra 2002, 276–95. The issue of term rather than life tenancy strongly impacted patronage practices among the upper echelon of the Congregation, whose mobility contributed to determining broader patterns of patronage among houses; for examples, see Cooper 1991; Beltramini 1995.

187 BUP, Potenza, 35r–v (41r–v), "ornamento del*le* lettere logica filosofia et theologia nelle quelle professione . . . essendo monaco, nelle altre scientie poi et principalmente al Architetura et Giometria per natural Inclinatione perche sia nato à quello et col occasione de questa fabrica dela chiesa diede tal saggio del suo Intelletto de felice et rara reuscita come effetualmente si e, visto in S. Paulo de Roma essendo sue cellario nella fabrica de Monte Cavallo, Ravenna, in S. Giustina havendo se puo dire renovata tutto il monastero con nova pianta et maggior benefitii se sperano et dentro et fuora del monastero," 39 (45), "In

questo monastero in honorarlo inalzarlo polirlo et arechirlo, ma hancora bisognerria dire quelli benefiti de fabriche de argenterie de debiti pagati et richezze aquistate in quelli monasteri dove e stato priore et Abbate in S. Paulo de Roma in S. Vidale de Ravenna in S. Giorgio de Venetia et quella bella faciata et prospettiva dela Chiesa honore et grandezza de quella Cita de Venetia, et finalmente qui in Sta. Justina benefiti signalati dentro et fuora del monastero."

188 ASV, SGM, B. 21, proc. 13, loose, dated 1 August 1571, the *ochio* "in mezo la fazada della chiesa supra la cornise grande" was executed by Bortolo di Domenico and Andrea dalla Vecchia "secondo la forma della sagoma" of Palladio. Cicogna 1969, 4: 331 n. 214 (*ochio*), 354 n. 272 (Tizianello); G. Zorzi 1967, 67, doc. 28. There is also an account of 1572 for the *ochio* in the same *processo*, included in the "Conti- Libro maestro della fabbrica (1566–72)." The discrepancy between the interior and exterior placement of the *ochio* has long troubled scholars, and been explained as a departure from a solution by Palladio for the façade, in which a portico was envisioned; for further discussion, see Ackerman 1977c, 12, who noted the *ochio* would interrupt the exterior inscription of the executed façade; Isermeyer 1980, 261–62, accommodated by a later solution for a portico and changed design of the retrochoir; Guerra 2002, 281–82, with the most recent explanation that a portico was part of Palladio's original design. It should be noted that Palladio was apparently untroubled by a similar discrepancy in the interruption of the exterior cornice of the transept by an internal window built under his supervision. A suggestive parallel in Palladio's treatment of the *ochio* exists at San Francesco della Vigna and has been analyzed by Foscari & Tafuri 1983, 155; as well as Morresi 2000, 150.

189 He describes the capitals as a mix of Ionic and Corinthian and the bases as a mix of Attic and Ionic, in Palladio 1997, 273, and for preparatory studies, see 374 n. 108; on London, RIBA XIV, 2, see Lewis 2000, 88–89 cat. 35 and fig. 38, with earlier literature, dating the drawing to 1541, and illustrating the prototype from the old narthex of the Baptistry later incorporated into the Chapel of Santa Rufina.

190 SPV, Olmo, 379, "Ma avanti partiamo di chiesa, è da ricordarsi, che vi sono molti nichi, ne' quali vi anderanno dentro le proprie statue, e che in tanto ne sono quattro di stucco, che rappresentano in tutta eccellenza i quattro Evangelisti, e sono opera di Alessandro Vittoria mai abbastanza lodati." The statues are signed on the base ALEXANDER VITTORIA F. and recorded in his account book in 1574 (between 2 and 30 October), on which see Cooper 1990b, 264–66, for further sources, with an account of the so-called rivalry over the commission of the high altar; most of the niche sculptures were filled in the mid-to-late

seventeenth century, see G. Rossi 1969, 268; Cicogna 1969, 4: 344–45 n. 245.

191 On this drawing and its identification with a Florentine project, (after Morrogh, 1985, 107–09 cat. 50), see Lewis 2000, 243–46 cat. 112; for the restoration of the drawing to a Venetian context, see Battilotti 1999, 489–90 cat. 97*. A philological analysis of Palladio's drawings for sepulchral monuments can be found in Burns 1979, 18–29; on the aedicule, see Burns 1980, 166–67 cat. VII, 7. For Vittoria's importance in the introduction of the bust-format, also externally from the 1580s, see T. Martin 1998.

192 Wittkower 1962, 94. There are widely diverging interpretations of the relationship of the drawing to the façade as first planned and as executed; see, for example, Isermeyer 1980, 261; Isermeyer 1972, 111–12, who assigns the project to the re-thinking of the church plan *circa* 1579; Frommel 1977, 111–14; Burns with Fairbairn & Boucher, 1975, 142–43; summarized in Lewis 2000, 246–48 cat. 113. The drawing is crucial to the recent argument put forward by Guerra 2002, 281–82, who persuasively demonstrates how Palladio would accommodate the *ochio* within a portico, although he places it in relation to the original project (whereas at the time of the completion of the circumference in 1575 the excavations did not provide for such an extension, as the documents indicate they strictly followed the foundation walls); Palladio was certainly thinking about porticoed temples in the mid-1570s, after the publication of the *Four Books*, and during his development of a solution for San Petronio in Bologna, in which he shifts from his earlier notion of the basilica, and which will be reflected in his project proposals for Il Redentore (on which see below, Part V). Although generally accepted as the only original drawing by Palladio for San Giorgio, evidence that has been cited against a strict association is the absence of correspondence with the internal system of the church, for the drawing shows both the major and minor orders as Corinthian, and does not differentiate the major order by placing it on high pedestals. In the upper left corner of the drawing, the pilaster group sketched there does not correspond with those executed, and their Doric capitals would seem to indicate that the group may belong to a different project altogether. Palladio's custom of considering diverse solutions to projects is demonstrated in the series of drawings for San Petronio in Bologna, see Timofiewitsch 1980, 237–38, who first compares London, RIBA XIV, 12 to a project *circa* 1579 for San Petronio (Oxford, Worchester College, H.T. 68 [further literature in Lewis 2000, 256–57 cat. 118]), which accords in many respects in style and conception of the temple.

193 Gaier 2002a, 21, for the program of the façade set into a general context, 21–27; and in

relation to the history and decoration of San Giorgio, see Cooper 1990a; Cooper 1990b, 389–412.

194 An influential view has been that of Wittkower 1962, 94, who felt that the two systems of major and minor orders were not well coordinated and therefore not by Palladio, but were an alteration of his design of "superimposed temple fronts" made by the later executor of the façade; cf., Burns with Fairbairn & Boucher 1975, 142, for a critical response to Wittkower's analysis, in which the correspondence to the internal system of the church is noted. It is instructive that a criticism commonly directed against the façade of San Francesco della Vigna – that the continuous high basement for both the major and minor orders causes problems in adapting their relative proportions (in the portal, for example) – is similar to that directed against San Giorgio; see Foscari & Tafuri 1983, 152. A predecessor is Giovanni Maria Falconetto's parish church at Codevigo, where the columns and pedimented aedicules of the first story are raised on high pedestals, while the niches flanked by pilasters on the upper story are set into the wall without supporting elements. See Forssman 1966, 60, and more recently, Boucher 1998, 170. On Palladio and this motif in antiquity, see Burns 1980a, 103–17; Guerra 2002, 279 and 291 n. 16, as being linked to triumphal architecture (291–92 n. 21, following Decio Gioseffi), with a convincing comparison to the alternate reading of the façade as intersecting temple fronts (278 and 290 n. 5, by Wittkower). The continuation of the minor entablature behind the major columns disrupts a reading of the area as an attic, found both at Palladio's San Francesco and San Pietro, as Guerra describes (289–90), a product of the executors' misunderstanding.

195 Cicogna 1969, 4: 354 n. 276, for del Moro, and 402–04 inscr. 1, for the central epigraph, inscr. 2–3, for Memo and Ziani, 413–51 inscr. 6, for Donà; Cooper 1990b, 396–97, with further documentary references for this period of the decoration in the decade following the completion of the façade in 1610 (begun under Abbot Perozzi, continued by Alvise Zuffo da Padova, 1612–17, and Pietro Aronzio di Valtellina, 1617–22), including the five statues on the pediment commissioned from Gian Battista Albanese of Vicenza on 4 September 1618 (also considered a *terminus ante quem* for Del Moro's works), in ASV, SGM, B. 21, proc. 10A "Libro," 52, to which there were later substitutions (410–11); and 402–04, for the sepulchral monument with an anonymous portrait-bust of Doge Leonardo Donà over the interior portal commissioned by his heirs after his death. See Gaier 2002a, 99–106, on the Maggior Consiglio 1523 prohibition of public dogal effigies and inscriptions.

196 Cooper 1990b, 404–08, the bust of Doge Marc'Antonio Memo's tomb on the interior

façade is also signed by Giulio del Moro; Gaier 2002a, 22, agrees that the historicizing costume reinforces the message of the renewal of the tradition of the "case vecchie dogali," and see 23–28, on the rights of families for the renewal of their sepulchers in the event of their destruction due to construction. The selective nature of the recognition of those rights at San Giorgio (which produced fascinating legal opinions on this point), as indicated by the absence of some former occupants of exterior memorials, notably the Civran and Michiel families, underlines the desire of new patrons to occupy areas of privilege, such as Memo and Donà, and the monks' willingness to accommodate current wielders of power as well as to express the history of their corporate identity through their association with these figures.

197 Cooper 2001, for the "myth of Venice," and the historian chosen to defend the Republic, Cassinese monk Fortunato Olmo, chronicler of San Giorgio; Cooper 1990b, 390–95, on Donà, whose proposed epitaph was "Here lie the remains of Leonardo Donato Doge. PUBLICAE LIBERTATIS APPRIME STUDIOSI," 408–10, on Ziani (this argument was also published in Cooper 1990a); Gaier 2002a, 21–22. See Bouwsma 1968, on this period and his formulation of the relation between the Renaissance and the concept of republican liberty; also Cozzi 1958, for an influential characterization.

198 Palladio 1997, 215. See the discussion above of the drawing in London, RIBA XIV, 12, regarding the *ochio*, for its relation to a porticoed project, esp. Guerra 2002, 281. Discussions of this project, as in Lewis 2000, 246–48 cat. 113, often refer to Palladio's study of the Temple of Serapis, London, RIBA XI/23r (232–33 cat. 105). It should be noted that there was not the clear view of the new church as we see it today, until the abbot who completed the façade, Domenico Perozzi, was compelled to tear down some warehouses due to the complaints made by Fortunato Olmo to Doge Donà, see Cooper 1990b, 390–93.

199 Timofiewitsch 1962, 160–63; Timofiewitsch 1980, 238–39, 243–44, reiterates a dating of *circa* 1579, as evidence of Palladio's late interest in porticoed churches, to be differentiated from his earlier projects for church façades, such as San Francesco della Vigna and, probably, the model and first project for San Giorgio.

200 It is probable that 857 is later than 857b since it shows the correct number of columns for the Cloister of the Cypresses; Isermeyer 1980, 267 n. 12, whose main focus is the *modello* of 1565, finding a portico to be a later solution by Palladio; Puppi 1986, 272–73, although differing in declaring the drawing autograph, had initially followed G. Zorzi 1967, 52, who had concluded that the portico seemed to be drawn in a lighter ink than the remainder of the plan and thus was a later addition, dating *circa* 1583. From observation of the original

drawing, its integrity can be maintained despite its appearance in photographs, which is due to water damage sustained in the lower left half of the folio that lightened the color of the ink in that area. For different reasons, C. Frommel 1977, 118, had earlier maintained the integrity of the drawing. Guerra 2002, maintains that the portico was part of Palladio's first design and model, as supported by an early role in the design process for London, RIBA XIV, 12, and that ASV, MM 857 (his 857/1) is a later architect's (possibly Scamozzi) "re-proposal" of Palladio's original portico project.

201 Most recently, see Guerra 2002, 285–87, who dates the drawing to 1581, during the period when Marc'Antonio Barbaro made his visits to San Giorgio, and notes the design characteristics that suggest Scamozzi, although possibly executed by Bortolo di Domenico. The planar style of the executed façade also has been seen as close to Scamozzi, active in Venice until his death in 1616, a theory first proposed by Tomaso Temanza in the mid-eighteenth century; Temanza 1966, 379, based this on a document he attributed to Scamozzi in the San Giorgio archives, but the existence of the document has subsequently been discredited. See Cicogna 1969, 4: 330–31 n. 214, and Magrini 1845, 64. Barbieri 1966, 341–42, attempts to conserve Temanza's position through the support of stylistic criteria, maintaining that the façade of San Giorgio was too important to be executed by a "minor" architect. Equally, the converse can be argued, that Scamozzi was too important an architect not to be mentioned in any document or history of the church, see further below.

202 SPV, Olmo, 383, "e seguendo nelle incominciate imprese preparò abbondante materia di marmi, per farne la facciata della chiesa, e ne furono condotti tanti dall'Istria a Venezia, ch'empirono tutta la piazza vecchia." On the construction, in addition see now Guerra 2002, 276–95, esp. 267 and 293 n. 55, where he identified the twenty-four columns (half each in bronze-colored and red-colored stone) ordered 2 June 1595 by Alabardi as intended for an atrium (the term in the document is "portego") closer to the type of four-sided porticoed enclosure of the old church, in ASV, SGM, B. 21, proc. 10, "Libro," 29, noting that nothing more is heard about this project; also Guerra 2001, 105–06, discusses the chromatic implications of these columns (and further notes that the 1597 agreement was also originally for a Veronese marble rather than the Istrian stone from which it was eventually made, see 110 n. 77), and for the interior in relation to Palladio's usage.

203 SPV, Olmo, 380v, described how Alabardi incurred the debt: "Nè perchè fosse l'anno della carestia cosi grande, qual fu il primo del suo governo restò di far ogni ordinaria limosina, e perchè conosceva conosceva [sic] esservene maggior bisogno, tanto più solenne

la ordinò. E si sa, che per ajutare i Contadini, o abitatori delle nostri ville, fu la prima impresa un debito, che addossò al Monastero di 6000"; and 383v, the effect it had on constructing the façade: "Ma lo ritardò che gli cominciarono a mancar danari, che non facesse quanto voleva, sebbene fatto un debito di sei mille ducati, cominciò quando potè." On the beginning of construction, BUP, Valle, "Breve chronichon," 90, "Iacobus S: Felicis Brixiensis Abbas. Hic marmoreum Templi Frontispicium e Lapidibus quos Michael Abbas paraverat, cepit à fundamentis haud parumque supra solum plurimis ~~solum~~ aliis marmoribus paratis sublimavit." Cicogna 1969, 4: 342 n. 236. Stringa, in his edition of Sansovino 1604, 168v, also remarked on the façade as already under construction, "S'è già cominciato il suo frontispicio ammirabile tutto di viva pietra istriana." See also Isermeyer 1972, 134 n. 12; and now Guerra 2001, 105–06; Guerra 2002, 287–88.

204 Sorella was proposed by R. Gallo 1955, 43–45, after the document in ASV, SGM, B. 21 (given as B. 89 bis, a provisionary collocation), proc. 13, not numbered, "Misure et quantità di Pietre vive che anderanno nella facciata della chiesa fatte da m. Simon Sorella Protho." Sorella had held the post of *proto* of San Marco since 21 June 1574 from the Procuratoria de Supra. Sorella counter-signed Palladio's recommendations of 27 December 1577 for the restoration of the Doge's Palace (Lorenzi 1868, 418; Cecchetti 1886, 82), see Part V. A lack of contemporary citations associating an architect of stature, such as Vincenzo Scamozzi, with San Giorgio first led some scholars to propose that Palladio's project was executed by a lesser known architect, i.e., Ricci 1859, 3: 380; Guerra 2002, 287–90, elaborates on Sorella's role at San Giorgio, and draws an important connection to his work for the abbess of San Lorenzo, Paola Priuli, sister of the patriarch of Venice.

205 ASV, SGM, B. 21, proc. 10A "Libro," 37, dated 6 June 1597 in the presence of Abbot Michele Alabardi, Procurator Leonardo Donà, *proto* Simone Sorella, sculptor Girolamo Campagna and stonemason Giovanni Giacomo. The agreement called for payment by the monastery to be made from time to time with an initial payment of 50 ducats; subsistence wages were set at 3 lire per day excluding holidays; necessary trips would be paid for, as well as materials, such as the wood and iron needed for cutting the stone. Cicogna 1969, 4: 341 n. 231. Guerra 2002, 289, also makes a good case that Donà's opposition to Marc'Antonio Barbaro's plans by Palladio for Il Redentore and by Scamozzi for the Marciana Library adaptation may reflect his similar influence at San Giorgio on the elimination of a portico. On Il Redentore, see Part V, and for the Marciana Library, see Cooper 1995.

206 ASV, SGM, B. 21, proc. 10A "Libro," 45v, 30 June 1607, an accord with Giulio di Bortolo

and Giovanni Giacomo di Pietro; see Cicogna 1969, 4: 334 n. 275; G. Zorzi 1967, 75, doc. 46. Further documents for the façade (and cloister), with dates between 1597–1603, in ASV, SGM, B. 22, proc. 13A–II, fasc. 4, unnumbered, do not give the names of the stonemasons assembling cut stone, but do provide another reference to a prototype being followed, referring to the "sagoma del proto" and "disegno et sagoma"; these refer to template drawings, such as the one by Giovanni Giacomo di Pietro Comini in ASV, MM, 857d, see Cooper 1994b, 500 cat. 118. Also see Burns with Fairbairn & Boucher 1975, 253–54. These were normally executed as the work progressed, so even if Palladio's model was being followed, such details would have to be produced by the current supervisor of the work. Guerra 2002, 287, interprets the model referred to in 1607 as one by Sorella reflecting his 1597 estimate for the materials needed (because he posits that Palladio's 1565 model was porticoed); however, no records reflect a new model being commissioned, and the word could be ambiguous in referring to a two- or three-dimensional prototype, so another explanation may be that the stonemasons were supplied with templates by the current supervisor (possibly one of them) after Sorella's estimate of a façade design that perforce reverted to Palladio's original model (prior to his re-design of the church when he added a portico). An example of a profile drawing for the pedestals is reproduced in Guerra 2002, 288 fig. 17, from 9 March 1601, in ASV, SGM, B. 22, proc. 13A–II, fasc. 4, unnumbered; there is another dated 4 April 1603 among these sheets.

207 As discussed above, Bortolo di Domenico, with his son Giulio, and Pietro Comini, with his son Giovanni Giacomo, were all involved in executing the stonework for the altars between 1592–96, based on Palladio's model for the Bollani chapel (Bortolo's last notice at San Giorgio is 1595); the two sons were later working together on the façade, documented between 1607–11, which reinforces the interdependence of the executed designs for the altars and façade, and their allegiance to Palladio. ASV, SGM, B. 21, proc. 10A "Libro," between 7v–24v. On the altars, see in Cicogna 1969, 4: 342 n. 238, 352–54 nn. 259–a, 267, 269; G. Zorzi 1967, 50 n. 95, 71–75, docs. 37–44 (as fasc. 13).

208 In the 25 June 1594 contract for the high altar, ASV, SGM, B. 21, proc. 10A, "Libro," 21. Cicogna 1969, 4: 242 n. 38; G. Zorzi 1967, 73, doc. 41; Timofiewitsch 1972, 260.

209 The particular profile of Palladio's cantiere has been drawn by Puppi 1980b; also Puppi 1986, 205–11. Antonio Paleari di Marcò muratore, who worked under Palladio both at Santa Maria della Carità and at San Giorgio, recounted how Palladio left the execution of his designs to the various specialists. Discussed in Zocconi 1978, 184–86. On his role as supervisor, see Burns with Fairbairn & Boucher 1975, 259–60; Burns 1991, on the Basilica organization.

210 BUP, Valle, "Breve chronichon," 90v, "Dominicus Perotius Abbas S. Georgii oppido Coloniensi oriundus quod est in Agro Vicentino, Frontispicio marmoreo absolvendo incubit, tum marmoreum ope quae sibi Iacobus Sanctfelicis paraverat, tum plurimis ipse coactis." Cicogna 1969, 4: 342 n. 236.

211 Sansovino 1968, 225; Cicogna 1969, 4: 405 inscr. 4. Isermeyer 1980, 260, interprets the inscription to mean that the church was begun (condidere), though not completed on Palladio's model of 1565.

212 Timofiewitsch 1980, esp. 243, on the shared typology of the façades of San Pietro and San Giorgio, as well as to the only one to be executed during his life at San Francesco della Vigna, and the role of the model of San Giorgio for Smeraldi at San Pietro; Guerra 2002, 288–89, as he identifies Palladio's 1565 model with a portico, sees Sorella as relying on San Pietro for the realization of his simplified solution for the façade of San Giorgio. Regardless of the sequence, both find a strong circulation of influence between Palladio's executed works, surviving project materials, and between executors and patrons, so that, as Guerra puts it, Palladio becomes both model and copy. In my view, this precedes the phase of Palladianism, where his work may be used as inspiration without his personal input and influence in the building process having been established as a contributory factor (and see Part VI, on Le Zitelle for an example).

213 Vasari 1966, 6: 195.

214 In 1134 the order was established in Venice by canons from Ravenna, first reformed by Pope Martin V in 1421 as the Congregazione di Santa Maria di Fregionaia, then attached to the Lateran by Pope Eugenius IV in 1445; for the Augustinians in Venice, see Pedani 1985, 46. Fogolari 1924, for the history of the Carità before Palladio; Bassi 1973 remains the fundamental monograph; with some essential revisions summarized in Puppi 1986, 175–78, notably the reassignment of two plans (in ASV, SMC, serie I, B. 29 [previously as B. 2], not numbered, parchment plan, and Serie III, B. 17, fasc. "Documenti relativi a lavori," not numbered, plan) as belonging to the phase of construction before Palladio, for which documents indicate activity between 1538 and 1555. This period also coincided with the Venetian cardinal Gasparo Contarini being named co-protector of the Canons (in 1540), together with Cardinal Ercole Gonzaga (from 1528), and Pope Paul III's desire for reform of their Chapter General; see McNair 1967, 183–88. On the Lateran Canons: Egger 1975; Widloecher 1929, 41–42; and the Carità, Asquini 1992.

215 Bassi 1973, 22 n. 8, suggests Gregorio, son of Doge Marco, and a Fra Gregorio "Nobili Veneto" (francesco diGabriele; Barbaro, "Albori, I, "F") bought property in the 1540s. The Barbarigos and Barbaros were key patrician connections for Palladio at the Carità and Il Redentore (see Part V), supporters of the insertion of a Romanist calssical style. For dispersed elements in church, esp. A. Zorzi 2001, 343–47.

216 In 1260 it began as a Scuola dei Battuti, and came to the Carità in 1344; see Pignatti, ed. 1981, 27–40; Gramigna Dian & Perissa Torrini, 1981a, 58–61. For more on the institution of the scuole, see Part VI.

217 Bassi 1973, 13; Fogolari 1924, 63–64; Widloecher 1929, 73–104, esp. 101–04 on privileges.

218 On the Doge's Palace cycle in the Great Council Hall, see Wolters 1987, 162–78, esp. 171; further bibliography on the "Peace of Venice" is in Cooper 2001. On the ritual observance, mentioned in Doglioni 1692, 47; Renier Michiel 1817, I: 305–29; and Tassini 1933, 141; see Muir 1981, 118, who gives manuscript sources; Fabris 1988, 77, the visit garnered a papal indulgence.

219 Logan 1995, ch. 17, 472–93, for an analysis of Fiamma's preaching and career, with biographical information based on Gradenigo, "Vita Gabriele Fiamma," 1871.

220 McGinnis 1995 compares to modern media, 66–67; contemporary descriptions of its ubiquity, 82–83.

221 McGinnis 1995, 29–30, 49–52.

222 Logan 1995, 473, describes as "works of art."

223 Trans. from Logan 1995, 481; from Fiamma 1574, 43v–44r.

224 Note the original plate was not corrected for being in reverse, although some of the later editors, such as Isaac Ware, took it upon themselves to do so. See a reoriented reproduction of the 1570 edition in Bassi 1973, fig. XXXIX.

225 Bassi 1973, 50–51, 134, argues convincingly that there was a means of access from the upper story to the barco above the choir; Fogolari 1924, 80–84, 105–18, documents the building of the barco between 1460 and 1463, but his comparisons for reconstruction refer to widely diverging types; A. Zorzi 2001, 343, notes some opinions that the barco was removed circa 1584.

226 Bassi 1973, 115–16; after Wittkower 1962, 80–81; Ackerman 1977b, 153–56; and Pane 1961, 293.

227 Temanza 1778, 312; given in full in Bassi 1973, 133–35, who had already begun to incline against the association; on the Accesi, see Part II, above.

228 Palladio 1570, Bk. 2, ch. 1, 3, "a Gentil' huomeni grandi, e massimamente di Republica," has been translated in Palladio 1997, 77, as "for great men and especially those in public office," whereas I would suggest that the use of the term "Republic" in the Venetian context was not accidental, and so would retain Isaac Ware's "for great men, and particularly those in a republic" of 1738 (Palladio 1965, 37).

229 Recevuto for 7 March 1561–14 March 1562

(with reference for salary to 1 June), and the "Sommario delle scritture" for 30 August 1569, and 13 June 1570 in ASV, SMC, Serie I, B. 29 (formerly Sala diplomatica Regina Margherita, LXXIV–13), and Serie III, B. 2, no. 3011, and no. 3024, respectively; in Bassi 1973, 141–42, doc. V, and 140, doc. I; G. Zorzi 1965, 245–46, doc. 1, doc. 2; Tiepolo et al. 1980, 46–47 cat. 103, cat. 105; Puppi 1986, 177, gives a citation for the original of the "Sommario" in ASP, Notarile, S. de Astori, B. 3576, 396r, and B. 3579, 902r. Piana 1998–99, 318 and fig. 12, notes of the remaining fourteen original of the thirty-one terracotta *bucrania* in the cloister frieze, beside four of them is the date "1562," coinciding with the date of Palladio's supervision. I would like to thank Mario Piana and Guido Beltramini for the opportunity of visiting the Carità with them and members of the Centro Palladiano and seeing the results of the conservation campaign.

230 Paleari was paid on 5 June 1569 for his work, with reference to the original *accordo* he entered on the same date as Palladio, 1 June 1561, in an arbitration settlement of 18 October 1569, "Inventario," in ASV, SMC, previously as Parte I, B. 26; in Bassi 1973, 142, doc. VII; G. Zorzi 1965, 246, doc. 3. For Paleari's allegiance to Palladio and further associations, see Cooper 1995, 112–14, 116; also see earlier in this chapter, under San Giorgio Maggiore, and in Part V, under the Doge's Palace fires.

231 Bassi 1973, 130.

232 Sansovino 1581, 96v; Bassi 1973, 131, notes that Sansovino is the only Venetian contemporary to mention it, and Vasari alone among Italians (83); she then analyzes the latter's statement in connection with what he might have seen in his week-long visit to Venice in May 1566, and concludes that it is primarily dependent on what Palladio would publish in the *Four Books*, and therefore misleading to later authors, who thought that more of the complex had been built, but that his mention of the stair and of materials do indicate a first-hand acquaintance.

233 Wotton 1968, 43–44, in Bassi 1973, 84.

234 Jones 1742, 71, pl. XXII; Jones 1970, I: 25 (transcription), 2: 29 (facsimile); his *Notes and Remarks* in Bassi 1973, 125 n. 3.

235 "Sommario delle scritture" for 30 August 1569, and 13 June 1570 in ASV, SMC, Serie III, B. 2, no. 3011, and no. 3024; in Bassi 1973, 140, doc. I; G. Zorzi 1965, 245–47, docs. 2 and 3; Tiepolo et al. 1980, 47 cat. 105; Puppi 1986, as in n.229 above.

236 Piana 1998–99, 311–12, discussing the still open question of whether the atrium capitals were of Istrian stone (not recorded in the documents), or terracotta painted in white with only the abacus in stone (used in other Palladian buildings, such as Il Redentore). Piana suggests that the use of various coverings, from refined plasters to crushed brick to *marmorino*, served several aesthetic and functional purposes, also varying according to their loca-

tions, including chromatic richness, protection of the surface, and homogenization of color and surface.

237 Giovanni Antonio Moschini, "Atrium and Cloister of the Convento della Carità in 1828," in Moschini 1847 (the engravings are missing from many copies). Bassi 1973, 75, was unable to verify Temanza's attribution of the new atrium to an abbot Gozzi.

238 Bassi 1973, 76–81, provides a sensitive account of the modifications according to nineteenth-century mores and of subsequent restorations; for recent conservation reports, see Piana 1998–99, 313–19, on the peristyle materials, "è in cotto, lavorato per rimanere a vista e rifinito con una cromia rossa." He also discusses Palladio's use of local techniques and structural approaches imported from the mainland.

239 Jones 1970, 1: 25; from the transcription of his *Notes and Remarks*, 29, in Bassi 1973, 125 n. 3, who also gives in full an important estimate of the stonework by the stonecutters Antonio da Bissone a San Vidal and Girolamo Testagrossa, 142–46, doc. VIII, of [1] March 1573, in ASV, SMC, previously as Parte I, B. 6.

240 Puppi 1986, 178, summarizes prior comparisons such as to the Theater of Marcellus, the Coliseum in Rome, the Arena in Pola, and the work of the architects Bramante, Michelangelo, and Antonio da Sangallo the Younger; many of these passages given in Bassi 1973, 111–16; Boucher 1998, 153, notes also the proposed reconstruction of the courtyard of the Theater of Marcellus by Baldassare Peruzzi, which thus combined ancient and modern in the same monument; Piana 1998–99, 313–14, notes three drawings by Palladio after the Portico of Pompey ("Crypta Balbi"), London, RIBA, XI, 1–2r–v, which show his familiarity with the monument, with its variety of covering materials from marble veneer to plaster to stucco.

241 Pane 1961, 293; Ackerman 1977b, 155. Note that Bramante's work in Milan prior to Rome did use brick and terracotta as materials in the Lombard tradition, e.g., the cloister of Sant'Ambrogio. De Angelis d'Ossat 1966, in making a convincing analysis to the courtyard of the Farnese Palace finds it necessary to downplay the influence of Bramante, as well as the Coliseum (43).

242 Bassi 1973, 31, 16, and 21; see now Asquini 1992, 233. Ackerman 1977b, 156, aptly described its Venetian reception as being due to a design that seemed "anachronistically classical in the unclassical mid-Cinquecento."

243 Widloecher 1929, 277–83 (15 September); Egger 1975, 105; Asquini 1992, 233.

244 Bassi 1973, 33, on contemporary use at San Giorgio; Puppi 1986, 175, on Santa Lucia. For the Palazzo Trevisan, see Part II; Asquini 1992, 235–36, proposes the meaningful influence of the Lateran Baptistery, with its apsidal narthex and octagonal nave; it is presented as the Baptistery of Constantine in the *Four Books*, Bk. 4, ch. 16, 61 [misprinted as 53], and is placed

immediately before Bramante's Tempietto, probably because Palladio thought it was "modern" (Palladio 1997, 273); for its use at San Giorgio, see above.

245 Palladio 1570, Bk. 2, ch. 6, 29 (Palladio 1997, 105).

246 Piana 1998–99, 311, 314, draws on his conservation campaigns of 1984 and 1994–95, subsequent to Bassi's publications, to revise knowledge of the materials from remaining traces liberated from earlier restorations: esp. 320 n. 7, believes that the pilasters behind the columns (sheathed in marble in 1948) might originally have matched the materials and coloration of the cornice (rather than the plaster of the walls as suggested by Bassi 1973, 80).

247 Palladio 1570, Bk. 2, ch. 6, 29 (Palladio 1997, 105).

248 Bassi 1973, 63, discusses discrepancies between the current disposition of spaces and openings with what was built, and between both of those with what was published in the *Four Books*, 1570, Bk. 2, ch. 6, 29–32 (Palladio 1997, 105–08) and differences even between the plan and elevation (her pl. 30), notably the openings into the sacristy, such as the current door (in plan as a door, in elevation and originally built as a window).

249 St. Augustine is shown writing: "Ante omnia fratres carissimi diligatur Deus deinde prosimus quia ista praecepta sunt [prima] ut observetis praecipumus in monasterio constituti, primum, propter quod in unum congregatis estis; ut unanimes habitetis in uno et sit vobis anima una et cor unum in Deo." Nepi Scirè 1995, 84–85, with earlier bibliography; the possible identification of the canon at St. Augustine's shoulder as Francesco da Venezia is after Bassi 1980, 20; Fogolari 1924, 92, "molti padri dei nostri della Carità."

250 Palladio 1570, Bk. 1, ch. 28, 61 (Palladio 1997, 67). See Bassi 1973, 59; who acknowledges Chastel 1965, 11.

251 For a concise history of the convent, see Franzoi & Di Stefano 1976a, 102–04, note some discrepancies in founding date (as in Sansovino 1968, 140, early date of 1192), it later came under the jurisdiction of Corpus Domini in 1444, before passing to the Augustinian nuns in 1476.

252 Stringa, in his edition of Sansovino 1604, 149, put the current population at "73." Comparative figures on the populations and comparative wealth of convents are taken from Sperling 1999, 26, who estimates three-quarters of nuns were patricians (tab. 1), in 244–45, tab. A.1, "Nuns per Convent," Santa Lucia in the years 1594–96 had a population of eighty-one, Santa Maria degli Angeli had ninety in 1564, the Vergini had sixty-five in 1564 and sixty-seven in 1594–96, and 258–59, tab. A.6, "Net Revenues of Venetian Convents, 1564," ranks them respectively no. 23 (income 852 ducats), no. 5 (3,254 ducats), and no. 4 (3,637 ducats [note the relation between population and income for the latter two]), with

264–65, tab. A.9, "The Composition of Revenues, 1564," placing the latter two in the first of four cohorts of convents and Santa Lucia in the third.

253 Magrini 1845, 262–64, is the source for this information on the starting date, which he saw in the convent archives. For previous literature and a summary of the history and attribution of the project, see Puppi 1986, 204–05.

254 Tassini 1885, 105; A. Zorzi 2001, 231–32. For the Venice train station of Santa Lucia: Uberti 1985. The inscription of the consecration of 1617 is in Sansovino 1968, 143, and quoted in most accounts of the church.

255 Pioneering article of R. Gallo 1955, esp. 25–27; significantly expanded in Puppi 1987, esp. 345–47, suggesting a date for Palladio's work as supervisor and provider of designs and details beginning prior to Leonardo's embassy to Vienna in September 1557 and shortly after his inheriting it in March, based on a letter sent to his cousin Pietro Capello on 9 April 1558 that first names Palladio there (in BCV, MS P.D. c 506/4, no. 1), and for a completion of Palladio's involvement around the date of the last document in which he is named on 26 July 1564 (in BCV, MS P.D. c 248, tomo 63, no. 13), although his activity as *proto* is primarily in early 1560 (4 January, in BCV, MS P.D. c 248 tomo 6, no. 3).

256 R. Gallo 1955, 27–29 on Marocco, 29–34 on Dolo, restored these to Palladio's built inventory. Magrini 1845, Annot., xxiv, n. 47, provides the building campaign for the villa at Marocco with *a terminus post quem* from an inscription of 14 July 1562; Lewis 2000, 130, 167, confirmed the villa at the site of present Villa Morosini-Gatterberg-Volpi, on property received from Leonardo's paternal grandmother in a division of her estate in 1560 between him and his uncle Francesco di Alvise, and believes only a modest portion of the design was constructed by 1570. The villa at Dolo may have evolved over a longer period than its actual construction, since scholars have identified several phases in the design from surviving drawings and the ideal version in the *Four Books*, which begs the question of how early Palladio met Leonardo Mocenigo. Lewis 2000, 129, hypothesizes a first phase following the marriage of Leonardo to Marina Capello on 26 November 1544 (in BCV, MS P.D. c 248, tomo 3, 9r–v, see in Puppi 1987, 343, noting the extraordinary dowry of 14,000 ducats); Lewis 2000, 164, describes a second phase as dating to when Palladio was in Venice in 1554, consistent with documentation of work by the Venetian stonemason Antonio da Bissone a San Vido paid for by Leonardo, although not naming Palladio (17 February 1553 *m.v.* [= 1554] and 14 August 1554, in BCV, MS P.D. c 248, tomo 63, fasc. 1 a–b; see in Puppi 1987, 344–45); Lewis 2000, 164–67, notes a delay in construction, since Palladio is later named with the same stonemason in 1560 (19 January 1559 *m.v.*, in BCV, MS P.D. c 248, tomo 63, no.

2, see in Puppi 1987, 346–47, who also notes parallel documentation in BCV, MS P.D. c 506/4, as given in R. Gallo 1955), suggesting the main phase of construction under Palladio, lasting until interior finishing work is noted in accounts between 24 September 1562 and 6 March 1564 (in BCV, MS P.D. c 248, tomo 63, no. 9 a-c, see in Puppi 1987, 347).

257 ASV, Dieci Savi sopra la Decima, Redecima 1566, San Marco, B. 127, no. 472, Condizione di decima di Leonardo Mocenigo, received a rent of 47 ducats and 22 grossi per year (see in Tiepolo et al. 1980, 41 cat. 82; Puppi 1987, 347–48).

258 ASV, Barbaro, "Albori," 5: 201, "Mocenigo-D." R. Gallo 1955, 29, first drew attention to the Mocenigo archives in the Correr as a source for the property transactions and building notices regarding the house in Padua and villas in Dolo and Marocco (BCV, MS P.D. c 506/4); the private archive was referred to in Lewis 2000, 164 (1st edn., 1981, 126); and greatly expanded in Puppi 1987, *passim*, who traced the main members and financial dispositions of the Foscari (BCV, MS P.D. c 506/12) and Mocenigo (BCV, MS P.D. c 248, identifying Lewis' source as vol. 63 [357 n. 44]) to establish the basis for the conditions of Leonardo's patronage of Palladio.

259 R. Gallo 1955, 34; Puppi 1987, respectively 339, 343 (23 August 1514, and 30 January 1554, in BCV, MS P.D. c 248, tomo 2, 1v–2r, and 130r–145r).

260 Puppi 1987, 343, 26 November 1544 (in BCV, MS P.D. c 248, tomo 3, 9r–v). Pellegrina's dowry was also impressive at 12,000 ducats, whereas Leonardo's mother, Elizabeth, had a respectable dowry of 6,000 ducats: Puppi 1987, respectively 339, 340 (3 January 1492 [= *m.v.* 1491], and 25 March 1522, in BCV, MS P.D. c 506/12, no. 1, and MS P.D. c 248, tomo 3, 6r–v). For comparison, a dowry of 10,000 ducats would be considered high.

261 Puppi 1987, 342, describes how Alvise directed benefits from the Foscari estate towards his son Antonio and his line (27 October 1541, in BCV, MS P.D. c 248, tomo 1, 27r–31v), so that an annual portion in lieu of the properties (equal to one-third) was settled on his other legitimate son, Francesco, and his son, Giovanni (a third son, Michele, seems to have been in disgrace), and was followed in the dispensations of Pellegrina (30 June 1543, in BCV, MS P.D. c 248, tomo 1, 33r–41r); cf. Lewis 2000, 130, cites an equal division of Pellegrina's estate between Leonardo and his uncle Francesco on 30 January 1560; note Part v below, the likely involvement of Francesco's son Alvise with the entry of Henri III.

262 Antonio died on 13 March 1557 (ASV, Barbaro, "Albori," 5: 201); Marina's will of 11 November 1545 was published on 9 May 1559 (in ASV, Notarile, Testamenti, Avidio Branca, B. 44, no. 301, see Puppi 1987, 357 n. 38); Giovanni Capello died on 20 September 1559 (see Lewis 2000, 130).

263 Information on Leonardo's political career can be found in Litta 1819–83, v. 14, "Manfredi-Pagani," pl. VIII, s.v. "Mocenigo–ramo Dalle Zogie," who states he was unable to find posts prior to the embassy; in R. Gallo 1955, 25; and references to his published ambassadorial relations in Puppi 1987, 357 n. 40. Grendler 1990, on power offices, 38–40, does not include Leonardo among the exclusive roster of "Great Office Holders."

264 Sansovino 1968, 336. On the surviving visual sources for the painting by Veronese, see Wolters 1987, 169–70, who discusses the commission of 7 January 1562 (= 1561 *m.v.*, for the allocation of the funds, in ASV, Consiglio dei Dieci, reg. 25, 69, and description, in Parti Comuni, filza 83), see in Pignatti 1976, 1: 253, doc. 20), noting that Giorgio Vasari was first to describe the painting in his *Le vite* of 1568 (1878–85, 6: 589).

265 Puppi 1987, 343, particularly laments the lack of information on Leonardo's education.

266 R. Gallo 1955, 25; Puppi 1987, 337; Lewis 2000, 129.

267 Puppi 1987, 337 and 353 n. 4, identifies the *scrigno* with one of two ebony medal cabinets mentioned in the inventory of 1573, for which he provides a partial transcription (in BCV, MS P.D. c 506/4, no. 6); for the "scrigno d'ebano *fatto a somiglianza dell'arco di Costantino*," see letter from Girolamo Bos to Nicolò Gaddi, 21 June 1578, in Bottari, ed. 1754, 1: 278; G. Zorzi 1965, 135; this letter and others testifying to the significance of the collection are transcribed in C. Brown with Lorenzoni 1999, see 74, doc. 50; on the cabinet, Thornton 1997, 72.

268 Puppi 1987, 344, as an appropriately tentative, yet plausible suggestion; Lewis 2000, 162–64, cat. 72–73, discussing London, RIBA, X/1r–v, proposes that Palladio had brought an earlier drawing of the Roman theater at Vicenza with him to Venice in 1554 to discuss it with Daniele Barbaro in relation to the Vitruvian theater, and drew a late plan on the *verso* for the villa at Dolo as he traveled via the Brenta.

269 Rental to Pinelli took place before the tax declaration of 1566 made by Leonardo, in ASV, Dieci Savi sopra la Decima, B. 127, San Marco, no. 472, 28 June 1566, see in Tiepolo et al. 1980, 41, cat. 82, in which he retains a house for his own use as well; 14–15, cat. 8, for the provenance from Pinelli of the *filza* containing Alvise Cornaro's proposal for a theater in the Venetian *laguna* (in ASV, Savi ed esecutori alle Acque, B. 986, filza 4). For Pinelli's letters to Fulvio Orsini regarding the collection, see C. Brown with Lorenzoni 1999, passim. On the intersecting circles of scientific thought between Pinelli and Jacopo Contarini, including Palladio, see Tafuri 1989, 130–35, and 251–52 n. 137; Lewis 2000, 129, proposes a congruence between the ideas represented in the Villa Vescovile supervised by Alvise Cornaro for Cardinal Bishop Francesco Pisani, Leonardo's uncle by marriage, and early designs for the villa at Dolo, dating this phase

to 1544/45 on his marriage to Marina Capello (prior to any documented work by almost a decade), and further noting his belief that Leonardo would also be related through this connection to Palladio's patron Vettor Pisani of Bagnolo (see esp. Parts I and II above). His brother-in-law, Pietro Capello, would act as his agent for the Padua house during Leonardo's embassy to Vienna, as evidenced by their correspondence in 1558 (9 and 16 April), in BCV, MS P.D. c 506/4, no. 1, see in R. Gallo 1955, 26; Puppi 1987, 337.

270 See the citation in note 269 above, "Io habito in contrà di San Vitale, in una casa delli magnifici messeri Francesco, Iacomo et Zuane Marcelli fo del magnifico messer Andrea." The Marcello Palace is actually near San Trovaso, see Bassi 1987, 507–09. I associated the figure of Giacomo di Andrea Marcello with the brothers named in the *decima*, see BMV, Cappellari Vivaro, s.v. Marcello "G."; BMV, Barbaro, "Albori," 3: 41r.

271 Grendler 1979, 330, traces Jacopo's offices in the Council of Ten and as *consigliere ducale*.

272 Sansovino 1968, 346, 371 (where Daniele Barbaro's library is mentioned). Bassi 1987, 307, hypothesizes a date for Tintoretto's frescoes with subjects from Ovid at the time of his work in the Sala Quadrato in the Doge's Palace (1565) or around the redecoration (which would be after Leonardo's death) and associates them with Jacopo Marcello's patronage (Pallucchini & Rossi 1982, I: 263, make a stylistic analogy to *Le lune e le ore* [formerly Berlin, Kaiser Friedrich Museum, destr.] of 1580–81, based, however, only on engravings by Andrea Zucchi in Lovisa 1720, 2: 15–16).

273 Michele Foscari had left 600 ducats for the construction of his sepulcher and chapel (20 May 1506, two copies of his will by the notary Alvise Talenti in BCV, MS P.D. c 506/12, no. 2, and MS P.D. c 248, tomo I, 7r–10v); Pellegrina also reiterated her own desire to be buried in Santa Lucia (30 June 1543, notary Bonifacio Soliano, in BCV, MS P.D. c 248, tomo I, 33r–41r), in Puppi 1987, 338. Magrini 1845, 263, is the source for Pietro Carpi, *provocator della fabbrica*, in 1562, who reported on problems with the façade porch, some altars, the sacristy, and the roof; see in M. Franco 1980, 258.

274 Pane 1961, 300; and see the section on the Carità above on the Corinthian atrium.

275 Sansovino 1581, 53; Sansovino 1968, 140–42. For a summary of attributions based on this early observation, see Puppi 1986, 204–05.

276 R. Gallo 1955, 36, noted the confusion caused by Temanza 1778, 495, as "Lazzaro," changed in later edition (Temanza 1966, 377) to "Bernardo Mocenigo"; the misappellation persists, although none of the ensuing descendents of Leonardo (his sixteen grandchildren by Alvise or grandson by Antonio who would have been chronologically feasible) is named either Bernardo or Lazzaro, see the entry for the bust of *Bernardo Mocenigo* in T. Martin

1998, 161, cat. 75, "Works not by Vittoria," with a summary of the attributions.

277 T. Martin 1998, 1, on the late arrival of this type in Venice in the 1550s, and 12–21, on the importance of Padua for the introduction of this classicizing phenomenon.

278 The Padua house was reacquired on 30 July 1576 (in ASV, Magistrato del Sopragastaldo, reg. 617, 115r–v), and then finally sold on 3 December 1619 (in ASV, Notarile, Testamenti, Domenico Adami, prot. 76, 651–52), see in R. Gallo 1955, 27; Tiepolo et al. 1980, 42, cat. 85.

279 Magrini 1845, 263; Puppi 1986, 204.

280 This was the Donato Baglione chapel, completed by 1592; in ASV, Senato, Terra, reg. 60, 40v, 14 June 1590 (the opinion of the Provveditori di Comun in ASV, Senato, Terra, filza 115), see in Magrini 1845, 264; G. Zorzi 1967, 120; Tiepolo et al. 1980, 63, cat. 162; Puppi 1986, 204. Note the strong foreign presence at Santa Lucia, with the Florentine nobleman Baglione, and, later, the chapel to the right of the *cappella maggiore* was acquired by Nicolò Perez (Peeters) from Antwerp nobility (inscription dated) 1628; inscriptions in Sansovino 1968, 141–42.

281 For the commemorative inscription, see Sansovino 1968, 143–44; On St. Lucy, see Niero 1962, 22–23; also in Niero & Tramontin, eds. 1965, 197.

282 For a full discussion of this work in the context of San Giorgio Maggiore, see Cooper 1990b, 352–57.

283 Sansovino 1968, 142–42, Polacco was personally devoted to St. Jerome and built a small oratory, or grotto, "Antro Bethlemitico," adjacent to the sacristy of Santa Lucia, which probably indicates a penitential nature.

284 Palma il Giovane's organ shutters (closed: *Annunciation*; open: *St. Lucy, St. Augustine*), are dated on the basis of style around 1620, shortly after the consecration of the church, by Mason Rinaldi 1984, 121, cat. 377–80. Traditional Augustinian spirituality venerated Mary as Mother of God for the mystery of the Incarnation, with the title "Nostra Signora di Grazia," after the words spoken by the Archangel Gabriel at the moment of the Annunciation, see Rano 1974b, 347, also for other invocations, as well as a special devotion to St. Joseph developed in the fifteenth century.

285 On the jurisdiction of Augustinian convents, see Rano 1974a, 171, for rules of *clausura* pre- and post-Trent, 174–79, as well as another means of control, the control of elections and limitation of abbesses' or prioresses' terms to three years. On Venice, see Sperling 1999, 144–47, on *clausura* laws from 1514, and the origins of the state magistracy, the Provveditori sopra i Monasteri di Monache, in 1528, which became part of the decision-making structure for each convent together with the patriarch of Venice, the convent's three procurators, and its chapter (formerly the sole agency), thus limiting "private" influence (such

as direct appeal to the papacy, family connections, etc.). Sperling argues that this contributed towards turning convents into civic institutions (120), over which the control of space and the nun's actions created social order (126–27); and now M. Laven 2002, 82–101.

286 See in Franzoi & Di Stefano 1976a, 515–17, without secure attribution. Other extant *barche* are at Santa Maria dei Miracoli and San Michele in Isola.

287 The Gothic church of Santa Lucia was reconsecrated in 1343, see Franzoi & Di Stefano 1976a, 100–02.

288 Magrini 1845, 24; trans. from Puppi 1986, 204, with reference to the nuns' petition of 12 August 1610, in ASV, Senato, Terra, reg. 80, 80.

289 Sansovino 1968, 143; see interpretations in R. Gallo 1955, 35; G. Zorzi 1967, 118; Puppi 1986, 204, who suggests that the senate petition reference of 1590 to its "quadra perfetta" – that the church retain a perfect square form – was made in relation to an existing model by Palladio, one followed in 1609, and alluded to in this inscription.

290 Excellent discussions of this problem in Puppi 1986, 205; Bassi 1997, 198–211, which reproduces drawings made by Visentini or his draftsmen of plans, interior elevations, altar and portal frames, façade. Both Muttoni (his preparation for the volumes of the architecture of Andrea Palladio, partially published as architect "N. N." vol. 1 in 1740 and vol. 4 in 1743) and Visentini (his project "Admiranda Urbis Venetae") were engaged in their projects ca. 1740.

291 For Le Zitelle and the issue of "Palladianism," see Part VI. Puppi 1986, 205, provides a sound analysis.

292 At the altar dedicated to the Madonna del Parto; Bassi 1997, 198, 210, for the frame. Its altarpiece of the subject (transferred to San Geremia) was commissioned from Palma il Giovane *circa* 1615–1618 by Primicerio di San Marco, later Patriarch, Giovanni Tiepolo, see Mason Rinaldi 1984, 121, cat. 375.

293 Sansovino 1968, 141. G. Zorzi 1967, 120, has an overly optimistic view of the reconstruction in San Geremia of the fragments as representing the destroyed Mocenigo chapel; on which see the judgment of Puppi 1986, 205.

294 On Palladio's contribution, see the summary in Puppi 1986, 239–40; and particularly the range of opinions between R. Gallo 1955, 36; and G. Zorzi 1967, 177–78.

295 Tassini 1885, 18; A. Zorzi 2001, 233–34; Bassi 1997, 242–51. Some of the monuments in the church were recorded in BCV, Gradenigo 1755, 1: VI no. 17, L no. 151, and BCV, Grevembroch 1759, 2: 47, 54, 3: 83, 84.

296 Sansovino 1968, 75. For more on the history of the convent, see Corner 1749, II: 236–38; Cicogna 1969, 3: 196–242; Mazzucco 1983, 79–80 cat. 49; Franzoi & Di Stefano 1976a, 463–65.

297 Sperling 1999, 244–45, tab. A.1, "Nuns per Convent," La Celestia in 1564 had a popula-

tion of 57, and 52 in the years 1594–96, San Lorenzo had 115 in 1564, San Zaccaria had 40 in 1564 and 67 in 1594–96; 258–59, tab. A.6, "Net Revenues of Venetian Convents, 1564," ranks them respectively no. 3 (income 4,556 ducats = 80 per capita), no. 2 (6,611 ducats = 57 per capita), and no. 1 (7,467 ducats = 187 per capita), with per capita expenditures respectively 84 ducats, 33 ducats, 105 ducats; and net revenue respectively 252 ducats, 2,854 ducats, and 3,275 ducats (note the relation between population, income, and per capita expenditures); 260–61, tab. A.7, "Expenditures, 1564," places La Celestia at the top, at 4,809 ducats, with San Lorenzo as fourth at 3,756 ducats, and San Zaccaria as second at 4,192 ducats.

298 Sperling 1999, 28–29.

299 Sanudo 1879–1903, 8: 25 May 1509, 31: 13 September 1521, 39: 25 August 1525; excerpted in Cicogna 1969, 3: 195; part. trans. in Sperling 1999, 120.

300 Sanudo 1879–1903, 31: 21 August 1521; trans. in Chambers & Pullan, eds. 1992, 202–03; Sperling 1999, 144–45.

301 Cicogna 1969, 3: 195–96; Mazzucco 1983, 79–80 cat. 49, illustrates the frontispiece of the *Rule* in *volgare*; excerpt trans. in Sperling 1999, 127.

302 Sansovino 1968, 367; Cicogna 1969, 3: 199, summarizes accounts.

303 Decided on 28 September 1569, in ASV, Collegio, Notatorio, reg. 38, 87v–88, see in Tiepolo et al. 1980, 72 cat. 193; Corner 1758, 156–57; R. Gallo 1955, 36.

304 San Giacomo (also dedicated to Santa Maria Novella), located near the future Redentore, was under the jurisdiction of the procurators of San Marco, which made it possible to impose upon by the State. Franzoi & Di Stefano 1976a, 276–77; Bassi 1997, 147, discounts Tommaso Temanza's theory that Palladio was responsible for the construction of the new church of San Giacomo, begun in 1603, now destroyed (in Ivanoff, ed. 1963, 7); A. Zorzi 2001, 227–28.

305 The information comes from one of the two inscriptions on the lateral walls of the destroyed Saler chapel in the Celestia, printed copies in BMV, "Arbori," not numbered, but inserted between 95 and 96, "Nella Chiesa dell'Illustrissime Monache della Celestia una Capella propria particolar della Famiglia de Signori Saler Cittadini Veneti Originarii," left and right; in Cicogna 1969, 3: 226–27, inscr. 8–9; note R. Gallo 1955, 36, wrongly gives a date for return as 14 March 1574, after Corner 1749, II: 238.

306 9 September 1570, in APV, Visite Trevisan, 38v, trans. in Sperling 1999, 337–38 n. 151.

307 Bassi 1997, 242.

308 ASV, Notarile, Testamenti, Pietro Contarini, prot. 2577, in Tiepolo et al. 1980, 72, cat. 194. R. Gallo 1955, 37, provides the only notice of the third procurator Gradenigo, otherwise unconfirmed, although it is tempting to specu-late a possible relation to Abbess Angela Gradenigo.

309 See Part VI.

310 27 November 1558, printed copy in BMV, "Arbori," not numbered, but inserted between 95 and 96, no. 3, "Terminatione di tutti Tre li Avogadori di Comun, quali approbano l'Elettione di Gastaldo Ducal fatta dal Serenissimo Priuli della persona di Zorzi Saler come Giuridica, e giusto le Leggi," note that one of the officials was Giovanni Battista Contarini, brother of Palladio's patron Jacopo, and an important contributor to the new charitable institutions, for which see Part VI. On cittadini, see Pullan 1971, 99–109; Zannini 1993; Grubb 2000.

311 Mutinelli 1978, 12–13, notes the role of the *gastaldo* in capital sentences was to give the sign to the executioner; Molmenti 1906, 1: 78, traces the role back to the tribunes; Da Mosto 1937, 1: 102.

312 30 January 1553, printed copy in BMV, "Arbori," not numbered, but inserted between 95 and 96, nos. 1–2, "Patenti in Bergamina del Magistrato di Proveditori di Comun della Cittadinanza Veneta Originaria Provata di Nicolò Saler q: Giacomo e suoi Figlioli, Zorzi, Zan Antonio, Zan Battista, Vicenzo, e Giacomo," and on 91v, s.v. "Saler," some brief notes concerning family origins, coat of arms, and a family tree that contradicts information in a printed one included with the other inserted material; also in BCV, Tassini, "Cittadini Veneziani," s.v. "Saler," 196 and insert.

313 Wills for two of the brothers, Giorgio and Giovanni Antonio, are respectively in ASV, Notarile, Testamenti, Galeazzo Secco, 1191/278, 19 May 1597 (twenty-six years after Giorgio's death, it is being vouched for its authenticity by notarial colleagues, beginning in 1587, from a "professor of handwriting," to a surviving brother, Vicenzo, in 1597), and ASV, Cancelleria Inferiore, Miscellanea notai diversi, B. 67.134, 21 August 1587 (proved 2 October 1587). The *Redecima* of 1582 provides information on properties of the brothers Giovanni Antonio and Vicenzo, including those variously inherited from their widowed mother, Cecilia, and Giorgio their brother: in ASV, Dieci Savi sopra la Decima, B. 159/ 86, 2 June 1581, Zuan Antonio Saler de Nicolò; B. 159/ 86, 30 June 1581, q. Cecilia vedova de Nicolò (presented by Zuan Antonio and Vicenzo Saler "e nipoti [sons of deceased brother Giovanni Battista]"); B. 160/ 444, 24 March 1582, Zuan Antonio and Vicenzo Saler de Nicolò; B. 160/ 461, 24 March 1582, q. Cecilia Saler vedova Nicolò (presented by Zuan Antonio and Vicenzo); B. 161/ 1055, 28 March 1582, q. Zorzi Saler q. Nicolò (presented by Zuan Antonio and Vicenzo), note the house in *contra* Santa Marina was jointly owned by the two brothers (valued at 40 ducats, along with a rental at 22 ducats), but it was inhabited by Vicenzo and family (wife Benetta Davanzo), whereas Giovanni Antonio and family (wife Isabetta di Francesco Spina, daughter Cecilia) rented from "magnifico" Luca Valareso in *contra* San Zuane Bragolla (San Giovanni in Bragora).

314 In ASV, Notarile, Testamenti, Galeazzo Secco, 1191/278, 19 May 1597, Giorgio Saler fu Nicolò, among many charitable bequests stipulates that 10 ducats in alms and 60 *doppieri* (large candles) be given to "la mia Scuola dela Carità," with 12 ducats for each of the *fratelli* who accompany the *scuola* on the day of his burial; one of the documents used to authenticate Giorgio's will was a *giornale* from 1561 when he was procurator at San Giovanni Elemosinario; for the Scuola dei Mercanti, see Part VI.

315 Puppi 1986, 240, while supporting some participation by Palladio as documented, describes the "very poor quality of the work – which reproduces without any attempt at interpretation the most obvious and usual models of cloister architecture."

316 ASV, Notarile, Testamenti, Pietro Contarini, prot. 2578, 9–10, in Tiepolo et al. 1980, 72–73 cat. 195, according to the archivists, this notary followed the "common style," misleading most scholars who have translated it as *more veneto* (therefore wrongly as 1571); as in R. Gallo 1955, 36; G. Zorzi 1967, 177; Puppi 1986, 239. The adjustment of the date provides a different schedule for the work, with less time allotted to a design phase, and more to the actual building.

317 11 January 1553 *m.v.*, in ASV, Provveditori al Sal, B. 68, Notatorio, reg. 16 (previously Serie II, Notatorio 17), 105v, in Tiepolo et al. 1980, 30, cat. 51; see also in Part V. G. Zorzi 1967, 178, remarks there is no notice before 1571 or after 1577, for which he refers to Cadorin 1838, 62–65.

318 Cicogna 1969, 3: 226–27, inscr. 8; Bassi 1997, 242–51, is the latest to recount the hypothesis for the church eventually built by Scamozzi, begun 1581 as a circular plan (supported by Stringa's description of 1604), but torn down and rebuilt as a Latin-cross plan, according to Martinioni, consecrated in 1611, and she puts it in relation to RIBA drawings (XIV, 13–14–15–16) discussed with the Redentore and Zitelle, Parts V (see figs. 242–45) and VI.

319 9 December 1571, inserted in a decree of 14 December, in ASV, Senato, Terra, filza 58, in Tiepolo et al. 1980, 73–74 cat. 196; R. Gallo 1955, 36.

320 Printed copy in BMV, "Arbori," not numbered, but inserted between 95 and 96, "Nella Chiesa dell'Illustrissime Monache della Celestia una Capella propria particolar della Famiglia de Signori Saler Cittadini Veneti Originarii," right side; in Cicogna 1969, 3: 226–27, inscr. 8, and reiterated in an inscription once located in the center of the chapel floor, by Giovanni Antonio's widow, Isabetta Spina (inscr. 10).

PART V

1 Howard 1987, called particular attention to the functioning of the Salt Office as patrons, for the Rialto, see 47–61; also Calabi & Morachiello 1987, pt. 2.

2 Concina 1995, 44–48, situates San Giacomo di Rialto in the broader context of the city's architectural development; also Howard 2002, 14–17; more fully elaborated in Calabi & Morachiello 1987, pt. 1; Calabi 2001c, 416–20.

3 Sinding-Larsen 1974, 3, defines the equivalent of *provveditori* as "Surveyors of Works."

4 ASV, Senato, Terra, Reg. 37, fol. 88r–v, 17 January 1550 *m.v.* (= 1551); G. Zorzi 1967, 247–48, doc. 6; Calabi & Morachiello 1987, 151 and 219: The three *provveditori* elected were Vettor Grimani, Antonio Capello, and Tommaso Contarini.

5 "Et come si vede nelli modelli fatti pur del 54, quando si trattò di far questo ponte, venuti Da Roma et altre parti, di mano di saldi architetti professori ben intendenti di quest'arte," ASV, Provveditori sopra la fabbrica del Ponte di Rialto, b. 3, Pareri, 29 August 1588, in Cessi & Alberti 1934, 413–14; letters from Benedetto Agnello to Guglielmo Gonzaga, Duke of Mantua, in 1551 confirm the participation, see Carpeggiani 1980, cat. 101–06; analyzed in Calabi & Morachiello 1987, 221. For his biography: Gaeta 1964, and the classic Yriarte 1874.

6 Palladio 1997, 187.

7 See Rigon, ed. 1980, esp. 7–9, 10–13, 17–19; Puppi & Romanelli, eds. 1985, esp. 59–60, 62–64; and Calabi & Morachiello 1987, 54–57. The rejection of Palladio's idealized solutions for their impracticability would recur, as the Scala d'Oro and Doge's Palace will show.

8 "Et ne tempi nostri si trattò di farlo di marmo, & essendosi perciò composti diversi modelli, quello del Sansovino prevalse à gli altri, come più commodo, & bello per tanto edificio, ma sopravenuta la guerra del Turco l'anno 1570. la impresa rimase imperfetta." Sansovino 1968, 364.

9 ASV, Consiglio dei Dieci, Comuni, Reg. 21, fol. 127v, 12 September 1554; in Cessi & Alberti 1934, 336–38. Calabi & Morachiello 1987, 220, note responsibilities of magistracy expanded to add to their title as "Provisores super ornamento civitatis," new slate elected on 24 November 1554: Giulio Contarini, procurator *de ultra*, Giovanni Capello, Francesco Sanudo; and again on 11 November 1559: Giulio Contarini, Antonio Capello, Andrea Barbarigo.

10 Doge's Palace: Vettor Grimani was elected with Gabriel Vendramin in March 1550, and Antonio Capello with Giulio Contarini (also on the Rialto magistracy, see above), and Francesco Venier, 19 August 1553, and Maffio Venier on 7 October, in Lorenzi 1868, 599, app. 32 (included here in Appendix II), from ASV, Secretario alle voci, Elezioni del Senato, Reg. 1–6.

11 Howard 1987, 41–42 and 169 nn. 26–30, 56, convincingly argues that Sansovino was not responsible for the third story of the Mint (begun 1558), since it was being built during the Council of Ten's investigation into a conflict between the Procurators of San Marco and the *provveditori di Zecca* from 1554 to 1559 over who was owed the shop rents on the Piazzetta; this reflects on the "precarious position" of architects employed by the Salt Office, due to the "instability," both of their contracts, and of the tenure of officials, who at this time were elected every six months, and so had no loyalty to their predecessors' choices; generally even when favorable in their patronage, these magistracies could be curtailed by the Senate or Council of Ten, as with Sansovino at the Rialto, see idem, 54–55. See also Cooper 1995, 115–16, 123 n. 30 (Calabi & Morachiello 1987, 143, 151–52, 154, 158, do not see such defined positions).

12 For the *proti al sal*, see Lorenzi 1868, 264–318, app. 32 and doc. 601 for the *concorso*, from ASV, Magistrato al Sal, Notatorio, b. 16, 105v.

13 In addition to the histories of the Rialto already cited, see Tafuri 1989, 162–66, who sees Marc'Antonio Barbaro's support for Scamozzi in opposition to Alvise Zorzi's successful backing of da Ponte as symptomatic of continuing differences over the architectural language – classicism or continuity – by which Venice would define itself in the second half of the sixteenth century: the three *provveditori* for the completion of the Rialto bridge had earlier been involved in the restoration of the Doge's Palace after the fire of 1577, on which see further below.

14 The best discussion of this is Tafuri 1987, xxvi, who hypothesizes that it caused Daniele Barbaro to "change tactics" and abandon the institutionalization of Palladio, one of the consequences of which was the architect's being associated with the papalists.

15 Lorenzi 1868, 264–318, appendix 32; see doc. 615 for the *concorso*, from ASV, Collegio, Notatorio, 1553–55 guigno, 122v.

16 Generally agreed to account for some of the opposition to his proposals and success in competitions for public projects in Venice, see Battilotti 1982, 179, 30. G. Zorzi 1965, 130, describes various such projects.

17 In addition to earlier references (in Part II above), see Besta 1899; Da Mosto 1937.

18 Burns 1979, whose acutely observed and careful attribution will be discussed in further detail below; and is also in Simane 1993, 65–81; Tafuri 1994, 438; Battilotti 1999, 508, cat. 162*.

19 See on this point most recently Pincus 2000, 223–24 n. 46, and who notes the role of the Dominicans in Venice as mediators between "ducality" and "nobility" (148–50). One author who refers to it as a "Pantheon veneziano" is Lorenzetti 1982, 340.

20 Characterized as the "paradoxical prince," in Muir 1981, esp. 251–63. Further see: Boholm

1990; Franzoi, ed. 1986; Knezevich 1986; Rendina 1984; Benzoni, ed. 1982.

21 The basis for modern biographies is Da Mosto 1960, 274–83, with primary sources; also salient is Grendler 1979, 312. Alvise first took office as *savio agli ordini* in 1532, then embarked on a public career primarily as governor and ambassador, earning a knighthood from Charles V during his embassy of 1546–48, and gaining election to the Procuratia de Ultra in 1566, when he was also *dogabile*, as he was again in 1567, preceding his election in May 1570. Alvise's mother was Lucrezia di Alvise di Piero Marcello.

22 From his speech made after his election, "Promettendo di administrar giustitia, et abondantia a tutto suo poter, ma per esser tempo de guerra non promesse la pace anci persuase tutti ad agiutar questa guerra che si havea col Turco per conservation et defesa del suo stato, et augmento della fede Cristiana," and described as an "homo de gran valor et pratica nel manezo della Repubblica," in BMV, Savina, 329; for the conclave through twelve *scrutini* (rounds of balloting), see Da Mosto 1960, 275–76. Alvise inherited a strong disposition to take action against Turkish incursions on Venetian possessions in the Levant from his father, Tomaso P., who had been *capitano generale da mar* in 1539, in addition to governorships and ambassadorial roles; in Grendler 1990, 65 (although the *ramo* is not San Stae, but San Samuele), as is also the case for Alvise's brother, Giovanni (Zuane, 1508–1580), see 70; it was another brother Nicolò (1512–1588), who established the San Stae branch that would produce three eighteenth-century doges, Alvise Mocenigo II, III, and IV). Regarding the fire of 1569 in the Arsenale, see under "La Celestia" above in Part IV.

23 One of Mocenigo's (and Palladio's) more severe critics: BMV, Molin, 80; trans. from Chambers & Pullan, eds. 1992, 76. On the collective mentality represented by Molin, see Preto 1991, 183.

24 Chroniclers (such as Molin) attributed the negative tone of Mocenigo's reputation in part to envy of his wealth, with 10,000 ducats reported by one chronicler, in Da Mosto 1960, 279–80, although his reported income for the tax return of 1566 was 1799 ducats, and together with his brother, Giovanni, another 1057 ducats, in ASV, Dieci Savi sopra la Decima, 1566, San Marco, 560, and Dorsoduro, 1102, and aggiunte 34, 37, 38, 1386. This would still place him in the top bracket, see W. Brown 1974, who compares a sample of twenty-five prominent political figures' real estate incomes in 1566 in Table IVa.

25 For the location of the painting seen by Ridolfi 1965, 2: 53, see Cooper 1998. For previous bibliography, see P. Rossi 1994, 148–53 cat. 135. The childless doge was in a *fraterna*, or family partnership, with his brother Giovanni, whose elder son Tomaso was his

heir, while his younger son, "Alviseto," was named heir to Doge Alvise, maintaining the partnership and residences; it should be noted that Giovanni was also father to six daughters, who married into some prominent *vecchi* families (Grimani, Foscarini, Contarini, Foscari); his wife was Daria di Agostino di Baldissera di Zuanne P. Moro.

26 BMV, Molin, 80; trans. from Chambers & Pullan, eds. 1992, 76. Also considered a dangerous sign of self-aggrandizement, he was the first to wear the *stola d'oro*, Da Mosto 1960, 276. Mocenigo's association with the elevation of nobility is reflected in the dedication to him of Girolamo Muzio's *Il gentilhuomo*, Venice, appresso gli heredi di Luigi Valvassori & Gio. Domenico Micheli, 1575, on which see Tenenti 1991, 113.

27 The identification of *vecchi* with *papalisti* is less clear in this decade than it would become; Grendler 1979, 312, discusses the inconclusive evidence for Mocenigo's position. Note a similarity to the problem of defining da Ponte as *giovani* or *vecchi*, in W. Brown 1974, 130–58, esp. 156, where he describes his policy as "defensive neutrality," responding to contemporary circumstances rather than taking a fixed ideological position associated with either faction (outlining the scholarly debate on the validity of these categories, generally speaking more accepted by Italian scholars following Gaetano Cozzi); Mocenigo was related through his sister Pasqual's marriage of 1542 to da Ponte's son Antonio Lazaro (26, Table 1A, no. 10); such a close familial tie would be a possible explanation for some of their shared stands.

28 For a survey of some of the cultural manifestations surrounding the War of Cyprus and particularly the Holy League victory at Lepanto of 1571, see Fenlon 1987; Sinding-Larsen 1974, 88 n. 37; Wolters 1987, 207–15. Intellectually, Mocenigo's participation in the Accademia Veneziana, or "della Fama," would identify him as a *vecchi*; for his membership, see Cicogna 1969, 3: 52 n. 1; Da Mosto 1960, 274; and the broader context in Rose 1969; Tafuri 1989, ch. 5, esp. 114; Hochmann 1992, 117–18; the homonymic Alvise di Francesco K. is another possible candidate, see n. 123.

29 Burns 1979, 24–27, with a reconstruction of the sketch in the side chapel site and discussion of its unrealized commission to Giovanni Antonio Rusconi (see as Palladio's collaborator below) in 1569, substituted by a design from Alessandro Vittoria in 1575, and executed by the two successive *proti* of Palladio's *cantiere* at San Giorgio Maggiore, Antonio Paliari da Marcò (also involved in the reconstruction after the fire of 1577 in the Doge's Palace, and at the Carità) and Bortolo di Domenico; see Cooper 1995, 116.

30 18 December 1572 and 5 January 1574 (chapter deliberations agreeing to the consignment), in ASV, SSGP, B. m.xlvii, fasc. 6, n. 26, 13 and 3 (also in Registri, Libro Instrumenti, 1542–86,

59 and 61v); in Simane 1993, 70; and ASV, Notarile, Testamenti, Cesare Ziliol, B. 1256, 12, 10 November 1574 (codicil to Alvise Mocenigo's will of 23 May 1562, made before he was doge and while his wife was still living, with a further codicil of 15 September 1576); in Da Mosto 1960, 280–82.

31 Burns 1979, 23–24, draws analogies to projects ranging from 1574 for the Palazzo Pubblico in Brescia, to 1577 for the Doge's Palace in Venice, and the *scenae frons* of 1580 for the Teatro Olimpico in Vicenza. His dating in the 1560s for the drawing of the Porta Aurea is discussed together with other opinions in Puppi 1990, 96 cat. 34. For another use of an antique prototype in an interior façade, see San Giorgio Maggiore, above in Part IV; and relations between tombs and bays, see the Grimani tomb monument in Part III.

32 Da Mosto 1960, 281; Zava Bocazzi 1965, 277–81 and 358 n. 192, discusses the attribution to Grapiglia, noting his academic and rationalizing approach to the poetics of Palladio's architectural innovations as responsible for negative critical evaluations of the realized monument; Simane 1993, 72–77, recognizes the Palladian typology (and acknowledges he was one of the *favoriti* of Doge Alvise), but concludes due to its conglomerate effect rather it is a homage to Palladio's style (which does not invalidate the argument that there was an intentional association of Palladio's architectural language with Mocenigo); Tafuri 1994, 438, finds merit in Burns's idea; for the documents relating to its later execution, see Simane 1993, 78–80, of particular interest are the indications that the armature was on site at least by early 1603 (27 January 1602 *m.v.*, ASV, Giudici del Proprio, Extraordinari, fasc. 100, 194); P. Rossi 2001, 194, mentions only Grapiglia and Contin, but while the latter certainly executed the systematization of the entire façade, the concept seems to be part of the original design, one that was extremely bold for its date.

33 Sansovino 1968, 60, 69, giving the names of the descendents who completed the tomb as the "fratelli Luigi Mocenighi," being Alvise I, Alvise II ("Leonardo"), Alvise III ("Antonio"), Alvise IV ("Pietro") di Alvise di Giovanni (the doge's brother); the proliferation of homonymic names of Doge Alvise was dictated by the terms of his will, by which means he ensured his symbolic succession through the family line, and which has led to much confusion over individual identities, see Cooper 1998, 67, for an example. On such family practices in the Venetian patriciate, see J. Davis 1975.

34 Pincus 2000, 174–75, calling this "ducal arms."

35 ASV, Notarile, Testamenti, Cesare Ziliol, B. 1256, 12, 10 November 1574; these warm sentiments are frequently repeated throughout his wills, and have been remarked by many scholars, such as Da Mosto 1960, 278–79, who

provides information about Loredana; Benzoni, ed. 1982, 180–81, compares esequies of the dogaresses.

36 Sansovino 1968, 59–60, the tomb monument of Doge Giovanni Mocenigo is attributed to Tullio Lombardo (completed 1522), and the tomb monument of Doge Pietro Mocenigo (1481–84) documented by Pietro Lombardo; Zava Bocazzi 1965, respectively 139–45, and 117–23, identifying two statues of *Sts. Mark and Theodore* as having been transferred to Alvise's tomb (but the cross on the shield would seem to indicate George rather than Theodore; Luchs 1995, 33). Debra Pincus (in a private communication) reminds us that there was also a *divisorio* later in the seventeenth century that may have been responsible for moving these statues, so any ascription of programmatic intention must be made with this caveat.

37 Pincus 2000, 223 n. 32; the author also generously shared with me an unpublished talk "Tomb as Trattato: Visions of Good Government in Fifteenth-Century Venice," given in "Venetian Art in its Cultural and Intellectual Context, 1400–1600," College Art Association, 1982, in which she corrects the identification of the first relief, usually described as the *Taking of Scutari* (or *Smyrna*); Manno 1995, 27, describes Pietro's tomb as "a significant rupture in the history of the representation of death at San Zanipolo."

38 Many scholars fix the interpretation to a single event, i.e., Simane 1993, 66–70, as the Peace of Cyprus; Zava Bocazzi 1965, 280, as Henri III, for whose visit, see below.

39 P. Rossi 2001, 194–98; previously the reliefs and, with more reservation, the standing figures on the upper story had been attributed to Girolamo Campagna, see Zava Bocazzi 1965, 281 and 358 n. 194, who notes a comparison to Campagna's work on the tomb monument of Doge Marino Grimani at San Giuseppe in Castello; Grapiglia also was engaged with Girolamo Campagna and his master Danese Cattaneo on the tomb monument of Doge Leonardo Loredan (1501–21) in the presbytery of Santi Giovanni e Paolo in 1572, which may have provided an opportunity for Campagna and Grapiglia to collaborate on the Mocenigo tomb; see Simane 1993, 30–48, with earlier bibliography and documented executants, and on the latter tomb, 66–70, following some previous authors, such as Da Mosto, identifies the left hand figure as Mark (rather than Peter), and thus makes an analogy between the doge as Mark and the "dogaressa" as Mary.

40 Sinding-Larsen 1974, 87–90 (see his correction of the identification of a *Victory* figure in the *modello*, in 1980, 40–49, esp. n. 15); accepted by Wolters 1987, 120; Pallucchini & Rossi 1982, 198 cat. 324, dating it between 1571 and 1574.

41 Sinding-Larsen 1974, 92, proposes that without the galleys, the *Victory* makes reference to relations with the Turks, and the Lion of St.

Mark's PAX TIBI MARCE provides the shift of iconography to refer instead to the Peace of Cyprus; Wolters 1987, 118–23, finds the reference to "pax" to be too generic; Pallucchini & Rossi 1982, 222 cat. 422, accept Sinding-Larsen's interpretation and date it to 1581–82.

42 The presence of *Christ the Redeemer* in both settings does not offer a conclusive association with a particular event, because, although that imagery became most strongly linked to the plague of 1576 that led to the dedication of the votive church of Il Redentore, this aspect of Christ had reference to Lepanto as well, with the banner of the Holy League commander, Don Juan of Austria, raised before the Christian forces; the statues of *St. Peter* and the *Virgin* on the tomb may even refer to the latter, representing Rome and Venice, and the memory of the Holy League whose victory at Lepanto was the greatest triumph of Alvise's reign. For Il Redentore, see below in this part; and on the imagery of Christ in this context, Sinding-Larsen 1974, 94–95, with a comparison to the tomb of Doge Marino Grimani at San Giuseppe in Castello, 85–86, discounting earlier interpretations alluding to the plague (note Simane 1993, 66–70, identifies the right-hand Mocenigo tomb relief as the plague Mass of 1576); Wolters 1987, 118–21, does not consider an iconography of the Redeemer in reference to Lepanto and the plague to be mutually exclusive.

43 On the election, see W. Brown 1974, 130–31. The brothers were first identified by Rodolfo Pallucchini, see Pallucchini & Rossi 1982, 222 cat. 422; on the rarity of such representation in dogal portraiture, see Wolters 1987, 123. According to ASV, Barbaro, "Albori," 187, ramo "D," Nicolò (1512–1588) was a member of the Council of Ten and *consigliere*, married to Paola di Marc'Antonio di Alvise Priuli. The presence of both brothers may indicate that the composition of the painting preceded Giovanni's death in August 1580 (a fourth brother, Francesco, had died much earlier in 1538, but he may account for the unidentifiable fourth saint with the other name saints, Louis of Toulouse, John the Baptist, and Nicholas of Bari; for unsupportable attempts to identify the unknown saint as a plague saint, see Sinding-Larsen 1974, 85–86). The great deeds of the Mocenigo family can be found in Quadri 1840, based on Abate Morlopino, *L'illustri azioni de' serenissimi principi della famiglia Moceniga*, Venice, Farri, 1572.

44 Logan 1972, 311–12, on his intervention in the decoration of the Maggior Consiglio and the architecture of San Marco.

45 BMV, Savina, 364v. The doge had first gone to the Procurator's apartment "in piazza" of Giovanni K. di Priamo da Lezze; also BMV, Molin, 53; ASV, Collegio, Cerimoniale I, 52, in Lorenzi 1868, 382–83, doc. 785. On the Mocenigo palaces at San Samuele, see above and Part II.

46 Sansovino 1968, 489.

47 Benzoni, ed. 1982, 272; and see Tafuri 1989, 179–84, for a similar initiative under Doge Pasquale Cicogna (1585–95).

48 BMV, Savina, 364v.

49 Puppi 1986, 251. Hochmann 1992, 147–68, examines the vexed question of programmatic advisors and literary intermediaries for Venetian painting in great depth, concluding that such practice differed from other centers (notably Florence): in Venice an expert might be consulted but it was as often not the case, since programs whether fluid or fixed were frequently devised by cultivated patricians and artists who were not on the margins of their intellectual circles as often assumed; such thinking can be applied to architecture, and Palladio seems to have been created for such collaboration. For a general study of this issue, see Hope 1981, with particular reference to the story of Benvenuto Cellini's Saltcellar (current location unknown, stolen from Vienna, Kunsthistorisches Museum).

50 ASV, Provveditori al Sal, B. 412 (other documents are in Lorenzi 1868, *s.a.*) largely published in G. Zorzi 1953; also G. Zorzi 1965, 137–51, with only the documents pertaining to Palladio; for references to other publications of selected documents, see Burns 2000, and Beltramini & Padoan, eds. 2000, 266–67.

51 Palladio and Rusconi appear together in documents on 20 August and 24 October 1574 (docs. 1–4), Rusconi on 20 February, 3 August, and 23 December 1575, and a "resto e saldo" 13 August 1576 (docs. 9–10, 13, 15), and Palladio on 17 September 1575, 1 January 1576, 14 July 1577 (docs. 12, 14, 22, the last co-signed by Marc'Antonio Barbaro), in G. Zorzi 1965, 149–51 (his dates translated from *more veneto*); Rusconi may have been included since he was working with Palladio in consultation on the Palazzo Comunale in Brescia at this time, and had participated in the estimate of Palladio's work at the Scuola dei Mercanti in 1573 (see Part VI); Calabi 2001b, 458, on his role as technical assistant and collaborator. Excellent discussions of the working process can be found in Wolters 1987, 33–45; and Sinding-Larsen 1974, 3–12.

52 Lorenzi 1868, doc. 786 and appendix 32, the election of the first three on 12 May 1574, and Barbaro on 9 May 1575, from ASV, Secretario alle voci, Elezioni del Senato, Reg. 4, Senato, Deliberazione, c. 74; in ASV, Provveditori al Sal, B. 412, Badoer is first documented on 16 June 1574 and last on 30 July 1575 (the most common two signatories for the *provveditori* were Foscari & Morosini), whereas Barbaro first appears on 12 August 1575, suggesting that Badoer and Barbaro overlapped following the latter's election.

53 Sansovino 1968, 389; and see the Conclusion for the visit of Henri III.

54 BMV, Molin, 118, after Lowry 1971, 286.

55 This concept of cultural genealogy is based on

the work of S. Chojnacki 2000a, 273, for "bilateral links"; S. Chojnacki 2000b, 3, has described Venetian women "as being so important to their families, and having such substantial legal and economic resources, that they could influence the behavior of their male kin, natal and marital, and on that basis contribute to the cohesion of the patriciate." Herlihy 1985, esp. 82–83, discusses the effect on "bilateral kindred" of agnatic lineage (or patrilineage) as being superimposed on the older system, and existing simultaneously to further differing aspects of family success. *Parentela*, or kinship has been a concern of Palladio scholars, particularly Giangiorgio Zorzi, but more usually explored in relation to single family patrons of individual monuments, such as the villa (although Lionello Puppi on the Badoer, Douglas Lewis on the Corner, for some examples pertinent to this discussion, certainly acknowledge the wider implications); the potential for identifying broader inter-family connections has been traced by Tafuri 1989; also Foscari & Tafuri 1983; and Foscari 1979, whose study of the Accesi (see above, Part II) is particularly relevant here. The expanded study of patronage networks for architecture was proposed by Lewis 1981. For a recent overview of patronage in Venice (focused on painting, but including architecture and other media), see Hochmann 1992, esp. 217–63, on the Corner, Grimani, Barbaro, and Jacopo Contarini; and Logan 1972, appendix 295–321, who remains an invaluable reference.

56 Foscari 1979, in his study of Gerolamo Foscari and the Accesi, went into the importance of Pietro's relations, including his brother Bishop Girolamo's connections to the church, linking him with Trissino, Ridolfi, Grimani; Gullino 2000, 139–40, has suggested this potential direction through his documentation of the career of Pietro's father, Marco Foscari, and his work shows political alliances cemented by marital ties during Marco's generation, i.e., especially with the Capello of Santa Maria Mater Domini, and Grimani of Santa Maria Formosa.

57 Gullino 2000, 145; for his posts, see Grendler 1990, 73; on the Mocenigo connection as influencing state culture, see Casini 1996, 304. The author of the program published an explanation: Betussi 1573, xv, on "nobility," explains the three ceiling canvasses (unlike the villa frescoes, these are in less well-preserved condition) as the three states of man, 1) *Monarchia*, like Rome; 2) *Nobile*, or a democracy like Athens; 3) *Aristocrathia*, like Venice, xxiii/v–xxiii, and names the figures that represent the "Venetian Republic and its enduring grandeur," as Doge Alvise Mocenigo, Senators Pietro Foscari, *capitano* of Padua, Vicenzo Morosini, Paolo Tiepolo K., Francesco Bernardo, Giovanni Donà "dalle Renghe," Jacopo Soranzo K., *provveditor generale*

dell'armata, Dolfin Valier, and Marc'Antonio Franceschi, secretary. This is a fascinating glimpse of the generation that had been represented in some of the sixteenth-century narrative paintings lost in the fires at the Doge's Palace, many of whom were linked by the action at Lepanto and subsequent diplomacy in the Mocenigo administration. Zelotti's portraits are unmistakably *dal vivo*, and several of our patrons can be identified either by costume or comparison to other portraits, including, most notably, the doge, and Vicenzo Morosini silhouetted against the sky, and since Pietro Foscari is one of the only two figures given a role, it may be he who holds the sword and gazes out at the viewer from the center, because in other portraits Jacopo Soranzo is represented as dark haired at this time. On Cataio, see Glaser 2003, 103–29; Kliemann 1993, 114–29; Fantelli 2003, 8. My thanks to the Signore Dalla Francesca and Caterina Pellizzari for their kind facilitation at Cataio.

58 See above, Part II, on the Accesi; esp. Foscari 1979, who explores both architects' productions for the Accesi.

59 Ventura 1963, 99. Alberto inherited both his father's and uncle Andrea's rights to the family chapel in San Francesco della Vigna, and became a significant art patron in his own right, see Humfrey & Holt 1995, 205–09; note the contingency at San Francesco della Vigna in relation to the Barbaro and Grimani spheres, and connecting to Pietro Foscari as well through his Grimani wife, Elena di Marco di Gerolamo (her mother Bianca di Gian Francesco K.P. di Alvise Foscari was also a more distant cousin, see Gullino 2000, 39, 115), niece of the patriarch of Aquileia, Giovanni. Alberto Badoer is discussed in relation to the importance of *parentela* (kinship), particularly his reinforcing links to the Corner, by Lowry 1970–71, 159–60.

60 Another son of Andrea's brother Gian Alvise, Marco, was married to Betta, the daughter of Palladio's cultured patron Leonardo K. di Antonio P. Mocenigo (see Part IV).

61 Francesco Badoer was married to Lucietta di Gian Francesco Loredan, whose mother was Cornelia di Giorgio (Zorzi) K.P. Corner, sister of Giovanni (Zuane) whose daughter Cecilia married Andrea Badoer, and one of whose nephews was the patron of Palladio's Villa Corner at Piombino Dese, Giorgio (Zorzon) di Girolamo (Hieronimo). Puppi 1975, 13–33, outlines connections between Francesco Badoer and the Loredan, Corner, Grimani, and Giustiniani. On the Cortesi-Accesi, see Maylender 1926–30, 2: 97; Venturi 1983, 140–41.

62 See Part II, above; Gullino 2000, 139–40, cautiously proposes that their father Marco Foscari was in a position to influence the 24-year-old orphaned Vettor in his choice of Palladio.

63 Foscari 1979; Gullino 2000, 38–39 and 115, on

Marco's generation and forging connections to the Capello and Grimani; also refer to Part III on the Grimani patriarchs of Aquileia.

64 Sansovino 1968, 371, notes that Stringa (Sansovino 1604) lists Vicenzo's brother Domenico K. as having a notable library, in the company of Giovanni Grimani, Daniele Barbaro, Jacopo Marcello, and Jacopo Contarini of San Samuele (the latter two authors of the decorative program in the Maggior Consiglio after the fire of 1577, see below).

65 On his patronage, see the excellent summary in Mozzetti & Santi 1997; see further in Part IV on San Giorgio Maggiore.

66 Hochmann 1992, 43.

67 A letter places Palladio in Morosini's palace in 1572 (G. Zorzi 1965, 132, 29 February; Fasolo 1938, 264), and it should be noted that Morosini's wife was Cecilia di Zuane P. Pisani, granddaughter of Alvise Pisani dal Banco of Santa Maria Zobenigo, whose first husband was Almorò Barbaro, brother of Daniele and Marc'Antonio, in Gullino 1996b, 72 (note, however, inconsistency in sources regarding Almorò's death date); see further in Part IV on San Giorgio Maggiore, and below on the triumphal entry of Henri III.

68 Vicenzo Morosini was made *generale sopra i lidi* in 1571 under Doge Mocenigo during the period culminating in the Battle of Lepanto (see Part IV on San Giorgio Maggiore). According to G. Zorzi 1965, 133–34, after 1570, when Palladio was in Venice, he was domiciled at San Samuele with Jacopo Contarini, who was *deputato della guardia et fortificazione* at San Nicolo al Lido, in 1572 (after ASV, Barbaro, "Albori"; Hochmann 1992, 254, with earlier sources), the same year that Palladio accompanied "li signori sopra le fortezze" to Chioggia (G. Zorzi 1965, 135 and n. 51, May 1572); in the preceding and following years another of his patrons, Alvise Foscari, was one of the *provveditore alle fortezze* (1570–71, 1573–74, and five more times; see Gullino 1997a; Palladio was again on the Lido in 1575 with Contarini and Andrea Bernardo (Tiepolo et al. 1980, 76–77 cat. 209.).

69 Yriarte 1874, 215–18; Gaeta 1964; Ventura 1963, 99. Tenenti 1974 elucidates the role of the French, who had not joined the Holy League, and subsequent to Lepanto were keen to block Spain by supporting the separate peace (and shows that although Venice accepted French intervention, it was largely superfluous to the negotiations). A contemporary account in Paruta 1605.

70 Sinding-Larsen 1974, 7, who notes the ceiling was finished by 1581 when it was described by Sansovino 1968, 324; there were payments to Veronese and for the soffit and cornice in 1577 when the account-book ends, and Schulz 1968, 105, hypothesizes that Venier's coat of arms in the frieze indicates that it was completed during his brief dogate, in 1578 (note the same *provveditori* were still in place then); for the documents, see G. Zorzi 1953; Wolters

1987, 248 and 252–53, remarks that the program reflects more the politics after Lepanto and the Peace of Cyprus than the Counter Reformation; Rosand 2001, 144–46, on the mode employed of "Venetian panegyric."

71 Trans. from Federico Badoer's *Supplica* (1560) in Tafuri 1989, 116 (on Mocenigo, also 114, 120–21, 246–47 n. 96); Wolters 1987, 35; Sinding-Larsen 1974, 7; Hochmann 1992, 117–18. The fundamental source remains Rose 1969, 191–235, his trans. reads: "the Academy has prepared for the Provveditori sopra le Fabbriche del Palazzo a programme for the paintings to be placed in the chambers of the Collegio, the Senate, the Consiglio dei X, and the Chancery, as well as being commissioned to choose the painter" (210); also in Chambers & Pullan, eds. 1992, 364–66: "in accordance with the will of the most serene Prince, the most eminent overseers of the Palace building works made a decision, set down in writing, that a scheme should be drawn up for the 'inventions'"; it should be noted that Francesco Badoer is listed as *provveditore sopra la fabbrica del Palazzo* in 1560 (Lorenzi 1868, app. 32, on 17 October), thus combining roles of *provveditore* and advisor.

72 "& l'inventione fu di Daniel Barbaro eletto d'Aquilea dottissimo gentilhuomo di questa età," Sansovino 1968, 325; Wolters 1987, 35; Sinding-Larsen 1974, 7; Hochmann 1992, 119, 121, 156–57. Many of these academic ties extended back to Padua, where the successor to the Infiammati of which Daniele Barbaro was a noted founder was the Elevati, with which Alvise Mocenigo was associated (when *podestà*, or governor, a post he also held in Vicenza, which raises the suggestive possibility of ties there as well, e.g., the Costanti, precursor to the famous Olimpica, has been connected to Barbaro and the Fama), see Maylender 1926–30, 1: 114–17, 2: 263–65, 3: 266–70. It should be noted with caution, however, that the identification of the Alvise Mocenigo associated with the Accademia della Fama may not be the doge as usually supposed, but a homonymic, who features in the development of the program for the entry of Henri III (see below), and first cousin to Leonardo K. Mocenigo.

73 For Palladio, see Part I above. Rusconi's own treatise *Dell'architettura* was only published posthumously (Venice, 1590); on distinguishing Rusconi's technically oriented approach, see Morresi 1998b, 276–80; Hajnoczi 1988; Bedon 1983; Fontana 1978. Cellauro 2001 now provides new insight on Rusconi's investment in a substantial library and analysis of his specific interests.

74 Lorenzi 1868, 384, doc. 786, 12 May 1574 election.

75 Puppi 1986, 250–51, admirably sums up opinions regarding the evidence for more cautious attributions (to which should be added Burns 2000, and Beltramini & Padoan, eds. 2000,

240) following the overly enthusiastic attributions of G. Zorzi 1965, 137–49, but whose earlier article, G. Zorzi 1953, however, reliably assigns the various craftsmen – carpenters, woodcarvers, stuccoists, gilders, etc. – to the concurrent projects in the rooms, giving an approximate chronology that associates Rusconi's presence in, and Palladio's absence from, Venice with payments predominantly being made in the Senato, and a coincidence of payments to workers with Palladio's documentation in the Collegio as the basis for respective responsibilities.

76 Some uncertainty exists as to whether the cornice referred to is the tribune or the upper wall, but most scholars accept only the former; see in G. Zorzi 1965, 139–41, for arguments associating several documents with the tribune, beginning with a payment on 15 January 1574 *m.v.* (= 1575), "A M.o Zuane intaiador a Santa Marina per haver intaiada la sagoma del cornise del Palladio lire otto" (150, doc. 8), which he correlates with other documents by the same master that specify work on the tribune and *banche*; also persuasive is a comparison to the *tribuna* illustrated in Barbaro's Vitruvius of 1556 (133).

77 The style has been contrasted to the compartmented framework of the Collegio ceiling, as well as to the tribune and *banche* in the Senato, see Puppi 1986, 50–251; for differing views, compare Wolters 1968a, 256–62, and Lewis 2000, 264–67 cat. 122, on the contract drawing (London, Victoria and Albert Museum, E.509–1937) of the ceiling compartmented framework in the Senato assigned to Cristoforo Sorte on 27 July 1578 (for its history, see Schulz 1968, 111–14 cat. 114; the "disegno" also given to Sorte by Sansovino 1968, 324–25; the inscription on it of one of the wood carvers to be provided with profiles "by Sorte and the two protos" indicates the complex collaborative environment, see trans. in Burns with Fairbairn & Boucher 1975, 160 cat. 280).

78 Sansovino 1968, 323–24. There is one other infrequently accepted attribution to Palladio that is close in time, by Girolamo Gualdo in 1629 (BMV, MS It. VI, 151 B, fol. 192), for the ceiling of the Anticollegio; but I believe this is a mistake, confusing it with the Sala delle Quattro Porte, which was also known as the "camera grande di Anticollegio"; G. Zorzi 1965, 143; on this and other doubtful attributions, such as the fireplaces, see Puppi 1986, 251.

79 G. Zorzi 1965, 144, on Bombarda, and 139, linking the documentation of Palladio's payment on 17 September 1575, a payment the same day for "carta fabriana per sagome e disegni," and the successive assignment of Marco "marangon" (carpenter) in October to "fare il volto della salla dell'Antipregadi."

80 Continuing: "but one cannot say there is a fixed and predetermined rule for doing this," Palladio 1997, 57; and later in describing the Corinthian Hall (Bk. 2, ch. 9, 38–39), the vault "had to be decorated with compartments of stucco and paintings," Palladio 1997, 114; collected in Wolters 1968a, 256–62; Wolters 2000, 255–63, on these stucco framework systems in the Doge's Palace; but cf. Lewis 2000, 199–201 cat. 89, recording Palladio's interest in elaborate compartment drawings based on an account-book for the Villa Godi ceilings.

81 The ceiling paintings by Jacopo Tintoretto and his workshop were begun by January 1577 (G. Zorzi 1953, 133, 150) and completed by 1581, when they were described by their inventor, Sansovino 1968, 323–24; Sinding-Larsen 1974, 242–44; Pallucchini & Rossi 1982, 95, 207–08, cat. 359–69; Wolters 1987, 59–66, aptly discusses the program under "The Foundation of the City and the Role of the Aristocracy."

82 2 September 1574, ASV, Senato, Terra, reg. 50, 40v, in Lorenzi 1868, 389–90, doc. 798.

83 He specifically alludes to the churches of San Gregorio and San Luca, but this raises the question as to whether marble was acquired from San Pietro in Castello at this time, see above Part III; 28 October 1574, in BCV, Cod. Cicogna 2583, "Variorum ad Venet. Eccles. Atque ipsius Ven. Cleri. Spectantia," 1: 104 bis, "Pro fabrica palatii Ducalis."

84 Other columns were acquired from Sant'Avian and the nuns at San Girolamo, see G. Zorzi 1965, 143, 147–48; G. Zorzi 1953; Puppi 1986, 251, generally accepts all the portals as by Palladio; Burns 2000, and Beltramini & Padoan, eds. 2000, 240.

85 Palladio 1997, 299, and 295, 296, respectively. These and other comparisons can be found in G. Zorzi 1965, 143, 147–48; Puppi 1986, 251.

86 BMV, Savina, 354–55. An "official" account of the fire and subsequent creation of posts and elections of officials through to 20 January 1578 can be found in ASV, Collegio, Cerimoniale I, 64v, in Lorenzi 1868, 413–14, doc. 842.

87 Quoted from BMV, Molin, 91, but a common phrase in instructions to painters, for example, indicating attitudes broadly shared about the notion of "restoration"; see Cooper 2001, 142.

88 Foscari 1983–87, 329.

89 For da Ponte's election, see under the Rialto bridge above, as well as the following discussion for the other *proti*, with more on Sorella below, and in Part IV under San Giorgio Maggiore; G. Zorzi 1965, 132, 151.

90 23 December 1577, in ASV, Senato, Terra, reg. 52, 30, in Lorenzi 1868, 415–16, doc. 844, Barbaro was supported by Maffeo Venier, and a compromise proposal that also failed was put forward by Vicenzo Tron; see Foscari 1983–87, 324.

91 For Jacopo Soranzo, who had preceded Barbaro as *bailò* in Constantinople, see Grendler 1990, 75; Grendler 1979, 322–23. For Paolo Tiepolo, see Grendler 1979, 316–17, of the Santi Apostoli branch, ambassador in Rome who had to break the unpopular news of the Peace of 1573 to Gregory XIII and was temporarily excommunicated (good account in W.

Brown 1974, 83–87); Lowry 1970–71, 176–81, hypothesizes a "formidable" political alliance between the Soranzos and Tiepolos, and in Lowry 1971, 294–95, suggests that the latter was the target of the reformers in 1582–83; see further on both diplomats below under Henri III and Il Redentore. For Alvise Zorzi, in Grendler 1979, 321–22; Lowry 1971, 302; see above on the Rialto. All three deputies were influential *vecchi* and leading *papalisti*, in addition, see Logan 1964, 54–57 (whom I thank for his generosity in sharing this earlier work with me with its invaluable prosopographical analyses); both Soranzo and Zorzi would subsequently serve again as *provveditori* for the restoration as well.

92 The voting on 27 December 1577 in ASV, Senato, Terra, reg. 52, 30v, with Palladio's report on the same day, together with Da Ponte's estimate of the construction expenses for the Canonica solution requested by Tiepolo, of 29 December, in idem, filza 72; in Lorenzi 1868, 416–18, doc. 845; Foscari 1983–87, 326–27.

93 Valier 1787, 399–400, then Morosini goes on to blame Venice's travails on God's anger and the need to renew "l'antica disciplina dei nostri Maggiori," a common appeal to the return to the traditional ways of Venetian forebears. There was animosity between Barbaro and Morosini (a reminder that strong relationships within a network, whether familial, affinal, or political, were not always positive), aggravated in 1581 by the latter's continuing support of Francesco Barbaro's incarceration, see Trebbi 1984, 81.

94 29 December 1577 in ASV, Senato, Terra, reg. 52, 32, with da Ponte's report on the Terra Nova site, in idem, filza 772; in Lorenzi 1868, 419–20, doc. 846, in which da Ponte remarks that the architects saw a "disegno" made for Marc'Antonio Barbaro, which has been proposed as possibly having been drawn by Palladio; Foscari 1983–87, 326–27.

95 Foscari 1983–87, 323–28, contrasts Barbaro's proposal of the Terra Nova site, as intended to be a permanent relocation of these government functions, to the consideration of sites, first, in the Piazza, and second, to the Arsenale—with its additional symbolic importance—as inherently temporary, and favoring the rebuilding of the status quo (in this respect, reading the negative parallels drawn in relation to the Canonica site, which would have had to be torn down, to the preservation of the Maggior Consiglio); he notes the voting strategy, in which Barbaro and his supporters disassociated themselves from votes on the opposing proposals, thus preserving the appearance of unanimity. If this was the case, then the prominent Priuli (see below) and Gritti (made procurator the same year; Grendler 1979, 324; Lowry 1971, 307–09) may be seen as having supported Barbaro and Venier as well.

96 20 January 1578 (*m.v.* 1577), in ASV, Secretario alle voci, reg. 5, Elezioni del Senato, 130v, in

Lorenzi 1868, 452, doc. 885a, this was the culmination of another series of contested proposals (see 422, doc. 849, with Barbaro again absenting himself, 422–23, doc. 850, 452, doc. 854); for a thorough analysis, see Foscari 1983–87, 327–28. Wolters 1987, 34, has suggested that the *provveditori alla restauratione* elected in early 1578 were subordinate to the already existing *provveditori sopra la fabbrica del Palazzo* from 1574 (who by this reasoning would have been responsible for commissioning the inventors of the decorative program of the Maggior Consiglio), but the replacement and merging of their distinct and separate roles are indicated in the call for the next election of 7 February 1579 (*m.v.* 1578) in ASV, Senato, Terra, reg. 52, 136, in Lorenzi 1868, 452–53, doc. 885.

97 See below for Henri III; Grendler 1979, 331, later procurator, at this time just returned from office as simultaneous *provveditore generale*, *sindaco*, and *inquisitore* in Candia, 1574–78; Zago 1997. Foscarini and Marc'Antonio Barbaro became father-in-laws with the marriage of Alvise Barbaro to Maria Foscarini (21 November 1574); see Gullino 1996b, 97. The political effects of a Grimani-Barbaro-Foscarini "consortium" are analyzed by Trebbi 1984, 383–84; as well as Lowry 1971, 304–05.

98 From the rich Priuli "da Scarpon di San Felice" branch with notable ecclesiastical connections; see Grendler 1990, 75; Lowry 1971, 290–91; Lowry 1970–71, 189–92; Logan 1964, 254 (with a family tree); elected 22 November 1578, overlapping with Zorzi who left on 20 January 1579, and serving only three months, until 21 February 1579; later re-elected a second time on 12 April 1580, in Lorenzi 1868, app. 32, for elections (see here Appendix II); also Logan 1972, 186–90; Wolters 1987, 34; Sinding-Larsen 1974, 8.

99 Hochmann 1992, 253–54, 359–63; his palace at the Carmini was visited by Henri III (see below), and Marc'Antonio Barbaro was resident there at his death; their closeness is indicated in their respective wills, see Gullino 1996b, 77.

100 Thus Priuli was closely related to the *provveditori del Palazzo* of 1574, notably Foscari and Barbaro, as well as Morosini and Badoer (through the Pisani and Corner); Gullino 1996b, 69, 71–72; and strongly connected to the church, see further in Grendler 1990, 75; Lowry 1971, 290–91; Logan 1964, 254, with a family tree. Girolamo must have been aware of Palladio's impact in Vicenza through the family bishoprical presence, and for the influence of his father's villa at Treville, see the important article by Battilotti 1985c, 37.

101 Foscari 1983–87, 327–28, sees the instructions as reflecting a wider impulse for reorganization of the governmental institutions, but one that was soon forestalled by the decisions of the Council of Ten.

102 Transcriptions of the oral depositions by Giacomo Bozzetto, Francesco Zamberlan (see the Scuola dei Mercanti), Antonio Paliari da Marcò (see San Giorgio Maggiore and the Carità), Simone Sorella (see San Giorgio), Francesco Malacrea, Giacomo Guberni, Paolo da Ponte and Andrea dalla Valle, Antonio da Ponte (see the Rialto and Il Redentore), Angelo Marco da Corticelle (see La Celestia), Cristoforo Sorte, Giovanni Antonio Rusconi (see the Scuola dei Mercanti), and Palladio are in ASV, Compilazione Leggi, B. 205, "Fabbriche pubbliche," fasc. "Pareri di diversi architetti sulla fabbrica del Palazzo," 349–76; the written statements by Rusconi, Palladio, Andrea dalla Valle and Paolo da Ponte, and Guglielmo de Grandi are in ASV, Senato, Secreta, Materie Miste Notabili, filza 55 (prev. Miscellanea MSS), "Della fabrica del Palazzo di San Marco"; Sorte's written statement is in BMV, Cod. It. IV, 169 (52625), 67–72 (including the questionnaire, published by G. Zorzi 1965, 153–54 n. 10); Francesco Sansovino published his opinion in *Del segretario libri VII* (Venice, Appresso Cornelio Arrivabene, 1584), 215–18. The redactions are analyzed in Puppi, ed. 1988, 141–59; Tiepolo et al. 1980, 77–79. Palladio's oral and written statements have been widely published, including G. Zorzi and Puppi, as cited here; the earliest collection of opinions was published by Cadorin 1838; additional sources in Lorenzi 1868, 423–31, docs. 851–53, 433–38, doc. 856; G. Zorzi 1956–57b; G. Zorzi 1956–57a.

103 See Lupo 1998; Wolters 1996, 327–33; Wolters 2004.

104 BMV, Molin, 91; trans. from Burns with Fairbairn & Boucher 1975, 158. Again, see Preto 1991, 191–92, on the climate of suspicion reflected by Molin.

105 From the transcription in Palladio 1988a, 157, in ASV, Senato, Secreta, Materie Miste Notabili, filza 55. Lupo 1998, 19–21, provides a detailed analysis, noting that Palladio differs from the others in explaining good principles to counter the defects, such as the "pyramidal form" (*Four Books*, Bk. 1, ch. 11, 14), being inverted in the thicker walls atop more slender columns, solids over voids, and so on, as well as recourse to theorists from Vitruvius to Alberti for analogies of the relation of the whole to the parts of the body; Palladio 1997, 17; also Boucher 2000. Sennett 1994, 236–37, discusses the fear of corruption of the body politic as represented by its physical fabric, and says of the sixteenth century: "A society profoundly uncertain of itself, as at this moment Venice was, fears that it lacks the powers of *resistance*." Defensive reactions to the critique of the Doge's Palace, such as Francesco Sansovino's, may reflect this underlying mentality. Foscari 1983–87, 329, sees Sansovino's publication as further support that Palladio intended a new palace (with symbolic parallels to governmental institutions).

106 Trans. from Lewis 2000, 12.

107 Burns with Fairbairn & Boucher 1975, 158–60, who also note discrepancies with Palladio's descriptions and measurements (e.g., number of bays); quotes here are from an early object description trans. by Magrini 1845, 309–12, in Lewis 2000, 262–63 cat. 121, with a recent detailed resumé of the scholarly controversy; cf. Calabi 2001c, 435 n. 19; the most sustained argument with this attribution and purpose was made by Tafuri 1990, whose alternative proposal as "Anonimo del Cinquecento" opens up his previous attribution to "Vicenzo Scamozzi (?)" to consider Cristoforo Sorte as another possible author, and retains his alternative suggestion for the drawing as a new dogal residence.

108 Burns with Fairbairn & Boucher 1975, 159, acknowledge the deviations between the drawing and Palladio's written reports: "But the drawing must be considered not as ready for execution and exactly tailored to the pre-existing structure, but as an 'invention' closely but not precisely reflecting the problems involved. Its purpose could either be to attract interest, or alternatively (like the *Four Books* Rialto project or the *Four Books* adjusted designs of Palladio's existing works) to offer an improved, regularized version of a design which the real situation prevented from achieving a total regularity and perfection."

109 G. Zorzi 1965, 90–109, for the history of Palladio's projects for Brescia, esp. 96–100 for the fire of 18 January, 105–09 and docs. 8–16; Puppi 1986, 251–52, other projects with which the drawing has been compared include the Teatro Olimpico and Loggia Capitaniato in Vicenza, San Petronio in Bologna; Burns with Fairbairn & Boucher 1975, 239–41.

110 Puppi 1986, 252, trans. from Palladio's letter of mid-February 1575 (G. Zorzi 1965, 108, doc. 16), sees the triple-order elevation as programmatically intended by a specific patronage group (previously unsuccessfully proposed in 1550), possibly explaining its divergence from Palladio's "cogent reasoning" and quotations not fully transposed into his style; could similar thinking be applied to Venice, and the problems of the Doge's Palace drawing in Chatsworth, as fulfilling patrons' concepts (rather than having reached the stage of producing a realizable, integrated project)?

111 Boucher 1998, 243 and 255, on this point.

112 Attribution made by Olivato 1980, Puppi 1986, 252, discusses the three-story order for Brescia in relation to antique examples as in London, RIBA 1, 2 and XI, 4, and modern works such as the Carità and Farnese Palace (Rome) courtyard elevations; Boucher 1998, 254–55, also notes the dependence on quotations in the Chatsworth elevation, such as the middle-story aedicules after the Pantheon, and more generally to the Coliseum and Arena of Verona (examples cited by many scholars).

113 Respectively, in ASV, Senato, Terra, reg. 52, 15, and Consiglio dei Dieci, Comuni, reg. 33, 120v, in Lorenzi 1868, 459, docs. 858 and 849; note that both Barbaro and Foscarini absented themselves from the former vote.

114 Lewis 2000, 263, puts the design into a broader context.

115 G. Zorzi 1965, 160–62, makes the case for Zamberlan's closeness to Palladio (see also Part VI for his role as Palladio's "agent" in the estimate of the Scuola della Misericordia) and execution of the work in the palace, as well as then going further than most scholars would accept in attributing it to Palladio (esp. the tribune and portals); Calabi 2001b, 458, on his relation to Palladio as collaborator not student; see Puppi 1986, 266–68, for a thorough dissection of opinions.

116 See above for the election of 21 February 1579. The *provveditori* were: Antonio (later procurator) di Andrea P. Bragadin (on whom, see more fully under his concurrent role for Il Redentore, but it should be noted here that his mother was Barbaro's paternal aunt and his first wife was the sister of Andrea Badoer's wife from the Corner della Regina family); Giorgio Corner (if di Giacomo P., then a member of the "della Regina" branch, known as Zorzetto and whose daughter was married to Bragadin's son; Grendler 1990, 73; Logan 1972, 303–06, with a family tree (i); Hochmann 1992, 219–29; Howard 1987, 132–46); and Giovanni Mocenigo (if "alla Carità," then a collector; Logan 1972, 314; Giovanni and his brother Giovanni Battista di Andrea, later procurator, in Grendler 1979, 324–25).

117 On 10 August 1579, in ASV, Secretario alle voci, reg. 5, Elezioni del Senato, 131, in Lorenzi 1868, 459, doc. 899a, the *provveditori* were: Francesco di Marc'Antonio Bernardo (a collector of antiquities and patron of Alessandro Vittoria; Grendler 1979, 315; Logan 1972, 187, 300; Hochmann 1992, 263, will, 358–59); Jacopo Soranzo K.P. (see as previous *deputato sopra l'informazioni di luoghi*); Paolo di Santo Tron (married to a Priuli; Grendler 1990, 76). Ridolfi 1965, I: 326, somewhat confuses the *provveditori* (naming only Bernardo and Soranzo) with the program advisors Contarini (see below under Henri III) and Marcello (see with Leonardo Mocenigo and Santa Lucia); see Hochmann 1992, 258; Wolters 1987, 35, for the program, passim, and as published by Bardi (1587) in app. 341–54; Sinding-Larsen 1974, 8, on the decoration, 45–82, 220–38, for Bardi, 282–84; Schulz 1968, 107–11.

118 Da Mosto 1960, 190, notes Venier's unchallenged election as doge and previous opposition to the Peace of Cyprus, having offered his patrimony (such as it was) to Venice to continue the war; he was contrasted to Mocenigo in the eyes of one chronicler as "having little gravity and attitude in sustaining and performing the majesty of the principate, and one has often desired the prudence and eloquence of prince Mocenigo," no doubt, the very qualities that other chroniclers (such as Molin) had found dangerously close to princely authority in Mocenigo (191). Doge Nicolò da Ponte (1578–85) had served as ambassador

extraordinary (in place of Jacopo Soranzo, one of the *deputati* and *provveditori* above) to placate Pope Gregory XIII, who had excommunicated the Venetian ambassador in Rome, Paolo Tiepolo (one of the *deputati* above), on learning of the separate peace; see W. Brown 1974, 83–88.

119 From the most complete study on the visit, de Nolhac & Solerti 1890, 60, from ASF, Riformagioni, Carteggio Urbani, filza 2983.

120 P. Brown 1990, on elements of Venetian ritual for the entry of foreign powers; she notes the specific case of Venice, where no sovereign prince entered in triumph in the Renaissance. On Venetian ritual generally, see Muir 1981; and the comparative study of Casini 1996, including a good bibliographical summary of the visit, 339 n. 194.

121 14–15 July 1574, ASV, Senato, Terra, reg. 50, 26v, in G. Zorzi 1965, 178–79, doc. 17; Casini 1996, 307–08 (as ASV, Senato, Terra, reg. 50, 52v–53r), considers this a victory for the *vecchi*, with whom he identifies Vicenzo Morosini. On Morosini's connections to Palladio, see above on the Doge's Palace, and Part IV on San Giorgio Maggiore. The adroit diplomacy of ceremonial expression is illustrated by the *podestà* of Treviso's reception of Henri III, who was presented with a "magnificent" horse trained to bow at the king's approach; de Nolhac & Solerti 1890, 85–86.

122 Henri III would formally nominate to universal acceptance the candidacy of Contarini to the Senate, recognition of the success of the *apparati*, as Doge Mocenigo verbally acknowledged, in de Nolhac & Solerti 1890, 140–41, on the selection of Barbaro, 62, on Contarini, 31–32, 140–41. Palladio was probably domiciled at San Samuele from 1570; G. Zorzi 1965, 133–34, discusses the evidence. On Contarini (whose brother, Giovanni Battista, was a patron of Palladio's charitable projects, see Part VI below) as a patron, see Hochmann 2002, 89–90; Hochmann 1992, 254–63; Logan 1972, 301–02; as the heir of Daniele Barbaro's scientific current in the intellectual life of Venice and renowned as a Galilean sponsor, Tafuri 1986; Tafuri 1989, 122–38, 262 n. 138; Rose 1976; a particularly telling situation was Contarini's relationship to Giovanni Battista Maganza (Magagnò), the Vicentine dialect poet and painter, who was also close to Trissino (accompanied them to Rome, 1545–47), and who celebrated the convivial intellectual gatherings at Contarini's San Samuele palace (as well as at Francesco P. di Giovanni Pisani's villa in Montagnana, at the Barbaros at Maser), and, further, he was the editor of the play performed in Palladio's temporary theater for the Accesi (G. Zorzi 1965, 133–34, 316–17; G. Zorzi 1969, 277); his library and collections were remarked in unusual detail by Sansovino 1968, 370–71; see Puppi 1990, 20, for the provenance of Palladio's drawings from Contarini, via Scamozzi, on Gualdo's (1619) authority (in Lewis 2000, 11–12, including the

following quote in the text on their intimacy); for his will and tax declarations, see Tiepolo et al. 1980, 18–20 cat. 20–26, 36 cat. 69.

123 Sansovino 1968, 339–441, Alvise Mocenigo is not identified by patronymic in sources, the difficulty of identification is generally bypassed in literature, an exception being Casini 1996, 309 n. 199, who proposes Alvise di Tomà of *ramo* San Barnaba, one of forty youths designated to serve the king during his stay; among these were another even more tempting candidate, the son of Palladio's patron Leonardo Mocenigo, Alvise (although only 27 years old, he had received the Padua house remodeled by Palladio and its collections of antiquities the year before), see above, Part IV; more likely, however, Sansovino (1968, 372) lists a "Luigi Mocenigo" among the possessors of notable Studi d'Antecaglie, being an antiquities collector would be an appropriate qualification for the type of expertise a Roman triumph might entail; Hochmann 1992, 263, assumes this is the case; as does M. Zorzi, ed. 1988, 65; probably the same "Luigi Mocenigo" Sansovino also identifies for a notable library (371, with a brother Marc'Antonio), and with one of the Venetian *literati* (613, "Scrittori veneti"), famous for his Aristotle *Rhetorica* and therefore able to devise erudite programs, son of Francesco K., and first cousin to Palladio's close patron Leonardo (above); in her otherwise excellent article, Fletcher 1994, 136 and 150 n. 39, errs in identification, since Mocenigo cannot be the father of Leonardo, who was Antonio P. di Alvise (died 1557), on whom see Part IV. De Nolhac & Solerti 1890, for a list of the forty youths, 58–59, on the selection of Barbaro, 62, on Contarini, 31–32, 140–41. As noted, Palladio may have been domiciled at San Samuele from 1570; G. Zorzi 1965, 133–34, discusses the evidence.

124 De Nolhac & Solerti 1890, 55, 228–29, doc. 9; G. Zorzi 1965, 178, doc. 16, from ASV, Senato, Terra, vol. 50, 25, 1 July. Note the adjacent Giustiniani palaces (originally the Foscari palace was owned by the Giustinian as well) belonged to Gian Francesco and Marc'Antonio. The de' Vescovi branch of the family was also connected to San Francesco della Vigna (see Part III), related by marriage to the Grimani, Corner, Loredan, and Badoer; their father, Girolamo P., was brother to Lorenzo P. (a *provveditore del Palazzo*), and Marc'Antonio, father of Giustiniana, wife of Marc'Antonio Barbaro

125 Sansovino 1968, 388, the four palaces were the Dolfin at San Salvador and Corner at San Maurizio (both by his father), Grimani at San Luca (by Sanmicheli), and Loredan at San Marcuola (designed by Mauro Codussi).

126 See the Conclusion, on Henri III's visit to Malcontenta; he also visited the Villa Contarini at Mira, on which Fletcher 1994, 150 n. 39, mistakes Jacopo Contarini as the patron, and Palladio as the architect, of the villa at Mira, later Contarini-Pisani "delle Leoni,"

actually belonging to Federico (later procurator) di Francesco Contarini dalle Due Torri of *ramo* San Luca, who was married to the niece of Doge Alvise Mocenigo, Lucrezia di Giovanni P. di Tommaso P. Mocenigo, and a strong *papalisti* as well as supporter of Le Zitelle (for which, see Part VI).

127 See Part II, above, for the Foscari; Gullino 1997a, Alvise Foscari was first elected to the Council of Ten in 1572–73, his career was curtailed subsequent to the reform of the Zonta, aligning him with the *vecchi*. In addition to Casini 1996, 307–08, on the *vecchi*; Casini 1995, 37 n. 75. The signed painting is dated by Mason Rinaldi 1984, 84 cat. 88, *circa* 1593–95, depending from the inscription on the print by Martin Preis (for which see below), and a preparatory drawing is in Vienna, Albertina (D196); an earlier date with a *terminus post quem* of 1578 and *ante quem* of 1589 has been proposed by Mozzetti & Sarti 1997, 155–57, who convincingly identify a portrait of Morosini (died 1589) wearing his procuratorial robes (elected *de citra* 1578) and cavalier's stole.

128 Casini 1996, 305–06 and 338 n. 185, negatively associated by Marin Sanudo with "monarchia" (1879–1903, 34, cols. 5–6); and see further, Tafuri 1984a and Muir 1984, 59–77.

129 Muir 1997, ch. 7, "Government as Ritual Process"; Mitchell 1986, ch. 1, "The Background and Occasions of Italian Renaissance Pageantry"; Strong 1984, pt. 1, ch. 3, "The Spectacles of State"; a fundamental resource is Jacquot, ed. 1956–75; and Mulryne 2002.

130 Barkan 1986, 221–31; Strong 1984, 7–11, on "les rois thaumaturges." Literature on the entries of Charles V is summarized in Mitchell 1986, 173–79; and Baldwin 1990; with useful reconstructions of the various entries in Fagiolo, ed. 1979. Gleason 2000 refocuses the political paradigm shift of Venice at this moment.

131 Mitchell 1986, 147, also notes Charles V's appreciation of the recently built Palazzo del Tè (such interests in the new architecture would be echoed by Henri III); Adorni 1989, 498–501.

132 Mitchell 1986, 29, the only other notice being for the *possesso* of Alexander VI (Rodrigo Borgia) in Rome in 1492, where one of the arches in the streets was modeled after the Arch of Constantine.

133 Mitchell 1986, 151.

134 Mitchell 1986, 160–65, notes a discrepancy with the actual practices as understood for ancient Rome, 7.

135 Ackerman 1986, 152; and see Part II above.

136 Mitchell 1986, 13.

137 Pastor 1969, 18: 432–33; Colonna was said to be quite popular in Venice.

138 *I trionfi feste et livree fatte dalli signori conservatori, & e popolo romano, & da tutte le arte di Roma, nella felicissima, & honorata entrata dell' illustrissimo signor Marcantonio Colonna*, Venice [Domenico Farri?], 1571, copy in the Marciana, which also has a copy of another *livret*,

by Francesco Albertonio, *L'entrata che fece l'Eccellentissimo Signor Marc'Antonio Colonna in Roma alli 4. di dicembre 1571*, Viterbo, n.p. [1571], showing the circulation of this event; the latter author noted in Mitchell 1986, 34.

139 This was regarding information for later depictions of the battle itself in the fresco in the Sala Regia in the Vatican Palace, see Partridge & Starn 1990, 49–50 n. 67; on the artistic nexus between Venice and Rome, see also Cooper 2001, 141–48.

140 De Nolhac & Solerti 1890, 100.

141 Documents in G. Zorzi 1965, 176, doc. 7; summary in Puppi 1986, 101.

142 Wolters 1979, 279–80, notes the unusual allowance for a dogal *stemma* to appear outside of the Doge's Palace on the "portoni" erected in Piazza San Marco for this occasion; for a new interpretation of this event, see Tondro 2002.

143 Benedetti 1571 [5r–6r]; Padoan Urban 1969, 148 and 155 n. 26, gives this passage, noting the imprecision of description; Wolters 1979, 279, cites Sansovino's passage, which is very close to Benedetti's (Sansovino 1968, 415). On Panvinio (1529/30–1568), see Partridge & Starn 1990, 24, for his contemporary influence.

144 Morsolin 1878, 187–99, for the years 1529–32; Gullino 2000, 139–41, discusses Marco Foscari's contact with the circle of Trissino and Ridolfi in Rome, where, as a Medici adherent, he was involved with cardinals Salviati and Ridolfi in proposals for Elena di Marco Grimani's marriage, eventually, however, marrying her to his son, Pietro (as explicated in his useful family trees on 39, 94, 115).

145 Morsolin 1878, 286, on the visit of 1541 to Bagnaia, 294–98 on Ridolfi's entry; G. Zorzi 1965, 167–79; Puppi 1986, 101.

146 G. Zorzi 1965, on Priuli, 170–71; Puppi 1986, 215, considers this entry to be a rehash of 1543.

147 Mitchell 1986, 211. See also Watanabe-O'Kelly 2002, 15–25.

148 Ivanoff 1972, 322, the source for the visit attributed to Carlo Ridolfi, whereas Marc'Antonio Michiel's claim is generally accepted (Michiel 1969, 133), that the king wanted to buy Paolo D'Anna's *Ecce Homo* by Titian (Vienna, Kunsthistorisches Museum) for 800 ducats; J. Brown 1994, 29, on its acquisition in Venice.

149 Verheyan 1990, 214 n. 4, arranges the most cited accounts by date (I have consulted the Benedetti edition of 20 November). For more, see de Nolhac & Solerti 1890, 3–27, who also correct the name of one of the procurators, substituting Giovanni K. di Priamo da Lezze for Ottaviano di Marc'Antonio Grimani (accounts, such as Sansovino's, that relied on Benedetti follow his list), 100 n. 1.

150 *L'Historia della publica et famosa entrata in Vinegia del serenissimo Henrico III re di Francia, et Polonia, Con la descrittione particolare della pompa, e del numero, & varietà delli Bregantini,*

Palaschermi, & altri vasselli armati, con la dechiaratione dell'edificio, & arco fatto al Lido, Venice, n.p., 1574, 12–15; trans. from Chambers & Pullan, eds. 1992, 64–65, although I have substituted for the translation where it is given as "44.5 feet [*sic*] 7 inches high"; the original measurements as given by della Croce are: "un quadrilatero, lungo piedi cinquanta cinque, largo quatordeci, & alto quaranta quattro, onzi sette, e mezo." Verheyan 1990, 214 n. 3, della Croce's publication follows by some months, on 1 December, those of Benedetti, Tommaso Porcacchi (30 September 1574) and Nicolò Lucangeli (30 October 1574).

151 Palladio 1554a, 8r, "De gli archi trionfali e a chi si facevano," with a description of the decorative elements both allegorical and historical, relating to Septimius' victory over the Parthians; see Puppi, ed. 1988, 18, and for other references.

152 Palladio 1997, 193. See the useful commentary on this passage with references to Barbaro's Vitruvius in Magagnato & Marini, eds. of Palladio 1980, 505–08; Puppi 1990, 93–94 cat. 22, regards this drawing as the penultimate stage prior to being ready for the printer, although dating it to the late 1540s–early 1550s (based on the autograph orthography), stating that the Arch of Septimius Severus "was one of the ancient ruins Palladio studied most closely," with four drawings in Vicenza, Museo Civico (D 2r–v and D 13r–v), and two in London, RIBA (XII, 6r–v), and noting after Erik Forssman that the Composite capital on D 13r–v is after the Arch of Titus. Some of the measurements on the sheet indicate the width of the central arch as "18 feet 10 inches," and side arches as "8 feet 3 inches – minutes."

153 All subsequent visual representations show the columns as Corinthian, as in G. Zorzi 1965, 172, describing Andrea Vicentino's Doge's Palace painting; and shown as clearly Corinthian as interpreted by Antonio Visentini's series for Consul Smith in 1750 (London, BL, Royal MS 146), on which see more below.

154 Padoan Urban 1980, with a thorough catalog of visual material related to the entry, on 161, cat. 158, both states are reproduced, including the second in BCV, Stampe Gherro, 1741; both states circulated, as can be seen in a copy of the first by Angelo Tramontin in Vicenza, MC, inv. 1669; also Padoan Urban 1969, 148; and see the important contribution of Wolters 1979, questioning the attribution of the loggia to Palladio, on which see further below.

155 The assumption of Palladio's authorship of the loggia is reflected in the translation in Chambers & Pullan, eds. 1992, 64–65, "By means of the arch one passed beyond to a loggia which faced it and was built by the honored and ingenious architect Palladio, supervised by the lords Luigi Mocenigo and Iacomo Contarini, who are most honorable noblemen and possess great spirit." The crucial phrase regarding an attribution of the loggia to Palladio is: "di passare per quello [the arch]

ad una loggia fabricata all'incontro dopò esso eretti da l'honorato & ingenioso architetto Paladio," della Croce 1574, 12. Puppi 1986, 248, translates only parts of the crucial sentence, stringing together the phrases "triumphal arch with three doorways," "beautiful large loggia," "of the Corinthian order with large pilasters," "somewhat apart opposite the arch" without questioning the attribution, but see now Battilotti 1999, 504, acknowledging the question, although retaining Palladio's authorship.

156 The remainder of the translation follows Chambers & Pullan, eds. 1992, 64–65. G. Zorzi 1965, 171–72, gives measurements of the arch in meters as: central arch 9 m. high and 5 m. wide, lateral arches 5.25 m. high and 2.50 m. wide; and of the loggia as: 28 m. long by 14 m. wide.

157 The quote continues from above after describing the scenes and inscriptions on the arch: "Alquanto discosto all'incontro dell'arco, era una bella & gran Loggia con dieci colonne d'ordine corinthio co [sic] suoi pilastroni." Sansovino 1968, 445. Wolters 1979, 275–76, adds to Sansovino and Benedetti another source that specifically names Palladio only as author of the arch: Porcacchi 1574, 24, and noting among modern authors that only Forssman 1964, 124, expressed doubts about the loggia due to its appearance.

158 Verheyan 1990, 214–15; Cooper 2001, 141.

159 The corroborating legend at lower left reads: "Henrico III Franciae atque Poloniae regi christianissimo ac invictissimo christianae religionis acerrimo propugnatori advenienti venetorum respublica ad veteris benevolentiae atque observantiae declarationem. Pro serenissima Foscarorum aede," in Padoan Urban 1980, 154–55, whose doubts on the traditional attribution to Andrea Vicentino are surely justified. Note also that della Croce's dedicatee (1574, 3–4) was another Foscari, Filippo Edvardo (who remains to be identified), to whom he explained that his intention in writing the account included "his desire to celebrate, exalt, and highlight with all his ability in every part, to increase Your greatness, glory, splendor, and exaltation, and then for particular obligation that I singularly bear towards the entire illustrious House of Foscari," noting the participation of the recipient's brother.

160 The arch (fol. 2r) and loggia (fol. 5v–6r) in elevation and plan from: "Pianta ed alzato del magnifico arco trionfale e loggia eretto dal celebre architetto Andrea Palladio, per ordine pubblico, in occasione della venuta a Venezia di Enrico terzo, Rè di Francia e Pollonia, l'anno MDLXXIV. Diligentemente dissegnato e sopra le giuste misure prese dalla relazione di Marsilio dalla Croce eseguito da Antonio Visentini, pittore ed architetto Veneziano, l'anno del Giubileo MDCCL," title page (fol. 1r). The other drawings are: fol. 3r, arch side elevations; fol. 5r, arch decorative panels; fol. 7r, loggia side elevation, fol. 8r, alternate arch ele-

vation and plan (added allegorical figures); fol. 9r, alternate loggia elevation and plan (added allegorical figures); fol. 10r, loggia side elevation without pediment (indicates Visentini's access to both states of Zenoni's print); reproduced in Padoan Urban 1980, 152–54 cat. 148.

161 The response from the interlocutor follows, "M. A.: This Arch of Septimius, for being made in the time that the Roman Empire had declined, doesn't have in it that perfection, and beauty in its parts, and in the goodness of the figures, that the Arch of Titus has at the head of the Comitio [Forum]: the latter is more ancient than all the others, but however, it is beautiful," Porcacchi 1574, 24, the passage is in Wolters 1979, 278, to explain the choice of the arch as an imperial reference. No one has remarked that Porcacchi is the only source to identify the order correctly. On the appearance of the arch, see Brilliant 1967, 36.

162 G. Zorzi 1965, 173.

163 Burns with Fairbairn & Boucher 1975, 150; Puppi 1990, 91 cat. 16, additional studies in London, RIBA, XI, 17r–v and 18r–v, and VII, 5v. Lewis 2000, 95–96 cat. 39–40, illustrates 17r and 18r, but makes no connection to the loggia, noting, however, the Severan patronage of this entrance portico, which would make it a historically appropriate model.

164 Wolters 1979, 287–88.

165 Chastel 1960, 31; Fagiolo 1979, 11, advances this concept since he declares it "the visual manifestation of a political manifesto."

166 Grendler 1990, 75; also Morin 1985, 229; to get a sense of why this branch of the family was known as the "Golden Touch," see W. Brown 1974, who compares a sample of prominent political figures' real estate incomes: in Table IVA, among 25 individuals in 1566, Soranzo's income was 2,641 ducats, second only to Girolamo Grimani's at 3,975, although in 1571 Soranzo's income rose to 3,236 ducats; in Table VIb, among seven individuals listed for 1580–83, Soranzo's remains second with 2,557 ducats, somewhat lower than the previous decade. On portraits of Jacopo Soranzo and his family, see P. Brown 2004, 16–19; Pilo 1997; P. Rossi 1974, 130. Soranzo is depicted as provveditore general dell'armata in his portrait in the Museo Storico Navale, Venice, attributed to Jacopo Tintoretto, circa 1575 (as is a version in Vienna, Kunsthistorisches Museum).

167 Gorse 1990, 195–96; similarly on such a transposition, Fagiolo 1979, 15–16.

168 Howard 1993, 8–9. The visit of Henri III would be commemorated by a marble inscription by the Scala dei Giganti, in Sansovino 1968, 320–21; voted on 12 March 1575, in ASV, Collegio, Cerimoniale II, 21–22; also ASV, Senato, Terra, reg. 50, 125v, in Lorenzi 1868, 395, doc. 808; de Nolhac & Solerti 1890, 169 and 254–55, doc. 33; G. Zorzi 1965, 179–80, doc. 20; the inscription itself became a commemorative object, executed by Marc'Antonio Palladio in Alessandro Vittoria's studio.

169 "Henrico III. Francia atque Poloniae Regi

Christianis. & invictiss. Christianae religionis acerrimo propugnatiori advenienti, Venetorum Resp. ad veteris benevolentiae, atque observantiae declarationem," in Sansovino 1968, 440, and on the inside face of the arch visible to the king as he returned from the loggia was a second inscription welcoming him to Venice: "Henrico III. Franciae & Poloniae Regi Optimo atque fortissimo, hospiti incomparabili, Venetorum Respub. ob eius adventum foelicissimum" (441).

170 Sansovino 1968, 445; following Benedetti 1574, 4v. Contrast the expanded descriptions in della Croce 1574, 13–13v, where the paintings are attributed to Paolo Veronese and Jacopo Tintoretto (but see Verheyen 1990, 220–21, who identifies Borghini 1584, 558, as the first to mention the king's interest in being portrayed by Tintoretto); Ridolfi 1965, 2: 207–08, adds that Antonio Vassilacchi ("Aliense") participated in the decoration of the arch, and is a reliable source for this artist who was his teacher; but once again caution must be advised, since Sansovino does not mention these painters well known to him. On the other hand, this was a prestigious commission that could well have engaged these prominent painters and their studios in the hurried production described by the Florentine ambassador and, since both worked for the Doge's Palace, their participation is conceivable; furthermore, the project called for the rapid execution that Tintoretto was known for. There is documentary evidence of Tintoretto's work for the king, because three unspecified paintings were listed in the expenses for the trip (de Nolhac & Solerti 1890, 115–16, 251, for 50 escuz), and it has been assumed that these include portraits of Henri III (P. Rossi 1974, 42; Verheyen 1990, 220), although the story of Tintoretto riding along in the Bucintoro to sketch the king, later visiting the Foscari Palace to finalize the portrait, may be less supportable; after Ridolfi 2:1965, 36–37.

171 Ventura 1963, elected in 1575 as ambassador to France, but died in Vercelli (11 September); Grendler 1979, 316, notes that Badoer was strongly anti-Spain (and thus had opposed the Holy League and favored a separate peace with the Turks); see above as provveditore sopra la fabbrica del Palazzo for the fire of 1574.

172 Grendler 1990, 75; Grendler 1979, 322–23, later procurator de citra; his brother Jacopo had been ambassador to France in the years 1555–58, Grendler 1990, 75. A portrait in P. Rossi 1974, 146, inscribed ANN. XLIX, with a depiction of Castel Sant'Angelo in the background; it commemorates Soranzo's role in the negotiations over the Holy League, he was 49 in 1569; his commission of the votive painting by Jacopo Palma "il Giovane" (Padua, Museo Civico) showed him as podestà of Padua (1589–91); it served also as a rehabilitation of his brother, Jacopo (podestà 1569–70), condemned to exile for treason in 1584 (revoked in 1586), and this position was Giovanni's

return to significant office; see Mason Rinaldi 1991; Pilo 1997.

173 Grendler 1990, 74, later procurator, was succeeded in France by Marc'Antonio Barbaro (see above), and again as ambassador extraordinary in 1572, ostensibly to prevent outright war between Spain and France, but covertly to explore support for a separate peace with the Turks; on which see Tenenti 1974, 404.

174 Grendler 1979, 331, later procurator, notes his unprecedented election to simultaneous *provveditore generale*, *sindaco* and *inquisitore* in Candia, 1574–78, when Crete was of immense strategic importance after the recent loss of Cyprus; in 1539 Foscarini (aged 16) was in the entourage of the Venetian ambassador extraordinary to France, see Zago 1997: 365, also noting his cautious anti-Spanish analysis post-Lepanto and support for peace with the Turks (367), although his later pragmatism would associate him with pro-Spanish positions identified with the *vecchi*. Only a few months after the king's visit, Foscarini and Marc'Antonio Barbaro became father-in-laws with the marriage of Alvise Barbaro to Maria di Jacopo P. Foscarini (21 November 1574); see Gullino 1996b, 97. The political effects of a Grimani–Barbaro–Foscarini "consortium" are analyzed by Trebbi 1984, 383–84; as well as by Lowry 1971, 304–05.

175 De Nolhac & Solerti 1890, 132–34.

176 De Nolhac & Solerti 1890, 143.

177 R. Davis 1999.

178 Strong 1984, 112–17; note only in Padua was there a depiction of this extreme event, not in Venice proper. A succinct statement of French policy in the Mediterranean as revolving around the containment of Spain is in Tenenti 1974, achieving a sort of *de facto* neutrality during the Holy League with the Ottomans, and encouraging Venetian rapprochement on its conclusion.

179 Strong 1984, 116, an indicator of this reform zeal was Henri III's introduction of the Order of the Holy Spirit, ironically a precious gift from Doge Mocenigo was a manuscript of its statutes; the doge also took an opportunity to counsel the young king on the virtues of peace, de Nolhac & Solerti 1890, 136.

180 Wolters 1979, 276, discovery of the date in Nagler led to the accepted redating of derived works, including Vicentino's, and he proposed rereading the subject in light of the political situation in the 1590s, culminating in its resolution with the Peace of Vervins, and celebrations of the wedding progress of 1598 of Margaret of Austria, consort of Philip III of Spain; see in Mitchell 1986, 165. For de Moustier, in BCV, MS P.D. 2416, see also in Padoan Urban 1980, 162.

181 Wolters 1987, 101–02.

182 Wolters 1979, 276, a *terminus ante quem* for Vicentino's painting is provided in an engraving by Martin Preiss (Preÿs) with an inscription of 1593; in BCV, MS P.D. 2417, see Padoan Urban 1980, 160.

183 Sansovino 1604, 225r–v. A similar strategy was probably employed in Palma il Giovane's portraits of the king's arrival at Palazzo Foscari: Mason Rinaldi 1984, 84 cat. 88, identifies the figures to the left of Henri III as the patriarch and Marc'Antonio Barbaro, and to the right as Doge Mocenigo and Pietro Foscari, but the latter seems to be ruled out by the French costume, next to a figure identified by Ivanoff 1972, 316, as Henri d'Angoulême, half-brother to the king.

184 Lowry 1971, for a cautionary revision of more dramatic conceptualizations of the debates over the dissolution of the Zonta of the Council of Ten in 1582–83 (i.e., Stella 1958b), showing through an analysis of the leading political figures in the next decades that many of the same *vecchi* retained power, but acknowledging, however, that the institutional changes effected a shift in areas of decision-making back to the more public bodies and out of the control of the more elite group in the Zonta (which had also been a means of avoiding *contumacia*, and assuring the continuous presence of this group); see Trebbi 1984, 61–62, for a moderated point of view of the effect on the Barbaro, especially Marc'Antonio and his son, later patriarch of Aquileia, Francesco, who was also associated with his father's activities in Constantinople.

185 Although Jacopo Soranzo was alive (died 1599), he had been sidelined following a political scandal in 1584, and Paolo Tiepolo had died in 1585; both, however, had powerful brothers who had succeeded to important offices; Grendler 1990, respectively 75, 80; Grendler 1979, 325, 316. Both men had been involved in the restoration of the Doge's Palace after the fire of 1577, see above, and Tiepolo in Il Redentore, which had been consecrated the preceding year, 1592 (Barbaro, Soranzo, and Tiepolo had served together as *sopra-provveditore alla sanità* in 1577, the year Il Redentore was begun and the plague was officially declared over), see further below.

186 The name was chosen by Marc'Antonio Barbaro to symbolize "Victory" (attribute: the palm branch), see Sinding-Larsen 1974, 88 n.1, on the commemoration of Lepanto. For more, see Pavan, ed. 1993. For Barbaro's and Foscarini's roles in the fires of 1574 and 1577 respectively, see above.

187 For example, the portrait *Marc' Antonio Barbaro, Knight, 1572* (Venice, Accademia, on deposit with the Fondazione Cini) of 1591 by Alberto d'Hollanda (Lambert Sustris), formerly in the Procuratia de Supra, Hopkins 2003, 220, cat. 12d; Burns with Fairbairn & Boucher 1975, 157–58, cat. 278, provides a summary of the literature and documentation; also P. Rossi 1980, 245, notes the confusion caused by identical inscriptions for this portrait and another in the same collection (with a copy in Vienna), which shows the younger Barbaro of the Peace of 1573, and was probably executed then, Rossi believes by the same

artist (see above, Part I), whereas the inscription here refers retrospectively to his election date, and clearly shows the features of the still vigorous 73-year-old, as "Alberto d'Hollanda" (Lambert Sustris) is documented as being paid on 30 March 1591 for the portrait, originally commissioned from Tintoretto.

188 See for Palladio's *cantiere*, Cooper 1995; and the fundamental study by Tafuri 1989, ch. 7, "Renewal and Crisis. The Debate on the *imago urbis* between 1580 and the Interdict"; Foscari 1983–87, 329, notes the more overt tenor of dissent in the case of the Rialto and Procuratie Nuove.

189 I would like to thank Deborah Howard warmly for her generosity in sharing with me prior to its publication in 2003 her important article "Marc'Antonio Barbaro and Palladio's Church of the Redentore," with new contributions regarding the genesis of the plan of the church; also now add Pizzigoni 2003, who brings to the debate the letter of Gabriele Fiamma (166), and several new useful graphic project reconstructions (on Fiamma, see above, Part IV). For Il Redentore, see the monograph by Timofiewitsch 1971; Timofiewitsch 1968; the most complete documents in G. Zorzi 1967, 121–41; a review of the literature in Puppi 1986, 262–66; earlier bibliography collected in Burns 2000, and Beltramini & Padoan, eds. 2000, 261–63.

190 Fundamental influences in the writing on its function and typology are: Wittkower 1962, 97–100; Wittkower 1963; Ackerman 1977b, 127–32; Isermeyer 1968.

191 I thank *bibliotecario* Padre Tellan for his assistance at the Archivio della Provincia Veneta dei Frati Cappuccini, Mestre (MAPC). The former archivist, P. Davide M. da Portogruaro, is fundamental for the history of the Capuchins at Il Redentore and for his archival researches: Portogruaro 1930 and Portogruaro 1957.

192 Puppi & Romanelli, eds. 1985; Puppi, ed., 1980b; Brusatin, ed. 1979; Cosgrove 1993.

193 Estimates run around a population loss of 30 percent for the plague of 1575–77; see *Venezia e la peste* 1979; Preto 1978; Preto 1991, 183–87, on the climate of fear; Pullan 1971, 314–25.

194 Valier 1719, 392; as cardinal bishop of Verona, Valier was directly involved in plague relief efforts, and well aware of the measures being undertaken by the Magistrato alla Sanità in Venice, e.g., Agostino Valier, *Lettera consolatoria*, Venice, n.p., 1575.

195 4 September 1576, in ASV, Senato, Terra, reg. 51, 2v, in G. Zorzi 1967, 130–31, the contributions as part of doc. 1 (also Tiepolo et al. 1980 80, cat. 222, as ASV, Senato, Secreta, Annali, 1594–79), the contributions not included in the version in Timofiewitsch 1971, 65, doc. 1, from ASV, Collegio, Cerimoniale I, 47.

196 8 September 1576, ASV, Collegio, Cerimoniale I, 48; in G. Zorzi 1967, 131, doc. 2; Timofiewitsch 1971, 65–66, doc. 2.

197 Trans. from the King James Bible (1611), Book II, also known as Book IV, an almost identical

198 phrase is used in the preceding chapter when the Lord delivers Jerusalem by smiting down the Assyrian army (another allusion, this time to Lepanto?), II, 19: 34. On Fra Cosmo, Portogruaro 1936, 47–49.

198 18 September 1576, in ASV, Senato, Terra, reg. 51, 114, in G. Zorzi 1967, 131–32, doc. 3; Timofiewitsch 1971, 66, doc. 3; on the combining of the provveditorial duties, 10 September and 18 November 1591, G. Zorzi 1967, 141, docs. 35 and 36; only the information relative to the Doge's Palace in Lorenzi 1868, 327–28, docs. 1021 and 1023.

199 See Tucci 1971, 663–64, with a careful distinction between the homonymic Antonio di Nicolò (active on Cyprus and at Lepanto), not made in the ASV, Barbaro, "Albori"; Grendler 1990, 318; Lowry 1971, 285, 301, 307–10; for income, in ASV, Dieci Savi sopra la Decima, B. 131, 894, and B. 161, 1114 (showing his *casa da statio* in *contra* Santa Marina in 1582), see W. Brown 1974, 181–83, Tables IVa and b (mislabeled as VIb), for a comparative declaration of income that shows Bragadin (as Zuan Antonio) as third wealthiest in 1566 (income 2,225 ducats, after Girolamo Grimani and Jacopo Soranzo), and first in 1582 (income 4,037 ducats); see Part VI on Le Zitelle, esp. noted by Foscari 1975; Frank 1992, 101, where she notes Bragadin's contribution. Bragadin was briefly *provveditore del Palazzo* in 1579 when Palladio's close patron Jacopo Contarini was selected as advisor for the program of the Maggior Consiglio, see above. Antonio's second wife was Maria di Alvise Dr. di Leonardo P. Mocenigo, and mother of their son Andrea, a senator, married first to Marietta di Domenico Priuli, and second to the daughter of "Zorzetto" (Giorgio) di Giacomo P. di Giorgio (Zorzi) K.P. Corner della Regina; on the Cortesi, Venturi 1983, 140.

200 See Ventura 1964a, with a careful distinction between the homonymic *provveditore general* of the fleet at Lepanto (*de facto* military strategist and commander of the left wing, dying of his wounds), not made in the ASV, Barbaro, "Albori"; Grendler 1990, 327; see Part VI on Le Zitelle, also Foscari 1975, 56; esp. noted by Frank 1992, 101, where she supports a claim for Barbarigo's Jesuit leanings; on the conclaves, Da Mosto 1960, 301, 307. Agostino's wife was the daughter of Vettor Pisani. There seem to be repeated marital links between the Barbarigo and Bragadin, but not directly between the branches concerned from what I have traced, although it may be enough to indicate that a closer look at alliances would be fruitful.

201 The proposal from the sisters at Santa Croce and its subsequent survey was announced prior to its presentation, that undated document inserted between 17 and 22 November 1576, in ASV, Senato, Terra, filza 70, in G. Zorzi 1967, 132, doc. 4; Tiepolo et al. 1980, 80 cat. 225. The church was suppressed in the nineteenth century and razed in the re-zoning of

the area for Piazzale Roma, the Rio Nuovo, and the Giardini ex-Papadopoli, across the Grand Canal from the Ferrovia Santa Lucia (some writers have confused the site with Santa Croce on the Giudecca, a Benedictine convent), see A. Zorzi 2001, 218–19; Franzoi & di Stefano 1976a, 84–86.

202 17 November 1576, in ASV, Senato, Terra, reg. 51, 133v–134, in G. Zorzi 1967, 132, doc. 5.

203 22 November 1576, in ASV, Senato, Terra, reg. 51, 134, in G. Zorzi 1967, 132–33, doc. 6; excerpts in Timofiewitsch 1971, 66, doc. 4; Foscari 1975, 56, noted the voters for this motion.

204 For Tiepolo, see above on the fire of 1577; for Donà, see Part IV, on San Giorgio Maggiore.

205 9 February 1577 (*m.v.* 1576), in ASV, Senato, Terra, reg. 51, 155–56, in G. Zorzi 1967, 133, doc. 7; Timofiewitsch 1971, 67, doc. 5; partial transcription in Tiepolo et al. 1980, 80 cat. 225. Howard 2003, 306 and 321 n. 3, corrects a persistent trend when she firmly notes that the proposal for two alternative three-dimensional models was not acted on.

206 17 February 1577 (*m.v.* 1576), in ASV, Collegio, Cerimoniale I, 50, in G. Zorzi 1967, 133, doc. 8 (as 16 February); Timofiewitsch 1971, 67, doc. 6 (as fol. 1); and in ASV, Collegio, Notatorio, reg. 42, 185v, in Tiepolo et al. 1980, 81, cat. 226. Some scholars have interpreted the term *quadrangolare* as used by Palladio to mean a centralized plan, thus an ideal geometrical form like the circular (indeed this is the thrust of Sinding-Larsen 1965a, whose argument rests on the longitudinal nave being an addition to the desired ideal form—much as at St. Peter's, between Michelangelo and Carlo Maderno), but this is no longer considered viable, see Howard 2003, 306 and 321 n. 3; although Schofield 1997, 408, noted a deliberately ambiguous use by Palladio (having his theoretical cake and eating it too).

207 In brief, the arraignment of pro- and anti-Jesuit forces that would characterize the later events of the Interdict are seen in nucleus in the debate over the San Vidal site, with Tiepolo and (less so) Barbaro versus Donà and (less so) Mocenigo, with Palladio's Jesuit patronage contacts transferring to Le Zitelle (although this summary fails to do justice to the more complex arguments made to support this general point, for which see Foscari 1975, 50, on the "alleanza del 'partito' gesuitico con quello 'palladiano'"; also Tafuri 1980, 25–26; Battilotti 1985b, 41–42); but, as will be seen, dating seems to exclude Palladio from association with the San Vidal site. Another problem with this polarization is that Barbaro, as is well known, was well disposed to the Franciscan Order, his family deeply involved in San Francesco della Vigna (see above, Part III), and, as will be seen below, Tiepolo was seen by the Capuchins as their protector; albeit, Donà was later in favor of banning the Jesuits from Venice, although his comments as Valier puts them are not all that inflammatory.

208 The sequence of Valier's speeches conflates separate responses by Barbaro and Donà to Tiepolo on the site (debated 22 November), and by Donà to Barbaro on the plan (debated 9 February), nor are Barbaro's words given as a quote, as are Tiepolo's and Donà's; Valier 1719, 392–95, the author's approach to historical narrative can be determined by analyzing the text for similarly chronologically compressed accounts.

209 Da Mosto 1960, 276, 279, his wife's funeral procession was accompanied by the nuns of Santa Croce alla Giudecca, who would also host the first procession to lay the foundation stone on 3 May 1577 (more below). Another hypothesis has been raised to explain Barbaro's support of the Jesuits at San Vidal, since he was not known for being a strong supporter of theirs, since the site was near the Palazzo Barbaro, but it should be remembered that he was no longer living there by 1566 (recorded in Cha Belegno at San Geremia), and a few years later, in 1581, he was living with his brother-in-law Leonardo Giustinian at San Stae; see Gullino 1996b, 73 (ASV, Dieci Savi sopra la Decima, 1566, B. 134, 180) and 77 (idem, 1581, B. 157, 296).

210 Timofiewitsch 1971, 17, proposes that the coins represent the doge's contribution, cites its provenance from the Mocenigo-Robilant collection, and suggests that it represents a model of the church made between 9 February and 3 May; Battilotti 1980a, 268 cat. 440, summarizes attributions and dating, and sees as probably inspired by the decision to build another votive church, La Salute; another example of the retrospective commemoration of the doge's role in saving Venice from the plague, probably commissioned by members of the Mocenigo family, is in Verona, Museo di Castelvecchio, *The Doge and Signoria Implore the Redeemer for Liberation from the Plague, circa* 1590, by Palma il Giovane, see Mason Rinaldi 1984, 149 cat. 598.

211 The document abstract is worded: "che detta chiesa sia fatta secondo il modello presentato in Collegio," whereas the body of the decree reads that the *provveditori* presented "un dissegno," but the term *modello* in the Renaissance could refer to either two- or three-dimensional designs, and without some descriptive qualification, such as *in relievo*, was more often a drawing. Sansovino 1968, 255, in 1581 recounts the "careful and diligent" progress of the church made according to Palladio's "modello" ("fabricando con sollecitudine & diligenza, sul modello d'Andrea Palladio)." For the term and the practice of models, see Millon 1994b, 70–72, if a model was made, it probably would have been as a construction guide, or "final model," 35, as an extreme, Antonio da Sangallo the Younger's model for St. Peter's, the largest extant wood model from the Renaissance, took seven years to build; Cooper 1994b, 500; Carpo 2001, 171–73.

212 Burns with Fairbairn & Boucher 1975, 147, does suggest two drawings also may be related to Il Redentore, London, RIBA, XIII, 18v, for a church interior, and Oxford, Ruskin School, for an altar tabernacle; Burns 1991, 193, 215–16, on his education of craftsmen.

213 Lord Burlington's acquisition of the drawings from the Trevisan descendents in 1719 was probably not at Maser as legend has it, but in Venice, where Puppi 1990, 13, traces it to the drawings left by Palladio with Jacopo Contarini (see also Lewis 2000, 16, and 249–57 cat. 114–17, for an up-to-date account of earlier literature), see further in Part VI, under Le Zitelle.

214 G. Zorzi 1965, 343–46, documents his presence in Vicenza through payments on the Basilica that he received in person.

215 Adding up the authorized payments, G. Zorzi 1967, 126–27, estimates expenditures during Palladio's lifetime at 29,000 ducats (4 September 1576–7 November 1579), with another 48,000 ducats advanced by the completion of most of the construction (6 May 1581–22 December 1586), 5,100 for pavement and altar furnishings (16 May 1588–11 November 1591), not counting expenses of 800 ducats yearly for the *ponte*; Portogruaro 1930, 222, estimates a higher total of 95,850 ducats, he adds payments made through to 29 May 1592, including construction on the convent (of which two deliberations do indicate payments by the Senate, 11 November 1581 and 26 February 1592 *m.v.* (=1593), for 6,020 ducats, see Portogruaro 1957, 416–18), and includes in his total the pledges of Mocenigo, Grimani, and Bragadin as over and above the initial sum of 12,000 ducats.

216 See the summaries in Lewis 2000, 249–55 cat. 114–17; although Burns with Fairbairn & Boucher 1975, 146 cat. 258, and Puppi 1986, 276–77, do not believe the drawings relate to the Tempietto, but do agree with projects "in forma rotonda" for Il Redentore on the Giudecca, following Pane's original suggestion (1961, 304–05), the latter more accepting of a subsequently mediated association with Le Zitelle; Isermeyer 1969, 476, agrees but assigns them to the San Vidal site transferred from the Jesuits there to the Jesuits at Le Zitelle (see above, for concurrences by Foscari, Tafuri, and Battilotti); Frank 1992, 106–09, sees the drawings (regardless of the site, although favoring a Jesuit connection) as another influence on a project already begun by 1574 (but see Lewis, as cited). An unanswered question about the transmission, given the hypothesis of a connection between the *provveditori* Bragadin and Barbarigo with both Giudecca sites, is how drawings in Barbaro's hands if used for the Tempietto were actually made available: here the affinal relationship between first cousins Barbaro and Bragadin may have served the circulation of these ideas; these drawings would have been available to both sites if they already were kept at the Contarini palace, see Le Zitelle in Part VI.

217 Howard 2003, for a background on this way of thinking; and more broadly, Howard 2000; I would also like to thank Oleg Grabar for his observations on Palladio and Sinan.

218 Howard 2003, 313–18.

219 Howard 2003, 310–11, sees the failure of the *sopraprovveditori alla sanità* (Barbaro, Jacopo Soranzo, and Paolo Tiepolo, with further references to their diplomatic activities; and see also above) as negatively impacting their political power.

220 I would like to thank Enrique Perez de Guzman for his kind hospitality at the Palazzo Mocenigo, where family tradition displays among other memories of Doge Alvise I the trowel said to be used in the laying of the stone on 3 May 1577. In ASV, Collegio, Cerimoniale I, 51, in G. Zorzi 1967, 34, doc. 11; Timofiewitsch 1971, 68, doc. 7. The doge with the Signoria and Collegio convened at the convent of Santa Croce alla Giudecca to hear Mass before processing for the doge and patriarch each to lay an inscribed stone on the foundation at the site (Sansovino 1968, 255; Magrini 1845, 213, for the inscription), which was then blessed by the patriarch; the iconography of the day chosen (Invention of the Cross) and of the choice of Santa Croce as host has been associated with the architectural symbolism of both the temporary activities and the built Redentore (as a *tau*, representing the Temple of Solomon, the *via triumphalis*, the way to Calvary, and the *Anastasis*, see: Sinding-Larsen 1965a, 431–37; Timofiewitsch 1971, 39–40; Puppi 1986, 263; recently summarized in Concina 1995, 316–23.

221 King James Bible, Samuel II, also called the Second Booke of Kings, 23: 25, the entire account of King David's penitence, 9–28; also found in Chronicles I, 21: 9–28; and in Joshua, 22: 11, the children of Gad build an altar in Canaan by Jordan at the passage of the Children of Israel. See Niero 1979, 289, on the rapport between sin and plague in the biblical episode of David.

222 Hopkins 2000, 144–53, for a comparison of the ducal ceremonials of Il Redentore and La Salute (similarly a government-sponsored votive church to combat the plague in 1630), where he makes the point that the doge and Signoria went by boat to the Giudecca for Low Mass, returning to the choir at San Marco, while the "public" led by the Scuole and clergy processed over the two bridges and through the church then returned to process in San Marco, as in the description by Sansovino 1968, 513 (trans. 147); the sources (ASV, Collegio, Cerimoniale I, 70, in G. Zorzi 1967, 135, doc. 14; Timofiewitsch 1971, 69, doc. 11) also make it clear that this was the case for the first thanksgiving procession on 20 July 1577, when the bridge extended from the Molo.

223 Dyer 1989, who describes the Old Testament as a "repertory of types fulfilled in the mission of Christ" (536), which indicates the creative possibilities. David Bryant has generously shared his research on the penitential songs, *lagrime* ("tears"), published in relation to these communally experienced events and reflecting contemporary spirituality. A relevant example is Scipione Manzano's *Le lagrime della Penitenza di David*, Venice, presso Altobello Salicato, 1592, dedicated to Agostino Valier in the year of the consecration of Il Redentore.

224 In relation to cultural production, Fenlon 1987, 220–21, discusses the flexibility of the liturgy as "particularly susceptible to political influence" and "a direct reflection of the changing fortunes of the Venetian state."

225 Candiani 1965. I would like to thank Marilyn Aronberg Lavin for sharing her knowledge of comparative iconography and confirmation of the unusual use of this aspect of David for the rest of Italy at this time (see Niero 1979, 289, for its specific use in Venice during plagues), and specifically discussing the allegorization of the Bacino as the Red Sea.

226 For a summary on Titian's woodcut, see Romanelli 1990, 42; and Olivato 1990, 166–67 cat. 10. Mason Rinaldi 1984, 121–22 cat. 387, describes *Il Passagio del Mar Rosso* by Palma il Giovane in San Giacomo dell'Orio (1580–81) as an allusion to Lepanto. In an earlier period the island of San Giorgio Maggiore was so dedicated to suggest the strait of the Dardanelles as a metaphor for the new Byzantium; Candiani 1965, 113–31; Muir 1981, 96. Discussing Palladio's work in the Bacino as a "theatre of nature," see Cosgrove 1993, 41, and ch. 9 (222–54), "Landscape as Theatre," 23, "as Palladio's words indicate, resemblance signified meaningful connection, and metaphors were considered to have efficacy, so that pictorial or architectural representation could express phenomena otherwise unable to be grasped"; after the *Four Books*, Bk. 4, 3, "Foreword to the Readers" (Palladio 1997, 213). The phenomenon of Venetian appropriation of other geographical and historical identities is well studied, see Part II above, in relation to the "myth of Venice" (esp. P. Brown 1996b); particularly relevant in this context is Howard 2000, 209–15, "The influence of pilgrimage on Venetian architecture," and the rhetorical practice of metonymy; also Grabar 1996, 340, adroitly understood as "Jerusalem Elsewhere." Rosand 2001, 80–81, notes instances of themes of salvation as coming from the sea as particularly Venetian.

227 Levey 1965, 718–20, "the perfect painted expression of the same emotion that led to the church of the Redentore"; Pallucchini & Rossi 1982, 201–02 cat. 332; Romanelli, ed. 1994; Manno 1994. For a comparative cycle by Palma il Giovane in San Giacomo dell'Orio, see Mason Rinaldi 1984, 121–22 cat. 387, who notes the Eucharistic connotations of the subjects and post-Tridentine context.

228 Levey 1965, 718–20; after A. Pallucchini 1972, 159–84, summarizing earlier articles; more recently Romanelli 1994, 30, and further bibliography; Nichols 1999, 192–93; but cf. Ros-

and 1997, 244 n. 98; and Aikema 1996, 200 n. 216. For a theoretical approach to interpretation based on the exegetical model, see Berdini 1997; also articles in Gentili, ed. 1995.

229 20 May 1592, in Mestre, MAPC, Annali BB, 11v, in Portogruaro 1957, 414, who believes the earlier phases beginning with the period of his definitorship can also be assigned to Bellintani. I thank Bernard Aikema for pointing me to Bellintani: Mattia was one of three brothers, all Capuchin friars, one of whom, Fra Paolo, had accompanied the papal forces at Lepanto, and was engaged in Milan during the plague of 1576, writing about his experiences in *Dialogo della peste* (Paccagnini, ed. 2001).

230 The main character of the play set to music was David, in Celio Magno, *Trionfo di Christo per la vittoria contra Turchi* (Venice, 1571, known in several variant editions), discussed in Fenlon 1987, 224–25; also published in celebration were paraphrases of selected Psalms of David (the example reproduced in Fenlon is anonymous, *Parafrasi poetica sopra alcuni salmi di David profeta. Molto accommode per render gratie à Dio della vittoria donata al Christianesimo contra Turchi*, Venice, Appresso Nicolò Bevilacqua, 1571, but it seems likely that this is by Gabriele Fiamma – a contemporary edition identifying the author published appresso Giorgio Angelieri – who we have met with the Lateran Canons at the Convento della Carità, see Part IV, and see now Pizzigoni 2003, 165–66), and music based on the Israelites crossing the Red Sea was also created for the occasion (Pietro Vinci, *Secondo libro di motetti a cinque voci*, Venice, 1572).

231 Lane 1973, 372. See also the discussion of Doge Mocenigo's votive painting above, esp. Sinding-Larsen 1974, passim. The dedication of Il Redentore is strikingly non-Franciscan (see Cataldi Gallo 1984, ch. 3, esp. 50–51; since it still reflects a Christological vs Mariological basis for public piety (cf. La Salute, for which, see Hopkins 2000, 3–7), "la linea cristocentrica del rinascimentale," see Niero 1992, 254–55.

232 Howard 2003, 323; following Burns with Fairbairn & Boucher 1975, 122 cat. 216d, obverse; cf. Battilotti 1980a, 267–68, cat. 438, who identifies the crowned female figure as *Venice*. Timofiewitsch's view (1971, 58–63, appendix II) is now widely accepted on the five variant commemorative *oselle* (four unique examples: two in London, British Museum, and two in Venice, Museo Civico Correr; a fifth in multiple copies) struck for Doge Mocenigo on the occasion of the vow: the reverses being possible designs for five different temple types made prior to choice of plan, and so, with little relation to the church as built (hence not foundation medals); and the deviation from standard iconography on the obverses with the substitution of the Redeemer for St. Mark (now represented by the Lion); see further in Sinding-Larsen 1965a, 431–37, on the Eucharistic implications for both sides of the medals.

233 24 April (3 galleys) and 13 May (1 galley) 1577, in ASV, Senato, Mar, reg. 43, 74 and 79, in G. Zorzi 1967, 133–34, docs. 10 and 12.

234 BMV, Molin, 80. 13 July 1577, in ASV, Collegio, Cerimoniale I, 59, and ASV, Senato, Terra, reg. 51, 148v, in G. Zorzi 1967, 134–35, docs. 13; Timofiewitsch 1971, 68, doc. 8.

235 The procession on 20 July and a description from 21 July 1577, in ASV, Collegio, Cerimoniale I, 70 and 60, in G. Zorzi 1967, 135, docs. 14 and 15; Timofiewitsch 1971, 69, docs. 11 and 9; the account of Muzio Luminis of 22 July 1577, *La Liberatione di Vinegia*, in G. Zorzi 1967, 135–36, doc. 16; Timofiewitsch 1971, 69, doc. 10.

236 18 February 1577, in ASV, Collegio, Cerimoniale IV, 5, in G. Zorzi 1967, 133, doc. 9 (as 17 February); Timofiewitsch 1971, 67, doc. 6 (from ASV, Collegio, Cerimoniale I, 1). For the monastery property, see Timofiewitsch 1971, 18, authorized 25 May 1577, after Portogruaro 1957, 412–14, who follows various negotiations for approval of the sale: from ASV, Maggior Consiglio, Deliberazioni, fol. 12, 8 April 1577; ASV, Collegio, Notatorio, fol. 62, 6 August 1577; ASV, Provveditori alla Zecca, reg. 44, 50 and 85, 11 August and 25 September 1577; an additional 200 square feet was ceded from the monastery property to the church (Portogruaro 1957, 414–16, referred to on 11 November 1581, when the Capuchins requested assistance from the state, in which Tiepolo was critical, in ASV, Senato, Terra, filza 83, and see above); also Sinding-Larsen 1965a, 427–30, and fig. 3, reconstructing the site; and see now Pizzigoni 2003, 169, fig. 7.

237 28 July and 7 November 1579, in ASV, Senato, Terra, reg. 52, 185 and 217, in G. Zorzi 1967, 137, docs. 17 and 18, inaugurating the regular series of requests for additional funds to finish the church throughout 1591, see above.

238 For example, Magrini 1845, 213, speaks of his "amorosa cura," but his account depends on a letter purported to be from Palladio in Venice, 1577, to Count Giulio Capra, but now universally acknowledged as a late eighteenth–early nineteenth-century fake. G. Zorzi 1967, 128; Puppi 1986, 264, agreed with G. Zorzi.

239 Burns 1991, 202–6, 215–16, describes in depth the necessary elements undertaken by the architect at the design and organizational stages, essentially setting up both the material and business practices for the project for the *cantiere* and patrons, also Puppi 1980b, 13–26.

240 13 February 1580, in ASV, Senato, Terra, reg. 52, 247, in G. Zorzi 1967, 137, doc. 19; 25 June 1582, in ASV, Senato, Terra, reg. 54, 32, in G. Zorzi 1967, 169, doc. 2. Portogruaro 1957, 416–17, with payments for the monastery construction (new wings on the east and south) from 27 February 1586–29 April 1587 (from Mestre, MAPC, Conto de Bartolomeo Bontempelli, 1585–1591), dates the completion to 1586 from the materials and wages.

241 Monaro gave his opinion on the Rialto bridge in 1589, see Cessi and Alberti 1934, 398, 425,

where he is identified specifically as "lavorado alla chiesa del Redentor"; G. Zorzi 1967, 128, who refutes attempts to attribute supervision to State *proti* Sorella (present at a 26 February 1593 [*m.v.* 1592] estimate, in ASV, Senato, Terra, filza 125 in Portogruaro 1957, 418–19, for the campaign for the west wing infirmary and additional cells completed by the next year and designed by Fra Mattia Bellintani) and da Ponte, instead, seeing them as occasional crucial consultants to the *provveditori* when their expertise was required for important decisions, or Vincenzo Scamozzi (no evidence and was occupied elsewhere). Among the workers Stefano Paliaga can be found at the site of Le Zitelle as well, see Part VI.

242 Burns 1991, 213. For their government experiences, see Ventura 1964a; Tucci 1971, the latter, for example, was co-author of a plan to amortize the public debt incurred over the War of Cyprus. Hochmann 1992, 171–77, on the competence of amateurs in Venice (more broadly than in regard to painting).

243 Padre Mario da Mercato Saraceno, *circa* 1580, in Portogruaro 1957, 408.

244 The documents in Portogruaro 1957, 576–78, docs. 67–70, respectively 21 December 1577 (from Antonio Tiepolo in Rome to the Senate, in ASV, Senato, Secreta, Dispacci di Roma, filza 12, 582), 28 December (from the Senate to Tiepolo, in ASV, Senato, Terra, Deliberazioni, filza 72), 31 December (Senate deliberation on Capuchin supplication, idem), 4 January 1578 (Tiepolo informs the Senate of the pope's concession to the Capuchins allowing them to officiate, ASV, Senato, Secreta, Dispacci di Roma, filza 12, 591). On Antonio Tiepolo (not a branch close to that of Santi Apostoli), see Grendler 1979, 326; he was Barbaro's replacement as *bailò* in Constantinople.

245 Burns with Fairbairn & Boucher 1975, 209, describe the building materials Palladio typically used, including the "pie-shaped bricks" for columns at San Giorgio and Il Redentore.

246 Timofiewitsch 1971, 21–30, with detailed measured drawings. Palladio 1997, 41–47, on the Corinthian order.

247 Timofiewitsch 1971, 30–31; Lingo 1998, for a comprehensive discussion of models used by the Order; Portogruaro 1957, 407–12.

248 On the Franciscan plan, see Burns with Fairbairn & Boucher 1975, 145 cat. 256; Howard 1987, 70–74, who provides an excellent summary of Franciscan elements in Sansovino's plan at San Francesco della Vigna (side chapels, aisle-less nave, extension of chancel behind the high altar for the monk's choir), earlier models and contemporary developments, and makes an important point that is relevant for Palladio at Il Redentore in regard to Sansovino's interior originally being "a brilliant white, creating an overall luminosity" unlike examples whose use of colored stone (such as the *pietra forte* of Il Cronaca's San Salvatore in Monte, Florence) provided a

contrasting "articulation"; also, Foscari & Tafuri 1983, 62–63; for further bibliography on Barbaro and Palladio at San Francesco della Vigna, see Part III, patriarch of Aquileia; on the retrochoir under Part IV, San Giorgio Maggiore.

249 For direct influences in sixteenth-century architecture to mutual responses by architects to reform phenomena in different centers (from Bramante to Raphael, Galeazzo Alessi to Girolamo Genga, Michelangelo to Vignola), see Ackerman 1977b, 129; Isermeyer 1968, 53; Timofiewitsch 1971, 41–44; Puppi 1986, 264–65; Burns with Fairbairn & Boucher 1975, 145; a good summary now in Boucher 1998, 172–75; and for cross-cultural influences from Milan to Constantinople, Howard 2003, 312–17.

250 For an illustration of a comparable seating plan for the dogal ceremony, see Hopkins 2000, 148–49, and 151, fig. 99, reconstructs the arrangements in the transept/presbytery.

251 On choir screens and the development of the "retrochoir," see the fuller treatment in Part IV, San Giorgio Maggiore.

252 Timofiewitsch 1971, 43–44 and 50 n. 83. Palladio 1997, 200–02, 219–21.

253 I should like to thank John Shearman for his insight regarding Santa Maria degli Angeli in relation to the general problem of the retrochoir. Ackerman 1986, 260–68, 331–34, fig. 137 (see here fig. 259), Pius IV made Santa Maria degli Angeli a titular church in 1565, after which access to the choir was opened up (the interior was substantially transformed in the eighteenth century). Ackerman 1977b, 171, makes the salient observation: "The Imperial baths came closest to Palladio's ideal. Actually, they were the only class of ancient structure that could stimulate solutions to many of his planning problems." Influentially, Wittkower 1962, 99–100, believed the "revolutionary feature" of the column screen derived from Roman thermae; noted by most scholars, for a detailed discussion, see Timofiewitsch 1971, 43–44, who sees the monopteral temple as referent in the curvature of the screen.

254 Wittkower 1962, 96. Detailed measured drawings and descriptions are in Timofiewitsch 1971, 31–39, 46–48.

255 Palladio 1997, 220.

256 Palladio 1997, 219–20.

257 Timofiewitsch 1971, 46, in reference to Wittkower 1962, 91, fig. 9 (in later editions, the author stated he had not intended for his diagram to be interpreted as a reconstruction of Palladio's creative procedure, responding specifically to Pane 1961, 88). See also Part IV above, on San Giorgio Maggiore.

258 Puppi 1986, 163, on San Pietro in Castello.

259 Burns with Fairbairn & Boucher 1975, 142, on a drawing associated with San Giorgio Maggiore (London, RIBA, XIV, 12), which Wittkower (1962, pl. 33b, 94–95 and n. 5) believed to be Palladio's original solution for the façade, not followed in its execution;

recent literature in Lewis 2000, 246–48, cat. 113. On the drawing in relation to the project of San Giorgio Maggiore, see above in Part IV, but it might be noted here that another scholar, in agreement with Wittkower and not with Burns, found his negative proof in a lack of correspondence between interior and exterior, focusing on different elements than Burns had, C. Frommel 1977, 109; and Kühbacher 1990, 178, 181; but cf. Timofiewitsch 1971, 46–48, with earlier references; Cooper 1990a, 136, 138. See now Guerra 2002, 281–82, who discusses antique precedents for the shift from external to internal orders, and further notes that, unlike Scamozzi, followed a "conceptual" rather than "rigid" correspondence (285), and on the drawing, Part IV above. Deborah Howard has observed Sansovino's concerns with correspondence at the Misericordia and Palazzo Corner.

260 Palladio 1997, 200. Palladio perfectly understood the function of the basilica "where justice was administered" (*Four Books*, Bk. 3, ch. 19, 38).

261 Palladio 1997, 217, "There is no trace left today of the first two appearances of temples" (*Four Books*, Bk. 4, ch. 3, 7).

262 "Quanto alla facciata di detta chiesa, il di fuori verso la piazza mi pare assai bella, ma chi in cima alla chiesa, mi piacerà molto più, et averia più bella presenza, e li anderia quattro di questi pilastri, che ornarebbono assai la facciata della chiesa che è all'incontro della nave di mezzo, e le faccie delle navi piccole averiano alcuni pilastri più piccoli a proporzion del modello, e toriano suso l'estrema cornice delle navi piccole e fariano un mezzo frontispicio per banda, et così mi pareva che stesse benissimo, et a questo modo è fatto il disegno," Palladio 1988a, 124; G. Zorzi 1967, 88–89, doc. 3. He further described a large window placed in the front and one at the head of the crossing. A translated excerpt may also be found in Puppi 1986, 227 cat. 104.

263 "Il portico ai nostri tempi non si ponga in uso, onde e per far quello che più non fosse istato fatto ai nostri giorni e perché certo riuscirebbe cosa bellissima, oltre le molte commodità, grandezza e meraviglia che apporterà, quasi quasi ch'io mi lascerei indurre a laudar l'opinione di quelli che desiderano il detto portico," *Lettera per la facciata di San Petronio a Bologna*, 12 January 1579, in Palladio 1988a, 134, doc. 4; G. Zorzi 1967, 113–14, doc. 19.

264 Vitruvius 1987, Bk. 3, ch. 1, 116–21.

265 "Lasciaremo le ombre, & lo empir i fogli di figure, & di cose minute, & facili, non affettando la quantità, & la sottilità delle figure adombrate in iscorzo, & prospettiva, perche la nostra intentione è di mostrare le cose, & non insegnare a dipingere," Barbaro 1987, 119.

266 "La maggior parte si facevano con li portici, e non solo in fronte ma anco tutto atorno," Palladio 1988a, 134 (San Petronio), doc. 4; G. Zorzi 1967, 113, doc. 19.

267 "Et per consequentia renderebbe gran maestà

non solamente alla chiesa di San Petronio et all piazza, ma ancora a tutta la città, G. Zorzi 1967, doc. 18, 113.

268 "Ma quando non ve fose altra, pigliassi la sua istessa nelle fabriche di Venetia, alle quali non ha fatto portici," G. Zorzi 1967, 116, doc. 26, 31 October.

269 This notion has a distinguished history, for example, Ackerman 1977b, 143, in speaking generally of Palladio's approach to the innovation of introducing into his façade design the "metaphor of space," says of Il Redentore: "The façade was designed as a relief."

270 See a discussion with earlier literature in Boucher 1998, 176–79; Puppi 1986, 276–77 cat. 142; Burns 2000, and Beltramini & Padoan, eds. 2000, 215–17, 283.

271 See above, Part III for San Pietro in Castello and San Francesco della Vigna, Part IV for San Giorgio Maggiore.

272 Palladio 1997, 164, discussing the order of subjects in Book 3, follows his description of piazzas, saying: "After which shall follow that on temples which are essential to religion, without which the maintenance of civilization of any kind is impossible" (*Four Books*, Bk. 3, 6, "Foreword to the Readers").

273 Timofiewitsch 1971, appendix 1, 54–55, whose interpretation of the iconographical program in relation to the ceremonial role of the church has formed the basis for most subsequent treatments; see Sinding-Larsen 1965a, 431–34, on the Christological aspect; also in agreement with the *via triumphalis*, Puppi 1986, 263; a general summary in A. Gallo & Spadavecchia 1994; Concina 1995, 316–23.

274 16 May 1588, in ASV, Senato, Terra, reg. 58, 54, in G. Zorzi 1967, 140, doc. 33.

275 Palladio 1997, 225.

276 Palladio 1997, 217.

277 Described in Ridolfi 1965, 2: 163; Portogruaro 1957, 421–25, with chronicles from Mestre, MAPC, Padre Francesco da Venetia, "Relatione delle fondationi," 66, and Annali BB, 79–80; Portogruaro 1930, 176–78, and 224–25, doc. 3, 29 September 1619, from ASV, Senato, Terra, filza 236; Portogruaro 1936, 47–48; Niero 1974 describes a later (1758) repainting of thirteen figures whose "nudity" was then considered indecorous (probably the *Sibyls*) and the dispersion of most of the figures.

278 Doge Antonio was the son of Girolamo Priuli, who served twice as *provveditore del Palazzo* for the fire of 1577, and closely related to Marc'Antonio Barbaro, so it is interesting that he brought Piazza to work there; see Grendler 1990, 84.

279 Humfrey 1990, on the concept of "coordinated" altarpieces. An excellent discussion on the regularization of the church and its effects on art in Venice is in Hochmann 1992, 267–91.

280 Schulz 1968, 47; see also on the *concorrentia* of commissions as leading to the heterogeneous character of the decoration, in Wolters 1987, 37–38.

281 Revisionist views can be found in Hall 1998; Hall 1999, 257–67; Ostrow 1996; Robertson 1992; Madonna, ed. 1993.

282 Fully illustrated discussions of the paintings as a cycle can be found in: Portogruaro 1930, 184–94; Timofiewitsch 1971, appendix 1, 53–55; Hochmann 1992, 302–05; Concina 1995, 316–23; A. Gallo & Spadavecchia 1994, 15–29.

283 M. Lavin 1990, 290–92, for examples.

284 In addition to discussions of the full cycle, see: Arslan 1960, 224; Rearick 1982; Rearick 1996–97, 80; Nodari 1992; Alberton Vinco da Sesso 1996. Continuity of these aims may be compared in Hopkins 2000, 69–75; see further in Part IV.

285 Ridolfi 1965, 1: 354. In addition to its discussion in the context of the cycle above, see Rearick 1988a, 200–03 cat. 104–05, with earlier literature on autograph related drawings and a proposed timetable for the cutting of the marble altar frames relative to the painting commissions in late 1587.

286 Mason Rinaldi 1984, 149 cat. 598, dates the work stylistically circa 1590, which would coincide with the consecration of 1592.

287 Assigned to Domenico Tintoretto by Pallucchini & Rossi 1982, 252–53 cat. A 104, despite Ridolfi's attribution to Jacopo (1965, 2: 60), agreeing with a dating contemporary to Veronese and heirs' Baptism.

288 See Part IV on San Giorgio Maggiore.

289 Palladio was in Vicenza on 24 April (when he was paid his salary on the Basilica for March through to June, indicating that he was not there to collect it earlier, and was probably returning to Venice with no plans to be in Vicenza until the summer, in fact, he did not return until December 1578, an absence of eighteen months, engaged in the campaigns in the Doge's Palace of 1574 and 1577, traveling to Bologna, and overseeing the foundations and setting up the Il Redentore cantiere, as well as overseeing other projects, such as San Giorgio), see G. Zorzi 1965, 343–46.

290 See above, and Timofiewitsch 1971, 35–40; Puppi 1986, 264.

291 24 March 1590, in ASV, Senato, Terra, reg. 60, 7, in G. Zorzi 1967, 140–41, doc. 34, "restando a far il pavimento, due figure di bronzo che vanno sopra l'altar grande," and other things for 4,000 ducats. On the marble pavements typical in Palladio's churches, see Wolters 2000, 226–29. On Campagna, the authoritative catalogue raisonné by Timofiewitsch 1972, 253–55 cat. 12; Timofiewitsch 1984; Hochmann 1992, 302–04; Boucher 1996, 531–34. On the seventeenth-century changes to the high altar, see Timofiewitsch 1971, 54–55; Portogruaro 1930, 180–83, 223–24, docs. 4–5; Portogruaro 1957, 425–27.

292 Wolters 1987, 37–38, on how artists got commissions through the recommendations of other artists (NB: the opposite could occur, as in the commission for the high altar at San Giorgio Maggiore), as well as patrons; Hochmann 1992, 261, on Contarini's ridotti and these artists' participation; Rearick 1996–97, 80, comments that until Veronese was dead, the Bassano family were not associated with Palladio's commissions, but, in this case, the choice of the provveditori seems to parallel the approach taken in the Doge's Palace, assigning works to the major Venetian studios (Bassano, Caliari, Robusti, Palma il Giovane) to ensure their timely and simultaneous execution; Boucher 1996 theorizes that Marc'Antonio Barbaro was influential in Campagna's obtaining a part in the Doge's Palace campaign after their successful collaboration on the now-dismantled tomb of Doge Nicolò da Ponte in the Carità; this is a viable and not mutually exclusive hypothesis to my supposing the importance of Contarini, and reinforces the notion of the mutual tastes that these patrons of the deceased Palladio must have shared and supported politically (i.e., Scamozzi).

293 Timofiewitsch 1971, 54, bases his reconstruction on Stringa's description (Sansovino 1604, 188r-v); Mason Rinaldi 1990, 191–92, notes the rare subject of David in one of the surviving panels by Francesco Bassano (now in the sacristy).

294 For an interesting discussion of the political ramifications of the development of the high altar in Milan, see Scotti 1977 (it should be remembered that Palladio's opinions were engaged regarding Milan Cathedral); and see now Repishti 1998; also with a good discussion of this altar-type development, see Ostrow 1996; particular to Venice, see Hochmann 1992, 302–05; Mason Rinaldi 1987. See also Part IV, San Giorgio Maggiore.

295 Mason Rinaldi 1984.

296 Hopkins 2000, 116. I would also like to thank Peter Brown for his insightful comments on this concept.

297 Palladio 1997, 215.

298 Stringa (Sansovino 1604, 188r-v), speaks of the intention to populate the niches of the façade with statues of marble or bronze (now with Sts. Mark and Francis), and other places on the pediment (now with Faith, two angels, St. Lorenzo Giustiniani and St. Anthony of Padua); for the late seventeenth-century statues, see Timofiewitsch 1971, 53; Portogruaro 1930, 173–76.

299 Sansovino 1604, 187v, "Hoe quanto bella, ricca, & nobile sia questa Chiesa, è cosa difficile il raccontare; poscia che per architettura, per altre sue nobili qualità non è punto inferiore a quella di San Giorgio maggiore. Ella è, come è detto, sù'l modello del Palladio, Architettore di molto nome a i nostri tempi; modello veramente degno di somma lode, perche apporta a' riguardanti vaghezza non picciola, e tale, che alletta gli animi di ciascheduno a rimirare così ben' intesa compositura. Ella può esser dalla Piazza di S. Marco lontana 500. buoni passa, che fanno poco più di meza miglio: vedesi stando in detta Piazza, il suo Frontispicio, che risguarda quasi verso tramontana: egli è tutto in vaga forma di pietra viva histriana fabricato."

PART VI

1 Pullan 1971 remains the outstanding work on this subject. Also useful are Pignatti, ed. 1981; and Gramigna and Perissa, eds. 1981.

2 Sansovino 1968, 1: 281.

3 Pullan 1971, 43–50. P. Brown 1988, 15–21, describes them as "miniature commonwealths," a notion that pervades texts of the period; for example, Antonio Milledonne, cittadino originario and secretary of the Council of Ten, in his "Ragionamento" of 1581, BMV, Milledonne, 52r-v, calls the scuole "Republichete"; discussed in Scarabello 1981, esp. 20. MacKenney 1994, 390, cautions against too much reliance on the "myth" in interpretation.

4 Sansovino 1968, 1: 282.

5 Pullan 1971, 33–38; Martinelli Pedrocco 1981; Gramigna Dian & Perissa Torrini 1981b, 25–28; Maschio 1981; MacKenney 1994, 392–94, esp. on the diversity of members; also Mackenney 1987, for an overview; P. Brown 1996a. Sansovino 1968, 290, simply says that there are "an incredible number" of scuole piccole. The provveditori del comune controlled the scuole piccole after 1508 (P. Brown 1996a).

6 P. Brown 1988, passim; Humfrey & MacKenney 1986.

7 Aikema & Meijers, eds. 1989; Ellero, ed. 1987; Semi 1983; Pullan 1971.

8 Meijers 1989.

9 Also called San Cristofalo dei Mercanti. Cicogna 1969, 2: 346–47 inscr. 121–23; Gramigna Dian & Perissa Torrini 1981b, 118–19 cat. 71/A; Martinelli Pedrocco 1981, 219–20.

10 The archival record is confusing when it comes to making a distinction between the closely named scuola piccola Scuola della Misericordia ai Frari and the Scuola Grande della Misericordia della Valverde, whose statutes date from 1308; Pullan 1971, 38 n. 23, sees no evidence of continuity between them. The first author to draw attention to this problem for the later period was Howard 1987 (orig. pub. 1975), 96–112, esp. 110; re-examining the issue in Howard 1999, 33–35, and 62–67 for documents. Howard's circumspect summation decides in favor of identifying the scuola piccola at the Frari with the Scuola Grande della Misericordia at the time of the former's merger with the Scuola dei Mercanti at Madonna dell'Orto. Evidence for Howard's identification is largely based on a "Mariegola riformata, 1564," in the ASV fondo of the Scuola Grande della Misericordia, B. 9, and which contains documents relating to the merger of 1570. As Howard duly cautions, there is an archival notation that indicates some doubt as to its presence in the fondo of the Scuola Grande.

The alternative explanation followed here, however, is that documents relating to the *scuola piccola* were mistakenly placed with those of the Scuola Grande at an earlier point in the organization of the ASV, which probably applies to several other *buste* in the *fondo* as well (for their helpful information I would like to thank the archivists Alessandra Sambo, Michela Dal Borgo, Edoardo Giuffrida, and Alessandra Schiavon). The interpretation here is also based on a different reading of some of the internal evidence of B. 9: there is never a direct reference as the Scuola Grande della Misericordia, except on a later label written in pen and pasted to the spine of the volume; the title page identifies it as "Matricola riformata in Essecution De la Parte presa Adi xxvi Febraio 1564," and further concludes with "La qual è stata ridotta al suo dovuto fine de ordine, et in tempo del Magnifico Giulio Ziliolo Governor de ditta scola. Et delli magnifici maestro Bortolamio Moro, et maestro Gasparo Dardani diffensori." The latter names match officers of the Scuola dei Mercanti for 1597–98 (ASV, Scuole piccole e suffrage, B. 435–436 bis, Scuola di S. Maria e S. Cristoforo dei Mercanti alla Madonna dell'Orto, B. 436 bis, "Elenco delle Cariche," not numbered, see under respective headings). Further comparison of the memberships of the united *scuole piccole* of the Misericordia and Mercanti and their officers for this period also suggests that they are distinct from the Scuola Grande della Misericordia (which also uses more conventional Venetian terms for its officers, such as *guardian grande*), although more thorough work needs to be done here (particularly since some individuals also belonged to several *scuole* so their multiple memberships and positions need to be clarified where there is overlap; on the composition of its members, see MacKenney 1987, 51–61). The declared aims of the Scuola della Misericordia to rival the *scuole grandi* contributes to the possibility of confusion. Manuela Morresi came to a similar conclusion; for the Misericordia, see Morresi 2000, 114–17, cat. 19.

11 R. Gallo 1955, 36–41, for partial transcription of documents; G. Zorzi 1967, 178–79; Puppi 1986, 240–41; Tiepolo et al. 1980, 74–75.

12 "Elenco delle Cariche," not numbered, translated here into common style, but see under the position by year in *more veneto* (e.g., a governor listed as "1566" would have served from February 1567 to January 1568 common style).

13 Howard 1987, 96–112; Howard 1999, 31–33; also Morresi 2000, 114–17 cat. 19.

14 On 9 July 1531, in ASV, Scuola Grande della Misericordia, B. 166, 238; in Howard 1987, 179 n. 37; Howard 1999, 24–26, 63.

15 On 4 September 1532, in ASV, Scuola Grande della Misericordia, B. 166, 255; in Howard 1987, 179 n. 42; Howard 1999, 26–27, 63–64. I thank Deborah Howard for the further observation that the Scuola di San Rocco

exploited this setback for the Misericordia by introducing free-standing columns to their own façade.

16 A new model was commissioned, on 16 and 26 April 1535, and criticized for introducing vaults, which required further models, 25 May 1544, in ASV, Scuola Grande della Misericordia, B. 166, 284–85, and 409–10; in Howard 1987, 179 nn. 43 and 51; Howard 1999, 30–31, 65.

17 Tafuri 1989, 94, and for the "Scuole Grandi," 81–102.

18 In addition to the above on *scuole*, see Wolters 1990, 104–14.

19 Sansovino 1968, 290.

20 The first offer was made on 25 January 1555 *m.v.* (= 1556), and the union on 31 October 1570 in "Mariegola riformata," 27 and 54v–55v; in Howard 1987, 180 n. 82; Howard 1999, 66.

21 "Mariegola riformata," 59, 10 December 1570.

22 Professor Paula Clarke has suggested in a personal communication that the terminology may be influenced by the presence of foreign merchants, notably Florentines; see Weissman 1982, 62–63, on the analogy between Florentine confraternity titles and government offices.

23 "Mariegola riformata," 58r–v, 7 December 1570; in Howard 1999, 66; a lengthier description from 21 January 1571 (common style), and the Valier heirs agreement from 24 March 1573, in ASV, Scuole piccole e suffragi, B. 436, 99r–100v, and 102r–v. The embedded wall and covered-up left window of the chapel now form part of a passageway between the church and the Scuola.

24 30 November 1572, in ASV, Scuole piccole e suffragi, B. 417, Scuola di S. Maria e S. Cristoforo dei Mercanti alla Madonna dell'Orto, fasc. C, 6r–v; in R. Gallo 1955, 37–39 (as 20 November); Tiepolo et al. 1980, 74.

25 Referred to on 29 October 1581, in ASV, Scuole piccole e suffragi, B. 413, Scuola di S. Maria e S. Cristoforo dei Mercanti alla Madonna dell'Orto, 50; see Cicogna 1969, 2: 347, inscr. 122 (citing another copy from the "Mariegola riformata," 63v–64r).

26 16 May 1572 and 13 July 1573, in ASV, Scuole piccole e suffragi, B. 417, fasc. C, 3r, and fasc. B, 17r; in R. Gallo 1955, 37–39 and 41; Tiepolo et al. 1980, 74–75.

27 13 October 1532, in ASV, Scuola Grande della Misericordia, B. 166, 256; in Howard 1987, 179 n. 39; Howard 1999, 64.

28 Quoting from the petition of 16 May 1572 (above), in which Palladio states that he worked for eight months, but the deposition of 1 December 1572 (ASV, Scuole piccole e suffragi, B. 417, fasc. C, 7r–v; in R. Gallo 1955, 39–41) indicates that this is the amount of time for which he was seeking compensation, since he had ceased work at the end of three months for lack of payment, whereupon a deputation of the Mercanti *provveditori* per-

suaded him to continue for another eight months. Eleven months is exactly the period between the initial building contracts and Saler's death, after which Palladio waited a further six months before demanding payment, and it was a further fourteen months before the final decision.

29 ASV, Scuole piccole e suffragi, B. 417, fasc. B, 9 (= *m.v.* 1570), on behalf of the Scuola were the governor Domenego Bonamor and procurators Giorgio (Zorzi) Saler and Antonio Cornoni (who signed as Antonio dela Vechia); the masons were Masters Jacopo de Stephano and Bernardo del Zanetto de Rohan murer, "metter le piere vivere dove sarano i lastri del balchoni, porte, et voli deli parti dele schalle . . . Et li pilastrelli se hano a far del fuora via dele fazzade." On the translation of *balchoni* as windows (*finestra*), and for *pilastrelli* as small piers or balusters (*pilastrino, balaustro*), see Concina 1988, 43, 114.

30 ASV, Scuole piccole e suffragi, B. 417, fasc. B, 10r–v (= *m.v.* 1570), the same signatories for the Scuola as above, except Domenego Bonamor became a procurator, following his term as governor; on the campo portal: "Et prima. La porta che va sul campo deve esser larga pie 6 in luse et alta pie dodese in luse con gli suoi adornamenti, cornise, over cartele, segondo la sagoma che li e sia data in tutti et per tutto si che sii ben, et polita, et ben fatta et lavorada, et questo per precio de lire sette el pie. Et sii detta porta dela grossezza del muro"; that it was a more elaborate design may be inferred from the fact that the *fondamenta* portal cost less at 5 lire per Venetian foot.

31 "Modest" is a word frequently used in conjunction with the building by commentators. Puppi 1986, 240–41, summarizes opinions on Palladio's authorship, and accepts his design of the moldings, noting that F. Barbieri 1966, 351, originally accepted only the lateral portal, an opinion that can now be confirmed. Hochmann 1992, 335–36, can be added as skeptical of Palladio's share. Howard 1999, 35, notes that the ample scansion and high plinths of the Tuscan columns may be compared to the Villa Badoer.

32 Voted on 15 April 1571, approved by the *provveditori del comune* on 30 May, in ASV, Scuole piccole e suffragi, B. 436, 101v; Cicogna 1969, 2: 346. The fifteenth-century relief came from the Scuola della Misericordia at the Frari, see Rizzi 1987, 274, who identifies the flanking saints as (?)Mark and Francis.

33 In the deposition of 1 December 1572, see above.

34 See Part IV, above, on Giovanni Antonio (Zuanantonio) Saler who continued the work at La Celestia; also an important figure in the Scuola dei Mercanti, he was not, however, on the Zonta in the critical years except in 1571 (later also in 1574, 1577, 1579, 1583, 1585, and 1587, from the "Elenco delle Cariche").

35 For the deposition of 30 November 1572, and the vote of 31 July 1573 (18–0), see above. Vicenzo is not mentioned in the recorded inscriptions of the family chapel at La Celestia. He was long prominent in the Scuola, holding office more than sixteen times from 1563 to 1598, eleven of those on the Zonta, which meant that the Saler family presence was more or less continuous (only out of office nine times in thirty-five years, from the "Elenco delle Cariche"), dying in 1612. According to a handwritten note (by Amadeo Svajer?) in BMV, "Arbori," 91v (see also the insert between 95 and 96), he was married to Benetta Davanzo; Nicolò, the son of his brother Giovasnni Basttista, became prior of the Ca' di Dio in 1600 (limited to *cittadini*), and a daughter, Marietta, married the patrician Tomà Donà.

36 ASV, Scuole piccole e suffragi, B. 413, 30; in Hadeln 1911, 129; Pallucchini & Rossi 1982, 1: 265–66. Borghini 1584, 556, was the first to ascribe the "Ascensione della Vergine con molti ritratti di naturale" to Jacopo Tintoretto; it was located opposite the door over the bench that gives the *banca* its name (although attributed to Domenico Tintoretto) by Boschini 1664, 453, "Nell'Albergo al diimpetto della porta, sopra il Banco, evvi Maria, che ascende al Cielo, accompagnata da molti Angeli; e nel piano, vi sono gli Apostoli; & è di mano di Domenico Tintoretto."

37 Payments for the woodwork of the soffit extended from 23 June 1575 to 16 June 1576, and the *banche* from 22 February 1579 *m.v.* (= 1580) to 17 September 1580, in ASV, Scuole piccole e suffragi, B. 417, fasc. B, 18–21. The document of 31 December 1577 for the *Nativity*, in ASV, Scuole piccole e suffragi, B. 413, 35, "Havendo il Magnifico Maestro Giacomo Grillo Governator passato con li suoi Colleghi questi sottoscritti fatti far un Quadro della Natività della Madona quello à Laude del nostro Signor Iddio donato alla nostra Scola. L'andera parte, che mette il Magnifico Maestro Angelo Tornimben Governor presente, che il detto Quadro sia accettato, et tenuto nel nostro albergo dove è messo, non potendo quello esser levato via se non de consentimento delli cinque sesti del Capitolo nostro ridotto al numero di 60 in sù. + 28 -6 Presa"; in Hadeln 1911, 146; the painting of this subject in the *albergo* on the wall to the left of the *banco* was identified as Benedetto Caliari by Boschini 1664, 453, "Dal lato sinistro, la nascita di Maria, di Benedetto, fratello di Paolo Veronese: opera stupenda, e copiosa di figure"; Moschini Marconi 1962, 2: 77–78, for its history and attributions.

38 Boschini 1664, 453, "Sopra la porta al dirimpetto del Banco, Maria Annonciata dall'Angelo, con molte architetture maestosissime, e da lati due statue di chiaro oscuro: l'una rappresenta la Fede, e l'altra la Carità: & alcune altre cartelle, e Puttini, veramente è un'opera, che hà più del divino, che dell'humano, e si può dire, che sia il condimento di tutte altre nominate; e basta poi dire, che sia di Paolo Veronese." The family arms are the Cadabrozzo and Cottoni; the architecture was compared to Palladio's San Francesco della Vigna by Nepi Scirè 1991, 156–57, who cites reflectographic examination as basis for a dating of 1578 and restoration to Paolo Veronese; it was flanked by grisaille panels of the *Madonna della Misericordia*, *St. Mark* (both in Milan, Brera), *Faith*, and *Charity* (Venice, Libreria Marciana, on deposit from the Accademia); Pignatti & Pedrocco 1995, 2: 369–70, for earlier literature. For a comparison to Palladio's Santa Maria Nova in Vicenza and its dating, see below.

39 The humble exteriors of a number of *scuole piccole* concealed richly decorated interiors from the fifteenth and early sixteenth centuries; see esp. P. Brown, "Le scuole," MS (I should like to thank the author for allowing me to read her original work in manuscript, see now in P. Brown 1996a), who notes that the Mercanti were unusual for this date. It was singled out for description in guidebooks, one of the most extensive being by Boschini 1664, 449–54. A target during the Napoleonic suppression, Pietro Edwards's inventory of 1819 lists ninety-two paintings of good quality, now mostly lost; see Martinelli Pedrocco 1981, 219–20; Gramigna Dian & Perissa Torrini 1981a, 118–19.

40 Wolters 1987, 157, makes this important point.

41 Part of the larger campaign in which Jacopo Tintoretto and Antonio Vassilacchi (Aliense) also participated in 1591–92, including the ceiling decoration of the upper hall; 19 and 24 October 1591, in ASV, Scuole piccole e suffragi, B. 413, 120, "due mezi quadri, che vanno dalle bande dell'Altare li Retratti di tutti quelli di Banca, et delli Xii presenti"; Hadeln 1911, 130–31; Ridolfi 1965, 2: 257–58; Moschini Marconi 1962, 2: 379–80, *Confratelli della Scuola dei Mercanti*; Nepi Scirè 1995, 85–88 cat. 44–45; to which add Hochmann 1992, 64–65; Fenlon 1996, 248–49. On the *Nativity*, first identified as a later work by Jacopo Tintoretto by Ridolfi 1965, 2: 64, said to be executed at his villa in Carpanedo, therefore from 1576, when the property was acquired; the altar was centrally located on the *fondamenta* wall between the windows, according to Boschini 1664, 452; Pallucchini & Rossi 1982, 1: 247–48 cat. A63 (works of uncertain or erroneous attribution), before 1591.

42 Hadeln 1911, 130, transcribed the *vicario*'s name as "Finetti." The third officer identified by the ducal sleeves is probably *cancellier* (chancellor, again an elevated title), Francesco Rosini, from the "Elenco delle cariche," for 1590.

43 Cicogna 1969, 2: 347, inscr. 123, after an eighteenth-century chronicle; the importance of the Dardani family at the Mercanti is amply testified to by the offices they held, Francesco's son Gasparo would be governor in 1596, see the "Elenco delle cariche." According to BMV, "Arbori," 36, Francesco's great-grandfather Alvise was knighted by Andrea Gritti for the recuperation of Padua. Other portraits in "Vesta Ducale" are described in the *sala del capitolo*, in Boschini 1664, 451 (by Paolo de Freschi and Domenico Tintoretto, also credited with a number of other portraits placed above some of the religious narratives).

44 "Elenco delle Cariche," under "De mezo anno, 1591, Domenego Robusti"; artists often contributed work rather than serve in office, and would then be listed as exempt, known as *nobeli*, or *huomeni da ben*, see an earlier *mariegola* in ASV, Scuole piccole e suffragi, B. 406, listing Giovanni Bellini, Alvise Vivarini, and Giovanni Bon, as well as both Nicolò and Giacomo Saler (father and grandfather to the brothers Giorgio, Vicenzo, and Giovanni Antonio), among others. On this status, see MacKenney 1987, 54. Domenico Tintoretto's mother was a *cittadina originaria*, Faustina di Marco Episcopi, and his family lived nearby on the Fondamenta dei Mori (Cannaregio 3399); see R. Gallo 1941. His ambitions in the expression of personal status may be contrasted to those of his father; on the latter's deliberate cultivation of *mediocritas*, see Nichols 1999, 12–27, "Introduction," and 137–47, for *scuole* patronage.

45 Wolters 1990, 105–06.

46 A variant drawing of the upper half is in London, RIBA, Burlington-Devonshire VIII, 12 (now in box Q 26). Howard 1999, 50–51, and 58 n. 242, provides a recent summary of their attributions, which now generally assign the architecture to Palladio (noting the typical use of orthogonal projection and incised lines, and details of the column treatment), and the figures of the RIBA drawing and the lower of the two sheets that make up the Vicenza drawing to another hand, Bernardino India. My thanks to David Ekserdjian for confirming this attribution.

47 Magrini 1845, 302–03. Following Magrini on the dating are Burns with Fairbairn & Boucher 1975, 154–55; and Lewis 2000, 236–37 cat. 107; On the provenance of the Vicenza drawings, see Puppi 1990, 11–23.

48 Howard 1999, 37–52, for a thorough analysis of the project and its sources, particularly in festive architecture, see esp. 48, on the elements particular to Sansovino, and 51, on a hypothesis that the drawing may have been used to create an ephemeral façade for the Mercanti on the occasion of the Carnival procession of 1572 for the victory of Lepanto (*Mascherata*) that began and ended at the Madonna dell'Orto, which, however, is less convincing without the union of the Misericordia, unless it can somehow be associated with that Scuola's participation; on the celebration, Fenlon 1996, 248–50.

49 Puppi 1990, 23. Tafuri 1985, 28–29, on publication as a possible purpose, dating the drawings as 1550s–1560s, following Puppi's revised dating in relation to others in the Vicenza group (implicit as well as the comparison in

50 Puppi 1990, 98, "Buildings of Modern Rome."

51 Palladio's intention is reported by Paolo Gualdo 2000, 11; Silla Palladio, 27 January 1581, in Vicenza, BBV, Archivio dell'Accademia Olimpico, B. 1, reg. D, by date; discussed by Puppi, ed. 1988, 61; Puppi 1990, 16.

52 A fundamental study for the spirituality of the Ospedaletto is the unpublished *tesi di laurea* of Ellero 1980–81, to whom I am indebted for its consultation; for further history and bibliography, see Pilo 1985; Aikema & Meijers, eds. 1989, 149–89. As Deborah Howard has discussed, at this time Venice had four main State hospitals (the Pietà, the Ospedaletto, the Incurabili, and the Lazzaretto – later the Mendicanti), of which the Pietà was exclusively an orphanage, and the Ospedaletto, Incurabili, and later Mendicanti had orphanages attached (only female orphans gave musical performances); see for comparison Sansovino's Incurabili, in Howard 1987, 88–95.

53 8 October 1575 and April 1576 (no day), in Venice, Archivio IRE, Derelitti, F 15 (previously G 2), no. 29: The document linking Palladio was first published by Bassi 1978, 126 n. 24; and in the contemporary exhibition and catalog, *Arte e musica all'ospedaletto* 1978, 99–100; more recently in Aikema & Meijers, eds. 1989, 183–84.

54 For a description of the alterations needed to fit Mazza's altarpiece to the proportions of the later high altar by Antonio Sardi in 1659, see Aikema & Meijers, eds. 1989, 170, with earlier literature (see esp. Pilo 1985, 93–95); the attribution rests on Ridolfi's description (1965, 1: 32, including a lost painting for the soffit of the *Assumption of the Virgin*); recent restorations have shown frescoes by Francesco Montemezzano, with a *Nativity of the Virgin* behind the high altar, carrying out the theme of the church dedication to the Virgin Mary.

55 2 December 1575 and 6 January 1575 m.v. (= 1576), in Venice, Archivio IRE, Derelitti, B 1, "Libro di parte," 69r–v; for a discussion of which I would like to thank Giuseppe Ellero; see Ellero 1982, 124–25. For more on the comparative difficulties of financing *ospedali*, see Aikema & Meijers, eds. 1989, 152.

56 Sansovino 1968, 1: 72. See Pullan 1989, 30–33; Ellero 1989, 109–14.

57 Ellero 1989, 109. St. Jerome Emiliani (1481–1537) was the Venetian founder of the Augustinian Clerks Regular Somaschi in 1532 (recognized in 1568), to minister actively to the poor, especially the young, through hospitals, orphanages, and education; see *San Girolamo Miani e Venezia* 1986. On French theologian Guillaume Postel in Venice, see Kunst, ed. 1981.

58 2 February 1572 m.v. (= 1573), and 2 February 1573 m.v. (= 1574), "Libro di parte," 61, and 62, remaining active in various capacities

among the governing board throughout his life; see Aikema & Meijers, eds. 1989, 153; Tafuri 1989, 252 n. 138; Pilo 1985, 10, with reference to Contarini's funeral oration in which he was praised as "pauper pauperum"; Ellero 1982, including his inventory of 17 March 1599, in Venice, Archivio IRE, Derelitti, E 73, fasc. 1 (previously E 1, fasc. K, 1–6).

59 On this point, see in particular Ellero 1989, 112, in addition to the above.

60 As discussed above, on 8 October 1575 and April 1576 (no day), in Venice, Archivio IRE, Derelitti, F 15 (previously G 2), no. 29.

61 This last phrase has proved particularly troubling, Pilo 1985, 11, reinterprets the wording thus: "il volto in mezzo del quale va [= andrà] la Pala," the vault (meaning ciborium, or arch, the latter interpretation supported by Pilo) in the center of which will go the altarpiece.

62 It is pertinent to recall that the retrochoirs of San Giorgio Maggiore and Il Redentore follow this project, see Parts IV and V above.

63 Cristinelli 1978, 26; Pilo 1985, 8; Aikema & Meijers, eds. 1989, 150.

64 Ellero 1989, 112, on the hierarchy of seating, beginning with the three presidents, next patricians, then merchants.

65 Bassi 1978, 12; Puppi 1986, 109–10, summarizes evidence starting from the seventeenth-century attribution to Palladio of the destroyed ciborium altar for the church of Santo Spirito in Sassia, with a less confident attribution for the workmanship of the extant ciborium altar in the hospital; Ellero 1982, 123, on the issue of visibility. On Santo Spirito, see now Bruschi 2000; Colonna 2000.

66 Franzoi & Di Stefano 1976a, 466–77, the church architecture was completed in 1602 by Simone Sorella (except for the still bare façade). On the relation to the Zitelle choir, see Bassi 1978, 12, and below.

67 Sardi's contract of 4 June 1659, in Venice, Archivio IRE, Derelitti, E 63 no. 9 (previously E 1, B. 37; see Ellero, ed. 1987, 80); in Bassi 1978, 119–20, 127 n. 29; *Arte e musica* 1978, 100–02; Pilo 1985, 13–15 and fig. 7 (see here fig. 294), reconstruction of Palladio's altar, with extrapolation of Palladian elements from the Sardi contract, noting many similarities from the *Four Books*, 25 and fig. 20, reconstruction of Sardi's altar, 32–33, for Baldassare Longhena's subsequent modifications in 1676–77, and 229–30, contracts; Aikema & Meijers, eds. 1989, 154–56, and 184 (as Der E 64, n. 9).

68 Aikema & Meijers, eds. 1989, 156 ff., who discuss the modifications to the choir; see references from 1597 to 1676, in Venice, Archivio IRE, Derelitti, G 1, filza F, no. 25, in *Arte e musica* 1978, 105; Battilotti 1999, 505 cat. 153*, finds this reconstruction most persuasive, comparing it with the transept altars of San Giorgio Maggiore (see Part IV).

69 Bassi 1978, 124–25; also Cristinelli 1978, 27, 30, sees a larger role possible for Palladio; more cautious are: Pilo 1985, 17, who also compares internal articulation to Santa Maria Nova, 27;

Aikema & Meijers, eds. 1989, 158, note that the undoubted Palladian elements in the church also must be balanced against incongruencies, such as a lack of socles with pilasters. Puppi 1986, 269, on Santa Maria Nova, for which a bequest for the building was given as early as 1578, but construction begun only *circa* 1583/85–1594 (Puppi notes a comparison to the Palladian architecture in the above-mentioned Paolo Veronese's *Annunciation* for the Scuola dei Mercanti).

70 Bassi 1978, 122, 124–25, notes that if Marchio is the "Marco" documented at the Doge's Palace after the fire of 1574, then da Ponte was present as *proto*, and Palladio in an advisory capacity and provider of some of the designs for stone and woodwork (see above, Part V); Aikema & Meijers, eds. 1989, 138, note Marchio and Pasqualin both at the Incurabili with da Ponte in 1573, 158, on da Ponte's realization of projects by Palladio, 228, note Marchio at the *casa* delle Zitelle in 1575, for which see further below; Puppi 1986, 228, notes Pasqualin may be the "Pasqualino da Venezia" in Vicenza in 1567 working on the shops for Basilica Palladiana.

71 Bassi 1978, 125; Bassi 1954, as a published source for documents for this later period, since lost; see Pilo 1985, 27, 39 n. 164; and Aikema & Meijers, eds. 1989, 161–62, 187 nn. 107–08.

72 M. Chojnacka 1998 proposes the introduction of different models of "community" as a result of female expansion from family and neighborhood, which helped to shape these institutions in new ways as they brought different experience to governance. Ellero 1989, 114, describes the role of the male *governatori* as delegating the life of the community to the female *governatrice* who acted as consultants to the *priora*.

73 On the Contarini of the Madonna dell'Orto, see Gleason 1993, 1–7, and appendix 1; Andriana was Vincenzo's second wife, they were married in 1533 and Vincenzo died in 1541; his male heirs were by his first wife, a Pisani, both sons predeceasing Andriana, but leaving a grandson to continue the *ramo*.

74 Ellero 1989, 110, for Valier, 114, on another important female figure at this time, Prioress Violante Canal (to whom Andriana Contarini left a bequest in 1593, see Archivio IRE, Patrimoniale 1 B 53), one supported by Giovanni Battista Contarini, and 114–17, on the female communities. Pilo 1985, 93, refers to "La chiesa contariniana nel Cinquecento," albeit in reference to Giovanni Battista.

75 See now Puppi, ed. 1992, with earlier references; for the announcement of the property acquisition: letter of Andriana Contarini, 30 August 1560, in Ellero & Lunardon 1992, 89.

76 In addition to Frank 1992, on the architectural program, and Maschio 1992, 163–218, a study of the visual records of the site, in *Le Zitelle*; see still the definitive archival investigation and summary by Lunardon 1982; and for diverse

Howard 1999, 50, to the Rialto drawings, although it would contradict the hypothesis that it was executed for the *Mascherata* of 1572).

conclusions on some points, Aikema & Meijers, eds. 1989, 225–39.

77 The most forceful re-statement of the Zitelle as "il primo esempio di tipo postpalladiano" and not attributable to Palladio himself, even if based on his drawings, is in Aikema & Meijers, eds. 1989, 229–30. For an excellent discussion of such examples of the post-Palladian type, see Frank 1992, 102–05, albeit in the service of a hypothesis in support of Palladio's paternity for the entire complex (105–10); in reopening the question of authorship, Foscari 1980c, expresses this contradictory dilemma confronting the interpreters of this site: "Più che luogo palladiano, in senso stretto, la chiesa delle Zitelle si può dunque considerare un luogo della critica palladiana ed una prova delle molte vicende del palladianesimo veneto"; Puppi 1986, 273–76, inclined towards accepting a more direct contribution by Palladio (and Puppi, ed. 1992, 3–8), summarizes earlier views.

78 Semi 1983, 293–97; Ellero 1989, 109–20; M. Chojnacka 1998.

79 Doglioni 1598, 940; recently in Frank 1992, 102.

80 A succinct chronology and documents for the materials are in Lunardon 1982, 115–20, from Venice, Archivio IRE, Zitelle, G 1, "Libro della Fabrica per le spese fatte dall'anno 1575 sin l'anno 1600," which includes several groups of documents, from 1575–76 (including the "Libro di madonna" of Marina Bernardo), 1589–91 and 1593, 1596–97; the grant of timber of 25 June 1582 in ASV, Senato, Terra, reg. 54, 32, in G. Zorzi 1967, 169; for the progress noted in 1583, in Archivio IRE, Zitelle, G 1, proc. B, "Rodolo de Benefattori concorsi alla Fabrica," in Lunardon 1982, 117, who includes other indications for the state of the building; also Aikema & Meijers, eds. 1989, 228–29; Frank 1992, 127; and for transcriptions of earlier documents, see also Gardani 1961.

81 The inscription is first recorded by Stringa, in Sansovino 1604, 191; in G. Zorzi 1967, 166; for Bartolomeo Marchesi's will of 12 July 1583, in Venice, Archivio IRE, Zitelle, C 1 (Catastico bianco no. 2), 141; in Gardani 1961, 24–25; also Aikema & Meijers, eds. 1989, 234, with a discussion of the altarpiece, its attribution (in some sources as Leandro) and iconography (234–37); for which also Mazza 1992.

82 The consecration of 8 May 1588 is recorded in an inscription in the sacristy, see Aikema & Meijers, eds. 1989, 229. For Francesco Barbaro and Giovanni Grimani, see Part III.

83 "È questa Chiesa fabricata su'l modello del Paladio [sic], ma fu fornita dal Bozetto," Sansovino 1604, 192; but the stakes are raised in Martinioni's edition of 1663 (Sansovino 1968, 1: 258), who adds: "Fù l'Architetto il famosissimo Andrea Palladio, terminato poi dal Bozetto sul modello del medesimo Paladio [sic]."

84 Most recently to argue this point of view and summarize the evidence is Frank 1992, 102, who hypothesizes an interruption due to the plague, 106–07; Lunardon 1982, 107, retains that uncertain finances prevented a sustained campaign; also Calabi 2001a, 441. Cf. Aikema & Meijers, eds. 1989, 229–30.

85 For example, a reference to Palladio's *modello* for the Redentore calls it a "dissegno" in the same document, which a subsequent suggestion to provide for a "modello di rilievo" indicates was two-dimensional; see Part V. On categories of models, see Millon 1994b.

86 Equally, a connection to Antonio da Ponte, who was in charge of the restorations; see Part V; G. Zorzi 1967, 166, connected Bozzetto with the mason named by Cadorin 1838, 72–76. Bozzetto's death in 1583 (Temanza 1762, 372) raised the issue of who would have completed the project: Magrini 1845, 261, looked to the *proti* present in the later building phases, Girolamo Gallo, from the Magis-

trato alle Acque, in 1589; and Lorenzetti 1929, 721, proposed Bartolomeo from San Rocco, identified as Bartolomeo Manopola, in 1596; Frank 1992, 109–10, suggested Simone Sorella, *proto* of the Procurators of San Marco, based entirely on secondary connections, and the apt comparison to San Trovaso (also showing Palladian forms, such as thermal windows).

87 Puppi 1986, 275, utilizes the notion of a "point of departure."

88 These drawings are fully discussed in Part V, Il Redentore.

89 Frank 1992, 101, on the dates of their association with Le Zitelle; see Part V, Il Redentore, for biographies of each *provveditore*.

90 Puppi 1990, 13; Lewis 2000, 16.

91 Burns with Fairbairn & Boucher 1975, 147.

CONCLUSION

1 Vasari 1966, 6: 198, *Life* of Jacopo Sansovino, "Non tacerò che a tanta virtù ha congiunta una sì affabile e gentil natura, che lo rende appresso d'ognuno amabilissimo."

2 G. Zorzi 1965, 132, in a letter of 17 May 1572, from the *provveditore alla fabbrica del San Petronio in Bologna*.

3 Sites visited by King Henri III in Venice noted in de Nolhac & Solerti 1890, 132–33 (Doge's Palace), 136–37 (Palazzo Grimani), 142 (San Giorgio Maggiore), Villa Foscari (159–60; he also visited Federico Contarini's villa at Mira, the fame of the visit recorded in Tiepolo's frescoes under later Pisani ownership, see Part V), 161 (Pietro Foscari and the Arena palace in Padua; further, see Gullino 2000, 16–17).

4 Carpo 2001, 171 n. 82, "The modern idea of a project conceived in its entirety prior to construction – visualized in the form of a drawing or model, and then realized without any deviations – is not a Renaissance invention."

MANUSCRIPT AND ARCHIVAL SOURCES

Venice

Archivio Patriarcale di Venezia [APV]
Visite Trevisan

Archivio di Stato di Venezia [ASV]
Archivio Gradenigo
Archivio private Grimani di S. Maria Formosa
Avogaria di Comun
   Cronaca Matrimoni dei nobili veneti ["Cronaca Matrimoni"]
   Libro d'Oro
    Nascite
Cancelleria Inferiore
   Miscellanea notai diversi
Collegio
   Cerimoniali
   Notatorio
Compilazione Leggi
Consiglio dei Dieci
   Capi del Consiglio dei Dieci
    Ambasciatori, Roma
     Concilio di Trento
     Notatorio
   Comuni
   Misti
   Secreta
Dieci Savi sopra la Decima
Giuseppe Giomo, "Matrimoni patrizi per nome di donna," 86 ter 1–2 [Giomo]
Giudici del Proprio
   Extraordinari
Maggior Consiglio
   Deliberazioni
Magistrato al Sal
   Notatorio
Magistrato del Sopragastaldo
Miscellanea Codici Serie 1, Storia Veneta, 17–23, Marco Barbaro, "Albori de' patrizi veneti" [Barbaro, "Albori"]
Miscellanea Mappe [MM]

Notarile
  Atti
    Domenico Adami
    Avidio Branca
    Antonio Callegarini
    Angelo Canal
    Marc'Antonio Cavanis
    Pietro Contarini
    Giovanni Maria Coradine
    Giovanni Figolin
    Marco Graziabona
    Vettor Maffei
    Antonio Marsilio
    Pietro Perazzo
    Marin Rhenio
    Galeazzo Secco
    Cesare Ziliol
    Giulio Ziliol
Procuratoria de Supra
   San Marco [SM]
Provveditori alla Sanità
   Necrologi
Provveditori alla Zecca
Provveditori al Sal
   Notatorio
Provveditori sopra la fabbrica del Palazzo
Provveditori sopra la fabbrica del Ponte di Rialto
Sala diplomatica Regina Margherita
Savi ed esecutori alle Acque
Scuola Grande della Misericordia
Scuole piccole e suffragi
   Scuola di S. Maria e S. Cristoforo dei Mercanti alla Madonna dell'Orto
Secretario alle Voci
   Elezioni del Senato
San Francesco della Vigna [SFV]
San Giorgio Maggiore [SGM]
Santa Maria della Carità [SMC)
Sant'Antonio di Castello (SAC)
Santi Giovanni e Paolo [SSGP]
Senato

  Mar
  Secreta
   Ambasciatori, Roma
   Annali
   Dispacci di Roma
   Materie Miste Notabili
  Terra
   Deliberazioni

Biblioteca del Museo Civico Correr di Venezia [BCV]
MS Cicogna 516 (2504), 6 vols., Marco Barbaro, "Genealogie delle famiglie patrizie venete" [Barbaro, "Genealogie"]
Cod. Cicogna 890
Cod. Cicogna 1195
Cod. Cicogna 2131, Marco Valle, "De Monasterio et Abbatia S. Georgii Maioris Venetiarum clara et brevis notitia ex pluribus M.S. praecipuae Fortunati Ulmi abbatis titulo Casin. Xcerpta . . . MDCXCIII," 1693 [Valle, C 2131]
Cod. Cicogna 2556, Alvise Michiel, "Annali," 1578–1588 [Michiel]
Cod. Cicogna 2558, 464–79, Giovanni Lippomano, "Istorie venete"; no. 465 as Zuane Lippomano, "Delle Historie Vinitiane dall'anno MDLI all'anno MDLXVIII divise in dieci libri, T. 1, libri I–V" [Lippomano]
Cod. Cicogna 2583, "Variorum ad Venet. Eccles. atque ipsius Ven. Cleri. spectantia," pt. 1, 104
Cod. Cicogna 2991
Cod. Cicogna 3341/3
MS Cicogna 3617
Cons. 33 D 76/4, Giuseppe Tassini, "Cittadini Veneziani," Venice, 1888, 5 vols. [Tassini, "Cittadini"]
MS Correr, Cl. 3, 158
MS Correr, Cl. 3, 906, *Commissione* of Antonio Grimani for procurator *de supra* in 1510 from Doge Leonardo Loredan
Cod. Donà delle Rose 132, "Primicerio di S. Marco e Dogado"

Cod. Gradenigo 49, Giovanni Grevembroch, "Gli abiti de veneziani de quasi ogni età," 1754, 4 vols. [Grevembroch 1754]

Cod. Gradenigo 228, Giovanni Grevembroch, "Monumenta veneta," 1759, 3 vols. [Grevembroch 1759]

Cod. Gradenigo-Dolfin 65, Pietro Gradenigo and Giovanni Grevembroch, "Varie venete curiosità sacre e profane," 1755, 3 vols. [Gradenigo 1755]

Cod. Gradenigo-Dolfin 110, Marco Valle, "De Monasterio et Abbatia S. Georgii Maioris Venetiarum Clara et Brevis Notitia Ex Pluribus M.S. Praecipuae Fortunati Ulmi Abbatis Titularis Casin.s Excerpta MDCXCIII," 1693 [Valle]

Cod. Gradenigo-Dolfin 155, "Funzione Pubbliche"

MS Morosini-Grimani 270, "Origini dalla famiglia Grimana havuta dall'anno 666," 1627

MS P.D. c 248

MS P.D. c 506

MS P.D. c 818/17, 1–2

MS P.D. c 857/3

MS P.D. 745 C

MS P.D. 2416

MS P.D. 2417

Stampe
  Gherro I-I, 185; I-I, 203
  Gherro II-I, 789
  Gherro 1741
  H 34/I
  M 2658, tav. 23
  Molin, 2293

Varie coll. 69/4A, 303

Biblioteca Nazionale Marciana di Venezia [BMV]

MS It. IV, 37 (5133)

MS It. IV, 65 (5068), 209, Anton Maria the Elder and Anton Maria the Younger Zanetti, "Disegni delle Statue, Busti e altri marmi antichi" [Zanetti]

MS It. IV, 152 (5106), "L'Architettura, col commento di Daniele Barbaro in volgare"

Cod. It. IV, 169 (52625)

MS It. VI, 151 B, Girolamo Gualdo, "Vicenza Tamisata MSS," 1629

MS It. VII, 90 (8029), "Arbori, e Croniche delli Cittadini Veneti, e d'alcune Case Patritie" ["Arbori"]

MS It. VII, 925–928 (8594–8597), Marco Barbaro, "Genealogie delle famiglie patrizie venete" [Barbaro, "Genealogie"]

Cod. It. VII, 15–18 (8304–8307), Girolamo Alessandro Cappellari Vivaro Vicentino, "Il campidoglio veneto" [Cappellari Vivaro]

MS It. VII, 137 (8462), Giuseppe Malatesta, "Relatione Historica, e Politica delle differenze nate trà Papa Paolo v., e li SS.ri Venetiani l'anno 1605" [Malatesta]

MS It. VII, 709 (8403), Antonio Milledonne, "Ragionamento di doi gentil huomeni . . . sopra il governo della Repubblica Venetiana," 1581 [Milledonne]

MS It. VII, 553 (8812), Francesco da Molin, "Compendio di me Francesco da Molino de Messer Marco delle cose, de reputerò degne di venerne particolar memoria, et che succederanno in mio tempo si della Republica Venetiana" [Molin]

MS It. VII, 1269 (9573), Giovanni Battista Pace, "Ceremoniale Magnum, sive raccolta universale di tutte le ceremonie spettanti alla ducal regia capella di San Marco," 1678 [Pace]

MS It. VII, 531 (7152), Marin Sanudo, "Vite dei dogi" [Sanudo]

MS It. VII, 134 (8035), Girolamo Savina, "Cronaca veneta sino al MDCXV" [Savina]

MS It. VII, 76 (9436), Giovanni Carlo Sivos, "Cronaca . . . 1595–1605" [Sivos]

MS It. VII, 1279 (8886), "Avisi notabili del Mondo, et deliberazioni più importanti di Pregadi, dal 4 marzo 1588 al 25 febbraio 1588 (m.v. = 1589)"

MS It. X, 73 (7097), 156–157, Paolo Gualdo, "Vita di Andrea Palladio" [Gualdo]

MS Lat. III, 172 (2276), "Rituum ecclesiasticorum cerimoniale," 1559–1564 (Doge Girolamo Priuli)

MS Lat. IX, 177 (2949), Fortunato Olmo, "Historiarum Insulae s. Georgii Maioris prope Venetias positae libri III" [Olmo]

Archivio Istituzzioni di Ricovero e di Educazione di Venezia [Archivio IRE]

Derelitti

Patrimoniale

Zitelle

Seminario Patriarcale di Venezia [SPV]

MS 602, Fortunato Olmo, "Istoria dell' isola di S. Georgio Maggiore di Venezia," 1619 [Olmo]

FLORENCE

Archivio di Stato di Firenze [ASF]

Riformagioni
  Carteggio Urbani

LONDON

British Library [BL]

Add. MS 18000

Add. MS 26107

King's Library, 146, Antonio Visentini, "Pianta ed alzato del magnifico arco trionfale e loggia eretto dal celebre architetto Andrea Palladio," 1750

71. i. I. Antonio Visentini, "Admiranda Urbis Venetae," 3 vols., 1755 [Visentini]

Public Record Office

State Papers 99, file 8, Sir Dudley Carleton

Sir John Soane's Museum

Vol. 143 (MS II), Marino Grimani, *Commentarii in Epistolas Pauli, Ad Romanos, et ad Galantas*

MESTRE

Annali BB

Conto de Bartolomeo Bontempelli, 1585–1591

P. Francesco da Venetia, "Relazione delle fondazioni"

MILAN

Biblioteca Ambrosiana

Cod. F 245 Inf., 78

MONTAGNANA

Archivio della Chiesa arcipretale

PADUA

Archivio di Stato di Padova [ASP]

Notarile
  S. de Astori
  Santa Giustina [SG]

Biblioteca Civica

Raccolta iconografia e topografica padovana, XLVIII. 4742, Praglia, Monastero, B.VIII

Biblioteca Universitaria di Padova [BUP]

Cod. 285, Fortunato Olmo, "Historiarum Insulae s. Georgii cognomento Maioris iuxta Venetias positae, antiquitate, situs amoenitate rerumque gestarum dignitate celeberrimas a primi temple structura anno DCCLXXXX ad annum MDCXIX" [Olmo]

MS 905, Girolamo da Potenza, "Cronica del mon.ro di S. Giustina fatta nell'anno 1614" [Potenza]

MS 1621, Marco Valle, "Breve Chronichon s. Georgii Maioris Venetis," 1685 [Valle]

MS 2213–2214

PARIS

Bibliothèque Nationale de Paris [BN]

Fonds Français

UDINE

Archivio Archivescovile di Udine [AAU]

Epistolario del cancellaria patriarcale Giovanni Bottana

Biblioteca Archivescovile di Udine [BAU]

Carteggio Maracco

VATICAN CITY

Biblioteca Apostolica Vaticana [BAV]

Cod. Barb. Lat. 5751

VICENZA

Biblioteca Bertoliana di Vicenza [BBV]

Archivio dell'Accademia Olimpica

BIBLIOGRAPHY

Ackerman 1977a

Ackerman, James. "L'architettura religiosa veneta in rapporto a quella toscana del rinascimento." *Bollettino del Centro internazionale di studi di architettura Andrea Palladio* 19 (1977): 135–64

Ackerman 1977b

——. *Palladio: The Architect and Society*, Harmondsworth, 1977 (orig. pub. 1966)

Ackerman 1977c

——. "Palladio e lo sviluppo della concezione della chiesa a Venezia." *Bollettino del Centro internazionale di studi di architettura Andrea Palladio* 19 (1977): 9–26

Ackerman 1980

——. "Observations on Renaissance Church Planning in Venice and Florence, 1470–1570." In *Florence and Venice: Comparisons and Relations.* Acts of Two Conferences at Villa I Tatti in 1976–77, Florence, 1980, 2: 287–307

Ackerman 1986

——. *The Architecture of Michelangelo*, Harmondsworth, 1986 (orig. pub. 1961)

Ackerman 1990

——. *The Villa: Form and Ideology in Country Houses*, Princeton, N.J. 1990

Ackerman 1991a

——. "Architectural Practice in the Renaissance." In *Distance Points*, Cambridge, Mass., 1991, 361–84 (orig. pub. in *Journal of the Society for Architectural Historians* 13 [1954]: 3–11)

Ackerman 1991b

——. *Distance Points: Essays in Theory and Renaissance Art and Architecture*, Cambridge, Mass., 1991

Ackerman 1991c

——. "The Geopolitics of Venetian Architecture in the Time of Titian." In *Distance Points*, Cambridge, Mass., 1991, 453–94 (orig. pub. in *Titian: His World and His Legacy*, ed. D. Rosand, New York, 1982, 41–71)

Ackerman 1991d

——. "Style." In *Distance Points*, Cambridge, Mass., 1991, 3–22 (orig. pub. in *Art and Archaeology*, with Rhys Carpenter, Englewood Cliffs, N.J., 1963, 164–86)

Ackerman 2002

——. "Daniele Barbaro and Vitruvius." In *Origins, Imitation, Conventions*, Cambridge, Mass., 2002, 217–34 (orig. pub. in *Architectural Studies in Memory of Richard Krautheimer*, ed. C. Stryker, Mainz, 1996, 1–5)

Acta Sanctorum 1940

Acta Sanctorum, 68 vols., Brussels, 1940 (orig. pub. Paris, 1863–1925)

Adorni 1983

Adorni, Bruno. "Alessio Tramello architetto della chiesa di San Sisto a Piacenza." In *La Madonna per San Sisto di Raffaello a la cultura piacentina della prima metà del cinquecento.* Atti del convegno: Piacenza, 10 dicembre 1983, ed. P. Ceschi Lavagetto, Parma, 1985, 49–83

Adorni 1989

——. "Apparati effimeri urbani e allestimenti teatrale." In *Giulio Romano*, Milan, 1989, 498–501

Aikema, 1996

Aikema, Bernard. *Jacopo Bassano and his Public: Moralizing Pictures in an Age of Reform,* ca. 1535–1600. Princeton, N.J., 1996

Aikema & Meijers, eds. 1989

Aikema, Bernard, and Dulcia Meijers, eds. *Nel regno dei poveri: arte e storia dei grandi ospedali veneziana in età moderna, 1474–1797,* Venice, 1989

Alberigo 1964

Alberigo, Giuseppe. "Barbaro, Daniele Matteo Alvise." In *Dizionario biografico degli Italiani,* Rome, 1964, 6: 89–95

Alberti 1986

Alberti, Leon Battista. *The Ten Books of Architecture of Leon Battista Alberti: The 1755 Leoni Edition*, New York, 1986

Alberti 1988

——. *On the Art of Building in Ten Books*, trans. J. Rykwert, N. Leach, and R. Tavernor, Cambridge, Mass., 1988

Alberton Vinco da Sesso 1996

Alberton Vinco da Sesso, Livia. "Francesco Bassano." In *Dictionary of Art*, ed. J. Turner, London, 1996, 3: 348–49

Albertonio [1571]

Albertonio, Francesco. *L'entrata che fece l'Eccellentissimo Signor Marc'Antonio Colonna in Roma alli 4. di dicembre 1571.* Viterbo [1571]

Alexander, ed. 1994

Alexander, Jonathan J. G., ed. *The Painted Page: Italian Renaissance Book Illumination, 1450–1550*. London and Munich, 1994

Anderson 1969

Anderson, Marvin. "Luther's Sola Fide in Italy, 1542–1551." *Church History* 38 (1969): 25–42

Aquilecchia 1980

Aquilecchia, Giovanni. "Pietro Aretino e altri poligrafi a Venezia." In *Storia della cultura veneta. 3/2: Dal primo Quattrocento al Concilio di Trento,* ed. G. Arnaldi and M. Pastore Stocchi, Vicenza, 1980, 61–98

Arbel 1988

Arbel, Benjamin. "A Royal Family in Republican Venice: The Cypriot Legacy of the Corner della Regina." *Studi veneziani* 15 (1988): 131–52

Arslan 1960

Arslan, Edoardo. *I Bassano.* 2 vols., Milan, 1960

Arte e musica 1978

Arte e musica all'Ospedaletto. Venice, 1978

Asquini 1992

Asquini, Massimo. "Palladio e i Canonici regolari lateranensi: per una ricerca sul Convento della Carità di Venezia." *Arte documento* 6 (1992): 231–37

Asquini & Asquini 1997

Asquini, Licia, and Massimo Asquini. *Andrea Pal-*

ladio e gli antonini: un palazzo "romano" nella Udine del Cinquecento, Gorizia, 1997

Attardi 2003

Attardi, Luisa. "Cat. entry." In *Pinacoteca civica di Vicenza: catalogo scientifico delle collezioni*. I: *Dipinti dal XIV al XVI secolo*, ed. M. E. Avagnina, M. Binotto, and G. C. F. Villa, Milan and Vicenza, 2003, 386–87

Azzi Visentini 1984

Azzi Visentini, Margherita. *L'Orto Botanico di Padova e il giardino del Rinascimento*. Milan, 1984

Azzi Visentini 1996

——. "Daniele Barbaro e il giardino: dall'Orto Botanico di Padova a Villa Barbaro a Maser." In *Una famiglia veneziana nella storia: i Barbaro*. Atti del Convegno di Studi in occasione del quinto centenario della morte dell'umanista Ermolao: Venice, 4–6 November 1993, ed. M. Marangoni and M. Pastore Stocchi, Venice, 1996, 397–434

Bacchi 1999

Bacchi, Andrea. "Girolamo Campagna." In *"La bellissima maniera": Alessandro Vittoria e la scultura veneta del Cinquecento*, ed. A. Bacchi, L. Camerlengo, and M. Leithe-Jasper, Trent, 1999, 399–416.

Baldoria 1891

Baldoria, Natale. *Il Briosco ed il Leopardi architetti della chiesa di S. Giustina di Padova*, Rome, 1891

Baldwin 1990

Baldwin, Robert. "A Bibliography of the Literature on Triumph." In *"All the world's a stage . . ."*: *Art and Pageantry in the Renaissance and Baroque*. I: *Triumphal Celebrations and the Rituals of Statecraft*, ed. B. Wisch and S. Munshower, University Park, Pa., 1990, 359–85

Ballarin 1971

Ballarin, Alessandro. "Un ritratto inedito di Bassano." *Arte veneta* 25 (1971): 268–71

Baluze 1762

Baluze, St. (Etienne). *Miscellanea*, Lucca, 1762

Banfi 1956

Banfi, Luigi. "Ermolao Barbaro, Venezia e il Patriarcato di Aquileia." *Nuova antologia* 91 (1956): 421–28

Barbaro 1556

Barbaro, Daniele. Commentary on *I dieci libri dell'architettura di M. Vitruvio, tradotti et commentati da Monsignor Barbaro eletto patriarca d'Aquileggia*, Venice, 1556

Barbaro 1557

——. *Della Eloquenza, Dialogo del Reverendiss. Monsignor Daniel Barbaro, eletto patriarca d'Aquileia. Nuovamente mandato in luce da Girolamo Ruscelli. Ai Signori Academici Costanti di Vicenza*, Venice, 1557

Barbaro 1567a

——. Commentary on *De architectura libri decem, cum commentariis Danielis Barbari, electi Patriarchae Aquileiensis, multis aedificiorum, horologiorum, et machinarum descriptionibus, et figuris*, Venice, 1567

Barbaro 1567b

——. Commentary on *I dieci libri dell'architettura di M. Vitruvio, tradotti et commentati da Mons. Daniele Barbaro eletto Patriarca d'Aquileia, da lui rivedi et ampliati; & hora in più commoda forma ridotta*, Venice, 1567

Barbaro 1569

——. *La Pratica della perspettiva, opera molto utile a pittori, a scultori, & ad architetti, di Daniel Barbaro*, Venice, 1569

Barbaro 1987

——. Commentary on *I dieci libri dell'architettura tradotti et commentati da Daniele Barbaro 1567. Con un saggio di Manfredo Tafuri e uno studio di Manuela Morresi*, Milan, 1987

F. Barbieri 1966

Barbieri, Franco. Review of *Le chiese e i ponti di Andrea Palladio di Giangiorgio Zorzi*, by Giangiorgio Zorzi. *Bollettino del Centro internazionale di studi di architettura Andrea Palladio* 8 (1966): 337–55

F. Barbieri 1970

——. *The Basilica of Andrea Palladio*, University Park, Pa., 1970

F. Barbieri 1980

——. "Giangiorgio Trissino e Andrea Palladio." In *Atti del convegno di studi su Giangiorgio Trissino: Vicenza, 31 March–1 April 1979*, ed. N. Pozza, Vicenza, 1980, 191–211

G. Barbieri 1983

Barbieri, Giuseppe. *Andrea Palladio e la cultura veneta del Rinascimento*, Rome, 1983

Barkan 1986

Barkan, Leonard. *The Gods Made Flesh: Metamorphosis and the Pursuit of Paganism*, New Haven and London, 1986

Bartolini, Bergamini, & Sereni 1983

Bartolini, Elio, Giuseppe Bergamini, and Lelia Sereni. *Raccontare Udine: vicende di case e palazzi*, Udine, 1983

Bassi 1954

Bassi, Elena. "Gli architetti dell'Ospedaletto." *Arte veneta* 8 (1954): 175–81

Bassi 1973

——. *The Convento della Carità*, University Park, Pa., 1973

Bassi 1978

——. "Attività del Palladio all'Ospedaletto." *Bollettino del Centro internazionale di studi di architettura Andrea Palladio* 20 (1978): 113–28

Bassi 1980

——. *Il complesso palladiano della Carità*, Milan, 1980

Bassi 1987

——. *Palazzi di Venezia: Admiranda Urbis Venetae*, 4th rev. edn., Venice, 1987

Bassi 1997

——. *Tracce di chiese veneziane distrutte: ricostruzione dai disegni di Antonio Visentini*, Venice, 1997

Battilotti 1980a

Battilotti, Donata. "La chiesa del Redentore." In *Architettura e utopia nella Venezia del Cinquecento*, ed. L. Puppi, Milan, 1980, 265–68

Battilotti 1980b

——. *Vicenza al tempo di Andrea Palladio*, Vicenza, 1980

Battilotti 1982

——. "Palladio a Venezia: regesti per un itinerario." In *Palladio e Venezia*, ed. L. Puppi, Florence, 1982, 175–218

Battilotti 1985a

——. "Palazzi per Venezia non realizzati (XV–XVI secolo)." In *Le Venezie possibili*, ed. L. Puppi and G. Romanelli, Milan, 1985, 34–40

Battilotti 1985b

——. "Progetti palladiani per il Redentore a San Vidal." In *Le Venezie possibili*, ed. L. Puppi and G. Romanelli, Milan, 1985, 41–44

Battilotti 1985c

——. "Villa Barbaro a Maser: un difficile cantiere." *Storia dell'arte* 53 (1985): 33–48

Battilotti 1990

——. *The Villas of Palladio*. Milan, 1995 (trans. of *Le ville di Palladio*, 1990)

Battilotti 1999

——. "Aggiornamento del catalogo del opera." In Lionello Puppi, *Andrea Palladio*, Milan, 1999, 512–15

Battilotti, ed. 1999

Battilotti, Donata, ed. *Andrea Palladio* by Lionello Puppi, Milan, 1999 (rev. edn. of *Andrea Palladio: L'opera completa*, 1973)

Battistella 1898

Battistella, Antonio. "La politica ecclesiastica della Repubblica Veneta." *Archivio veneto* 16 (1898): 386–420

Bauer 1975

Bauer, Linda Freeman. "On the Origins of the Oil Sketch: Form and Function in Cinquecento Preparatory Techniques." PhD dissertation, New York University, 1975

Bauer 1978

——. "*Quanto si disegna, si dipinge ancora*: Some Observations on the Development of the Oil Sketch." *Storia dell'arte* 32 (1978): 45–57

Bedon 1983

Bedon, Anna. "Il 'Vitruvio' di Giovan Antonio Rusconi." *Ricerche di storia dell'arte* 19 (1983): 84–90

Bellavitis 1980

Bellavitis, Giorgio. "L'invenzione palladiana di un palazzo a Venezia. Due ipotesi sul 'sito': un'ipotesi per San Luca." In *Architettura e utopia nella Venezia del Cinquecento*, ed. L. Puppi, Milan, 1980, 270–73

Bellavitis 1982

——. "I progetti di Palladio per due palazzi a Venezia." In *Palladio e Venezia*, ed. L. Puppi, Florence, 1982, 55–70

Bellodi 1974

Bellodi, Rosolino. *Il monastero di San Benedetto in Polirone nella storia e nell'arte*, San Benedetto Po, 1974 (orig. pub. Mantua, 1905)

Bellori 1672

Bellori, Gian Pietro. *Vite de' pittori, scultori et architetti moderni*, Rome, 1672

Beltrami 1956

Beltrami, Daniele. *Saggi di storia dell'agricoltura nella Repubblica di Venezia durante l'età moderna*, Florence, 1956

Beltramini 1991

Beltramini, Guido. "Andrea Moroni e la chiesa di Santa Maria di Praglia." *Annali di architettura* 3 (1991): 70–89

Beltramini 1995

———. "Architetture di Andrea Moroni per la Congregazione Cassinese: due conventi bresciani e la basilica di Santa Giustina a Padova." *Annali di architettura* 7 (1995): 63–94

Beltramini & Padoan, eds. 2000

Beltramini, Guido, and Antonio Padoan, eds. *Andrea Palladio: atlante delle architecture*, intro. H. Burns, Venice, 2000

Benedetti 1571

Benedetti, Rocco. *Ragguaglio delle allegrezze, solennità, e feste fatte in Venetia per la felice vittoria*, Venice, 1571

Benedetti 1574

———. *Le feste et trionfi fatti dalla Sereniss. Signoria di Venetia nella felice venuta di Henrico III. Christianiss. re di Francia, et di Polonia*, Venice, 1574

Bentmann & Müller 1992

Bentmann, Reinhard, and Michael Müller. *The Villa as Hegemonic Architecture*, trans. T. Spence and D. Craven, Atlantic Highlands, N.J., and London, 1992 (trans. of *Die Villa als Herrschaftsarchitektur*, Frankfurt am Main, 1970)

Benzoni 1961

Benzoni, Gino. "Una controversia tra Roma e Venezia all'inizio del '600: la conferma del patriarca." *Bollettino dell'Istituto di storia della società e dello stato veneziano* 3 (1961): 121–38

Benzoni 1987

———. "I papi e la 'corte di Roma' visti dagli ambasciatori veneziani." In *Venezia e la Roma dei papi*, Milan, 1987, 75–104

Benzoni 1997

———. "Comportamenti e problemi di comportamento nella Venezia di Giovanni Grimani." In *Lo Statuario Pubblico della Serenissima: due secoli di collezionismo di antichità, 1596–1797*, ed. I. Favaretto and G. L. Ravagnan, Cittadella, 1997, 17–37

Benzoni, ed. 1982

Benzoni, Gino, ed. *I dogi*, Milan, 1982

Berdini 1997

Berdini, Paolo. *The Religious Art of Jacopo Bassano: Painting as Visual Exegesis*, Cambridge, 1997

Bertotti Scamozzi 1785

Bertotti Scamozzi, Ottavio. *Le terme dei Romani disegnate da Andrea Palladio: e rippublicate con la giunta di alcune osservazioni di Ottavio Bertotti Scamozzi, giusta l'esemplare del lord co. di Burlingthon impresso in Londra l'anno 1732*, Vicenza, 1785

Bertotti Scamozzi 1796

———. *Le fabbriche e i disegni di Andrea Palladio: raccolti ed illustrati da Ottavio Bertotti Scamozzi*, 4 vols. in 1, Vicenza, 1796

Bertotti Scamozzi 1968

———. *Le fabbriche e i disegni di Andrea Palladio: raccolti ed illustrati da Ottavio Bertotti Scamozzi, Vicenza 1796*, intro. J. Quentin Hughes, London, 1968

Besta 1899

Besta, Enrico. *Il Senato Veneziano (origine, costituzione, attribuzione e riti)*, Venice, 1899

Bettagno, ed. 1997

Bettagno, Alessandro, ed. *Venezia da stato a mito*, Venice, 1997

Betussi 1573

Betussi, Giuseppe. *Ragionamento di M. Giuseppe Betussi sopra il Cathaio, luogo dello ill. S. Pio Enea Obizzi*, Padua, 1573

Biasutti 1958

Biasutti, Guglielmo. *Storia e guida del Palazzo Arcivescovile di Udine*, Udine, 1958

Bigi 1964

Bigi, Emilio. "Barbaro, Ermolao (Almoro)." In *Dizionario biografico degli Italiani*, Rome, 1964, 6: 96–99

Boholm 1990

Boholm, Åsa. *The Doge of Venice: The Symbol of State Power in the Renaissance*, Gothenburg, 1990

Boito, ed. 1880–93

Boito, Camillo, ed. *La Basilica di San Marco in Venezia illustrata nella storia e nell'arte dalle scrittori veneziani*. 8 vols. in 15, Venice, 1880–93

Borghini 1584

Borghini, Raffaello. *Il Riposo*, Florence, 1584

Boschini 1664

Boschini, Marco. *Le minere della pittura*, Venice, 1664

Bossi 1953

Bossi, Franco. *La Chiesa di S. Pietro in Gessate*, Milan, 1953

Bossi da Modena 1983

Bossi da Modena, Arcangelo. *Matricula monachorum congregationis casinensis ordinis S. Benedicti. 1: 1409–1699*, ed. L. Novelli and G. Spinelli, Cesena, 1983

Botero 1640

Botero, Giovanni. *Delle relationi universali di Giovanni Botero . . . divise in quattro parte . . . aggiuntovi la Ragion di Stato del medesimo*, Venice, 1640

Bottari, ed. 1754

Bottari, Giovanni Gaetano, ed. *Raccolta di lettere sulla pittura, scultura e architettura*, Rome, 1754

Boucher 1979

Boucher, Bruce. "The Last Will of Daniele Barbaro." *Journal of the Warburg and Courtauld Institutes* 42 (1979): 277–82

Boucher 1986

———. "Il Sansovino e i procuratori di San Marco." *Ateneo Veneto* n.s., 24/1–2 (1986): 59–74

Boucher 1991

———. *The Sculpture of Jacopo Sansovino*, 2 vols., New Haven and London, 1991

Boucher 1994

———. "L'architettura." In *Storia di Venezia. Temi: L'arte*, 2 vols., ed. R. Pallucchini, Rome, 1994, 1: 609–84

Boucher 1996

———. "Campagna, Girolamo." In *Dictionary of Art*, ed. J. Turner, London, 1996, 5: 531–34

Boucher 1998

———. *Andrea Palladio: The Architect in his Time*, New York and London, 1998 (orig. pub. 1994)

Boucher 2000

———. "Nature and the antique in the work of Andrea Palladio." *Journal of the Society of Architectural Historians* 59 (2000): 296–311

Bouwsma 1968

Bouwsma, William. *Venice and the Defense of Republican Liberty: Renaissance Values in the Age of the Counter-Reformation*, Berkeley and Los Angeles, 1968

Braudel 1958

Braudel, Fernand. "La vita economica di Venezia nel secolo XVI." In *La civiltà veneziana del rinascimento*, Storia della civiltà veneziana 4, Florence, 1958, 81–102

Braudel 1982

———. *Civilization and Capitalism, 15th–18th Century. 2: The Wheels of Commerce*, New York, 1982

Bresciani Alvarez 1970

Bresciani Alvarez, Giulio. "La Basilica di Santa Giustina nelle sue fasi storico-costruttive." In G. Fiocco et al., *La Basilica di Santa Giustina: arte e Storia*, Castelfranco Veneto, 1970, 65–166

Bresciani Alvarez 1977

———. "Le fasi costruttive e l'arredo plastico-architettonico della cattedrale." In *Il Duomo di Padova e il suo battistero*, Trieste, 1977, 80–136

Brilliant 1967

Brilliant, Richard. *The Arch of Septimius Severus in the Roman Forum*, Memoirs of the American Academy in Rome 29, Rome, 1967

Bristot 2001

Bristot, Annalisa. "Dedicata all'amore per l'antico: il camerino di Apollo a Palazzo Grimani." *Arte veneta* 58 (2001): 42–93

Bristot & Piana 1997

Bristot, Annalisa, and Mario Piana. "Il Palazzo dei Grimani a Santa Maria Formosa." In *Lo Statuario Pubblico della Serenissima: due secoli di collezionismo di antichità, 1596–1797*, ed. I. Favaretto and G. L. Ravagnan, Cittadella, 1997, 45–52

C. Brown with Lorenzoni 1999

Brown, Clifford, with A. M. Lorenzoni. "The 'Studio del Clarissimo Cavaliero Mozzanico in Venezia.'" *Jahrbuch der Berliner Museen* 41 (1999): 55–76

D. Brown 1990

Brown, David. Cat. entry in *Titian, Prince of Painters*, ed. S. Biadene and M. Yakush, Venice, 1990, 252–54

J. Brown 1994

Brown, Jonathan. *Kings & Connoisseurs: Collecting in Seventeenth-Century Europe*, Washington, D.C., and Princeton, N.J., 1994

P. Brown 1988

Brown, Patricia Fortini. *Venetian Narrative Painting in the Age of Carpaccio*, New Haven and London, 1988

P. Brown 1990

——. "Measured Friendship, Calculated Pomp: The Ceremonial Welcomes of the Venetian Republic." In *"All the world's a stage . . . ": Art and Pageantry in the Renaissance and Baroque.* I: *Triumphal Celebrations and the Rituals of Statecraft*, ed. B. Wisch and S. Munshower, University Park, Pa., 1990, 136–86

P. Brown 1991

——. "The Self-Definition of the Venetian Republic." In *Athens and Rome, Florence and Venice: City-States in Classical Antiquity and Medieval Italy*, ed. A. Molho, K. Rauflaub, and J. Emlen, Ann Arbor, Mi., 1991, 511–48

P. Brown 1996a

——. "Le 'Scuole.'" In *Storia di Venezia: dalle origini alla caduta della Serenissima.* 5: *Il rinascimento, società ed economia*, ed. A. Tenuti and U. Tucci, Rome, 1996, 307–54

P. Brown 1996b

——. *Venice and Antiquity: The Venetian Sense of the Past*, New Haven and London, 1996

P. Brown 2004

——. *Private Lives in Renaissance Venice: Art, Architecture, and the Family*, New Haven and London, 2004

W. Brown 1974

Brown, William. "Nicolò da Ponte: the Political Career of a Sixteenth-century Venetian Patrician." PhD dissertation, New York University, 1974

Brunetti 1933

Brunetti, Mario. "Da un carteggio di Leonardo Donà, ambasciatore a Roma, col fratello Nicolò (1581–1583)." In *Miscellanea di studi storici in onore di Alessandro Luzio*, Florence, 1933, I: 121–46

Brusatin, ed. 1979

Brusatin, Manlio, ed. *Venezia e lo spazio scenico*, Venice, 1979

Bruschi 1994

Bruschi, Arnaldo. "Religious Architecture in Renaissance Italy from Brunelleschi to Michelangelo." In *The Renaissance from Brunelleschi to Michelangelo: The Representation of Architecture*, ed. H. Millon and V. Lampugnani, Milan and London, 1994, 133–81

Bruschi 2000

——. "Palladio architetto a Roma e la sua attività per l'ospedale di Santo Spirito." In *Studi in onore di Renato Cevese*, ed. G. Beltramini, A. Ghisetti Giavarina, and P. Marini, Vicenza, 2000, 61–82

Buddenseig 1969

Buddenseig, Tilman. "Zum Statuenprogramm im Kapitolsplan Pauls III." *Zeitschrift für Kunstgeschicte* 32 (1969): 177–228

Buffa 1997

Buffa, Elisabetta. "Delle pagine dei viaggiatori stranieri a Venezia: antologia di brani sullo studio." In *Lo Statuario Pubblico della Serenissima: due secoli di collezionismo di antichità, 1596–1797*, ed. I. Favaretto and G. L. Ravagnan, Cittadella, 1997, 310–14

Burke 1992

Burke, Peter. "The language of Orders in Early Modern Europe." In *Social Orders and Social Classes in Europe since 1500: Studies in Social Stratification*, ed. M. L. Bush, New York and London, 1992, 1–12

Burns 1979

Burns, Howard, "Le opere minori del Palladio." *Bollettino del Centro internazionale di studi di architettura Andrea Palladio* 21 (1979): 9–34

Burns 1980a

——. "L'antichità di Verona e l'architettura del Rinascimento," in *Palladio e Verona*, ed. P. Marini, Milan, 1980, 103–17

Burns 1980b

——. Cat. entries in *Palladio e Verona*, ed. P. Marini, Milan, 1980, 165–67

Burns 1982

——. "The Lion's Claw." *Daidalos* 5 (1982): 73–80

Burns 1987

——. "A Tomb Designed by Andrea Palladio and an Early Sentimental Attachment of Daniele Barbaro." Talk given at College Art Association Annual Meeting, 12–14 February 1987, abstract published in *Abstracts of the 75th Annual Meeting of the College Art Association of America*, New York, 1987

Burns 1991

——. "Building and Construction in Palladio's Vicenza." In *Les chantiers de la renaissance*. Actes des colloques tenus à Tours en 1983–1984, ed. J. Guillaume, Paris, 1991, 191–226

Burns 2000

——. Intro. to *Andrea Palladio: atlante delle architecture*, ed. G. Beltramini and A. Padoan, Venice, 2000

Burns, with Fairbairn & Boucher 1975

Burns, Howard, with Lynda Fairbairn and Bruce Boucher. *Andrea Palladio 1508–1580: The Portico and the Farmyard*, London, 1975

Burns, Frommel, & Puppi, eds. 1995

Burns, Howard, Christoph Frommel, and Lionello Puppi, eds. *Michele Sanmicheli: architettura, linguaggio e cultura artistica nel Cinquecento*, Milan, 1995

Byam Shaw 1976

Byam Shaw, James. *Drawings by Old Masters at Christ Church, Oxford*, 2 vols., Oxford, 1976

Cadorin 1838

Cadorin, Giuseppe. *Pareri di XV architetti e notizie storiche intorno al Palazzo Ducale di Venezia*, Venice, 1838

Cairns 1976

Cairns, Christopher. *Domenico Bollani, Bishop of Brescia*, Niewkoop, 1976

Cairns 1980

——. "Diocesan Studies of the Venetian Terraferma (apropos of recent studies of Treviso)." *Studi veneziani* 4 (1980): 79–97

Calabi 2001a

Calabi, Donatella. "Le chiese di Palladio." In *Storia dell'architettura italiana.* 4: *Il secondo cinquecento*, ed. C. Conforti and R. Tuttle, Milan, 2001, 436–53.

Calabi 2001b

——. "La terraferma veneta e l'opera del Palladio." In *Storia dell'architettura italiana.* 4: *Il secondo cinquecento*, ed. C. Conforti and R. Tuttle, Milan, 2001, 454–81.

Calabi 2001c

——. "Venezia e Veneto: città e progetti." In *Storia dell'architettura italiana.* 4: *Il secondo cinquecento*, ed. C. Conforti and R. Tuttle, Milan, 2001, 406–35.

Calabi & Morachiello 1987

Calabi, Donatella, and Paolo Morachiello. *Rialto: le fabbriche e il ponte, 1514–1591.* Turin, 1987

Calquhoun 1981

Calquhoun, Alan. "Form and Figure." In *Essays in Architectural Criticism: Modern Architecture and Historical Change*, Cambridge, Mass., 1981, 190–202, 207 (orig. pub. in *Oppositions* 12 [1978]: 28–37)

Calvillo 2000

Calvillo, Elena. "*Romanità* and *Grazia*: Giulio Clovio's Pauline Frontispieces for Marino Grimani." *Art Bulletin* 82 (2000): 280–97

Camerlengo & Piva 1980

Camerlengo, Lia, and Raffaella Piva. "Cronologia: il cantiere architettonico e urbanistico a Venezia nel Cinquecento." In *Architettura e utopia nella Venezia del Cinquecento*, ed. L. Puppi, Milan, 1980, 277–81

Candiani 1965

Candiani, Carlo. "Antichi titoli di chiese." In *Il culto dei santi a Venezia*, ed. S. Tramontin, Venice, 1965, 99–131

Candussio 1992

Candussio, Aldo. "Il tesoro di Pertéole." In *Storia e arte del patriarcato di Aquileia*, Antichità Altoadriatiche 38, Udine, 1992, 377–92

Caniato & Dal Borgo, eds. 1990

Caniato, Giovanni, and Michela Dal Borgo, eds. *Le arti edili a Venezia*, Rome, 1990

Carcereri 1907

Carcereri, Luigi. *Giovanni Grimani Patriarca d'Aquileia accusato d'eresia*, Rome, 1907

Carile & Fedalto 1978

Carile, Antonio, and Giorgio Fedalto. *Le origini di Venezia*, Bologna, 1978

Carpeggiani 1980

Carpeggiani, Paolo. Cat. entries in *Architettura e utopia nella Venezia del Cinquecento*, ed. L. Puppi, Milan, 1980, 123–24

Carpo 2001

Carpo, Mario. *Architecture in the Age of Printing: Orality, Writing, Typography, and Printed Images in the History of Architectural Theory*, Cambridge, Mass., 2001 (trans. of *L'architettura dell'età della stampa: Oralità, scrittura, libro stampato e riproduzione meccanica dell'immagine nella storia delle teorie architettoniche*, Milan, 1998)

Casini 1995

Casini, Matteo. "*Triumphi* in Venice in the Long Renaissance." In *Italian History and Culture*, Florence, 1995, 23–41

Casini 1996

——. *I gesti del principe: la festa politica a Firenze e Venezia in età rinascimentale*, Venice, 1996

Casini 2002

——. "Fra città-stato e stato regionale: riflessioni politiche sulla repubblica di Venezia nella prima età moderna." *Studi veneziani* 44 (2002): 15–36

Cataldi Gallo 1984

Cataldi Gallo, Marzia. "Cenni sull'iconografia dei dipinti della Gentilissima Concezione con riferimento all'iconografia cappuccina nei secoli XVII e XVIII." In *Vita e cultura Cappuccina: La chiesa della SS. Concezione a Genova*, Genoa, 1984, 49–53

Cavazza 1996

Cavazza, Silvano. "La riforma del patriarcato d'Aquileia gruppi eterodossi e comunità luterana." In *Il patriarcato d'Aquileia tra riforma e controriforma*. Atti del convegno di studio, Accademia Udinese di SS. LL. ed AA., Deputazione della Storia Patria per il Friuli: Udine, 9 dicembre 1995, Udine, 1996, 9–60

Caye 1995

Caye, Pierre. *Le savoir de Palladio: architecture, métaphysique et politique dans la Venise du Cinquecento* [Paris], 1995

Cecchetti 1872

Cecchetti, Bartolomeo. "I nobili e il popolo." *Archivio veneto* 3 (1872): 428–32

Cecchetti 1874

——. *La Repubblica di Venezia e la Corte di Roma nei rapporti della religione*, 2 vols., Venice, 1874

Cecchetti 1886

——. "Preface." In *Documenti per la storia dell'augusta ducale basilica di San Marco in Venezia*, ed. C. Boito, Venice, 1886, vii–xv

Cellauro 1998

Cellauro, Louis. "Palladio e le illustrazioni delle edizioni del 1556 e del 1567 di Vitruvio." *Saggi e memorie di storia dell'arte* 22 (1998): 55–128

Cellauro 2000

——. "Daniele Barbaro and his Venetian Editions of Vitruvius of 1556 and 1567." *Studi veneziani* 40 (2000): 87–134

Cellauro 2001

——. "La biblioteca di un architetto del Rinascimento: la raccolta di libri di Giovanni Antonio Rusconi." *Arte veneta* 58 (2001): 224–36

Ceriani Sebregondi 2002

Ceriani Sebregondi, Giulia. "Un doge e il suo manifesto: il palazzo di Leonardo Donà (1536–1612) alle Fondamenta Nuove a Venezia." *Annali di architettura* 14 (2002): 231–50

Ceschi Lavagetto, ed. 1985

Ceschi Lavagetto, Paola, ed. *La Madonna per San Sisto di Raffaello e la cultura piacentina della prima metà del cinquecento*. Atti del convegno: Piacenza, 10 dicembre 1983, Parma, 1985

Cessi 1957

Cessi, Roberto. "Paolinismo Preluterano." *Rendiconte della sedute dell'Accademia nazionale dei Lincei* 8/12 (1957): 3–30

Cessi & Alberti 1934

Cessi, Roberto, and Annibale Alberti. *Rialto: L'isola–Il ponte–Il mercato*, Bologna, 1934

Cevese 2002

Cevese, Renato. "Contributi palladiani." *Annali di architettura* 14 (2002): 163–70

Chabod 1958

Chabod, Frederick. "Venezia nella politica italiana ed europea del Cinquecento." In *La civiltà veneziana del Rinascimento*, ed. V. Branca, Florence, 1958, 29–55

Chambers 1970

Chambers, David. *The Imperial Age of Venice*, London, 1970

Chambers 1997

——. "Merit and Money: The Procurators of St. Mark and their *Commissioni*, 1443–1605." *Journal of the Warburg and Courtauld Institutes* 60 (1997): 23–88

Chambers & Pullan, eds. 1992

Chambers, David, and Brian Pullan, eds., with Jennifer Fletcher. *Venice: A Documentary History*, Oxford, 1992

Chastel 1960

Chastel, André. "Palladio et l'art des fêtes." *Bollettino del Centro internazionale di studi di architettura Andrea Palladio* 2/2 (1960): 29–33

Chastel 1965

——. "Palladio et l'éscalier." *Bollettino del Centro internazionale di studi di architettura Andrea Palladio* 7/1 (1965): 11–12

Chastel 1969

——. *Le Mythe de la Renaissance*, Geneva, 1969

Chastel 1983

——. *The Sack of Rome, 1527*, Princeton, N.J., 1983

Chastel & Cevese, eds. 1990

Chastel, André, and Renato Cevese, eds. *Andrea Palladio: nuovi contributi*, Milan, 1990

Cheney 1963

Cheney, Iris. "Francesco Salviati's North Italian Journey." *Art Bulletin* 45 (1963): 337–44

Chiappini di Sorio 1988

Chiappini di Sorio, Ileana. "Palladio e la 'Vigna' Pisani del Lido." *Notizie da Palazzo Albani* 17/2 (1988): 49–54

Chiari Moretto Wiel, Gallo, & Merkel 1996

Chiari Moretto Wiel, Maria Agnese, Andrea Gallo, and Ettore Merkel. *Chiesa di Santo Stefano: arte e devozione*, Venice, 1996

M. Chojnacka 1998

Chojnacka, Monica. "Women, Charity and Community in Early Modern Venice: The Casa delle Zitelle." *Renaissance Quarterly* 51 (1998): 68–91

M. Chojnacka 2001

——. *Working Women of Early Modern Venice*, Baltimore, Md., 2001

S. Chojnacki 1973

Chojnacki, Stanley. "In Search of the Venetian Patriciate: Families and Factions in the Fourteenth Century." In *Renaissance Venice*, ed. J. R. Hale, London, 1973, 47–90

S. Chojnacki 1994

——. "Social Identity in Renaissance Venice: The Second *Serrata*." *Renaissance Studies* 8/4 (1994): 341–58

S. Chojnacki 2000a

——. "Identity and Ideology in Renaissance Venice: The Third *Serrata*." In *Venice Reconsidered: The History and Civilization of an Italian City-State, 1297–1797*, ed. J. Martin and D. Romano, Baltimore, Md., 2000, 263–94

S. Chojnacki 2000b

——. *Women and Men in Renaissance Venice*, Baltimore, Md., and London, 2000

Cicogna 1969

Cicogna, Emanuele. *Delle inscrizioni veneziane*, 6 vols. in 7, Bologna, 1969 (orig. pub. Venice, 1824–53)

Cicognara, Diedo, & Selva 1858

Cicognara, Leopoldo, Antonio Diedo, and Giantonio Selva. *Le fabbriche e i monumenti più cospicui di Venezia*, 2 vols., ed. F. Zanotto, Venice, 1858

Cipolla 1947

Cipolla, Carlo. "Comment c'est perdue la propriété ecclésiastique dans l'Italie du Nord entre le XIe et le XVIe siècle." *Annales* 2 (1947): 317–27

Cocke 1980

Cocke, Richard. "The Development of Veronese's Critical Reputation." *Arte veneta* 34 (1980): 96–111

Cocke 1984

——. *Veronese's Drawings*, Oxford, 1984

Cocke 2001

——. *Paolo Veronese: Piety and Display in an Age of Religious Reform*. Aldershot, Hampshire, and Burlington, Vt., 2001

Coffin 1979

Coffin, David. *The Villa in the Life of Renaissance Rome*, Princeton, N.J., 1979

Collett 1985

Collett, Barry. *Italian Benedictine Scholars and the Reformation: The Congregation of Santa Giustina of Padua*, Oxford, 1985

Colonna 2000

Colonna, Flavia. "Il ciborio di corsia sestina, l'organo e il ciborio della chiesa di Santo Spirito in Sassia: nota storico-cronologica." In *Studi in onore di Renato Cevese*, ed. G. Beltramini, A. Ghisetti Giavarina, and P. Marini, Vicenza, 2000, 83–92

Concina 1981

Concina, Ennio. *Structure urbaine et fonctions des Bâtiments du XVIe au XIXe siècle, une recherche à Venise*, Venice, 1981

Concina 1983

——. *La macchina territoriale: La progettazione*

della difesa del '500 veneto, Rome and Bari, 1983

Concina 1984a
——. *L'Arsenale della repubblica di Venezia: Tecniche e istituzioni dal medioevo all'età moderna*, Milan, 1984

Concina 1984b
——. "Fra Oriente e Occidente: gli Zen, un palazzo e il mito di Trebisonda." In *'Renovatio Urbis,' Venezia nell'età di Andrea Gritti (1523–1538)*, ed. M. Tafuri, Rome, 1984, 265–90

Concina 1988
——. *Pietre, parole, storia: Glossario della costruzione nelle fonti veneziane (secoli XV–XVIII)*, Venice, 1988

Concina 1991
——. "La casa del Arsenale." In *Storia di Venezia* 12. *Temi: Il mare*, ed. A. Tenenti and U. Tucci, Rome, 1991, 147–210

Concina 1993
——."Arca del seme antico, 'res publica' e 'res aedificatoria' nel Lungo Rinascimento veneziano." In *Venedig und Oberdeutschland in der Renaissance*, Sigmaringen, 1993, 209–22

Concina 1995
——. *Storia dell'architettura di Venezia, dal VII al XX secolo*. Milan, 1995 (trans. as *A History of Venetian Architecture*, Cambridge, 1998)

Contarini 1572
Contarini, Giovanni Pietro. *Historia delle cose successe dal principio della Guerra mossa da Selim Ottomano a venetiani fino al dì della gran giornata vittoriosa contra turchi*, Venice, 1572

Conte 2001
Conte, Tiziana. "Note biografiche." In *Cesare Vecellio, 1521–c.1601*, ed. T. Conte, Belluno, 2001, 13–22

Cooper 1990a
Cooper, Tracy E. "La facciata commemorativa di S. Giorgio Maggiore." In *Andrea Palladio: nuovi contributi*, ed. A. Chastel and R. Cevese, Milan, 1990, 136–45

Cooper 1990b
——. "The History and Decoration of the Church of San Giorgio Maggiore in Venice." PhD dissertation, Princeton University, 1990. Ann Arbor, Mi., 1990

Cooper 1991
——. "Un modo per 'la riforma cattolica'? La scelta di Paolo Veronese per il refettorio di San Giorgio Maggiore." In *Crisi e rinnovamenti nell'autunno del Rinascimento a Venezia*, ed. V. Branca and C. Ossola, Florence, 1991, 272–92

Cooper 1994a
——. Review of *The Villa as Hegemonic Architecture*, by Reinhard Bentmann and Michael Müller. *The Sixteenth Century Journal* 25-2 (1994): 455–56

Cooper 1994b
——. "Template Drawings: i modani." In *The Renaissance from Brunelleschi to Michelangelo: The Representation of Architecture*, ed. H. Millon and

V. Lampugnani, Milan and London, 1994, 494–500

Cooper 1995
"Expert Opinion: *Proto* and *perizia* in the case of the Libreria Marciana and the Procuratie Nuove." *Annali di architettura* 7 (1995): 111–24

Cooper 1996a
——."'Locus meditandi et orandi': Architecture, Liturgy and Identity at San Giorgio Maggiore." In *Musica, scienza e idee nella Serenissima durante il Seicento*, ed. F. Passadore and F. Rossi, Venice, 1996, 79–105

Cooper 1996b
——."*Mecenatismo* or *Clientelismo*? The Character of Renaissance Patronage." In *The Search for a Patron in the Middle Ages and the Renaissance*, Medieval and Renaissance Studies 12, ed. D. Wilkins and R. Wilkins, Lewiston, N.Y., 1996, 19–32

Cooper 1998
——. "The Trials of David: Triumph and Crisis in the Imagery of Doge Alvise Mocenigo I (1570–1577)." *Center* 18 (1998): 64–68

Cooper 2001
——. "Prolegomenon to a Quarrel of Images." In *Coming About . . . A Festschrift for John Shearman*, ed. L. Jones and L. Matthew, Cambridge, Mass., 2001, 141–48

Corner 1749
Corner, Flaminio. *Ecclesiae venetae antiques monumentis*, 13 vols. in 7, Venice, 1749

Corner 1758
——. *Notizie storiche delle chiese e monasteri di Venezia e di Torcello*, Padua, 1758

Cornet 1859
Cornet, Enrico. *Paolo V e la Reppublica Veneta: Giornale dal 22 ottobre 1605–9 guigno 1607*, Vienna, 1859

Coryat 1905
Coryat, Thomas. *Coryat's Crudities. Hastily gobbled up in five Moneths travels in France, Savoy, Italy, Rhetia*, vol. 1 of 2, Glasgow, 1905

Cosgrove 1993
Cosgrove, Denis. *The Palladian Landscape: Geographical Change and its Cultural Representations in Sixteenth-Century Italy*, University Park, Pa., 1993

Cowan 1982
Cowan, Alexander. "Rich and Poor among the Patriciate in Early Modern Venice." *Studi veneziani* 6 (1982): 147–60

Cozzi 1958
Cozzi, Gaetano. *Il Doge Nicolò Contarini: ricerche sul patriziato veneziano agli inizi del seicento*, Venice and Rome, 1958

Cozzi 1961
——. "Federico Contarini, un antiquario veneziano tra Rinascimento e Controriforma." *Bollettino dell'Istituto di storia della società e dello stato veneziano* 3 (1961): 190–220

Cozzi 1963–64
——. "Cultura politica e religione nella 'pubblica

storiografia' veneziana del '500." *Bollettino dell'Istituto di storia della società e dello stato veneziano* 5/6 (1963–64): 215–94

Cozzi 1973
——. "Authority and the Law in Renaissance Venice." In *Renaissance Venice*, ed. J. R. Hale, London, 1973, 293–345

Cozzi 1984
——. "Ambiente veneziano, ambiente veneto, governanti e governati nel Dominio di qua dal Mincio nei secoli XV–XVIII." In *Storia della cultura veneta. 4/2: Dalla Controriforma alla fine della Repubblica*, ed. G. Arnaldi and M. Pastore Stocchi, Vicenza, 1984, 495–539

Cozzi 1987
——. "Stato e Chiesa: vicende di un confronto secolare." In *Venezia e la Roma dei papi*, Milan, 1987, 11–56

Cozzi 1990
——. "I rapporti fra Stato e Chiesa." In *La chiesa di Venezia tra riforma protestante e riforma cattolica*, ed. G. Gullino, Venice, 1990, 11–36

Cristinelli 1978
Cristinelli, Giuseppe. "Nota sulle fabbriche dell'Ospedaletto." In *Arte e musica all'Ospedaletto*, Venice, 1978, 23–34

Crollalanza 1886–90
Crollalanza, Giovanni Battista di. *Dizionario storico-blasonico delle famiglie nobili e notabili Italiane estinte e fiorenti*, 3 vols., Pisa, 1886–90

Cross & Livingstone, eds. 1983
Cross, F. L., and E. A. Livingstone, eds., *The Oxford Dictionary of the Christian Church*, Oxford, 1983

Crouzet-Pavan 1992
Crouzet-Pavan, Elisabeth. *Espaces, pouvoirs et société à Venise à la fin du Moyen Age*, Rome, 1992

Crouzet-Pavan 1996
——. "Immagini di un mito." In *Storia di Venezia: dalle origini alla caduta della Serenissima. 4: Il rinascimento, politica e cultura*, ed. A. Tenenti and U. Tucci, Rome, 1996, 579–601

Crouzet-Pavan 2002
——. *Venice Triumphant: The Horizons of a Myth*, Baltimore, Md., and London, 2002 (trans. of *Venise triomphante: les horizons d'un mythe*, Paris, 1999)

Cultura, scienze e techniche 1987
Cultura, scienze e techniche nella Venezia del Cinquecento, Venice, 1987

da Bergamo 1575
da Bergamo, Giacopo Filippo. *Sopplimento delle Croniche Vniversali del Mondo di F. Giacopo Filippo da Bergamo, tradotto nuovamente da M. Francesco Sansovino*, Venice, 1575

Dacos & Forlan 1987
Dacos, Nicole, and Caterina Forlan. *Giovanni da Udine, 1481–1561* [Udine], 1987

Dale 1997
Dale, Thomas. *Relics, Prayer, and Politics in Medieval Venetia*, Princeton, N.J., 1997

Dalla Pozza 1943
Dalla Pozza, Antonio. *Andrea Palladio*, Vicenza, 1943

Damerini 1956

Damerini, Gino. *L'isola e il cenobio di San Giorgio Maggiore*, Venice, 1956

Da Mosto 1937

Da Mosto, Andrea. *L'Archivio di Stato di Venezia: Indice generale, storico, descrittivo, ed analitico*, 2 vols., Bibliothèque des "Annales Institutorum" 5, Rome, 1937

Da Mosto 1960

———. *I dogi di Venezia nella vita pubblica e private*, Milan, 1960

Daniels 1976

Daniels, Jeffrey. *Sebastiano Ricci*, Hove, Sussex, 1976

D'Arco 1842

D'Arco, Carlo. *Storie della vita e delle opere di Giulio Pippi Romano*, Mantua, 1842

J. Davis 1962

Davis, James. *The Decline of the Venetian Nobility as a Ruling Class*, Baltimore, Md., 1962

J. Davis 1975

———. *A Venetian Family and its Fortune, 1500–1900: The Donà and the Conservation of their Wealth*, Memoirs of the American Philosophical Society 106, Philadelphia, 1975

R. Davis 1999

Davis, Robert. "The Spectacle Almost Fit for a King: Venice's *Guerra de canne* of 26 July 1574." In *Medieval and Renaissance Venice*, ed. E. Kittrell and T. Madden, Urbana and Chicago, 1999, 181–212

De Angelis d'Ossat 1956

De Angelis d'Ossat, Guglielmo. "Un palazzo veneziano progettato da Palladio." *Palladio* 4 (1956): 158–61

De Angelis d'Ossat 1966

———. "I Sangallo e Palladio." *Bollettino del Centro internazionale di studi di architettura Andrea Palladio* 8/2 (1966): 43–51

De Jonge 1989

De Jonge, Krista. "La serliana di Sebastiano Serlio: appunti sulla finestra veneziana." In *Sebastiano Serlio*, ed. C. Thoenes, Milan, 1989, 50–56

De Leva 1880–81

De Leva, Giuseppe. "Giovanni Grimani, Patriarca d'Aquileja, Memoria." *Atti del reale Istituto Veneto di SS. LL. ed AA.* 39/1 (1880–81): 407–54, 647–49

della Croce 1574

della Croce, Marsilio. *L'historia della publica et famosa entrata in Vinegia del serenissimo Henrico III. Re di Francia, et Polonia, Con la descrittione particolare della pompa, e del numero, & varietà delli Bregantini, Palaschermi, & altri vasselli armati, con la dechiaratione dell'edificio, & arco fatto al Lido*, Venice, 1574

del Torso 1978

del Torso, Enrico. "Contributi." In *Araldica civica del Friuli*, ed. G. M. Del Basso, Udine, 1978, 40–45

Demus 1960

Demus, Otto. *The Church of San Marco in Venice*, Washington, D.C., 1960

Dengel 1909

Dengel, Philipp. *Der Palazzo di Venezia in Rom*, Vienna, 1909

de Nolhac & Solerti 1890

de Nolhac, Pier, and Angelo Solerti. *Il viaggio in Italia di Enrico III re di Francia e le feste a Venezia, Ferrara, Mantova e Torino*, Turin, 1890

De Paoli 2002

De Paoli, Marcella. "Die Restaurierung der Antiken der Sammlung Grimani." In *Venezia! Kunst aus der venezianischen Palasten Sammlungsgeschicte Venedigs vom 15. bis 19. Jahrhundert*, Ostfildern-Ruit, 2002, 131–34

De Renaldis 1888

De Renaldis, Girolamo. *Memorie storiche dei tre ultimi secoli del Patriarcato d'Aquileia (1411–1751)*, Udine, 1888

De Tolnay 1965

De Tolnay, Charles. "A Forgotten Architectural Project by Michelangelo: The Choir of the Cathedral of Padua." In *Festschrift für Herbert von Einem*, Berlin, 1965, 247–51

D'Evelyn 1996

D'Evelyn, Margaret. "Venice as Vitruvius's City in Daniele Barbaro's Commentaries." *Studi veneziani* 32 (1996): 83–104

D'Evelyn 1998–99

———. "*Varietà* and the Caryatid Portico in Daniele Barbaro's *Commentaries* on Vitruvius." *Annali di architettura* 10–11 (1998–99): 157–74

de Voragine 1494

de Voragine, Jacobus. *Legendario de Sanctis (Le legende de sancti)*, Venice, 1494

de Voragine 1969

———. *The Golden Legend of Jacobus de Voragine*, trans. G. Ryan and H. Ripperberger, New York, 1969 (orig. pub. 1941)

de Voragine 1993

———. *The Golden Legend: Readings on the Saints*, 2 vols., trans. W. Ryan. Princeton, N.J., 1993

Doglioni 1598

Doglioni, Giovanni Nicolò. *Historia Venetiana scritta brevemente da Gio. Nicolò Doglioni delle cose successe dalla prima fondation di Venetia sino all'anno di Christo MDXCVII*, Venice, 1598

Doglioni 1692

———. *Le cose notabili et maravigliose della città di Venetia, di Nicolò Doglioni, con nuova aggiunta di cose nuove, poste in quella ultima impressione nel fine*, Venice, 1692

Dolce 1557

Dolce, Lodovico. *Dialogo della pittura di M. Lodovico Dolce intitolato l'Aretino*, Venice, 1557

Dorigo 1983

Dorigo, Wladimir. *Venezia origini: fondamenti, ipotosi, metodi*, Milan, 1983

Dyer 1989

Dyer, Joseph. "The Singing of Psalms in the Early Medieval Office." *Speculum* 64 (1989): 535–78

Egger 1975

Egger, Carlo. "Canonici regolari della Congregazione del SS. Salvatore Lateranense." In

Dizionario degli istituti di perfezione, Rome, 1975, 2: 101–07

Elam 1992

Elam, Caroline. "Drawings as Documents: The Problem of the San Lorenzo Façade." In *Michelangelo Drawings*, Studies in the History of Art 33, ed. C. H. Smyth with A. Gilkerson, Washington, D.C., 1992, 99–116

Ellero 1980–81

Ellero, Giovanni. "Un ospedale della riforma cattolica veneziana: i Derelitti ai SS. Giovanni e Paolo." Tesi di laurea, Università degli Studi di Venezia, 1980–81

Ellero 1982

———. "Interventi di Palladio sui luoghi pii. L'Ospedaletto." In *Palladio e Venezia*, ed. L. Puppi, Florence, 1982, 121–32

Ellero 1989

———. "Personaggi e momenti di vita." In *Il regno dei poveri: arte e storia dei grandi ospedali veneziana in età moderna 1474–1797*, ed. B. Aikema and D. Meijers, Venice, 1989, 109–20

Ellero, ed. 1987

Ellero, Giuseppe, ed. *L'Archivio I. R. E.: Inventari dei fondi antichi degli ospedali e luoghi pii di Venezia*, Venice, 1987

Ellero & Lunardon 1992

Ellero, Giuseppe, and Silvia Lunardon. "Appendice" to Giuseppe Ellero, "Vergini cristiane e donne di valore." In *Le Zitelle: Architettura, arte e storia di un'istituzione veneziana*, ed. L. Puppi, Venice, 1992, 49–96

Elliott 1985

Elliott, J. H. "Yet Another Crisis?" In *The European Crisis of the 1590s*, ed. P. Clark, London, 1985, 301–12

Fabbri, ed. 1999

Fabbri, Gianni, ed. *La Scuola Grande della Misericordia di Venezia: storia e progetto*, Milan, 1999

Fabris 1988

Fabris, Antonio. "Esperienza di vita comunitaria: i canonici regolari." In *La chiesa di Venezia nei secoli XI–XIII*, Contributi alla storia della chiesa veneziana 2, ed. F. Tonon, Venice, 1988, 73–108

Fagiolo 1979

Fagiolo, Marcello. "L'effimero di Stato: strutture e archetipi di una città di illusione." In *La città effimera e l'universo artificiale del giardino: La Firenze dei Medici e l'Italia del '500*, Rome, 1979, 9–21

Fagiolo, ed. 1979

Fagiolo, Marcello, ed. *La città effimera e l'universo artificiale del giardino: la Firenze dei Medici e l'Italia del '500*, Rome, 1979

Fairbairn [1981–]

Fairbairn, Lynda. "The Palladio Drawings: Detailed Summary of Contents." In *Palladio–Smythson–Adam*, The Royal Institute of British Architects, The Drawings Collection: Phase, London [1981–], D, 1–15

Fantelli 2000

Fantelli, Pier Luigi. *Il Castello del Catajo e i suoi giardini*, Battaglia Terme, 2000

Fasolo 1938

Fasolo, Giulio. "Notizie di arte e di storia vicentina." *Archivio veneto* ser. 5, 22 (1938): 261–301

Favaretto 1984

Favaretto, Irene. "'Una tribuna ricca di marmi . . .': appunti per una storia delle collezioni dei Grimani di Santa Maria Formosa." *Aquileia nostra* 15 (1984): 206–39

Favaretto 1997a

——. "*Un notabilissimo ornamento*: La vita dello Statuario tra XVII e XVIII secolo." In *Lo Statuario Pubblico della Serenissima: due secoli di collezionismo di antichità, 1596–1797*, ed. I. Favaretto and G. L. Ravagnan, Cittadella, 1997, 53–60

Favaretto 1997b

——. "*Per la memoria delle cose antiche* . . . La nascita delle collezioni e la formazione dello Statuario Pubblico." In *Lo Statuario Pubblico della Serenissima: due secoli di collezionismo di antichità, 1596–1797*, ed. I. Favaretto and G. L. Ravagnan, Cittadella, 1997, 38–44

Favaretto & Ravagnan, eds. 1997

Favaretto, Irene, and Giovanna Luisa Ravagnan, eds. *Lo Statuario Pubblico della Serenissima: due secoli di collezionismo di antichità, 1596–1797*, Cittadella, 1997

Fedalto 1991

Fedalto, Giorgio. "La diocesi nel medioevo." In *Patriarcato di Venezia: storia religiosa del Veneto*, ed. S. Tramontin, Padua, 1991, 47–90

Fenlon 1987

Fenlon, Iain. "Lepanto: The Arts of Celebration in Renaissance Venice." *Proceedings of the British Academy* 73 (1987): 201–35

Fenlon 1996

——. "Public and Private: The musical world of Jacopo Tintoretto." In *Jacopo Tintoretto nel quarto centenario della morte*, ed. P. Rossi and L. Puppi, Venice, 1996, 247–55

Fenster & Smail, eds. 2003

Fenster, Thelma, and Daniel Smail, eds. *Fama: The Politics of Talk and Reputation in Medieval Europe*, Ithaca, N.Y., and London, 2003

Fiamma 1574

Fiamma, Gabriele. *Discorsi sopra l'epistole e vangeli di tutto l'anno*, Venice, 1574

Finlay 1980

Finlay, Robert. *Politics in Renaissance Venice*, New Brunswick, N.J., 1980

Finlay 1984

——. "Al servizio del Sultano: Venezia, i Turchi e il mondo Cristiano." In *'Renovatio Urbis,' Venezia nell'età di Andrea Gritti (1523–1538)*, ed. M. Tafuri, Rome, 1984, 78–118

Fiocco 1928

Fiocco, Giuseppe. *Paolo Veronese*, Bologna, 1928

Fletcher 1994

Fletcher, Jennifer. "Fine Art and Festivity in Renaissance Venice: the Artist's Part." In *Sight & Insight: Essays on Art and Culture in Honor of E. H. Gombrich at 85*, ed. J. Onians, London, 1994, 128–51

Fogolari 1924

Fogolari, Gino. *La Chiesa di Santa Maria della Carità di Venezia*, Venice, 1924 (extract from *Archivio veneto-tridentino* 5 [1924]: 57–119)

Fois 1979

Fois, Mario. "L' 'osservanza' come espressione della 'Ecclesia semper renovanda.'" In *Problemi di storia della Chiesa nei secoli XV–XVII*, Naples, 1979, 13–107

Fois 1980

——. "Osservanza." In *Dizionario degli istituti di perfezione*, Rome, 1980, 6: 1035–57

Fontana 1978

Fontana, Vincenzo. "'Arte' e 'Esperienza' nei trattati d'architettura veneziana del Cinquecento." *Architectura* 8 (1978): 49–72

Fontana 1985

——. "Il 'Vitruvio' del 1556: Barbaro, Palladio, Marcolini." In *Trattati scientifici nel Veneto fra il XV e il XVI secolo*, Vicenza, 1985, 39–72

Fontana 1989

——. "Il mestiere di architetto secondo Vincenzo Scamozzi." In *L'architettura a Roma e in Italia (1580–1621)*, ed. G. Spagnesi, Rome, 1989, 2: 233–42

Forssman 1964

Forssman, Erik. *Palladios Lehrgebaude*, Stockholm, 1964

Forssman 1966

——. "Palladio and Daniele Barbaro." *Bollettino del Centro internazionale di studi di architettura Andrea Palladio* 8/2 (1966): 68–81

Forssman 1973

——. *Visible Harmony: Palladio's Villa Foscari at Malcontenta* [Stockholm], 1973

Foscari 1975

Foscari, Antonio. "Per Palladio: note sul Redentore a San Vidal e sulle Zitelle." *Antichità viva* 14 (1975): 44–56

Foscari 1979

——. "Ricerche sugli 'Accesi' e su 'questo benedetto theatro' costruito da Palladio in Venezia nel 1565." *Notizie da Palazzo Albani* 8 (1979): 68–83

Foscari 1980a

——. "Un'altare di Palladio nella vecchia chiesa di San Pantalon (1555)." In *Architettura e utopia nella Venezia del Cinquecento*, ed. L. Puppi, Milan, 1980, 255–56

Foscari 1980b

——. "L'invenzione palladiana di un palazzo a Venezia: due ipotesi sul 'sito': Un'ipotesi per San Samuele." In *Architettura e utopia nella Venezia del Cinquecento*, ed. L. Puppi, Milan, 1980, 270–73

Foscari 1980c

——. "Le Zitelle." In *Architettura e utopia nella Venezia del Cinquecento*, ed. L. Puppi, Milan, 1980, 269–70

Foscari 1982

——. "Palladio a San Pantalon." In *Palladio e Venezia*, ed. L. Puppi, Florence, 1982, 89–94

Foscari 1987

——. "Un dibattito sul foro marciano allo scadere del 1577 e il progetto di Andrea Palladio per il palazzo ducale di Venezia." In "Saggi in onore di Guglielmo De Angelis d'Ossat," *Quaderni dell'Istituto di storia dell'architettura*, n.s. 1/10 (1983–87), Rome, 1987, 323–32

Foscari & Tafuri 1981a

Foscari, Antonio, and Manfredo Tafuri, "Un progetto irrealizzato di Jacopo Sansovino: il palazzo di Vettor Grimani sul Canal Grande." *Bollettino dei Civici Musei Veneziani d'arte e di storia* 26 (1981): 71–87

Foscari & Tafuri 1981b

——. "Un progetto del Sansovino per il palazzo di Vettor Grimani a S. Samuel." *Ricerche di storia dell'arte* 15 (1981): 69–82

Foscari & Tafuri 1982

——. "Sebastiano da Lugano, i Grimani e Jacopo Sansovino: artisti e committenti nella chiesa di Sant'Antonio di Castello." *Arte veneta* 36 (1982): 100–23

Foscari & Tafuri 1983

——. *L'armonia e i conflitti: la chiesa di San Francesco della Vigna nella Venezia del '500*, Turin, 1983

G. Franco 1610

Franco, Giacomo. *Habiti d'uomeni et donne venetiane con la processione della ser.ma signoria et altri particolari, cioè trionfi feste cerimonie publiche della nobilissima città di Venetia*, Venice, 1610, pt. 1 (published together with Giovanni Nicolò Doglioni, *La città di Venezia con l'origine e governo di quella*, Venice, 1614, pt. 2)

M. Franco 1980

Franco, Maria Teresa. "Chiesa di Santa Lucia." In *Architettura e utopia nella Venezia del Cinquecento*, ed. L. Puppi, Milan, 1980, 258–60

Frank 1992

Frank, Martina. "Il luogo delle Zitelle: segni e forme di un pensiero palladiano." In *Le Zitelle: Architettura, arte e storia di un'istituzione veneziana*, ed. L. Puppi, Venice, 1992, 97–128

Franzoi, ed. 1986

Franzoi, Umberto, ed. *Il Serenissimo doge*, Treviso, 1986

Franzoi & Di Stefano 1976a

Franzoi, Umberto, and Dina Di Stefano. *Le chiese di Venezia*, Venice, 1976

Franzoi & Di Stefano 1976b

——. "I rapporti tra la Chiesa e la Repubblica." In *Le chiese di Venezia*, Venice, 1976, xx–xxvi

Frattini 1983

Frattini, Adriano. "Documenti per la committenza nella chiesa di S. Pietro in Gessate." *Arte lombarda* 65 (1983): 27–48

H.-W. Frey, ed. 1940

Frey, Herman-Walther, ed. *Neue Briefe von Giorgio Vasari*, Munich, 1940

K. Frey, ed. 1941

Frey, Karl. *Il carteggio di Giorgio Vasari, dal 1563 al 1565*, Arezzo, 1941

Frey & Frey, eds. 1923–30

Frey, Karl, and Herman-Walther Frey, eds. *Das literarische Nachlass Giorgio Vasaris*, 2 vols., Munich, 1923–30

Frizzoni, ed. 1800

Frizzoni, Gustavo, ed. *Notizia d'opere di disegno nella prima metà del secolo XVI*, Bologna, 1800

C. Frommel 1977

Frommel, Christoph. "Palladio e la chiesa di San Pietro a Roma." *Bollettino del Centro internazionale di studi di architettura Andrea Palladio* 19 (1977): 107–24

C. Frommel 1982

——. *Der Palazzo Venezia in Rom*, Opladen, 1982

C. Frommel 1989

——. "Serlio e la scuola romana." In *Sebastiano Serlio*, ed. C. Thoenes, Milan, 1989, 39–49

C. Frommel 1994

——. "Reflections on the Early Architectural Drawings." In *The Renaissance from Brunelleschi to Michelangelo: The Representation of Architecture*, ed. H. Millon and V. Lampugnani, Milan and London, 1994: 101–21

S. Frommel 2003

Frommel, Sabine. *Sebastiano Serlio: Architect*, Milan, 2003 (trans. of *Sebastiano Serlio: architetto*, 1998)

Fulin 1865

Rinaldo Fulin, *Relazione della repubblica di Venezia scritta da Raffaele de'Medici nel MDLXXXIX*, Venice, 1865

Gaeta 1963

Gaeta, Franco. "Badoer, Andrea Biagio." In *Dizionario biografico degli Italiani*, Rome, 1963, 5: 98–99

Gaeta 1964

——. "Barbaro, Marcantonio." In *Dizionario biografico degli Italiani*, Rome, 1964, 6: 110–12

Gaeta 1981

——. "L'idea di Venezia." In *Storia della cultura veneta. 3/3: Dal primo Quattrocento al Concilio di Trento*, ed. G. Arnaldi and M. Pastore Stocchi, Vicenza, 1981, 565–641

Gaeta 1984

——. "Venezia da 'stato misto' ad aristocrazia 'esemplare.'" In *Storia della cultura veneta. 4/2: Dalla Controriforma alla fine della Repubblica*, ed. G. Arnaldi and M. Pastore Stocchi, Vicenza, 1984, 437–94

Gaeta, ed. 1958

Gaeta, Franco, ed. *Nunziature di Venezia* 1, Rome, 1958

Gaier 2002a

Gaier, Martin. *Facciate sacre a scopo profane: Venezia e la politica dei monumenti dal quattrocento al settecento*, Studi di arte veneta 3, ed. F. Valcanover and G. Pavanello, Venice, 2002

Gaier 2002b

——. "Königen in einer Republik. Projekte für ein Grabmonument der Caterina Corner in Venedig." *Mitteilungen des Kunsthistorischen Institutes in Florenz* 46 (2002): 197–234

A. Gallo 1566

Gallo, Agostino. *Le dieci giornate della vera agricoltura e piaceri della villa*, Venice, 1566

A. Gallo & Spadavecchia 1994

Gallo, Andrea, and Fiorella Spadavecchia. *Chiesa del Redentore: arte e devozione*, Venice, 1994

R. Gallo 1934

Gallo, Rodolfo. "Reliquie e Reliquiari veneziani." *Rivista di Venezia* 12 (1934): 187–214

R. Gallo 1941

——. "La famiglia di Jacopo Tintoretto." *Ateneo Veneto* 132 (1941): 73–92

R. Gallo 1944

——. "Una famiglia patrizia: i Pisani ed i palazzi di Santo Stefano e di Stra." *Archivio veneto* ser. 5, 34–35 (1944): 65–228

R. Gallo 1952

——. "Le donazione alla Serenissima di Domenico e Giovanni Grimani." *Archivio veneto* ser. 5, 50–51 (1952): 34–77

R. Gallo 1955

——. "Andrea Palladio e Venezia, di alcuni edifici del Palladio ignoti o mal noti." *Rivista di Venezia* 1 (1955): 23–48

Ganz 1968

Ganz, Jurg Peter. *Alessio Tramello: Drei Sakralbauten in Piacenza und die oberitalienische Architektur um 1500*, Frauenfeld, 1968

Gardani 1961

Gardani, Dante. *La chiesa di S. Maria della Presentazione (delle Zitelle) a Venezia*, Venice, 1961

Gaston 1977

Gaston, Robert. "A Drawing by Battista Franco and its Venetian Context." *Art Bulletin of Victoria* 18 (1977): 25–32

Gentili, ed. 1995

Gentili, Augusto, ed. "Tintoretto e la Scuola di San Rocco." *Venezia cinquecento* 5/no. 9 (1995)

Gerulitas 1976

Gerulitas, Leonardas. *Printing and Publishing in Fifteenth-Century Venice*, Chicago and London, 1976

Ghedini 1997

Ghedini, Francesca. "Le sculture romane dello Statuario: copie, originali, ritratti e rilievi." In *Lo Statuario Pubblico della Serenissima: due secoli di collezionismo di antichità, 1596–1797*, ed. I. Favaretto and G. L. Ravagnan, Cittadella, 1997, 97–106

Gianighian & Pavanini 1984

Gianighian, Giorgio, and Paola Pavanini. *Dietro i palazzo: Tre secoli di architettura minore a Venezia, 1492–1803*, Venice, 1984

C. Gilbert 1967

Gilbert, Creighton. "When Did a Man in the Renaissance Grow Old?" *Studies in the Renaissance* 14 (1967): 172–84

F. Gilbert 1968

Gilbert, Felix. "The Venetian Constitution in Florentine Political Thought." In *Florentine Studies*, ed. N. Rubenstein, London, 1968, 463–500

F. Gilbert 1973

——. "Venice in the Crisis of the League of Cambrai." In *Renaissance Venice*, ed. J. R. Hale, London, 1973, 274–92

Gilmore 1973

Gilmore, Myron. "Myth and Reality in Venetian Political Theory." In *Renaissance Venice*, ed. J. R. Hale, London, 1973, 431–45

Glaser 2003

Glaser, Sabine. *Il Cataio: Die Ikonographie einer Villa im Veneto*, Munich and Berlin, 2003

Gleason 1993

Gleason, Elisabeth. *Gasparo Contarini: Venice, Rome, and Reform*, Berkeley and Los Angeles, 1993

Gleason 2000

——. "Confronting New Realities: Venice and the Peace of Bologna, 1530." In *Venice Reconsidered: The History and Civilization of an Italian City-State, 1297–1797*, ed. J. Martin and D. Romano, Baltimore, Md., 2000, 168–84

Goi 1989

Goi, Paolo. *Guida didattica: Sebastiano Ricci*, Milan, 1989

Goldthwaite 1993

Goldthwaite, Richard. *Wealth and the Demand for Art in Italy, 1300–1600*, Baltimore, Md., 1993

Golzio 1936

Golzio, Vincenzo. *Raffaello nei documenti, nelle testimonianze dei contemporanei e nel letteratura del suo secolo*, Vatican City, 1936

Gombrich 1966

Gombrich, Ernst. "Leonardo's Method for Working Out Compositions." In *Norm and Form: Studies in the Art of the Renaissance*, London, 1966, 58–63

Gorse 1990

Gorse, George. "Between Empire and Republic: Triumphal Entries into Genoa During the Sixteenth Century." In *"All the World's A Stage . . .": Art and Pageantry in the Renaissance and Baroque. 1: Triumphal Celebrations and the Rituals of Statecraft*, ed. B. Wisch and S. Munshower, University Park, Pa., 1990, 188–256

Gould 1975

Gould, Cecil. *The Sixteenth-Century Italian Schools*, London, 1975

Goy 1989

Goy, Richard. *Venetian Vernacular Architecture: Traditional Housing in the Venetian Lagoon*, Cambridge, 1989

Grabar 1996

Grabar, Oleg. "Jerusalem Elsewhere." In *City of the Great King: Jerusalem from David to the Present*, ed. N. Rosovsky, Cambridge, Mass., and London, 1996, 333–43

Gradenigo 1771

Gradenigo, Giovanni Antonio. "Vita Gabriele Fiamma." In Gabriele Fiamma, *La rima di Mons. Gabriel Fiamma canonico lateranense e poi vescovo di Chioggia, illustrate cogli argomenti di*

Pietro Petracci e con la vita di esso Fiamma scritta da Mons. D. Gian Agostino Gradenigo vescovo di Ceneda, Treviso, 1771

Gramigna Dian & Perissa Torrini 1981a

Gramigna Dian, Silvia, and Annalisa Perissa Torrini. Cat. entries in *Scuole di arti: mestieri e devozione a Venezia*, ed. S. Gramigna and A. Perissa, Venice, 1981, 31–125

Gramigna Dian & Perissa Torrini 1981b

——. "Le scuole a Venezia." In *Scuole di arti: mestieri e devozione a Venezia*, ed. S. Gramigna and A. Perissa, Venice, 1981, 25–30

Gramigna & Perissa, eds. 1981

Gramigna, Silvia, and Annalisa Perissa, eds. *Scuole di arti: mestieri e devozione a Venezia*, Venice, 1981

Grendler 1977

Grendler, Paul. *The Roman Inquisition and the Venetian Printing Press*, Princeton, N.J., 1977

Grendler 1979

——. "The Tre Savii sopra Eresia 1507–1605: A Prosopographical Study." *Studi veneziani* 3 (1979): 283–340

Grendler 1990

——. "The Leaders of the Venetian State, 1540–1609: a Prosopographical Analysis." *Studi veneziani* 19 (1990): 35–86

Grimani 1880

Grimani, Marino. *Lettere del Cardinale Marino Grimani a Giangiorgio Trissino: Per nobili nozze Papadopoli-Hellenbach*, intro. A. Morsolin, ed. A. and A. da Schio, Schio, 1880

Grubb 1986

Grubb, James. "When Myths Lose Power: Four Decades of Venetian Historiography." *Journal of Modern History* 58 (1986): 43–94

Grubb 1988

——. *Firstborn of Venice: Vicenza in the Early Renaissance State*, Baltimore, Md., 1988

Grubb 2000

——. "Elite Citizens." In *Venice Reconsidered: The History and Civilization of an Italian City-State, 1297–1797*, ed. J. Martin and D. Romano, Baltimore, Md., 2000, 339–64

Gualdo 1958–59

Gualdo, Paolo. "Vita di Andrea Palladio." Ed. G. Zorzi. *Saggi e memoria di storia dell'arte* 2 (1958–59): 93–104

Gualdo 2000

——. "Life of Andrea Palladio." In Douglas Lewis, *The Drawings of Andrea Palladio*, New Orleans, 2000, 3–4

Guerra 2001

Guerra, Andrea. "Quel che resta di Palladio: eredità e dispersione nei progetti per la chiesa di San Giorgio Maggiore di Venezia." *Annali di architettura* 13 (2001): 93–110

Guerra 2002

——. "Movable Façades: Palladio's Plan for the Church of San Giorgio Maggiore in Venice and Its Successive Vicissitudes." *Journal of the Society of Architectural Historians* 61 (2002): 276–95

Gullino 1980

Gullino, Giuseppe. "I patrizi veneziani di fronte alla proprietà feudale (secoli XVI–XVIII). Materiale per una ricerca." *Quaderni storici* 43 (1980): 162–93

Gullino 1984

——. *I Pisani dal banco e moretta: storia di due famiglie veneziane in età moderna e delle loro vicende patrimoniali tra 1705 e 1836*, Rome, 1984

Gullino 1986

——. "Da Mula, Marcantonio." In *Dizionario biografico degli Italiani*, Rome, 1986, 32: 383–87

Gullino 1991

——. "Diedo, Vincenzo." In *Dizionario biografico degli Italiani*, Rome, 1991, 39: 781–84

Gullino 1994

——. "Quando il mercante costruisce la villa: le proprietà dei Veneziani nella Terraferma." In *Storia di Venezia: dalle origini alla caduta della Serenissima. 6: Dal rinascimento al barocco*, ed. G. Cozzi and P. Prodi, Rome, 1994, 875–924

Gullino 1996a

——. "L'evoluzione costituzionale." In *Storia di Venezia: dalle origini alla caduta della Serenissima. 4: Il rinascimento, politica e cultura*, ed. A. Tenenti and U. Tucci, Rome, 1996, 345–78

Gullino 1996b

——. "Il patrimonio dei Barbaro di San Vidal: proprietà privata e benefici feudali." In *Una famiglia veneziana nella storia: i Barbaro*. Atti del Convegno di Studi in occasione del quinto centenario della morte dell'umanista Ermolao: Venice, 4–6 November 1993, ed. M. Marangoni and M. Pastore Stocchi, Venice, 1996, 67–100

Gullino 1996c

——. "Il patriziato." In *Storia di Venezia: dalle origini alla caduta della Serenissima. 4: Il rinascimento, politica e cultura*, ed. A. Tenenti and U. Tucci, Rome, 1996, 379–414

Gullino 1997a

——. "Foscari, Alvise." In *Dizionario biografico degli Italiani*, Rome, 1997, 49: 294–95

Gullino 1997b

——. "Foscari, Marco." In *Dizionario biografico degli Italiani*, Rome, 1997, 49: 328–33

Gullino 2000

——. *Marco Foscari (1477–1551): l'attività politica e diplomatica tra Venezia, Roma, e Firenze*, Milan, 2000

Habert et al. 1992

Habert, Jean, et al. *Le Noces de Cana de Véronèse: une oeuvre et sa restauration*, Paris, 1992

Hadeln 1911

Hadeln, Detlev Freiherr von. *Italienische Forschungen: Archivalische Beiträge zur Geschicte der venezianischen Kunst aus dem Nachlass G. Ludwigs*, Berlin, 1911

Hadeln 1922

——. *Zeichnungen des Giacomo Tintoretto*, Berlin, 1922

Hadjinicolaou 1995

Hadjinicolaou, Nicos. "Portrait of a Man." In *O Greko stin Italia kai i italiki techni*, ed. N. Hadjinicolaou, Athens, 1995, 368–73 and 538–40

Hajnoczi 1988

Hajnoczi, Gàbor. "Un traité vitruvien le *Della Architettura* de Giovan Antonio Rusconi." In *Les traités d'architecture de la renaissance*, ed. J. Guillaume, Paris, 1988, 75–81

Hale 1994

Hale, J. R. *The Civilization of Europe in the Renaissance*, New York, 1994

Hale, ed. 1973

Hale, J. R., ed. *Renaissance Venice*, London, 1973

Hall 1979

Hall, Marcia B. *Renovation and Counter-Reformation: Vasari and Duke Cosimo in Sta Maria Novella and Sta Croce, 1565–1577*, Oxford, 1979

Hall 1998

——. "Sixtus V: A Program for the Decorum of Images." *Arte cristiana* 86, fasc. 784 (1998): 41–48

Hall 1999

——. *After Raphael: Painting in Central Italy in the Sixteenth Century*, Cambridge, 1999

Hallman 1985

Hallman, Barbara McClung. *Italian Cardinals, Reform, and the Church as Property*, Berkeley and Los Angeles, 1985

Hartt 1958

Hartt, Frederick. *Giulio Romano*, 2 vols., New Haven, 1958

Herlihy 1985

Herlihy, David. *Medieval Households*, Cambridge, Mass., 1985

Hirst 1963

Hirst, Michael. "Three Ceiling Decorations by Francesco Salviati." *Zeitschrift für Kunstgeschicte* 26 (1963): 146–56

Hochmann 1992

Hochmann, Michel. *Peintres et commanditaires à Venise (1540–1628)*, Collection de l'Ecole Française de Rome 155, Rome, 1992

Hochmann 2002

——. "Kunstsammeln im 15. und 16. Jahrhundert – zwischen privater Leidenschaft und öffentlicher Aufgabe." In *Venezia! Kunst aus der venezianischen Palasten Sammlungsgeschicte Venedigs vom 15. bis 19. Jahrhundert*, Ostfildern-Ruit, 2002, 82–91

Holberton 1990

Holberton, Paul. *Palladio's Villas: Life in the Renaissance Countryside*, London, 1990

Hope 1981

Hope, Charles. "Artists, Patrons, and Advisors in the Italian Renaissance." In *Patronage in the Renaissance*, ed. G. Lytle and S. Orgel, Princeton, N.J., 1981, 293–343

Hope 1993

——. "The Early Biographies of Titian." In *Titian 500*, Studies in the History of Art 45, ed. J. Manca, Washington, D.C., 1993, 167–97

Hope 1995

——. "Can You Trust Vasari?" Review of *Giorgio*

Vasari: Art and History, by Patricia Rubin. *New York Review of Books* (5 October 1995): 10–13

Hopkins 2000

Hopkins, Andrew. *Santa Maria della Salute: Architecture and Ceremony in Baroque Venice*, Cambridge, 2000

Hopkins 2003

——. "Procuratie Nuove in Piazza San Marco (1581)." In *Vincenzo Scamozzi (1548–1616): architettura e scienza*, ed. F. Barbieri, and G. Beltramini, Venice, 2003, 210–20

Hoppenbrouwers 1980

Hoppenbrouwers, Henricus W. "Observantia." In *Dizionario degli istituti di perfezione*, Rome, 1980, 6: 679–83

Howard 1977

Howard, Deborah. "Le chiese di Jacopo Sanso-vino a Venezia." *Bollettino del Centro internazionale di studi di architettura Andrea Palladio* 19 (1977): 49–67

Howard 1980

——. "Four Centuries of Literature on Palladio." *Journal of the Society of Architectural Historians* 39/3 (1980): 224–41

Howard 1987

——. *Jacopo Sansovino: Architecture and Patronage in Renaissance Venice*. rev. edn., New Haven and London, 1987 (orig. pub. 1975)

Howard 1993

——. "Ritual Space in Renaissance Venice." *Scroope: Cambridge Architecture Journal* 5 (1993): 4–11

Howard 1996a

——. "Barbaro, MarcAntonio." In *Dictionary of Art*, ed. J. Turner, London, 1996, 3: 203

Howard 1996b

——. "Gritti, Andrea." In *Dictionary of Art*, ed. J. Turner, London, 1996, 13: 678

Howard 1999

——. "La Scuola Grande della Misericordia di Venezia and appendice documentaria." In *La Scuola Grande della Misericordia di Venezia: storia e progetto*, ed. G. Fabbri, with P. Piffaretti, Milan, 1999, 13–70

Howard 2000

——. *Venice and the East: The Impact of the Islamic World on Venetian Architecture, 1100–1500*, New Haven and London, 2000

Howard 2002

——. *The Architectural History of Venice*, rev. edn. New Haven and London, 2002 (orig. pub. 1980)

Howard 2003

——. "Venice between East and West: Marc'Antonio Barbaro and Palladio's Church of the Redentore." *Journal of the Society of Architectural Historians* 62 (2003): 306–25

Howard, ed. 1995

Howard, Deborah, ed. and intro. *Architecture in Italy, 1500–1600* by Wolfgang Lotz, New Haven and London, 1995 (orig. pub. as *Architecture in Italy, 1400–1600*, Harmondsworth, 1974)

Humfrey 1990

Humfrey, Peter. "Co-ordinated Altarpieces in Renaissance Venice: The Progress of an Ideal." In *The Altarpiece in the Renaissance*, ed. P. Humfrey and M. Kemp, Cambridge, 1990, 190–211

Humfrey 1994

——. "Some Thoughts on Writing a History of Venetian Altarpieces." In *New Interpretations of Venetian Renaissance Painting*, ed. F. Ames-Lewis, London, 1994, 9–16

Humfrey & MacKenney 1986

Humfrey, Peter, and Richard MacKenney. "Venetian Trade Guilds as Patrons of Art." *Burlington Magazine* 128 (1986): 317–30

Humfrey & Holt 1995

Humfrey, Peter, and Stephen Holt. "More on Veronese and his Patrons at San Francesco della Vigna." *Venezia cinquecento* 5/no. 10 (1995): 187–214

Huse 1974

Huse, Norbert. "Palladio und die Villa Barbaro in Maser: Bemerkungen zum Problem der Autorschaft." *Arte veneta* 28 (1974): 106–22

Huse 1979

——. "Palladio am Grand Canal." *Städel Jahrbuch* 7 (1979): 61–99

Huse & Wolters 1993

Huse, Norbert, and Wolfgang Wolters. *The Art of Renaissance Venice: Architecture, Sculpture, and Painting, 1460–1590*, Chicago, 1993 (orig. pub. 1990; trans. of *Venedig: Die Kunst der Renaissance – Architektur, Skulptur, Malerei 1460–1590*, Munich, 1986)

Inglott 1980

Inglott, Peter. "Appunti sulla chiesa palladiana: il rapporto tra stile, simbolismo e funzionalità." *Arte cristiana* 70 (1980): 153–68

Ippolito 1987

Ippolito, Antonio. "Ecclesiastici veneti, tra Venezia e Roma." In *Venezia e la Roma dei papi*, Milan, 1987, 209–34

Isermeyer 1968

Isermeyer, Christian-Adolf. "Le chiese di Palladio in rapporto al culto." *Bollettino del Centro internazionale di studi di architettura Andrea Palladio* 10 (1968): 42–58

Isermeyer 1969

——. "'Die sakrale Architektur Palladios,' di Wladimir Timofiewitsch." *Bollettino del Centro internazionale di studi di architettura Andrea Palladio* 11 (1969): 472–76

Isermeyer 1972

——. "La concezione degli edifici sacri Palladiani." *Bollettino del Centro internazionale di studi di architettura Andrea Palladio* 14 (1972): 105–35

Isermeyer 1980

——. "Il primo progetto del Palladio per S. Giorgio secondo il modello del 1565." *Bollettino del Centro internazionale di studi di architettura Andrea Palladio* 22 (1980): 259–68

Ivanoff 1972

Ivanoff, Nicola. "Henri III a Venise." *Gazette des Beaux-Arts* 80 (December 1972): 313–30

Ivanoff, ed. 1963

Ivanoff, Nicola, ed. *Zibaldon*, Venice and Rome, 1963

Jacquot, ed. 1956–75

Jacquot, Jean, ed. *Les fêtes de la Renaissance: études réunies et présentées par Jacques Jacquot*, 3 vols., Paris, 1956–75 (vol. 3, ed. Jean Jacquot and Elie Koningston)

Jameson 1864

Jameson, Anna Brownell. *Legends of the Madonna as Represented in the Fine Arts*, London, 1864

Jameson 1890

——. *Legends of the Monastic Orders*, London, 1890

Jedin 1947

Jedin, Hubert. *Papal Legate at the Council of Trent, Cardinal Seripando*, St. Louis and London, 1947

Jedin 1972

——. "Venezia e il Concilio di Trento." *Studi veneziani* 14 (1972): 137–57

Jones 1742

Jones, Inigo. "Notes and Remarks of Inigo Jones upon the plates of the Second Book of Palladio's Architecture: Taken from the Manuscript of the said Inigo Jones in the Library of Worcester College, Oxford, June 23, 1741." In *The Architecture of A. Palladio in Four Books*, ed. G. Leoni, London, 1742, 70–72

Jones 1970

——. *Inigo Jones on Palladio: Being the Notes by Inigo Jones in the Copy of Il Quattro libri dell'architettura di Andrea Palladio, 1601, in the Library of Worcester College, Oxford*, Newcastle upon Tyne, 1970

Jones & Penny 1983

Jones, Roger, and Nicholas Penny. *Raphael*, New Haven and London, 1983

Kettering 2002

Kettering, Sharon. *Patronage in Sixteenth- and Seventeenth-Century France*, Aldershot, Hampshire, 2002

King 1986

King, Margaret. *Venetian Humanism in an Age of Patrician Dominance*, Princeton, N.J., 1986

Klein 1970

Klein, Robert. "L'imagination comme vêtement de l'âme chez Marsile Ficin et Giordano Bruno." In *La Forme et l'intelligible: écrits sur la Renaissance et l'art moderne*, ed. A. Chastel, Paris, 1970, 65–88 (orig. pub. in *Revue de métaphysique et de morale* [1956], 18–39)

Klein 1979

——. "Judgement and Taste in Cinquecento Art Theory." In *Form and Meaning: Writings on the Renaissance and Modern Art*, Princeton, N.J., 1979, 161–69 (trans. of "Giudizio et gusto dans la théorie de l'art au Cinquecento." *Rinascimento* 12 [1961], 105–16)

Kliemann 1993

Kliemann, Julian-Matthias. *Gesta dipinte: la grande*

decorazione nelle dimore italiane dal Quattrocento al Seicento, Cinisello Balsamo (Milan), 1993

Knapton 1986

Knapton, Michael. "Lo Stato Veneziano fra la battaglia di Lepanto e la guerra di Candia (1571–1644)." In Venezia e la difesa del levante da Lepanto a Candia 1570–1670, Venice, 1986, 233–41

Knapton 1992

——. "Tra Dominante e Dominio (1517–1630)." In Gaetano Cozzi, Michael Knapton, and Giovanni Scarabello, La Repubblica di Venezia nell'età moderna. 2: Dal 1517 alla fine della Repubblica, Turin, 1992, 203–549

Knapton 1998

——. "Nobiltà e popolò e un trentennio di storiografia veneta." Nuova rivista storica 1 (1998): 167–92

Knezevich 1986

Knezevich, Michela. Il magnifico principe di Venezia: norme e tradizioni legate al dogado, Venice, 1986

Kolb 1984

Kolb, Carolyn. "New Evidence for the Villa Pisani at Montagnana." In Interpretazione veneziane: Studi di storia dell'arte in onore di Michelangelo Muraro, ed. D. Rosand, Venice, 1984, 227–39

Kolb 1997

——. "The Sculptures of the Nymphaeum Hemicycle of the Villa Barbaro at Maser." Ed. M. Beck. Artibus et historiae 35 (1997): 15–33

Kostof, ed. 1977

Kostof, Spiro, ed. The Architect: Chapters in the History of the Profession, Oxford, 1977

Kruft 1986

Kruft, Hanno-Walter. Geschicte der Architekturtheorie, Munich, 1986

Kryza-Gersch 1999

Kryza-Gersch, Claudia. "Tiziano Aspetti." In "La bellissima maniera": Alessandro Vittoria e la scultura veneta del Cinquecento, ed. A. Bacchi, L. Camerlengo, and M. Leithe-Jasper, Trent, 1999, 417–31

Kubelik 1977

Kubelik, Martin. Die Villa im Veneto: Zur typologischen Entwicklung im Quattrocento, 2 vols., Munich, 1977

Kühbacher 1990

Kühbacher, Sabine. "Il principio della corrispondenza nell'architettura del Serlio e del Palladio." In Andrea Palladio: nuovi contributi, ed. A. Chastel and R. Cevese, Milan, 1990, 166–81

Kunst, ed. 1981

Kunst, Marion, ed. Postello, Venezia e il suo mondo, Florence, 1981

Kunst 1999

——. Venice, Myth, and Utopian Thought in the Sixteenth Century: Bodin, Postel, and the Virgin of Venice. Aldershot, Hampshire, and Brookfield, Vt., 1999

Lane 1973

Lane, Frederic C. Venice: A Maritime Republic, Baltimore, Md., 1973

Lanfranchi, ed. 1968

Lanfranchi, Luigi, ed. S. Giorgio Maggiore, 2 vols., Venice, 1968

M. Laven 2003

Laven, Mary. Virgins of Venice: Broken Vows and Cloistered Lives in the Renaissance Convent, New York, 2003

P. Laven 1957

Laven, Peter. "Daniele Barbaro, Patriarch Elect of Aquileia, with Special Reference to his Circle of Scholars and to his Literary Achievement." PhD dissertation, University of London, 1957

P. Laven 1967

——. "The Causa Grimani and its Political Overtones." Journal of Religious History 4/3 (1967): 184–205

M. Lavin 1990

Lavin, Marilyn Aronberg. The Place of Narrative: Mural Decoration in Italian Churches, 431–1600, Chicago, 1990

S. Lavin 1992

Lavin, Silvia. Quatremère de Quincy and the Invention of a Modern Language of Architecture, Cambridge, Mass., 1992

Law & Lewis, 1996

Law, John, and Douglas Lewis. "Grimani." In Dictionary of Art, ed. J. Turner, London, 1996, 13: 656–59

Leccisotti 1962

——. "La condizioni economiche dei Monasteri cassinesi di Toscana alla metà del '600." In Studi in onore di Amintore Fanfani, Milan, 1962, 5: 289–312

Leccisotti ed. 1939

Leccisotti, Tommaso, ed. and intro. Congregationis S. Justina de Padua O.S.B. ordinationes capitulorum generalium, 2 vols., Montecassino, 1939

Lee 1967

Lee, Rensselaer. "Ut pictura poesis": The Humanistic Theory of Painting, Princeton, N.J., 1967

Leonardi 1983

Leonardi, Giovanni Giacomo. Libro delle fortificazioni. In Ennio Concina, La macchina territoriale: la progettazione della difesa nel Cinquecento Veneto, Bari, 1983, 55–60

Levey 1965

Levey, Michael. "Tintoretto and the Theme of Miraculous Intervention." Journal of the Royal Society of Arts 713–14 (1965): 707–25

Lewine 1960

Lewine, Milton J. "The Roman Church Interior, 1527–1580." PhD dissertation, Columbia University, 1960

Lewis 1972a

Lewis, Douglas. "La datazione della villa Corner a Piombino Dese." Bollettino del Centro internazionale di studi di architettura Andrea Palladio 14 (1972): 381–93

Lewis 1972b

——. "Un disegno autografo del Sanmicheli e la notizia del committente del Sansovino per San Francesco della Vigna." Bollettino dei musei civici veneziani 17 (1972): 7–36

Lewis 1972c

——. Paper delivered to the Washington Renaissance Colloquium, in typescript in the Library of the National Gallery of Art. Washington, D.C., 1972

Lewis 1973

——. "Disegni autografi del Palladio non pubblicati: le piante per Caldogno e Maser, 1548–1549." Bollettino del Centro internazionale di studi di architettura Andrea Palladio 15 (1973): 369–79

Lewis 1981

——. "Patterns of Preference: Patronage of Sixteenth-Century Architects by the Venetian Patriciate." In Patronage in the Renaissance, ed. G. Little and S. Orgel, Princeton, N.J., 1981, 353–80

Lewis 1982

——. "Palladio, Andrea." In MacMillan Encyclopedia of Architects, 4 vols., ed. A. Placzek, New York, 1982, 3: 345–62

Lewis 1996

——. "Cornaro [Corner]." In Dictionary of Art, ed. J. Turner, London, 1996, 7: 861–63

Lewis 1997

——. "Postscript with an Excursus on Recent Historiography." Artibus et Historiae 35/18 (1997): 35–40

Lewis 2000

——. The Drawings of Andrea Palladio, New Orleans, 2000 (orig. pub. Washington, D.C., 1981)

Liberali 1971a

Liberali, Giuseppe. Le "dinastie ecclesiastiche" nei Cornaro della Chà Granda, Treviso, 1971

Liberali 1971b

——. Il "Papalismo" dei Pisani "dal Banco," Treviso, 1971

Lingo 1998

Lingo, Stuart. "The Capuchins and the Art of History: Retrospection and Reform in the Arts of Late Renaissance Italy." PhD dissertation, Harvard University, 1998

Liruti 1749

Liruti, Gian Giuseppe. Della moneta propria, e forstiera ch'ebbe corso nel ducato di Friuli dalla decadenza dell'imperio romano sino al secolo XV, Venice, 1749

Litta 1819–83

Litta, Pompeo. Famiglie celebri d'Italia, 16 vols., Milan, 1819–83

Logan 1964

Logan, Oliver. "Studies in the Religious Life of Venice in the Sixteenth and Early Seventeenth Centuries: The Venetian Clergy and Religious Orders 1520–1630." PhD dissertation, Cambridge University, 1964

Logan 1972

——. Culture and Society in Venice, 1470–1790, London, 1972

Logan 1984

——. "La committenza artistica pubblica e privata." In *Cultura e società nel rinascimento, tra riforme e manierismi*, ed. V. Branca and C. Ossola, Florence, 1984, 271–89

Logan 1995

——. *The Venetian Upper Clergy in the Sixteenth and Early Seventeenth Centuries: A Study in Religious Culture*, Salzburg, 1995

Lorenzi 1868

Lorenzi, Giambattista. *Monumenti per servire alla storia del Palazzo Ducale in Venezia. 1: Dal 1253 al 1600*, Venice, 1868

Lorenzetti 1929

Lorenzetti, Giulio. *Venezia e il suo estuario*, Venice, 1929

Lorenzetti 1982

——. *Venezia e il suo estuario: Guida storico-artistico*, Trieste, 1982 (orig. pub. 1926; rev. edn. 1963)

Lotto 1962

Lotto, Lorenzo. *Lettere inedite*, ed. L. Chiodi, Bergamo, 1962

Lotz 1995

Lotz, Wolfgang. *Architecture in Italy, 1500–1600*, rev. edn. and intro. D. Howard, New Haven and London, 1995 (orig. pub. as *Architecture in Italy 1400–1600*, Harmondsworth, 1974)

Lotz 1981a

——. "The Rendering of the Interior in Architectural Drawings of the Renaissance." In *Studies in Italian Renaissance Architecture*, Cambridge, Mass., 1981, 1–65 (trans. of "Das Raumbild in der Architekturzeichnung der italienischen Renaissance." *Mitteilungen des Kunsthistorischen Instituts in Florenz* 7 [1956]: 193–226)

Lotz 1981b

——. "The Roman Legacy in Jacopo Sansovino's Venetian Buildings." In *Studies in Italian Renaissance Architecture*, Cambridge, Mass., 1981, 140–51 (orig. pub. in *Journal of the Society for Architectural Historians* 22 [1963]: 3–12)

Lovisa 1720

Lovisa, Domenico. *Il gran teatro di Venezia*, Venice, 1720

Lowry 1970–71

Lowry, Martin. "The Church and Venetian Political Change in the Later Cinquecento." PhD dissertation, University of Warwick, 1970–71

Lowry 1971

——. "The Reform of the Council of Ten, 1582–1583: An Unsettled Problem?" *Studi veneziani* 13 (1971): 275–310

Lucangeli 1574

Lucangeli, Nicolò. *Successi del viaggio di Enrico III. Re di Francia e di Polonia dalla sua partita di Cracovia fino al'sue arrivo in Torino*, Venice, 1574

Luchs 1995

Luchs, Alison. *Tullio Lombardo and Ideal Portrait Sculpture in Renaissance Venice, 1490–1530*, Cambridge, 1995

Luminis 1577

Luminis, Muzio. *La Liberatione di Vinegia*, Venice, 1577

Lunardon 1982

Lunardon, Silvia. "Interventi di Palladio sui luoghi pii. Le Zitelle." In *Palladio e Venezia*, ed. L. Puppi, Florence, 1982, 103–20

Lupo 1998

Lupo, Giulio. "Principio murario e principio dei concatenamenti: I pareri sul restauro di Palazzo Ducale di Venezia dopo l'incendio del 1577." *Rassegna di architettura e urbanistica* 32 (1998): 17–34

Luzio 1917

Luzio, Alessandro. *La congiuro spagnola contra Venezia nel 1618 secondo i documenti dell'Archivio Gonzaga*, Venice, 1917 (orig. pub. in *Miscellanea di storia veneta* ser. 3a, vol. 13, 1917)

Luzzato 1938

Luzzato, Gino. *Storia economica dell'età moderna e contemporanea. L'età moderna*, Padua, 1938

Luzzato 1961

——. *Storia economica di Venezia dall'XI al XVI secolo*, Venice, 1961

MacColl 1924

MacColl, D. S. "Tintoretto's Vincenzo Morosini." *Burlington Magazine* 44 (1924): 266–71

MacKenney 1987

MacKenney, Richard. *Tradesmen and Traders*, London, 1987

MacKenney 1994

——. "Continuity and Change in the *scuole piccole* of Venice, *c.*1250–*c.*1600." *Renaissance Studies* 8 (1994): 388–403

Madonna 1979

Madonna, Maria Louisa. "L'ingresso di Carlo v a Roma." In *La città effimera e l'universo artificiale del giardino*, ed. M. Fagiolo, Rome, 1979, 63–68

Madonna, ed. 1993

Madonna, Maria Louisa, ed. *Roma di Sisto V: le arti e la cultura*, Rome, 1993

Magagnato & Marini, eds. 1980

Magagnato, Licisco, and Paola Marini, eds. *I quattro libri dell'architettura*, by Andrea Palladio. Trattati di architettura 6, Classici italiani di scienze techniche e arti, intro. L. Magagnato, Milan, 1980 (orig. pub. Venice, 1570)

Magno 1571

Magno, Celio. *Trionfo di Christo per la vittoria contra i Turchi, rappresentato al Principe di Venezia il dì di Sto. Stefano*, Venice, 1571

Magrini 1845

Magrini, Antonio. *Memorie intorno la vita e le opere di Andrea Palladio*, Padua, 1845

Mancini 1999

Mancini, Vincenzo. "Tintoretto, Parrasio Michiel e i ritratti di Andrea Dolfin." *Venezia cinquecento* 9/no. 17 (1999): 77–90

Manno 1994

Manno, Antonio. "La Sala superiore." In *Tintoretto: la Scuola Grande di San Rocco*, ed. G. Romanelli, Milan, 1994, 172–75

Manno 1995

——. "I monumenti funerari." In *Basilica dei Santi Giovanni e Paolo: arte e devozione*, Venice, 1995, 26–37

Manzano 1592

Manzano, Scipione. *Le lagrime della Penitenza di David*, Venice, 1592

Marani & Perina 1965

Marani, Ercolano, and Chiara Perina. *Mantova: le arti*, vol. 2, Mantua, 1965

Maranini 1931

Maranini, Giuseppe. *La costituzione di Venezia dopo le Serrata del Maggior Consiglio*, Venice, 1931

Marchesi 1978

Marchesi, Pietro. *Il Forte di San Andrea a Venezia*, Rome, 1978

Marchesi 1984

——. *Fortezze veneziane, 1508–1797*, Milan, 1984

Marchesi 1993

——. "Lambert Sutris [*sic*], *Ritratto di Marc'Antonio Barbaro*." In *Palmanova, fortezza d'Europa 1593–1993*, ed. G. Pavan, Venice, 1993, 90

Marcucci 1978

Marcucci, Laura. "Regesto cronologico e critico delle edizioni, delle traduzioni e delle ricerche più importanti sul trattato latino 'De Architettura libri 10' di Marco Vitruvio Pollione." *Studi e documenti di architettura* 8 (1978): 11–185

Maretto 1992

Maretto, Paolo. *La casa veneziana nella storia della città dalle origini all'ottocento*, Venice, 1992 (orig. pub. 1986)

Margarini 1650–70

Margarini, Cornelio. *Bullarium Casinense*, 2 vols., Venice and Todi, 1650–70

Marini, ed. 1980

Marini, Paola. ed. *Palladio e Verona*, Milan, 1980

J. Martin 1993

Martin, John. *Venice's Hidden Enemies: Italian Heretics in a Renaissance City*, Berkeley and Los Angeles, 1993

T. Martin 1988

Martin, Thomas. "The Portrait Busts of Alessandro Vittoria." PhD dissertation, Columbia University, 1988

T. Martin 1998

——. *Alessandro Vittoria and the Portrait Bust in Renaissance Venice: Remodelling Antiquity*, Oxford, 1998

Martinelli Pedrocco 1981

Martinelli Pedrocco, Elisabetta. "Altre scuole." In *Le scuole di Venezia*, ed. T. Pignatti, Milan, 1981, 217–26

Marpillero 1937

Marpillero, Vico. "L'opera di Giovanni da Udine nel Palazzo Grimani a Santa Maria Formosa." *La Panerie* 74 (1937): 106–18

Marx 1978

Marx, Barbara. *Venezia – altera Roma? Ipotesi sull' umanesimo veneziano*, Centro Tedesco di Studi Veneziani, Quarterni 10, Venice, 1978

Maschio 1981

Maschio, Ruggiero. "Le Scuole Grandi a Venezia." In *Storia della cultura veneta. 3/3: Dal primo Quattrocento al Concilio di Trento*, ed. G. Arnaldi and M. Pastore Stocchi, Vicenza, 1981, 193–206

Maschio 1992

——. "Il tempo delle Zitelle: immagini di un luogo palladiano." In *Le Zitelle: Architettura, arte e storia di un'istituzione veneziana*, ed. L. Puppi, Venice, 1992, 163–218

Mason 1996

Mason, Stefania. "Intorno al soffitto di San Paternian: gli artisti di Vettor Pisani." In *Jacopo Tintoretto nel quarto centenario della morte*, ed. P. Rossi and L. Puppi, Venice, 1996, 71–75

Mason Rinaldi 1984

Mason Rinaldi, Stefania. *Palma il Giovane: L'opera completa*, Milan, 1984

Mason Rinaldi 1987

——. "'Hora di nuovo vedesi,' immagini della devozione eucaristica alla fine del Cinquecento." In *Venezia e la Roma dei papi*, Milan, 1987, 171–96

Mason Rinaldi 1990

——. "Un percorso nella religiosità veneziana del Cinquecento attraverso le immagini eucaristiche." In *La chiesa di Venezia tra riforma protestante e riforma cattolica*, Contributi alla storia della chiesa di Venezia 4, ed. G. Gullino, Venice, 1990, 183–94

Mason Rinaldi 1991

——. Cat. entry in *Da Bellini a Tintoretto: dipinti dei Musei Civici di Padova dalla metà del Quattrocento ai primi del Seicento*, ed. A. Ballarin and D. Banzato, Rome, 1991, 240–41

Maylender 1926–30

Maylender, Michele. *Storia delle accademie d'Italia*, 5 vols., Bologna, 1926–30

Mazza 1992

Mazza, Barbara. "Committenti e artisti nell'èta delle riforme: l'arredo della chiesa di Santa Maria della Presentazione." In *Le Zitelle: Architettura, arte e storia di un'istituzione veneziana*, ed. L. Puppi, Venice, 1992, 129–62

Mazzucco 1982

Mazzucco, Gabriele. *Monasteri benedettini nella laguna veneziana*, Venice, 1983

McGinnis 1995

McGinnis, Frederick. *Right Thinking and Sacred Oratory in Counter-Reformation Rome*, Princeton, N.J., 1995

McNair 1967

McNair, Philip. *Peter Martyr in Italy*, Oxford, 1967

McTavish 1981

McTavish, David. "Giuseppe Porta called Giuseppe Salviati." PhD dissertation, Courtauld Institute of Art, University of London, New York, 1981

Meijers 1989

Meijers, Dulcia. "L'architettura della nuova filantropia." In *Nel regno dei poveri: arte e storia dei grandi ospedali veneziana in età moderna*

1474–1797, ed. B. Aikema and D. Meijers, Venice, 1989, 43–70

Merkel 1981

Merkel, Ettore. "Battista Franco detto il Semolei." In *Da Tiziano a El Greco: per la storia del Manierismo a Venezia*, Milan, 1981, 202–07

Merkel 1990

——. Cat. entry in *Titian, Prince of Painters*, ed. S. Biadene and M. Yakush, Venice, 1990, 364–67

Michiel 1969

Michiel, Marc'Antonio. *The Anonimo: Notes on Pictures and Works of Art in Italy Made by an Anonymous Writer in the Sixteenth Century*, New York, 1969 (orig. pub. 1903, trans. from *Notizia d'opere di disegno nella prima metà del secolo XVI*, ed. G. Frizzoni, Bologna, 1800)

Millon 1988

Millon, Henry. "The façade of San Lorenzo." In *Michelangelo Architect*, ed. H. Millon and C. H. Smyth, Milan, 1988, 2–89

Millon 1994a

——. "Michelangelo and the Façade of S. Lorenzo in Florence." In *The Renaissance from Brunelleschi to Michelangelo: The Representation of Architecture*, ed. H. Millon and V. Lampugnani, Milan and London, 1994, 565–72

Millon 1994b

——. "Models in Renaissance Architecture." In *The Renaissance from Brunelleschi to Michelangelo: The Representation of Architecture*, ed. H. Millon and V. Lampugnani, Milan and London, 1994, 18–73

Mitchell 1986

Mitchell, Bonner. *The Majesty of the State, Triumphal Progresses of Foreign Sovereigns in Renaissance Italy (1494–1600)*, Florence, 1986

Mitrović 2004

Mitrović, Branko. *Learning from Palladio*, New York and London, 2004

Molmenti 1888

Molmenti, Pompeo. "I Procuratori di San Marco." In *La Basilica di San Marco in Venezia illustrata nella storia e nell'arte dalle scrittori veneziani*, ed. C. Boito, Venice, 1888, 29–37

Molmenti 1906

——. *Venice, Its Individual Growth from the Earliest Beginnings to the Fall of the Republic. 1: The Middle Ages*, trans. H. Brown, Chicago, 1906 (trans. of *La storia di Venezia nella vita privata dalle origini alla caduta della repubblica*, Turin, 1880)

Montenari 1749

Montenari, Giovanni. *Del Teatro Olimpico di Andrea Palladio in Vicenza*, Padua, 1749

Monticolo & Besta, eds. 1905–14

Monticolo, Giovanni, and Enrico Besta, eds. *I capitolari delle art veneziane*, 3 vols., Rome, 1905–14

Mor 1978

Mor, Carlo Guido. "Problematica storica dell'araldica civica in Friuli." In *Araldica civica del Friuli*, ed. G. M. Del Basso, Udine, 1978, 12

Morachiello 1991

Morachiello, Paolo. "Fortezze e lidi." In *Storia di*

Venezia 12. Temi: Il mare, ed. A. Tenenti and U. Tucci, Rome, 1991, 111–34

Morando di Custoza 1979

Morando di Custoza, Eugenio. *Libro d'Arme di Venezia*, Verona, 1979

Morin 1985

Morin, Marco. "La battaglia di Lepanto." In *Venezia e i Turchi: scontri e confronti di due civiltà*, Milan, 1985, 210–31

Morlopino 1572

Morlopino, Abate. *L'illustri azioni de' serenissimi principi della famiglia Moceniga*, Venice and Farri, 1572

Morresi 1987

Morresi, Manuela. "Le due edizioni dei commentari di Daniele Barbaro, 1556–1567." In Vitruvius Pollio, *I dieci libri dell'architettura tradotti et commentati da Daniele Barbaro 1567: con un saggio di Manfredo Tafuri e uno studio di Manuela Morresi*, Milan, 1987, xli–lviii

Morresi 1998a

——. *Piazza San Marco: istituzioni, poteri e architettura a Venezia nel primo Cinquecento*, Milan, 1998

Morresi 1998b

——. "Treatises and the Architecture of Venice in the Fifteenth and Sixteenth Centuries." In *Paper Palaces: The Rise of the Renaissance Architectural Treatise*, ed. V. Hart and P. Hicks, New Haven and London, 1998, 263–80

Morresi 2000

——. *Jacopo Sansovino*, Milan, 2000

Morrogh 1985

Morrogh, Andrew. *Disegni di architetti fiorentini 1540–1640*, Florence, 1985

Morsolin 1984

Morsolin, Bernardo. *Giangiorgio Trissino, monografia d'un gentiluomo letterato nel secolo XVI*, Florence, 1984 (orig. pub. Vicenza, 1878)

Moschini 1847

Moschini, Giovanni Antonio. *Nuova Guida di Venezia*, Venice, 1847

Moschini Marconi 1962

Moschini Marconi, Sandra. *Gallerie dell'Accademia di Venezia: Opere d'arte del secolo XVI*, Rome, 1962

Mozzetti & Santi 1997

Mozzetti, Francesco, and Giovanna Santi. "Biografia, immagine e memoria: storia di Vincenzo Morosini." *Venezia cinquecento* 7/no. 13 (1997): 141–58

Mueller 1971

Mueller, Reinhold. "The Procurators of San Marco in the Thirteenth and Fourteenth Centuries: A Study of the Office as a Financial and Trust Institution." *Studi veneziani* 13 (1971): 106–220

Muir 1975

Muir, Edward. "The Ritual of Rulership in Sixteenth-Century Venice." PhD dissertation, Rutgers University, 1975

Muir 1979

——. "Images of Power: Art and Pageantry in

Renaissance Venice." *American Historical Review* 84 (1979): 16–52

Muir 1981

———. *Civic Ritual in Renaissance Venice*, Princeton, N.J., 1981

Muir 1984

———. "Manifestazioni e ceremonie nella Venezia di Andrea Gritti." In *'Renovatio Urbis,' Venezia nell'età di Andrea Gritti (1523–1538)*, ed. M. Tafuri, Rome, 1984, 59–77

Muir 1991

———. "Introduction: Observing Trifles." In *Microhistory and the Lost Peoples of Europe*, ed. E. Muir and G. Ruggiero, Baltimore, Md., 1991, vii–xxviii

Muir 1997

———. *Ritual in Early Modern Europe*, Cambridge, 1997

Muir 2000

———. "Was There Republicanism in Renaissance Republics? Venice after Agnadello." In *Venice Reconsidered: The History and Civilization of an Italian City-State, 1297–1797*, ed. J. Martin and D. Romano, Baltimore, Md., 2000, 137–67

Mulryne 2002

Mulryne, J. R. Intro. to *Court Festivals of the European Renaissance: Art, Politics and Performance*, ed. J. R. Mulryne and E. Goldring, Aldershot, Hampshire, and Burlington, Vt., 2002, 1–12

Muraro 1986

Muraro, Michelangelo. *Venetian Villas*, Udine, 1986

Murray 1966

Murray, Peter. "Palladio's Churches." In *Arte in Europa: scritti di storia dell'arte in onore di Edoardo Arslan*, ed. G. C. Argan et al., Milan, 1966, 1: 597–608

Musolino 1965

Musolino, Giovanni. "Feste religiose popolari." In *Culto dei santi a Venezia*, ed. A. Niero and S. Tramontin, Venice, 1965, 209–37

Musolino 1972

———. "I santi nel Folklore." In *Santità a Venezia*, ed. S. Tramontin, Venice, 1972

Mutinelli 1978

Mutinelli, Fabio. *Lessico veneto*, Bologna, 1978 (orig. pub. Venice, 1851)

[Muttoni] 1740–48

[Muttoni, Francesco Antonio]. *Architettura di Andrea Palladio . . . di nuovo ristampata. E di figure in rame . . . arricchita . . . con le osservazioni dell'Architetto N. N.*, 8 vols. in 4, Venice, 1740–48

Muzio 1575

Muzio, Girolamo. *Il gentilhuomo*, Venice, 1575

Nardi 1958

Nardi, Bruno. *Saggi sull'aristotelismo padovano dal secolo XIV al XVI*, Florence, 1958

Nepi Scirè 1991

Nepi Scirè, Giovanna. *Treasures of Venetian Painting: The Gallery of the Accademia*, New York, 1991

Nepi Scirè 1995

———. *Guida alla Quadreria*, Venice, 1995

Newerow 2002

Newerow, Olga. "Die Sammlung des *Studiolo Grimani*." In *Venezia! Kunst aus den venezianischen Palasten Sammlungsgeschicte Venedigs vom 15. bis 19. Jahrhundert*, Ostfildern-Ruit, 2002, 145–47

Nichols 1999

Nichols, Tom. *Tintoretto: Tradition and Identity*, London, 1999

Niero 1961

Niero, Antonio. *I patriarchi di Venezia da Lorenzo Giustiniani ai nostri giorni*, Venice, 1961

Niero 1962

———. *Saint Lucy Virgin and Martyr*, trans. E. Mitchell, Dentford, 1962

Niero 1965

———. "Reliquie e corpi di santi." In *Culto dei Santi a Venezia*, ed. A. Niero and S. Tramontin, Venice, 1965, 181–208

Niero 1974

———. "Un episodio controriformistico di arte veneziana: l'espurazione post mortem del capp. P. Paolo Piazza." *Arte veneta* 28 (1974): 296–97

Niero 1979

———. "Pietà ufficiale e pietà popolare in tempo di peste." In *Venezia e la peste 1348/1797*, Venice, 1979, 287–93

Niero 1982

———. "I pergoli palladiani di San Zulian." In *Palladio e Venezia*, ed. L. Puppi, Florence, 1982, 133–38

Niero 1992

———. "Spiritualità popolare e dotta." In *La Chiesa di Venezia nel Seicento*, Contributi alla storia della chiesa di Venezia 5, ed. B. Bertoli, Venice, 1992, 253–90

Niero, ed. 1996

Niero, Antonio, ed. *San Marco: aspetti storici e agiografici*. Atti del Convegno Internazionale di Studi: Venezia, 26–29 aprile 1994, Venice, 1996

Niero & Tramontin, eds. 1965

Niero Antonio, and Silvio Tramontin, eds. *Culto dei santi a Venezia*, Biblioteca Agiografica Veneziana 2, Venice, 1965

Nodari 1992

Nodari, Francesca. "Alcuni disegni di Francesco Bassano." *Arte documento* 6 (1992): 271–76

Nussdorfer 1992

Nussdorfer, Laurie. *Civic Politics in the Rome of Urban VIII*, Princeton, N.J., 1992

Oechslin 1987

Oechslin, Werner. "'Rendering.' The representative and expressive function of architectural drawing." *Daidalos* 25 (1987): 68–73, 76–77

Olivato 1980

Olivato, Loredana. Cat. entry in *Architettura e utopia nella Venezia del Cinquecento*, ed. L. Puppi, Milan, 1980, 102

Olivato 1982

———. "Il luogo del teatro palladiano per gli 'Accesi.'" In *Palladio e Venezia*, ed. L. Puppi, Florence, 1982, 95–102

Olivato 1990

———. Cat. entry in *Titian: Prince of Painters*, ed. S. Biadene and M. Yakush, Venice, 1990, 166–69

Olivieri 1981

Olivieri, Achille. *Palladio, le corti e le famiglie: simulazione e morte nella cultura architettonica del '500*, Vicenza, 1981

Olivieri 1985

———. "La città 'commoda' e utile: cultura e sensibilità religiosa nel patriziato mercantile fra' '400 e '500." In *Mercanti e vita economica nella Repubblica Veneta*, ed. G. Borelli, Verona, 1985, 2: 362–67

Olivieri 1992

———. *Riforma ed eresia a Vicenza nel Cinquecento*, Rome, 1992

Olivieri 1998

———. "La porpora e il dogado di Andrea Gritti (1523–1538). Intorno al Doge, principe o 'Rex.'" In *La porpora: realtà e immaginario di un colore simbolico*. Atti del convegno di studio: Venice, 24–25 October 1996, ed. O. Longo, Venice, 1998, 373–88

Olmo 1612

Olmo, Fortunato. *Vita s. Cosmae eremitae cujus corpus Venetiis in Templo s. Georgii majoris quiescit*, Venice, 1612

Onians 1988

Onians, John. *Bearers of Meaning: The Classical Orders in Antiquity, the Middle Ages, and the Renaissance*, Princeton, N.J., 1988

Ongania 1888–93

Ongania, F. *La Basilica di San Marco in Venezia illustrata nella storia e nell'arte dalle scrittori veneziani*, 8 vols. in 15, ed. C. Boito, Venice, 1888–93

Ongpin 2004

Ongpin, Stephen. "A Group of Ten Drawings by Federico Zuccaro after Correggio and other Artists." In Jean-Luc Baroni Ltd., *An Exhibition of Master Drawings and Oil Sketches, New York & London 2004*, London, 2004

Ordo 1527

Ordo benedictionis sive consecrationis virginum secundum consuetudinem monialium sancte Marie de Celestibus ordinis sancti Bernardi per reverendum Beatum Laurentium Iustinianum venetiarum patriarcam, Venice, 1527

Ostrow 1996

Ostrow, Steven. *Art and Spirituality in Counter-Reformation Rome: The Sistine and Pauline Chapels in Santa Maria Maggiore*, Cambridge, 1996

Paccagnini, ed. 2001

Paccagnini, Ermanno, ed. *Dialogo della peste* by Paolo Bellintani, Milan, 2001

Pace 1678

Pace, Giovanni Battista. *Ceremoniale Magnum, sive raccolta universale di tutte le ceremonie spettanti alla ducal regia capella di San Marco. Biblioteca Nazionale Marciana, MS. It. VII, 1269 (9573)*, Venice, 1678

Padoan Urban 1968

Padoan Urban, Lina. "La festa della Sensa nelle arti e iconografia." *Studi veneziani* 10 (1968): 291–353

Padoan Urban 1969

——. "Apparati scenografici nelle feste veneziane cinquecentesche." *Arte veneta* 33 (1969): 145–55

Padoan Urban 1980

——. "Gli spettacoli urbani e l'utopia." In *Architettura e utopia nella Venezia del Cinquecento*, ed. L. Puppi, Milan, 1980, 144–66

Padoan Urban 1998

——. *Processioni e feste dogali: "Venetia est mundus,"* Vicenza, 1998

Palladio 1554a

Palladio, Andrea. *L'antichità di Roma*, Rome, 1554

Palladio 1554b

——. *Descritione de le Chiese, Stationi, Indulgenze & Reliquie de Corpi Sancti, che sonno in la Citta di Roma*, Rome, 1554

Palladio 1555

——. *L'antichità di Roma*, Venice, 1555

Palladio 1570

——. *I quattro libri dell' architettura di Andrea Palladio*, Venice, 1570

Palladio 1575

——. *I Commentari di C. Giulio Cesare, con le figure in rame de gli' Allogiamenti, de' fatti d' arme, delle circonvallatione delle città, & di molte altre cose notabili scritte in essi*, Venice, 1575

Palladio 1965

——. *The Four Books of Architecture*, intro. A. Placzek, New York, 1965 (orig. pub. London, 1738)

Palladio 1976

——. *I quattro libri dell' architettura di Andrea Palladio*, Milan, 1976 (orig. pub. Venice, 1570)

Palladio 1980

——. *I quattro libri dell' architettura*, Trattati di architettura 6, Classici italiani di scienze techniche e arti, ed. L. Magagnato and P. Marini. Milan, 1980 (orig. pub. Venice, 1570)

Palladio 1988a

——. *Andrea Palladio: scritti sull'architettura (1554–1579)*, ed. L. Puppi, Vicenza, 1988

Palladio 1988b

——. "Proemio ai 'Discorsi' di Polybio." In *Andrea Palladio: scritti sull'architettura*, ed. L. Puppi, Vicenza, 1988, 195–96 (orig. pub. Venice, 1579)

Palladio 1997

——. *The Four Books on Architecture*, trans. R. Tavernor and R. Schofield, Cambridge, Mass., 1997 (orig. pub. Venice, 1570)

A. Pallucchini 1972

Pallucchini, Anna. "Venezia religiosa nella pittura del Cinquecento." *Studi veneziani* 14 (1972): 159–84

R. Pallucchini 1981

Pallucchini, Rodolfo. "Per la storia del Manierismo a Venezia." In *Da Tiziano a El Greco: Per la storia del Manierismo a Venezia*, Milan, 1981, 11–68

R. Pallucchini 1983

——. "Un nuovo ritratto di Jacopo Tintoretto." *Arte veneta* 37 (1983): 184–87

R. Pallucchini 1984

——. *Veronese*, Milan, 1984

Pallucchini & Rossi 1982

Pallucchini, Rodolfo, and Paola Rossi. *Jacopo Tintoretto: le opere sacre e profane*, 2 vols., Milan, 1982

Palme 1959

Palme, Per. "Ut architectura poesis: Idea and Form, Studies in the History of Art." *Figura* 1 (1959): 95–107

Pane 1961

Pane, Roberto. *Andrea Palladio*, Turin, 1961

Panofsky 1968

Panofsky, Erwin. *Idea: A Concept in Art Theory*, Columbia, S.C., 1968 (orig. pub. Leipzig, 1924)

Panofsky 1972

——. "The Neoplatonic Movement and Michelangelo." In *Studies in Iconology: Humanistic Themes in the Art of the Renaissance*, New York, 1972, 171–230 (orig. pub. Oxford, 1939)

Pantoni 1974

Pantoni, Angelo. "Barbo, Ludovico." In *Dizionario degli istituti di perfezione*, Rome, 1974, 1: 1044–47

Paoletti 1839

Paoletti, Ermolao. *Il fiore di Venezia: ossia i quadri, i monumenti, le vedute, ed i costume veneziani*, vol. 2 of 4, Venice, 1839

Partridge & Starn 1990

Partridge, Loren, and Randolf Starn. "Triumphalism and the Sala Regia in the Vatican." In *"All the World's A Stage . . .": Art and Pageantry in the Renaissance and Baroque*. 1: *Triumphal Celebrations and the Rituals of Statecraft*, ed. B. Wisch and S. Munshower, University Park, Pa., 1990, 22–81

Paruta 1599

Paruta, Paolo. *Della perfettione della vita politica di M. Paolo Paruta, libri tre*, Venice, 1599

Paruta 1658

——. "Historia vinetiana . . . divisa in due parti." In *The History of Venice . . . Likewise the Wars of Cyprus*, trans. Henry Carey, Earl of Monmouth, London, 1658 (orig. pub. Venice, 1605)

Paschini 1927

Paschini, Pio. "Le collezioni archeologiche dei prelati Grimani nel Cinquecento." *Rendiconti della pontificia accademia romana di archeologia* 5 (1927): 149–90

Paschini 1933

——. "Breve storia del Patriarcato." In *La Basilica di Aquileia*, Bologna, 1933, 3–36

Paschini 1936

——. *Storia del Friuli*, Udine, 1936

Paschini 1943

——. *Domenico Grimani, Cardinale di S. Marco (1523)*, Rome, 1943

Paschini 1948

——. "La nomina del patriarca di Aquileia e la repubblica di Venezia nel secolo XVI." *Rivista di storia della Chiesa in Italia* 2 (1948): 61–76

Paschini 1951

——. *Eresia e riforma Cattolica al confine orientale d'Italia*, Lateranum n.s. 17, Rome, 1951

Paschini 1952–53

——. "La questione del feudo di Tajedo e le peripezie di un patriarca." *Memorie Storiche Forogiuliesi* 40 (1952–53): 76–137

Paschini 1956

——. "Il mecenatismo artistico del patriarca Giovanni Grimani." In *Studi in onore di Aristide Calderini e Roberto Paribeni*, Milan, 1956, 851–62

Paschini 1957

——. *Tre illustri prelati del rinascimento: Ermolao Barbaro, Adriano Castellesi, Giovanni Grimani*, Lateranum n.s. 23, Rome, 1957

Paschini 1958

——. "Il mecenatismo artistico del Cardinale Marino Grimani." In *Miscellanea in onore di Roberto Cessi*, Rome, 1958, 2: 79–88

Paschini 1962

——. "Daniele Barbaro letterato e prelato veneziano nel Cinquecento." *Rivista di storia della Chiesa in Italia* 16 (1962): 73–107

Pastor 1969

Pastor, Ludwig Freiherr von. *The History of the Popes from the Close of the Middle Ages*, 6th edn., 40 vols., Nendeln (Liechtenstein), 1969 (orig. pub. as *Geschichte der päpste seit dem ausgang des mittelalters*, 16 vols. in 21, Freiburg im Breisgau, 1891–1933)

Pavan, ed. 1993

Pavan, Gino, ed. *Palmanova: fortezza d'Europa 1593–1993*, Venice, 1993

Pedani 1985

Pedani, Maria. "Monasteri di Agostiniane a Venezia." *Archivio veneto* ser. 5, 125 (1985): 35–78

F. Pellegrini 1880

Pellegrini, Federico. *I Benedettini a Venezia con speciale riguardo all'isola di S. Giorgio Maggiore*, Venice, 1880

R. Pellegrini 2003

Pellegrini, Roberta. "Il monumento del doge Marino Grimani a San Giuseppe di Castello, Venezia (1598–1604)." In *Vincenzo Scamozzi (1548–1616): architettura e scienza*, ed. F. Barbieri and G. Beltramini, Venice, 2003, 384–85

Penco 1961

Penco, Gregorio. *Storia del Monachesimo in Italia*, 2 vols., Rome, 1961

Pepi 1970

Pepi, Ruperto. "Cenni storici sulla Basilica e sulla Badia di Santa Giustina." In Giuseppe Fiocco et al., *La Basilica di Santa Giustina: arte e storia*, Castelfranco Veneto, 1970, 347–428

Perry 1972

Perry, Marilyn. "The Statuario Publico of the Venetian Republic." *Saggi e memorie di storia dell'arte* 8 (1972): 75–150

Perry 1981

——. "A Renaissance Showplace of Art: The Palazzo Grimani at Santa Maria Formosa, Venice." *Apollo* 113 (1981): 215–21

Pertusi 1965

Pertusi, Agostino. "Quedam regalia insignia: Ricerche sulle insegne del potere ducale a Venezia durante il medioevo." *Studi veneziani* 7 (1965): 3–123

Pertusi 1977

——. "La presunta concessione di alcune insegne regali al doge di Venezia da parte del Papa Alessandro III." *Ateneo Veneto* 15 (1977): 133–55

Pesce 1969

Pesce, Luigi. *Ludovico Barbo, vescovo di Treviso (1437–1443)*, Italia sacra 9–10, Padua, 1969

Petrucci 1993

Petrucci, Armando. *Public Lettering: Script, Power, and Culture*, Chicago and London, 1993 (trans. of *La scrittura: ideologia e rappresentazione*, Turin, 1980)

Piana 1998–99

Piana, Mario. "Il Convento della Carità: materiali, tecniche, strutture." *Annali di architettura* 10–11 (1998–99): 310–21

Picasso 1975

Picasso, Giorgio. "Commenda." In *Dizionario degli istituti di perfezione*, Rome, 1975, 2: 1246–50

Pignatti 1976

Pignatti, Teresio. *Paolo Veronese*, 2 vols., Venice, 1976

Pignatti, ed. 1981

Pignatti, Teresio, ed. *Le scuole di Venezia*, Milan, 1981

Pignatti & Pedrocco 1995

Pignatti, Teresio, and Filippo Pedrocco. *Veronese*, Milan, 1995

Pillinini 1969

Pillinini, Giovanni. "Bollani, Domenico." In *Dizionario biografico degli Italiani*, Rome, 1969, 11: 291–93

Pilo 1985

Pilo, Giuseppe. *La chiesa dello "Ospedaletto" in Venezia*, Venice, 1985

Pilo 1991

——. "Postilla a Jacopo Tintoretto." *Arte/Documento* 5 (1991): 108–47

Pilo 1997

——. "Il procuratore di San Marco Jacopo Soranzo Jr e il ritratto recuperate di Jacopo Tintoretto già in Procuratia 'De Supra.'" In *Storia dell'arte marciana: i mosaici*. Atti del Convegno internazionale di studi: Venezia, 11–14 October 1994, ed. R. Polacco, Venice, 1997, 209–21

Pincus 1982

Pincus, Debra. "Tomb as Trattato: Visions of Good Government in 15th-Century Venice." Talk given in "Venetian Art in its Cultural and Intellectual Context, 1400–1600," College Art Association, 1982

Pincus 1992

——. "Venice and the Two Romes: Byzantium and Rome as a Double Heritage in Venetian Cultural Politics." *Artibus et Historiae* 26 (1992): 101–14

Pincus 2000

——. *The Tombs of the Doges of Venice*, Cambridge, 2000

Piovene 1963

Piovene, Guido. "Trissino e Palladio nell'Umanesimo vicentino." *Bollettino del Centro internazionale di studi di architettura Andrea Palladio* 5 (1963): 13–23

P. Piva 1980

Piva, Paolo. *Da Cluny al Polirone*, pref. F. Zuliani, San Benedetto Po, 1980

P. Piva, ed. 1981

Piva, Paolo, ed. *I secoli di Polirone*, 2 vols., Mantua, 1981

P. Piva & Pavesi 1975

Piva, Paolo, and Giancarlo Pavesi. "Giulio Romano e la chiesa abbaziale di Polirone: documenti e proposte filologiche." In *Studi su Giulio Romano*, ed. Accademia Polironiana, San Benedetto Po, 1975, 53–119

R. Piva 1980

Piva, Raffaella. "L'immagine ideale." In *Andrea Palladio: il testo, l'immagine, la città*, ed. L. Puppi, Milan, 1980, 102–13

V. Piva 1938–60

Piva, Vittorio. *Il patriarcato di Venezia e le sue origini*, 2 vols., Venice, 1938–1960

Pizzati 1997

Pizzati, Anna. *Commende e politica ecclesiastica nella Repubblica di Venezia tra '500 e '600*, Venice, 1997

Pizzigoni 2003

Pizzigoni, Vittorio. "I tre progetti di Palladio per il Redentore." *Annali di architettura* 15 (2003): 165–77

Plesters 1979

Plesters, Joyce. "Tintoretto's Paintings in the National Gallery." *National Gallery Technical Bulletin* 3 (1979): 3–24

Plesters 1980

——. "Tintoretto's Paintings in the National Gallery." *National Gallery Technical Bulletin* 4 (1980): 32–48

Plesters 1984

——. "Tintoretto's Paintings in the National Gallery." *National Gallery Technical Bulletin* 8 (1984): 24–35

Poppone 1997

Poppone: L'età d'oro del patriarcato di Aquileia, Rome, 1997

Porcacchi 1574

Porcacchi, Tommaso. *Le attioni d'Arrigo Terzo Re di Francia e Quarto di Polonia, descritte in dialogo*, Venice, 1574

Portogruaro 1930

Portogruaro, Padre Davide M. da. "Il tempio e il convento del Redentore." *Rivista [della città] di Venezia* 9–4/5 (April–May 1930): 141–224

Portogruaro 1936

——. *Paolo Piazza ossia P. Cosmo da Castelfranco, Pittore Cappuccino, 1560–1620*, Venice, 1936

Portogruaro 1957

——. *Storia dei Cappuccini Veneti 2: primi sviluppi, 1560–1580*, Venice and Mestre, 1957

Pratesi 1964

Pratesi, Allesandro. "Barbo, Ludovico." In *Dizionario biografico degli Italiani*, Rome, 1964, 6: 244–49

Predelli, ed. 1876–1914

Predelli, Riccardo, ed. *I libri commemoriali della Repubblica di Venezia: regesti*, 8 vols., Venice, 1876–1914

Preto 1978

Preto, Paolo. *Peste e società a Venezia nel 1576*, Vicenza, 1978

Preto 1991

——. "Le grandi paure di Venezia nel secondo '500: le paure naturali (peste, caresti, incendi, terremoti)." In *Crisi e rinnovamenti nell'autunno del Rinascimento a Venezia*, ed. V. Branca and C. Ossola, Florence, 1991, 177–92

Priuli 1992

Priuli, Girolamo. *Diarii*. In *Venice: A Documentary History, 1450–1630*, ed. D. Chambers and B. Pullan, Oxford, 1992, 161 (from *I diarii*, ed. R. Cessi, Bologna, 1938, 4: 15–17)

Le Procuratie nuove 1994

Le Procuratie nuove: in Piazza San Marco, Rome, 1994

Le Procuratie vecchie 1994

Le Procuratie vecchie: in Piazza San Marco, Rome, 1994

Prodi 1965

Prodi, Paolo. "Ricerche sulla teorica delle arti figurativa nella riforma cattolica." *Archivio italiano per la storia della pietà* 4 (1965): 121–212

Prodi 1973

——. "The Structure and Organization of the Church in Renaissance Venice: Suggestions for Further Research." In *Renaissance Venice*, ed. J. R. Hale, London, 1973, 409–40

Prodi 1977

——. "Istituzione ecclesiastiche e mondo nobiliare." In *Patriziati e aristocrazie nobiliari*, ed. C. Mozzarelli and P. Schiera, Trent, 1977, 64–77

Pullan 1965

Pullan, Brian. "Service to the Venetian State: Aspects of Myth and Reality in the Early Seventeenth Century." *Studi secenteschi* 5 (1965): 95–148

Pullan 1968

——. "Wage Earners and the Venetian Economy, 1550–1630." In *Crisis and Change in the Venetian Economy in the Sixteenth and Seventeenth Centuries*, ed. B. Pullan, London, 1968, 146–74 (orig. pub. in *Economic History Review* 16 [1964]: 407–26)

Pullan 1971

——. *Rich and Poor in Renaissance Venice: The Social Institutions of a Catholic State, to 1620*, Oxford, 1971

Pullan 1973

——. "The Occupations and Investments of the Venetian Nobility in the Middle and Later Sixteenth Century." In *Renaissance Venice*, ed. J. R. Hale, London, 1973, 379–408

Pullan 1989
——. "La nuova filantropia." In *Il regno dei poveri: arte e storia dei grandi ospedali veneziana in età moderna 1474–1797*, ed. B. Aikema and D. Meijers, Venice, 1989, 19–34

Pullan 1999
——. "'Three Orders of Inhabitants': Social Hierarchies in the Republic of Venice." In *Orders and Hierarchies in Late Medieval and Renaissance Europe*, ed. J. Denton, Toronto and Buffalo, N.Y., 1999, 147–58, 190–95

Pullan, ed. 1968
Pullan, Brian, ed. *Crisis and Change in the Venetian Economy in the Sixteenth and Seventeenth Centuries*, London, 1968

Puppi 1971
Puppi, Lionello. *Michele Sanmicheli, architetto di Verona*, Padua, 1971

Puppi 1973
——. *Scrittori vicentini d'architettura del secolo XVI*, Vicenza, 1973

Puppi 1975
——. *The Villa Badoer at Fratta Polesine*, Corpus Palladianum 7, University Park, Pa., 1975

Puppi 1980a
——. "Alvise Cornaro e Andrea Palladio padovani." In *Alvise Cornaro e il suo tempo*, ed. L. Puppi, Padua, 1980, 10–16

Puppi 1980b
——. "Palladio in cantiere." In *Palladio: ein Symposium*, ed. K. Forster and M. Kubelik, Padua, 1980, 13–26

Puppi 1981
——. "La teoria artistica del Cinquecento." In *Storia della cultura veneta. 3/3: Dal primo Quattrocento al Concilio di Trento*, ed. G. Arnaldi and M. Pastore Stocchi, Vicenza, 1981, 134–86

Puppi 1982
——. "Verso Gerusalemme." In *Verso Gerusalemme: immagini e temi di urbanistica e di architettura simboliche tra il XIV e il XVIII secolo*, ed. L. Puppi, Rome and Reggio Calabria, 1982, 62–76

Puppi 1986
——. *Andrea Palladio: The Complete Works*, New York and Milan, 1986 (trans. of *Andrea Palladio: l'opera completa*, 2 vols., Milan, 1973)

Puppi 1987
——. "Palladio e Leonardo Mocenigo. Un palazzo a Padova. Una villa 'per un . . . sito sopra la Brenta'; e una questione di metodo." In *Klassizismus, Epoche e Probleme, Festschrift für Erik Forssman zum 70. Geburtstag*, ed. J. Meyer zur Capellen and G. Oberreuter-Kronabel, New York, 1987, 337–61

Puppi 1990
——. *Palladio Drawings*, New York, 1990

Puppi 1999
——. *Andrea Palladio*, ed. D. Battilotti, Milan, 1999 (rev. edn. of *Andrea Palladio: l'opera completa*, 1973)

Puppi, ed. 1980a
Puppi, Lionello, ed. *Alvise Cornaro e il suo tempo*, Padua, 1980

Puppi, ed. 1980b
——. *Architettura e Utopia nella Venezia del Cinquecento*, Milan, 1980

Puppi, ed. 1982a
——. *Palladio e Venezia*, Florence, 1982

Puppi, ed. 1982b
——. *Verso Gerusalemme: Immagini e temi di urbanistica e di architettura simboliche tra il XIV e il XVIII secolo*, Rome and Reggio Calabria, 1982

Puppi, ed. 1988
——. *Andrea Palladio: scritti sull'architettura (1554–1579)*, Vicenza, 1988

Puppi, ed. 1992
——. *Le Zitelle: Architettura, arte e storia di un'istituzione veneziana*, Venice, 1992

Puppi & Romanelli, eds. 1985
Puppi, Lionello, and Giandomenico Romanelli, eds. *Le Venezie possible*, Milan, 1985

Quadri 1831
Quadri, Antonio. *Il Canal Grande di Venezia*, Venice, 1831

Quadri 1840
——. *Serto de' dogi Mocenigo per l'imeneo Mocenigo-Spaur*, Venice, 1840

Queller 1986
Queller, Donald. *The Venetian Patriciate: Reality versus Myth*, Urbana and Chicago, Ill., 1986

Rano 1974a
Rano, Balbino. "Agostiniane, monache." In *Dizionario degli istituti dei perfezione*, Rome, 1974, 1: 155–90

Rano 1974b
——. "Agostiniani." In *Dizionario degli Istituti dei Perfezione*, Rome, 1974, 1: 278–358

Ravagnan 2002
Ravagnan, Giovanna Luisa. "Der Familie Grimani und ihre archäologischen Sammlungen." In *Venezia! Kunst aus der venezianischen Palasten Sammlungsgeschicte Venedigs vom 15. bis 19. Jahrhundert*, Ostfildern-Ruit, 2002, 92–94

Rearick 1959
Rearick, W. R. "Battista Franco and the Grimani Chapel." *Saggi e memorie di storia dell'arte 2* (1959): 107–39

Rearick 1982
——. "Leandro Bassano, Italian 1557–1622, *Adoration of the Shepherds, ca. 1592–1594*." *Bulletin of the Rhode Island School of Design. Museum Notes* 69 (1982): 22–27

Rearick 1988a
——. *The Art of Paolo Veronese 1528–1588*, Cambridge and Washington, D.C.: 1988

Rearick 1988b
——. "Catalogo dei dipinti." In *Paolo Veronese: Disegni e dipinti*, Vicenza, 1988, 49–109

Rearick 1991
——. "The 'Twilight' of Paolo Veronese." In *Crisi e rinnovamenti nell'autunno del Rinascimento a Venezia*, ed. V. Branca and C. Ossola, Florence, 1991, 237–53

Rearick 1996–97
——. "I clienti veneziani di Jacopo Bassano." In *Jacopo Bassano (1510–c.1592)*, Bollettino del Museo civico di Bassano 17–18, ed. M. Guderzo (1996–1997), 51–82

Rendina 1984
Rendina, Claudio. *I dogi: storia e segreti*, Rome, 1984

Renier Michiel 1817
Renier Michiel, Giustina. *Le origine delle feste veneziane*, 6 vols., Milan, 1817

Renier Michiel 1829–1916
——. *Origine delle feste veneziane*, 3 vols., Venice, 1829–1916

Repishti 1998
Repishti, Francesco. "Il tabernacolo di Pio IV (1561–1567)." *Civiltà ambrosiana* 15 (1998): 61–65

Ricci 1859
Ricci, Amico. *Storia dell'architettura in Italia dal secolo IV al XVIII*, vol. 3 of 3, Modena, 1859

Richardson 1994
Richardson, Brian. *Print Culture in Renaissance Italy: The Editor and the Vernacular Text, 1470–1600*, Cambridge, 1994

Richardson 1999
——. *Printing, Writers and Readers in Renaissance Italy*, Cambridge, 1999

Riccoboni 1947
Riccoboni, Alberto. *Quattrocento pittura inedite*, Venice, 1947

Ridolfi 1965
Ridolfi, Carlo. *Le Maraviglie dell'arte*, 2 vols., Rome, 1965 (reprint of D. von Hadeln, ed., Berlin, 1914–1924; orig. pub. Venice, 1648)

Rigon, ed. 1980
Rigon, Fernando, ed. *I ponti di Palladio*, Milan, 1980

Rio, ed. 1840
Rio, Nicolò da, ed. *Notizie d'antiche costumanze dei dogi di Venezia*, Padua, 1840 (orig. pub. 1559)

Rizzi 1983
Rizzi, Aldo. *Udine, tra storia e leggenda nell'arte e nell'iconografia*, Friuli Venezia Giulia (Udine), 1983

Rizzi 1987
——. *Scultura esterna a Venezia*, Venice, 1987

Rizzi, 1989
——. *Sebastiano Ricci*, Milan, 1989

Robertson 1992
Robertson, Clare. *"Il gran cardinale": Alessandro Farnese, Patron of the Arts*, New Haven and London, 1992

Rösch 2000
Rösch, Gerhard. "The *Serrata* of the Great Council and Venetian Society, 1286–1323." In *Venice Reconsidered: The History and Civilization of an Italian City-State, 1297–1797*, ed. J. Martin and D. Romano, Baltimore, Md., 2000, 67–88

Romanelli 1990
Romanelli, Giandomenico. "Titian's Politics Between the Republic and Empire." In *Titian: Prince of Painters*, ed. S. Biadene and M. Yakush, Venice, 1990, 34–42

Romanelli 1994
——. "Tintoretto a San Rocco: Pittura, teologia,

narrazione." In *Tintoretto: La Scuola Grande di San Rocco*, ed. G. Romanelli, Milan, 1994, 7–50

Romanelli, ed. 1994
Romanelli, G., ed. *Tintoretto: La Scuola Grande di San Rocco*, Milan, 1994

Romanin 1857
Romanin, Samuele. *Storia documentata di Venezia*, vol. 6, Venice, 1857

Romano 1987
Romano, Dennis. *Patricians and Popolani: The Social Foundations of the Venetian Renaissance State*, Baltimore, Md., 1987

Romano 1996
——. *Housecraft and Statecraft: Domestic Service in Renaissance Venice,* Baltimore, Md., 1996

Roochnik 1998
Roochnik, David. *Of Art and Wisdom: Plato's Understanding of Technē*, University Park, Pa., 1998

Rosand 1970a
Rosand, David. "The Crisis of the Venetian Renaissance Tradition." *L'Arte* 11–12 (1970): 5–53

Rosand 1970b
——. "Palma il Giovane as Draughtsman: The Early Career and Related Observations." *Master Drawings* 8 (1970): 148–61

Rosand 1997
——. *Painting in Cinquecento Venice: Titian, Veronese, Tintoretto*, rev. edn., Cambridge, 1997 (orig. pub. New Haven and London, 1982)

Rosand 2001
——. *Myths of Venice: The Figuration of a State*, Chapel Hill, N.C., and London, 2001

Rosand & Muraro 1976
Rosand, David, and Michelangelo Muraro. *Titian and the Venetian Woodcut*, Washington, D.C., 1976

Rose 1969
Rose, Paul. "The Accademia Venetiana: Science and Culture in Renaissance Venice." *Studi veneziani* 11 (1969): 191–242

Rose 1976
——. "Jacomo Contarini (1536–1595): a Venetian Patron and Collector of Mathematical Instruments and Books." *Physis* 18 (1976): 117–30

G. Rossi 1969
Rossi, Giovanni. "Storia del monastero di San Giorgio Maggiore." In Emmanuele Cicogna, *Delle inscrizioni veneziane*, vol. 4, Bologna, 1969, 241–80 (orig. pub. Venice, 1834)

P. Rossi 1974
Rossi, Paola. *Jacopo Tintoretto. 1: I ritratti*, Venice, 1974

P. Rossi 1975a
——. *I disegni di Jacopo Tintoretto*, Florence, 1975

P. Rossi 1975b
——. "Per la grafica di Domenico Tintoretto." *Arte veneta* 29 (1975): 205–11

P. Rossi 1980
——. "I protagonisti." In *Architettura e utopia nella Venezia del Cinquecento*, ed. L. Puppi, Milan, 1980, 235–48

P. Rossi 1984
——. "Per la grafica di Domenico Tintoretto." *Arte veneta* 38 (1984): 57–71

P. Rossi 1994
——. "I ritratti di Jacopo Tintoretto" and cat. entries in *Jacopo Tintoretto: Ritratti*, Milan, 1994, 13–38 and 71–165

P. Rossi 2001
——. "La decorazione scultorea del Monumento al doge Alvise Mocenigo della chiesa dei Santi Giovanni e Paolo: l'ultima fase dei lavori." *Arte veneta* 58 (2001): 194–98

Rykwert 1980
Rykwert, Joseph. "Palladio chiese veneziane/Venetian church façades." *Domus* 609 (1980): 28–31

Saccocci 1992
Saccocci, Andrea. "La circolazione monetaria nel Patriarcato dal X al XIII secolo." In *Storia e arte del patriarcato di Aquileia*, Antichità Altoadriatiche 38, Udine, 1992, 359–76

Sagredo 1957
Sagredo, Agostino. *Sulle consorterie delle arti edificative in Venezia,* Venice, 1857

Sagredo 1865
——. "Leggi venete intorno agli ecclesiastici sino al secolo XVIII." *Archivio storico italiano* ser. 3, 2 (1865): 92–133

Salimbeni, ed. 1977
Salimbeni, Fulvio, ed. *Le lettere di Paolo Bisanti, vicario generale del patriarca di Aquileia (1577–1587)*, Rome, 1977

Sambin 1970
Sambin, Paolo. "L'abate Giovanni Michiel (+1430) e la riforma di S. Giorgio Maggiore di Venezia." In *Miscellanea Gilles Gérard Meersman*, Italia sacra 16, Padua, 1970, 2: 483–548

Sambò 1990
Sambò, Alessandra. "Esperimenti d'archivio: itinerari di ricerca, verifiche, documenti." In *Andrea Palladio: nuovi contributi*, ed. A. Chastel and R. Cevese, Milan, 1990, 44–48

San Girolamo Miani e Venezia 1986
San Girolamo Miani e Venezia nel V centenario della nascità, Venice, 1986

Sansovino 1581
Sansovino, Francesco. *Venezia città nobilissima et singolare*, Venice, 1581

Sansovino 1584
——. *Del Segretario libri VII*, Venice, 1584

Sansovino 1604
——. *Venezia città nobilissima et singolare*, ed. G. Stringa, Venice, 1604

Sansovino 1663
——. *Venezia città nobilissima et singolare*, ed. G. Martinioni, Venice, 1663

Sansovino 1968
——. *Venezia città nobilissima et singolare*, ed. L. Moretti, Venice, 1968 (orig. pub. G. Martinioni, ed., Venice, 1663)

Sanudo 1879–1903
Sanudo, Marin. *I Diarii di Marin Sanuto*, 58 vols., ed., R. Fulin et al., Venice, 1879–1903

Sartori 1970
Sartori, Antonio. "Regesto di Santa Giustina." In Giuseppe Fiocco et al., *La Basilica di Santa Giustina: Arte e storia*, Castelfranco Veneto, 1970, 429–62

Sbriziolo 1973–74
Sbriziolo, Lia. "Note di storia monastica medievale in Padova." *Atti e memorie dell'Accademia patavina di SS. LL. ed AA.* 86/3 (1973–74): 5–27

Scamozzi 1964
Scamozzi, Vincenzo. *L'idea della architettura universale, di Vincenzo Scamozzi, divisa in x libri. Venetiis, expensis auctoris, 1615*, 2 vols., Ridgewood, N.J., 1964 (orig. pub. Venice, 1615)

Scarabello 1981
Scarabello, Giovanni. "Caratteri e funzioni sociopolitiche dell'associazionismo a Venezia sotto la Repubblica." In *Scuole di arti: mestieri e devozione a Venezia*, ed. S. Gramigna and A. Perissa, Venice, 1981, 5–24

Schiavon 2001
Schiavon, Alessandra. "Appendice documentaria." *Arte veneta* 58 (2001): 88–93

Schlosser 1977
Schlosser, Julius, Ritter von. *La letteratura artistica: manuale delle fonti della storia dell'arte moderna*, 3rd edn., Florence, 1977 (trans. of *Die Kunstliteratur: ein Handbuch zur Quellenkunde der neueren Kunstgeschicte*, Vienna, 1924)

Schofield 1997
Schofield, Richard. "English and Italian Glossary." In *The Four Books on Architecture*, by Andrea Palladio, trans. R. Tavernor and R. Schofield, Cambridge, Mass., 1997

Schofield 2003
——. "Architettura, dottrina e magnificenza nell'architettura ecclesiastica dell'età di Carlo e Federico Borromeo." In Richard Schofield and Francesco Repishti, A*rchitettura e controriforma. I dibatti per la facciata del Duomo di Milano, 1582–1682*, Milan, 2003, 125–250

Schulz 1968
Schulz, Juergen. *Venetian Painted Ceilings of the Renaissance*, Berkeley and Los Angeles, 1968

Schutte 1989
Schutte, Anne. "Periodization of Sixteenth-Century Italian Religious History: The Post-Cantimori Paradigm Shift." *Journal of Modern History* 61 (1989): 269–84

Scotti 1977
Scotti, Aurora. "L'architettura religiosa di Pellegrino Tibaldo." *Bollettino del Centro internazionale di studi di architettura Andrea Palladio* 19 (1977): 221–50

Selmi 1973
Selmi, Paolo. "Perché 'Venezia città del libro'? La politica della Veneta Repubblica per il libro." In *Venezia: città del libro*, Venice, 1973, 103–08

Semi 1983
Semi, Franca. *Gli "Ospizi" di Venezia*, Venice, 1983

Seneca 1959
Seneca, Federico. *Il Doge Leonardo Donà: la sua*

vita e la sua preparazione politica prima del dogado, Padua, 1959

Seneca 1962
——. *Venezia e Papa Giulio II*, Padua, 1962

Sennett 1994
Sennett, Richard. *Flesh and Stone: The Body and the City in Western Civilization*, New York, 1994

Serlio [1559–62]
Serlio, Sebastiano. *Libro primo[-quinto] di architettura, di Sebastiano Serlio Bolognese*, Venice [1559–62]

Serlio 1982
——. *The Five Books of Architecture: An Unabridged Reprint of the English Edition of 1611*, New York, 1982 (orig. pub. London, 1611)

Serlio 1996
——. *On Architecture*. 1: *Books I–V of "Tutte l'opere d'architettura et prospettiva" by Sebastiano Serlio*, trans. V. Hart and P. Hicks, Cambridge, Mass., 1996

Serlio 2001
——. *On Architecture*. 2: *Books VI–VII of "Tutte l'opere d'architettura et prospettiva" with "Castramentation of the Romans" and "The Extraordinary Book of Doors" by Sebastiano Serlio*, trans. V. Hart and P. Hicks, New Haven and London, 2001

Severin 1992
Severin, Ingrid. "Baumeister und Architekten: Studien zur Darstellung eines Berufsstandes in Porträt und Bildnis." PhD dissertation, Rheinisch-Westfälischen Technischen Hochschule, Aachen, 1987, Berlin, 1992

Shapley 1979
Shapley, Fern Rusk. *Catalogue of the Italian Paintings*, 2 vols., Washington, D.C., 1979

Shearman 1975
Shearman, John. "The Florentine *entrata* of Leo X, 1515." *Journal of the Warburg and Courtauld Institutes* 38 (1975): 136–54

Simane 1993
Simane, Jan. *Grabmonumente der Dogen: Venezianische Sepulkralkunst im Cinquecento*, Centro Tedesco di Studi Veneziani Studi 11, Sigmaringen, 1993

Sinding-Larsen 1965a
Sinding-Larsen, Staale. "Palladio's Redentore: A Compromise in Composition." *Art Bulletin* 47 (1965): 419–37

Sinding-Larsen 1965b
——. "Some Functional and Iconographical Aspects of the Centralized Church in the Italian Renaissance." *Acta ad archaeologiam et artium historiam pertinentia* 2 (1965): 203–52

Sinding-Larsen 1974
——. "Christ in the Council Hall: Studies in the Religious Iconography of the Venetian Republic." *Acta ad archaeologiam et artium historiam pertinentia* 5 (1974)

Sinding-Larsen 1980
——. "L'immagine della Repubblica di Venezia." In *Architettura e utopia nella Venezia del Cinquecento*, ed. L. Puppi, Milan, 1980, 40–49

Smith 1977
Smith, Graham. *The Casino of Pius IV*, Princeton, N.J., 1977

Soccal 2002
Soccal, Eva. "Hypothesen zur Rekonstruktion der Tribuna im Palazzo Grimani: Die Methodologie." In *Venezia! Kunst aus der venezianischen Palasten Sammlungsgeschicte Venedigs vom 15. bis 19. Jahrhundert*, Ostfildern-Ruit, 2002, 130

Socol 1986
Socol, Carlo. *La visita apostolica del 1584–85 alla diocesi di Aquileia e la riforma dei regolari*, Udine, 1986

Soranzo 1857
Soranzo, Girolamo. "Relazione di Rome, letta in Senato 14 giugno 1563." In Eugenio Alberì, *Le relazioni degli ambasciatori veneti al senato durante il secolo decimosesto*, Florence, 1857, 65–120

Sparrow 1969
Sparrow, John. *Visible Words: A Study of Inscriptions in and as Books and Works of Art*, Cambridge, 1969

Sperling 1999
Sperling, Jutta Gisela. *Convents and the Body Politic in Late Renaissance Venice*, Chicago, 1999

Speroni 1984
Speroni, Sperone. *Dialoghi*. 2: *La Fortuna* (Padua, 1790). In B. Morsolin, *Giangiorgio Trissino, monografia d'un gentiluomo letterato nel secolo XVI*, Florence, 1984, 263–42 (orig. pub. Vicenza, 1878)

Stefani Mantovanelli 1984
Stefani Mantovanelli, Marina. "Giovanni Grimani patriarca di Aquileia e il suo palazzo di Venezia." *Quaderni Utinensi* 3–4 (1984): 34–54

Stella 1956
Stella, Aldo. "La crisi economica veneziana nella seconda metà del secolo XVI." *Archivio veneto* ser. 5, 58–59 (1956): 17–69

Stella 1958a
——. "La proprietà ecclesiastica nella Repubblica di Venezia dal secolo XV al XVII." *Nuova rivista storica* 42 (1958): 50–77

Stella 1958b
——. "La regolazione delle pubbliche entrate e la crisi politica veneziana del 1582." In *Miscellanea in onore di Roberto Cessi*, Rome, 1958, 2: 157–71

Stella 1964
——. *Chiesa e Stato nelle relazioni dei nunzi pontifici a Venezia: ricerche sul giurisdizionalismo veneziano del XVI al XVIII secolo*, Studi e testi 239, Vatican City, 1964

Stella 1976
——. "Gli eretici a Vicenza." In *Vicenza illustrata*, ed. N. Pozza, Vicenza, 1976, 253–61

Stinger 1990
Stinger, Charles. "The Campidoglio as the Locus of *Renovatio Imperii* in Renaissance Rome." In *Art and Politics in Late Medieval and Early Renaissance Italy, 1250–1500*, ed. C. Rosenberg, Notre Dame, Ind., 1990, 135–56

Stockdale 1980
Stockdale, Rachel. "Benedictine Libraries and Writers." In *The Benedictines in Britain*, London, 1980, 62–81

Strong 1984
Strong, Roy. *Art and Power: Renaissance Festivals, 1450–1650*, Woodbridge, Suffolk, 1984

Suida [1933]
Suida, Wilhelm. *Tiziano*, Rome [1933]

Summers 1981
Summers, David. *Michelangelo and the Language of Art*, Princeton, N.J., 1981

Tafuri 1972
Tafuri, Manfredo. *Jacopo Sansovino e l'architettura del '500 a Venezia*, Padua, 1972

Tafuri 1980
——. "'Sapienza di Stato' e 'atti mancanti': architettura e technica urbana nella Venezia del '500." In *Architettura e utopia nella Venezia del Cinquecento*, ed. L. Puppi, Milan, 1980, 16–39

Tafuri 1982
——. "La 'nuova Constantinopoli': La rappresentazione della 'renovatio' nella Venezia dell'Umanesimo (1450–1509)." *Rassegna* 4/9 (1982): 25–38

Tafuri 1984a
——. "Il problema storiografico." In *"Renovatio Urbis," Venezia nell'età di Andrea Gritti (1523–1538)*, ed. M. Tafuri, Rome, 1984, 9–57

Tafuri 1984b
——. "Progetto per la facciata della chiesa di San Lorenzo, Firenze, 1515–1516." In *Raffaello architetto*, ed. C. Frommel, S. Ray, and M. Tafuri, Milan, 1984, 165–70

Tafuri 1985
——. "Tempo veneziano e tempo del 'progetto': continuità e crisi nel Venezia del Cinquecento." In *Le Venezie possibili*, ed. L. Puppi, Milan, 1985, 23–33

Tafuri 1986
——. *Humanism, Technical Knowledge and Rhetoric: The Debate in Renaissance Venice*, Walter Gropius Lecture, Cambridge, Mass., 1986

Tafuri 1987
——. "La norma e il programma: il Vitruvio di Daniele Barbaro." In *I dieci libri dell'architettura tradotti et commentati da Daniele Barbaro 1567: con un saggio di Manfredo Tafuri e uno studio di Manuela Morresi*, Milan, 1987, xi–xl

Tafuri 1989
——. *Venice and the Renaissance*, Cambridge, Mass., 1989 (trans. of *Venezia e il Rinascimento*, Turin, 1985)

Tafuri 1990
——. "Il disegno di Chatsworth (per il palazzo Ducale di Venezia?) e un progetto perduto di Jacopo Sansovino." In *Andrea Palladio: nuovi contributi*, ed. A. Chastel and R. Cevese, Milan, 1990, 100–11

Tafuri 1992
——. *Ricerca del Rinascimento: principi, città, architetti*, Turin, 1992

Tafuri 1994
——. "Il pubblico e il privato. Architettura e committenza a Venezia." In *Storia di Venezia*

dalle origini alla caduta della Serenissima. 6: Dal rinascimento al barocco, ed. G. Cozzi and P. Prodi, Rome, 1994, 367–477

Tafuri, ed. 1984
Tafuri, Manfredo, ed. *"Renovatio Urbis," Venezia nell'età di Andrea Gritti (1523–1538)*, Rome, 1984

Talvacchia 1996
Talvacchia, Bette. "Notes for a Job Description to be Filed Under 'Court Artist.'" In *The Search For a Patron in the Middle Ages and the Renaissance*, ed. D. Wilkins and R. Wilkins, Lewiston, N.Y., 1996, 179–90

Tamassia Mazzarotto 1980
Tamassia Mazzarotto, Bianca. *Le feste veneziane*, 2nd edn., Florence, 1980

Tassi 1951
Tassi, Ildefonso. "La crisi della congregazione di S. Giustina tra il 1419 e il 1434." *Benedictina* 5 (1951): 95–111

Tassi 1952
——. *Ludovico Barbo (1381–1443)*, Rome, 1952

Tassini 1863
Tassini, Giuseppe. *Curiosità veneziane*, Venice, 1863

Tassini 1885
——. *Edifici di Venezia distrutti o vôlti ad uso diverso da quello a cui furono in origine destinata*, Venice, 1885

Tassini 1933
——. *Curiosità veneziane*, Venice, 1933

Tassoli 1571
Tassoli, Domenico. *I trionfi feste et livree fatte dalli signori conservatori, & popolo romano, & da tutte le arte di Roma, nella felicissima, & honorata entrata dell'illustrissimo signor Marcantonio Colonna*, Venice, 1571

Tavernor 1997
Tavernor, Robert. Intro. to *The Four Books on Architecture*, by Andrea Palladio, trans. R. Tavernor and R. Schofield, Cambridge, Mass., 1997 (orig. pub. Venice, 1570)

Temanza 1762
Temanza, Tommaso. *Vita di Andrea Palladio*, Venice, 1762

Temanza 1778
——. *Vite dei più celebri architetti, e scultori veneziani*, Venice, 1778

Temanza 1966
——. *Vite dei più celebri architetti, e scultori veneziani*, Milan, 1966 (orig. pub. Venice, 1778)

Tenenti 1973
Tenenti, Alberto. "The Sense of Space and Time in the Venetian World." In *Renaissance Venice*, ed. J. R. Hale, London, 1973, 17–46

Tenenti 1974
——. "La Francia, Venezia, e la sacra lega." In *Il mediterraneo nella seconda metà del '500 alla luce di Lepanto*, ed. G. Benzoni, Florence, 1974, 393–408

Tenenti 1991
——. "Il nobile veneziano." In *Crisi e rinnovamenti nell'autunno del Rinascimento a Venezia*, ed. V. Branca and C. Ossola, Florence, 1991, 105–18

Tentori 1988
Tentori, Francesco. *Udine*, Rome and Bari, 1988

Testi 1909–15
Testi, Laudedeo. *La storia della pittura veneziana*, 2 vols., Bergamo, 1909–15

Thornton 1997
Thornton, Dora. *The Scholar in his Study: Ownership and Experience in Renaissance Italy*, New Haven and London, 1997

Tiepolo 1996
Tiepolo, Maria Francesca. "Il linguaggio dei simboli: le arme dei Barbaro." In *Una famiglia veneziana nella storia: i Barbaro*. Atti del Convegno di Studi in occasione del quinto centenario della morte dell'umnaista Ermolao: Venice, 4–6 November 1993, ed. M. Marangoni and M. Pastore Stocchi, Venice, 1996, 133–92

Tiepolo et al. 1980
Tiepolo, Maria Francesca, et al. *Testimonianze veneziane di interesse palladiano: mostra documentaria*, Venice, 1980

Tietze-Conrat 1946
Tietze-Conrat, Erica. "Titian's Workshop in his Late Years." *Art Bulletin* 28 (1946): 76–88

Tietze & Tietze-Conrat 1944
Tietze, Hans, and Erica Tietze-Conrat. *The Drawings of the Venetian Painters in the 15th and 16th Centuries*, New York, 1944

Timofiewitsch 1962
Timofiewitsch, Wladimir. "Eine Zeichnung Andrea Palladios für Klosteranlage von S. Giorgio Maggiore." *Arte veneta* 16 (1962): 160–63

Timofiewitsch 1963
——. "Eine neuerbautrag zu der Baugeschicte von San Giorgio Maggiore." *Bollettino del Centro internazionale di studi di architettura Andrea Palladio* 5 (1963): 330–39

Timofiewitsch 1963–65
——. "Quellen und Forschungen zum Punkgrab des Dogen Marino Grimani in S. Giuseppe di Castello zu Venedig." *Mitteilungen des Kunsthistorischen Institutes in Florenz* 11 (1963–65): 33–54

Timofiewitsch 1968
——. *Die sakrale Architektur Palladios*, Munich, 1968

Timofiewitsch 1969
——. *The Chiesa del Redentore*, Corpus Palladianum 3, University Park, Pa., and London, 1971 (trans. of *La Chiesa del Redentore*, Vicenza, 1969)

Timofiewitsch 1972
——. *Girolamo Campagna: Studien zur Venezianischen Plastik um das Jahr 1600*, Munich, 1972

Timofiewitsch 1980
——. "Delle chiese palladiane: alcune osservazioni in rapporto alle facciate." *Bollettino del Centro internazionale di studi di architettura Andrea Palladio* 22 (1980): 237–46

Timofiewitsch 1984
——. "Campagna, Girolamo." In *Dizionario biografico degli Italiani*, Rome, 1984, 17: 300–06

Tondro 2002
Tondro, Maximilian. "The First Temporary Triumphal Arch in Venice (1557)." In *Court Festivals of the European Renaissance: Art, Politics and Performance*, ed. J. R. Mulryne and E. Goldring,

Aldershot, Hampshire, and Burlington, Vt., 2002, 335–62

Tramontin 1967
Tramontin, Silvio. "La visita apostolica del 1581 a Venezia." *Studi veneziani* 9 (1967): 453–533

Tramontin 1968
——. "La figura del vescovo secondo il Concilio di Trento ed i suoi riflessi nell'interrogatorio del patriarca Trevisan." *Studi veneziani* 10 (1968): 90–114

Tramontin 1970
——. "Realtà e leggenda nei racconti marciani veneti." *Studi veneziani* 12 (1970): 35–58

Tramontin 1975
——. "Canonici Secolari di San Giorgio in Alga." In *Dizionario degli istituti di perfezione*, Rome, 1975, 2: 154–58

Tramontin 1987
——. "Origini e sviluppi dalla leggenda marciana." In *Le origini della Chiesa di Venezia*, Contributi alla storia della chiesa veneziana 1, ed. F. Tonon, Venice, 1987, 167–86

Tramontin 1989
——. "Dall'episcopato castellano al patriarcato veneziano." In *La Chiesa di Venezia tra Medioevo ed età moderna*, Contributi alla storia della chiesa veneziana 3, ed. G. Vian, Venice, 1989, 55–90

Tramontin 1991a
——. "Fondazione e sviluppo della diocesi." In *Patriarcato di Venezia*, Storia religiosa del Veneto 1, ed. S. Tramontin, Padua, 1991, 19–46

Tramontin 1991b
——. "Venezia tra riforma cattolica e riforma protestante." In *Patriarcato di Venezia*, Storia religiosa del Veneto 1, ed. S. Tramontin, Padua, 1991, 91–130

Tramontin, ed. 1991
Tramontin, Silvio, ed. *Patriarcato di Venezia*, Storia religiosa del Veneto 1, Padua, 1991

Trebbi 1984
Trebbi, Giuseppe. *Francesco Barbaro, patrizio veneto e patriarca di Aquileia*, Udine, 1984

Trebbi 1996
——. "Francesco Barbaro (1546–1616) o la scelta romana." In *Una famiglia veneziana nella storia: i Barbaro*. Atti del convegno di studi in occasione del quinto centenario della morte dell'umanista Ermolao: Venice, 4–6 November 1993, ed. M. Marangoni and M. Pastore Stocchi, Venice, 1996, 435–60

Trincanato 1984
Trincanato, Egle Renata. *Dietro i palazzi: tre secoli di architettura minore a Venezia, 1492–1803*, ed. G. Gianighian and P. Pavanini, Venice, 1984

Trolese 1983
Trolese, Francesco G. B. *Ludovico Barbo e S. Giustina, contributo bibliografico, problemi attinenti alla riforma monastica del quattrocento*, Rome, 1983

Trolese, ed. 1984
Trolese, Francesco G. B., ed. *Riforma della chiesa, cultura e spiritualità nel Quattrocento veneto. Atti del Convegno per il VI centenario della nascita

di Ludovico Barbo (1382–1443): Padova, Venezia, Treviso, 19–24 settembre 1982, Cesena, 1984

Tucci 1971

Tucci, Ugo. "Bragadin, Antonio." In *Dizionario biografico degli Italiani*, Rome, 1971, 13: 663–64

Uberti 1985

Uberti, Carla. "Il ponte ferroviario e la stazione." In *Le Venezie possibili: da Palladio a Le Corbusier*, ed. L. Puppi and G. Romanelli, Milan, 1985, 228–38

Ughelli 1720

Ughelli, Ferdinand. *Italia sacra*, Venice, 1720

Urbani de Gheltof 1890

Urbani de Gheltof, Giuseppe Marino. *Il palazzo de Camillo Trevisan a Murano*, Venice, 1890

Valier 1719

Valier, Agostino. *Bernardi Navagerii vita*, Padua, 1719

Valier 1787

——. *Dell'utilità che si può ritrarre dalle cose operate dai Veneziani, libri XIV*, Padua, 1787

Vasari 1568

Vasari, Giorgio. *Le vite de' più eccellenti pittori, scultori et architettori*, 3 vols., Florence, 1568

Vasari 1878–85

——. *Le vite de' più eccellenti pittori scultori ed architettori*, vols. 1–7 of *Le opere di Giorgio Vasari*, 9 vols., ed. G. Milanesi, Florence, 1878– 85

Vasari 1960

——. *Vasari on Technique*, ed. L. Maclehose, New York, 1960 (orig. pub. 1907)

Vasari 1966

——. *Le vite de' più eccellenti pittori scultori ed architettori: nelle redazioni del 1550 e 1568*, 6 vols., ed. R. Bettarini and P. Barocchi, Florence, 1966[–1967]

Vasari 1987

——. *Lives of the Artists*, 2 vols., trans. G. Bull, London and New York, 1987

Vasoli 1991

Vasoli, Cesare. "Alle origini della crisi delle 'tradizioni': Francesco Patrizi e la cultura veneta degli anni sessanta." In *Crisi e rinnovamenti nell'autunno del rinascimento a Venezia*, ed. V. Branca and C. Ossola, Florence, 1991, 155–76

Venezia e la peste 1979

Venezia e la peste, 1348/1797, Venice, 1979

Ventura 1984

Ventura, Angelo. "Scrittori politici." In *Storia della cultura veneta. 4/2: Dalla Controriforma alla fine della Repubblica*, ed. G. Arnaldi and M. Pastore Stocchi, Vicenza, 1984, 513–63

Ventura 1963

——. "Badoer, Andrea Biagio." In *Dizionario biografico degli Italiani*, Rome, 1963, 5: 98–99

Ventura 1964a

——. "Barbarigo, Agostino." In *Dizionario biografico degli Italiani*, Rome, 1964, 6: 49–50

Ventura 1964b

——. *Nobiltà e popolo nella società veneta del '400 e '500*, Bari, 1964

Ventura 1980

——. Intro. to *Relazione degli Ambasciatori Veneti al Senato*, Rome and Bari, 1980

Ventura 1983

Venturi, Lionello. *Le Compagnia della Calza (sec. XV–XVI)*, Venice, 1983 (orig. pub. 1909)

Verheyan 1990

Verheyan, Egon. "The Triumphal Arch on the Lido: On the Reliability of Eyewitness Acounts." In *The Verbal and the Visual: Essays in Honor of William Sebastian Heckscher*, ed. K.-L. Selig and E. Sears, New York, 1990, 213–21

Da Villa Urbani & Mason 1994

Da Villa Urbani, Maria, and Stefania Mason. *Chiesa di San Pantalon*, Venice, 1994

Vinci 1572

Vinci, Pietro. *Di Pietro Vinci siciliano della citta di Nicosia maestro di cappella in S. Maria Maggiore Bergamo il secondo libro di motetti a cinque voci*, Venice, 1572

Vitruvius Pollio 1556

Vitruvius Pollio, Marcus. *I dieci libri dell'architettura di M. Vitruvio, tradotti et commentati da Monsignor Barbaro eletto patriarca d'Aquileggia*, Venice, 1556

Vitruvius Pollio 1567a

——. *De architectura libri decem, cum commentariis Danielis Barbari, electi Patriarchae Aquileiensis, multis aedificiorum, horologiorum, et machinarum descriptionibus, et figuris*, Venice, 1567

Vitruvius Pollio 1567b

——. *I dieci libri dell'architettura di M. Vitruvio, tradotti et commentati da Mons. Daniele Barbaro eletto Patriarca d'Aquileia, da lui rivedi et ampliati; & hora in più commoda forma ridotta*, Venice, 1567

Vitruvius Pollio 1960

——. *The Ten Books on Architecture*, trans. M. H. Morgan, New York, 1960 (orig. pub. Cambridge, Mass., 1914)

Vitruvius Pollio 1987

——. *I dieci libri dell'architettura tradotti e commentati da Daniele Barbaro 1567: con un saggio di Manfredo Tafuri e uno studio di Manuela Morresi*, Milan, 1987

Vitruvius Pollio 1999

——. *Ten Books on Architecture*, ed. I. Rowland and T. Howe, Cambridge, 1999

Voelker 1977

Voelker, Evelyn. "Charles Borromeo's Instructiones Fabricae et supellectilis Ecclesiasticae, 1577: A Translation with Commentary and Analysis." PhD dissertation, Syracuse University, 1977

Warnke 1993

Warnke, Martin. *The Court Artist: On the Ancestry of the Modern Artist*, Cambridge, 1993 (trans. of *Der Hofkünstler. Zur Vorgeschichte des modernen Künstlers*, Cologne, 1985)

Watanabe-O'Kelly 2002

Watanabe-O'Kelly, Helen. "Early Modern European Festivals – Politics and Performance, Record and Event." In *Court Festivals of the European Renaissance: Art, Politics and Perfor-*mance, ed. J. R. Mulryne and E. Goldring, Aldershot, Hampshire, and Burlington, Vt., 2002, 15–25

Weissman 1982

Weissman, Ronald. *Ritual Brotherhood in Renaissance Florence*, New York, 1982

Widloecher 1929

Widloecher, Nicolà. *La Congregazione dei Canonici Regolari Lateranensi*, Gubbio, 1929

Wilinski 1965–69

Wilinski, Stanislaw. "La serliana." *Bollettino del Centro internazionale di studi di architettura Andrea Palladio* 7 (1965): 103–25; 11 (1969): 399–429

Wilinski 1972

——. "La finestra termale." *Bollettino del Centro internazionale di studi di architettura Andrea Palladio* 14 (1972): 327–37

Williams 1997

Williams, Robert. *Art, Theory, and Culture in Sixteenth-Century Italy: From Techne to Metatechne*, Cambridge, 1997

Wittkower 1949

Wittkower, Rudolf. *Architectural Principles in the Age of Humanism*, rev. edn., New York, 1962 (orig. pub. 1949)

Wittkower 1963

——. "L'influenza del Palladio sullo sviluppo dell'architettura veneziana del Seicento." *Bollettino del Centro internazionale di studi di architettura Andrea Palladio* 5 (1963): 61–72

Wittkower 1992

——. *Ricerca del Rinascimento: principi, città, architetti*, Turin, 1992

Wolters 1968a

Wolters, Wolfgang. "Andrea Palladio e la decorazione dei suoi edifici." In *Bollettino del Centro internazionale di studi di architettura Andrea Palladio* 10 (1968): 255–78

Wolters 1968b

——. *Plastische Deckendekorationen des Cinquecento in Venedig und im Veneto*, Berlin, 1968

Wolters 1979

——. "Le architetture erette al Lido per l'ingresso di Enrico III a Venezia nel 1574." *Bollettino del Centro internazionale di studi di architettura Andrea Palladio* 21 (1979): 273–89

Wolters 1987

——. *Storia e politica nei dipinti di Palazzo Ducale: aspetti dell'autocelebrazione della Repubblica di Venezia nel Cinquecento*, Venice, 1987 (trans. of *Der Bilderschmuck des Dogenpalastes: Untersuchungen zur Selbstdarstellung der Republik Venedig im 16. Jahrhundert*, Wiesbaden, 1983)

Wolters 1990

——. "Scuole." In Norbert Huse and Wolfgang Wolters, *The Art of Renaissance Venice*, Chicago, 1990, 104–14

Wolters 1996

——. "Überlengen zum Wiederaufbau stark zerstörter Gebäude im Cinquecento: Die Gutachten nach dem Brand des Dogenpalasts vom 20. Dezember 1577." In *Ars naturam adiuvans: Festschrift für Matthias Winner zum 11. März 1996*, ed. V. Flemming and S. Schütze, Mainz am Rhein, 1996, 327–33

Wolters 2000
——. *Architektur und Ornament Venezianischer Bauschmuck der Renaissance*, Munich, 2000

Wolters 2004
——. "Le perizie sulle ricostruzione del Palazzo dopo l'incendio del 20 dicembre 1577." In *Palazzo Ducale: storia e restauri*, ed. G. Romanelli, Verona, 2004, 193–204

Woolf 1968
Woolf, S. J. "Venice and the Terraferma: Problems of the Change from Commercial to Landed Activities." In *Crisis and Change in the Venetian Economy in the Sixteenth and Seventeenth Centuries*, ed. B. Pullan, London, 1968, 175–203 (orig. pub. in *Bollettino dell'Istituto di storia della società e dello stato veneziano* 4 [1962]: 415–41)

Wotton 1968
Wotton, Henry. *The Elements of Architecture*, ed. F. Hard, Charlottesville, Va., 1968 (orig. pub. London, 1624)

Yates 1966
Yates, Frances. *The Art of Memory*, Chicago, 1966

Yriarte 1874
Yriarte, Charles. *La vie d'un patricien de Venise au seizième siècle*, Paris, 1874

Zago 1997
Zago, Roberto. "Foscarini, Giacomo (Jacopo)." In *Dizionario biografico degli Italiani*, Rome, 1997, 49: 365–70

Zannini 1993

Zannini, Andrea. *Burocrazia e burocrati a Venezia in età moderna: i cittadini originari (sec. XVI–XVIII)*, Venice, 1993

Zaupa 1990
Zaupa, Giovanni. *Andrea Palladio e la sua committenza: denaro e architettura nella Vicenza del Cinquecento*, Rome, 1990

Zava Bocazzi 1965
Zava Bocazzi, Franca. *La Basilica dei Santi Giovanni e Paolo in Venezia* [Venice], 1965

Zocconi 1978
Zocconi, Mario. "Il Palladio nel processo produttivo del cinquecento veneto." *Bollettino del Centro internazionale di studi di architettura Andrea Palladio* 20 (1978): 171–201

A. Zorzi 2001
Zorzi, Alvise. *Venezia scomparsa*, 3rd edn., Milan, 2001 (orig. pub. 1972 in 2 vols.)

Zorzi 1534
Zorzi (Giorgio), Fra Francesco. *De harmonia mundi totius Cantica tria*. In *aedibus Bernardini de Vitalibus*, Venice, 1534 (orig. pub. 1525)

G. Zorzi 1924
Zorzi, Giangiorgio. "Andrea Palladio in Friuli." *Archivio veneto tridentino* ser. 4, 5 (1924): 120–45

G. Zorzi 1953
——. "Nuove rivelazioni sulla ricostruzione delle sale del piano nobile del Palazzo Ducale di Venezia dopo l'incendio dell'maggio 1574." *Arte veneta* 7 (1953): 123–51

G. Zorzi 1954
——. "Progetti giovanili di Andrea Palladio per palazzo e case in Venezia e terraferma." *Palladio* n.s. 4 (1954): 105–21

G. Zorzi 1956–57a
——. "Altre due perizie inedite per il restauro del Palazzo Ducale di Venezia dopo l'incendio del 20 dicembre 1577." *Atti del Istituto Veneto di SS. LL. AA.* 115 (1956–57): 133–74

G. Zorzi 1956–57b
——. "Il contributo di Andrea Palladio e di Francesco Zamberlan al restauro di Palazzo Ducale di Venezia dopo l'incendio del 20 dicembre 1577." *Atti dell'Istituto Veneto di SS. LL. AA.* 115 (1956–57): 11–68

G. Zorzi 1959
——. *I disegni delle antichità di Andrea Palladio*, Venice, 1959

G. Zorzi 1963
——. "Quattro monumenti sepolcrali disegnati da Andrea Palladio." *Arte veneta* 27 (1963): 96–103

G. Zorzi 1965
——. *Le opere pubbliche e i palazzi privati di Andrea Palladio* [Venice], 1965

G. Zorzi 1967
——. *Le chiese e i ponti di Andrea Palladio* [Venice], 1967

G. Zorzi 1969
——. *Le ville e i teatri di Andrea Palladio* [Venice], 1969

M. Zorzi 1987
Zorzi, Marino. *La Libreria di San Marco*, Milan, 1987

M. Zorzi, ed. 1988
Zorzi, Marino, ed. *Collezioni di antichità a Venezia nei secoli della repubblica*, Rome, 1988

INDEX

Bortolo di Domenico, 115, 121, 144, 316nn40, 42, 324n188, 325n201, 326n207, 332n29

Bortolo, *proto* of the Scuola Grande di San Rocco, 283

Botero, Giovanni, 134, 322n157

Boucher, Bruce, ix, x, 134

Bourdieu, Pierre, x

Boyle, Richard, 3rd Earl of Burlington (Lord Burlington), 21, 209, *284*, 285

Bozzetti, Camillo, 312n104

Bozzetto, Jacopo (Giacomo), 282, 336n102, 349nn83, 86

Bragadin, Andrea di Antonio P., 230, 341n199

Bragadin, Antonio di Nicolò, 341n199

Bragadin, Antonio P. di Andrea P., 229–32, 285, 292, 337n116, 341n199, 342nn215, 216
  wealth of, 341n199

Bragadin, Bartolomeo, 191

Bragadin family, 191, 230, 301n24, 341n200

Bragadin, Laura di Daniele Barbaro, 230

Bragadin, Maria di Alvise Dr. di Leonardo P. Mocenigo, 230, 341n199

Bragadin, Maria di Giovanni di Giorgio K.P. Corner, 230, 337n116, 341n199

Bragadin, Marietta di Domenico Priuli, 341n199

Bramante, Donato, 10, 13, 47, 79, 148, 297n26, 299n68, 301n17, 304n80, 311n102, 327n240, 344n249
  and choir at Santa Maria del Popolo, 316n36, 317n65
  and cloister of Santa Maria della Pace, 156
  Sala Regia, 44, *45*
  Tempietto (San Pietro in Montorio), 19, *21*, 270, 327n244
  see also Belvedere Courtyard, St. Peter's *under* Vatican

Brescia
  Palazzo Comunale (Pubblico), drawings for, *17*, 209–11, *210*, 332n31, 336nn102, 112
  Palazzo Comunale (Pubblico), Palladio advice on, 47, 124, 209, 333n51, 336n102
  cathedral, Bollani tomb in, 312nn110, 115, 319n86
  cathedral, Palladio advice on, 124, 230

Bristot, Annalisa, 86

Brown, Patricia Fortini, x, xi

Brunelleschi, Filippo, 315n32

Bucintoro, 220–21, 224, 339n170

Budapest, *see* Szépművészti Museum

Burckhardt, Jacob, x

Burns, Howard, ix, xi, 16–17, 54, 191, 209, 223, 239, 248, 285

Cadabrozzo family, 347n38

Ca' Dario, 309n66

Ca' di Dio, 347n35

Caliari, Benedetto: *Nativity of the Virgin*, 268, 347n37

Caliari, Carlo: *St. Augustine Giving the Rule to the Lateran Canons*, 157–59, *158*

Caliari, Carlo and Gabriele: *Doge Sebastiano Ziani's Recognition of Pope Alexander III at the Monastery of the Carità*, 147–48, *147*

Caliari family and studio, 253

Caliari, Paolo, *see* Veronese, Paolo

Calvinism, increase in, 31

Calvo, Marco Fabio, 297n23

Campagna, Girolamo, 253, 325n205, 345nn291, 292
  Christ on the Cross, Sts. Mark and Francis, 253, *254*, 345nn291, 292

God the Father Standing on the Globe of the World Supported by the Four Evangelists, 116
  high altar and choir grills of San Lorenzo, 276, *277*
  tomb monument of Doge Leonardo Loredan in San Giovanni e Paolo, 332n39
  tomb monument of Doge Marino Grimani in San Giuseppe in Castello, *90*, 332n39, 333n42

Campanile, 44, 46

Canal, Antonio di Girolamo, 216

Canaletto, Antonio
  Capriccio with Palladian Buildings, 185–86, *186*
  Caprice View of the Monastery of the Lateran Canons, 148, *151*

Canal, Violante, 348n74

Candia, 36

Canons Regular, *see* Lateran Canons

Capello, Antonio P. di Giambattista, 42, 44, 186, 215, 292, 331nn4, 9

Capello family, 75, 208, 295, 305n111, 333n56, 334n63

Capello, Filippo di Giovanni P., 202, 294–95

Capello, Giovanni, 331n9

Capello, Giovanni K. di Lorenzo, 165, 328n262

Capello, Maria di Zaccaria K.P. Barbaro, 63, 202, 294–95

Capello, Marina di Giovanni K., *see under* Mocenigo

Capello, Orsa di Filippo, *see under* Foscari

Capello, Pietro di Giovanni K., 328nn255, 269

capi del Consiglio dei Dieci, *see* Council of Ten, heads of

capi della Quarantia, *see* Council of Forty, heads of

Caporali, Giovanni Battista, 297n23

capriccio, genre of, 187
  see also Canaletto; Guardi

Capuchin order, 107, 229, 237, 239–40, 244–45, 343n229
  see also Il Redentore

Cardinal of San Sisto, Filippo Buoncampagni, 227

Careni, Abbot Giuliano, 115–19, 316n39, 317nn52, 58

Carleton, Sir Dudley, 32, 39–40

Carlevariis, Luca: view of Sant' Antonio di Castello, *80*

Carmini, church of the (Santa Maria del Carmelo), 225

Carpi, Pietro, 329n273

Carthusian order, 245

case
  apostoliche, 36
  ducali, 36, 38, 191, 301n26, 324n196
  grandi, 36
  nuove, 13, 36, 301n26, 302n37
  nuovissime, 36
  vecchie, 36, 55, 126, 301n24, 26, 302n37, 319n88
  see also longhi, curti, evangelisti under San Giorgio Maggiore

Casini, Matteo, x, xi

Catena, Vicenzo: portrait of Giangiorgio Trissino, *5*

Caterino, Maestro: lost panel painting by, 134, 322nn161, 163

Catholic Reform (pre-Tridentine), 83, 100–103, 107, 109–110, 122, 148, 245, 273–74, 279, 315nn13, 31

Cattaneo, Danese, 332n39

Cavrioli, Francesco: figures for Mocenigo tomb at Santi Giovanni e Paolo, *192*, 193

Cedin, Alessio, and sons, 144

La Celestia (Santa Maria Assunta in Cielo or Santa Maria Celeste), 175, 263, 267, 330n301, 336n102, 346n34, 347n35

Cistercian nuns at, 107, 175–79, *177*, 283, 329nn296, 297
  church of (destroyed), 329n295, 330n318
  cloister, *174*, *176*, 291, 330nn315, 316
  under direction of the Columba, 176
  fire of 1569, 175, 177, *177*, 178–179, 331n22
  plan of, *178*
  Saler chapel (destroyed), 178, 330n305

"il Celestro," 303n57

Cellini, Benvenuto, 333n49

ceremony, *see apparati*; processions; ritual and

Centro internazionale di studi di architettura Andrea Palladio, ix

Cervelli, Federico, 124, 319nn92–94

Cesariano, Cesare, 10, 18

Cesaro, Valentin di Filippo, 265, 268

Cevese, Renato, ix, 49–53

Chancery (Cancellaria), 261

charitable institutions, 261, 281–83, 273–74, 277–79, 281–83, 288
  see also scuole; ospedale

charity, 273–74, 277, 281–82, 345n1

Charles V, 46, 126, 214–17, 306n12, 331n21, 338nn130, 131

Chastel, André, ix, 46

Chatsworth, *see* The Devonshire Collection

Chigi, Agostino, 311n92

Chojnacka, Monica, xi

Chojnacki, Stanley, xi, 32

Christopher, Saint, 263, 265

Christ the Redeemer, 230–31, 236–37, 251–57, 333n42, 343nn231, 232, 344n273
  see also Il Redentore

church reform, 74, 91, 100–104, 107, 109–111, 253, 285, 288, 314n133, 316n36, 45, 326n214, 344n249
  see also Catholic Reform; Council of Trent; individual Orders

Cicogna, Doge Pasquale, 302n37, 321n150, 333n47

Cicogna, Emmanuele, 126

Cistercian order, 107, 176, 283
  see also La Celestia

cittadini, 32, 155, 261, 300n8, 330n310
  cittadini originari, 32, 178, 300n9, 330n312, 345n3, 347n44
  as patrons, 175, 178–79, 261, 263, 269, 273, 277

civic piety, xii, 148, 229, 246, 257, 273–74, 279, 343n231, 348n72
  see also processions; ritual

Cividale, 65
  Palazzo Pretorio, 85, 305n116, 310n80

Civran family, 325n196

Clement VII Medici, 4

Clement VIII Aldobrandini, 306n16

Clovio, Giulio: *Commentarii in Epistolas Pauli, Ad Romanos, et ad Galatas*, 101, *102*, 312n116, 314n135

Codevigo: parish church at, 324n194

Codussi, Mauro, 337n125

Collegio, 39, 82, 176–77, 179, 187, *199*, 230, 232, 234, 239
  Pien Collegio, 187

Colombo, Ignatius: "Fire in the Arsenale," *177*

Colonna, Marc'Antonio, 215–16, 338nn137, 138
  see also processions

Comini, Giovanni Giacomo di Pietro, 124, 128, 134, *137*, *142*, 144, 325nn205, 206, 326n207

Tempietto, 99, 234, 313n128, 342n216

Villa Contarini at Mira, *see* Mira

Villa Contarini at Piazzola sul Brenta, 301n17

Villa Corner at Piombino Dese, 5, 31, 294, 333n55, 334n61
  in *Four Books*, 6

Villa Foscari ("La Malcontenta") at Gambarare, 31, 59, 214, 288, 304n97, 309n70, 349n3
  in *Four Books*, 59

Villa Mocenigo at Dolo, 31, 167, 294, 328nn256, 258, 269
  in *Four Books*, 163, 165

Villa Mocenigo at Marocco, 31, 294, 306n5, 328nn256, 258
  in *Four Books*, 163, 165

Villa Pisani at Bagnolo di Lonigo, 4–5, 31, 202, 295, 334n62
  in *Four Books*, 6

Villa Pisani at Montagnana, 7, 31, 65, 301n13, 337n122
  in *Four Books*, 6

Villa Priuli, *see* Treville

villegiatura, 33, 300n10, 301n13

Vinci, Pietro: *Secondo libro di motetti a cinque voci*, 343n230

Visentini, Antonio, 71, 306n3
  drawings of arch and loggia for entry of Henri III, 221, *223*, 338n153, 339n160
  Santa Lucia, 173, 329n290

Viterbo: villa of Cardinal Ridolfi at Bagnaia (near), 217, 301n10, 338n145

Vitruvius Pollio, Marcus, 42, 43, 91
  I dieci libri, 10–18, *11*, 16–17, 148–49, *150*, 167, 248, *249*, 290–91, 294, 297nn22, 23, 26, 298n42, 304n83, 328n268
  see also Barbaro, Daniele; Palladio

Vittoria, Alessandro, 22, 313n119, 324n190, 332n29, 337n117, 339n168
  bust of Giovanni Battista Ferretti, 54, 55, 304n85
  bust of Leonardo Mocenigo (lost), 169, 329n276
  Four Evangelists (at San Giorgio Maggiore), *138*, 139–40, *140*, 324n190
  Morosini Chapel sculptural ensemble (at San Giorgio Maggiore), 126–28, *129*, 320nn111, 126, 127
  and Palazzo Thiene in Vicenza, 54
  and Palazzo Trevisan on Murano, 54
  Risen Christ, *Faith* and *Charity*, 319n86

Vitturi family, 250

Vivarini, Alvise, 347n44

Ware, Isaac, *21*, 326n224

War of Chioggia, 36, 40

War of Crete, 301n24

War of Cyprus, 36, 40, 59, 60, 186, 189, 193, 203, 224, 309n68, 331n8, 332n28, 340n173, 343n242

War of the League of Cambrai, 31, 43–44, 46–47, 69, 72, 303n63, 306n13, 320n115

War of the Morea, 301n24
  see also Morea

Wars of Religion, 40, 183

waterfront palace type, 44, 49–53, 58–59, *58*, 269

Wittkower, Rudolf, 14, 21, 91, 100, 140, 246, 248, 344n257

Wolters, Wolfgang, xi, 220, 223

women
  monachization of, 163, 176
  public role of, in Venice, 273, 277–79, 348n72
  see also female governance of convents; La Celestia; Santa Lucia; Le Zitelle; patronage, aspects of

women's choirs, *106*, 170–73, *171*, 276, *277*, 278, 281, *282*, 284

Worcester College, Oxford (H. T. 68), 324n192

Wotton, Sir Henry, 155

Zamberlan, Francesco, 336n102, 337n115
  drawings for the Brescia Palazzo Comunale, 209–11, *210*

Zanetti, Anton Maria the Elder and Anton Maria the Younger, 313n119

La Zecca, *see* Mint

Zelotti, Giam Battista
  Allegory of "Aristocrazia," Castello "il Cataio" (Battaglia Terme), *200*, *201*, 333n57
  painting cycle at Castello "il Cataio" (Battaglia Terme), 202

Zen, Nicolò (humanist), 303n67, 304n88

Zeno, Caterino di Nicolò, 215

Zeno, Nicolò di Caterino, 215

Zenoni, Domenico: *Triumphal Arch for the Entry of Henri III*, 219–21, *219*, 224–26, 338n154, 339n160

Zeri, Federico, 253

Ziani, Doge Pietro, 109, 314n7

Ziani, Doge Sebastiano, 43–44, 140–41, *143*, 147–48, *147*, 205, 324n195, 325n197

Ziletti, Lodovico: engraving after Cesare Vecellio, *Tribune Wall in the Sala del Collegio Before the 1574 Fire*, 198

Ziliol, Prioress Chiara, 169

Le Zitelle (Santa Maria delle Presentazione), 173, 230, 234, 239, 261, *280*, 281–85, *282*, *283*, 288, 291, 326n212, 329n291, 330n314, 337n126, 341nn199, 207, 343n241, 348nn66, 75, 76, 349nn77, 80–84, 86–89
  casa delle Zitelle, 348n70
  consecration of, 349n82
  deputato sopra la fabbrica, 283
  drawings associated with, 342n216, 349nn77, 88, 89
  façade of, 281–82, 284
  governance of, 281–85
  plan of , 281, *281*, 284–85

Zonta, 39
  see also Council of Ten

Zorzi, Alvise P. di Benedetto, 208, 292, 309nn61, 62, 335n91, 336n98

Zorzi di Vicenzo, 266, *267*

Zorzi, Doge Marino, 32

Zorzi, Fra Francesco, 91
  Da harmonia mundi, 298n39
  Memoriale (also as *relazioni*), 79, 100, 307n44, 313nn129, 132

Zorzi, Gerolamo, 231

Zorzi, Giangiorgio, ix, xi, 23, 124

Zuane a Santa Marina, Maestro, 335n76

Zuan Maria di Pietro ("il Monaro"), 239, 343n241

Zuccaro, Federico, 65, 85, 305n116, 309nn74, 75, 310nn79, 80
  Casino of Pius IV in Vatican gardens, decoration of, 85, 309nn74, 75, 313n121
  drawing of the "Antiquario del Ill.mo Patriarca Grimani," 97, *98*, 313n119
  figures in Palladio's drawing for a tomb monument (Vicenza, Museo Civico, D 17), 89, *94*, 312n108
  Grimani chapel in San Francesco della Vigna, 85, 309nn75, 76
  scenes for *L'Antigono*, 65
  stairway of Grimani Palace, 85, 309n75, 310n76, 312n116
  study after Veronese's destroyed *Frederick Barbarossa Kissing the Ring of the Schismatic Pope Victor IV*, 166

Zuccaro, Taddeo, 305n107, 309nn74, 75

Zucchi, Andrea: engravings after Tintoretto, 329n272

Zuffo da Padova, Abbot Alvise, 324n195

PHOTOGRAPH CREDITS